THROWING THUNDERBOLTS

A Wargamer's Guide to the War of the First Coalition, 1792-1797

Garry David Wills

HELION & COMPANY

Helion & Company Limited
Unit 8 Amherst Business Centre
Budbrooke Road
Warwick
CV34 5WE
England
Tel. 01926 499 619
Email: info@helion.co.uk
Website: www.helion.co.uk
Twitter: @helionbooks
Visit our blog http://blog.helion.co.uk/

Published by Helion & Company 2023
Designed and typeset by Mary Woolley, Battlefield Design (www.battlefield-design.co.uk)
Cover designed by Paul Hewitt, Battlefield Design (www.battlefield-design.co.uk)

Text and maps © Garry David Wills 2023
Illustrations as individually credited © Helion & Company 2023
Front cover artwork drawn by Giorgio Albertini © Helion & Company 2023

Every reasonable effort has been made to trace copyright holders and to obtain their permission for the use of copyright material. The author and publisher apologise for any errors or omissions in this work and would be grateful if notified of any corrections that should be incorporated in future reprints or editions of this book.

ISBN 978-1-804512-03-6

British Library Cataloguing-in-Publication Data.
A catalogue record for this book is available from the British Library.

All rights reserved. No part of this publication may be reproduced, stored in a retrieval system, or transmitted, in any form, or by any means, electronic, mechanical, photocopying, recording or otherwise, without the express written consent of Helion & Company Limited.

For details of other military history titles published by Helion & Company Limited contact the above address or visit our website: http://www.helion.co.uk.

We always welcome receiving book proposals from prospective authors.

Contents

Acknowledgements

I would like to thank my friend Jorge Planas Campos for his help in finding Coronel Luis Ariza. I would also like to thank Dr Stephen Summerfield for his help on the Austrian and Sardinian artillery. Thanks are also due to Paul Demet and Geert van Uythoven, who have both generously shared their research with me. I would like to thank the members of the Sons of Simon de Montfort wargames club who have helped by playtesting some of the scenarios. I would also like to thank Colin Ashton for generously providing photographs of his excellent 28mm collection to illustrate this book and for reviewing the text. Finally, this project has involved my family, my wife Susan organised my visit to Linselles and took some important photographs, my son James helped me in presenting the wargames at several shows, my daughter Jennifer helped by obtaining some key references for me and my son George helped with translations. Thanks to one and all.

1

Introduction

Peoples do not judge in the same way as courts of law ... they throw thunderbolts! – *Maximilien de Robespierre*

I cannot remember a time when I was not a wargamer of some sort, but I have been a Napoleonic wargamer since 1971. After starting with Airfix HO/OO scale plastic figures, I caught the wave of the Miniature Figurines 15mm strips which were just being introduced, and I have, although not exclusively, stuck with 15mm figures ever since. Since 2006 I have become increasingly interested in the conflicts that preceded the Napoleonic Wars; those associated with the French Revolution.

My first book, which I self-published in 2011, was '*Wellington's First Battle*' which dealt with the then Arthur Wesley's exploits at the battle of Boxtel in 1794, during the Duke of York's unsuccessful campaign in Flanders and Holland. Since then, I have researched several scenarios which feature in this volume. This research has taught me that, while the wars of the French Revolution have been dominated in wargaming terms by the magnificence, splendour, and tragedy of the wars of Napoleon's First Empire, they have an underappreciated appeal all their own. For example, the 'great men' of the wars of the First Empire are, during the revolution, more junior officers making their way in the world and can be more credibly placed on the average wargamer's table in a battalion scale game. Napoleon himself at Toulon or Augereau as a division commander at Castiglione are two examples. Likewise, Chassé was a battalion commander fighting for the French at Boxtel, which also featured Generals Byng, Cooke, Maitland and Vandeleur, all of Waterloo fame, as regimental officers. Furthermore, it was during the War of the First Coalition, that the art of war was undergoing the changes that we read so much about in the days of the First Empire.

At the start of the war, Britain's Guards Brigade set out for Flanders without any light companies to face the demi-brigades of the revolutionaries who were similarly without specific voltigeur companies in their line battalions. Similarly, while the French *artillerie légère* (horse artillery) was making an impact, their British opponents had to rely on their Hanoverian allies to provide a similar capability as the newly formed (and soon to be Royal) Horse Artillery were kept at home. Meanwhile, the Prussian infantry and cavalry were feared, while the Austrian artillery and light troops were widely admired. Similarly in naval warfare, Nelson's breaking of the Franco-Spanish line of battle at Trafalgar is predated by Admiral William Howe's direct assault on the French at the Glorious First of June in 1794.

The response of the monarchies of Europe to the French Revolution was, eventually, to promote and deliver a counter-revolution, which was greatly assisted by the French revolutionary government declaring war on them. The counter-revolution took the form of a series of coalitions of which the government of Great Britain was a prime mover and sponsor. The coalitions are known to history by their numbers, the First Coalition lasted from 1792 to 1797, the Second from 1798 to 1802, the Third from 1803 to 1806, the Fourth from 1806 to 1807, the Fifth just 1809, the Sixth from 1813 to 1814, with Napoleon's final defeat achieved by the Seventh Coalition in 1815, during the Hundred Days. The focus of this volume, the War of the First Coalition, 1792–1797, involved at least 280 battles and actions. These actions took place on all of France's borders, as well as the internal counter-revolution and overseas. These theatres of war will all feature in this volume along with some aspects of the conflict at sea. At the same time, I have chosen to exclude the detail of the internal politics of France between 1789 and 1792, the Second Partition of Poland (1792–1793) and the Third Anglo-Mysore War (1790–1792), all of which are strictly not part of the War of the First Coalition. Likewise, the story of the coup d'état of 18 Fructidor (4 September 1797) is better seen as the first step towards the War of the Second Coalition.[1]

This guide to wargaming the War of the First Coalition is intended to be enjoyable and useful to the beginner and experienced wargamer, new to the period, alike. This is a book for wargamers based on history rather than a history book, which will explain how the battles of the French revolution can be recreated by some of the different wargame systems available at an appropriate scale.

A brief history of the War of the First Coalition will be provided complete with notes on each of the protagonists. Within this context the various chapters will describe a process for deciding how to start out in wargaming the period, including choosing scales, games systems, designing scenarios, building forces, selecting figures and terrain, and painting. A guide will also be provided to various information resources that are available both in hard copy and online.

Ten scenarios are provided to illustrate this process covering the different scales of game and the different protagonists and theatres in the war.

There are dozens and dozens of sets of rules or game systems for the period from 1750–1850, each of which could be applied to the games depicting the War of the First Coalition. Some of these rulesets are new and fashionable and some are old but still in regular use. One way of structuring this diversity is to look at what is represented by the basic unit in the game, which is the smallest group into which most of the miniatures or figures in the game are organised. Some rules use the individual figure representing one man as this basic unit, others group the figures into a company or platoon, many rules use the battalion, while others use the brigade and the division as the basic unit. This is the model that I will use in describing how to game our period.

With this cornucopia of options, it is inevitable that my own preferences will shine through. However, I believe that it is important to remember the words of the late Stuart Asquith who wrote in the 1987 'Military Modelling Guide to Wargaming' that 'it is important to realise that wargaming is … all things to all men [or women]. No

1 Timothy Charles William Blanning, *The French Revolutionary Wars, 1787–1802* (London: Arnold, 1996), pp.56–58; Blanning provides the wargamer with a pithy and succinct guide to the wider political situation across Europe leading up to the Revolution.

one approach … is necessarily right or wrong'.[2] This book is written in this spirit but obviously I cannot and never intended to give a comprehensive review of the market in detail, so please forgive me if you feel your favourite game system or figure scale has been neglected.

The War of the First Coalition is an exciting period for wargamers as the art of war was undergoing continual transformation, which was reflected in the way the different armies fought. The 280 battles and actions of the War of the First Coalition can each provide inspiration for an exciting wargame scenario.[3] This guide aims to capture this excitement and enable you to bring it to your own wargames table.

2 Henry Hyde, *The Wargames Compendium* (Barnsley: Pen and Sword Military, 2013), Kindle edition location 1394.

3 Digby Smith, *The Greenhill Napoleonic Wars Data Book* (London: Greenhill Books, 1998), pp.19–135.

2

A Brief History of the French Revolution[1]

The space available does not enable a detailed description of the complex phenomenon that was the French Revolution. What follows is an attempt to provide a sense of the main events that led to the War of the First Coalition.

It has been said that war begets war, and this is certainly the case with the French Revolution. In some ways the origins of the revolution can be traced to the American War of Independence and specifically to King Louis XVI's decision to enter that war on the side of the Americans.[2] While he was successful in humiliating his number one enemy, Great Britain, he also ran out of money. Furthermore, the king was in turn humiliated by his failure to intervene in support of his allies in the Dutch revolution of 1787, during which the United Provinces were easily occupied by the Prussian army in support of the Stadtholder.[3] In 1789 Louis was compelled to call on his *États généraux* (Estates General), a representative body, to raise taxes.

The Estates General began its meeting 5 May 1789, the first such meeting since 1614. It was divided into three equally represented Estates, the 'First Estate', representing approximately 100,000 clergy, the 'Second Estate', representing 400,000 nobles, and the 'Third Estate' representing the rest of the population of 25 million people. The Third Estate actually paid most of the tax in what was an intrinsically unfair system. Unsurprisingly, the elected representatives of the Third Estate, who were themselves wealthier members of the middle class, inspired in part by the *philosophes* of the Enlightenment, preferred to discuss the rights of the people rather than the tax to be paid to the king, consequently the talks degenerated into a stalemate. The impasse was broken by the representatives of the Third Estate declaring themselves a National Assembly (17 June 1789), which some members of the other two Estates joined. Famously, on 14 July 1789, following several days of violent unrest, the Bastille in Paris was stormed by the 'mob' and the world changed forever, starting with the stone-by-stone demolition of the Bastille itself as this symbol of oppression was razed to the ground. In October a shortage of bread

1 Gregory Freemont-Barnes, *The French Revolutionary Wars* (Oxford: Osprey Publishing, 2001), pp.12–16; Alistair Horne, *The French Revolution* (London: Carlton Publishing, 2009), pp.14–36; Duncan Townson, *France in Revolution* (Sevenoaks: Hodder and Stoughton, 1990), pp.39, 64, 95; Colin Jones, *Longman Companion to the French Revolution* (Harlow: Longman, 1988), pp.10–29.

2 For a more in-depth discussion of the full eighteenth-century context of the revolution, see Charles J. Esdaile, *The Wars of the French Revolution 1792–1801* (Oxon: Routledge, 2019), pp.1–28.

3 Blanning, *Revolutionary Wars*, p.26.

provoked the lynching of an unfortunate baker and the subsequent march on the Palace of Versailles, where the *sans culottes* (working class revolutionary extremists who specifically wore trousers rather than knee-breeches – *culottes* – to distinguish themselves from the nobility and bourgeoisie) forced the king to give his assent to the declarations of the National Assembly including that of 'the Rights of Man'.

The king and queen were then taken to the Tuileries Palace in Paris, effectively prisoners of their own people. After unsuccessful attempts to establish a constitutional monarchy, during the night of the 20 June 1791 the king and queen attempted to escape but were captured at Varennes and brought back to Paris. Meanwhile, in response to Queen Marie-Antoinette's appeal for help, Prussia and Austria stated their intent to create a coalition to reinstate Louis in the Declaration of Pillnitz (27 August 1791). Back in Paris, the king had no choice but to give his assent to a new constitution (13 September 1791), which removed virtually all his power. In February 1792 troops from Austria and Prussia began to advance on the borders of France. Meanwhile in Paris, in the assembly of deputies, now called the Legislative Assembly, the Girondin leader, Jacques-Pierre Brissot proposed that a limited war would both solve France's internal problems and export the revolution across Europe. Consequently, on 20 April 1792, following an unacceptable ultimatum, France declared war on Austria, King Louis XVI thus declaring war on his wife's nephew.

In May, Prussia declared war on France, in support of Austria. After an unsuccessful skirmish against the Austrians near Valenciennes on the border with the Austrian Netherlands (now Belgium), *Maréchal de Camp*[4] Théobald Dillon was accused of treason and murdered by his own troops (29 April 1792). On 20 June 1792, 8,000 Gardes Nationales and *sans culottes* invaded the Tuileries Palace in protest at Louis' use of his veto. In response the Duke of Brunswick,[5] at the head of the Allied army, issued his 'Manifesto', stating his intent to enable King Louis to 'exercise once more the legitimate authority that belongs to him'. This merely fanned the flames of revolution. On 5 July 1792 the Legislative Assembly declared '*La Patrie en danger*' and assumed emergency powers. At this time 5,000 *Fédérés* (*Garde Nationale Volontaires* from the regions of France) arrived in Paris bringing with them *La Marsaillaise*. On 10 August 1792 the Tuileries Palace was again attacked this time by several thousand *Gardes Nationales* and *Fédérés*. The 3,000 troops guarding the royal family included 2,000 *Gardes Nationales* who promptly joined the attackers. Having been ordered to cease fire by the king, his 600 Swiss Guards were promptly massacred, and the royal family escaped to the Legislative Assembly for protection. However, the insurgents invaded the assembly forcing it to recognise the revolutionary commune which the *sans culottes* had established in the Hotel de Ville the previous day. The royal family was then imprisoned by the *Commune* in the Temple, previously a fortified monastery of the Templars and now a prison.

On the northern border, Luckner's foray towards Ghent, capturing Menin and Courtrai along the way, yielded some success for the French before an Austrian victory at Harlebeke, and the absence of a popular rising by the inhabitants, forced Luckner to retire back to Lille (23 June).[6]

4 This rank became *Général de Brigade* in 1793.

5 *Generalfeldmarschall* Karl Wilhelm Ferdinand, Duke of Brunswick-Lüneburg, Prince of Brunswick-Wolfenbüttel.

6 Smith, *Data Book*, p.23; *Maréchal de France* Nicolas Luckner, commanding the Armée du Nord.

In the southeast war was declared on the Kingdom of Sardinia-Piedmont (27 July 1792).

The Duke of Brunswick led the Prussian army across the French frontier and captured the fortresses of Longwy (23 August) and Verdun (2 September 1792). In Paris the 'September Massacres' (2–6 September) followed, during which the mob murdered 1,200 prison inmates including Marie-Antoinette's First Lady of the Bedchamber.

At the battle or 'cannonade' of Valmy (20 September 1792), 156 miles from the Rhine, the Armée du Centre, commanded by Kellermann,[7] and the Armée du Nord, now commanded by Dumouriez,[8] faced down the Duke of Brunswick's Prussian Army. When the French stood their ground, the Duke of Brunswick retired back to the Rhine. The casualties were light, the French lost 300 men of the 32,000 engaged, and the Prussians suffered 180 casualties out of 34,000. The poet Goethe, who was present at the action, afterwards wrote 'here and today, a new epoch in the history of the world has begun'.[9] In pursuing the Prussians, the French retook Verdun, and subsequently Custine,[10] with the Armée des Vosges, captured the city of Mainz (21 October) on the Rhine. Custine then crossed the Rhine to capture Frankfurt am Main (22 October) only to lose it again before the year was out (2 December 1792).

Following a campaign championed by the Jacobin leader Maximilien de Robespierre, the Legislative Assembly was replaced by the *Convention Nationale* (21 September 1792), based on universal male suffrage. On the same day the *Convention Nationale* voted to abolish the monarchy and France was declared a republic (25 September 1792).

Just across the frontier, in the Austrian Netherlands, Dumouriez, commanding both the Armée du Nord and the Armée des Ardennes, then beat an inferior Austrian force at the battle of Jemappes (6 November 1792). At Jemappes, Dumouriez outnumbered his opponents by a margin of three to one, but the attacks of his enthusiastic troops were uncoordinated. The pursuit after Jemappes was briefly halted by Ferdinand in command of the Austrian rearguard (20,000 men) at Anderlecht on the outskirts of Brussels, but he was forced back by Dumouriez (35,000 men) with the loss of 500 men (13 November).[11] Dumouriez was then free to occupy Brussels. Miranda then led the Armée du Nord in the capture of the port of Antwerp in the Austrian Netherlands (27 November).

The last act of 1792 was the siege of the fortress city of Namur by the Armée des Ardennes, commanded by Valence, from 6 November to its capture on 2 December 1792.[12] The victory at Jemappes thus concluded a campaign season in the Austrian Netherlands that had begun with cross-border raiding and a series of clashes won by the Austrians but ended with the French occupation of the Austrian Netherlands.

---

7 Jacques de Roussel, *État Militaire de France* (Paris: Onfroy, 1793), p.9; *Général d'Armée* François-Étienne-Christophe Kellermann.

8 *Général d'Armée* Charles-François du Périer Dumouriez.

9 Esdaile, *Wars*, pp.63–5; the French outnumbered the Prussians and their Austrian allies but were divided between two positions.

10 Jones, *Companion*, p.135; *Lieutenant Général* Adam Philippe, Comte de Custine.

11 *Feldmarschallleutnant* Duke Ferdinand Frederick Augustus of Württemberg.

12 *Lieutenant Général* Jean-Baptiste Cyrus de Timbrune de Thiembronne, Comte de Valence.

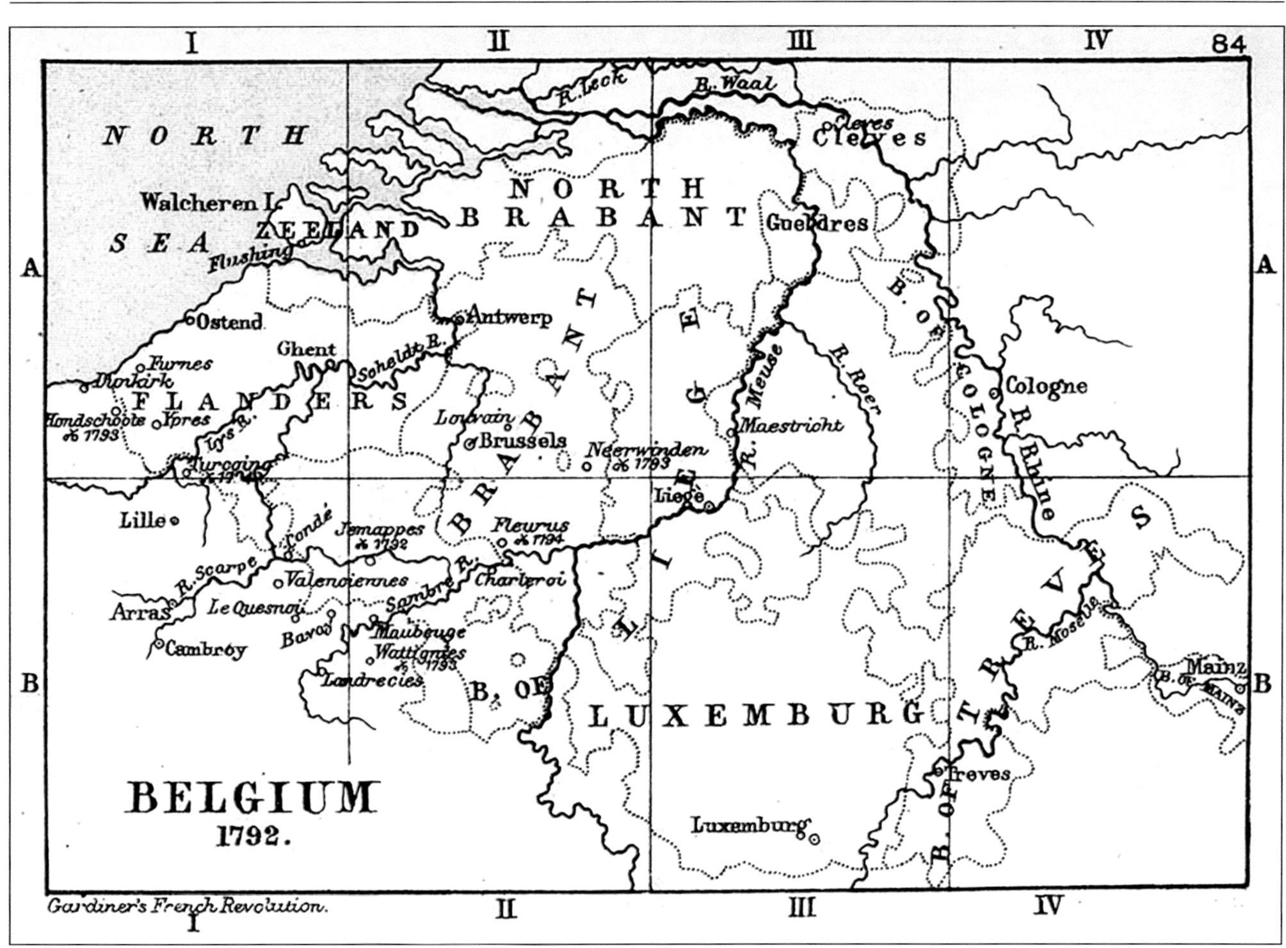

Map 1 – Austrian Netherlands

The French Republic annexed Savoy on its southeast frontier (27 November) following their raid on Oneglia (23 September) and defeat in the clash of Sospello (18 November) against the forces of the Kingdom of Sardinia-Piedmont.[13]

At the end of 1792, despite some early difficulties, the French armies had established themselves in some outposts beyond their own frontiers. During 1792 the French army had fought in seven engagements or battles involving more than 20,000 combatants, winning six and losing only one. The French also fought in 29 lesser actions, winning 12 but losing 17. The disorganised French army had held its own and consequently the allies failed to make a significant contribution towards fulfilling the Pillnitz Declaration.[14]

Back in Paris, King Louis, now just Louis Capet, was put on trial in front of the *Convention Nationale*, accused of high treason (11 December 1792). Having convicted Louis (18 January 1793) and inspired by Louis-Antoine St. Just, the *Convention Nationale* sentenced Louis to death by a margin of 366 to 288 votes. Louis was guillotined on the Place de la Révolution (Concorde), 21 January 1793. Marie-Antoinette followed him to the guillotine later in the same year. France then annexed Nice (31 January 1793), the Principality of Monaco (15 February) and then the Bishopric of Basle and the region of Porrentruy (23 March 1793).

13 At the beginning of the century Savoy was an independent county but had been part of the Kingdom of Sardina-Piedmont since 1720.

14 Smith, *Data Book*, pp.21–35.

Map 2 – Key Actions and Battles, 1792

France widened the conflict by further declarations of war against Great Britain and the United Provinces (1 February 1793) and Spain (7 March 1793).

The *Convention Nationale* decree of 21 February 1793 had a significant impact on the organisation of the French army, firstly by changing the ranks of the senior officers.

Ranks before 21 Feb 1793	Ranks after 21 Feb 1793
Maréchal de France	Removed
Général d'Armée	*Général en Chef*
Lieutenant Général	*Général de Division*
Maréchal de Camp	*Général de Brigade*
Colonel	*Chef de Brigade*
Lieutenant-Colonel	*Chef de Bataillon/d'Escadron*

Secondly the decree initiated the process of creating the *demi-brigades* (the word *régiment* being replaced to create a break from the *ancien régime*) by combining one battalion of the old royal army with two battalions of *Gardes Nationales* volunteers. This process had administrative, political and tactical benefits.[15] A similar process would create the *demi-brigades légère* from the various light infantry battalions. Although this process was begun immediately it was paused on 31 March 1793, before being resumed in the first *amalgame* of 1794 and the second *amalgame* in 1796. In another break with the past, the decree also set out the methods by which the officers of the new demi-brigades were elected by their subordinates. The *Convention Nationale* again entered new ground by conscripting 300,000 men to reinforce the army (24 February).

The *Représentants du Peuple en Mission*, deputies sent from the Convention to the *départements* to rally everyone behind the war effort, were created on 9 March 1793, followed by similar *Représentants* sent to each of the armies to 'supervise' the generals (9 April 1793).

Maximilien Robespierre came to power via the *Comité du Salut Public* (Committee of Public Safety), which was established on 6 April 1793, with powers to cover 'all measures necessary for the internal and external defence of the republic'. Robespierre joined the committee in July 1793 and Lazare Nicolas Marguerite Carnot (the 'Organiser of Victory') in August 1793.

During 1793, France completed its collection of countries with which it was at war. Besides Austria, Great Britain, Prussia, Sardinia-Piedmont, Spain and the United Provinces, France was now at war with the Kingdom of Naples (12 July 1793), Portugal (26 September 1793) and from the Holy Roman Empire the states of Baden, Bavaria, Hanover, Hesse-Cassel, Hesse-Darmstadt, Saxony and Württemberg.[16]

15 Jean Paul Bertaud and R.R.Palmer, *The Army of the French Revolution* (Guildford: Princeton University Press, 1988), pp.81–84, 86–88.

16 Freemont-Barnes, *French Revolutionary Wars*, p.30.

3

A Military Chronology of the War of the First Coalition

This chapter provides a military history chronology of the fighting, summarising the main offensive movements, the commanders and the size of their forces, the major battles, actions and sieges, together with the campaign outcomes, in each theatre of war. This chronology is intended to provide the wargamer with a series of starting points for researching and developing their own scenarios and perhaps campaigns.[1] The organisation and nomenclature of the French armies during this period was extremely fluid and no attempt is made to track all these changes in the narrative, so apologies if your favourite, albeit short-lived, force is not mentioned.[2] It has not been possible to provide maps for all of these campaigns but the majority of places named can be found on Google maps, using the directions in the text.

The War in 1793

The campaign of 1793 was marked by the Allied armies mustering 350,000 men on the north, east, southeast, and southwest frontiers of France. It was also the year of significant counter-revolutionary action within the borders of France, both to the west and the southeast.

The North

In the north, the French had some 122,000 troops, divided into five commands, and the garrisons of the Austrian Netherlands.[3] On 1 February, Dumouriez, commanding the Armée du Nord, was ordered to invade the United Provinces.[4] Dumouriez duly invaded two weeks later (16 February), advancing from Antwerp with 17,000 men.[5] The fortress of Breda surrendered (26 February), quickly followed by Klundert and

1 To see this chronology in the full context of the French revolution readers are guided to Professor Esdaile's '*The Wars of the French Revolution, 1792–1801*'.

2 Jones, *Companion*, pp.147–155, citing Charles Clerget's *Tableaux des armées Françaises pendant les guerres de la Révolution* (Paris: Chapelot, 1905).

3 Ramsay Weston Phipps, *The Armies of the First French Republic, and the Rise of the Marshals of Napoleon I—The Armée du Nord*, (Godmanchester: Ken Trotman, 2011), p.150.

4 Phipps, *Armée du Nord*, p.152.

5 John William Fortescue, *A History of the British Army* (Uckfield: The Naval & Military Press Ltd, 2004), vol. IV, pt.1, p.65.

Gertruydenburg. Bergen op Zoom, Steenburgen and Willemstadt were blockaded or besieged. Meanwhile he had ordered Miranda to advance with 30,000 men to besiege Maastricht on the southern tip of the United Provinces.[6] Dumouriez was soon ready to attempt the passage of the Hollands Diep[7] to advance on Rotterdam and Amsterdam, however the allies were now ready to oppose him.

Succour for the Dutch arrived in the form of three battalions of British Foot Guards, the first battalions of each of the three regiments, which comprised 2,000 men. They disembarked at Helvetoetsluis (1 March) and four days later were in Dort ready to oppose Dumouriez's force. Here they were supported by Dutch gunboats crewed by British sailors on the river Meuse.

However, the bigger threat to the French was provided by the Austrians; 40,000 men commanded by Coburg.[8] On 1 March, these men left their cantonments on the river Roer to retake the Austrian Netherlands, attacking through Aldenhoven. Within four days Coburg had chased Miranda's routed men back to Leuven/Louvain, 16 miles east of Brussels, but fortunately for the French, Coburg chose to halt his pursuit for 10 days. Reluctantly Dumouriez left his expedition into the United Province to assume command at Louvain where the remainder of the Armée du Nord, des Ardennes and de la Belgique were gathered. Having restored French morale, but fearing his army would be routed if it assumed a defensive posture, Dumouriez advanced with 48,000 men and attacked Coburg's 40,000 men at Neerwinden (18 March), where he was defeated, losing 5,000 men when his left was repulsed. The Austrians lost 3,000 men. Having withdrawn to Louvain, where he was defeated again (21 March), Dumouriez withdrew through Brussels back to France, sheltering behind the fortresses of Valenciennes and Condé.[9] Dumouriez also lost another 10,000 men, who simply deserted. Meanwhile 8,000 Prussians under Brunswick had advanced from the Rhine to Bois-le-Duc to attempt to cut off the French forces in the United Provinces, in collaboration with the 5,000 British and Dutch troops.

Disillusioned, Dumouriez then formulated a plan to lead his army to Paris and overthrow the Convention. Thwarted in this by, among others, *Chef de Bataillon* Louis-Nicolas Davout, Dumouriez himself deserted to the Austrians (5 April), accompanied by Valence and the Duc de Chartres (the future King Louis-Philippe).

Dumouriez was replaced as commander of the Armée du Nord by Dampierre (6 April), who was killed in action at the Battle of Raismes (8 May), and then by Custine (28 May).[10] At this time Coburg had amassed an Allied army of 105,000 men (55,000 Austrians, 15,000 Dutch, 12,000 Hanoverians, 8,000 Hessians, 8,000 Prussians and 7,000 British, including a total of 21,300 cavalry).[11] With part of this force (53,000 men) he attacked the fortress of Valenciennes, fighting the battle of Famars (23 May), which pushed the French army of 27,000 men away from the fortress. Following a successful siege, the fortress fell 27 July. The defeat at Famars proved catastrophic for Custine, who was

6 *Lieutenant Général* Sebastiàn Francisco de Miranda y Rodríguez de Espinoza: a Venezuelan who served Spain in the American Revolutionary War and went on to be one of the leaders of the independence movement in Venezuela.

7 The estuary of the Rhine and Meuse rivers.

8 *Feldmarshall* Prince Josias of Saxe-Coburg-Saalfeld.

9 Fortescue, *History*, vol. IV, pt.1, pp.66–67; Phipps, *Nord*, pp.153–155; Paddy Griffith, *The Art of War of Revolutionary France, 1789–1802* (London: Greenhill, 1998), p.183.

10 Phipps, *Nord*, pp.180–181; *Général de Division* Auguste Marie Henri Picot de Dampierre, *Général de Division* Adam Philippe, Comte de Custine.

11 Fortescue, *History*, vol. IV, pt.1, p.90.

accused of treason and went to the guillotine 28 August 1793. Thus, a terrible precedent had been set.

Kilmaine subsequently took command of the Armée du Nord (17 July) and following the fall of Valenciennes, the allies had a choice to make.[12] They could have advanced directly on Paris a mere 126 miles away, but the involvement of the British in the attack on Valenciennes had been conditional on Coburg agreeing to subsequently attack Dunkerque. Consequently, the Duke of York, commanding the British contingents, led his troops to the coast to besiege Dunkerque, fighting an insignificant but famous action, the Battle of Lincelles (18 August),[13] along the way. Houchard, who had replaced Kilmaine (11 August), then launched an attack on the positions around Dunkerque (6–8 September). The Duke of York's covering force of Hanoverians and Hessians was defeated at Hondschoote, which in turn forced the Duke to abandon the siege.[14] Despite this victory, Houchard was accused of cowardice for not pursuing with more vigour and he also went to the guillotine (17 November). The allies also failed to take the fortress of Maubeuge, 22 miles east of Valenciennes, a failure hastened by the Battle of Wattignies (15–16 October), where the new commander of the Armée du Nord, Jourdan, with 60,000 men defeated the 30,000 strong Austrian covering force.[15]

The Rhine

On the Rhine frontier, 1792 had ended quietly as the French chose to allow Brunswick to withdraw his forces from Valmy without serious challenge. The campaign on the Rhine in 1793 began with a reorganisation of the French forces, with Custine being given command of the Armée du Rhin, enlarged by the absorption of his own Armée des Vosges in the process (1 March). In the last quarter of 1792, Custine had captured Mainz/Mayence on the west bank of the Rhine, consequently his main concern was to employ his 45,000 men in its defence. On 21 March, Brunswick led his army, comprised of Prussian, Austrian, Saxon and Hessian troops (37,000 men), across the Rhine and proceeded to lay siege to Mainz (10 April) which was garrisoned by 22,000 French commanded by d'Oyre.[16]

Custine retired with the rest of his army to the 'Lines of Wissembourg' along the river Lauter, a tributary of the Rhine. There followed another reorganisation (30 May) with Beauharnais taking command of the Armée du Rhin (60,000 men) under the command of Houchard, who also commanded the Armée de la Moselle (40,000 men).[17] However, these two men were too tardy in their attempt to save Mainz, which fell to the allies on 23 July (they also omitted to inform the garrison that they were coming).[18] The garrison however was released on parole conditions that allowed 16,000 men to be used against the counter-revolutionary forces in the Vendée and elsewhere within France.[19]

12 Jones, *Companion*, p.152; Phipps, *Nord*, p.193; Phipps has Kilmaine taking command 30 July.

13 For more detail on the Battle of Lincelles, see Scenario 1.

14 *Général de Division* Charles-Édouard-Saül Jennings de Kilmaine, suspended because he was of Irish descent; *Général de Division* Jean-Nicolas Houchard.

15 *Général de Division* Jean-Baptiste Jourdan, one of Napoleon's future marshals.

16 *Général de Division* François-Ignace Ervoil d'Oyre.

17 Jones, *Companion*, p.152; *Général de Division* Alexandre François Marie de Beauharnais, first husband of the future Empress Josephine.

18 Ramsay Weston Phipps, *The Armies of the First French Republic, and the Rise of the Marshals of Napoleon I—The Armées de la Moselle, du Rhin, de Sambre-et-Meuse, du Rhin-et-Moselle* (Godmanchester: Ken Trotman, 2012), pp.42–47.

19 Phipps, *Moselle*, p.55.

Beauharnais subsequently lost the confidence of his army and resigned (21 August). He too would be sent to the guillotine (23 July 1794) only a few days before the fall of Robespierre and the end of the 'Terror'. Landremont replaced Beauharnais as commander of the Armée du Rhin (18 August) and began a series of skirmishes with the Austrians and Prussians along the Rhine, particularly around the Lines of Wissembourg (20 August).[20] At the battle of Pirmasens (14 September), Moreaux led 12,000 men of the Corps des Vosges (part of the Armée de la Moselle) in an assault on 8,000 Prussians in prepared positions, command by Brunswick.[21] Despite their significantly superior numbers the three French columns were repulsed. Subsequently, Landremont, a 'suspect' noble was arrested (29 September) and accused of treason. After months of skirmishing and minor clashes, Wurmser led 34,000 Austrians in a successful assault on the Lines of Wissembourg (13 October) and the French fell back to Hagenau.[22] Landremont was replaced by Pichegru (27 October) with Hoche assuming command of the Armée de la Moselle (31 October).[23]

Prussians Calmly Await the French Onslaught

20 *Général de Division* Charles Hyacinthe Leclerc de Landremont.
21 Jean Colin, *Campagne de 1793 en Alsace et dans le Palatinat* (Paris: Chapelot, 1902), vol. I, p.397; Griffith, *Art of War*, p.186; *Général de Division* Jean René Moreaux.
22 *General der Kavallerie* Dagobert Sigmund von Wurmser.
23 *Général de Division* Jean-Charles Pichegru; *Général de Division* Louis Lazare Hoche.

On 17 November Hoche led 36,000 men from the line of the river Sarre with the intention of relieving the garrison of Landau on the west bank of the Rhine. Initially Brunswick's Prussians (26,000 men) fell back before him, but at the Battle of Kaiserslautern they defeated Hoche's three assaults on consecutive days (28–30 November) and by 3 December Hoche had retired to Zweibrücken.[24] Meanwhile Pichegru had thrown his Armée du Rhin at the Austrians to his front and then in collaboration with Hoche drove them back again to the Lines of Wissembourg (22 December).[25] The Prussians then abandoned the blockade of Landau and by Christmas Day the allies were back on the line of the river Rhine.

The Southeast

Our tour of the war in 1793 now moves to the southeast of France, where the most significant events were the counter-revolutionary movements in the three biggest cities Lyon, Marseilles and Toulon. In April 1792 the south of France, both east and west, was relatively undefended, consequently the Armée du Midi was created with responsibility for the vast tracts of France between Lake Geneva and Bordeaux (340 miles as the crow flies). By the end of April 1793, this army had become four, the Armée des Alpes (also known as the Armée de Savoie for a short time), Armée d'Italie (initially the Division du Var of the Armée du Midi), Armée des Pyrénées Orientales and the Armée des Pyrénées Occidentales.[26]

The Armée des Alpes, commanded by Kellermann, started the year guarding against the non-existent threat offered by the Swiss. However, Brunet, in temporary command of the Armée d'Italie (then less than 22,000 men present under arms), launched an attack on the island of Sardinia (8 January), but returned defeated before the end of February.[27] The expedition was marked both by the indiscipline of the volunteer battalions and the presence of *Capitaine* Napoleone di Buonaparte, serving as *lieutenant-colonel en seconde* of the *2e Bataillon Volontaires de la Corse*, who was part of the unsuccessful assault on the island of Maddalena, off the northern coast of Sardinia.[28]

Biron took command of the Armée d'Italie (8 February) and began to push along the coast establishing his right at Sospel.[29] In March the Armée d'Italie had been reduced to 17,000 men present under arms, before undergoing another change of command when Biron was sent to the *Vendée* (4 May) and replaced by Brunet (8 May). Meanwhile having been accused of anti-republican sentiments, the acquitted Kellermann was given overall command of both the Armée des Alpes and the Armée d'Italie (24 May).

In Paris, the 2 June was marked by popular unrest, including the *Gardes Nationales de Paris*, demanding the expulsion and arrest of the 29 Girondin deputies from the Convention. When this was enacted, a wave of unrest swept most of France, protesting the over centralisation of the government in Paris. In the south, this 'Federalist' movement was particularly strong in Lyon, Marseilles and Toulon. In Lyon the

24 Phipps, *Moselle*, p.87.
25 Phipps, *Moselle*, p.99.
26 Ramsey Weston Phipps, *The Armies of the First French Republic, and the Rise of the Marshals of Napoleon I—3. The Armies in the West 1793 to 1797 and the Armies in the South 1792 to 1796* (Godmanchester: Ken Trotman), pp.67, 71.
27 *Maréchal de Camp* Gaspard Jean-Baptiste Brunet.
28 Phipps, *West*, p.80.
29 *Lieutenant Général* Armand Louis de Gontaut, Duc de Biron.

Federalists executed the Jacobin ex-mayor, Chalier (on the guillotine he had himself brought from Paris) and seceded from the Republic.[30] In response Dubois-Crancé, a *Représentant du Peuple en Mission* to the Armée des Alpes, ordered Kellermann to retake Lyon.[31] Kellermann assembled 38,000 men to undertake the siege of Lyon, which began on 9 August. Meanwhile Carteaux led another force, 3,830 men strong, which retook Avignon (27 July), where he was joined by Capitaine Buonaparte, before moving on to retake Marseilles (25 August).[32]

In Toulon the revolt took a different turn, denied food by the Convention in Paris and threatened by the vengeance visited upon Marseille, the Federalists opened negotiations with Vice Admiral Samuel Hood, commanding the Royal Navy's Mediterranean Fleet, and surrendered the port to the British (29 August) along with France's own Mediterranean Fleet. The British demanded that Toulon declared for King Louis XVII.[33]

On the frontier with Piedmont, Brunet launched the Armée d'Italie in a series of attacks on Mont-Authion (approximately 10 miles north of Sospel) during May and June, culminating in the Battle of Saorgio (8–12 June), where the Sardinian defences barred the route through the mountains from Nice to Turin via the Colle di Tenda. Despite some early French success, which gained André Masséna and Sérurier promotions to *général de brigade*, the Sardinians, commanded by the Austrian de Vins, were triumphant, repelling three assaults.[34] As the attacking forces retired having suffered 1,500 casualties, some new French levies in the second line threw down their arms and ran crying 'treason!' Following this failure Brunet was suspended (8 August) by the *Représentants* Barras and Fréron, and Dumerbion took his place.[35] Eventually the *Représentants* Ricord and Robespierre joined the condemnation of Brunet, unfairly describing him as the 'soul of the counter-revolution in the south' to the *Comité du Salut Public*.[36] Consequently, Brunet was sent to the Abbaye prison in Paris, put on trial by the *Tribunal Révolutionnaire* and taken to the guillotine the next day (15 November).[37]

Taking advantage of the internal 'distractions' that the French faced, the forces of Sardinia-Piedmont took the offensive, the Duke of Montferrat advanced down the Little Saint Bernard pass into the valley of the river Isère, while on his left the Marquis de Cordon passed over Mont Cenis into the Maurienne valley of the river Arc (14 August).[38] The defenders from Dubourg's division fell back but further withdrawal would have threatened the French hold on Savoy.[39] Consequently Kellermann, after the usual debate with the *Représentants* and one false start, left the siege of Lyon (31 August) to take charge of the defence of Savoy. Fortunately for the French, the Sardinians lacked coordination and a sense of urgency. Cordon advanced down the Arc to attack the French, expecting to be supported by Montferrat (10 September). Kellermann, with

30 Jones, *Companion*, pp.29–30; Horne, *French Revolution*, p.40.

31 Jones, *Companion*, p.340; Edmond Louis Alexis Dubois-Crancé, a former *Mousquetaire du roi*.

32 Phipps, *West*, p.92; *Général de Brigade* Jean-Baptiste François Carteaux.

33 Townson, *Revolution*, p.77; Sam Willis, *The Glorious First of June, Fleet Battle in the Reign of Terror* (London: Quercus, 2012), p.23.

34 *Feldzeugmeister* (lieutenant-general) Joseph Nikolaus de Vins.

35 Jones, *Companion*, p.111; Paul François Jean-Nicolas, Comte de Barras; Louis Stanislas Fréron (*Représentants* to the Armée des Alpes); *Général de Division* Pierre Jadart du Merbion.

36 Jones, *Companion*, p.110; Jean-François Ricord; Augustin Bon Joseph de Robespierre (the younger brother) (*Représentants* to the Armée d'Italie).

37 Phipps, *West*, pp.85, 95–96.

38 Phipps, *West*, pp.98–99; Prince Maurizio of Savoy, Duke of Montferrat; Victor Amédée Sallier de La Tour, Marquis de Cordon.

39 *Général de Brigade* François Joseph Thorillon Dubourg.

8,000 men, met Cordon's 6,000 men at Epierre (15 September), 33 miles northeast of Grenoble, and following the absence of any support from Montferrat, Cordon was forced to retire having lost 1,000 men (the French losses were 500). By 8 October the Sardinians had been driven back up the Little Saint Bernard and Mont Cenis respectively. Despite this success, having already been replaced by Doppet in the command of the siege of Lyon (25 September), Kellermann was denounced by the *Représentants*, arrested and sent to Paris (11 October).[40] Inconclusive skirmishing along the frontier continued through October, but after Lyon fell to the Republic on 9 October, the focus inexorably moved onto the Siege of Toulon. Throughout the last quarter of 1793 the French massed troops around the port of Toulon, rising from 9,000 (9 September) to 38,000 (11 December), aided by the terms of the surrender of Valenciennes. The garrison of this fortress were released and barred from being employed against the Allied field armies, but they were free to be used against the republic's internal enemies. The besiegers had several commanders, but eventually Dugommier and his artillery commander Du Teil came together and successfully implemented Buonaparte's plan.[41] In a night attack, the key position of Fort Mulgrave was stormed (16/17 December), which prompted Hood to evacuate the port (19 December) and Toulon was reclaimed for the republic. Buonaparte was subsequently promoted *général de brigade*.[42]

The Southwest

The southwest of France was relatively quiet until the declaration of war against Spain (7 March 1793). The Armée des Pyrénées having been formed in 1792 was divided into two forces, the Armée des Pyrénées Orientales and the Armée des Pyrénées Occidentales, covering the frontier with Spain divided by the left bank of the river Garonne (30 April). Both armies were thus responsible for approximately 125 miles of the frontier. The Armée des Pyrénées Occidentales was commanded by Servan, the original commander of the Armée des Pyrénées, who initially had only 10,000 men including only two regular army battalions amongst the 14½ battalions of line infantry.[43] The Armée des Pyrénées Orientales, commanded by de Flers, began the campaign with a field force of 10,800 men, of whom only 2,000 were regulars. A further 10,300 men were on garrison duty.[44]

The Spanish mirrored the French organisation, on their left Caro y Fontes commanded 8,000 regulars and 10,000 militia, covering the provinces of Navarre and Gipuzkoa.[45] In the east, the Ejército de Cataluña, commanded by Ricardos, comprised of some 50,000 men based around Figueras, which reflected the wish of the government to remain on the defensive in the west, while invading France from the east.[46] As a reserve, the Principe de Castelfranco commanded 4,000–5,000 men guarding Aragón.[47] The three Spanish forces were coordinated from the distant Madrid by Godoy, the *capitán general* of the

40 Phipps, *West*, pp.104–105, 108; *Général de Division* François Amédée Doppet, commanded the *Armée des Alpes*.

41 *Général de Division* Jean Coquille Dugommier; *Général de Brigade* Jean Du Teil de Beaumont.

42 Phipps, *West*, pp.110–129: for more detail on the Siege of Toulon, see Scenario 3.

43 Phipps, *West*, p.134; *Général de Division* Joseph Marie Servan de Gerbey, twice briefly minister of war in 1792.

44 Phipps, *West*, p.138; Jones, *Companion*, p.149; *Général de Division* Louis-Charles de La Motte-Ango, Vicomte de Flers.

45 Phipps, *West*, p.244; Alberto Martín-Lanuza Martinez, *Diccionario Biografico del Generalato Espanol: Reinados De Carlos IV y Fernando VII (1788–1833)* (Madrid: Pinares Impresores, 2012), p.177; *Capitán General* Ventura de Caro y Fontes (uncle of Romana of Peninsular War fame).

46 *Capitán General* Antonio Ramón Ricardos y Carrillo de Albornoz.

47 *Teniente Generale* Pablo Sangro Gaetani de Aragón y Merode, Principe de Castelfranco.

army.[48] What followed also became known as the War of Roussillon, named after the region around the French city of Perpignan on the Mediterranean coast at the eastern end of the frontier. The war was known to the Spanish as the War of the Convention.

The city of Bordeaux on the Atlantic Coast declared itself in insurrection as an early adopter of the Federalist movement (9 May). However, despite widespread support across the region, the Federalists could still only raise 400 men for their proposed march on Paris, and the movement petered out (2 August). The government in Paris then sent its avengers who ultimately issued 294 death sentences of which 104 were carried out before the Terror ended.

At the western end of the Pyrenees, Caro y Fontes began the campaign on his left and drove the panicked French volunteers back from the river Bidassoa and captured the *Camp de Jolimont* in the rear.[49] After this failure, with Servan absent, his deputy Duverger was arrested and sent to Paris.[50] Arriving at the front (2 May) Servan pulled his troops back behind the river Nivelle, to give time to organise and train his new troops. Caro y Fontes followed up this success by pushing his right forward towards Château Pignon, six miles south of Saint-Jean-Pied-de-Port (6 June). Despite a successful counterattack on his right which regained the line of the Bidassoa (22 June), Servan was dismissed (4 July) and replaced temporarily by Labourdonnaie, and then by d'Elbhecq, who promptly died (31 August).[51] Desprez-Crassier, who had commanded the Armée du Rhin before Custine, then took command but after the failure of an attack across the Bidassoa at Biriatou, he was also arrested. Stable leadership of the Armée des Pyrénées Occidentales was finally provided by Muller, a favourite of thc *Représentants* (5 October).[52] To prepare for winter, Muller pushed his army, numbering 30,000 men in July, forward on his right to the heights overlooking the Bidassoa, establishing the fortified *Camp des Sans Culottes* (11 November). The centre remained on the river Nivelle at Saint-Pée and Ainhoa, while the left held Saint-Jean-de-Luz. In this position he faced some 20,000 Spanish.[53]

On the Mediterranean coast, before de Flers took command, La Houlière was in command at Perpignan when Ricardos advanced through St Laurent de Cerdans (17 April).[54] A French force of 1,800 men were routed by 4,400 Spaniards at the battle of Céret on the river Tech (20 April).[55] Suspended by the *Représentants*, La Houlière committed suicide (18 June).[56] The command of the army was provisionally given to Chameron (1 May) and then Grandpré before de Flers arrived to take command (14 May).[57] Ricardos, with 15,000 men, attacked Dagobert's division of 5,000 men at the Battle of Mas Deu, approximately 5 miles southwest of Perpignan, driving them back

48 Manuel de Godoy Álvarez de Faria Ríos Sánchez Zarzosa, duque de Alcudia y de Succa.
49 Phipps, *West*, p.145.
50 *Général de Division* Joseph Duverger.
51 *Général de Division* Anne François Augustin de Labourdonnaie; *Général de Division* Pierre-Joseph du Chambge d'Elbhecq; *Général de Division* Jean Étienne Philibert de Prez de Crassier.
52 *Général de Brigade* Jacques Léonard Muller.
53 Phipps, *West*, pp 147–149.
54 *Général de Division* Mathieu Henri Marchant de La Houlière.
55 Smith, *Data Book*, p.45.
56 Stéphane Berthe, *Les représentants du peuple en mission près l'armée des Pyrénées Orientales (1793–1795)* in Jean Sagnes (ed.), *L'Espagne et la France à l'époque de la Révolution française (1793–1807)* (Perpignan: Presses Universitaires, 1993), pp.53–74; the *représentants* at this time were Claude Dominique Côme Fabre, Augustin Jacques Leyris, Pierre François-Dominique Bonnet and Joseph-Étienne Projean.
57 *Général de Brigade* Claude Souchon de Chameron; *Général de Brigade* Louis d'Arut de Grandpré.

in disorder (20 May).[58] Dagobert's fleeing men swept away de Flers' reinforcements advancing from Perpignan. This success allowed Ricardos to besiege and capture the fortress of Bellegarde on the main road (24 June). De Flers formed the fortified *Camp de l'Union*, under the walls of Perpignan, where he was allowed to spend six weeks training his 12,000 men. Ricardos then attempted to assault this camp with a frontal assault but was repulsed (17 July). It was not all good news for de Flers as two battalions of *Garde Nationale* volunteers had to be disbanded for attempting to desert en masse.[59] Ricardos created an armed camp of his own at Ponteilla, six miles southwest of Perpignan and captured Villefranche de Conflent on the river Têt, to the west of Perpignan (4 August).

When in a subsequent conference with his generals, de Flers declared that he had no alternative but to act on the defensive, the *Représentants* arrested him (16 August) and sent him to Paris, where he was guillotined (22 July 1794). Barbatane was then appointed to command the Armée des Pyrénées Orientales but when Ricardos advanced to almost surround Perpignan, Barbatane panicked and abandoned his army.[60] Dagobert was placed in temporary command (18 September) and soon won two small victories, at Puigcerdà (28 August) and Peyrestortes (17 September). However, he and his 22,000 men were then defeated by 17,000 men commanded by Ricardos at the battle of Trouillas (22 September), seven miles southwest of Perpignan. Dagobert then resigned his position as army commander, preferring to command his division instead. The *Représentants* then appointed the inexperienced, 30-year-old d'Aoust to the command (29 September).[61] Further, ultimately indecisive, fighting occurred throughout October including at Boulu, where Ricardos with 15,000 men defeated d'Aoust's 16,000 troops (3 October) and at the *Batterie du Sang* (14 October). Reinforced by 5,000 Portuguese troops, Ricardos took the defensive works at Saint Férréol to the north of Céret (26 November). Doppet, fresh from the siege of Lyon, then arrived to assume command of the Armée des Pyrénées Orientales (28 November). Ricardos then attacked and captured the French works at Villalongue while its garrison of 3,000 men was absent trying to attack the Spanish positions.

The French garrison, finding themselves potentially cut off by Spanish cavalry, broke and ran for the ford over the Têt at Brouilla (7 December). Doppet now planned to draw back his troops to the *Camp de l'Union* and covered this withdrawal by an assault on the Spanish fortifications at Villalongue dels Monts, 12 miles south of Perpignan. D'Aoust led 2,000 men in this assault, which was a great success, and the Portuguese garrison was ejected with great loss. The future *Maréchal* Lannes led 500 grenadiers in the attack.[62] Following this attack Doppet took to his sick bed for 10 weeks and d'Aoust formally took command of the army. However, the Spanish soon counter-attacked, La Cuesta, at the head of 8,000 Spaniards and Portuguese, attacked Delattre, at the head of 5,000 troops and seized the fort at Saint Elme and the major fort at Collioure, 15 miles southeast of Perpignan, thus driving the French from the coast (20 December).[63] During these events *Représentant* Fabre was killed in action at Port Vendres.[64] These

58 Phipps, *West*, p.152: *Général de Division* Luc Siméon Auguste Dagobert de Fontenille.

59 Smith, *Data Book*, p.49; Skirmish at Niel.

60 *Général de Division* Hilarion Paul Puget de Barbantane.

61 Eustache Charles Joseph d'Aoust; *Général de Brigade* 2 June 1793, *Général de Division* 7 August 1793.

62 *Capitaine* Jean Lannes commanded the advance guard of *Général de Brigade* Jean-Jacques de Laterrade's brigade.

63 *Teniente General* Gregorio García de la Cuesta y Fernández de Celis, of Peninsular War fame; *Général de Brigade* Louis Pierre François Delattre.

64 Jones, *Companion*, p.346.

events forced d'Aoust to retire on Perpignan once again, and 1793 ended with the Spanish holding a bridgehead inside France. Unfortunately, success at Villalongue was insufficient to offset the loss of Collioure, and d'Aoust, denounced by Turreau and Doppet, was arrested by a fresh batch of *Représentants* (10 January 1794), who sent him to Paris and the guillotine (2 July 1794, aged 31).[65]

The West

In the west of France, the war was altogether of a different nature, comprising as it did of a profoundly serious counter-revolution and its bloody suppression. At the beginning of the revolution, the National Assembly had taken the principles of the revolution to the church, confiscating the church lands, dissolving the monasteries, and removing the privileges of the clergy. The Civil Constitution of the Clergy (July 1790) split the clergy between 'constitutionalists' and 'dissidents'. It has been described as the point when the revolution 'went wrong', beginning a civil war, and gave every other power in Europe *casus belli* supported by the Pope.[66]

The Vendée in Western France became a hotbed of dissent, largely ignoring the Constitution of the Clergy. This dissent broke out into armed rebellion when the Convention announced the conscription of 300,000 men (24 February). When the news of this conscription spread to the departments in the west in the first week of March, people gathered in great numbers throughout the countryside. The spark came in the capital town of *Les Mauges*, when 500–600 young men gathered and swore to disobey the new laws (4 March). The following day bands of men scoured the countryside for weapons. A week later the first shot was fired when the authorities in *Saint-Florent le Vieil* attempted to proceed with the drawing of lots for the conscription (12 March).[67] The countryside in the west, with its many woods, thick hedges and deep ditches provided the perfect terrain for an insurrection. The early months of the conflict were characterised by many small-scale clashes between small groups of rebels and the scattered and ill-prepared Republican *Garde Nationale*.[68] For example, Marcé led 2,400 Republican troops with nine guns from La Rochelle towards Nantes. When they tried to storm the *Pont de Gravereau* across the *Petit Ley*, his men, unable to stand the fire of the rebels shooting at them from the behind the thick hedges, fled (19 March).[69] Small though this defeat was, it was enough for Marcé to be sent to the guillotine (19 January 1794).

The *Convention Nationale* created the Armée des Côtes de la Manche, under the command of Labourdonnaie, with responsibility for the Atlantic coast between the Gironde and the Somme, thus including the Vendée (1 March 1793).[70] This was however a temporary arrangement and after a short-lived intermediate measure, the army was reorganised as the Armée des Côtes de La Rochelle responsible for the region from the mouth of the Gironde to that of the Loire, the Armée des Côtes de Brest covering the

65 Jones, *Companion*, p.149; *Général de Division* Louis-Marie Turreau; on paper he was the commander of the army from 12 October to 21 November, but he was not favoured by the *représentants* and was unable to take command.

66 Horne, *French Revolution*, p.22; Blanning, *Revolutionary Wars*, p.50.

67 Michael Ross, *Banners of the King, the War of the Vendée 1793–1794* (London: Seeley Service & Co., 1975), pp.58–63.

68 Phipps, *West*, p.6; Ross, *Banners*, pp.66–109.

69 Ross, *Banners*, pp.96–99; *Général de Division* Louis Henri François de Marcé, commanding the *12e Division Militaire*.

70 Phipps, *West*, p.9; *Général de Division* Anne François Augustin de Labourdonnaie.

coast from the Loire to Saint Malo and the Armée des Côtes de Cherbourg covering the coast from Saint Malo to the mouth of the Authie, the river beyond the Somme.[71] When the Federalist revolt erupted in May, Wimpffen, the commander of the Armée des Côtes de Cherbourg, declared for the rebels.[72] Wimpffen was unable to rally many men to his cause, but in July his deputy Puisaye, led 3,000 volunteers from Caen towards Paris.[73] The march was stopped at Château de Brécourt outside of the city of Vernon on the river Seine, by 1,200 Republican troops led by Sepher and his chief of staff, the future *Maréchal* Brune.[74] The sound of the Republican's artillery alone was sufficient to rout the Federalist volunteers. The collapse of the Federalist revolt in Normandy sent Wimpffen into hiding but he survived to serve the First Empire.

The response of the Republic to the insurrections was brutal, and the death penalty without appeal was introduced for any rebels found carrying arms (19 March).[75]

In April 1793 three rebel or Royalist armies were active in the region; the Armée d'Anjou et du Haut-Poitou (also known as the Grande Armée), recruited largely from *Les Mauges*, the Armée du Centre, recruited largely from the *Bocage Vendéan*, and the Armée de Bas Poitou (also known as the Armée de Marais). Initially, each of these armies were under the joint command of their senior leaders or *divisionnaires*.[76] Each of the armies would also assume the prefix *Armées catholique et royale* signalling their joint goals of restoring the church and the monarchy.

The Republican Armée des Côtes de La Rochelle was commanded by Biron after he arrived from the Armée d'Italie (29 May). A division of this army, the Armée de Saumur, was commanded by Menou with another future *maréchal*, Berthier, as his chief of staff. Menou held the city of Saumur with 7,000–8,000 men, when he was attacked by Jacques Cathelineau at the head of 25,000–30,000 *Vendéan* rebels (11 June).[77] Many of the Republicans panicked and ran in the face of the rebel charges, who were then able to occupy Saumur. Casualties were 4,500 Republicans against less than 400 for the rebels.

Cathelineau (the elected generalissimo), d'Elbée, De la Rochejaquelein, Stofflet and Donnissan led 40,000 Royalists against Nantes, supported by a further 10,000 commanded by Charette (29 June). The city was defended by its military governor, Beysser, with 12,000 men and when Cathelineau was fatally wounded the Royalists were repulsed, despite having advanced to the city centre.[78] This victory has been described as a second Valmy, saving the revolution.[79] Within a few days of this victory, Beysser sided with the Federalists, which ultimately led him to the guillotine in 1794.

At Châtillon-sur-Sèvre (5 July) de la Rochejaquelein, at the head of 20,000 Royalists, defeated Westermann's similar-sized Republican force, inflicting 5,000 casualties and losing only 2,000.[80]

---

71 Phipps, *West*, p.10.

72 Phipps, West, p.10; *Général de Division* Georges Félix de Wimpffen.

73 *Lieutenant-Colonel* Joseph-Geneviève, Comte de Puisaye.

74 *Général de Brigade* Charles Guillaume Sepher; *Chef de Brigade* Guillaume Marie-Anne Brune.

75 Jones, *Companion*, p.196.

76 Ross, *Banners*, p.103.

77 Phipps, *West*, p.15; *Général de Brigade* Jacques-François de Menou, Baron of Boussay; *Général de Brigade* Louis-Alexandre Berthier.

78 Ross, *Banners*, pp.157–165; Jacques Cathelineau; Maurice-Joseph-Louis Gigost d'Elbée; Henri du Vergier, Comte de la Rochejaquelein; Jean-Nicolas Stofflet, Marquis de Donnissan; François Athanase de Charette de la Contrie; *Général de Brigade* Jean-Michel Beysser.

79 Esdaile, *Wars*, p.188.

80 Smith, *Data Book*, p.48; *Général de Division* François Joseph Westermann.

Vive le Roi! Vendéan Counter-Revolutionaries

Frustrated with the local politics, Biron resigned his command (13 July), but in so doing, fatally criticised the *Représentants* who arrested him. Biron, accused of treason and complicity with Brunet, went to guillotine before the year was out (31 December). Rossignol, who replaced Biron (24 July), was a 'true patriot' but he was totally unfit for this command, as he had only been a *chef de bataillon* until as recently as April.[81] La Barolière, commanding the Armée de Saumur now reorganised by Berthier, determined to move from Saumur towards the centre of the revolt, and began to advance, repelling *Vendéan* attacks (15 and 17 July).[82] At Vihiers, 12,000 *Vendéans*, led by Piron, launched another general assault, again routing the 14,000 Republican troops, who fled back to Saumur losing 5,000 men against *Vendéan* losses of 1,000 (18 July). Davout tried to cover the routing troops with his cavalry.[83]

By the end of July, the Royalist armies had captured towns across four *departements*, Beaupréau, Saint-Florent, Vihiers and their neighbouring parishes in the department of Maine-et-Loire, Châtillon in Deux-Sèvres, Mortagne, Montaigu, Chantonnay, Saint Fùlgent, les Herbiers and Pouzages in the Vendée itself and Machecoul, Clisson, Saint Philbert, l'Ile Bouin and Bourgneuf in Loire-Inférieure.

At Lucon (14 August), Tuncq, commanding 10,000 Republicans, defeated d'Elbée at the head of 35,000 men. However, fortune smiled on d'Elbée at Chantonnay (5 September), where his 20,000 Royalists defeated Lecomte's 8,000 men.[84]

81 Phipps, *West*, p.22; *Général de Division* Jean Antoine Rossignol.

82 Phipps, *West*, p.18; *Général de Division* Jacques-Marguerite Pilotte de La Barollière.

83 Dominique Piron de la Vienne; *Général de Brigade* Louis-Nicolas Davout.

84 Smith, *Data Book*, pp.51, 53; *Général de Division* Augustin Tuncq, *Général de Brigade* René François Lecomte.

The Armée des Côtes de Brest, commanded by Canclaux was reinforced by the paroled garrison of Mainz and embarked on the strategy, also proposed by Biron, of using converging columns designed to keep the Royalist forces from the coast where they could communicate with the Royal Navy, as had happened at Toulon. To complete the isolation of the rebels, the French fleet at Brest was stationed in Quiberon Bay.[85] Canclaux was unsuccessfully attacked in Nantes by the *Vendéans* (4 September) but attempts to advance against the Royalists were defeated as much by the lack of support from Rossignol as from the fighting qualities of the rebels, who were able to fight each Republican force in turn (19 September).[86]

De la Rochejaquelein won another victory at Saint Fulgent (22 September) when his 11,000 men destroyed Mieszkowski's 6,000 strong force, causing 50 percent casualties.[87] In October the Republic's armies were reorganised and the Armée de l'Ouest was created from the Armée du Côtes de La Rochelle, Armée Côtes du Brest and the troops from the Mainz garrison, the new army being commanded by Léchelle (2 October). d'Elbée was one of the killed amongst his 8,000 casualties at the battle of Cholet (17 October), when his 40,000 strong force was defeated by the 25,000 strong Armée de l'Ouest, commanded by Léchelle. The Royalists subsequently retired south across the Loire.[88] However, de la Rochejaquelein was victorious over the pursuing Republicans at Entrames on the river Jouanne (27 October), where his 31,000 men defeated the 25,000 men under Westermann. Following this defeat, the army commander, Léchelle, resigned and took to his sick bed in Nantes, where he died, perhaps by his own hand (11 November).[89]

The victorious rebels then determined on an advance across the Loire into Normandy, advocated by the noted Royalist, Talmont.[90] The plan was to seize a port on the Channel coast from which they could be resupplied by the Royal Navy. The army, some 60,000 strong, well supplied with ammunition, met no resistance as it advanced through Mayenne, Ernée and Fougères, indiscriminately killing the fleeing Republican officials and soldiers as it went (5 November).[91]

De la Rochejaquelein was then beaten by Peyre's 5,000 men from the Armée des Côtes de Cherbourg, at the heavily fortified port of Granville on the Gulf of St. Malo (14–15 November).[92] Following this defeat the decision was made to withdraw the Royalist army south across the Loire, but en route they managed to inflict further defeats on the Republicans at a series of actions at Dol-en-Bretagne(29 miles north of Rennes), Pontorson and Antrain (20–22 November). By this time the Republicans were again commanded by Rossignol, who had taken command of the Armée de l'Ouest (14 November) as well as the Armée des Côtes de Brest. Rossignol managed to lose 8,000 of his 25,000 troops, while the victor de la Rochejaquelein lost only 2,000 of his 20,000 men.[93] The Republicans fell back to Rennes and the Royalists marched southeast with the intention of crossing the Loire at Angers. However, the Republican garrison of

85 Phipps, *West*, p.22; Willis, *Fleet Battle*, p.25; *Général de Division* Jean-Baptiste-Camille de Canclaux.
86 Phipps, *West*, p.26.
87 Smith, *Data Book*, p.56; *Général de Brigade* Jean Quirin de Mieszkowski.
88 Smith, *Data Book*, p.59; Jones, *Companion*, pp.150,155; *Général de Division* Jean Léchelle.
89 Ross, *Banners*, pp.245–248.
90 Ross, *Banners*, p.251; Antoine Philippe de La Trémoïlle, Prince de Talmont.
91 Ross, *Banners*, pp.255–256; Phipps, *West*, p.29.
92 Smith, *Data Book*, p.61; *Général de Brigade* André Pacifique Peyre.
93 Smith, *Data Book*, p.62; Jones, *Companion*, p.148, 155; Ross, *Banners*, pp.276–293.

Angers repelled the ill-prepared Royalist assault with ease (3 December). Frustrated, de la Rochejaquelein lead his now demoralised men 49 miles northeast towards Le Mans. Meanwhile, Rossignol resigned his command of the Armée de l'Ouest (4 December) and in the interim was replaced by Marceau.[94]

Having sailed from Portsmouth (1 December) Rear Admiral MacBride's squadron of the Royal Navy belatedly arrived off Cherbourg and Saint-Vaast-la-Hougue, with Moira's force of eight battalions and one hundred gunners to support the Royalist forces, but failing to contact them, withdrew.[95]

As the Republicans attempted to concentrate their forces on Le Mans, Westermann determined to surprise the unfortified town with a force of only 1,500 men. The surprise attack routed the dispirited Royalists, who fled *en masse* (12–13 December) retreating in the direction of Nantes at the mouth of the Loire. Marceau concentrated his 20,000 men beyond Blain confronting the remnants of the Royalist army, now numbering only 1,000 men, a mile from Savenay. The Armée Catholique et Royale d'Anjou et du Haut-Poitou was about to fight its last battle, with the result never in doubt, although these last few stood their ground until overwhelmed (23 December). In the aftermath, thousands of those *Vendéans* following their army were killed in the vengeful pursuit, including in the infamous mass drownings in Nantes. The crossing of the Loire had been a strategic mistake and now perhaps 80,000–100,000 dead littered the roads of Mayenne, La Sarthe and Brittany.[96] The vengeance of the Republic would continue into the new year.

Overseas

Away from Metropolitan France, there were no major fleet actions during 1793. However, the effects of the revolution were immediately felt in France's West Indian colonies. The declaration of *liberté*, *égalité* and *fraternité* was clearly disruptive to these colonies, whose economies were based on slavery. Furthermore, the owners of these slaves were largely from the same noble families who were key targets of the revolutionaries. In March a French fleet sent from Brest to the West Indies got no further than the Bay of Biscay. Once Britain was at war, the American born Cuyler with 500 men, transported from Barbados by Laforey's squadron, captured Tobago, with only a 'trifling loss' in the assault (14 April). This success was not repeated when Cuyler's successor, Bruce, led 1,100 men, transported by Gardner's squadron, against Martinique. Promised Royalist levies panicked when the assault began and Bruce was forced to re-embark for Barbados (21 June).[97] In Saint Domingue (modern day Haiti), the nobles appealed to the British for protection and Whitelocke, with a force of 700 men, left Jamaica in Ford's squadron of frigates, arriving off Jérémie on the southern peninsular (19 September). Subsequently, Môle-Saint-Nicolas and Léogâne were also occupied.[98]

---

94 Jones, *Companion*, p.155; Ross, *Banners*, p.301; *Général de Division* François Séverin Marceau-Desgraviers.

95 Fortescue, *History*, vol. IV, pt.1, pp.154–155; Rear Admiral John MacBride, Major-General Francis Edward Rawdon-Hastings, Earl of Moira.

96 Ross, *Banners*, pp.318–321.

97 Fortescue, *History*, vol. IV, pt.1, pp.134–135; Colonel Sir Cornelius Cuyler (55th Foot), Commander-in-Chief, West Indies; Vice Admiral Sir John Laforey; Major-General Thomas Bruce, Rear Admiral Gardner. Laforey and Gardner were consecutive commanders-in-chief of the Leeward Islands station.

98 Fortescue, *History*, vol. IV, pt.1, pp.330–331; Lieutenant-Colonel John Whitelocke, 13th Foot of Buenes Aires fame; Commodore John Ford, Commander-in-Chief, Jamaica station.

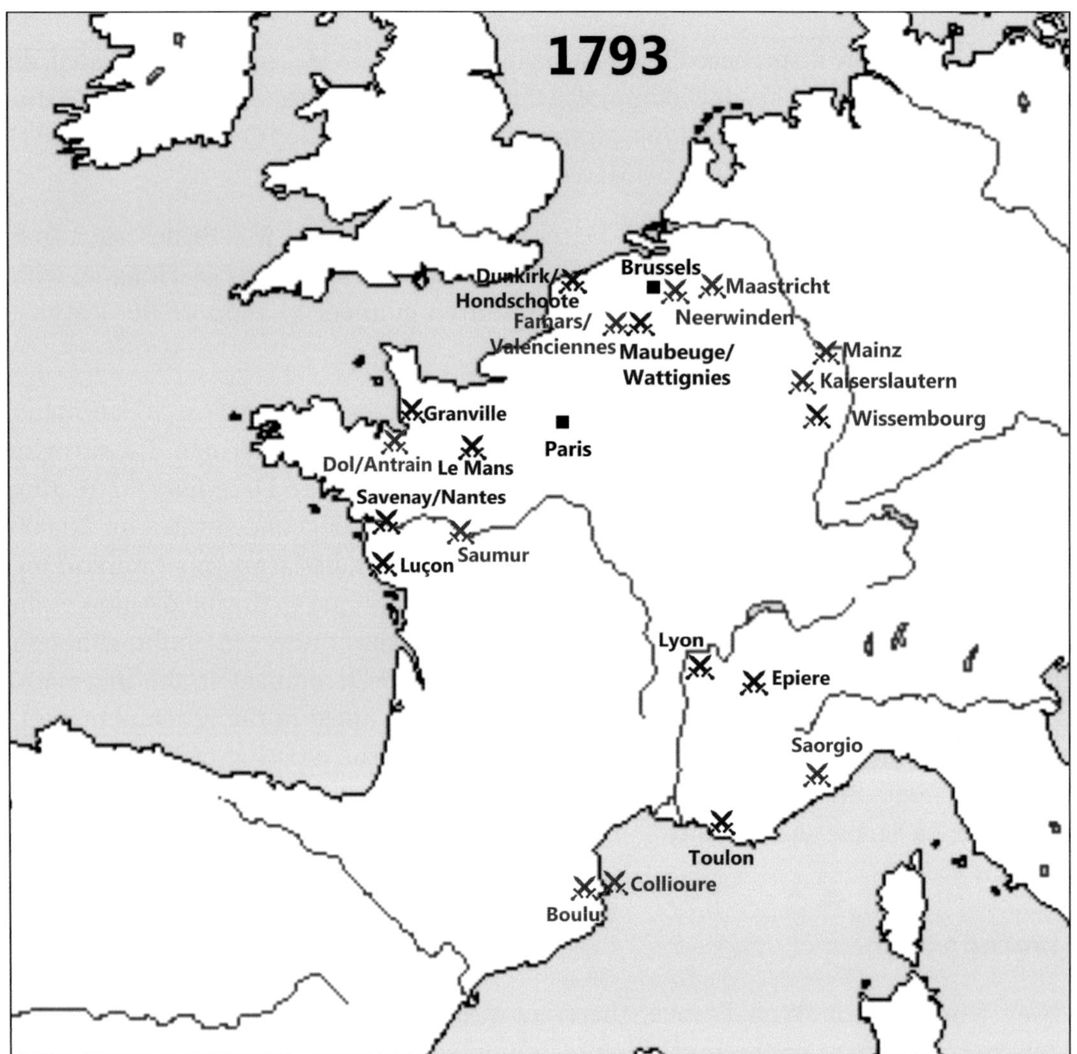

Map 3 – Key actions and battles, 1793

Further north, Captain William Affleck (HMS *Alligator*) transported Brigadier General James Ogilvie and 300 men to seize from the French the oft disputed island fishing bases of Saint Pierre and Miquelon, off Newfoundland (14 May).[99]

In November Sir Charles Grey's expedition set out from Portsmouth for the West Indies, targeting the key French colonies of Martinique, Saint Lucia and Guadeloupe.[100]

Nearer to home, the first major French ship captured during the war, the frigate *Cléopâtre* (40) was taken by HMS *Nymphe* (36), off the Devon coast (18 June). For this action the victorious captain, Edward Pellew, was knighted.

99 Willis, *Fleet Battle*, p.6; Ogilvie was lieutenant-colonel in the 4th Foot, and his report to Dundas is available at: <http://grandcolombier.com/2010/10/09/1793-letters-from-brigadier-general-ogilvie-and-captain-william-affleck-about-the-surrender-of-st-pierre-and-miquelon/>, accessed 14 February 2022.

100 Fortescue, *History*, vol. IV, pt.1, p.351; Lieutenant-General Sir Charles Grey, 2nd Earl Grey.

Other naval engagements during 1793 include:[101]

Theatre	Date	Action
Home waters	13 March	HMS *Scourge* (8) captured the privateer *San Culotte* (12), in the Channel.
	11 April	HMS *Bedford* (74) and HMS *Leopard* (50) fired on each other at night off Scilly.
	20 October	HMS *Crescent* (36) captured the *Réunion* (36) off Cape Barfleur.
	24 October	HMS *Thames* (32) captured by the *Uranie* (38), *Carmagnole* (42), *Résolue* (32) and *Sémillante* (32) 154 miles southwest of Brest.
	19 November	HMS *Latona* (36) engaged two French frigates in the Channel.
Mediterranean	13 May	HMS *Iris* (32) dismasted by the French privateer *Citoyenne Française* (34).
	22 October	HMS *Agamemnon* (64) commanded by Captain Horatio Nelson engaged a French frigate squadron of the *Melpomène* (40), *Minerve* (40), *Fortunée* (36), *Mignonne* (28) and the *Hasard* (14) off Sardinia.
North America	25 July	HMS *Pluto* (14) captured the French brig *Lutin* (16) off Newfoundland.
	31 July	HMS *Boston* (32) engaged the *Embuscade* (34) off Newfoundland.
West Indies	25 May	The French frigate *Concorde* (40) captured HMS *Hyaena* (24) off Hispaniola.
	25 November	HMS *Penelope* (32) and HMS *Iphigenia* (32) captured the French frigate *Inconstante* (36)

In summary, during 1793 the French Republic eventually deployed 983,000 men in its armies to defy their internal and external enemies.[102] The armies of the Republic had fought 35 battles involving 20,000 men or more, winning 14 and losing 21. They had also fought 45 lesser actions, winning 15 and losing 30.[103] In the process, nine generals commanding these armies had been or were about to be sent to the guillotine. Despite their disorganised, poorly supplied and under trained armies losing most of the actions in the war, the Republic had survived by winning key battles at key moments, bringing large numbers of volunteers and conscripts to the field. The First Coalition was thus frustrated, and the war continued.

101 Isaac Schomberg, *Naval Chronology or, an Historical Summary of Naval and Maritime Events from the Time of the Romans, to the Treaty of Peace 1802* (London: T. Egerton, 1802), vol. II, pp.230–231, 233–236, 253; William James, *The Naval History of Great Britain from the Declaration of War by France In 1793 to the Accession of King George IV* (London: Richard Bentley, 1859), vol. I, p.117); these lists given above are not exhaustive but focus on ship to ship actions largely involving ships with more than 20 guns as recorded in Schomberg. Numerous other actions including commerce raiding are listed in James.

102 Jones, *Companion*, p.156.

103 Smith, *Data Book*, pp.39–66; clearly this list is understandably not exhaustive and other, particularly minor, actions could have been included. However, the picture created is a good representation of the war in 1793.

Hussards de la Mort and 25e or 31e Infanterie

The War in 1794

The North

For the Armée du Nord, 1794 began inauspiciously, with its commander, Jourdan, summoned to Paris to defend his inability to prevent minor incursions across the border by the allies. With Jourdan in domestic exile, Pichegru was sent to replace him at the head of the Armée du Nord, taking command 8 February 1794.[104] During the first quarter of the year the French made 45 small but harassing attacks across the border with the Austrian Netherlands, ensuring that Coburg's army gained little rest during the winter.[105] In March 1794, Pichegru commanded 126,000 men in the field army of the Armée du Nord, with a further 69,000 dispersed in the various garrisons, plus the 33,000 men of the Armée des Ardennes of which 7,000 men were available as a field force.[106] Against this force the allies could bring but 120,000 men into the field with a further 40,000 dispersed in garrisons.

These armies were deployed across an extensive front, with the allies stretching from Nieuwpoort on the Channel coast through Ypres, Menin and Tournai, Valenciennes in the centre, Dinant and Namur on the river Meuse and onto Trier on the river Moselle on the Allied left. In all the front extended more than 210 miles.[107] Carnot proposed

104 Phipps, *Nord*, pp.272–273, 275; *Général de Division* Jean-Charles Pichegru.
105 Fortescue, *History*, vol. IV, pt.1, pp.223–224.
106 Phipps, *Nord*, p.284.
107 Fortescue, *History*, vol. IV, pt.1, pp.226–227.

to Pichegru that the superior French force should execute a double envelopment of the allies, advancing both through Ypres to Ghent on the left and through Namur and Liège on the right. However, after 30,000 of his men were repulsed at Le Cateau (29 March), Pichegru ceased offensive operations claiming that 'it was dangerous to match his young troops against the enemy so soon'.[108] Consequently the allies struck the first serious blow of the campaign by advancing to besiege the fortress of Landrecies, 58 miles southwest of Brussels (17 April). With Pichegru absent with the left wing of his army, Ferrand led the divisions of the right wing of the Armée du Nord in an attempt to relieve Landrecies.

As the French advanced, a mixed force of Austrian and British cavalry broke 3,000 French infantry and their supporting cavalry at Villers-en-Cauchies (24 April). As three divisions of French infantry (100,000 men) attempted to converge on Landrecies they were defeated in detail during the Battle of Le Cateau (26 April), the worst fate befalling Chapuis at Troisvilles, who was captured with thousands of his men when the Austrian and British cavalry charged into their open flank.[109] The French also lost 40 guns.[110] While these events were unfolding, Pichegru led the French left forward to threaten Menin. Clerfayt attempted to support Menin but was beaten back by Souham at Mouscron (28/29 April) and nothing could then prevent the fall of Menin (30 April).[111] However, Landrecies fell to the allies that same day and they were now free to fall on Pichegru's left. However, screening Clerfayt with Moreau's division,[112] Pichegru sent

British Light Dragoons Charging French Chasseurs à Cheval in the Flank

108 Fortescue, *History*, vol. IV, pt.1, p.229.

109 *Général de Brigade* René-Bernard Chapuis or Chapuy.

110 Phipps, *Nord*, pp.286–288; Fortescue, *History*, vol. IV, pt.1, pp.237–243.

111 Smith, *Data Book*, p.76; *Feldmarschallleutnant* François Sébastien Charles Joseph de Croix, Count of Clairfeyt (or Clerfayt); *Général de Division* Joseph Souham.

112 *Général de Division* Jean-Victor Moreau.

two columns along the axis provided by the Lille – Tournai Road, to attack the Duke of York's position between Lamain and Hertain (four miles west of Tournai). However, this attack was unsuccessful, with the French withdrawing to their start line behind the river Lys near Menin.

The day has gone down in history for the action at Willems, where the Duke of York sent his strong cavalry against the retiring French infantry. Unlike in previous actions, the French infantry proved capable of forming steady squares and held off the cavalry, firmly resisting nine charges. Eventually the battalion guns of the supporting British infantry arrived, and their fire proved the decisive factor, causing the French infantry to waver. The British cavalry, having already seen off their opposite numbers, were then able to successfully charge the French infantry riding down three squares inflicting 1,000–2,000 casualties and taking 400 prisoners and 13 guns (10 May).[113]

The action at Willems was part of the larger Battle of Courtrai and having blocked Clerfayt's attempt to capture Courtrai (10 May), Souham forced Clerfayt's Anglo-Austrian force from his position at Lendelede and drove them back eight miles northeast to Tielt (11 May). The Duke of York himself also retired to Tournai, in the face of the superior French numbers.[114] The Austrian chief of staff Mack then put into motion a grand concentric attack by six separate columns, totalling 74,000 men, with the goal of encircling the divisions of Souham and Moreau.[115] However, this Battle of Tourcoing turned into a disaster for the allies when Souham, in the absence of Pichegru, decided on a counterstroke. With some of the other columns failing to get into position promptly, the Duke of York's column, 10,500 men strong, became isolated and was overwhelmed losing 19 of its 28 guns. At one point the Duke of York himself was almost captured (17–18 May).[116] The British were spared greater losses by Clerfayt's advance from the north, which demanded Souham's attention.[117] Returning from his army's right wing, Pichegru then ordered an attack on Tournai which was beaten off (22 May).

The allies followed up this victory with another gained by Kaunitz's Austro-Dutch force of 24,000 men, the left wing of Coburg's army, who defeated Charbonnier's attempt to lead the Armée des Ardennes across the river Sambre at Erquelinnes, 16 miles southwest of Charleroi (24 May).[118] This was only one of several French attacks across the Sambre between 11 May and 3 June, each of which was repulsed.[119] Mack, dejected after the defeat at Tourcoing resigned from his post as chief of staff and the emperor began to consider abandoning the Austrian Netherlands altogether.

The French then attacked the Allied right flank, advancing to besiege Ypres (1 June), before again attacking their left at Charleroi (3 June). Three Allied attempts to relieve Ypres were defeated at Vry-Bosch (6 June), Roeselare (10 June) and Hooglede (13 June), before the fortress surrendered (18 June). In the centre, Jourdan advanced to besiege the fortified town of Charleroi on the river Sambre. Advancing across the river he began the siege and advanced to cover it with 58,000 men. However, the Prince of Orange attacked with 43,000 men (both Austrians and Dutch) and drove the French

113 Phipps, *Nord*, p.294–295; Fortescue, *History*, vol. IV, pt.1, pp.248–250.
114 Fortescue, *History*, vol. IV, pt.1, pp.250–251.
115 *Generalmajor* Karl Freiherr Mack von Leiberich.
116 Fortescue, *History*, vol. IV, pt.1, pp.256–269.
117 Phipps, *Nord*, p.305.
118 Smith, *Data Book*, p.81; *Feldmarschallleutnant* Franz Wenzel, Graf von Kaunitz-Rietberg; *Général de Division* Louis Charbonnier.
119 Phipps, *Moselle*, p.147.

Compagnie Aérostiers and their Balloon

back across the Sambre at the Battle of Lambusart (16 June). Undeterred, Jourdan recrossed the Sambre to continue the siege of Charleroi (18 June).[120] Coburg attempted to relieve Charleroi but was repulsed by Jourdan commanding his own Armée de la Moselle as well as the Armée des Ardennes and elements of the Armée du Nord at the Battle of Fleurus (26 June). This battle turned out to be decisive for the campaign but was also noteworthy for the first battlefield use of an observation balloon, the *Entreprenant*, although its observations did not impress Jourdan and his generals. Charleroi fell the same day.[121]

On the Channel coast, some British reinforcements arrived in Ostend, (25 June), including Lieutenant-Colonel Arthur Wesley (33rd Foot), the future Duke of Wellington. Meanwhile, Pichegru's left wing both threatened Ostend and advanced to threaten Oudenarde on the river Scheldt, behind the Duke of York's position at Tournai (28 June). With Pichegru's Armée du Nord extended over a 180-mile front from Dunkerque to Longwy, there was now a reorganisation of the French armies. The units that had won the battle of Fleurus, the Armée des Ardennes and elements of the right wing of the Nord and the Armée de la Moselle were united to form the new Armée du Sambre-et-Meuse, commanded by Jourdan (29 June).[122]

On the coast, Ostend was evacuated (28 June) and Pichegru's men then took Mons (1 July). The Duke of York began his withdrawal from the line of the river Scheldt and the Austrians retired from Tournai (2 July). At a council of war held at Waterloo, Coburg and the Duke of York agreed to defend a new line from Antwerp to Namur via Wavre (5 July), however the next day Jourdan launched attacks along the Austrian line from Braine-le-Comte to Gembloux, pushing the Austrian right back from Braine-le-Comte and Nivelles to Waterloo. Coburg consequently cancelled the outcome of the Waterloo conference and determined to retire further to Tirlemont, 25 miles east of Brussels (7 July), which the French were able to occupy (11 July).[123]

While the Duke of York and the Dutch covered Antwerp, the Armée du Nord and the Armée de Sambre-et-Meuse now occupied a line from Malines through Brussels to Namur, with only the fortresses of Landrecies, Le Quesnoy, Valenciennes and Condé behind them still held by the allies (11 July). Continuing their advance up the coast the French, under Vandamme, took Nieuwpoort, executing the 500 French *émigrés* amongst

120 Phipps, *Moselle*, pp.153–155.

121 Phipps, *Moselle*, pp.159–164, 170–171; Smith *Data Book*, p.85; Smith gives the allies only 41,000 men and gives Jourdan 73,000 men, by including those that were directly involved in the siege.

122 Phipps, *Nord*, pp.314–315.

123 Fortescue, *History*, vol. IV, pt.1, p.287.

the garrison in the ditch of the fortress (18 July).[124] Pressed by superior French numbers the Austrians continued their retirement from Tirlemont to Landen, a further seven miles to the southeast. This uncovered the Duke of York's left flank, and he abandoned Antwerp retiring north to Roosendaal in the United Provinces (24 July). The Austrians retreated still further, crossing the Meuse at Maastricht, to 's-Gravenvoeren and thus the British and Austrians were finally separated.[125]

The transformation in the fortunes of war in the Austrian Netherlands had been brought about, in part, by the *levée en masse*. In July 1794, Pichegru's Armée du Nord, had approximately 83,000 men and Jourdan's Armée de Sambre-et-Meuse had approximately 90,000 men, against these numbers Coburg's Austrian army numbered approximately 48,000 men, the Duke of York's British Army, including its Hanoverian and Hessian auxiliaries, had less than 40,000 men, while the Prince of Orange's Dutch army numbered only 12,000 men or thereabouts. The allies were thus outnumbered by almost two to one. Coburg's defeat at Fleurus led to his replacement by Clerfayt. It was also at this juncture that Maximilien Robespierre fell from power in Paris and went to the guillotine (24 July). His declaration that all British prisoners of war were to be executed could then be more openly ignored by the commanders in the field.[126]

The next task for the French, at the direction of the *Comité du Salut Public*, was to recapture the fortresses on the French border and they duly fell; Landrecies (16 July), Le Quesnoy (16 August), Valenciennes (27 August) and Condé (29 August). In another first, the news of the fall of Le Quesnoy was transmitted the 111 miles to Paris in an hour using the new Chappe telegraph system of semaphore stations.[127]

Meanwhile the French advance continued, Moreau with his division of the Armée du Nord took Sluis, 10 miles northeast of Bruges from a Dutch/Hanoverian garrison (24 August). Pichegru subsequently began to march further northeast from Antwerp to Hoogstraten, driving the Dutch before him and uncovering the Duke of York's flank. The Duke of York consequently was obliged to retire to a line between the fortress of Bois-le-Duc ('s-Hertogenbosch) and the Peel morass, along the river Aa with his outposts forward along the river Dommel, centred on Boxtel (30 August).[128] Despite a successful sortie by its garrison (6 September), Breda, 30 miles northeast of Antwerp, was bypassed by Pichegru's Armée du Nord. Pichegru assailed the position at Boxtel (14 September) which was held by Hammerstein's advanced guard of the Duke of York's army, mainly Hanoverian and Hessian

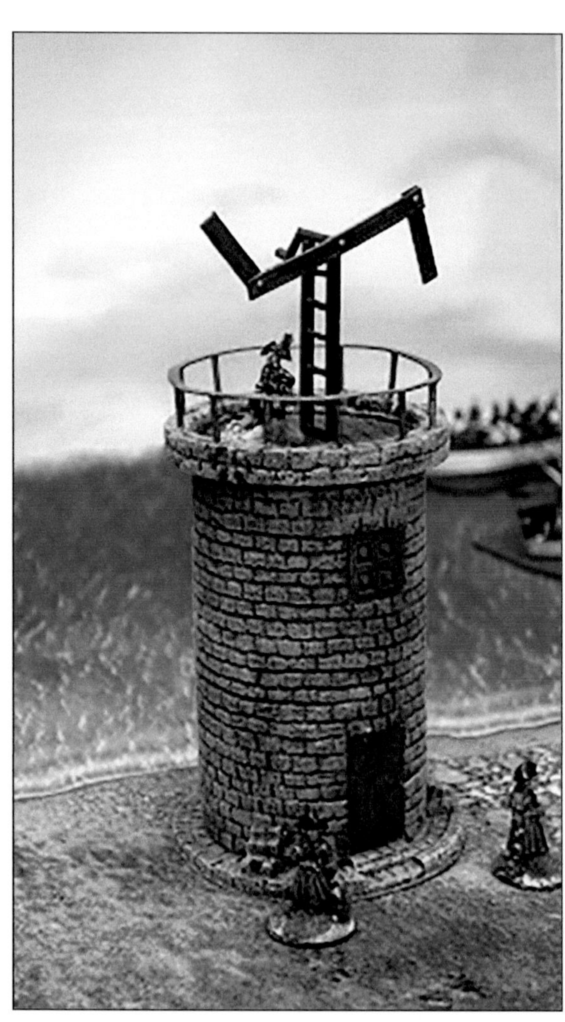
French Telegraph Relay Station

124 Fortescue, *History*, vol. IV, pt.1, p.286; *Général de Brigade* Dominique Joseph René Vandamme.
125 Fortescue, *History*, vol. IV, pt.1, p.290.
126 Phipps, *Nord*, p.322.
127 Phipps, *Moselle*, p.179.
128 Fortescue, *History*, vol. IV, pt.1, p.304; Smith, *Data Book*, pp.87–90.

troops. Hammerstein's force, some 12,000 men, were attacked from multiple directions by up to 60,000 men from Pichegru's army. Positioned too far from the Duke of York's main body to be properly supported, Hammerstein's force was thrown back from the Dommel with heavy losses.[129] Overnight the Duke of York despatched Abercromby with the reserve of his army (approximately 5,000 men) to attempt to retake Boxtel at dawn (15 September), but he was intercepted between Boxtel and Schyndel by Delmas's division and abandoned his attack, retiring to the main camp on the river Aa. This attack is noteworthy as Lieutenant-Colonel Arthur Wesley was commanding one of Abercromby's brigades and helped cover the withdrawal, when the Guards Brigade was hard pressed by the French pursuit.[130]

When Abercromby and his men reached the main British camp at Berlicom on the river Aa, he found that the Duke of York was already in full retreat to the Meuse at Grave. Pichegru used the division of Delmas to prosecute the siege of 's-Hertogenbosch which promptly surrendered (9 October).

In support of Pichegru's advance, Jourdan brought the Armée de Sambre-et-Meuse, now 160,000 men strong, forward to approach Maastricht. Forcing the line of the river Ourthe (14 September), and after defeating Clerfayt at Sprimont (18 September), he was able to advance to the river Roer. Here Clerfayt occupied a position with his right at Roermond on the Meuse then along the Roer from Linnich to Nideggen on his left, thereby screening Cologne. Jourdan attacked Clerfayt's 76,000 men all along this line in the Battle of the Roer. Clerfayt was menaced on both wings, so retired across the Rhine (2 October). Consequently, Jourdan was able to advance further and occupy Cologne (6 October). There Jourdan faced Clerfayt's army extended along the Rhine from Duisburg to Bonn. Along the way, Jourdan left detachments to besiege Venloo and Maastricht.[131]

With Clerfayt now behind the Rhine, the Duke of York was forced to retire from the river Meuse to the river Waal. This line extended from the island of Bommelwaert, held by the Hessians, through Geldermalsen, where the British took over, to the road between Nijmegen and Arnhem, and the Hanoverians guarded the rest of the line to the river Lek. The Austrian line started at Emmerich (3 October).[132] However the Duke of York still held Grave, seven miles further forward, on the Meuse, which fell when Pichegru forced the line of that river (18 October). As they then advanced to the Waal some French hussars, Gendarmerie and light infantry managed to deceive and surprise the 37th Foot at Druten, 12 miles west of Nijmegen along the Waal, effectively destroying the regiment, taking both their colours and battalion guns (19 October, Battle of Puiflijk).[133] In response to Pichegru's growing ill health, Moreau took command of the Armée du Nord (19 October).[134]

129 Paul Demet, *We are Accustomed to do our Duty, German Auxiliaries with the British Army 1793–1795* (Warwick: Helion, 2018), pp.88–93; *Generalmajor* Rudolph Georg Wilhelm von Hammerstein of the Hanoverian service.

130 Garry David Wills, *Wellington's First Battle, Combat for Boxtel, 15 September 1794*, (Grantham, Caseshot Publishing, 2011), pp.13, 22; Lieutenant-General Sir Ralph Abercromby; *Général de Division* Antoine Guillaume Maurailhac Delmas de la Coste.

131 Fortescue, *History*, vol. IV, pt.1, pp.310–311; Phipps, *Moselle*, pp.182–183, 186–187; the Battle of the Roer is also known as the Battle of Aldenhoven.

132 Fortescue, *History*, vol. IV, pt.1, p.309.

133 Fortescue, *History*, vol. IV, pt.1, p.311; Pierre David, *A history of the campaigns of General Pichegru: containing the operations of the armies of the North, and of the Sambre and the Meuse, from March 1794 to March 1795* (London: G.G.J. and J. Robinson, 1796), pp.122–125; G-J.A.N. Derksen, *De Slag bij Puiflijk, oorlog en politiek overschreden een drempel in het land van Maas en Waal* (Soest: Boekscout, 2015), pp.55–61.

134 Jones, *Companion*, p.152; other sources place it a few days earlier.

Bataille d'Aldenhoven, 2 October 1794

With Bernadotte and Ney in the lead Jourdan crossed the Rhine to take Düsseldorf (7 October).[135] While three divisions were sent back to complete the siege of Maastricht, the Armée de Sambre-et-Meuse occupied the line of the Rhine from Bonn on its right through Cologne to Düsseldorf on its left.[136] Venloo fell to the French (27 October) followed promptly by Maastricht (4 November).[137] The Armée du Nord then attacked Nijmegen and despite a successful sortie by the garrison (6 November) the town fell the next day.

The Duke of York was called home for 'consultations' (27 November) and he left Wallmoden as the senior general in the British and Allied army, commanding the Hanoverians, while his junior Harcourt commanded the British troops (2 December).[138] Under pressure from Paris to further eschew winter quarters, Moreau attacked across the river Waal (11 and 13 December) before Pichegru resumed command of the Armée du Nord (15 December). The Waal then froze over (22 December) and the 12,000 French attacked and captured the Fort Sint Andries on the eastern tip of the Bommelerwaard, the 'island' between the Meuse and the Waal, 26 miles west of Nijmegen. The French crossed the Waal to capture Tuil (27 December) but were thrown back across the river by a counterattack led by Dundas (30 December).[139]

135 Phipps, *Moselle*, pp.176–177, 202; *Chef d'Escadron, Adjudant-Général* Michel Ney on the staff of *Général de Division* Jean-Baptiste Kléber's division (he was promoted *chef de brigade*, 10 December); *Général de Brigade* Jean-Baptiste Bernadotte leading the advanced guard of Kléber's division.

136 Phipps, *Moselle*, p.187.

137 Smith, *Data Book*, p.94.

138 Steve Brown, *The Duke of York's Flanders Campaign: Fighting the French Revolution 1793–1795* (Barnsley: Frontline Press, 2018), p.233; Lieutenant-General Johann Ludwig Reichsgraf von Wallmoden-Gimborn; Lieutenant-General William Harcourt, 3rd Earl Harcourt.

139 Brown, *Flanders Campaign*, pp.237–239; Major-General David Dundas.

Massed French Cavalry

The Rhine

On the Upper Rhine frontier, the two French armies, the Armée de la Moselle, 48,000 men (19 February) commanded by Hoche, and the Armée du Rhin, commanded by Michaud, who had taken over from Pichegru (14 January), now separated following the successful relief of Landau. The two changes ended the fractious relationship between Pichegru and Hoche. The Armée du Rhin was deployed along the river from Germersheim, 120 miles south to Basel. Ordered to take Mannheim and Kehl, Michaud refused because his army was exhausted and went into cantonments instead.[140]

The Armée de la Moselle began the year on the river Pfrimm, a left bank tributary of the Rhine, which it joins near the city of Worms, some 30 miles north of Germersheim. Ordered to advance to the northwest on Trier, the army advanced on Birkenfeld before going into cantonments on the river Saar and its tributary, the Blies. However, the successful Hoche, deemed too much of a threat by the government, was arrested and sent to prison in Paris. He was replaced as the commander of the Armée de la Moselle by Jourdan (19 March). Jourdan discovered that of his 100,000-man paper strength, only 48,000 were present under arms. He also had no maps and requested copies of the Ferrari maps. The government in Paris, envisaged that the Armée de la Moselle would advance to take Trier and Liège on its way to assist the Armées du Nord and des Ardennes in the assault on the Netherlands. Jourdan began this movement by occupying Arlon, 16 miles northwest of Luxembourg, with his left, while his right under Moreaux threatened Trier (15 April). Eventually Jourdan marched off to join the Armées du Nord and des Ardennes with just his left wing of four divisions; those of Lefebvre, Championnet, Morlot and Paillard (21 May).[141] Thus, Moreaux remained on the Rhine frontier in command of the rump of the Armée de la Moselle.

Jourdan's departure left the French armies on the Rhine frontier very weak. Moreaux's Armée de la Moselle was on the left, the 25,000 men present under arms were thinly

140 Phipps, *Moselle*, p.119; *Général de Division* Claude Ignace François Michaud.

141 Phipps, *Moselle*, pp.119–121, 127; *Généraux de Division* François Joseph Lefebvre, Jean-Étienne Vachier Championnet, Antoine Morlot and *Général de Brigade* Nicolas-Augustin Paillard.

stretched along the 89 miles from Longwy to Kaiserslautern. Nineteen miles to their right, Michaud's Armée du Rhin had only 30,000 men present under arms, deployed on a short 13-mile line from Neustadt along the river Speyerbach to Speyer on the Rhine, 12 miles south of Mannheim. Moreaux was confronted by the Austrians from Trier and Luxembourg and the right and centre of Möllendorf's Prussians, the left wing of which confronted Michaud.[142] The fighting restarted at Kaiserslautern, where Ambert's division of the Armée de la Moselle, 5,000 strong, was attacked by Möllendorf's Prussian and Saxon force of 46,000 men. It was overwhelmed and thrown back 18 miles to Pirmasens, having lost 1,000 men, 17 guns and two colours (23 May).[143] On the same day, a force of 30,000 Prussians and Austrians, commanded by Hohenlohe, attacked the Armée du Rhin at Schifferstadt, 6 miles northwest of Speyer, however the 20,000 French repelled the attack (23 May). Despite these mixed results Moreaux and Michaud decided to retire, the Armée de la Moselle to the line of the river Saar and the Armée du Rhin back 20 miles to Landau and the lines of the river Queich.[144]

After a failed attack which left Desaix's division dangerously exposed (2 July), both French armies advanced to take Trippstadt, after outflanking the Prussian position on the Schänzel or Steigerkopf mountain (12–13 July). Kaiserslautern was taken (17 July) and the French occupied the line of the river Speyerbach. The Prussians fell back to Mainz and the Austrians returned to the Rhine.[145] Reinforced by 15,000 men from the Vendée, after leaving a flank guard for the Armée du Rhin, Moreaux advanced with 48,000 men northwest towards Trier, which he occupied on 9 August. In the middle of September, Hohelohe led a force of Austrian, Prussian, and Hessen-Darmstadt troops, occupying Kaiserslautern again, and driving off Schaal's 16,000 defenders from the Armée du Rhin (17–20 September).[146] However, the retirement of Clerfayt's Austrians from the Austrian Netherlands to Cologne (2 October), exposed Hohelohe's right flank and he withdrew behind the Rhine.

In the last quarter of the year the French armies on the Rhine were intermingled, and having reached the Rhine, faced a new task. For this purpose, the *Représentants* divided the Armée de la Moselle and the Armée du Rhin into three corps, one for each of three sieges: the Armée devant Luxembourg, the Armée devant Mayence and the Armée devant Mannheim (29 November). To enable this, troops from the Armée de Sambre-et-Meuse took over responsibility for the Rhine from Andernach to Rheinfels from the divisions of the Armée de la Moselle.[147]

Moreaux had taken it upon himself to command this army, and the siege of Luxembourg began 24 November 1794. The Armée devant Luxembourg comprised four divisions of the Moselle, those of Ambert, Debrun, Péduchel and Taponier, giving it a strength of 23,500 men (20 December).[148]

Mayence, or Mainz, on the left bank of the Rhine was the toughest nut to crack, being garrisoned by 22,000 men. Kléber commanded the besieging force of 44,150 men, which was comprised of the divisions of Desaix, Saint-Cyr, Reneaud, Tugnot and

142 Phipps, *Moselle*, p.129; *Generalfeldmarschall* Wichard Joachim Heinrich von Möllendorf.
143 Phipps, *Moselle*, pp.130–131; Smith, *Data Book*, p.81; *Général de Division* Jean-Jacques Ambert.
144 Smith, *Data Book*, p.80; Phipps, *Moselle*, p.132; *Generalmajor Friedrich Ludwig Fürst zu Hohenlohe-Ingelfingen.*
145 Phipps, *Moselle*, p.133; Smith, *Data Book*, p.87; *Général de Division* Louis-Charles Antoine Desaix.
146 Phipps, *Moselle*, p.134; Smith, *Data Book*, p.92; *Général de Brigade* François-Ignace Schaal.
147 Phipps, *Moselle*, p.197; a frontage of 24 miles either side of Coblenz, south of Cologne.
148 Phipps, *Moselle*, p.198; *Généraux de Division* Jean-Baptiste Debrun, Alexandre Camille Taponier and Laurent Gouvion Saint-Cyr; *Général de Brigade* Guillaume Lepéduchelle.

Desbureaux (1 December). Without access to the right bank of the Rhine, the siege was barely a blockade.[149]

Mannheim stood on the right bank of the Rhine with a *tête-de-pont* on the left bank garrisoned by 3,000 men detached from the total garrison of 15,000. The two divisions of Vachot and Vincent comprised Michaud's attacking force. After a bombardment the *tête-de-pont* was evacuated by the garrison and taken by Vachot's division, subsequently Vincent's division was sent to join the Armée devant Mayence (25 December).[150]

The Southeast

In the southeast of France, having cleared the valleys of the rivers Arve (around Faucigny 12 miles southeast of Geneva), Tarentaise and Maurienne, the Armée des Alpes held the line from Montgènevre and Monte Viso to the Camp de Tournoux and onto Isola, a total front of 145 miles. From Isola the Armée d'Italie held the 35-mile-long line through Utelle to Nice on the coast. On the Coalition side, the Piedmontese still held the Little Saint Bernard pass and Mont Cenis.[151] After only four weeks in command of the Armée des Alpes, Carteaux was arrested and imprisoned (22 December 1793). Dumas arrived to take command of the army from its temporary commander Pellapra (21 January).[152] The Armée d'Italie was commanded by the infirm Dumerbion with Masséna and Macquard as his only *généraux de division*. *Général de Brigade* Buonaparte was appointed as the artillery commander (7 February). The Armée des Alpes had less than 40,000 men (4 April), while the Armée d'Italie had 50,000 men. Against these, Sardinia-Piedmont could only field some five to six thousand troops and a thousand militia.[153]

The Armée d'Italie launched its offensive against Colli's Austro-Sardinian defenders, by capturing Oneglia on the coast, 40 miles east of Nice (9 April).[154] This was following a campaign plan devised by Buonaparte, who was influential with the *Représentants*, the intention being to outflank the mountain positions by an advance along the coast.[155] In the mountains, beginning on 5 April and despite some delays, the army advanced to capture Saorge (24 April), Colle Ardente (24 April), La Brigue (27 April), the Colle di Finestre, the Colle di Tenda and the fortified camps of Authion and Mille Fourchies, by the end of May. The Armée d'Italie thus held the main line of the mountains with the routes to the plains of Piedmont now open. Given Dumerbion's infirmity, credit for this success has largely been attributed to Masséna.[156]

Once the snow had gone, after a small setback at Cerisiera on 6 April at the hands of one Sardinian and two Austrian battalions and two squadrons of Austrian dragoons, Dumas led the Armée des Alpes forward to take the Little Saint Bernard (24 April), La

149 Phipps, *Moselle*, p.201; Charles-Pierre-Victor Pajol, *Kléber, sa vie, sa correspondance* (Paris: Firmin-Didot, 1877), p.132; *Généraux de Division* Michel Reneaud and Charles-François Desbureaux; *Général de Brigade* Jean-Henri Tugnot de Lanoye.

150 Phipps, *Moselle*, pp.200–201; *Généraux de Division* Rémy Vincent and Martial Vachot.

151 Phipps, *West*, p.217.

152 Phipps, *West*, p.219; *Généraux de Division* Thomas-Alexandre Dumas Davy de la Pailleterie and Jean-Louis Pellapra.

153 Phipps, *West*, pp.220–222; *Généraux de Division* André Masséna and François Macquard. Macquard's rank was provisional and was not confirmed until January 1795.

154 *Feldmarschallleutnant* Michelangelo Alessandro Colli-Marchi de Vigevano.

155 Phipps, *West*, pp.221, 228.

156 Phipps, *West*, pp.224, 226; Smith, *Data Book*, pp.74–75.

Thuile (25 April) and then Mont Cenis (14 May), the French enthusiastically applying their bayonets in the close combat of mountain warfare.[157]

At a conference at Colmars (25 May) the French commanders and the *Représentants* from both armies attempted to agree a plan for a joint advance into the plains of Piedmont but the Armée des Alpes refused to merge with the Armée d'Italie. The younger Robespierre brother instead took the plan for the invasion of Piedmont to Paris to seek the approval of the *Comité du Salut Public*. Dumas was subsequently relieved of his command, handing over command of the Armée des Alpes to Petitguillaume (4 July). However, the plan became part of the collateral damage following the fall of the older Robespierre brother. On the same day that the Robespierre brothers went to the guillotine (28 July), the *Comité* decided that the Armée d'Italie was to confine itself to the defence of the coast and to providing adequate garrisons for Toulon and Marseille.[158]

With the deliberations in Paris ongoing, the Armée d'Italie advanced further in June to Demonte on the river Stura di Demonte, 56 miles southwest of Turin, with the Sardinians driven back down the river to Cuneo.[159] An indirect consequence of the fall of Robespierre was the suspension and arrest of Buonaparte at the request of the *Représentants* Saliceti, Albitte and Laporte, due to his 'suspicious behaviour' (9 August). Buonaparte was imprisoned in *Fort Carré* in Antibes until the *Représentants* cleared and released him (24 August).[160]

In September the Austro-Sardinians attempted to capture the port of Savona, 25 miles southwest of Genoa, thereby interrupting the French supply line from that city. Advancing down the valley of the Bormida, the Austro-Sardinians paused at Carcare, and a recovered Dumerbion, determined to attack, attempted to surrounded them. Although defeated Wallis slipped away with his Austro-Sardinians at the first battle of Dego (21 September), Dumerbion entered the town the next day and then occupied the port of Vado Ligure, three miles west of Savona. This proved to be Dumerbion's swansong, and he was replaced by Schérer (5 November). A month later Petitguillaume was replaced as the commander of the Armée des Alpes by Moulin and the snow ended the campaign (5 December).[161]

The Southwest

In the southwest of France, Dugommier, fresh from his success at Toulon, arrived to take temporary command of the Armée des Pyrénées Orientales (16 January), in place of the unwell Doppet. The *Représentants* were also replaced by Soubrany and Milhaud who arrived with Dugommier, who also brought 10,500 men with him from the troops at Toulon. Dugommier reported to Paris that his new command was very incomplete, with for example half his men unarmed, and that 70 percent of the muskets had no bayonets.[162]

157 Phipps, *West*, p.223; Smith, *Data Book*, pp.72, 74, 79; Smith states that Masséna led the unidentified and unsuccessful French troops at Cerisiera, but given the proximity to the Mont Cenis passes, they were more likely to have been from the Armée des Alpes.

158 Phipps, *West*, pp.227, 229, 230; *Général de Division* Pierre Petitguillaume.

159 Phipps, *West*, p.227.

160 Phipps, *West*, pp.231–232.

161 Phipps, *West*, pp.234–235; Smith, *Data Book*, p.92; *Feldmarschallleutnant* Oliver Remigius, Count von Wallis, *Général de Division* Barthélemy Louis-Joseph Schérer, *Général de Division* Jean-François Moulin.

162 Phipps, *West*, pp.168, 170; Jones, *Companion*, pp.149, 392: Édouard Jean-Baptiste Milhaud (later commander of Napoleon's IV Corps de Cavalerie de Reserve at Waterloo); Pierre-Amable de Soubrany.

The Armée des Pyrénées Occidentales was still commanded by Muller when the first serious fighting in the southwest began. Urrutia, with 13,000 Spaniards advancing from Hendaye on the border, attacked the *Camp des Sans Culottes*, behind the river Bidassoa. However, after a seven-hour battle, Dubouquet drove off the Spaniards (5 February). Muller was finally promoted to *général de division* (14 April).[163]

On the eastern front, the Spanish were also in the throes of a change of command, the successful Ricardos was recalled to Madrid to consult on the plan for the campaign but died there (13 March). Amarillas took command of the Ejército de Cataluña on a temporary basis before the arrival of the Conde de La Unión (4 April).[164]

After a period of resupply, reinforcement, and reorganisation, Dugommier had 28,000 men he could rely on to fight, plus 5,000 new recruits, the *force d'inertie*, who were kept in reserve, while a further 25,000 men were in garrisons and in the training camps in the rear. With his field army Dugommier advanced against La Unión's position at the *Camp de Boulu*, sending Pérignon's division through an undefended gap to outflank the position. On the second day the Spanish, pressed on all sides by the divisions of Augereau, Pérignon and Sauret, broke and fled to the frontier losing all 150 of their guns (30 April–1 May).[165] With his orders from the *Comité* in mind, Dugommier chose to besiege the coastal fortresses rather than launching a full-blown offensive into Spain.

The siege of Collioure began on 2 May, while Pérignon blockaded the fortress of Bellegarde (5 May) which guarded the main road into Spain.[166] Without orders Augereau led his division against the Spanish position at Sant Llorenç de la Muga, capturing an artillery foundry there (6 May). Augereau was still in this exposed position with his 6,000 men when La Unión assailed him with 15,000 men but divided into seven columns. Using their central position, Augereau's well-trained troops defeated each of the Spanish columns, who were thrown back in rout (19 May).[167] Collioure surrendered to the French on 26 May.[168] Dugommier now had 38,000 men in the field 9,000 on each flank and 16,000 under Pérignon in the centre. While Bellegarde still resisted the French siege, La Unión attempted to force Augereau from his position on the French right at Sant Llorenç de la Muga. This time La Unión led 22,000 men in six columns converging on the foundry. Augereau was equal to the task and despite initially losing some ground, drove off the Spanish. On the left Sauret was equally successful in beating the attack made on him, and the reserve brigade led by Victor from his position on the *Col de Banyuls* defeated an amphibious assault on the coast four miles distant (13 August). A few weeks later, Bellegarde, the last post held by the Spanish on French territory, surrendered after a siege of more than four months (17 September).[169]

Meanwhile on the Atlantic coast, Muller and his Armée des Pyrénées Occidentales of 30,000 men faced Caro y Fontes, who had only 20,000, half of whom were militia.

---

163 Phipps, *West*, pp.149–155; Smith, *Data Book*, p.72; Martinez, *Diccionario*, pp.893–894; *Général de Division* Louis Dubouquet; *Teniente General* José de Urrutia y de las Casas.

164 Phipps, *West*, pp.171–172; Martinez, *Diccionario*, pp.190, 378, 653; *Teniente General* Jerónimo Morejón Girón y Moctezuma, Marqués de las Amarillas; *Teniente General* Don Luis-Fermín de Carvajal y Vargas, Conde de La Unión was given the command when the chosen successor, *Capitán General* Alejandro O'Reilly y Macdowell, Conde de O'Reilly also died.

165 Phipps, *West*, pp.175–177; Smith, *Data Book*, p.77; *Généraux de Division* Charles Pierre François Augereau, Catherine-Dominique de Pérignon, Pierre François Sauret de la Borie.

166 Phipps, *West*, p.178.

167 Phipps, *West*, pp.180–181; Smith, *Data Book*, pp.77, 80.

168 Smith, *Data Book*, p.81.

169 Phipps, *West*, pp.184–185; Smith, *Data Book*, pp.83, 91; *Général de Brigade* Claude-Victor Perrin.

Against such odds, Caro y Fontes wanted either to be reinforced or to evacuate the valley of the river Baztán, a tributary of the river Nive, between San Sebastian and St Jean Pied de Port. Muller began his offensive by taking the Casa Fuorte, a fortified position blocking the pass of Ispéguy into the valley of the river Nive des Aldudes and, on the same day, successfully assaulting the ridges of Ispéguy and Maya (3 June).[170] Caro y Fontes attempted an assault with 8,500 men on the fortified position of Mont Calvari, near Vera/Bera on the Bidassoa, but was repulsed (23 June).[171] From his foothold in the Baztán valley, Muller then ordered Moncey with his own division and those of Delaborde and Frégeville to take the valley. The fortified hilltop of Mont Arquinzu was taken by Digonet, who subsequently shot 49 French emigres in the garrison from the Légion Royale des Pyrénées (10 July).[172]

Caro y Fontes went to Madrid to plead his case for reinforcements or permission to withdraw from the Batzán valley. However, Caro y Fontes resigned when the court would not countenance such a retirement and he was replaced by the 71-year-old Colomera (25 July).[173]

Moncey, with 10,000 men, advanced over the Col de Maya (24 July), seizing the Baztán valley the next day. To the west Delaborde, with 6,000 men crossed the lower Bidassoa marching from Biriatou to Vera and drove the Spaniards from their entrenchments (25 July). Moncey and Delaborde then joined forces at Lesaka (8 miles southeast of Irun). The combined force of 12,000 men marched west to support the attack of the right column of 6,000 men under Frégeville on the Spaniard's fortified camp of San Martial. The Spaniards were aware that Moncey was in their rear, so destroyed their works and retired, also surrendering the fortress of Fuenterrabia (1 August). Moving further west to San Sebastian which promptly surrendered (4 August), Frégeville then occupied Tolosa, 14 miles southwest of San Sebastian and 42 miles west of Saint-Jean-Pied-de Port (5 August). Exploiting his success, Muller resigned his command (30 August) and was replaced by Moncey (1 September).[174] Now reinforced to 52,000 men by the arrival of troops from the Vendée, Moncey began another offensive this time focussing on the valley of the river Irati. However, his attempt to encircle various Spanish detachments around the village of Orbaizeta, was not entirely successful, despite inflicting 4,000 casualties and capturing 50 guns (15–17 October).

Meanwhile, as part of the same offensive, Delaborde successfully assaulted the Mezkiritz hills, nine miles to the east (15 October). The French went on to capture Villanueva de Araquil which is only 15 miles northeast of Pamplona. The *Représentants* prevented a further advance on Pamplona by diverting the siege train to Strasbourg.[175] In the final fighting of the year on this section of the frontier, Marbot, holding the line between Lecunberri and Olague, fought a severe action and got the worst of the first day's fighting, but the next day the Spaniards were attacked in the rear by Harispe and his 2e Bataillon

---

170 Smith, *Data Book*, p.83.

171 Smith, *Data Book*, p.85.

172 mith, *Data Book*, p.87; Phipps, *West*, pp.186–187, 190; *Généraux de Division* Bon-Adrien Jeannot de Moncey, Henri François Delaborde and Jean-Henri Guy Nicolas de Frégeville; *Général de Brigade* Antoine Digonet; Phipps has Moncey responsible for the fight at Arquinzu and dates it to 16 July.

173 Phipps, *West*, p.186; Martinez, *Diccionario*, pp.42–43; *Capitán General* Martin Antonio Álvarez de Sotomayor, Conde de Colomera.

174 Phipps, *West*, pp.186–187; Jones, *Companion*, p.155, Smith, *Data Book*, p.88; Smith has San Sebastian surrendering on 2 August.

175 Smith, *Data Book*, p.93; Ian Beckett, *An Honest Man – Moncey* in David G. Chandler (ed.), *Napoleon's Marshals* (London: Weidenfeld and Nicolson, 1987), p.300.

de Chasseurs Basque who had marched over the mountains from Zubiri to the east.[176] The Spaniards fled, leaving some 600 dead on the field of battle (24–25 November), including prisoners murdered by their French captors. The French lost 400 men killed, wounded and missing. On the same day, 29 miles to the west, Frégeville, executing one of Moncey's favoured encircling moves from Lecunberri, appeared behind the Marqués de Rubi's 4,000 men on the heights of Bergara, on the main road from France to Vitoria. The Spanish were routed, leaving 150 dead on the field of battle, one cannon and four flags (26 November).[177]

The onset of winter stopped the fighting in the Western Pyrenees, and Moncey withdrew his army closer to his supplies, so that Frégeville was at Tolosa on the right, Marbot commanded his centre at Lesaka and the hills of Les Cinco Villas de Montaña, and Delaborde was in the Baztán valley, on his left. Moncey's reserve, commanded by Mauco, was in the valley of the river Nive des Aldudes (29 November).[178]

Meanwhile on the Mediterranean coast, to shield the port of *Roses*, La Unión built a series of 97 forts and redoubts, the Lines of Figueres, containing 250 guns and garrisoned by 46,000 men. Against this position, Dugommier brought 24,200 men plus a further 12,500 less well-trained men that he kept in the rear. The French attack stretched along a seven-and-a-half-mile front from Sant Llorenç de la Muga on the right, where Augereau led the advance, through Mont Roig in the centre, where Pérignon led the way, to Capmany on the left where Sauret commanded. The resulting battle of Montagne Noire, or the Lines of Figueres, was remarkable because both commanders-in-chief were killed in action, Dugommier while eating breakfast on the first day and La Unión in the chaotic retreat on the final day. On the first day Pérignon took command in Dugommier's place and stabilised a difficult situation in which Augereau's success on the right was counterbalanced by the repulse of Sauret on the left. (17 November). After two days of reconnaissance, Pérignon launched a second attack, during which Augereau with 11,400 men delivered the main blow by storming the great redoubt at Monestir de Santa Maria del Roure, one mile northwest of Pont de Molins. As the routed Spanish were falling back to Figueres, La Unión was killed. Over the four days the Spanish lost 10,000 men, 80 positions and 200 guns, while the French lost 3,000 men. The Castell de San Ferran in Figueres quickly surrendered enabling Pérignon to begin the siege of *Roses* (29 November). This siege continued for the rest of the year, as the garrison of 4,000 to 5,000 men, could be resupplied by a supporting Spanish squadron.[179] Urrutia replaced La Unión as the Spanish commander in this theatre, as *Capitán General de Cataluña* (23 December).[180]

176 Citoyen Beaulac, *Mémoires sur la Dernière Guerre entre La France et l'Espagne dans les Pyrénées Occidentales* (Paris: Truttel and Würtz, 1801), p.145, this work is anonymous, but Beaulac is identified as the author by Worldcat.org; Jean H.E. Labouche, *Le Chef de Brigade Harispe et Les Chasseurs Basques* (Pau: Vve Léon Ribaut, 1894), p.79; *Chef de Brigade* Jean-Isidore Harispe.

177 Phipps, *West*, p.193; Smith, *Data Book*, p.95; Martinez, *Diccionario*, p.710; Beaulac, *Mémoires*, pp.142–148; Smith dates this action to the 7 November, but Martinez, Phipps and Smith's source have it as the 25 November; *Teniente General* Cayetano Pignatelli Rubi Aymerich, Marqués de Rubi.

178 Phipps, *West*, p.193; Beaulac, *Mémoires*, pp.142–148; *Général de Division* Jean Antoine Marbot; *Général de Division* Jean Mauco.

179 Smith, *Data Book*, p.96; Phipps, *West*, pp.195–200.

180 Martinez, *Diccionario*, p.894.

Bataille de la Montagne Noire, 20 November 1794

The West

In the west of France, 1794 saw the conclusion of the *Vendéan* uprising. Turreau took command of the Armée de l'Ouest, while Rossignol retained command of the Armée de Côtes de Brest (30 December 1793).[181] Turreau's plan for the conclusion of the campaign against the *Vendéans* involved the destruction of the region by the '*promenade civique des colonnes infernales*'. To this end Turreau divided his 80,000 men into 12 columns, which were to scour the countryside, removing all grain and burning villages, farms, and houses. All rebels and even suspected rebels were to be bayonetted to death, including women and children. This campaign to snuff out the rebellion began 24 January 1794.[182] The campaign soon yielded results and d'Elbée was captured when the island of Noirmoutier, near the mouth of the river Loire, was re-occupied by Republican troops. Unable to stand, d'Elbée was strapped to an armchair and executed by firing squad along with three other Royalist officers (6 January). Talmont, who had been captured 31 December 1793, was condemned to death and went to the guillotine in Laval, at the very gates of his ancestral home (27 January). Henri de la Rochejacquelein died in a skirmish near Cholet (29 January).

The campaign was not however a complete success, as Charette and Stofflet evaded capture for two more years and continued to gather recruits, enraged by the activities of the *colonnes infernales*.[183] It has been estimated that between 150,000 and 200,000

181 Phipps, *West*, p.31; Jones, *Companion*, p.155; Turreau was appointed 26 December but arrived to take command only on 30 December.

182 Phipps, *West*, p.32; Esdaile, *Wars*, pp.190–191; some have described this campaign as a genocide, but this is very controversial in France, counterarguments being that the campaign took place in a civil war and only Royalist Vendéans were targeted, in some cases by Vendéan Republicans.

183 Ross, *Banners*, p.322.

individuals perished in the *Vendéan* revolt in the period 1793–1794, including those who died of hunger, disease as well as at the hands of both the Republican and Royalist forces.[184] Turreau was suspended by the *Comité* (13 May) before being sent to command the division at Belle Île en Mer. Vimeux took temporary command until Dumas was appointed (7 September). Its job done, the Armée de l'Ouest was reduced from its strength in April of 103,800 men, of whom 50,000 were available for field operations, to just 30,000 men. Large drafts had been sent to the other armies of the Republic.[185] Elsewhere in the west, Hoche arrived to replace Vialle in command of the Armée des Côtes de Cherbourg (1 September) before also being given command of the Armée des Côtes de Brest (10 November), when Dumas left to command a division in the Armée de Sambre-et-Meuse. Eventually, in Paris, the *Convention Nationale* declared an amnesty to end the conflict in the west, at least for now (2 December). This resulted in separate peace conferences, in early 1795, between the *Représentants* and the Vendéan Charette in Nantes, and with the Chouan Cormatin in Rennes.[186]

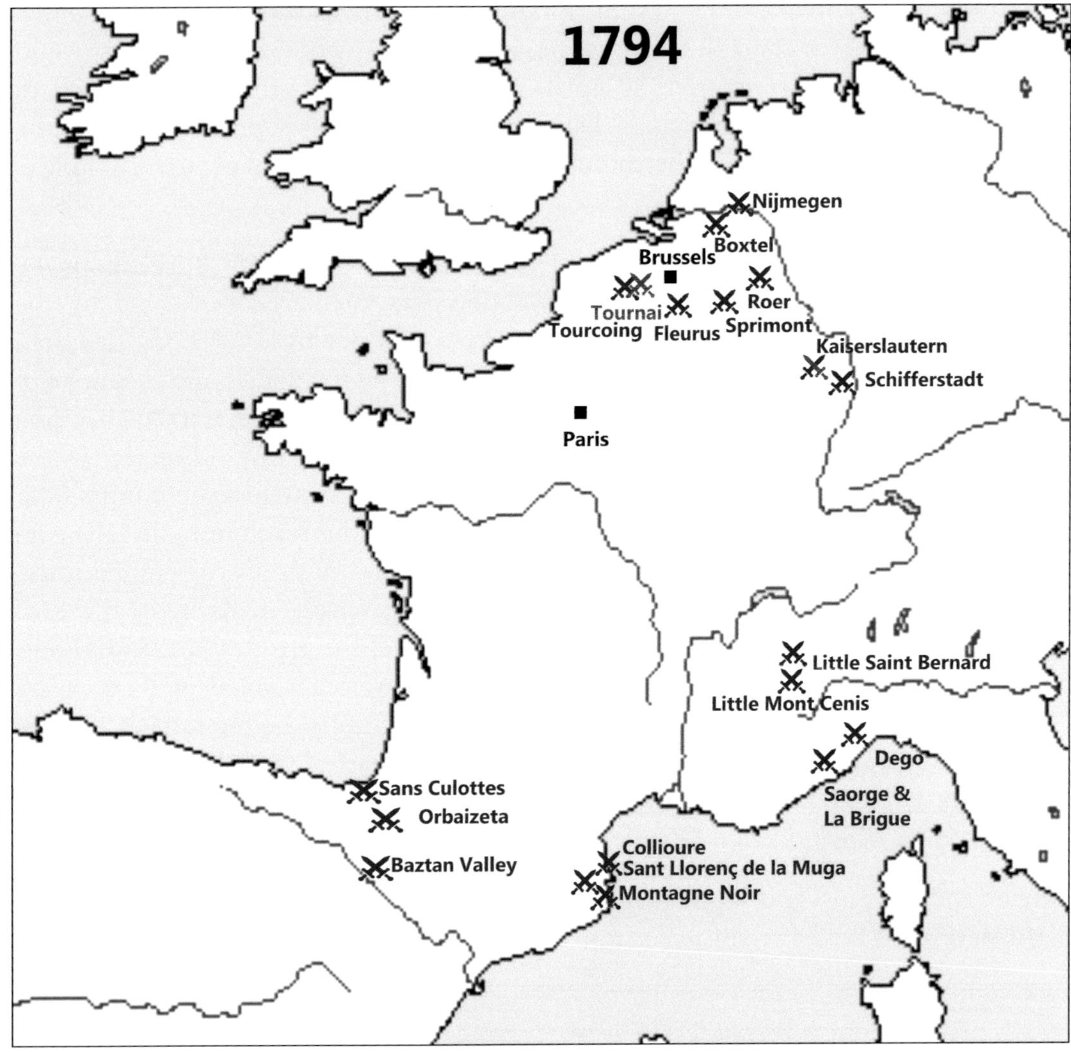

Map 4 – Key actions and battles, 1794

184 Jones, *Companion*, pp.114–115; c.f. the 35,000–40,000 deaths attributed to the 'Terror'.

185 Phipps, *West*, pp.34–35; *Général de Division* Louis-Antoine Vimeux.

186 Phipps, *West*, pp.36–38; Jones, *Companion*, p.148; *Major Général* Pierre Marie Félicité Dezoteux, Baron de Cormatin second in command to *Lieutenant Général* Joseph de Puisaye in the Armées Catholiques et Royales de Bretagne.

Overseas

Beyond the frontiers of Metropolitan France, Grey's expedition to the West Indies arrived in the Caribbean early in 1794. Grey with 6,500 men, in an example of excellent collaboration with Vice Admiral Sir John Jervis and his squadron, captured Martinique after a seven week-long campaign against the 3,000 men of Rochambeau's stubborn but scattered garrison (5 February–24 March).[187] Saint Lucia, 20 miles south of Martinique, became the next target of Grey's expedition. The island was garrisoned by only 400 men under the command of its governor, Ricard. Arriving with seven battalions off the northern tip of Saint Lucia (1 April), Grey soon overwhelmed Ricard (3 April). Given the state of politics in France both Ricard and Rochambeau chose new lives in the United States of America.[188] Guadeloupe, 80 miles north of Martinique, was the next target and offered a much more significant obstacle as it was garrisoned by 5,900 men, supported by 187 artillery pieces in 20 batteries, led by Collot. Nevertheless, Grey with fewer than 3,000 troops, supported by a reinforced Jervis with five ships of the line, nine frigates and five unrated ship-sloops, attacked the island, arriving off *Pointe-à-Pitre* on 10 April. In contrast to the aggression and energy of Grey, Collot was timid and inept, and soon surrendered (20 April).[189] Thus, the three great French targets of the expedition were in British hands, before the campaigning had to stop due to the arrival of the 'sickly season'. Furthermore, Port-au-Prince the capital of *Saint Domingue* was also occupied (4 June).[190]

The British had been assisted throughout the campaign by French Royalists in the islands, whose relationship with the Revolution was further complicated by the abolition of slavery.[191] However the British success was not to last, having departed Rochefort (23 April), Leissègues's small squadron arrived off Guadeloupe (3 June). On board were two companies of artillery and the *Bataillon Sans Culottes*, 1,300 men strong (actually two battalions), led by *Généraux de Brigade* Aubert and Royer, overseen by the *commissaire délégués* Victor Hugues.[192] Two days later Hugues and his co-commissioner Pierre Chrétien waded ashore at Pointe-à-Pitre to spread the revolution, declaring an end to slavery, and setting up their brand-new guillotine. With overwhelming force, the French stormed Fort Fleur d'Epée dispersing the garrison, made up of the 43rd Foot and some Royalist militia (6 June). Unable to defend the posts of Fort Saint Louis and Morne Gouvernment, the British evacuated the western island of Basse Terre (10 June). Grey arrived with reinforcements but an attempted counterattack at night was a disaster and Grey also withdrew from the greater part of the other major island, Grande Terre. This left only a garrison at Camp Berville, opposite Pointe-à-Pitre across the river Salée, which divided Grande Terre from Basse Terre (5 July).[193]

Hugues spent August and September recruiting new battalions of volunteers including freed slaves and further reinforced from France, launched a successful assault on the

187 Steve Brown, *By Fire and Bayonet, Grey's West Indies Campaign of 1794* (Solihull: Helion and Company, 2018), pp.70–111, 207; *Général de Division* Donatien-Marie-Joseph de Vimeur, Vicomte de Rochambeau.

188 Brown, *By Fire and Bayonet*, pp.116–119; *Général de Brigade* Nicolas Xavier de Ricard.

189 Brown, *By Fire and Bayonet*, pp.128–129, 133, 228–229; *Général de Brigade* Georges Henri Victor Collot.

190 Nicholas Andrew Martin Rodger, *The Command of the Oceans, A Naval History of Britain, 1649–1815* (London: Penguin, 2006), pp.428–429; Fortescue, *History*, vol. IV, pt.1, p.339.

191 Jones, *Companion*, p.37.

192 *Capitaine de Vaisseau* Corentin Urbain Leissègues; *Généraux de Brigade* Claude Aubert and Charles Étienne Rouyer.

193 Brown, *By Fire and Bayonet*, p.141; Fortescue, *History*, vol. IV – Maps, *Guadeloupe 1794*.

sickly garrison of Camp Berville which resulted in its surrender (6 July). Hugues had the 300 Royalist prisoners, who had fought with the British, executed either using the guillotine, by firing squad while some were buried alive. The last British-held post on Guadeloupe, Fort Matilde, was evacuated on the night of 10 December and Hugues's victory was complete. However, Yellow Fever was the greater victor as over 4,000 of Grey's initial force of 7,000 men had perished during the campaign.[194] Grey returned home sick with some significant military success achieved but with a reputation for looting and extortion, such that inhabitants of Martinique, Saint Lucia and Guadeloupe viewed the coming of the British as the exchange of one set of oppressors for another.[195]

The upheaval associated with the revolution had amongst other factors caused a failure of the harvest and with France at war with all its neighbours, she had to look elsewhere to import replacement food supplies. Consequently in 1794 a single large convoy was gathered in Chesapeake Bay which set sail on 2 April to bring grain and other foods to France. For Admiral Richard, Viscount Howe, commander of the Royal Navy's Channel Fleet, the major benefit of the French convoy was the opportunity it offered to bring the *Marine Nationale's Grand Flotte*, based in Brest, to battle and destroy it. The French fleet was commanded by 46-year-old *Contre-Amiral* Louis Thomas Villaret de Joyeuse, overseen by the *Représentant en Mission* Jean Bon Saint-André.[196] For his part Villaret de Joyeuse received his orders directly from Robespierre, and he was not to allow the grain convoy to fall into the hands of the British or else he would lose his head![197] The fleets met in the middle of the Atlantic, 560 nautical miles from Brest, and fought several actions from 28 May to 1 June. The Battle of the Glorious First of June, the only fleet action between the French and the British during the War of the First Coalition, in which Viscount Howe's 25 British ships of the line attacked 28 French ships of the line, was undoubtedly a British tactical victory with six French ships captured and another sunk. However, Villaret de Joyeuse had succeeded in screening the convoy and ensured its safe arrival in France, he had also demonstrated some skill in handling his fleet, which, in turn, had shown a great willingness to fight for the Republic.

Meanwhile in the Mediterranean, Hood led an expedition to take the island of Corsica, arriving in the Baia di San Fiorenzo (now the Golfe de Saint-Florent), to the west of and at the base of the long promontory at the north of the island, which could provide a safe base for the operation. As reported by Moore, the defences of the bay comprised the tower mounting two guns on the western Mortello Point (a model for the future Martello towers), a similar tower at Fornali covering two shore batteries and the larger Convention Redoubt, housing 21 guns, on a hill 250 feet above sea level (7 February). David Dundas was leading the army locally, in collaboration with some Corsicans keen to throw off the French yoke and stormed these positions with the support of naval guns brought ashore (17 February). Preferring a blockade until reinforcements arrived, Dundas and his successor, D'Aubant, refused to support Hood's planned assault on Bastia. Undeterred, Hood went ahead with his attack on Bastia using only his available naval assets (4 April). The starving garrison of Bastia surrendered just as D'Aubant

194 Brown, *By Fire and Bayonet*, pp.161–167, 176, 191.
195 Rodger, *Command*, p.429.
196 Willis, *Fleet Battle*, pp.32–35; the convoy has been variously described as being comprised of 107, 117, 160 and 170 ships.
197 Willis, *Fleet Battle*, p.121.

belatedly brought his men overland in support of the operation (15 May).[198] When Stuart arrived to assume the local army command, he cooperated, with bad grace, in the subsequent siege of Calvi.[199]

Other, lesser naval engagements during 1794 include:[200]

Theatre	Date	Action
Home waters	23 April	Warren's squadron of HMS *Flora* (36), HMS *Arethusa* (38), HMS *Melampus* (36), HMS *La Nymphe* (36) and HMS *Concorde* (36) engaged and captured the *Pomone* (44), *Engageante* (36) and the *Babet* (22) of Desgarceaux's squadron off Guernsey. The *Résolue* (36) escaped.
	10 May	HMS *Castor* sailing from Jersey and Guernsey was taken by a French squadron.
	17 May	HMS *Swiftsure* (74) captured the *Atlante* (38).
	29 May	HMS *Castor* (32) recaptured by HMS *Carysfort* (28).
	21 October	The *Revolutionnaire* (44) captured by HMS *Artois* (38).
	6 November	HMS *Alexander* (74) dismasted and captured by a squadron of five French 74's.
Mediterranean	17 June	HMS *Romney* (50) took the *Sybelle* (46) in the Mykonos roads.
East Indies	5 May	HMS *Orpheus* (32) took the privateer *Duguay-Trouin* (34) off Mauritius.
	22 October	HMS *Centurion* (50) and HMS *Diomede* (44) engaged *Cybèlle* (40), *Prudente* (32), the privateer *Jean-Bart* (22) and *Le Courier* (14) off Mauritius.

In summary, during 1794 the armies of the Republic, although smaller than in 1793, still deployed unheard of numbers in modern warfare, 730,000 men, and fought 36 battles involving 20,000 men or more, winning 23 and losing 13. They had also fought 44 lesser actions, winning 32 and losing 12.[201] During 1794 the French armies became more organised and better trained and consequently managed to win the key battles and push the allies across France's natural frontiers. The First Coalition was thus again frustrated, with Austrian giving up the Austrian Netherlands, Spain, having attempted to invade France, being itself invaded and any Allied successes did not have a lasting effect on the war.

198 Fortescue, *History*, vol. IV, pt.1, pp.181–183; Lieutenant-Colonel John Moore, 51st Foot; Colonel Abraham D'Aubant, Royal Engineers; Lieutenant-General Charles Stuart (local rank for the Mediterranean).

199 Rodger, *Command*, pp.430–431.

200 Schomberg, *Naval Chronology*, vol. II, pp.264, 266, 273, 281, 282, 294; *Capitaine de Vaisseau* Georges Desgarceaux; Commodore Sir John Borlase Warren.

201 Smith, *Data Book*, pp.72–97; Jones, *Companion*, p.157.

The War in 1795

The North

On France's northern frontier the war was fast approaching its climax. The final unhappy conference of the Dutch, British and Austrian commanders took place in Utrecht (7 January). The next day Macdonald crossed the river Waal on the still stable ice above and below Nijmegen, as he saw the British begin their retirement (8 January). As a result of the Utrecht conference, the Stadtholder and the Hereditary Princes of Orange-Nassau left for England in a fishing boat (18 January) and the United Provinces withdrew from the First Coalition, becoming a French client state. The Dutch army withdrew to its fortresses, which soon surrendered and Pichegru was able to advance unopposed to Amsterdam (20 January). The French victory over the Dutch was complete when Lahure, a former Belgian revolutionary, leading three battalions of infantry and some hussars advanced north from Amsterdam to Den Helder, where he accepted the surrender of the Dutch fleet frozen in the ice (23 January).[202]

Meanwhile, the British with their German auxiliaries had retired in the face of the constant attacks of the French masses. Forced back from the river Waal the British were attacked along the line of the river Nederrijn, from Arnhem, 14 miles west to Rhenen (14 January). Despite the Guards Brigade repulsing their assailants at Rhenen, that night the British began a retreat to the sea every bit as traumatic as the later retreat to Coruña. The French marched on through the United Provinces to Groningen, in pursuit of Cathcart's detached brigade of four infantry regiments and the 15th Light Dragoons, attacking and being repulsed from Cathcart's fortified headquarters at Winschoten (27 February). However, when Reynier attacked Cathcart a second time, the British general withdraw eastwards towards Bremen. Meanwhile, the main British columns retired, suffering temperatures of minus 12° Celsius and torrential rain, across the river Ijssel (15 January), 70 miles northeast to the river Ems, pausing in the town of Ems (5 February).

The army took a position behind the river Ems, the right commanded by Dundas and the left by Abercromby (23 February). The German column retired eastwards towards Münster. At the end of February Wesley, after repeated requests for leave, went home, having learnt 'how not to do it'. The British cabinet decided to withdraw the British troops from Germany, leaving the Hanoverians and Hessians to their own devices (8 March). A further retreat of 70 miles was required to reach the port of Bremen. The British army, under renewed French pressure, left their cantonments on 22 March and began arriving in Bremen three days later, severely weakened by both disease and desertion. There they met the 100 ships sent from England to take them home. Embarkation began in early April and the last of the British troops embarked on 1 June. In all 15,000 men embarked, suggesting that 6,000 men had been lost since leaving the river Waal.[203] The winter campaign had been just as difficult for the pursuing French.

202 Brown, *Flanders Campaign*, p.244; Phipps, *Nord*, pp.328–329; *Général de Division* Jacques Étienne Joseph Alexandre Macdonald; *Chef de Bataillon* Louis-Joseph Lahure.

203 Brown, *Flanders Campaign*, pp.252, 254–257; Major-General William Schaw Cathcart, 1st Earl Cathcart; *Général de Brigade* Jean-Louis Ebénézer Reynier.

Wallmoden, in command of the Hanoverian, Hessian and now Brunswick force, was left in a precarious position, having just 8,000 men to defend 100 miles of frontier.[204]

Having cleared the United Provinces without a single major battle, the Armée du Nord turned southeast near Bentheim, where a Prussian force had replaced the Austrians. Pichegru, the victorious commander, had already left for Paris (29 March) where he took charge of the *Gardes Nationales* in suppressing, via the imposition of martial law, the Jacobin insurrection of *12 Germinal An III* (1 April) brought on by poverty and hunger. Moreau succeeded Pichegru to the command of the Nord (21 March), which was reduced to an army of occupation, 136,000 men strong with 67,000 available for operations in the field. The Peace of Basel was signed between the French and Prussians on 5 April 1795, removing the Prussians from the First Coalition, and secretly recognising French hegemony on the west bank of the Rhine. Hesse-Kassel, Saxony and Hanover quickly followed Prussia's example.[205] Consequently, Wallmoden retired to the line of the river Weser to protect Hanover. Pichegru then moved on to the Rhine to take command of the newly formed Armée de Rhin-et-Moselle at Mainz (16 April). The Armée du Nord was subsequently prevented from cooperating with Pichegru's new command by the intervening territory of the now neutral Prussia.[206]

The Rhine

On the Upper Rhine frontier, the first quarter of 1795 was taken up with the sieges of Luxembourg, and, on the river itself, of Mannheim and Mainz. Moreaux in command at the siege of Luxembourg died of a fever (9 February) and was replaced by Ambert.[207] However Ambert and the divisions of the Armée de la Moselle were sent to Mainz and Hatry succeeded him, commanding three divisions of the Armée de Sambre-et-Meuse. Starved out, the garrison of Luxembourg surrendered on 7 June and Hatry's men re-joined their army.[208]

Without access to the right bank of the Rhine, the Armée devant Mannheim could only observe the city, having agreed in the terms of the capitulation of the *tête-du-pont* to refrain from bombarding the city from the left bank until they were able to access the right bank. The Armée devant Mayence comprised five divisions, three from the Moselle and two from the Rhin, and when Kléber left the army for health reasons (13 February), there was a hiatus before Pichegru arrived to take command of the forces, now the Armée de Rhin-et-Moselle (16 April). Pichegru had 11 divisions in total, seven stationed above Mainz and four blockading Mainz itself. This was reduced to three when Desaix was sent upriver with his division, and he was also given command on the Upper Rhine.[209]

Pichegru had his headquarters at Strasbourg and his army stretched from Huningue (Hüningen) in the south, 165 miles to Bingen in the north, 15 miles west of Mainz. For this frontage his army had a nominal strength of 193,000 men but in fact only 96,000 men were under arms. Amongst this army, five future *maréchals de France* were serving,

204 Brown, *Flanders Campaign*, p.256.

205 Freemont-Barnes, *French Revolutionary Wars*, p.36; Demet, *Duty*, pp.113–116; although the Hessians and Hanoverians remained in British pay for several months.

206 Phipps, *Nord*, pp.332–335, 340; Jones, *Companion*, p.152.

207 Phipps, *Moselle*, p.197; Smith, *Data Book*, p.96.

208 Phipps, *Moselle*, p.200; *Général de Division* Jacques-Maurice Hatry.

209 Phipps, *Moselle*, pp.202, 206, 209.

including Davout, Marmont, Oudinot and Saint-Cyr. Opposing Pichegru across the Rhine stood Wurmser with 79,000 Austrians, with his right resting on Mannheim, his left at Lörrach, near Basel, and his headquarters at Freiburg im Breisgau. Further down the Rhine, Jourdan's Armée de Sambre-et-Meuse, with 91,000 men held the line from Bingen down the river 106 miles to Büderich, near Düsseldorf, where it linked with the Armée du Nord. Jourdan's army also included its share of future *maréchals*; Bernadotte, Lefebvre, Mortier, Ney and Soult. Opposite Jourdan was the Austrian Commander-in-Chief Clerfayt, who commanded 96,000 men including the 15,000 strong garrison of Mainz, his bridgehead to the left bank of the Rhine. Of this force only 34,000 faced Jourdan, the rest being beyond the river Lahn facing Pichegru. In Paris the war was now being directed by Letourneur, who had replaced Carnot on the *Comité* (2 March). However, Carnot was a friend of Letourneur and retained his influence over the direction of the war.[210] This influence resulted in a plan to turn the flanks of the Austrian line, Pichegru was to cross the Rhine high up the river at Breisach opposite Freiburg. However, Jourdan moved first, having spent a month training his men for the crossing, and he organised his divisions into three 'corps' under Marceau, Hatry and Kléber. The crossing was to take place on the left opposite Hamm just above Düsseldorf, and at Ürdingen below it, towards Duisberg. The centre was to cross at Neuwied, below Coblenz (Koblenz).

The operation began at 9:00 p.m. on 5 September when, under the personal direction of Jourdan and Kléber, Lefebvre led his division across the Rhine to occupy Düsseldorf forcing the Austrian defenders led by Erbach back onto the Line of Neutrality agreed between France and Prussia. Ney led the advanced guard across the Line, violating Prussia's neutrality to strong Prussian protests. While Erbach fell back to Frankfurt, Kléber swept up the right bank pressing Werneck beyond the river Sieg and Colaud's division secured Düsseldorf. Werneck attempted to hold the line of the Sieg at Hennef, eight miles northeast of Bonn, but Ney found some fords to outflank Werneck's redoubts, forcing him to retreat further to Altenkirchen.

Turning Werneck again, Lefebvre cleared the right bank of the Rhine opposite Neuwied, allowing Hatry to lead the divisions of Bernadotte, Poncet and Marceau across the great river unopposed (15 September). Jourdan pushed on 25 miles southeast towards Mainz, to cross the river Lahn on a front of 35 miles from Wetzlar on the right to Nassau on the left, while leaving Marceau's division to blockade the fortress of Ehrenbreitstein overlooking Coblenz (20–21 September). Another 26-mile advance brought Jourdan to Kastel across the Rhine from Mainz. Thus, Jourdan and his Armée de Sambre-et-Meuse was able to blockade Mainz from the right bank of the Rhine deployed from Mosbach east of Mannheim to the river Liederbach near Höchst, while Pichegru and the Armée de Rhin-et-Moselle did the same from the left bank (29 September).[211] Meanwhile, with the Austrians focused on the action around Mainz, Pichegru sent two divisions from before Mainz to attack Mannheim, which, poorly defended, surrendered to a simple summons (20 September). Pichegru then pushed Ambert with two divisions (10,000 men) from Mannheim along the river Neckar, towards Heidelberg, with Dufour's division on the right bank and Ambert's own division on the left bank (23 September).

210 Phipps, *Moselle*, pp.211–213; Étienne-François-Louis-Honoré Letourneur.

211 Phipps, *Moselle*, pp.216–219; Joseph Frister, *Oesterreichischer Militär Almanach für das Jahr 1796* (Vien: Author, 1796); *Feldmarschallleutnant* Karl Eugen zu Erbach-Schönberg; *Feldmarschallleutnant* Franz Freiherr von Werneck; *Général de Division* Claude-Sylvestre Colaud; *Général de Division* André Poncet.

From the hills above the French, Quosdanovich massed his men against Dufour's division at Handschuhsheim, broke it and captured many prisoners including Dufour himself. Ambert was forced to withdraw his own division back to Mannheim (24 September). In not concentrating his force for a mass crossing at Mannheim, Pichegru thus missed an opportunity to separate Wurmser from Clerfayt.[212] Jourdan met with Pichegru and the *Représentants* of the two armies at Ober-Ingelheim (4 October). Jourdan urged Pichegru to bring the Armée de Rhin-et-Moselle through Mannheim to support him on the line of the river Main. However, Pichegru, the *Comité*'s favoured commander and therefore supported by the *Représentants*, preferred to focus on the reduction of Mainz. This left Jourdan's Armée de Sambre-et-Meuse in a vulnerable position as they could be outflanked on his left at Höchst by an Austrian turning movement across the Line of Neutrality through Prussian territory. Consequently, four divisions of the Armée de Rhin-et-Moselle were temporarily placed under Jourdan's command, to provide a unity of command for the forces besieging Mainz and Kléber was placed in command of the siege. Kléber had six divisions besieging Mainz, 18,000 men on the right bank and 21,000 on the left bank, however Reneauld's division on the left bank had to be moved to the right bank to reinforce Jourdan's men on the river Main (11 October).[213] Clerfayt, assured that Wurmser was marching down the right bank of the Rhine to support him, ignoring the Line of Neutrality, crossed the river Main at Seligenstadt and Offenbach am Main (10 October) and on the next day crossed the river Nidda at Vilbel (now Bad Vilbel), northeast of Frankfurt, threatening Lefebvre's rear.

With his rear and communications threatened, Jourdan withdrew to the line of the river Lahn and sent Reneauld back to the Armée de Rhin-et-Moselle (12 October). Clerfayt continued his advance north on Wetzlar and Weilburg, again disregarding the Line of Neutrality, turning Jourdan's left and forcing him to retreat further, recrossing the Rhine to the left bank at Neuwied, Bonn and Cologne such that his entire army was back behind the Rhine with the exception of Lefebvre's division (21 October).

By 1 November only the armed camp at Düsseldorf provided Jourdan with a bridgehead on the right bank of the Rhine.[214] Meanwhile further up the Rhine, through a heavy fog, Wurmser attacked Pichegru's 13,000 troops under Desaix, on the right bank before Mannheim, forcing them back into Mannheim (18 October).[215] Clerfayt advanced no further in his pursuit of Jourdan than the river Lahn before turning his attention on the French troops besieging Mainz. Leaving one third of his men under the Duke of Württemberg to observe Jourdan, Clerfayt attacked through Mainz (28 October) driving back the blockading force 27 miles to line of the river Pfrimm (31 October). The assault included an enterprising crossing of the Rhine at Bodenheim and Nackenheim by 1,000 Austrians facilitated by an Englishman, Captain Williams, commanding seven gunboats on the Rhine. The Austrians landed behind the rightmost French division, Courtot's, and panicked it into a retreat of 21 miles, back to Kirchheimbolanden. However, the other blockading French divisions including Saint-Cyr's, managed to

212 Phipps, *Moselle*, pp.220–222; *Feldmarschallleutnant* Peter Vitus Freiherr von Quosdanovich; *Général de Division* Georges Joseph Dufour.

213 Phipps, *Moselle*, pp.225–227; *Général de Division* Michel Reneauld.

214 Phipps, *Moselle*, pp.231–234.

215 Phipps, *Moselle*, pp.239–240.

withdraw in good order, even taking with them some of their siege artillery. Courtot was court-martialled and sentenced to three months in prison for his panic.[216]

In the aftermath of this disaster for the French, Pichegru's Armée de Rhin-et-Moselle occupied a line from the Donnersberg behind Kirchheimbolanden along the river Pfrimm to Worms on the Rhine (four divisions numbering 37,000 men in total) and then from Frankenthal to Basel, along the Upper Rhine (four divisions numbering 66,000 men). Mannheim was held by two further divisions (12,000 men). Pichegru hoped to hold this front of some 164 miles if Jourdan could extend his Armée de Sambre-et-Meuse up the Rhine to secure the flank of his position along the river Pfrimm. Jourdan made two attempts to do this (6 and 9 November), however Clerfayt with 75,000 men and 150 guns attacked Pichegru around Pfeddersheim near Worms on the river Pfrimm (10 November). The significantly outnumbered Pichegru determined to withdraw 30 miles up the river Rhine to Landau and the lines of the Queich, which was achieved very competently, especially by Desaix. Clerfayt, concerned about the Armée de Sambre-et-Meuse in his rear, pressed Pichegru no further. However, in retiring this far, Pichegru effectively abandoned the 9,000 men who were garrisoning Mannheim. While the fighting had been continuing a new government assumed office in Paris, the Directory (3 November), including Letourneur and Carnot as two of the five Directors. Wurmser soon opened his trenches before Mannheim (11 November), which quickly surrendered (21 November). Jourdan had attempted to march to the relief of Mannheim (27 November), advancing with four divisions and d'Harville's cavalry (40,000 men) from Simmern to the line of the river Nahe from Bingen on the left, Kreuznach (now Bad Kreuznach) in the centre and Kirn on the right (29 November). However, learning of the fall of Mannheim (28 November), Jourdan had no wish to face the full might of the Austrian army and withdrew 15 miles to the northern side of the Soonwald mountains. Thus, in just two months, the situation on the Rhine had been dramatically changed in favour of the Austrians who now occupied the left bank of the river, Wurmser at Mannheim facing upstream confronting Pichegru's Armée de Rhin-et-Moselle, while at Mainz, Clerfayt faced downstream confronting Jourdan's Armée de Sambre-et-Meuse.

The campaign of 1795 ended on the Rhine when the Austrians felt unable to take advantage of this central position and skirmishing along the 25-mile front, from Stipshausen to Bacharach on the river Rhine (17 December), convinced them that Jourdan was not about to withdraw the Armée de Sambre-et-Meuse behind the river Moselle. Negotiations between the two sides resulted in an armistice being concluded (10 January 1796).[217]

The Southeast

In the southeast of France, the war progressed very quietly, the government nominated Kellermann to take overall command of both the Armée des Alpes and the Armée d'Italie (3 March), which he executed by leaving Moulin in command of the Armée des Alpes while taking personal command of the Armée d'Italie. In the meantime, a

216 Phipps, *Moselle*, pp.235–237, 240; Edward Cust, *Annals of the Wars of the Eighteenth Century* (London: John Murray, 1869), vol. IV, p.296; *Général de Division* Pierre Antoine Courtot; *Feldmarschallleutnant* Duke Ferdinand Frederick Augustus of Württemberg.

217 Phipps, *Moselle*, pp.240–247; Smith, *Data Book*, p.108; *Général de Division* Louis-Auguste Jouvénel des Ursins d'Harville.

maritime expedition was prepared in Toulon comprising 15,000 men of the Armée d'Italie. The fleet, 15 sail of the line, put to sea, carrying 3,000 soldiers, with the intention of driving off the British fleet commanded by Hotham (and including Nelson amongst his captains), which was blockading the port (11 March). The two fleets met off Cape Noli (30 miles southwest of Genoa) and while the French captured HMS *Berwick*, they lost two of their own ships and were forced to retire into Genoa (13 and 14 March). The expedition was abandoned, and the troops returned to the army.[218]

Arriving to take up his command Kellermann with his new chief of staff, Berthier, met Buonaparte in Marsaille (1 May), before joining the army (5 May). Kellermann's army was weak, disorganised and 'destitute', only 25,000 of a nominal 80,000–90,000 men were available for operations.[219] The division commanders of the Armée d'Italie were Garnier on the left, Macquard in the centre and Masséna and Sérurier on the right.[220] Suddenly the population of Toulon rose again, marching on Marsaille in support of the Jacobin cause, Freytag was detached with 4,000 men to Toulon to suppress the rebellion, but arrived after it was over (23 May).[221] Kellermann was also ordered to prepare a detachment of 12,000 or 18,000 men to be ready to march on Lyons. Thus, Kellermann was forced to defend France's borders against a reinforced Austro-Sardinian army, commanded by De Vins, while always looking over his shoulder towards the counter-revolutionary activity in the Rhone valley and elsewhere in the southeast. Furthermore, Kellermann had to achieve this task with his two armies totalling only 45,000 men, while being directed by Paris to take the offensive.

The Armée d'Italie was less than 30,000 men strong (19 June) and its battalions varied in strength from 68 men up to 541 men, with a mean of only 320 men per battalion. The line held by Kellermann ran from Savona on the coast 73 miles northeast of Nice, up to the crest of the hills. The right of the Armée d'Italie held the strong positions from Monte Alto, San Giocomo, Melogno, and Monte Settepani, the centre held the upper basin of the river Roja and the Colle di Tenda, while the left held the line to Belvédère, a frontage of some 57 miles. While awaiting reinforcements from the Rhine armies, Kellermann relied on his fortifications for his defence, although the multiple points that needed garrisons dissipated his combat power further. De Vins determined to use his Austrian troops to attack along the coast, while the Sardinians under Colli advanced by the upper reaches of the river Tanaro. The Austrians were observed massing in front of Masséna's men on 18 June. De Vins attacked Masséna but was held by Laharpe's brigade in the valley of the Torrente Segno, two miles southwest of Savona (24 June). However, further inland, the posts held by Cervoni's brigade, Monte Alto and San Giacomo, were taken by the Austrians, their task made easier by Masséna's failure to fortify them as ordered by Kellermann (25 June).

San Giacomo was briefly retaken by the French but then lost again the following day. Furthermore, d'Argenteau took Monte Settepani and occupied it with 4,000 men, who were able to beat off an attempt by Masséna to retake it. Another counterattack by reinforcements from the left wing of the Armée d'Italie was also defeated (27 June). The same day Austrian attacks all along the French front were defeated except at the

218 Phipps, *West*, pp.235–237; Rodger, *Command*, p.433; Vice Admiral William Hotham.

219 Phipps, *West*, pp.238–240; *Général de Division* Jean-Mathieu-Philibert Sérurier.

220 George Nafziger, *Order of battle for the Armée d'Italie, 19 June 1795*, accessed 22 July 2022, available at: <https://usacac.army.mil/sites/default/files/documents/carl/nafziger/795FAH.pdf>; *Général de Division* Pierre Dominique Garnier.

221 Jones, *Companion*, p.41; *Général de Division* François Xavier Jacob Freytag.

post of Monte Spinarda, which was taken by Colli, the commander of the Austro-Sardinian right. In response to the Austrian assault, Kellermann withdrew his right 17 miles back to the line running northwest from Borghetto Santo Spirito (5 July). Masséna, with 14,000 men, held the line from the sea through Monte Alpe towards Monte Galero, while Sérurier, with 6,000 men, held the hills on the left bank of the river Tanaro, with his reserve at Ormea. Sérurier threw back an attack on the Colle dei Termini, three miles northwest of Ormea (5 July). Kellermann evacuated his magazines at Vado and Finale Ligure by sea, despite the proximity of the British Mediterranean Fleet, based 111 miles away in Saint-Florent, Corsica. Admiral Hotham sent Nelson in the Agamemnon and with some smaller ships to assist the Austrians, but he was chased back to Saint-Florent by a French squadron. The Austrians, surprised by the French withdrawal, slowly followed up and there followed a stalemate of several weeks as both sides fortified their positions along the new line. The French troops, now cut off from Genoa, were short of supplies with the Royal Navy often intercepting supplies sent by sea. Thus, Kellermann was both considering a withdrawal into the Var and planning for a renewed advance once reinforcements from Spain or the Rhine arrived. However, the *Comité* nominated Schérer to take command of the Armée d'Italie while Kellermann was to be restricted to the command of the Armée des Alpes (31 August).[222]

When Schérer assumed command of the Armée d'Italie on 29 September, Kellermann, taking Berthier with him, moved to Gap to take command of the Armée des Alpes on 8 October.[223] Augereau arrived from the Pyrenees with 6,921 men to join the Armée d'Italie as a senior division commander. His division was deployed on the right by the sea.

In the centre, Masséna commanded the divisions of Charlet and Laharpe, together with the reserve under Bizanet, 13,276 men in total. On the left Sérurier commanded 5,155 men and the army thus totalled approximately 25,000 men. Facing these troops, the Austro-Sardinians had 18,000 men.[224] Although Schérer agreed with Kellermann's plan to advance down the valley of the river Tanaro, attacking the junction between the Sardinian and Austrian armies, snow arrived to prevent this approach, consequently Schérer chose to attack the Austrians further towards the coast, breaking through their centre to attack Wallis on the coast in both the front and rear.[225] As the Austrians were preparing to take up winter quarters, with the ill De Wins replaced by Wallis, Sérurier launched a diversionary attack on Colli down both banks of the river Tanaro (22 November). Despite leading the assault on the works of San Bernardo himself, Sérurier was repulsed but rallied his troops before Colli's positions, having achieved Schérer's preliminary objective.[226]

---

222 Phipps, *West*, pp.241–245, 248, 250, 255; Nafziger, *Order of battle for the Armée d'Italie, 19 June 1795*; *Feldzeugmeister* Joseph Nikolaus Freiherr de Vins; *Généraux de Brigade* Amédée Emmanuel François Laharpe and Jean-Baptiste Cervoni; *Generalmajor* Eugen Gillis Wilhelm Graf Mercy d'Argenteau.

223 Jones, *Companion*, pp.147, 150.

224 Smith, *Data Book*, p.108; Phipps, West, p.262; Nafziger, *French Army at the Battle of Loano, 22/23 November 1795*, at: <https://usacac.army.mil/sites/default/files/documents/carl/nafziger/795KAF.pdf>, accessed 28 July 2022: Phipps has the French infantry alone totalling 25,392 men, while Smith gives the French 25,000 men of all arms, including 16 regiments of cavalry, Nafziger's unattributed order of battle totals 24,400 infantry but no cavalry.

225 Phipps, *West*, pp.261–263; *Général de Division* Étienne Charlet; *Général de Brigade* Guilin-Laurent Bizanet.

226 Ignazio Thaon di Revel and Genova Giovanni Thaon di Revel, *Mémoires sur la guerre des Alpes et les événements en Piémont pendant la révolution française tirés des papiers du comte Ignace Thaon de Revel de St-André et de Pralungo* (Turin: Bocca, 1871), pp.290–291.

Following Schérer's plan, at 4:00 a.m. on the same day, Masséna attacked the ridge to the east and south of San Bernardo, held by d'Argenteau. In this attack Charlet was killed at the head of his division and Masséna took his place in leading the division on to capture the Rocca Barbena, whose defenders fell back to Bardineto. Attacked again two hours later by Masséna at the head of Charlet's division, d'Argenteau's men, with their right flank turned, retired in confusion northwards three and half miles down the Western Bormida to Calizzano. Leaving a garrison in Bardineto, Masséna raced northeast to capture Melagno and Monte Settepani before d'Argenteau could get there. Meeting Cervoni's brigade at Melagno at 11:00 p.m., Masséna pressed on at midnight southeast to the heights around Gorra above Finale Ligure, in the rear of the Austrian force on the coast. Masséna thereby completed a 15-mile right hook through the mountains.[227] Meanwhile before daybreak (sunrise was at 7:21 a.m.) on 22 November, the four brigades of Augereau's division, with their right protected by a small flotilla, attacked Wallis's fortified lines before Loano, five miles southwest of Finale Ligure. In leading his brigade through Toirano, on the left, Banel was wounded and replaced by his friend *Chef de Brigade* Jean Lannes.[228] In the Varatella valley the *Certosa di Toirano*, a monastery, was the focus of an Austrian counterattack, led by Ternyey to retake the battery in front of the monastery, but Augereau sent Dommartin's brigade to drive Ternyey's men back into the monastery, where they subsequently surrendered.[229]

Several Austro-Sardinian posts became similarly surrounded and forced to surrender, but the French did not have it all their own way. In one example, Augereau with Victor's brigade behind deployed in column, demanded that Rukavina, the commander of the now isolated post of 'Greater Castellaro', surrender. However, Rukavina refused and instead led his garrison of 1,000 men in close column directly through Victor's much stronger brigade to re-join Wallis. Rukavina's daring paid off and he escaped although at the cost of half of his column.[230]

The day ended with a great deal of uncertainty amongst the commanders on both sides. Colli, unclear as to the fate of the Austrians to his left and having heard nothing from Wallis, determined to hold his ground and further fortify in preparation for further attacks by Sérurier.[231] Wallis only heard of the defeat of d'Argenteau during the night but had withdrawn to the heights overlooking Finalborgo, close to Finale Ligure, approximately four and a half miles northeast of Loano. On the other hand, unclear as to the extent of Masséna's progress, Schérer had halted Augereau's attack at 4:00 p.m. more than an hour before dusk which was at 5:15 p.m. The next day (23 November) Masséna could see Wallis deployed on the heights below him but had only 2,000 men and sent for Laharpe to bring forward reinforcements, which by noon brought

227 Phipps, *West*, p.266; the heights around Gorra are referred to as the heights of San Panteleone, a French description of the heights running southeast from Monte Settepani via Monte Collerina to Gorra and Finalburgo little over a mile from Finale Ligure.

228 Phipps, *West*, p.264: *Général de Brigade* Pierre Banel.

229 Phipps, *West*, p.264: *Generalmajor* Michael Joseph Ternyey de Kis-Ternye.

230 Phipps, *West*, p.265: *Generalmajor* Mathias Rukavina von Boynograd; it is not clear where the redoubt referred to by Phipps as 'Greater Castellaro' was. The village of Castellaro is 27 miles southwest of Loano, whereas the more likely height of Castellari is less than one and a half miles north of Loano itself. In June 1795, Rukavina commanded two battalions of Carlstädt Grenzers and one battalion of the Nadasdy regiment (N.39) (Revel, *Mémoires*, p.273).

231 Revel, *Mémoires*, p.291.

Masséna's strength up to 4,300 men. Wallis attempted to send his artillery to the rear, but 19 guns were captured by part of Masséna's force, under the command of Joubert.[232]

On the rest of the front the day was taken up with minor skirmishing and manoeuvres. Overnight Wallis began his retreat and, in the morning (24 November), Augereau, advancing in two columns, and Masséna advancing from the hills, set off in pursuit. Wallis disabled his guns and reached Savona (25 November) where the full extent of the defeat of his right wing became clear and he consequently marched via Montenotte to Acqui, covered by Rukavina's rearguard (29 November). Shortages of food prevented Augereau and Masséna advancing much beyond Savona. In total the Austro-Sardinians lost 3,500 men killed and wounded plus a further 4,000 men taken prisoner, with French losses reported as 1,700 killed and wounded.[233] Meanwhile Colli had held his ground until the French advanced during the night of 27 November, when he pulled back from his strong positions. While Joubert and Ménard prepared to attack Monte Spinarda, two miles southwest of Calizzano, Sérurier advanced down the valley of the river Tanaro, driving Colli into the entrenched camp at Ceva. The French halted three miles short of Ceva, desperate for food.[234] The victory of Loano enabled the French to end 1795 holding a line with Masséna on the right, with two divisions occupying Savona and the crest of the Apennines to Melogno, in the centre Augereau guarded the gorges of the river Bormida, and Sérurier held the valley of the Tanaro, while on the left Macquard held the Colle di Tenda with Garnier to his left.[235]

Bataille de Loano, 24 November 1795

232 Phipps, *West*, p.266; Phipps places the capture of the guns at the Colle di San Giacomo, 17 miles to the northwest of Finale Ligure, but it may have been at the much closer Tovo di San Giacomo, three miles west of Finale Ligure; *Chef de Brigade* Barthélemy Catherine Joubert, promoted *général de brigade* on the basis of his performance at Loano.

233 Phipps, *West*, p.267.

234 Phipps, *West*, p.269: Revel, *Mémoires*, pp.292–293; *Général de Brigade* Philippe Romain Ménard.

235 Phipps, *West*, p.270.

The Southwest

In Spain, at the eastern end of the Pyrenees, 1795 began with the continuing siege of Roses by Pérignon's Armée des Pyrénées Orientales, which ended with the capitulation of the port after most of the 4,000–5,000-man garrison had been evacuated by the Spanish navy on 3 February.[236] Pérignon then planned to drive the new Spanish commander, Urrutia, into Girona before laying siege to Barcelona. However, the *Comité* in Paris decided that his army would adopt a defensive stance, while the Armée des Pyrénées Occidentales took the offensive. Furthermore, the *Comité* determined that Pérignon was to be replaced by Schérer (3 March). There was only desultory fighting until Schérer joined the army (31 May).

When Schérer embarked on a reconnaissance on the line of the river Fluvià, approximately halfway between Figueres and Girona, to gather food for his army, Urrutia mistook this for an attack, and concentrated his army before driving the French centre back from Bàscara on the river Fluvià (14 June), until Augereau was able to force the Spanish to retire (15 June).[237] Meanwhile, Moncey had completed the *embrigadement* of his infantry in the Armée des Pyrénées Occidentales. The regiments now had two 'field battalions', the third battalions, comprised of the less fit and able men, were used for garrison duties. He also reformed the converged battalions of grenadiers, which were to be used as a reserve body in each division. Moncey's target was to besiege the city of Pamplona, and, in preparation, a siege train was gathered at Bayonne under the command of Marescot, fresh from the siege of Maastricht.[238] The *Comité* ordered 12,000 men from the Vendée to reinforce Moncey and these men began arriving 25 June, enabling him to begin his offensive. Moncey's opponent was Colomera's replacement, Castelfranco, who commanded the armies of Aragón, Navarra and Guipúzcoa. Of this force, two corps, each 9,000 men strong, faced Moncey, Filanguieri at Lekunberri held the hills protecting Pamplona, while Crespo held the line from Bergara, east of Bilbao, along the river Deva to the sea.[239]

Crespo was the first to feel the effect of Moncey's offensive when Raoul, leading five and a half battalions, crossed the river Deva near its mouth to threaten Crespo's left (28 June). The next day, two further columns each of five battalions moved on the front and left of Crespo's position, while Merle, leading a third column, set out from Tolosa for Villareal de Álava (now Legutia) 15 miles beyond Bergara, to cut Crespo's line of retreat. However, sensing the danger, Crespo withdrew through Villareal de Álava to Salinas de Léniz (now Leintz Gatzaga), 10½ miles north of Vitoria on the main road to Madrid, closer to Filanguieri (29 June). Moncey next moved on Filanguieri and the centre of the Spanish position (2 July). Three columns of between 16 and 21 battalions (11,500 to 14,000 men), left Tolosa to attack the front and flanks of the Spanish position at Lekunberri, while a further column of seven battalions left San Esteban to attack Lekunberri from the rear. With the four attacks simultaneously delivered at daybreak, the town quickly fell as the Spanish defenders left their entrenchments, retiring south to Irurtzun, 11½ miles northwest of Pamplona on the road to Vitoria, maintaining the

236 Phipps, *West*, p.199.

237 Phipps, *West*, pp.201–202; Smith, *Data Book*, p.103.

238 Phipps, *West*, pp.202–203: *Général de Division* Armand Samuel de Marescot.

239 Phipps, *West*, pp.203; Martinez, *Diccionario*, pp.235, 330, 815; *Capitán General* Pablo Sangro Gaetani de Aragón y Merode, Principe de Castelfranco; *Mariscal de Campo* Frey Antonio Filanguieri; *Teniente General* José Simón Crespo Álvarez.

connection with Crespo (3 July).[240] Moncey, with 16,000 men, followed up Filangueiri, sending 13 battalions in four columns to take Irurtzun and thereby intercepting the main route of communication between Filangueiri and Crespo (6 July).

Moncey then turned his attention on Crespo, sending Dessein with 4,500 men and two light guns from Elgoibar 12 miles across the mountains to Durango, on the road from Bilbao to Vitoria, throwing back Crespo's left along the way and taking 25 Spanish guns (12 July). Moncey also sent Willot with a further 3,500 men via Salvatierra (Agurain in Basque) to gain Crespo's rear at Vitoria (13 July). Moving on via Villareal de Álava, Dessein reached the hills above Vitoria (14 July) and entering the town the next day. Willot reached Salinas de Léniz apparently trapping Crespo (15 July). However, Crespo found the road north to Bilbao clear of French troops and marched to Durango leaving the two French columns 20 miles in his wake.[241] In response Dessein and Willot followed, marching through Orduña (Urduña in Basque) to Bilbao, which they entered without resistance (19 July). Crespo, reduced to less than 7,000 men, had doubled back through the mountains to the defile of Pancorbo, again blocking the road from Vitoria through Miranda de Ebro to Burgos.

Moncey responded by sending Miollis with a brigade across the river Ebro to occupy Miranda de Ebro, but the Spanish drove this brigade out the same evening (22 July). Bringing Dessein and Willot forward from Bilbao to Miranda de Ebro, Moncey now concentrated his forces at Puente la Reina to cover the siege of Pamplona. However, on 5 August, Moncey then received news that peace had been signed with Spain at Basel, 22 July, ending the war.[242] Schérer had received the same news six days earlier (30 July) to his great relief as his army, ravaged by fever, had been driven from the Cerdagne by La Cuesta, who captured the towns of Puigcerdà, on the frontier 49 miles southwest of Perpignon (26 July), and Beliver de Cerdanya, 11 miles further on, along the way (27 July).[243] The war in the Pyrenees thus ended with victory for France and Spain forced from the First Coalition.

The West

In the west of France 1795 began with the peace conferences between the *Représentants* and the surviving leaders of the rebellion. The conference between the *Représentants* with the Armée de l'Ouest and Charette, at the manor of La Jaunaye, Saint-Sébastien-sur-Loire near Nantes, successfully achieved the first 'pacification' granting the rebels religious freedom and exemption from military service in return for recognising the Republic (17 February 1795). Likewise, the *Représentants* with the Armée des Côtes de Brest and the Armée des Côtes de Cherbourg, both commanded by Hoche, agreed a similar convention with Cormartin at the Château de la Prévalaye, Rennes (20 April). Finally, after a failed attack on two Republican columns, commanded by Canuel, at Saint-Florent le Vieil, near Angers (22 March), Stofflet agreed a similar convention with the *Représentants* there (2 May). Much to the disgust of the Republican generals, the *Représentants* also agreed that the Republic's forces would withdraw from the region

240 Phipps, *West*, p.204; *Généraux de Brigade* Charles-François Raoul and Pierre-Hugues-Victoire Merle.

241 Phipps, *West*, p.205; *Général de Division* Bernard Dessein; *Général de Brigade* Amédée Willot.

242 Phipps, *West*, pp.205–206; Georges Six, *Dictionnaire Bibliographic des Généraux et Amiraux Français de la Révolution et de l'Empire, 1792–1814* (Paris: Librairie Historique et Nobiliaire, 1934), vol. II, p.202; *Général de Brigade* Balthazard de Miollis.

243 Phipps, *West*, p.202; Smith, *Data Book*, p.104.

and be replaced by two groups of 2,000 *garde territoriale* commanded by the *Vendéan* leadership, which had the potential to become the nucleus of future revolts.[244]

However, the revolt north of the river Loire, the *Chouannerie*, was continuing to cause trouble for the Republicans and in response Hoche was ordered to concentrate on commanding the Armée des Côtes de Brest, his other army, the Armée des Côtes de Cherbourg, passing to Aubert-Dubayet (20 April). Hoche was then ordered to arrest Cormartin and set his troops in motion (1 June). Soon Charette in the Vendée broke the peace and war erupted on both banks of the Loire (25 June).[245] The rebellion was reinforced by the landing in Quiberon Bay of an *émigré* army transported from England by the Royal Navy, despite the presence of *Vice Amiral* Villaret de Joyeuse's squadron from Brest.

The Brest squadron of nine ships of the line initially fell into contact with Cornwallis' squadron of five ships of the line, but Cornwallis managed to skilfully disengage without loss (16 June). Villaret de Joyeuse then contacted the troop convoy and the immediate escorts provided by Warren's three ships of the line (22 June) but alerted by Cornwallis, Bridport commanding the Channel Fleet at sea, with 17 ships of the line, including Warren's ships, intercepted the French off the Île de Groix, four miles off Lorient and 18 northwest of Quiberon (23 June). Bridport's fastest ships, HMS *Irresistible* (74), HMS *Orion* (74), HMS *Queen Charlotte* (100), HMS *Russell* (74), HMS *Collosus* (74) and HMS *Sans Pareil* (80) brought the French to battle and captured *L'Alexandre* (74), *Le Tigre* (74) and *Le Formidable* (74). Villaret de Joyeuse was chased into Lorient with his remaining ships of the line.[246]

The *émigré* army was commanded by Puisaye under the orders of the Comte d'Artois. The army comprised 5,500 *émigré* troops of all ranks under d'Hervilly in command of the first division and Sombreuil leading the second. Some of these men were *émigrés* brought to Great Britain from Coblenz, but others were prisoners of war taken from the Republican armies in the Netherlands. Hervilly's division of approximately 3,500 men landed largely unopposed at Carnac, 75 miles northwest of Nantes, covered by the Chouan rebels (27 June). Hervilly's division comprised four regiments of infantry, the Loyal Emigrant Regiment, and the freshly raised Régiment d'Hervilly (1,442 men, also known as the Régiment Saint Louis, after those of its men evacuated from Toulon in December 1793), the Régiment Hector and the Régiment du Dresnay, together with half a battalion of emigrant artillery.

On landing, Hervilly distributed arms to the Chouans and Bretons who had rallied to the Royalist cause, before forming a 10-mile-long defensive line from Auray to Landévant, seven miles inland from Carnac, with an advanced guard at Vennes, 15 miles northeast of Carnac (28 June). However, having gathered his forces, Hoche arrived and soon retook Auray and Landévant (30 June). Grouchy also repulsed a Royalist attempt to land on the Rhuys peninsula, 14 miles southeast of Carnac. Consequently, Hervilly decided

244 Phipps, *West*, pp.38–39; Bertrand Poirier de Beauvais, *Mémoires inédits de Bertrand Poirier de Beauvais, commandant général de l'artillerie des armées de la Vendée* (Paris: Plon, 1893), p.347; Six, *Dictionnaire*, vol. I, p.189: *Général de Division* Simon Canuel; *Maréchal de Camp* Pierre Dezoteux de Cormatin.

245 Phipps, *West*, pp.41–43; Six, *Dictionnaire*, vol. I, p.25; *Général de Division* Jean-Baptiste Annibal Aubert-Dubayet.

246 Rodger, *Command*, p.432; Schomberg, *Naval Chronology*, vol. II, pp.326–327; Smith, *Data Book*, p.103; Smith refers to the battle as Quiberon Bay, but it is also known as the battle of Groix; Vice Admiral William Cornwallis; Vice Admiral Alexander Hood, Baron Bridport (younger brother of Admiral Samuel Hood); Commodore Sir John Borlase Warren.

to retire to create a beachhead around the Quiberon peninsula, which included two small ports to allow resupply by the Royal Navy plus space to train the new volunteers. The peninsula was defended by a small fort, Fort Penthièvre, which was attacked and taken by Hervilly. The garrison of the fort and peninsula, some five to six hundred men, were taken prisoner and recruited into the Royalist regiments (3 July). The peninsula however was quite cramped and congested, only 10 miles long and barely one and a half miles wide. Hoche with 13,000 men attacked and retook Carnac, establishing himself at Sainte Barbe at the foot of the peninsula (7 July). Hervilly probed Hoche's defences at Sainte Barbe on both 7 July and 11 July.

Having just been evacuated from Stadt near Hamburg on 29 June, Sombreuil's second division of Puisaye's army, 1,500 men strong, left Portsmouth on 11 July and four days later, on 15 July, arrived in Quiberon Bay. Sombreuil's division comprised the weak regiments of Damas, Rohan, Salm and Perigord. Before the second division could disembark, Puisaye and Hervilly launched a major but poorly coordinated attack on Hoche at Sainte Barbe, which was repulsed with losses of 730 men, including Hervilly who was mortally wounded, on16 July. Over the next two days the second division was disembarked around the village of Saint Julien on the east of the peninsula. At this point Hoche had 12,000 men and 64 guns arrayed around Saint Barbe while Puisaye could only muster 4,500 regular troops plus 5,400 volunteers, women and children of whom perhaps half could bear arms, giving a total of 7,255 under arms.

The Royalist force had already been weakened by desertion, from which Hoche was able to garner useful intelligence. Hoche made his move late on 20 July, when his grenadiers, assisted by more deserters inside the position, captured Fort Penthièvre by 1:30 a.m. on 21 July. The Royalist response to Hoche's continued attack on the peninsula was confused, inhibited by a lack of ammunition, and marked by mass desertions. Rather than lead the defence, Puisaye joined the rout to Port d'Orange, only one and a half miles south of the fort, where he took a boat to Warren's flagship. Sombreuil deployed his division at Le Roch, one mile south of the fort at 5:00 a.m., before retiring to a position above Saint Julien, two miles further down the peninsula. Outnumbered and low on ammunition, Sombreuil withdrew his men to Fort Neuf and the adjacent bay, the Plage du Porigo, on the east of the peninsula. It was here, after a brief stand-off during which two small ships gave supporting fire to the Royalists, that Sombreuil surrendered to Hoche. The confusion and heavy seas prevented any mass evacuation of the Royalist forces by the Royal Navy, however 1,000 troops and 2,000 civilians managed to escape to the British fleet. In all Hoche, took 4,000–5,000 prisoners. Of these he executed 748 by firing squad (27 July), including Sombreuil, whose father and elder brother had gone to the guillotine in 1794.[247]

A footnote to the fiasco at Quiberon was provided by Great Britain's belated plan to send Moira's expedition of 3,300 men to occupy the Quiberon peninsula, providing a base for future operations with a plan to pay up to 15,000 local recruits. Moira was ordered to embark the 12th, 78th, 80th and 90th Foot together with a detachment of the 14th Light Dragoons and an appropriate amount of artillery. These troops were to

247 Phipps, *West*, pp.42–43; Fortescue, *History*, vol. IV, pt.1, pp.412–415; Hughes de Bazouges and Alistair Nichols, *For God and King, A History of the Damas Legion (1793–1798): a Case study of the Military Emigration during the French Revolution* (Warwick: Helion and Company, 2021), pp.177, 183–198; *Lieutenant Général* Joseph-Geneviève, Comte de Puisaye; *Maréchal de Camp* Louis-Charles Comte d'Hervilly; *Maréchal de Camp* Charles Eugène Gabriel de Vidot de Sombreuil; *Général de Division* Emmanuel de Grouchy, Hoche's chief of staff.

capture islands of Hoedic and the Île d'Houat, 10 miles southeast of Quiberon. The intention was to move 50 miles further southeast to the Île de Noirmoutier, south of the Loire estuary, from where they could support the Vendéan rebels under Charette, who had again taken up arms (25 June). This time the Comte d'Artois, younger brother of Louis XVI, was to accompany the expedition. After lengthy delays during which a disillusioned Moira resigned his command, being replaced by Brigadier Doyle, the expedition sailed on 30 August, arriving in Quiberon Bay on 12 September. The British disembarked on Hoedic where they joined the survivors of the Quiberon expedition.[248]

Meanwhile, with his victory at Quiberon increasing his prestige in Paris, Hoche was given the additional command of the Armée de l'Ouest (29 August) and renewed his efforts to suppress the rebellions on both banks of the river Loire. After discussions with Charette, Doyle determined that the planned capture of Noirmoutier was impractical and instead occupied the Île d'Yeu, a short distance further south (29 September). At d'Artois's request Charette marched his 15,000 rebels to the coast (10 October), but d'Artois refused to leave the relative safety of the Île d'Yeu. On the island Doyle was struggling, due to poor weather, to provide sufficient provisions for his men.[249] Hoche's task was eased by the arrival of reinforcements from the Armée de Pyrénées Orientales in October and the Armée du Nord in December.[250] The whole sorry episode ended when Doyle's expedition was reembarked between 3–15 December and returned to England by the Royal Navy.[251] The Directory then took the step of merging the three western armies into one force, the Armée des Côtes de l'Océan commanded by Hoche (26 December). The new army was nominally 183,000 men strong but had just 100,000 men present under arms.[252] However the rebellion in the west was not over as the year ended with the Chouans and *Vendéans* still waging their guerrilla campaign.

Paris

We cannot complete our survey of the war within and on the borders of Metropolitan France without summarising the events of the *13 Vendémiaire, An IV* (5 October) in Paris. Following more bad harvests and bread riots the *Convention Nationale* in Paris was shown to be ineffective in dealing with the problems of France and a new constitution proved unpopular. Royalist agitators brought about open rebellion in Paris in early October. The rebels were called *Sectionnaires* after the 48 *sections* into which Paris had been divided by the *Convention Nationale*. The *Sectionnaires* were led by Danican, who, from his headquarters at the convent *Filles Saint Thomas d'Aquin*, in *Section Le Peletier*, half a mile north of the Tuileries Palace, called Paris to arms to overthrow the *Convention Nationale* (4 October).[253]

In response on the same day, the commander of the Armée de l'Intérieur, Menou, was ordered to disarm *Section Le Peletier*. However, having marched on the convent he was faced down by the *Sectionnaires* and retired. Consequently, Menou was arrested

248 Fortescue, *History*, vol. IV, pt.1, pp.416–419; Bazouges, *God and King*, p.203; Lieutenant-Colonel John Doyle, 87th Foot.
249 Fortescue, *History*, vol. IV, pt.1, pp.421–422.
250 Phipps, *West*, pp.44–47.
251 Bazouges, *God and King*, p.207.
252 Phipps, *West*, p.49.
253 Michael John Sydenham, *The First French Republic, 1792-1804* (London: Batsford, 1974), pp.74–79: Six, *Dictionnaire*, vol. I, p.285; *Général de Brigade* Louis Michel Auguste Thévenet, called Danican.

and replaced by Barras, with Duvigneau as his chief of staff.[254] Overnight the Tuileries Palace was turned into a fortress to defend the seat of government, the theatre in the Tuileries Palace, where the *Convention Nationale* met. The call to arms resulted in a force of 25,000–30,000 *Sectionnaires*, while the government could count on a force of only 4,000 regulars, supported by 2,000 armed police, pensioners from Les Invalides and irregulars. With the *Sectionnaires* marching on the Tuileries Palace, Barras, asked his protégé Buonaparte to help defend the *Convention Nationale* (5 October). Buonaparte's role has been controversial with 30 other generals known to have been involved in the defence of the *Convention Nationale*. These men include several generals who were more senior to Buonaparte, suggesting that he was an aide-de-camp to Barras (as later claimed by Barras), or the artillery commander (although this role was held by d'Urtubie), rather than second in command.[255] However, Buonaparte wrote to his brother Joseph the next day (6 October), clearly describing his role as Barras's second in command, which is supported by other documents in the *Archives Nationales*.[256]

In Barras's name, Buonaparte sent Murat with 300 cavalry to retrieve some artillery from the *Camp des Sablons*, three miles away to the west-northwest. Murat arrived before a competing group of *Sectionnaires* and returned with 40 guns, which were deployed in the defensive ring around the Tuileries Palace, including near the *Eglise Saint Roch* on the *Rue Saint Honoré*. Most of the *Sectionnaires* remained in their own sections, but it is estimated that 7,000–8,000 *Sectionnaires* attempted to march on the Tuileries Palace. When they approached, the guns opened fire and the government troops held firm. Three hundred *Sectionnaires* were killed or wounded as were a similar number of government troops, in what Thomas Carlyle, in 1837, christened the 'whiff of grapeshot' and the *Convention Nationale* was saved and a new executive body, the *Directoire* was installed, led by Barras. Buonaparte, now a national figure, was rewarded with the command of the Armée de l'Intérieur (27 October) and subsequently the Armée d'Italie (27 March 1796).[257] This was the first time the regular army had been used in Paris to suppress rebellion against the government since 1789.

Overseas

Beyond Metropolitan France the scope of the war expanded still further in 1795. As early as January 1795 concerns were being raised in Great Britain regarding the need to safeguard the colonies of the United Provinces in case the French went on to conquer them. Consequently, permission was gained from the exiled Stadtholder to admit British troops into his colonies (7 February). Blankett was given command of a squadron of four ships, which transported the 2/78th Foot (500 men), under the command of Craig, to the Cape of Good Hope, South Africa. Arriving there, Blankett met Elphinstone's squadron, which had overtaken them and was carrying the 2/84th, 95th and 98th Foot

254 Six, *Dictionnaire*, vol. I, p.419; *Général de Brigade* Bernard Étienne Marie Duvigneau.

255 Six, *Dictionnaire*, vol. I, pp.50, 89, 114, 122–123, 167, 196, 221–222, 254–255, 408–409, 434; vol. II, p.62–63, 112, 128, 216, 237, 408, 520, 540.

256 J.M.Thompson, *Napoleon's Letters* (London: Prion, 1998), p.16; Henry Zivy, *Le Trieze Vendémiaire An IV* (Paris: Germer Baillière, 1898), p.75; Joachim Murat, *Murat, Lieutenant de l'empereur en Espagne, 1808* (Paris: E. Plon, Nourrit et Cie, 1897), p.33; *Général de Brigade* Paul Barras; *Général de Brigade* Napoleone di Buonaparte; *Chef d'Escadron* Joachim Murat, 21e Chasseurs à Cheval.

257 Horne, *French Revolution*, p.50; Esdaile, *Wars*, p.128; Jones, *Companion*, pp.149–150.

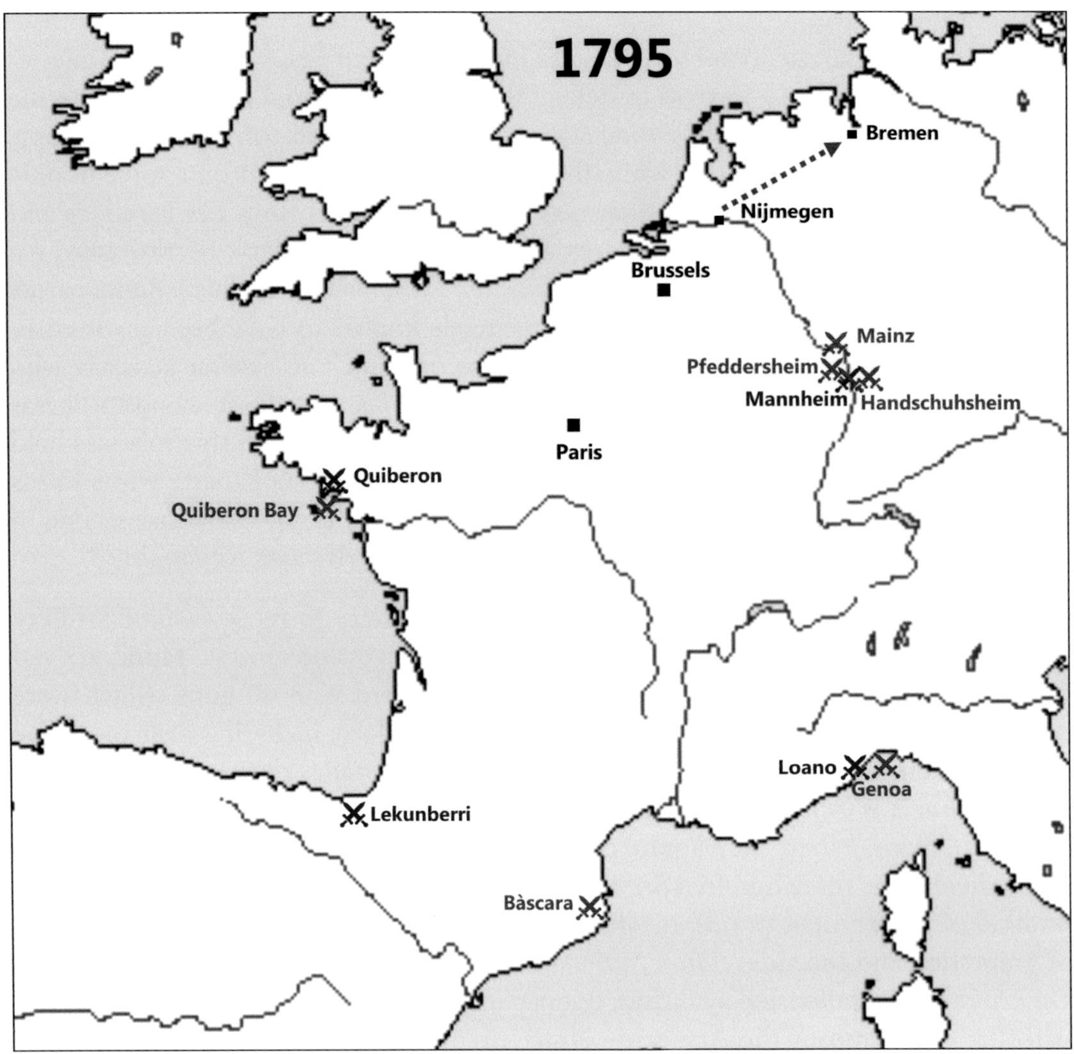

Map 5 – Key actions and battles, 1795

(2,000 men), commanded by Clarke, to secure the Dutch possessions in the East Indies (10 June).[258]

The combined fleet anchored in False Bay (12 June) but the Dutch colonists, including a significant and powerful group with sympathy for the French cause, rejected the instructions from the Stadtholder and the British decided that the colony needed to be taken by force of arms, despite a lack of field artillery. The governor of the colony then refused to supply the British ships with fresh provisions (27 June). Having occupied Simonstown (14 July) Craig and Elphinstone determined to open the road to Cape Town. With Clarke's men on their way to Bahia, Brazil, Craig led 1,600 soldiers and seamen up the road from Simonstown to Cape Town, 12 miles away, supported by artillery fire from Royal Navy gunboats in the bay (7 August). The artillery fire from the fleet forced the defenders from the defile formed by the Muizenberg hill. Craig repulsed a counterattack the next day (8 August). Then, although reinforced by 400 troops and nine guns from St Helena, Craig failed in an attempt to create panic in the defending militia (27 August). As the Dutch forces prepared for another assault on

258 Fortescue, *History*, vol. IV, pt.1, pp.392–396; Robert Gardiner (ed.), *Fleet Battle and Blockade, the French Revolutionary War, 1792–1797* (London: Chatham Publishing, 1996), p.70; Commodore John Blankett with HMS *America* (64), HMS *Stately* (64), HMS *Ruby* (64) and HMS *Echo* (16); Major-General James Henry Craig; Rear Admiral George Keith Elphinstone, with HMS *Monarch* (74), HMS *Arrogant* (74), HMS *Victorious* (74) and HMS *Rattlesnake* (16); Major-General Alured Clarke.

Craig, they hesitated when a large fleet arrived carrying Clarke's men, recalled from Bahia (3 September).[259]

With these reinforcements the British now had enough men to compel the Dutch to surrender Cape Town (15 September). Leaving Blankett's squadron and Craig with 3,000 infantry to hold Cape Town in the face of a hostile population, Elphinstone and Clarke sailed for Madras (15 November).[260] Similar combined operations in the East Indies led to the capture of the Dutch colonies of Malacca (17 August) and Trincomalee (26 August), at little cost.

In the West Indies, while their forces were being ravaged by Yellow Fever, the British faced slave revolts on the islands of Grenada, St. Vincent and St. Lucia, inspired and materially assisted by Victor Hugues on Guadeloupe, and a further rebellion broke out on the island of Jamaica.[261]

A convoy of British reinforcements arrived in Barbados (30 March) but comprised just five battalions (2nd, 25th, 29th, 34th and 45th Regiments of Foot, five further battalions had been too sick to join the convoy) totalling just 2,700 men. Many of these men were raw and young, with clothing unsuited to the climate. Within two weeks 200 were listed as sick. The British garrisons launched operations against the rebel 'brigands' but St. Lucia had to be abandoned (18 June); of the 1,400 men evacuated, 600 were sick. Meanwhile on the island of Grenada the British were reduced to holding only the main town of St. George's. Despite the closeness of the French, 40 miles away on St. Lucia, the British garrison of St. Vincent held out until the end of the year assisted by a local black militia and three weak battalions (40th, 54th and 59th Regiments of Foot) which had arrived from Flanders (2 October).[262]

Consequently, the government spent the latter part of 1795 preparing a further expedition to reinforce the island colonies, commanded by Rear Admiral Hugh Christian and Lieutenant-General Ralph Abercromby. The expedition sailed in November 1795, but severe gales forced it back into port (29 January).[263]

Other naval engagements during 1795 include:[264]

259 Schomberg, *Naval Chronology*, vol. II, p.410, Fortescue, *History*, vol. IV, pt.1, pp.403–404.
260 Fortescue, *History*, vol. IV, pt.1, pp.397–402.
261 Rodger, *Command*, pp.434–435.
262 Fortescue, *History*, vol. IV, pt.1, pp.430–431, 436, 441.
263 Fortescue, *History*, vol. IV, pt.1, pp.424–427; Schomberg, *Naval Chronology*, vol. II, p.413.
264 Schomberg, *Naval Chronology*, vol. II, pp.317–318, 334, 336–337, 391–292, 394–396, 399–400, 402–405; vol. IV (1815), p.496.

Theatre	Date	Action
Home waters	18 February	Warren's squadron intercepted the French frigate *Néréide* (36) with a convoy of 20 sail off the *Île d'Aix* capturing or destroying 19 sail loaded with provisions for the French army.
	2 March	HMS *Lively* (32) captured *L'Espion* (18) off Ushant and then the *La Tourterelle* (30) on 13 March.
	10 April	HMS *Astraea* (32) took *La Gloire* (36) in the Soundings and HMS *Hannibal* (74) took *La Gentile* (24) of the same force the next day.
	22 August	Off the Norwegian coast, HMS *Reunion* (36), HMS *Isis* (50), HMS *Stag* (32) and HMS *Vestal* (28) captured the Dutch (i.e., Batavian Republic) frigate *Alliantie* (36), while the frigate *Argo* (36) and the cutter *Nelly* (16) escaped.
	7 October	A French squadron (*Victoire* (80), *Barra* (74), *Résolution* (74), *Berwick* (74), *Jupitre* (74), *Duquesne* (74) and supporting frigates) intercepted the annual British Levant convoy escorted by HMS *Fortitude* (74), HMS *Bedford* (74), HMS *Censeur* (74), HMS *Lutine* (32) and HMS *Tisiphone* (14) from the Mediterranean off Cape St. Vincent, capturing HMS *Censeur* and 30 ships from the convoy.
Mediterranean	14 February	The Spanish ship of the line *Reina Maria Luisa* (112) chased and captured the French frigate *Iphigenie*, in the Gulf of Roses.
	8 March	The *Alceste* (32), *Minerve* (40) and *Vestale* (32), of the French fleet out of Toulon, captured the jury-rigged HMS *Berwick* (74), which was en route to Cap Corse to join the British fleet.
	13–14 March	Lord Hotham's British Mediterranean Fleet (14 ships of the line, including three from Naples) chased *Contre-amiral* Pierre Martin's French fleet (13 ships of the line) off Genoa capturing the *Ça Ira* (80) and the *Censeur* (74), while HMS *Illustrious* was heavily damaged and later wrecked on the Italian coast, near Avenza.
	24 June	Off the *Îles d'Hyères* near Toulon, HMS *Dido* (28) and HMS *Lowestoffe* (32) pursued and captured the *Minerve* (40), while her companion *L'Artémise* (32) escaped.
	13 July	Hotham with 23 ships of the line gave chase to Martin's French Mediterranean Fleet, 19 ships of the line, off the *Îles d'Hyères.* The French escaped with loss of one ship, *L'Alcide* (74), destroyed by fire.
N. America	17 May	HMS *Thetis* (38) and HMS *Hussar* (18) cruising off Chesapeake captured two *flûtes*, *La Prévoyante* (38 reduced to 24) and *La Raison* (24 reduced to 18), while three others escaped.
West Indies	4 January	HMS *Blanche* (32) captured *La Pique* (32) off Point-à-Pitre, Guadeloupe.
	25 May	HMS *Thorn* (16) captured *La Courier National* (18).
	10–14 October	HMS *Mermaid* (32) captured the *Brutus* (10) and the *Republicaine* (18) off Grenada.

During 1795 the French Republic still had 484,000 men to guard its frontiers and attack its enemies.[265] These armies fought 10 battles involving 20,000 or more men, winning only three and losing seven. They also fought 11 lesser actions, winning six and losing five. However, despite the lack of tactical battlefield success the French had conquered the Netherlands, forcing the Dutch from the First Coalition, followed by Prussia, Spain, Saxony, Hanover, Hesse-Kassel and Hesse-Darmstadt and Brunswick. Britain fought on but with its broken European expedition forced back home. Austria and the Holy Roman Empire remained the major force fighting the French.

The War in 1796

The Rhine

On France's Rhine frontier, during the armistice with the Austrians, Jourdan, commander of the Armée de Sambre-et-Meuse, went to Paris to garner support and resources from the Directory. When he returned to his headquarters in Cologne on 29 February, Jourdan set about preparing his army for the coming campaign, completing the amalgamation of the volunteer and regular battalions into the new *demi-brigades*, strengthening the line of the river Moselle, and completing the entrenched camp at Düsseldorf. The army now comprised 63,100 infantry, 11,400 cavalry and 3,300 artillery, divided into an advanced guard, six divisions and reserves of both infantry and cavalry. Among the army's officers were Bernadotte, Lefebvre, Mortier, Ney and Soult.[266]

Pichegru's Armée du Rhin-et-Moselle, spent the armistice freezing in the lines of Queich and in the Annweiler valley on the Upper Rhine, with the headquarters at Hagenau. The conditions were so bad and food so scarce that Saint-Cyr, without orders, withdrew his division 30 leagues to better cantonments centred on Zweibrücken. The army was separated from the Armée de Sambre-et-Meuse by the Austrians in Mannheim and Mainz. Pichegru resigned his command of the Rhin-et-Moselle, accused of treacherous communications with Royalist agents (5 March), and was initially replaced by Desaix, who immediately withdrew the troops to better cantonments, but ultimately by Jean-Victor Moreau (appointed 25 March, took up command 23 April). Moreau promptly reorganised his army into three corps and a small reserve. Férino commanded the two divisions on the right, where 20,400 men were deployed along the Upper Rhine from Bâle to Lauterbourg. Desaix commanded the two divisions in the centre, where 17,300 men held Landau and the lines of Queich. Saint-Cyr commanded the two divisions on the left, where 19,900 men held the line from Landau to Limbach on the river Blies, then following that river to Neunkirchen, where they contacted the Armée de Sambre-et-Meuse. Finally, Bourcier commanded the small infantry reserve and the heavy cavalry reserve of 7,500 men. In total the army had 65,100 men plus a further 12,100 men in various garrisons.[267]

Facing the two French armies were two Austrian armies. Wurmser commanded 82,800 men guarding a line that ran along right bank of the river Rhine from Bâle to

265 Jones, *Companion*, p.157.

266 Phipps, *Moselle*, pp.258–259.

267 Phipps, *Moselle*, pp.261, 267, 269–270, 272–273; *Général de Division* Pierre Marie Bartholomé Férino; *Général de Division* François-Antoine Louis Bourcier.

Mannheim before crossing the river and continuing westwards to Kaiserslautern.[268] Lower down the river, the Archduke Charles, in place of Clerfayt, commanded 71,100 infantry and 20,700 cavalry, whose line stretched from Wurmser's right along the river Nahe to Kirn, due east to Mainz. The line then ran northwards along the right bank of the Rhine to Altenkirchen and on to the river Seig. Thus, the Austrian centre formed a wedge between the two French armies. The French were further disadvantaged by the inability of the Armée de Rhin-et-Moselle to easily transfer troops to the right bank of the river Rhine.

The armistice was denounced by the Austrians (20 May) and hostilities soon resumed (1 June). Kléber with the left wing of the Armée de Sambre-et-Meuse – 21,000 men – advanced from Düsseldorf, crossing the river Wupper at midnight on 31 May. From here Kléber advanced up the right bank of the river Rhine, driving the Austrians from Altenkirchen to cover the crossing of the other French divisions (4 June). Kléber then advanced onto the river Lahn (6 June). At this juncture the Austrian high command ordered Wurmser to Italy with 25,000 men to join the fight against Bonaparte, and consequently the Archduke Charles withdrew his men across the river Rhine via Mainz to the right bank. Seeing the Austrians withdrawing, Jourdan chose to mask Mainz with Marceau's corps of 22,300 men, while he crossed to the right bank of the Rhine with the rest of the Armée de Sambre-et-Meuse at Neuwied (6 June). Jourdan then positioned his main body of 48,000 men along the river Lahn, with his headquarters 21 miles northeast of Coblenz at Hadamar (12 June).

Rather than divide the two French armies by attacking Marceau before Mainz, the Archduke Charles chose to focus on Jourdan's army. Consequently, when Jourdan, preparing to advance from the river Lahn, sent Lefebvre forward to Wetzlar and then Werdorf to cover his left flank, Lefebvre found himself with 6,000–7,000 men fighting the Archduke's 15,000 and was forced to retreat to the river Lahn (15 June). Soult's brigade at Herborn was now exposed and he was attacked, initially by 4,000 Austrians, and cut off from his line of retreat. Forming his men into squares Soult was forced to retire six miles across country and ultimately 29 miles to Altenkirchen. With his left defeated Jourdan ordered the Armée de Sambre-et-Meuse to withdraw down the right bank of the river Rhine (16 June). During this withdrawal Kléber ignored Jourdan's orders, and chose to turn and attack his pursuers, Kray's division of 14,000 men, at Uckerath and Kircheib. Both sides suffered heavy casualties, but the Austrians successfully beat off Kléber's attack and forced a further retreat, although Kléber also claimed victory by checking Kray's pursuit (19 June). Thereafter, Jourdan's retirement continued unmolested to Düsseldorf (22 June).[269]

Meanwhile, with the Archduke Charles focused on Jourdan, Moreau swung the left wing of the Armée de Rhin-et-Moselle eastwards to the river Rhine in line with the rest of the army, while Marceau advanced his corps to the river Nahe. Moreau sent Saint-Cyr and Desaix to attack the tête-du-pont at Mannheim (15 and 20 June), before bringing Saint-Cyr's men back from Alsenborn and Kaiserslautern. Appearing himself before Mannheim, to distract the Austrian commanders, Moreau then passed his army across

268 Wurmser was promoted *feldmarschall* 11 December 1795.

269 Phipps, *Moselle*, pp.274–275, 278, 280–285; Smith, *Data Book*, pp.114–115; *Feldzeugmeister* Erzherzog Karl Ludwig Johann Josef Lorenz von Österreich, Herzog von Teschen, younger brother of Francis II, the Holy Roman Emperor; *Feldmarschallleutnant* Paul Freiherr Kray von Krajova und Topola; at Wetzlar Smith gives Lefebvre 11,000 men against the archduke's 36,000 men.

the Rhine via Strasbourg on 24 June. While diversionary crossings were attempted at Strasbourg and below Gambsheim, 10 miles northeast of Strasbourg, Desaix and Férino led the main crossing at Strasbourg capturing Kehl on the right bank opposite, where 10,100 French drove back the 7,000 men of the *Schwäbisches-Kreis-Contingent* of the Holy Roman Empire. Desaix followed up the crossing with another victory at Renchen against Sztáray, commanding 9,000 Imperial troops from Württemberg and Kurpfalz-Bayern. At this point in the campaign although Jourdan had been forced by the Archduke Charles's superior numbers to retreat from the Lahn across to the left bank of the river Rhine, Moreau had taken the opportunity to establish a crossing point to the right bank. That the two French armies now both held a crossing point over the river Rhine was seen as a successful start by Carnot and the Directory in Paris.[270]

Wurmser, on his way to Italy, was replaced by Latour (18 June) under the overall command of the Archduke Charles, who thereby commanded all the Austrian troops on the Rhine, a total of 151,300 men, positioned between Jourdan (77,800 men) and Moreau (79,600 men). Once he was confident that Jourdan had crossed to the right bank, the Archduke Charles began to send troops up the Rhine. Hearing at Wallmerod that Moreau had crossed at Strasbourg (26 June) the Archduke Charles hurried south to attack him, leaving Wartensleben with 36,300 men (the Army of the Lower Rhine) to confront Jourdan.

Moreau deployed his army such that Desaix and his corps, in the valley of the Rhine, faced downstream while Férino faced upstream, with Saint-Cyr to the east in the hills, ready to support either body of troops in the valley. The Austrians facing Moreau formed a semicircle with the émigré corps of Condé, at Riegel am Kaiserstuhl, the Duc d'Enghien commanding the *avant-garde* and the Duc de Berry, the cavalry. The future King Louis XVIII was present with these troops until the Austrians asked him to leave at the end of June.[271] Moreau moved slowly but eventually led his left and centre north against Latour, who was advancing up the right bank of the river Rhine from Mannheim towards him. Moreau (19,000 men) attacked Latour (6,000 men) at Rastatt and forced him back across the river Murg (5 July).

Latour retired to Ettlingen where he was joined by Archduke Charles with 24 battalions and 39 squadrons, a total force of 32,000 men. Meanwhile Saint-Cyr had advanced from Oberkirch in the valley of the river Rench and captured the Austrian positions on Kniebis mountain (2 July), then through Oppenau to Freudenstadt at the head of the valley of the river Murg (3 July). Saint-Cyr's assault had cut through the Austrian line separating Fröhlich from the Archduke Charles and opening the way to Württemberg, Swabia and the road to the Danube. Moreau then attacked the combined Austrian force at Ettlingen, with Desaix's divisions, Bourcier's reserve and Saint-Cyr's cavalry and artillery (36,000 men), while Saint-Cyr brought his infantry down the right bank of the river Murg. Desaix's divisions were repulsed, and the Archduke Charles began to advance himself only to be halted, in turn, by the success of Saint-Cyr's infantry in the hills above, where he had forced the Austrian left, under Kaim, from the hills between the Murg and Enz valleys and after a heavy combat from the position of Rothenzholl,

270 Phipps, *Moselle*, pp.288–289; Smith, *Data Book*, pp.114–115; clashes of Maudach (in the outskirts of Mannheim) and Kehl; *Feldmarschallleutnant* Anton Graf Sztáray de Nagy-Mihály et Sztára.

271 Phipps, *Moselle*, pp.290–291; *Feldmarschallleutnant* Gustav Wilhelm Ludwig Count Wartensleben; Louis-Antoine de Bourbon, Duke of Enghien; Charles Ferdinand d'Artois, Duke of Berry; Louis-Joseph de Bourbon, Prince of Condé; *Feldmarschallleutnant* Maximilian Anton Karl Baillet de Latour.

northwest of Dobel (9 July). Moreau waited until 15 July before moving forward again with an attack on Pforzheim on the river Enz, however he discovered that the Archduke had, the day before, abandoned the valley of the river Rhine and marched eastwards. Reaching the river Neckar, 25 miles east of Pforzheim, Moreau's men drove 8,000 Austrians from Bad Cannstadt, opposite Stuttgart (21 July).[272] The Archduke Charles has since been criticised for surrendering his central position between the two French armies, so readily.

Meanwhile, once Jourdan was assured that the Armée de Rhin-et-Moselle was established on the right bank of the river Rhine, he advanced again. Kléber with the left wing of the Armée de Sambre-et-Meuse marched out of Düsseldorf to the river Lahn once more. Grenier's division and Bonnaud's infantry reserve crossed at Cologne on 28 June, while the divisions of Championnet and Bernadotte crossed at Neuwied (during night of 1–2 July). Bonnaud crossed with his cavalry reserve at Bonn (2 July) and this left only Marceau's 12,800 men on the left bank observing Mainz. The outnumbered Austrians led by Wartensleben and Kray conducted a steady fighting withdrawal. When Colaud's division was stopped at the river Sieg, Ney swam the river with a regiment of Chasseurs à Cheval to save the bridge at Buisdorf and advance to Uckerath (30 June). Lefebvre then had to dislodge Kray from a strong position at Wilnsdorf, by an attack in four columns, one of which turned Kray's right and forced him back to the Lahn, at the cost of 600 prisoners of war (4 July). Wartensleben, threatened by this development, also retired to the river Lahn, Jourdan was thus able to deploy his army along that river (7 July), surprising and driving off the garrison at Gleissen on the Lahn (8 July).[273] When Jourdan launched his army across the Lahn on 9 July, Archduke Charles ordered Wartensleben to hold Friedberg as a means of protecting Frankfurt, 15 miles to the south. However, Wartensleben was driven back by Lefebvre and Colaud (10 July).

Kléber led the left wing of the Armée de Sambre-et-Meuse towards Frankfurt and began to bombard the city on 13 July, creating many fires. Frankfurt surrendered and the French occupied it (16 July), Jourdan gathering his army around the city. Although Archduke Charles had been driven from the river Rhine, he had left 30,000 men in garrisons behind, at Mainz (15,000 infantry and 1,200 cavalry), Ehrenbreitstein (3,000 infantry), Mannheim (8,800 infantry and 300 cavalry) and Philippsburg (2,500 infantry). The French army commanders had to protect themselves against this threat to their rear echelons. Jourdan gave Marceau 28,500 men to blockade Mannheim and Ehrenbreitstein, with his headquarters at Wiesbaden on the right bank. Moreau left only 2,800 infantry and 240 cavalry to observe both Mannheim and Philippsburg. Further down the river Rhine the Armée du Nord, commanded by Beurnonville, had little to do as it guarded the new *République Batave* but supported its sister armies further up the river Rhine, by extending the line it held up to Düsseldorf.[274]

Carnot now determined that the two French armies should operate on the flanks of the Austrian army, with the Armée de Rhin-et-Moselle attacking the Archduke's left, while the Armée de Sambre-et-Meuse operated against Wartensleben driving him into Bohemia and then taking Ratisbon on the river Danube. At this point Jourdan's

272 Phipps, *Moselle*, pp.291–294; Smith, *Data Book*, pp.116–117; *Feldmarschallleutnant* Michael, Freiherr von Fröhlich; *Generalmajor* Konrad Valentin Ritter von Kaim; the battle of Ettlingen is also known as the battle of Malsch.

273 Phipps, *Moselle*, pp.295–296; Smith, *Data Book*, p.116.

274 Phipps, *Moselle*, pp.296–297, 299–300; Smith, *Data Book*, pp.116–117; *Généraux de Division* Jacques Philippe Bonnaud, Paul Grenier and Pierre Riel de Beurnonville.

Armée de Sambre-et-Meuse had 46,200 men, while his opponent Wartensleben had 36,300 men. While Wartensleben had marched 60 miles southeast from Frankfurt to Würzburg, Jourdan left Hanau, crossed the river Kinzig (18 July) and his advanced troops occupied Gemünden on 20 July and Schweinfurt on 22 July before Würzburg surrendered to Championnet's division three days later. Meanwhile, Moreau had 'groped' his way forward, Desaix reaching Gmünd (27 July), 65 miles almost due south of Würzburg, and Moreau expected to enter the valley of the Danube from thence by 1 August.

The Directory once again ordered its armies to operate on the flanks of Archduke Charles's army. Consequently, once Moreau was thus abreast of him, Jourdan resumed his march against Wartensleben, attempting to outflank his right. Jourdan and Lefebvre were almost captured when on reconnaissance between Schweinfurt and Hassfurt on the right back of the river Main (28 July). For his part, Wartensleben had marched to Zeil-am-Main, 32 miles northeast of Würzburg, on the right bank of the river Main such that Jourdan's army was between him and Archduke Charles. Kléber, commanding the Armée de Sambre-et-Meuse in place of the sick Jourdan, attacked Wartensleben at Zeil, while his right wing attempted to seize Bamberg, thereby obliging Wartensleben to retire into Bohemia. However, the operation was a failure as Wartensleben was able to slip away eastwards through Bamberg up the river Regnitz towards Nürnberg (3 August). Colaud's division advanced up the right bank of the river Regnitz from Hirschaid to attack Wartensleben at Forchheim. After some heavy fighting and threatened by the rest of the Armée de Sambre-et-Meuse, Wartensleben retired and the fortress at Forchheim surrendered to the French on 7 August. It was during this fighting that the enterprising, bold and energetic Michel Ney earned his promotion to *général de brigade.*

Instead of proceeding to Nürnberg as ordered, Wartensleben instead marched southeast to Amberg, with the rest of the army following. Ney was thus able to march on Nürnberg, until relieved by Bernadotte's division, from whence he captured the fortress of Rothenburg, 15 miles northeast of Nürnberg near Schnaitach. Jourdan pushed on, and after heavy fighting forced Wartensleben from Amberg on 18 August. The Armée de Sambre-et-Meuse then took up a position on the river Naab, from Schwandorf to Nabburg and Wernburg-Köblitz, with Bernadotte's division detached 25 miles to the west-southwest at Deining (21 August).[275]

Meanwhile, Archduke Charles had been withdrawing before Moreau and the Armée de Rhin-et-Moselle. The Archduke drew up his army of 43,000 men along a line of 22 miles from Nördlingen to the Danube (10 August). Facing him, Moreau, with 44,700 men, was deployed on an extended front of 96 miles from Bopfingen to Lindau on Lake Constance. As Moreau's men approached this line, Saint-Cyr (30,400 men) in Moreau's centre with only Taponier's division beyond the Egge stream drove the Austrians to his front from Eglingen (10 August). Intending to repulse Moreau before joining Wartensleben to crush Jourdan, Archduke Charles attacked Saint-Cyr in the battle of Neresheim (11 August).

Saint-Cyr's cavalry was thrown back from Eglingen, 13 miles across the Egge to Heidenheim. Moreau's army was scattered and in a bad position. Saint-Cyr could face the Archduke with only 12 battalions, nine of which he positioned either side of Dunkstelkingen, just over a mile west of Eglingen, while Lecourbe with the other

275 Phipps, *Moselle*, pp.301–303, 305–306, 309, 312–313, 315–316.

three battalions guarded the bridge at Dischingen. Nevertheless, when the Austrians attacked at 9:00 a.m., they were repulsed, but not without their artillery setting fire to Dunkstelkingen. Meanwhile Moreau was organising the rest of his army, ordering Desaix on his left to attack the Austrian right once Delmas's division, on Desaix's own left had re-joined him. While Desaix was preparing his advance, Archduke Charles sent a column against his extreme left at Bopfingen, also attacking him at Schweindorf and Kösingen.

With the Austrian attack thus spread over some seven-and-a-half miles, Desaix had no difficulty in beating it off. Meanwhile on Saint-Cyr's right, in the valley of the river Danube, Archduke Charles had sent another column under Mercandin (7,000 infantry and 2,400 cavalry) against Duhesme's division (5,000 infantry and 640 cavalry), almost surrounding it, capturing some of its guns and driving it away from Saint-Cyr. Consequently, Saint-Cyr's artillery park, was forced to withdraw from Heidenheim, 11 miles north to Aalen. Discovering Moreau's reserve under Bourcier between Frikinge and Weinacht-Hof between Saint-Cyr and Desaix, Archduke Charles chose not to renew his attack and the battle died out at around 1:00 p.m., with the French reoccupying Heidenheim from whence the Austrians retired on Dillingen, 17 miles southeast on the river Danube.

The battle of Neresheim was thus tactically inconclusive, with both sides missing opportunities for significant victory, and furthermore Archduke Charles had failed to achieve his goal of fending off Moreau so that he could focus his efforts on Jourdan. Moreau suspended Duhesme from his command for his performance in the battle, only to reinstate him a few days later at Saint-Cyr's urging. Archduke Charles initially held his ground expecting Moreau to withdraw, but when Moreau, despite cancelling Desaix's planned attack, held firm, the Austrians withdrew southeast across the Danube at Donauwörth (13 August). This move drew Moreau after them to the right bank of the Danube further away from Jourdan's Armée de Sambre-et-Meuse (14 August). Leaving Latour with 30,300 men and Condé's émigré corps of 5,000–6,000 men to screen and delay Moreau, Archduke Charles took his army of 28,000 men back across the Danube at Ingolstadt and Neuburg to join Wartensleben before Jourdan (17 August).

On that day Jourdan was six and a half miles northwest of Amberg, in front of Sulzbach-Rosenberg, where Kléber defeated Kray's 8,000 men, while Bernadotte was at Neumarkt in der Oberplaz, 21½ miles to the southwest of Amberg. Moreau having repaired the broken bridges at Münster, Blindheim and Höchstädt an der Donau, sent detachments across to the left bank of the river Danube which discovered that Archduke Charles had also crossed to the left bank (18 August).[276] Nevertheless, Moreau continued his advance on Augsberg, crossing to the right bank of the river Danube at Dillingen, 15 miles southwest of Donauwörth (19 August) and then forming his centre and left on the line of the lower reaches of the river Schmutter, a tributary on the right bank of the Danube, running north-south from Donauwörth (20 August). Moreau seems to have conducted this march without seriously considering the risk of leaving Jourdan's Armée de Sambre-et-Meuse on the left bank, facing Archduke Charles alone. As Moreau was crossing at Dillingen, Archduke Charles had reached Schamhaupten, almost 13 miles northeast of Ingolstadt and 22 miles due south from Deining, where Bernadotte

276 Phipps, *Moselle*, pp.317–326; Smith, *Data Book*, p.120; *Général de Brigade* Claude-Jacques Lecourbe, Taponier's division; *Général de Division* Philibert Guillaume Duhesme; *Feldmarschallleutnant* Ignaz Karl Graf von Mercandin.

formed Jourdan's left flank (19 August). Despite this, Moreau continued his advance on the right bank of the Danube, with Saint-Cyr ordered to occupy Augsberg (22 August).

Saint-Cyr managed to convince the citizens of Augsberg to shut the gates to all troops, enabling the French to drive the Austrians around the walls of the town and across the river Lech. In so doing Saint-Cyr joined up with Férino commanding the right wing of Moreau's army. Férino's men had enjoyed a relatively quiet advance from the Rhine, advancing to Lindau and Brégentz on the north shore of Lake Constance before marching to re-join the army, successfully defeating the Condé's night attack at Oberkammlach (13 August) and then following them through Mindelheim to the river Lech. The Condé's émigré corps re-joined Latour's Austrians at Munich (24 August). Moreau was now again in position to choose whether to march after Archduke Charles in support of Jourdan, but instead he chose to attack Latour's 30,000 men to his front, in the hope that the Archduke would be drawn towards him. Latour's men were scattered along a 120-mile front from Rain, on the river Lech, near the Danube, where Mercandin had 7,300 men, through Friedberg where Latour had 6,000 troops, and Landau am Lech, where the Condé's émigré corps was posted, then on to Fröhlich, who commanded 11,800 men at Schongau, thence to the Voralberg by Lake Constance. Consequently, Moreau, with 59,000 men, attacked across the river Lech, either side of Augsberg, a crossing that was made difficult by the state of the rising river (24 August). Latour watched the crossing from the heights of Friedberg, with only 6,000 men of his extended army. When Saint-Cyr cut the road to Ingolstadt and Férino that to Munich, Latour had to scramble away, with significant loss of both prisoners and guns.[277]

Meanwhile Archduke Charles had advanced from Ratisbon towards Jourdan's Armée de Sambre-et-Meuse arrayed along the river Naab. Jourdan was disabused of his belief that Moreau was still on the left bank of the river Danube by a message from Bernadotte on his right and by a despatch from Moreau himself (21 August). Advancing from Ingolstadt and Ratisbon, the Archduke then attacked, with 28,000 men, the 6,000 men of Bernadotte's division deployed behind Deining (22 August). Bernadotte held his ground throughout the day before withdrawing in good order overnight. The Archduke followed Bernadotte, attacking him again at Neumarkt on 23 August and at Berg, before Bernadotte, after a fighting withdrawal of over 40 miles, reached Forchheim, where Jourdan joined him (27 August). Jourdan had rejected the option to attack Wartensleben to his front and chosen to withdraw his army from the river Naab, briefly holding Amberg, against Austrian attacks, to allow the cavalry reserve to re-join, before moving off towards Sulzbach in the west. This withdrawal allowed Wartensleben to join up with Archduke Charles (23 August).[278]

Thus, in the evening of 24 August, Archduke Charles had defeated Jourdan's army at Amberg but Latour had been defeated by Moreau at Friedberg, across the Lech from Augsberg, 85 miles away. Hearing of Latour's defeat, Archduke Charles sent back 10,000 men, under Nauendorf, from Neumarkt, across the river Danube at Ingolstadt to check Moreau's Armée de Rhin-et-Moselle. Moreau was slow to pursue Latour's force, by 30 August, Saint-Cyr reached Pfeffenhofen an der Ilm only 29 miles from the Lech. Latour exploited Moreau's slowness to march across the front of the Armée de Rhin-et-Moselle to unite with Nauendorf between Siegenburg and Neustadt an der Donau.

277 Phipps, *Moselle*, pp.327, 330–331, 334–335; Smith, *Databook*, pp.119–121; Smith has the French at Neresheim with 50,000 men facing 20,000 Austrians.

278 Phipps, *Moselle*, pp.337–341; Smith, *Data Book*, p.120.

When Desaix advanced to attack Ingolstadt, the two Austrian generals intercepted him between Geisenfeld and Reichertshofen. Desaix repulsed this attack without help from Moreau who remained ignorant of the attack (1 September). In the meantime, Jourdan had withdrawn the Armée de Sambre-et-Meuse, joined Bernadotte's flank guard at Forchheim and formed up along the line of the river Regnitz (28 August). However, Archduke Charles had divided his force at Neumarkt sending Hotze with his left wing to Eltmann on the river Main, 11 miles northwest of Bamberg and 24 miles northwest of Forchheim. Jourdan initially planned to attack Hotze but, fearing that he had been joined by Archduke Charles, abandoned this plan, and marched through Bamberg and down the right bank of the river Main to Schweinfurt, 33 miles west-northwest of Bamberg (31 August). This proved unnecessary as Archduke Charles was at this point focused on Kléber with Jourdan's rearmost troops on his left.[279]

Instead of continuing his march down the right bank of the river Main, Jourdan now chose to leave Lefebvre at Schweinfurt with 12,000 men and marched south to reach Wurzberg, which he still believed was garrisoned by his own men. He then headed for Dettelbach and Kitzingen, where he could dispute the passage of the river Main if the Archduke approached with his main force. However, at noon on 2 September, Bonnaud's cavalry reached Wurzberg to find it occupied by Hotze's Austrians, with the 600 strong French garrison confined to the citadel. Archduke Charles sent a force to observe Lefebvre and then crossed the river Main at Schwarzach during the night of 2 September, heading for Jourdan's flank.

The battle of Wurzberg (3 September) began with an overwhelming attack by the Austrian heavy cavalry, which despite an initial repulse, captured the road to Schweinfurt. Jourdan was forced to retreat with the loss of 2,000 men, seven guns and the observation balloon, *l'Intrépide*. Jourdan retreated north through Hammelburg before reaching Bad Brückenau (6 September). Lefebvre, having retired from Schweinfurt by Bad Kissingen, formed the rearguard. Continuing its retreat, the Armée de Sambre-et-Meuse crossed the river Lahn at Wetzlar and formed along the line of that river. Rather than pursuing Jourdan, Archduke Charles had turned west heading via Aschaffenburg for Frankfurt. The Archduke then approached Marceau's force blockading Mainz and Kastel (6 September). Marceau had little choice but to raise the blockades (8 September), fighting a rearguard action at Wiesbaden (9 September) before joining Jourdan on the river Lahn (10 September). Jourdan was thus reinforced by Marceau's 12,000 men, but Archduke Charles gained the relieved garrisons, 27,800 men, including those of Mannheim and Philippsburg. During the retreat Jourdan had offered his resignation and the Directory accepted it, sending him to command the Armée du Nord while Beurnonville assumed command of the Armée de Sambre-et-Meuse.[280]

The retreat of the Armée de Sambre-et-Meuse to the river Rhine, left Moreau and his Armée de Rhin-et-Moselle in somewhat of a quandary, whether to turn to support Jourdan by attacking Archduke Charles or to continue his advance east into Austria. The centre and left of Moreau's army reached the river Abens, which joins the river Danube 18 miles downstream of Ingolstadt, where Saint-Cyr captured two Austrian guns at Mainburg, 18 miles southeast of Ingolstadt (7 September). Moreau was faced by two separate Austrian forces those of Nauendorf and Latour. While Nauendorf chose

279 Phipps, *Moselle*, pp.341–345; Smith, *Data Book*, pp.120–121; *Generalmajor* Friedrich August Joseph Graf von Nauendorf; *Feldmarschallleutnant* Friedrich von Hotze.

280 Phipps, *Moselle*, pp.349–355; Smith, *Data Book*, pp.121–123.

to stay on the river Danube. Latour preferred to form his army in a cordon defending Austria and he retired from the river Isar to the line of the river Inn, 30 miles east of Munich. However, Moreau gave up any idea of moving further east and moved on the river Danube.

Desaix and Saint-Cyr crossed the Danube at Neuburg an der Donau, 12 miles west of Ingolstadt (10 September), while Férino, with the right wing abandoned his attempts to cross the Isar at Munich and was drawn back to Friedberg, just east of Augsburg and 27 miles south-southwest of Neuburg. (Munich was held by the Bavarians against both the French and Austrians.) Once across the Danube, Desaix pressed on to Eichstätt and then Heideck, 28 miles north of Neuburg. Nauendorf followed Desaix marching on Eichstätt, while Latour, reinforced by Condé's émigré corps, fell on Delmas's small force holding the bridgehead at Ingolstadt, around Zell, almost 11 miles southeast of Ingolstadt. Although outnumbered, the French managed to hold on long enough despite the wounding of both Delmas and his successor Oudinot, for Moreau to come to their aide with reinforcements from Saint-Cyr's corps and repel the attack. Desaix, who had been unsuccessful in finding either Jourdan or Archduke Charles, was recalled to Neuburg just as Nauendorf was about to attack him (14 September). Saint-Cyr was brought back across the river Danube via Neuburg (15 September) followed by Desaix and the reserve (16 September). Marching south Moreau deployed his whole army to a position to the east of Augsburg, centred on Aichach, 25 miles south-southwest of Ingolstadt (18 September).[281]

Meanwhile Archduke Charles was slowly advancing on Jourdan's new position on the river Lahn, reaching Weilmünster, 14 miles east of Limburg on the river Lahn, only on 14 September. Jourdan having already been turned by his left on the line of the Lahn, loaded his left with troops at the expense of his right. Archduke Charles sent Kray to attack Jourdan's left which prompted Jourdan to commit his cavalry reserve and Lefebvre's division to this flank. Archduke Charles then attacked Jourdan's much weakened right, and after a day of heavy fighting managed to take one of the lesser crossing points of the river Lahn at Diez, two and a half miles southeast of Limburg (16 September). This then prompted Castelverd's division of the Armée du Nord with Jourdan to retire unnecessarily and against orders at 10:00 p.m.

In despair, Marceau ordered his corps to retire to Malzberg the next morning (17 September). Thus compromised Jourdan withdrew his army from Wetzlar northwest up the river Dill to Herborn and then westwards to Altenkirchen. During this retreat, Marceau was mortally wounded by a Tyrolean skirmisher. Although Jourdan's army was safely ensconced behind the river Wied, around Altenkirchen, with Castelverd holding the entrenched camp at Neuwied, he determined on a further retreat. Jourdan fell back to a position in front of Cologne, from Bonn and Portz on the river Rhine northeast through Rath to Bensberg, eight miles east of Cologne. Archduke Charles halted his pursuit at Uckerath and then leaving more than 30,000 men to watch Jourdan he marched up the river Rhine with 16,000 men to join the force facing Moreau. At this point Jourdan handed over his command to Beurnonville (22 September).[282]

All this left the Armée de Rhin-et-Moselle in a rather exposed position. Moreau had some 64,000 men under his command, to his immediate front Latour had 17,000

281 Phipps, *Moselle*, pp.356–359; *Général de Brigade* Nicolas Charles Oudinot, commanded a brigade of cavalry.
282 Phipps, *Moselle*, pp.359–366; *Général de Division* Jean Castelbert de Castelverd.

men, with a further 10,900 men under Fröhlich on the upper Iller and in the Tyrol. Nauendorf was also marching up the left bank of the river Danube with 5,800 men to occupy Ulm in Moreau's rear. A further 5,600 men under Petrasch were deployed from the river Neckar to the river Rhine, also in Moreau's rear, as were the 13,300 men released from the garrisons on the Rhine following Jourdan's retreat. Moreau's communication with France was blocked when Petrasch occupied Stuttgart and closed the road hub at Freudenstadt. When Archduke Charles brought his 16,000 men up the right bank of the river Rhine to join Petrasch, Moreau's retreat was now blocked, he was facing superior forces and the local population also rose against him. Moreau began his retreat, crossing the rivers Lech (145 miles from the Rhine) and Iller (19 September). Desaix was sent across the Danube through Ulm to the right bank of the river Blau, while Saint-Cyr was on the lower Iller and Férino was further south at Memmingen, also on the river Iller, a front of some 33 miles.

In response, the two Austrian forces had advanced in pursuit either side of the river Danube with Nauendorf reaching the heights behind Ulm and Latour reaching Pfühl (24 September). After a pause during which Moreau expected the Austrians to offer battle, he began a further withdrawal to the southwest (27 September). Desaix marched some 25 miles up the left bank of the river Danube crossing at Ehingen to a position between the Danube and the Federsee. Saint-Cyr was to the south of the Federsee while, 12 miles further south, Férino occupied a line from Waldsee to Lake Constance (29 September). Rather than uniting with Latour, Nauendorf, following his orders, had marched further west for Tübingen on the river Neckar. Undeterred Latour launched his forces against the French only to be repulsed by Lacourbe's brigade (30 September). Moreau in turn launched Desaix and Saint-Cyr (39,000) men at Latour (26,000 men) at the battle of Biberach (an der Riss). Saint-Cyr, on the right, sent forward a battery of 24 guns to cover the advance of his infantry against Latour's main body, while Desaix attacked further north. The outnumbered Austrians were driven back on the river Riss and pinned against it, while attempting cut a way through Desaix's men to escape to the north or finding the difficult passages across the river.

The French lost 500 men but the Austrians lost more than 4,000 men in prisoners alone, however had Férino reached the battlefield in time the Austrian casualties would have been higher still (2 October).[283] After this victory, Moreau continued his retirement along both banks of the river Danube (4 October), reaching Möhringen, four miles north of Stockach, with Férino between there and Lake Constance (9 October). Moreau then chose to reach the river Rhine and Kehl via the wider valley of the river Kinzig, sending Desaix from Tuttlingen to drive Petrasch from Villingen but here he was prevented from entering the valley. With Petrasch and Nauendorf's 16,300 men somewhat dispersed, Moreau persevered, and Saint-Cyr's leading elements took Neustadt (10 October) and forced the Höllental (Hell's Valley) reaching Zarten the next day, 38 miles west of Tuttlingen and just 15 miles from the river Rhine. Saint-Cyr's advanced guard then marched through Freiburg im Breisgau before turning northeast to Waldkirch, while contact was made with other French troops on the left bank of the river Rhine at Alt Breisach (12 October). Rather than get the Armée de Rhin-et-Moselle promptly across the river Rhine, Moreau, preferring to cross lower down at Kehl, went to Strasbourg (13 October), leaving his army around Waldkirch.

283 Phipps, *Moselle*, p.371; Smith, *Data Book*, p.125; Smith gives the respective armies as 35,000 French versus 15,000 Austrians.

This delay allowed Archduke Charles to concentrate his forces in front of and to the north of Moreau's army. It was only on 17 October that Saint-Cyr began to reconnoitre the roads that would take the army northwards down the valley of the river Elz. With his army (38,000 men) posted on both banks of the river Elz around Emmendingen, Moreau was attacked by Archduke Charles with 24,000 men (19 October). In addition, Frölich with 13,000 men on the Austrian left attacked the French right, under Férino, in the hills. Moreau's men were thrown back across the river Elz with considerable loss. This Austrian success was not repeated in a further attack the next day, but Moreau abandoned his planned crossing of the river Rhine at Kehl. Instead, Moreau sent Desaix's division across at Alt Breisach from whence they marched 38 miles north to Strasbourg (24 October). Meanwhile Moreau went to Schliengen, 19 miles south of Alt Breisach, with the corps of Saint-Cyr and Férino, along with his reserve (22 October). Here Moreau was again attacked by Archduke Charles but managed to hold his ground (24 October) before retiring again to cross the river Rhine at Huningue and Rheinfelden, either side of Basel (25/26 October). With both French armies now driven across the Rhine, Archduke Charles received further orders to besiege and capture the bridgeheads across the Rhine at Kehl and Huningue. Latour with 29,000 infantry and 5,900 cavalry faced Saint-Cyr at Kehl, while Férino's corps held Huningue. Moreau launched a sortie from Kehl with 16,000 infantry and 3,000 cavalry, led by Desaix. The sortie was initially successful in capturing 800 prisoners and some of the beseiger's cannon and spiking many more, but was eventually repulsed by the Austrian reserves, losing 3,000 men (22 November). The French resisted the Austrian sieges of Kehl and Huningue throughout the rest of the year.[284]

Further down the river Rhine the Directory appointed Kléber to the command of the Armée de Sambre-et-Meuse in place of Beurnonville, who returned to the command of the Armée du Nord, but Kléber refused the command (12 October). At this point Beurnonville's command, the Armée de Sambre-et-Meuse was divided into two wings, Macdonald's on the left, comprising four divisions, holding Düsseldorf, Neuwied, and the right bank of the Rhine as far as the river Wupper, which joins the Rhine near Leverkusen. The right wing, commanded by Kléber, held the left bank of the river Rhine from Mainz northwards, in all the army held a frontage of some 110 miles. There was a lot of fighting in this sector and Kléber beat off a determined attack by the Austrians on Neuwied (20–21 October).[285]

Beurnonville concluded an armistice for his army, withdrawing his artillery from the right bank of the river Rhine and declaring Neuwied as neutral (9 December), an action which promptly released 13 Austrian battalions to reinforce the besiegers of Kehl. Ill health forced Beurnonville to hand his command over temporarily to Kléber (14 December). Finally, the Directory decided that the Armée de Sambre-et-Meuse would be placed under Moreau's command in addition to the Armée de Rhin-et-Moselle (25 December).[286]

284 Phipps, *Moselle*, pp.367–383, 390, 393; Smith, *Data Book*, pp.125–126; *Feldmarschallleutnant* Franz von Petrasch; *Général de Brigade* Claude-Jacques Lacourbe; Smith lists the French at Emmendingen as only 32,000 men against 10,000 Austrians engaged of 28,000).

285 Phipps, *Moselle*, pp.387–389.

286 Phipps, *Moselle*, pp.391–392.

Italy

In Italy, January 1796 provided a pause in the fighting after the French victory at Loano. Schérer rewarded Masséna with the command of the advanced guard of the Armée d'Italie, comprised of the divisions of Laharpe and Meynier (who had replaced Charlet, killed in the recent fighting). The army had a nominal strength of 100,000 men but only 60,000 were 'present under arms', while the four most readily available divisions in the valley of the Tanaro and on the *riviera de Gênes*(Genoa), the two of Masséna and those of Augereau and Sérurier had only 30,700 men present under arms. However, the *amalgame* or *embrigadement* had been completed, during which 63 demi-brigades each of three battalions and 19 independent battalions (208 battalions in all, some only 50 men strong) were reduced to 14 *demi-brigades de ligne* and six *demi-brigades légère*, a total of only 60 battalions.

This process released two thirds of the cadres, who either went home or formed depot companies to supply the demi-brigades with replacements. At the same time, Kellermann's Armée des Alpes had been reduced to the size of a division (18,000 men). Both armies were described as 'destitute', lacking pay and money to repair equipment and even to buy the paper and books for company records. Schérer's health was suffering as a result of the pressures of keeping his army together and he requested help from Paris. Bonaparte who, in Paris, had been drawing up plans for the advance of the Armée d'Italie, was nominated by Carnot and named as Schérer's replacement (2 March). After Bonaparte left Paris (11 March), Schérer gathered 9,000 men at Savona for an operation, ordered by the Directory, to capture the fortress of Gavi (20 miles north-northeast of Genoa). Pijon then advanced to Voltri, 8 miles west of Genoa (26 March). *Général de Division* Napoleon Bonaparte, having stopped in Marsaille to visit his family, travelled through Toulon (24 March) and arrived to take command of the Armée d'Italie on 27 March. Bonaparte was 26 years old, and his staff included the aides-de-camp Junot, Murat and Marmont and his chief of staff was Berthier. Bonaparte's division commanders were Masséna, Laharpe, Meynier, Augereau, Macquard, Garnier and Sérurier, on whom he made a good impression immediately.[287]

Masséna with the advanced guard (the divisions of Laharpe and Meynier) held the coast from Vado Ligure to Savona and along the crest of the Apennines from Colla di San Giacomo to Colle del Melogno, a frontage of 12 miles. He also had outposts at Cadibona, five miles northwest of Savona and at Monte Negino, five and a half miles north-northwest of Savona. On Masséna's left, Augereau held the line five miles west to Calizanno and down the coast to Alassio, 23 miles southwest of Savona, with his headquarters at Pietra Ligura halfway between Savona and Alassio. Sérurier held the upper Tanaro valley, with his headquarters at Ormea, and Macquard held the Colle di Tenda, while Garnier held the extreme left of the line above Nice. The extreme right of the line still extended to Voltri, 17 miles up the coast from Savona. In all the Armée d'Italie comprised 63,100 men present under arms, but of these 16,500 men were in

287 Phipps, *West*, pp.270, 273–274, 276–277; Ramsay Weston Phipps, *The Armies of the First French Republic, and the Rise of the Marshals of Napoleon I—4. The Army of Italy 1796 to 1797, Paris and the Army of the Interior 1792 to 1797 and the Coup d'État of Fructidor, September 1797* (Godmanchester: Ken Trotman), pp.5, 7, 10–12; Leónce Krebs and Henri Moris, *Campagnes dans les Alpes pendant la Revolution 1794, 1795, 1796* (Paris: E.Plon, Nourrit et Cie, 1895), p.358; *Général de Division* Jean-Baptiste Meynier; Laharpe was promoted to *général de division* in August 1795; *Général de Brigade* Jean-Joseph Magdeleine Pijon; Napoleon changed his name on his marriage to Josephine (9 March 1796).

the various garrisons. Of the remainder 6,200 men guarded the coast (the divisions of Garnier and Macquard), leaving about 40,000 men as an available field force, 35,400 infantry, 3,400 cavalry and 1,800 artillery (manning initially only 24 mountain guns).[288]

Facing the French were the armies of Austria, on the left, and Sardinia-Piedmont, on the right. The main Austrian force commanded by Beaulieu, comprised 25,000–30,000 men, withdrawn into Lombardy somewhat. In the centre Provera commanded an auxiliary Austrian force around Dego, 13 miles northwest of Savona. On the right, the Sardinia-Piedmont force, commanded by Colli, comprised 20,000–25,000 men around Ceva, 14 miles southwest of Dego, and Mondovi, 17 miles west of Ceva.[289]

The fighting began when Beaulieu, with 7,000 men, attacked Cervoni's brigade, of Laharpe's division, at Voltri, in all 5,000 men, supported by a British squadron under Captain Horatio Nelson anchored offshore. Cervoni, following Bonaparte's orders, withdrew down the coast allowing the Austrians to enter Voltri (10 April). Attempting to cut off Laharpe's division from Savona, Beaulieu sent his right column of 7,000 men under d'Argenteau through the hills but after forcing the French from Montenotte Superiore they were checked by the redoubts at the summit of Monte Negino. Surprised by Cervoni's withdrawal and anxious about d'Argenteau's absence, Beaulieu, after consulting Nelson, withdrew 24 miles to Novi and Acqui, in preparation for a counterattack (11 April).[290]

Bonaparte having arrived in Savona (9 April) now prepared to insert his army into the centre of the Allied line, which Beaulieu's retirement had extended to 58 miles. Consequently, Masséna with the 10,000–11,000 troops around Savona, Cadibona and Vado Ligure attacked d'Argenteau at Montenotte, who was routed and retired 10 miles northwards through Mioglia to Pareto (12 April). Meanwhile Augereau had set off in support with the 10,000–11,000 troops around Finale Ligure and Loano, marching through the Colle di San Giacomo and the eastern Bormido, reaching Carcare, nine miles northwest of Savona. Meynier's division had been disbanded for this operation and Dommartin's brigade followed Augereau but was three miles further back at Montefreddo. Masséna with Laharpe's division marched towards Dego, with the intention of keeping the Austrians from interfering in the next phase of the operation. Bonaparte arriving in Carcare, sent Augereau with his own men and the brigades of Joubert and Ménard from Masséna's division due west towards Millesimo, attacking Provera's 900 Sardinian troops driving them into the ruined castle on the hill of Cosseria, one mile east of Millesimo. Augereau twice unsuccessfully assaulted Provera's position (13 April) but the defenders, out of ammunition, food and water were forced to surrender the next day (14 April). Provera's defence had however been successful in delaying Bonaparte's offensive and Joubert's brigade was so shattered by the failed assaults that it had to be relieved.[291]

Masséna, having advanced to the hills above and to the east of Cairo (now Cairo Montenotte) down the Eastern Bormida, attacked Dego with his two divisions, Laharpe's and elements of Meynier's. His 8,000–9,000 men quickly took Dego, routing

288 Phipps, *Italy*, pp.13–14.
289 Phipps, *Italy*, p.14; *Feldmarschallleutnant* Johann Marquis Provera.
290 Phipps, *Italy*, pp.14–15; Malcolm Boycott-Brown, *The Road to Rivoli, Napoleon's First Campaign* (London: Cassell, 2001), pp.194–197, 200, 204–208; Novi is now Novi Ligure and Acqui is Acqui Terme.
291 Phipps, *Italy*, pp.15–18; Smith, *Data Book*, p.111; Boycott-Brown, *Road to Rivoli*, p.230; *Général de Brigade* Philippe Romain Ménard.

the 3,000–4,000 Austro-Sardinian defenders, eventually commanded by d'Argenteau, and capturing many prisoners, as well as at least 16 guns. Bonaparte left Masséna to hold Dego but sent one of his divisions (Laharpe's) to support Augereau (14 April).[292] The next day the small French garrison of Dego, under the command of Lasalcette, was surprised and broken by an Austrian column commanded by Vukassovich, which was on its way to belatedly reinforce d'Argenteau at Dego. Masséna, arriving hurriedly from Cairo, rallied his routing troops on the plateau that had formed his start line on the previous day.

Bonaparte, from his headquarters at Carcare, sent Laharpe's division back to support Masséna's new assault on Dego along with other available troops, before moving to Dego himself. In all Bonaparte had 15,000 men almost surrounding the 3,500 Austrians garrisoning Dego and Vukassovich had little option but to evacuate the town and retire, pursued by the French cavalry.[293] Meanwhile Beaulieu, marching from Voltri reached Acqui, 17 miles northeast of Dego, (14 April) and was in no position to support Vukassovich. Rather than marching to the assistance of his allies Beaulieu asked Colli to come to his aid. Bonaparte's left now came into line with Augereau's left, Sérurier on the extreme left had advanced down both banks of the river Tanaro to Bagnasco, 17 miles southwest of Dego. Rusca with 2,000 men moved along the hills between the rivers Tanaro and Bormida capturing the redoubt at the chapel of San Giovani della Langa in Murialdo, six miles to the east of Bagnasco, linking with Joubert and forming Augereau's left.[294]

Bonaparte, with 15,000 men, now continued with his plan to attack the 13,000 Sardinia-Piedmont troops under Colli who were positioned around Ceva, five and a half miles north of Bagnasco. Augereau and Sérurier reconnoitred Colli's position but were repulsed (16 April). Bonaparte then moved his headquarters from Carcare four miles west to Millemiso and moved his line of communications, which had run via Savona, through Bardineto, 12 miles south of Millemiso, to Loano, 15 miles closer to France. Masséna, including Laharpe's division and Dommartin's brigade, then moved to Mombarcaro, six miles northeast of Ceva, turning Colli's entrenched camp at Ceva to the north, while Augereau, with Sérurier in support, attacked the camp from the south (17 April). However, Colli (11,000 men) slipped away, four miles northwest across the Torrente Corsaglia to a strong position with his right resting on the mountains and his left on the river Tanaro, near Castellino Tanaro, with the raging torrent that was the Corsaglia to his front. Colli also left a small garrison in the fort in Ceva under the command of the Count di Tornaforte.

From his new headquarters at Saliceto, four miles north of Millemiso, Bonaparte (15,500 infantry and 2,000 cavalry) ordered an assault on Colli's position, but Augereau failed in an attempt to cross the river Tanaro and although Sérurier managed to cross the Corsaglia and capture San Michele Mondovi, his troops dispersed to pillage the village and he could proceed no further, before Colli arrived to force him back across the Corsaglia (19 April). Faced with a further assault and alarmed that Augereau might cut him off from Cherasco, Colli chose to retreat again, six miles further west to Mondovi,

292 Phipps, *Italy*, pp.18–19: Smith, *Data Book*, p.112; Boycott-Brown, *Road to Rivoli*, p.248; Smith gives the forces as 12,000 French and 5,700 Austro-Sardinians of whom 3,000 were captured, while Boycott-Brown puts the number of prisoners in the range 1,500–4,400; Phipps puts the number of captured guns as 19.

293 Phipps, *Italy*, pp.20–22; *Général de Brigade* Jean-Jacques Bernardin Colaud de la Salcette, on Bonaparte's staff; *Oberst* Joseph Philipp Freiherr von Vukassovich, promoted to *generalmajor* in May 1796.

294 Phipps, *Italy*, p.23; *Général de Brigade* Jean-Baptiste-Dominique Rusca, one of Augereau's brigade commanders.

during the night of 20–21 April. Supported by Masséna, Sérurier led the pursuit described by Marmont as 'form[ing] his men in three columns, … himself at the head of the central one, throw[ing] out a cloud of skirmishers, and march[ing] at the double, sword in hand, 10 paces ahead of his column'. Sérurier, pushing back their light troops, caught up with the Sardinia-Piedmont rearguard at Vicoforte at 10:00 a.m., three miles southeast of Mondovi, before Colli was able to fully form his defensive line. Disordered by the speed of the French pursuit, Colli's army was soon retreating in disorder beyond the river Ellero, pursued by the French cavalry commanded by Stengel.

Reaching Mondovi, Sérurier parleyed with the garrison commander, while Fiorella took advantage of the cease fire to capture the Sardinia-Piedmont stronghold at Bricheto. Marmont turned the guns on the town and the garrison promptly surrendered and Bonaparte made his first triumphal entry into a captured town at 7:00 p.m. (21 April). As Colli continued his withdrawal, Bonaparte followed into the plains of Piedmont reaching Fessano and Cherasco, aiming to open communications with Kellermann's Armée des Alpes (25 April). Colli had requested an armistice (23 April) but Bonaparte rebuffed him and continued his advance forcing Colli's headquarters back to La Loggia, only five miles from Turin (27 April).

The next day King Victor Amadeus III agreed to Bonaparte's terms, surrendering the Piedmontese fortresses and taking Sardinia out of the First Coalition (28 April). Beaulieu had determined that he could do nothing to help his allies and turned back towards Alessandria and Tortona (27 April).[295] Beaulieu had his headquarters at Oviglio, seven miles southwest of Alessandria and 42 miles from Bonaparte's headquarters, with his rearguard under Vukassovich at Castelnuovo Belbo, five miles further southwest towards Nizza Monferrato. Meanwhile Schubirž, the new commander of the Austrian Auxiliary Corps, was attempting to extricate his men from the defeat of Sardinia-Piedmont towards Asti, 20 miles west of Alessandria, via Carmagnola, Poirino and Villanova di Asti.

Preparing to fall back behind the river Po, Beaulieu pulled Lipthay back behind Acqui on the river Bormido and sent detachments to secure the crossing of the river Po at Valenza, seven miles north of Alessandria (28 April). The next day Beaulieu fell back further, placing his headquarters and the main body, under Sebottendorf, in and around Marengo, four miles east of Alessandria, with a detachment at Tortona, eight miles further east. Vukassovich's rearguard was at Oviglio, while Schubirž was at Felizzano, nine miles west of Alessandria, and Lipthay was at Cassine, 11 miles south of Alessandria. Valenza and Alessandria are Piedmont towns and the former featured in Bonaparte's terms for the surrender of the Piedmontese fortresses, and he sent Masséna, now commanding Meynier's division, and Sérurier to demonstrate before Valenza. Beaulieu moved his headquarters to Valenza with Sebottendorf's men, while Lipthay retired through Alessandria, stopping close to Valenza. Vukassovich took post at Solario, two and a half miles west of Alessandria. Beaulieu's left wing under Roszelmini was at Tortona, with his rearguard at Orba (30 April). Meanwhile, with Beaulieu moving west, Bonaparte brought the rest of his army, the divisions of Augereau and Laharpe, and the cavalry under Kilmaine, east towards Piacenza, 51 miles east of Valenza. Masséna soon followed the main body of the army eastwards (2 May).

295 Phipps, *Italy*, pp.24–28; Boycott-Brown, *Road to Rivoli*, pp.260–261, 265–266, 270–272, 274, 278; Smith, *Data Book*, pp.112–113; *Général de Brigade* Pascual Antoine Fiorella; *Général de Division* Henri Christian Michel de Stengel, who was mortally wounded during a Piedmontese counterattack.

Beaulieu now was most concerned to prevent Bonaparte from taking Milan and formed a new line from Lomello through Ottobiano to Sommo, 30 miles west of Piacenza, observing the river Po from Valenza to Pavia (4 May). Hearing that the French were moving east Beaulieu extended his line by sending Lipthay (5,000 men) to Belgioioso, five miles east of Pavia (5 May). The same day Masséna began building bridges at Sale in front of the Austrian position, eight miles east of Valenza. After some fast-marching Bonaparte arrived at Piacenza and a pontoon bridge was then laid across the river Po near the confluence with the river Trebbia and Lannes led the advanced guard (3,500 infantry and 1,500 cavalry) across against little opposition followed by Laharpe's division (6,500 men). Augereau also led his division (7,000 men) across the river Po at a point four and a half miles east of Castel San Giovanni, eight miles west of Piacenza (7 May). The next day Dallemagne, with the advanced guard of elite grenadiers and carabiniers, met and overthrew a body of Lipthay's Austrians at the fortified village of Fombio, five miles northwest of Piacenza on the road to Milan. Lipthay retired east to Pizzighettone on the river Adda (8 May). Bonaparte then sent Laharpe's division towards Casalpusterlengo, 11 miles north-northwest of Piacenza, from whence he expected an attack from Beaulieu.

The Austrian general's 20,700 infantry and 5,400 cavalry were not in a great position to respond to the French crossing. Beaulieu reached Chignolo, 12 miles northwest of Piacenza, and decided that he had to force his way through to Lipthay. Consequently at 10:00 p.m. Schubirž led the Austrian advanced guard, 1,000 infantry and 600 *ulans*, towards Laharpe at Codogno, seven miles north of Piacenza (8 May). Schubirž's attack during the night caused great confusion amongst the French in Codogno, during which Laharpe was accidentally shot dead by his own men. Dallemagne restored order and Berthier replaced Laharpe. Beaulieu, discovering that Lipthay had withdrawn to Pizzighettone, drew off northwards pursued by Berthier towards Lodi on the river Adda, while Colli was ordered to garrison the citadel in Milan (9 May).[296]

Bonaparte's army was still divided by the river Po, Masséna's division only crossed to the north bank during the late afternoon on 9 May and Sérurier was still at Tortona and would not cross until 10 May. The passage of the river Adda at Lodi was held by 7,000 infantry and 2,500 cavalry under Sebottendorf, part of this force was on the right bank in front of Lodi itself. This force was Beaulieu's rearguard, he had decided to march to Mantua and having reached Lodi at midday 9 May, he ordered a concentration at Cremona, 28 miles southeast of Lodi, on the river Po and on the direct route to Mantua.

Bonaparte directed his army to Lodi with Masséna's division including Dallemagne's advanced guard in the lead, followed by Augereau, while Laharpe's division, under the command of Ménard, watched Lipthay on the Adda at Pizzighettone. Unable to destroy the bridge due to the necessary evacuation of his own troops from Lodi, Sebottendorf defended the bridge, some 200 yards long and 20–25 feet wide, with 12 guns, six directly sweeping the bridge and three either side. Dallemagne's men led the charge across the bridge and with the support of Masséna's division and some of Kilmaine's cavalry which had crossed by a ford. The assault column faltered under the fire of the Austrian guns and it required the inspirational presence of Masséna, Berthier, Dallemagne and Cervoni to make progress but the column was still thrown back. Realising that the river

296 Phipps, *Italy*, pp.33–34; Boycott-Brown, *Road to Rivoli*, pp.276, 286–288, 292, 298–305; *Feldmarschallleutnant* Karl Philipp Sebottendorf van der Rose; *Generalmajor* Anton Schubirž von Chobinin; *Generalmajor* Anton Lipthay de Kisfalud; *Generalmajor* Gerhard Roszelmini; *Général de Brigade* Claude Dallemagne.

was quite shallow, Masséna and Cervoni led some troops into the water by the bridge and forced the crossing with the help of the cavalry. The Austrians lost 2,000 men and 14 guns, while French losses are variously reported as 5,000–9,000 men.[297]

Following Lodi, Bonaparte again reorganised his army into the four active divisions under Augereau, Masséna, Ménard and Sérurier, with the reserve cavalry under Kilmaine, who also commanded the advanced guard including Dallemagne's eight battalions of grenadiers. Behind the active divsions, Macquard held the area around Cuneo, Hacquin the area around Cherasco and Meynier the area around Tortona. Masséna's division went to occupy Milan (13 May) before Bonaparte's triumphal entry (15 May).

Leaving the siege of the citadel of Milan to Despinoy, Bonaparte's army marched east through Lodi to Crema, nine miles east of Lodi and only 56 miles from the great fortress at Mantua (24 May). The advance continued under Berthier a further 10 miles east to Soncino, while Bonaparte was absent repressing revolts in his rear at Pavia and Tortona (26 May). When Bonaparte returned to the army it had arrived near Brescia, 49 miles due east of Milan and the campaign now passed into the territory of the neutral state of Venice. Beaulieu's army now stood on the line of the river Mincio, with his right, under Lipthay, holding Peschiera del Garda on the southern shore of Lake Garda, his headquarters at Vallegio sul Mincio and with his left under Colli at Goito, a frontage of 13 miles, eight and a half miles northwest of Mantua. Bonaparte attacked this line by sending Sérurier lower down the river Mincio to make demonstrations, distracting the Austrians, while Masséna's men, fording the river Mincio a little below the broken bridge at Borghetto, entered Vallegio sul Mincio and forced Beaulieu into a hurried retreat. Meanwhile Augereau turned north to occupy Peschiera, but his advanced guard was beaten back by Lipthay, who then withdrew two and a half miles east to Castelnuovo del Garda.

The right and centre of the Austrian army retired from a difficult situation by bridging the Adige at Chuisa and via Verona, while Colli on the left called off an attack on the French right flank and sent his infantry and guns into Mantua and his cavalry north to join Beaulieu at Villafranca di Verona (30 May). During this fighting Bonaparte was almost captured by two Neapolitan cavalry regiments from Beaulieu's army, who surprised his headquarters near Vallegio sul Mincio. Masséna entered Villafranca the next day, while Beaulieu retired up the river Adige, 38 miles north to Rovereto at the head of Lake Garda and then a further 13 miles to Trento, in the Tyrol where he hoped to reform his army. Lipthay was left with the rearguard of 5,600 men near the pontoon bridge at Dolcè, in the valley of the Adige, 13 miles northwest of Verona. There was a skirmish between Lipthay and Victor's brigade which resulted in the bridge being taken up by the Austrians and the two sides cannonading each other across the river Adige (31 May).[298]

Bonaparte could now focus on the fortress of Mantua, Masséna marched further east to occupy the Venetian town of Verona, with his own division, including Victor's brigade, and Sauret's division, in all 19,000 men (1 June). Meanwhile Sérurier went

297 Smith, *Data Book*, p.113; Phipps, *Italy*, pp.34–36; Boycott-Brown, *Road to Rivoli*, pp.305–309, 315.

298 Phipps, *Italy*, pp.45–47, 49, 50; Boycott-Brown, *Road to Rivoli*, pp.351, 360; *Général de Division* Honoré Alexandre Hacquin; *Général de Division* Hyacinthe François Joseph Despinoy; after the scare at Vallegio, *Capitaine* Jean-Baptiste Bessières was given command of a squadron of Guides, which together with two battalions of grenadiers formed a headquarters guard under the command of *Chef de Brigade* Jean Lannes (5 June).

south towards Mantua, occupying La Favorita, immediately across Lago Superiore to the north of the town. Augereau also marched south from Peschiera down the left bank of the river Mincio to hold Cerese, three miles south of Mantua.[299]

Mantua derived its strength not from the fortress walls but from the lakes and marshes which surrounded it, which was a deadly source of fever to the besiegers and the besieged alike. The Austrian garrison was 10,700 men strong, under the command of Canto d'Yrles. In the first operations against the fortress Dallemagne took the Saint-Georges suburb and Fort St Georges, the *tête-du-pont* to the east of the fortress (3 June).[300]

June was also marked by Bonaparte's response to rebellion in his rear. Lannes was sent to Tortona with some light infantry and, when Bonaparte himself arrived, Lannes was sent with 1,400 men to Pozzolo Formigaro and then Arquata Scrivia, where the insurgents were mercilessly punished. Similar columns were also despatched to the south, Augereau was sent with 4,800 men to Bologna (18 June) and Bonaparte and Vaubois with 7,600 men from the Armée des Alpes went to Modena before moving to Livorno (Leghorn, 154 miles north of Rome), where Vaubois was left in command, while Bonaparte went onto Florence, securing some siege artillery to be used against Mantua. Augereau was also despatched to suppress an insurrection of 15,000–20,000 men at Lugo, 28 miles east of Bologna on the eastern coast of the Italian peninsula (5 July).[301]

While Augereau was away from Mantua, Dallemagne, under Sérurier's command, covered the south of the fortress. Sérurier having fully reconnoitred the fortress recommended, with the aid of the engineer Chasseloup, that 54 siege guns, 22 mortars and 20,000–25,000 infantry, 1,000 cavalry and 1,000 artillery would be needed to capture Mantua (8 June).[302]

Facing an expected Austrian offensive from the Tyrol, Bonaparte with 42,000 men had positioned Masséna to the east of Lake Garda with Augereau on his right in the valley of the river Adige. Sauret's division was on the right of the lake with Despinoy's division at Peschiera del Garda to the south of the lake. Kilmaine with the reserve cavalry was at Valeggio sul Mincio, six miles south of Peschiera, providing the link to Sérurier's division before Mantua. Bonaparte tried to take the fortress by *coup de main* before the Austrian relief columns could arrive. However, the garrison moved first, launching a sortie which was beaten back (16 July). The next day Sérurier began an assault from the south, which was repulsed, as was a further attempt the day after. Bonaparte then summoned the place to surrender (18 July). The governor replied that the honours of war required him to hold out to the last extremity.[303]

Wurmser with 46,900 men, began his advance from the Tyrol in four columns, his main force of 23,800 men, which he accompanied, advanced to the east of Lake Garda in two columns, one down the shore of the lake and the other down the valley of the river Adige, (29 July). These columns quickly forced Joubert's brigade of Masséna's division back. Meanwhile Quosdanovich, with 17,600 men advanced down the western shore of Lake Garda pushing Sauret's division out of Salò, on the shore of the lake and only 15 miles northeast of its target, Bonaparte's headquarters at Brescia. The

299 Phipps, *Italy*, p.50.
300 Phipps, *Italy*, p.57–59; *Feldmarschallleutnant* Josef Canto d'Yrles.
301 Phipps, *Italy*, pp.52–55; *Général de Division* Charles-Henri Vaubois.
302 Phipps, *Italy*, p.59; *Chef de Brigade* François de Chasseloup-Laubat.
303 Phipps, *Italy*, pp.59–60.

smaller fourth column of 5,000 men was directed on Verona via Vicenza, 27 miles to the northeast of its target and 39 miles east of Lake Garda. Quosdanovich continued his advance capturing Brescia and thereby cutting Bonaparte's line of communication (30 July). Sauret defended stoutly and retook Salò, while Despinoy, sent to support him, held Lonato del Garda, 14 miles southeast of Brescia. In response to this threat Bonaparte sent Masséna and Augereau westwards, slipping away from Wurmser who, after crossing the Adige, advanced via Castelnuovo del Garda to Vallegio sul Mincio.[304]

With the Austrian offensive down the river Adige gaining momentum, Bonaparte ordered Sérurier to raise the siege and retire westward 13 miles to the bridge over the river Oglio at Macaria, which he did after a heavy cannonade of the fortress (31 July). In so doing Sérurier, despite Bonaparte's orders, left 40 guns in the entrenchments around the fortress, not all of which had been spiked and another 139 pieces of all types in the park.[305]

Relief for Sauret and Despinoy, came in the form of Augereau's division which marched from Roverbella, east of the river Mincio, through Montichiari to Brescia (1 August). Surprising the Austrians occupying Brescia, Augereau was able to release a number of prisoners held there, including the sick Joachim Murat. Leaving Masséna to face Quosdanovich, Augereau fell back southeast in readiness to face Wurmser's column. Thus, Quosdanovich and Wurmser were converging on Castiglione delle Stiviere from opposite directions. Meanwhile Bonaparte had managed to concentrate the divisions of Sauret, Masséna, Augereau and Despinoy with Kilmaine's reserve cavalry between the two Austrian forces. In a series of severe combats around Lonato, Masséna, Despinoy and Sauret resisted Quosdanovich's advance, sending his disparate columns reeling back to Desenzano del Garda and Salò, with some heading east for the Mincio. Meanwhile Wurmser who had reached Castelnuovo del Garda (31 July), hearing that the siege of Mantua had been lifted, moved westwards to Vallegio sul Mincio where he stayed throughout the next day (1 August).

Wurmser then marched south for Goito, increasing the distance from Quosdanovich (2 August), before marching northwest for Castiglione delle Stiviere, which he occupied and where he met Augereau fully deployed to meet his advanced troops (3 August). Advancing from Montichiari, Augereau's division attacked Wurmser's advanced troops taking the *château* of Castiglione and driving Wurmser back to his position before Solferino and preventing any junction with Quosdanovich. At Lonato, the French with 20,000 men managed to outnumber the 15,000 engaged Austrians, inflicting 3,000 casualties for the loss of 2,000 men. For his victory on 3 August, Bonaparte later gave Augereau the title *Duc de Castiglione*. Bonaparte spent the next day bringing Masséna's and part of Despinoy's divisions to Castiglione to face Wurmser. Quosdanovich was forced to withdraw up the Chiese valley, leaving a rearguard under Knorr at Lonato but finding all routes through and around Lonato blocked by the French, Knorr surrendered his 2,000 men on 4 August.[306]

Unaware of the extent of his defeat, Wurmser sent orders to Quosdanovich to march to join him and waited at his position around Solferino. Wurmser's position stretched from

304 Phipps, *Italy*, pp.62–63; Bernhard Voykowitsch, *Castiglione 1796* (Maria Enzersdorf: Helmet Military Publications, 1998), pp.48–50.

305 Phipps, *Italy*, pp.61–62.

306 Phipps, *Italy*, pp.64–69; Smith, *Data Book*, p.119; *Oberst* Carl Knorr von Rosenroth (Infanterie Regiment N.42).

the tower in Solferino to a redoubt on the Medolano mound in front of Medole, four miles to the southwest. In this position Wurmser had 16,000 infantry and cavalry with a further 3,000 infantry on the march to the battlefield under Weydenfeld. Bonaparte brought Masséna's division to face Wurmser's left and Augereau's division was moved to face the Austrian right, the cavalry, under Beaumont were to Augereau's right along with all of the horse artillery under the command of Marmont. Despinoy's division was still marching to the battlefield from Brescia.

Meanwhile to the south, Sérurier's division, under the command of Fiorella with Sérurier absent sick, was now marching from Marcaria onto Wurmser's left rear at Quidizolo, three miles east of Medole, arriving there at 6:00 a.m. 5 August. Wurmser had ordered his fourth column and elements of the Mantua garrison to intercept Sérurier, but the French successfully eluded them. In all Bonaparte managed to concentrate 26,700 men to face Wurmser's significantly smaller army on the battlefield between Solferino and Castiglione. However before launching his main attack Bonaparte had to await Fiorella's final approach and ordered Masséna and Augereau to launch feints against Wurmser's line to pin it in position. The first attack proper was on the Medolano redoubt by Marmont and his artillery advancing to close range. The Austrian guns were suppressed, and the redoubt taken. Beaumont then led the cavalry around the Austrian left flank in the direction of San Cassiano. Wurmser, surprised by Fiorella's appearance in his rear, hesitated before pulling his left back to the hill *en potence* to his right to cover a retreat to the east. At this point Bonaparte sent Augereau and Masséna against the Austrian front line, while Despinoy's division turned the Austrian right. In confusion, Wurmser's men retreated to the river Mincio at Vallegio, leaving behind 20 guns and 1,000 prisoners as well as 2,000 killed and wounded. Bonaparte's loss was 1,100 men killed, wounded and missing.[307]

Bataille de Castiglione, 5 August 1796

307 Phipps, *Italy*, pp.70–72; Smith, *Data Book*, p.119; Voykowitsch, *Castiglione 1796*, pp.74–75; *Oberst* Karl Philippi von Weydenfeld; *Général de Brigade* Marc-Antoine Bonin de La Boninière, Comte de Beaumont.

Following the battle of Castiglione, the French were deployed with Augereau's division on the left, with Kilmaine and the cavalry to his right, then Masséna's division, with Sérurier's division on the right, while Sauret's division observed Quosdanovich. On 6 August Masséna then marched to Peschiera where a small French garrison still held out, and arriving there the next day he attacked the Austrian entrenchments, capturing them after a severe struggle. Bonaparte led Sérurier's, now Fiorella's, division through Peschiera to Verona where he blew open the gates (7 August). Fiorella then led his division south to recommence the blockade of Mantua. Masséna took up his old position between Lake Garda and the river Adige, while Augereau occupied Verona. To the west of Lake Garda, Sauret continued to press Quosdanovich. Meanwhile Wurmser had taken the opportunity to send two brigades of reinforcements into Mantua, while withdrawing other sickly troops, and to replenish the food supplies in the fortress. Wurmser then retired up the river Adige crossing it using a bridge of boats at Volargne, 11 miles northwest of Verona, (6 August) before moving on to Ala and then Trento.[308]

The Castiglione campaign was over, the significantly more numerous Austrian army (50,000 men compared to 35,000 French) had been defeated on the battlefield and forced back to the Tyrol losing 16,800 killed, wounded and prisoners, while the French had lost just 6,000 killed and wounded and 4,000 prisoners. Nevertheless, Wurmser had prevented the fall of Mantua and had successfully reinforced and revictualled the fortress. Now the fighting had died down Bonaparte made some changes amongst his division commanders. Sérurier whose health had been wrecked before Mantua, was sent to command at Livorno (15 August) and Sauret was sent to command the reserve at Brescia. Vaubois was given command of Sauret's division and Despinoy was sent to command the garrison at Alessandria. Bonaparte also wrote a summary of the merits of his division commanders to the Directory. Masséna and Augereau were strongly endorsed and complimented, Sauret less so and Sérurier worse still, but special approbrium was reserved for Despinoy, Abbatucci, Garnier, Meynier, Casabianca and Macquard who were not seen fit for field commands as general officers (14 August).[309]

With the blockade of Mantua resumed by Sahuguet with 10,000 men (Sérurier's old division), Bonaparte could now contemplate a counterstroke against Wurmser, thereby supporting the activities of the two armies on the Rhine which had advanced deep into the Holy Roman Empire. Bonaparte's plan was to march on Trento via both sides of Lake Garda and planned to start 2 September. Bonaparte assembled 33,000 men for the advance. Vaubois, who had replaced Sauret, would advance with his division of 11,000 troops to the west of Lake Garda. Masséna would lead his division of 13,000 men up the valley of the river Adige with Augereau's division of 9,000 men to his right in the mountains marching up the valley of the Fiume Astico, via Lugo di Vicenza, 14 miles north of Vicenza and 32 miles northeast of Verona. Dubois commanded the cavalry in this strike force. In support, Kilmaine, with 2,500–3,000 men, was to hold Verona and the valley of the river Adige.[310]

Meanwhile, Wurmser was preparing his second attempt to relieve Mantua. His main body of 20,900 men was to advance via Bassano del Grappa along the river Brenta,

308 Phipps, *Italy*, pp.78–79.

309 Phipps, *Italy*, pp.81, 83, 85–86; Boycott-Brown, *Road to Rivoli*, p.412; *Généraux de Division* Jacques-Pierre Abbatucci and Raphaël, Comte de Casabianca.

310 Phipps, *Italy*, pp.89–90; *Général de Division* Jean-Joseph-François-Léonard Damarzit de Laroche Sahuguet; *Général de Division* Paul Alexis Dubois.

which runs southeast from Trento, before turning south to cross the river Adige at Legnago, 22 miles southeast of Verona, and then onto Mantua. Wurmser's right, 25,200 men under Davidovich, at the northern end of Lake Garda would defend the Tyrol.[311]

When Bonaparte's advance began (2 September) contact was soon made with Wurmser's right. Vaubois's division reached the northern end of Lake Garda pushing the Austrian outposts back at Torbole and Nago-Torbole at the northeast corner of the lake. Likewise, Masséna's division reached Ala in the valley of the river Adige engaging the Austrian outposts there under the command of Vukassovich and pushed them back to Serravalle All'adige. That evening Pijon led his brigade of Masséna's division in an assault on that village, which drove Vukassovich further back to Marco, three and a half miles south of Rovereto (3 September).

The next day, Vaubois was ordered to send a detachment to Serravalle but otherwise continue his advance on Rovereto. Likewise, Augereau, some way to the southeast in the mountains, was ordered to march to Rovereto. Masséna, whose main body was still at Ala and Santa Margherita – three miles south of Marco and six from Rovereto – was tasked with leaving at 3:00 a.m. to reach Rovereto by 9:00 a.m. At daybreak, Davidovich arrived with Spork's brigade at Marco and prepared to defend the defiles at Marco and the entrenched camp at Mori. Bonaparte had managed to concentrate 20,000 men to attack the 10,000 men that Davidovich had available. Vaubois attacked Mori while Masséna's division attacked Marco, with Victor's brigade making a frontal assault along the road and Pijon's brigade turning the position through the heights on the right. With his position turned, Davidovich retreated to Rovereto where Vukassovich resisted Masséna until midday, before falling back to Davidovich's next position at Calliano, four miles further up the valley of the river Adige. In this battle of Rovereto, the Austrians lost 3,000 men, 25 guns and seven colours, while the French losses were 750 men killed, wounded and missing. The French cavalry commander Dubois was one of those killed in action (4 September). The Austrians attempted to stand at Castel Pietra and Calliano but were quickly broken by the pursuing French from Masséna's division and the next day Masséna entered Trento (5 September).[312]

At this point Bonaparte's army and Férino's force on the river Isar were only 163 miles apart, but having thrown back Davidovich into the Tyrol, Bonaparte determined to follow Wurmser down the valley of the river Brenta, assuming that Wurmser was moving to cover Trieste. However, before doing this, Bonaparte needed to drive Davidovich further into the Tyrol and Vaubois therefore advanced towards Lavis, four and a half miles further north. In the evening of 5 September Vaubois drove Davidovich out of Levis at the second attempt. Davidovich retreated through San Michele All'adige to Salorno, where he was observed by Vaubois from Levis (6 September). Wurmser had been confident that Davidovich would be able to hold Bonaparte at bay and continued with his advance down the valley of the Brenta. However, Bonaparte had ordered Augereau to march east to Levico in the valley of the Brenta, to begin the pursuit of Wurmser's main force. The first fighting between Wurmser's rearguard and Bonaparte's advanced troops took place at Primolano, 14 miles north of Bassano del Grappa and 29 miles east-southeast of Trento. Augereau's division attacked the Austrian rearguard of 2,800 men from Quosdanovich's division, capturing the small fort of Covelo along with most of the garrison and five guns. Pushing quickly on, Bonaparte reached Cismon del

311 Phipps, *Italy*, p.90; Boycott-Brown, *Road to Rivoli*, pp.416, 418.

312 Smith, *Data Book*, p.122; Boycott-Brown, *Road to Rivoli*, pp.422–425; Phipps, *Italy*, p.90.

Grappa by the end of the day (7 September). Meanwhile, Wurmser's advance down the river Brenta continued and Mészáros, commanding his vanguard, attacked Verona that day but was repulsed by Kilmaine.[313]

Bonaparte continued his advance, setting off from Cismon at 2:00 a.m. with the divisions of Augereau and Masséna on the left and right banks of the river Brenta respectively. At 7:00 a.m. they met the Austrian rearguard of 3,800 men, posted in the gorges that marked the entrance to the plains below. Outflanking the position via the heights and by repeated attacks the Austrians were broken and driven through Bassano del Grappa. During the rout that was the battle of Bassano, the French captured a further 30 guns, 200 wagons including two bridging trains, inflicting casualties of 600 men, and capturing 2,000 more for the cost of 400 men, killed, wounded and missing (8 September).[314]

Following the defeat at Bassano, the majority of Quosdanovich's division was scattered with many men fleeing east towards Treviso, consequently Wurmser ordered him to march via Venice to Gorizia, gathering his men along the way. Wurmser reached Montebello Vicentino, nine miles southwest of Vicenza, before dawn on 9 September, where he had just 16,000 men ready for further action. Determined not to turn back to Trieste himself, he sent a detachment to Legnago to secure the crossing over the river Adige, the most direct route to Mantua. Wurmser reached Legnago, pursued at some distance by Masséna's division, who crossed the river Adige at Ronco all'Adige, 10 miles further north (10 September). Bonaparte was concerned that Wurmser would head for Trieste and sent Augereau towards Padua to block that road. Leaving a small garrison to hold the crossing at Legnago, Wurmser marched to Nogara in front of Mantua, but had to fight his way through when his advanced guard commanded by Ott was stopped by Masséna's advanced troops under Pijon at Cerea, five miles west of Legnago. Ott counter-attacked, retaking Cerea and driving Pijon back towards Ronco, thereby keeping the road to Mantua open (11 September). Masséna arrived at Due Castelli, near Castel Belforte, the next day, joining Sahuguet's division that was already blockading the fortress at La Favorita. Meanwhile, Augereau's division, at this time commanded by Bon in the absence of its sick commander, attacked the garrison of Legnago, capturing the crossing (12 September) before being sent to Governolo on the river Mincio near its confluence with the river Po.[315]

Wurmser's 14,000 men formed a line in front of San Giorgio and were attacked by Bonaparte and 17,000 men with Sahuguet attacking at La Favorita and Bon driving towards San Giorgio from the south, before Masséna attacked the Austrian centre. After some heavy fighting in which the Austrians lost 2,500 men and the French lost 1,500 men, Wurmser withdrew into Mantua and Masséna captured Fort San Giorgio. Wurmser was thus blockaded in the fortress he was trying to relieve (15 September).[316]

313 Phipps, *Italy*, pp.91, 93; Boycott-Brown, *Road to Rivoli*, pp.428–430; Smith, *Data Book*, p.123; Smith puts the garrison of Primolano at 4,000 of whom 1,500 were captured; Phipps names the small fort Cavolo, Italian for cabbage; *Generalmajor* Johann Mészáros de Szoboszló.

314 Phipps, *Italy*, pp.93–94; Boycott-Brown, *Road to Rivoli*, pp 431–432; Smith, *Data Book*, p.123; Phipps gives the number of Austrian prisoners as 3,000.

315 Boycott-Brown, *Road to Rivoli*, pp.432–433; Phipps, *Italy*, p.96; various strengths for Wurmser at Montebello are given in the sources, Boycott-Brown gives 9,000 infantry and 3,000 cavalry, but Phipps cites Berthier for his figures of 10,000 infantry and 6,000 cavalry; *Général de Brigade* Louis André Bon; *Generalmajor* Peter Karl Ott, Freiherr von Bátorkés.

316 Boycott-Brown, *Road to Rivoli*, pp.434–435; Phipps, *Italy*, pp.99–100: Smith, *Data Book*, p.124.

Bonaparte ordered a closer investment of Mantua, which was completed by 29 September, but it soon became clear that the Austrians would send another army to force the lifting of the siege. In preparation for the coming campaign Bonaparte sent Masséna's division (5,500 men) to Bassano del Grappa, while Bon brought Augereau's division (5,400 men) to Verona to replace him. Vaubois's division (8,000 men) still held Trento, while Kilmaine (9,000 men) prosecuted the blockade of Mantua with the troops of Sahuguet and Dallemagne and the engineer Chasseloup. In addition to these 27,900 troops Bonaparte had another 4,000 men in garrisons in the rear, 4,000 wounded men and 14,000 men sick. The weakness of the Armée d'Italie was shown by the fact that Masséna and Vaubois were not in direct communication because the Austrians had managed to occupy the Valsugana, the direct route between them (7 October).[317]

With Wurmser blockaded in Mantua, Alvinczi was appointed in his place. The plan for the third attempt to relieve Mantua called for Davidovich to advance from the Tyrol to the east of Lake Garda, while Quosdanovich advanced 84 miles west from Cividale del Fruili to Bassano del Grappa. Quosdanovich was then to offer battle near Verona, where Davidovich would hopefully join him. However, it would take time to rebuild the Austrian forces and, in the meantime, Bonaparte offered Wurmser the opportunity to surrender Mantua, which yielded no response (16 October). When the Austrian offensive began on 22 October, Quosdanovich had assembled 26,400 men and 74 guns at Fruili, while Davidovich had 16,800 men and 60 guns in the Tyrol. The rebuilding of Quosdanovich's force was not without cost as the reinforcements were largely made up 15 newly raised Grenzer battalions, full of untrained men and short of officers.[318]

At this time Bonaparte had been further south in Rome but after visiting Modena, Bologna and Ferrara, he arrived in Verona the day after the Austrian operation began (23 October). On his return the Armée d'Italie, 41,600 men strong, was deployed such that Vaubois (10,500 men) held Trento with his forward troops lining the *Torrente Avisio* near Lavis, six miles further north. Masséna (9,500 men) held Bassano del Grappa and Treviso, 24 miles to the southeast near Venice while Augereau (8,300 men) was on the river Adige. Macquard commanded the infantry reserve (2,700 men) at Villafranca di Verona and Dumas commanded the cavalry reserve (1,600 men) in Verona, leaving Kilmaine and 8,800 men besieging Mantua.[319]

The Austrian column advancing 24 miles from Fruili crossed their first obstacle, the river Tagliamento, by wading through the rapidly rising waters swelled by torrential rain (25 October). After a further advance of 28 miles the column crossed the river Piave over a bridge of boats near Campagne, 36 miles east of Bassano del Grappa, where Masséna had now assembled most of his division (1 November). Meanwhile Davidovich in the Tyrol, attacked Vaubois's outposts (27 October) and attacked the Castello di Segonzano, 10 miles northeast of Trento on the Avisio (29–30 October).

By now Davidovich had been reinforced to 19,500 men, significantly outnumbering Vaubois. Despite this Vaubois attacked Davidovich at San Michele All'adige, Crembra and Segonzano, but was repulsed after several hours of heavy fighting (2 November). The next day Davidovich advanced again using an outflanking manoeuvre to force Vaubois back to Calliano, 10 miles south of Trento (3–4 November). At this time, Alvinczi ordered

317 Phipps, *Italy*, pp.106–107; Boycott-Brown, *Road to Rivoli*, p.441.

318 Boycott-Brown, *Road to Rivoli*, pp.440–445; *Feldzeugmeister* József Alvinczi Borbereky.

319 Phipps, *Italy*, p.108; Boycott-Brown, *Road to Rivoli*, p.448.

the Fruili column to advance to the river Brenta, with Hohenzollern and Mittrowsky on the right directed to Bassano del Grappa and Lipthay and Brabeck on the left directed to Treviso. Masséna evacuated Bassano at 5:00 a.m. heading for Vicenza, and Hohenzollern entered the town the same day (4 November). Arriving in Vicenza with Augereau and anxious about the pressure on Vaubois, Bonaparte sent Joubert's brigade from Legnago to support him (5 November). The next day Bonaparte sent Augereau's division forward towards Bassano del Grappa and Masséna's division towards Fontaniva, nine miles south of Bassano, with the intention of crossing the river Brenta. However, Alvinczi had also decided to advance, and Hohenzollern crossed the river Brenta with the advanced guard at Bassano, followed by the rest of the Quosdanovich's division.

The first fighting occurred between Masséna's men and the Austrian left under Lipthay, which were defending the river line. On the Austrian right Augereau encountered them in a line stretching from the village of Marchesane on the river Brenta through Marostica, three miles west of Bassano to Nove on the river Brenta, three miles down the river from Bassano. Through some heavy fighting in which Quosdanovich lost more than 1,600 men and the village of Nove changed hands several times, the French were repulsed (6 November). This second battle of Bassano had seen Bonaparte's 19,500 men defeated by Alvinczi's 28,000, losing 3,000 men killed, wounded and missing against total Austrian losses of 2,800 men. Meanwhile on the other arm of the Austrian pincer movement, Davidovich attacked Vaubois at Calliano but was unable to dislodge him (6 November), but he attacked again the next day and, after Calliano changed hands several times, forced a weakened Vaubois back to beyond Rovereto (7 November). The Austrian pursuit was slow, Davidovich had lost 3,500 men in the two days of fighting, a fifth of his force. Vaubois, having lost 4,400 men killed, wounded and missing, managed to reform his division in the strong positions around Rivoli Veronese, but this was only 13 miles northwest of Verona, where Bonaparte, abandoning Vicenza, had positioned the divisions of Masséna and Augereau together with the reserve, following their withdrawal from Bassano del Grappa (8 November).[320]

Alvinczi followed Bonaparte's retiring divisions through Montebello Vincentino to Villanova, on the outskirts of San Bonifacio, 13 miles east of Verona. The French outposts were at San Martino Buon Albergo, just five miles east of Verona (10 November). Augereau had placed his headquarters at Ronco All'adige on the river Adige, four miles south-southwest of San Bonifacio. Bonaparte then attacked the Austrian positions around Caldiero, nine miles east of Verona, with Augereau's division on the right and Masséna's on the left. Masséna's men made good progress initially but, outflanked by Austrian reserves, they were forced back with losses of 1,700 men. The Austrians lost 1,300 men but Bonaparte had to withdraw both divisions to Verona (12 November).[321]

Both sides spent the next day resting and reorganising. Alvinczi, at Vago and Gombion, seven miles east of Verona, with Quosdanovich, Provera and Mittrowsky, now had 23,000 men, while Davidovich, before Rivoli Veronese had 14,000 men, although some were detached to guard the area north of Lake Garda (13 November). Bonaparte had reinforced Vaubois from the Mantua blockading force such that he now had 8,000 men, while the blockading force had 13,000 fit men. Leaving 3,000 men in Verona, Bonaparte had a field

320 Phipps, *Italy*, pp.108–109; Boycott-Brown, *Road to Rivoli*, pp.446–454; Smith, *Data Book*, pp.126–127; *Generalmajor* Friedrich Franz Xaver von Hohenzollern-Hechingen; *Generalmajor* Anton Ferdinand Graf Mittrowsky von Mittrowitz und Nemyšl; *Generalmajor* Adolph Balduin von Brabeck.

321 Phipps, *Italy*, p.109; Smith, *Data Book*, p.127.

force facing Alvinczi of 18,000 men, comprising Masséna (7,900 men), Augereau (6,000 men) and the reserve (2,600 men) with the cavalry making up the balance.

The next day Alvinczi planned to bridge the river Adige eight miles below Verona at Zevio, and ordered Davidovich to restart his advance on Verona, in support (14 November). However, delays meant that Alvinczi had to postpone his crossing of the river Adige until the night of 15–16 November. In the meantime, Vaubois was instructed to hold his position and in particular the bridge over the river Adige near the Chiusa.[322] Bonaparte then withdrew the divisions of Augereau and Masséna through Verona and marched them down the right bank of the river Adige to Ronco where they recrossed the river to the left bank, poised to strike Alvinczi's line of communications. However, the direct route north to Caldiero was impeded by marshy terrain and Bonaparte had to send Augereau's division two and a half miles east-northeast towards the crossing of the river Alpone at the village of Arcole, along a single narrow road leading to a bridge 27 yards long and 12 feet wide.

Masséna's division was directed towards Belfiore, three and a half miles to the northwest, where he could prevent Alvinczi advancing on Ronco All'adige. Alvinczi was aware of the threat to his rear and had deployed Mittrowsky with three battalions to Cologna Veneta, seven miles east-southeast of Ronco All'adige and Brigido with four battalions to Arcole. Augereau spent the day driving the Austrian outposts back to Arcole and made several unsuccessful attempts to storm the bridge and take the village. Surprised by the French offensive, Alvinczi sent Gavasini's brigade to Belfiore with Brabeck's brigade following, while Mittrowsky was ordered to Arcole. Gavasini's men were soon in contact with Masséna's division, but some confusion in the Austrian ranks allowed Masséna to take Belfiore. In the afternoon, back at Arcole both Augereau and Bonaparte unsuccessfully attempted to inspire their men in two further attempts to carry the bridge by personally leading them onto the causeway, flag in hand. Bonaparte ended his attempt in the dyke. Meanwhile Bonaparte, trying a different approach, had sent Guieu with two demi-brigades to cross the river Alpone at its confluence with the river Adige before approaching Arcole along the left bank of the river Alpone. In the evening, Guieu, at the second attempt, successfully drove Brigido from Arcole to San Bonifacio. Despite this success, Bonaparte was concerned that Vaubois might have been defeated by Davidovich, who would then have threatened Verona and consequently he withdrew his army across the river Adige, abandoning the hard-won bridge and village of Arcole (15 November).

The next day Alvinczi launched a counterattack, after sending another summons to Davidovich to move on Verona, he ordered Hohenzollern to observe Verona, while Provera attacked through Belfiore with two brigades of six battalions and two squadrons and Mittrowsky launched a separate attack through Arcole. The two attacks were launched at daybreak with the intention of driving the French back to Ronco All'adige. However, Provera's column suffered a bloody repulse at the hands of Masséna's division and they were pursued back to Caldiero, losing five guns in the process. Mittrowsky was more successful, driving Augereau's division almost back to the river Adige. However, seeing that Provera had been defeated, Mittrowsky's men fell back to Arcole where they were rallied. Augereau followed up in pursuit but stopped short of Arcole and all attempts to advance further were thwarted. Deciding on the

322 Phipps, *Italy*, p.110; it is not clear where this bridge was, perhaps Chizzola, six miles south of Rovereto.

indirect approach, Bonaparte bridged the river Alpone near its confluence with the river Adige during the night. Despite the respective fears and expectation of the two army commanders, Davidovich made no attempt to force Vaubois back to Verona during the day (16 November). In the morning of the next day, Augereau used the bridge to cross the Alpone under fire from the Austrian artillery, driving the defenders from their first position, while Masséna held the left and advanced frontally on Arcole.

By 3:00 p.m. the reinforced defenders of Arcole were being attacked both from their front across the bridge, where Robert led two demi-brigades, and along the left bank of the river Alpone by Augereau's division. However, an Austrian counterattack drove Robert's men back to the bridge at Ronco All'adige, a reverse that in turn caused Augereau's men to fall back to and across their bridge over the river Alpone. However, facing little other opposition Masséna was able to renew his attack and crossed the bridge at Arcole at 5:00 p.m, by which time Augereau had again recrossed the river Alpone and was approaching Arcole again. At twilight Mittrowsky retired from Arcole towards San Bonifacio pursued by the French who were in turn forced back towards Arcole by Alvinczi himself at the head of Schubirž's brigade. Now in an indefensible position, overnight Alvinczi retreated towards Montebello Vicentino. Meanwhile Davidovich had finally launched his attack on Vaubois forcing him back to Affi, before pushing him further back in disorder to Piovezzano, only10 miles northwest of Verona, and capturing both Fiorella and Valette. At the battle of Arcole the French suffered 1,200 men killed and 2,300 wounded, with Austrian losses numbering 600 men killed, 1,600 wounded and 4,000 prisoners. (15–17 November).[323]

The day after the battle, Bonaparte ordered an advance northward on Villanova using both banks of the river Alpone with Augereau's division on the left and Masséna's on the right. However, they discovered that Alvinczi had retired through Montebello Vicentino to Olmo, three miles southwest of Vicenza. This enabled Bonaparte to concentrate his forces on Davidovich and leave only a screening force to face Alvinczi. Masséna's division was directed through Verona southwest towards Villafranca di Verona to join Vaubois retiring from Castelnuovo del Garda. Meanwhile Augereau's division went through Verona and then turned north through the mountains and down into the valley of the river Adige at Dolce, behind Davidovich's force (18 November). However, Davidovich having heard of Alvinczi's retirement, pulled his own column back to the position at Rivoli Veronese, only for Augereau's flank march to force him further back to Trento (19 November). Deciding that he needed to support Davidovich or see him destroyed, Alvinczi advanced again reaching Colognola ai Colli, 10 miles east of Verona (21 November). The way to Mantua was now open but believing that the French were stronger than they were and hearing of Davidovich's withdrawal, Alvinczi withdrew to Montebello di Vicentino (23 November) and onto Vicenza (24 November). The hard-fought campaign, marred by mistakes on both sides, was over and Mantua remained blockaded by the French, although Alvinczi's force, now at Bassano del Grappa still threatened. In the aftermath Vaubois was sent to Livorno to replace Sérurier who was recalled to the active army and Joubert assumed the command of Vaubois's division. Sérurier resumed command of the blockade of Mantua, replacing the sick Kilmaine, his two divisions commanded by Dumas and Dallemagne (27 December).[324]

323 Smith, *Data Book*, p.127; Boycott-Brown, *Road to Rivoli*, pp.458–476; Phipps, *Italy*, pp.113–119; *Oberst* Wenzel Karl Freiherr von Brigido; *Général de Brigade* Jean-Joseph Guieu; *Général de Brigade* Jean Gilles André Robert; *Général de Brigade* Antoine Joseph Marie Valette.

324 Phipps, *Italy*, pp.118–120, 123.

The West

In the west of France, Hoche, benefitting from commanding the Republic's single army in the region, the Armée des Côtes de l'Océan, adopted a more tolerant stance towards the remaining rebels in the Vendée. His columns maintained a constant pressure on the rebels such that the struggle in the Vendée on the left bank of the river Loire was over. Hoche then took 15,000 infantry and two cavalry regiments across the river to tackle the Chouans, whose leaders were either captured or surrendered. Thus, by May both banks of the river Loire were pacified. There was a price, the rebel's priests were to be left in peace and conscription was not to be enforced. The Directory then declared on 25 August that the Armée des Côtes de l'Océan was to be disbanded on 22 September. Strong detachments were sent to the Rhine and Italy leaving just 73,100 men in the region under Hoche's continued command. Hoche spent the rest of the year preparing for an expedition to Ireland.[325]

On 16 December a French fleet of 17 ships of the line, several frigates and other armed vessels sailed from the Brest roads, carrying 25,000 troops under the command of *Vice Amiral* Justin Bonaventure Morard de Galles and Hoche destined for Ireland. The object of the expedition was to aid the United Irishmen in rebellion against British rule. The fleet soon lost *Le Séduisant* (74), driven onto the rocks, while leaving Brest. The French fleet was discovered off the coast of Ireland on 22 December before being dispersed by a heavy gale the following day. Part of the fleet, comprising six ships of the line, three *razées*, four frigates, two brigs and two luggers, anchored in Bantry Bay on 24 December. These ships were soon driven out to sea by a violent gale (27 December), and *L'Impatiente* (44) was wrecked near Crookhaven (30 December). After a tempestuous battle against the elements, the French fleet struggled back to Brest and Rochefort reaching there in the middle of January 1797.[326]

Overseas

In the Mediterranean in 1796, the success of Bonaparte in Northern Italy had a negative impact on the British fleet operating on that coast now they were denied access to the ports of Genoa and Leghorn for victualling. At the latter port Bonaparte assembled a body of Corsican refugees and sent agents to Genoa to foment unrest on Corsica. Discontent on the island became so concerning that Nelson was sent to seize the island of Elba as an alternative base (10 July). However, the situation worsened when Spain was pressed by the Directory in Paris to declare war on Great Britain, the subject of a treaty signed 19 August. The Admiralty in London sent orders to Jervis to evacuate Corsica, Elba and the Mediterranean in general (31 August), which Jervis received on 25 September. Spain duly declared war on Great Britain (5 October).[327] However, with better news from the fighting on the Rhine, the British government countermanded these orders, instructing Jervis to hold Elba and Corsica if possible (21 October). However, Nelson had already evacuated the British troops from Corsica (19 October). Jervis and the British Mediterranean Fleet sailed for Gibraltar (2 November), although

325 Phipps, *West*, pp.51–53.
326 Schomberg, *Naval Chronology*, vol. II, p.429–431; Phipps, *West*, pp.53–59.
327 Jones, *Companion*, p.134.

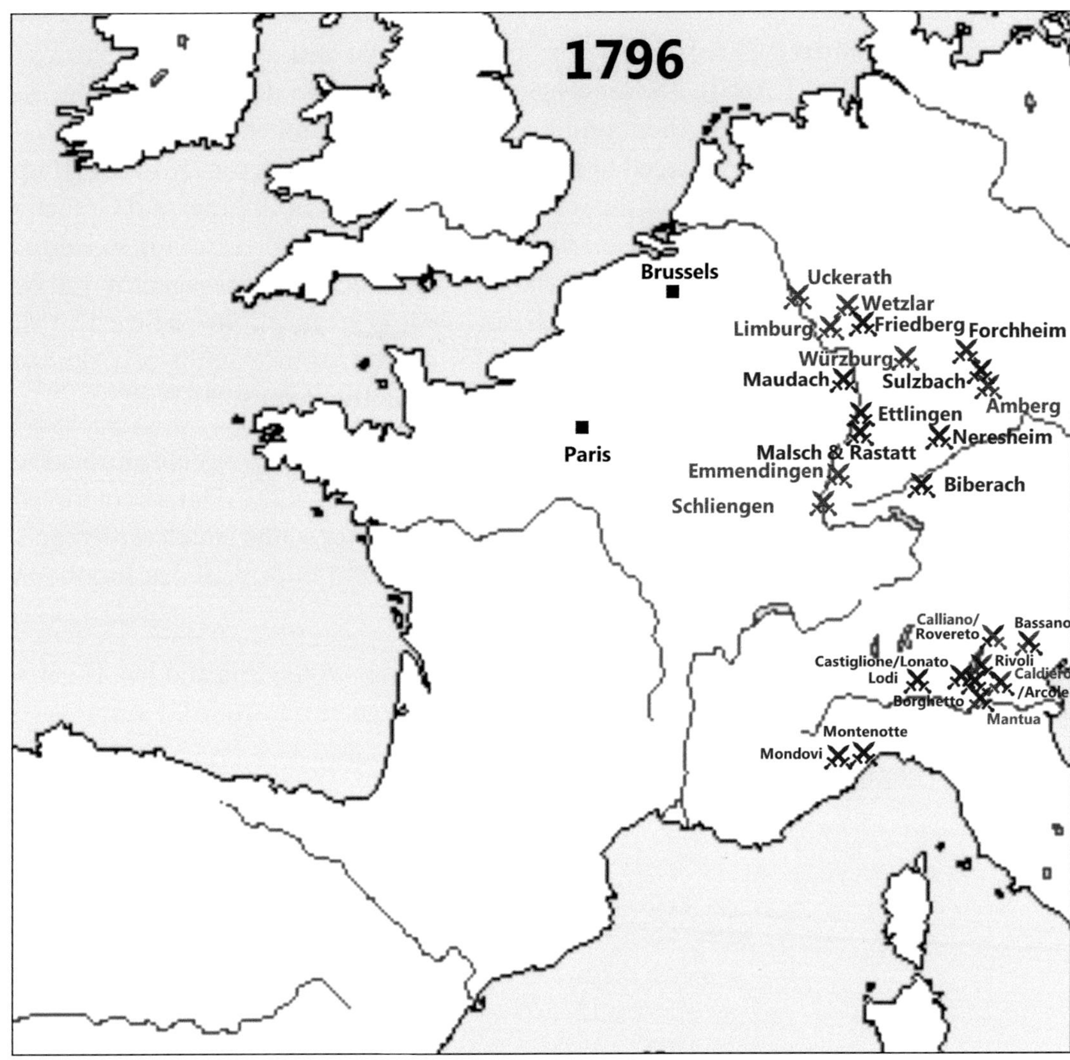

Map 6 – Key actions and battles, 1796

de Burgh continued to hold Elba until January 1797 as he had had no orders from London to evacuate.[328]

Abercromby's delayed expedition to the West Indies eventually set sail again at the end of February although Abercromby sailing separately arrived in Barbados ahead of the fleet (17 March). Abercromby's first action was to reinforce Nicolls fighting the insurrection on Grenada (24 March). The first of the troops from Abercromby's expedition, under Whyte, arrived from Cork on 1 April.[329] British Admiral John Laforey, commanding the Leeward Islands station, despatched Captain Thomas Parr with a small squadron (HMS *Malabar* (56), HMS *Scipio* (64), HMS *Undaunted* (38), HMS *Pique* (32) and HMS *Babet* (20)) carrying Whyte and 1,200 troops, (15 April) to attack the Dutch colonies in Guyana, South America, which were promptly captured, Demerara on 22 April and Berbice on 2 May.[330]

Further troops arrived bringing Abercromby's available troops to 8,000 men (14–15 April). Abercromby was now ready to attack St. Lucia and Laforey's successor, Rear

328 Fortescue, *History*, vol. IV, pt.1, pp.509–512; Schomberg, *Naval Chronology*, vol. II, p.429; Major-General John Thomas de Burgh, who had commanded the British troops on Corsica.

329 Fortescue, *History*, vol. IV, pt.1, pp.482–483, 485; Major-General John Whyte.

330 Schomberg, *Naval Chronology*, vol. II, pp.440–441; Fortescue, *History*, vol. IV, pt.1, p.486.

Admiral Hugh Cloberry Christian sailed from Martinique with Abercromby's troops to attack that island (21 April). The landings were made in two divisions, the first led by Moore and the second by Abercromby (26 April). The French put up a spirited resistance but were ultimately forced to surrender (26 May). Abercromby followed up this success with the suppression of the rebellions on St. Vincent (9 June) and Grenada (18 June). This concluded the campaign for the year and a sick Abercromby sailed for home in August, leaving Graham in command and his men to be ravaged by yellow fever. The three campaigns in the West Indies in 1794, 1795 and 1796 cost the British perhaps 40,000 dead and another 40,000 unfit for service from wounds or sickness, exceeding the British losses in Wellington's campaigns in the Peninsular War.[331]

In the East Indies, Captain Alan Hyde Gardner led a small British squadron to seize Colombo (16 February) thereby completing the conquest of the Dutch colony of Ceylon. Meanwhile, British Rear Admiral Peter Rainier captured the Dutch settlements of Amboyna (16 February, Ambon Island) and Banda Aceh, in present day Indonesia (8 March).[332]

In Saldanha Bay, South Africa, a Dutch fleet of three ships of the line and five frigates surrendered to the larger fleet of Rear Admiral Lord George Elphinstone (17 August).[333]

Other naval engagements during 1796 include:[334]

331 Schomberg, *Naval Chronology*, vol. II, pp.441–443; Fortescue, *History*, vol. IV, pt.1, pp.487–496; Colonel John Moore, 51st Foot; Major-General Charles Graham.

332 Schomberg, *Naval Chronology*, vol. II, pp.441–443.

333 Schomberg, *Naval Chronology*, vol. II, p.446; Fortescue, *History*, vol. IV, pt.1, pp.508–509.

334 Schomberg, *Naval Chronology*, vol. II, pp.415–416, 418, 421–426, 433–437, 439–440, 443–444; John William Norie, *The Naval Gazetteer, Biographer, and Chronologist; Containing a History of the Late Wars, from Their Commencement in 1793, to Their Conclusion in 1801; and from Their Re-commencement in 1803, to Their Final Conclusion in 1815* (London: author, 1827), p.410; the Gazetteer is a more detailed list than Schomberg but includes a lot of actions involving ships of less than 10 guns.

Theatre	Date	Action
Home waters	20 March	Warren with HMS *La Pomone* (44), HMS *Artois* (38), HMS *Anson* (44) and HMS *Galatea* (32), cruising close to the Saints near Brest, chased the *Proserpine* (38), *Unité* (38), *Coquille* (40), *Tamise* (32), *Étoile* (30), *Cygnone* (20) and *La Manche* (20), capturing *L'Étoile* plus four brigs from their accompanying convoy.
	13 April	HMS *Révolutionnaire* (40) captured *L'Unité* (38) off Ushant.
	15 April	HMS *La Pomone* (44) captured *La Robuste* (22) off the Saints.
	20 April	HMS *Indefatigable* (44), HMS *Amazon* (36) and HMS *Concorde* (32) chased down and captured the *Virginie* (40) near the Lizard.
	12 May	Admiral Duncan's squadron pursued a Dutch squadron from Norway. HMS *Phoenix* (36) captured the Dutch frigate *Argo* (36). HMS *Pegasus* (28) and HMS *Sylph* (16) drove the brigs *Echo* (18) and *Gier* (12) on shore east of Texel. HMS *Sylph* then captured the final brig *Mercury* (16).
	8 June	West of the Isles of Scilly, HMS *Unicorn* (32) and HMS *Santa Margarita* (36) chased down and captured *La Tribune* (36) and *La Tamise* (32).
	13 June	HMS *Dryad* (36) encountered and captured the *Proserpine* (38) off Cape Clear.
	22 June	HMS *Apollo* (38) and HMS *Doris* (36) captured the *Légère* (22) off Cape Clear.
	16 July	HMS *Glatton* (56) engaged six French frigates (50, 2x36, 3x28), a brig and a cutter off Texel. The superior British gunnery forced the French to retire into Flushing.
	22 August	Warren's squadron (specifically HMS *Galatea* (32) and HMS *Sylph* (16)) drove *L'Andromaque* (32) on shore near the mouth of the river Gironde.
Mediterranean	9 March	HMS *Barfleur* (90), HMS *Egmont* (74), HMS *Bombay Castle* (74) and HMS *Zealous* (74) captured the *Sardine* (22) and recaptured HMS *Nemesis* (28), in the neutral harbour of Tunis.
	20 April	HMS *Inconstant* (36) captured *L'Unité* (32, later HMS *Surprise* (28)) off Cape Bon, Tunisia.
	9 June	HMS *Southampton* (32) captured *L'Utile* (24) under the guns of *Fort de Brégançon* near Toulon.
	13 October	HMS *Terpsichore* (32) captured the Spanish frigate *Mahonesa* (34) off Cartagena.
	13 December	HMS *Terpsichore* (32) captured *La Vestale* (32) off Cadiz, but its crew overwhelmed the prize crew, retook it and got safely into Cadiz.
	19 December	Commodore Horatio Nelson with HMS *Minerve* (40) captured the Spanish frigate *Santa Sabina* (40), while HMS *Blanche* (32) set off in pursuit of the frigate *Ceres* (40) forcing it to surrender. The *Santa Sabina* was retaken by the Spanish when two ships of line and two frigates arrived. The *Ceres* was not secured and escaped.
N. America	28 August	HMS *Topaze* (32) pursued and captured the armed merchantman *L'Elizabeth* (36) off Bermuda.
	28 August– 5 September	Franco-Spanish expedition (*Contre-Amiral* Joseph de Richery with 17 ships of the line and three frigates) arrived off Newfoundland, although failing to take St. Johns, the British fishing fleet was severely damaged.
West Indies	25 November	HMS *Lapwing* (28) sailed from St. Kitts to prevent the French capturing Anguilla, capturing *Le Decius* (24) and destroying the brig *La Valliante* (4).

During 1796, the French Republic had 396,000 men in the field to guard its frontiers and attack its enemies. The French armies fought 34 battles involving 20,000 combatants or more, winning 21 and losing 13, plus 19 smaller actions, winning 12 and losing seven, with one additional drawn encounter.[335]

The War in 1797

The Rhine

Along the river Rhine, 1797 opened with the ongoing sieges of the *têtes du pont* at Kehl and Huningue. Moreau, against the wishes of the Directory, who were keen to keep Archduke Charles busy on the river Rhine, initiated talks for an armistice. When the Directory relented Kehl was surrendered to the Austrians (10 January). After a gallant defence the garrison of Huningue also evacuated the *tête-du-pont* on the right bank (5 February). Although the Armée de Sambre-et-Meuse held Düsseldorf, the Armée de Rhin-et-Moselle had been swept from the right bank of the river Rhine. Despite this, the two French armies had held considerable Austrian forces on the Rhine front, thereby facilitating Bonaparte's campaign in Italy.[336]

Moreau, now commanding both armies on the Rhine, was ordered to send 20,000 infantry and 2,000 cavalry to reinforce Bonaparte's Armée d'Italie. In response Moreau sent four infantry demi-brigades and two cavalry regiments (12,000 men) from the Armée de Sambre-et-Meuse and eight infantry demi-brigades and two cavalry regiments (9,500 men) from the Armée de Rhin-et-Moselle. Delmas led the contingent from the Armée de Rhin-et-Moselle, while Bernadotte led that from the Armée de Sambre-et-Meuse. Bernadotte left for Italy sometime between 7–10 January. Meanwhile, Delmas left after the fall of Kehl to the Austrians (10 January) and the head of his column reached Milan on 12 February.[337]

Beurnonville, commanding the Armée de Sambre-et-Meuse, was left with just Grenier and Championnet as *généraux de division* and to fill the vacancies Bonnard replaced Bernadotte, while Souham was brought in to replace Ligniville who was sick. Ney replaced Lefebvre in command of the advance guard. However, the Directory, sending Beurnonville back to the Armée du Nord, decided that Hoche should command the Armée de Sambre-et-Meuse and he soon arrived at Coblenz (25 February), prompting Kléber to leave the army the next day, but Lefebvre returned to command his division.

Hoche moved to reinforce his army bringing in the divisions of Macdonald (10,700 men) and Watrin (9,400 men) from the Armée du Nord and a further 8,000 men from the troops of the expedition to Ireland. By the beginning of April, he had 78,000 men present under arms, another 8,500 were sick and 3,000 were prisoners of the Austrians. Hoche then formed his six fighting infantry divisions into three corps, Lefebvre commanded the right with his own division and that of Lemoine and the cavalry division of Richepanse, in all 19,000 men. The centre was commanded by Grenier and made up of his own division and that of Olivier together with Ney's hussar division, totalling in the region of 16,600 men. The left was commanded by Championnet with his own

335 Jones, *Companion*, p.157; Smith, *Data Book*, pp.111–128.
336 Phipps, *Moselle*, pp.393–395.
337 Phipps, *Moselle*, pp.405–406.

division and that of Bonnard together with Klein's dragoon division and numbered 18,600 men. D'Hautpoul commanded the cavalry reserve, while Colaud commanded the Corps de Hunsrück, comprising the divisions of Macdonald and Watrin, 20,100 men in total. Within this organisation each infantry division included a regiment of chasseurs à cheval. Ney's division was charged with reconnaissance and with screening the front and flanks of the army.[338]

The Armée de Rhin-et-Moselle was also reorganised along similar lines. On the right, Dufour held the Upper Rhine from Huningue, with his own division and that of Férino (17,900 men in all). In the centre, Desaix held Strasbourg with his own division and that of Duhesme (15,200 men) and on the left Saint-Cyr, with the divisions of Sainte-Suzanne and Ambert, held the Lower Rhine down to Mannheim where it joined the Armée de Sambre-et-Meuse. Bourcier commanded the cavalry reserve of six heavy regiments and one of dragoons numbering 2,200 horsemen. In total the strength of the army was 57,400 men. However, Moreau withdrew the army away from the Rhine to rest and replenish their supplies.[339]

After some debate in Paris, the Directory determined that Hoche should cross the river Rhine and advance to the river Danube but no further than Donauwörth, before focussing on completing the sieges of the Rhine fortresses rather than advancing on Vienna (17 April). Facing the combined total of 142,600 men of the two French armies, was Latour, who had replaced Archduke Charles on 2 February, commanding just 93,000 men. Facing Hoche, the Austrian right, comprising 28,800 men commanded by Werneck, was positioned between the rivers Lahn and Sieg. Of these men, Kray commanded 8,100 men opposite Neuwied. In the centre, Staader commanded 29,000 men with the main body at Mannheim and the reserve under Simbschen at Rüsselsheim am Main. The Austrian left facing Moreau comprised 35,300 men under the command of Sztáray and was positioned along the river Rhine from the river Murg to the Swiss border. Along the Rhine, the Austrians held Ehrenbreitstein, Mainz, Mannheim and Philippsburg, whose garrisons numbered an additional 20,000 men.[340]

Hoche denounced the armistice on 13 April, enabling him to begin hostilities on 16 April. Championnet advanced southeast from Düsseldorf across the river Wupper, 16 miles away, while the centre and right closed on Neuwied. Starting at Mülheim, near Cologne, Championnet then marched to the river Seig, 15 miles further southeast (17 April). As Kray moved to support Werneck, Hoche then started his crossing of the Rhine at Neuwied, 28 miles further up the river Rhine (18 April). Lefebvre led the way with one infantry division and Richepanse's *chasseurs à cheval*, Grenier followed with the centre and Ney's hussars, while d'Hautpoul's heavy cavalry and Watrin's division crossed last. This meant that the entire army was on the right bank of the river Rhine apart from Macdonald's division watching the Hunsrück (an area of upland).

Hoche thus had 50,000 men concentrated against Kray's 8,100 men, who had been ordered back to Neuwied, reaching the forts there only at 6:00 a.m. on 18 April. Two

338 Phipps, *Moselle*, pp.409–410, 412–415; *Général de Division* Ennemond Bonnard; *Général de Division* Jean-Baptiste Olivier; *Général de Brigade* François Watrin; *Général de Division* Louis Lemoine; *Général de Brigade* Antoine Richepanse; *Général de Division* Jean-Joseph-Ange d'Hautpoul; *Général de Division* René Charles Élisabeth de Ligniville, who had replaced Marceau only in October 1796.

339 Phipps, *Moselle*, pp.416–417; suggests St. Cyr had 22,100 men by difference; *Général de Division* Gilles Joseph Martin Bruneteau de Sainte-Suzanne.

340 Phipps, *Moselle*, pp.419–420; *Feldmarschallleutnant* Josef Heinrich Staader von Adelsheim; *Generalmajor* Joseph Anton von Simbschen.

hours later Hoche attacked the Austrian line from Heddesdorf on the left to Engers on the right, which was two miles back from the crossing point covered by six redoubts. Further back on the Heddesdorf plateau there were three other works. Lefebvre turning upstream took Engers and Mühldorf, but a mile further on, before Bendorf, was delayed by the stubborn defenders. The defenders of Bendorf were then routed by Richepanse's cavalry and pursued 11 miles eastwards beyond Montabaur, which Lefebvre occupied that evening. Meanwhile Grenier's first assaults on the redoubts failed. But Ney, with cavalry and horse artillery, advanced around the end of the line and attacked the gorges of the redoubts, exploding the magazines and causing such disorder that the French infantry was able to storm the redoubts before noon. Kray retreated northwards to Dierdorf, 12 miles northeast of Neuwied. Hoche launched three columns of cavalry in pursuit, which were stopped by the Austrian reserve of 6,000 men at Dierdorf. However, when Grenier's infantry arrived the Austrians were routed, losing some 5,000 men, five colours and 15 guns.[341]

Bataille de Neuwied, 18 April 1797

Meanwhile in front of Werneck's main body, Championnet advanced from the river Sieg towards Altenkirchen. Championnet's advanced guard under Soult clashed with Werneck's rearguard near Uckerath, 11 miles east of Bonn, but the Austrians retired 12 miles further east to Altenkirchen. Learning of Kray's defeat at Neuwied, Werneck cancelled a planned attack on Championnet at Weyerbusch, four miles west of Altenkirchen, and retired through Hachenburg 10 miles further east to Stein-Neukirch, Kray's men having re-joined him at the former place. Championnet now formed the left of Hoche's army at Altenkirchen, Grenier in the centre, 10 miles south, at Dierdorf and Lefebvre holding the right at Montabaur, 11 miles to the southeast (18 April). Lefebvre then moved 11 miles southeast to Limburg on the river Lahn, with Watrin's division on his right.

341 Phipps, *Moselle*, pp.421–423; Smith, *Data Book*, p.134.

Instead of following Lefebvre's march with his whole army Hoche sent only Grenier's division from the centre, and instead, with Olivier's division, Ney's hussar division and d'Hautpoul's heavy cavalry, he marched northeast through Hachenburg to join Championnet at Altenkirchen (19 April). Belatedly, Latour had sent Simbschen with the Austrian reserve of 5,500 men to Limburg, but finding Lefebvre already there, Simbschen withdrew towards Höchst, six miles west of Frankfurt on the river Main. Lefebvre then advanced on Frankfurt pushing Simbschen before him (21 April). Meanwhile Hoche with his centre and left attempted to strike Werneck, but, misdirecting his attack, could only pursue Werneck's rearguard as it marched eastwards to Roth, 18 miles east of Hachenburg, where it was attacked by Ney's cavalry. Although the Austrian cavalry were overthrown, their infantry held firm and enabled a further retirement of four miles northeast through Herborn before turning southeast down the river Dill towards Wetzlar on the river Lahn, 30 miles north of Frankfurt. Werneck was retiring in three parts, his main column crossed the Lahn at Wetzlar and his left flank column crossed seven miles to the east at Giessen, while his right flank column crossed at Braunfels, six miles west of Wetzlar (20 April).

The next day, despite Werneck starting late, Hoche again misdirected his attack towards Giessen and therefore only contacted the rearguard of Elsnitz's flank column there. Reinforced by Werneck, Elsnitz's cavalry managed to capture Ney in the subsequent fighting at Giessen while Werneck made good his withdrawal of 13 miles across the river Wetter. Meanwhile Lefebvre had continued his advance from Limburg reaching Königstein, 11 miles northwest of Frankfurt (21 April). Pursuing Werneck to Frankfurt, Hoche learnt of the armistice agreed in Italy (22 April).[342]

In the meantime, Moreau arrived with the Armée de Rhin-et-Moselle (40,000 men) in time to take command of a new crossing of the river Rhine, which had been planned by Desaix and Reynier (19 April). The crossing began at 6:00 a.m. the next day, 10 miles below Strasbourg where the river Ill joins the Rhine, opposite Diersheim. Vandamme and Davout both led parties across the river in boats and secured Diersheim, only to be thrown out of it by the Austrian defenders, commanded by Sztáray (24,000 men). Davout, at the head of a demi-brigade, retook the village but the fierce struggle for the village continued for some time. Towards the end of the day a furious Austrian counterattack retook the village again, but Davout and Desaix took Honau, a mile to the southwest of Diersheim, and a final French attack retook Diersheim once more (20 April). This action covered the building of the bridge of boats and Desaix's corps was soon across the river, followed by the right of the army and the cavalry reserve. Saint-Cyr's left wing was also approaching the bridge led by Lecourbe's brigade. Before Moreau could launch his next attack, the Austrians launched their own assault on Diersheim with troops they had massed overnight.

The French artillery was dismounted by their opposite numbers and most of the French defenders were routed by this assault and fled for the bridge. However, Lecourbe used his own men to occupy the bridge and to threaten the fugitives with the bayonet, which helped restore order. Davout then led two demi-brigades from the right into the flank of the Austrians, prompting them to withdraw. Moreau then went on the offensive. On the right Kehl was easily captured, in the centre Vandamme advanced up the river Kinzig to Offenburg and Gengenbach, 15 miles southeast of Strasbourg, while on the

342 Phipps, *Moselle*, pp.423–428; *Generalmajor* Franz Anton von Elsnitz.

left Lecourbe's advanced guard reached the river Rench, beyond Rheinau (21 April). Both sides lost 3,000 men but Moreau also captured 3,000 prisoners, 20 guns and many carriages, including one which contained evidence which would incriminate both Pichegru and Moreau himself. The rest of Saint-Cyr's corps reached the bridge at Diersheim at noon 22 April, while Moreau continued his advance. Moreau's right under Dufour, advanced up the river Rhine towards Ettenheim, 23 miles south of Kehl, while the centre advanced up the river Kinzig to Biberach, 20 miles southeast of Kehl, and Vandamme marched up the river Rench to Freudenstadt, 28 miles east of Kehl. On the left Saint-Cyr sent Lecourbe across the river Rench to Lichtenau, 13 miles north-northeast of Kehl. In front of him Latour was marching up the valley of the river Rhine with 15,000 infantry and 3,000 cavalry to reinforce Sztáray's troops (22 April). Rather than attack Moreau's somewhat over extended army, the Austrians announced the armistice signed by Bonaparte in Italy, bringing the campaign to an end.[343]

Italy

At the end of 1796, Bonaparte's army was deployed such that Joubert (10,250 men) held the Rivoli Veronese position in the valley of the river Adige, Masséna (8,900 men) held Verona and along the river Adige to Bussolengo, Augereau (8,700 men) held the lower Adige at Legnago, while Sérurier (10,200 men) blockaded Mantua. In addition, Victor with the infantry reserve (1,800 men) was posted at Castelnuovo del Garda and Goito, while Dugua led the cavalry reserve (700 men) at Villafranca di Verona. Rey's new division (4,200 men) guarded the western shores of Lake Garda to Salò. In all Bonaparte had a field force of 34,400 men in addition to Sérurier's men blockading Mantua. In the rear Lannes (2,000 men) held Bologna and four more divisions (*Divisions des pays conquis*, 9,300 men) performed garrison duties. While Bonaparte was in Bologna agreeing a convention with the Duke of Tuscany (11 January), the Austrians (Provera with 9,000 men) advancing from Padua attacked Augereau and drove him from Legnago (9 January). Alvinczi had learnt from Graham, who had escaped from Mantua, that Wurmer's men were in a critical condition, and in addition to Provera, he sent Bajalics (6,200 men) against Verona from Bassano del Grappa, while he led the main body of the army (28,000 men) down the valley of the river Adige to crush Joubert, pushing him back to Rivoli Veronese (13 January).

Leaving Augereau to deal with Provera, Bonaparte concentrated his army in support of Joubert. Masséna leaving a small garrison in Verona, advanced to form up on Joubert's left, with the 18e Demi-Brigade advancing along the shore of Lake Garda. Victor marched from Castellaro to Villafranca and Rey advanced through Castelnuovo del Garda, following the crests of the hills to the left of Rivoli Veronese. Finally, Murat from Rey's division led his cavalry through Castelnuovo del Garda reconnoitring northwards.

Bonaparte managed to gather together 22,000 men, and with this force joined Joubert to find his division deployed on the Rivoli plateau, between Monte Baldo on the left and the valley of the river Adige on the right. In front of Joubert were three of the six Austrian columns totalling 12,700 men. On the French left was Lusignan's first column, whose advance had caused Joubert's withdrawal to Rivoli Veronese, and on the French right were the fifth and six Austrian columns advancing down both banks of the river Adige.

343 Phipps, *Moselle*, pp.429–432.

Most of the Austrian artillery was by necessity in the valley of the river Adige with the fifth and sixth columns. Bonaparte ordered Joubert to attack immediately. Masséna advancing to Joubert's support, yielded immediate results on the French left where the 18e and 75e Demi-Brigades and Murat with the 12e Demi-Brigade Légère manage to capture Lusignan's column. Meanwhile, Joubert successfully repelled the Austrian attempts to gain the plateau (14 January). Having been informed that Provera had advanced to the river Adige with a bridging train, Bonaparte left Joubert, reinforced by Rey's division, to continue the fight against Alvinczi and then marched south with Masséna's division and three cavalry regiments to support Augereau on the lower Adige. Joubert was ordered to attack Alvinczi who was still trying to advance. Joubert's attack overthrew the three central columns, routing them. In all over the two days of fighting during the Battle of Rivoli, the Austrians lost 4,000 men in killed and wounded and a further 8,000 men as prisoners of war, together with eight guns and 11 colours, double the French losses of 2,200 men killed and wounded and 1,000 prisoners (15 January).[344]

On the lower Adige, despite having pushed Augereau back to Legnago and Bonavigo, five miles up the river towards Verona (9 January), Provera was terribly slow to exploit his success. It was only four days later that Provera made his next move, feinting in one direction, he crossed the Adige via his pontoon bridge laid opposite Angiari, two miles upriver from Legnago (14 January). Counterattacks by both Bon and Guieu were beaten off. While Provera headed for Mantua, Augereau busied himself with trying to cut his line of retreat, back across the Adige, including destroying the pontoon bridge at Angiari (14 January). Having passed the night at Nogara, 11 miles west of Angiari, Provera marched on Mantua, his advanced guard arriving before Fort San Giorgio, defended by Miollis, having captured a wagon of Bonaparte's correspondence along the way. Within Mantua Wurmser was alerted that Provera's relief column was close at hand (15 January). The next day the battle of La Favorita was fought. Provera attacking from the Due Castelli road advanced towards La Favorita, a palace of the Dukes of Mantua, one and a half miles north of the city. Here he was joined by two columns – 1,000 and 1,200 men respectively – sent from the garrison of Mantua by Wurmser to Sant'Antonio on his left and Montala on his right. Sant'Antonio was defended by Dumas, but he was forced out by the Austrians attacking from Mantua. However, together with Dumas, Victor recaptured Sant'Antonio and drove the Austrian column back into the citadel. In the centre Sérurier held La Favorita with 1,500 men against Provera's advance. Provera soon found that both his flanks were being attacked by Masséna on the French right and Miollis from San Giorgio on the French left. In addition, Augereau had now reached the battlefield from the river Adige and attacked Provera's rear. In a hopeless situation Provera was forced to surrender the remains of his column of 7,000 men, 22 guns and the convoy of food intended for Mantua. The final Austrian attempt to relieve Mantua had failed and Bonaparte now moved to exploit the victory.[345]

The three fighting divisions were sent forward, Augereau marched from Legnago through Este and Padua to Cittadella on the left bank of the river Brenta, nine miles south of Bassano del Grappa (21 January), before marching east towards Treviso. Masséna marched through Vicenza and occupied Bassano del Grappa (26 January),

344 Phipps, *Italy*, pp.126–131; Boycott-Brown, *Road to Rivoli*, p.491; Smith, *Data Book*, p.131; Brevet Colonel Thomas Graham (90th Foot) attached to Wurmser; *Général de Division* Charles-François Joseph Dugua; *Général de Division* Gabriel Venance Rey; *Generalmajor* Adam Bajalics von Bajaháza; *Generalmajor* Franz Joseph Marquis de Lusignan.

345 Phipps, *Italy*, pp.134–139; Smith, *Data Book*, pp.131–132.

he then marched 30 miles up the valley of the river Brenta, through Primolano before reaching Borgo Valsugana (31 January). Separately Dumas, leading Masséna's advanced guard, had been sent up the river Piave to Feltre, 20 miles north-northeast of Bassano del Grappa, but was later withdrawn. Finally, Joubert led his division up the river Adige from Rivoli Veronese against little opposition occupying Trento (30 January) and then up the river Lavis to Segonzano, 10 miles northeast of Trento, with Murat further west as a flank guard (2 February).[346]

At the end of January, Wurmser opened talks with Bonaparte regarding the surrender of Mantua (31 January). The negotiations were completed by Sérurier, such that the surrender took place with Wurmser allowed to leave the fortress for Austria with an all-arms force of less than a thousand men, paroled not to fight against France for one year (2 February). The rest of the garrison, some 16,300 men, all that remained of 30,500 men, became prisoners of war.[347] Meanwhile Bonaparte had turned his attention south, sending Victor with a division of 4,000 men to Bologna, where Bonaparte himself soon arrived (1 February) and the force, now joined by Lahoz's division from the new Cisalpine Republic, headed south.

Having marched through Imola, Bonaparte (9,000 men) found the Pope's forces (7,000 men), including some hastily raised levies, entrenched behind the river Senia, three miles outside Faenza near Castel Bolognese (the ensuing combat is known by both names). The Pope's men were commanded by Colli, the erstwhile commander of the Sardinia-Piedmont army. While Lahoz frontally attacked the Papal forces, Victor forded the river to get behind them. The Pope's men lost 800 men killed and wounded and 1,200 captured, at least 20 times the French casualties (3 February).[348] Bonaparte continued his advance reaching Forli, 40 miles southeast of Bologna (4 February), before continuing 84 miles further south along the Adriatic coast towards Ancona. Three miles short of that town the French met the Pope's entrenched regular forces (1,200 men), which Victor (4,000 men) attacked, turning both flanks and capturing all the defenders (9 February). The citadel of Ancona was occupied with no resistance and that night Marmont was sent 12 miles further south to seize the treasures of the *Santuario della Santa Casa di Loreto*, although Colli had removed most of them. Leaving the coast, the French force now advanced southwest up the valley of the river Chienti through Macerata and Toletino and across the Apennines to Foligno, where Victor halted, the road to Rome open before him. Bonaparte concluded a treaty with the Pope, which ceded Bologna, Ferrara, Romagna, Avignon and Ancona along with 30,000,000 Francs. (19 February). While Victor occupied Rome, Bonaparte returned north via Bologna (24 February) to Mantua (2 March).[349]

The Austrian response to the loss of Mantua and north Italy was to appoint Archduke Charles to command the army facing Bonaparte. However, they were slower than the French to reinforce their new commander, which placed him at a significant disadvantage. In the first half of February the French reinforcements from the Armée du Sambre-et-Meuse (12,900 men) and the Armée de Rhin-et-Moselle (10,000 infantry plus two cavalry regiments) began to arrive in Verona under the respective command

346 Phipps, *Italy*, p.146.

347 Phipps, *Italy*, pp.152–154; Smith, *Data Book*, pp.132–133.

348 Phipps, *Italy*, pp.147–149; Smith, *Data Book*, p.133; *Général de Brigade* Giuseppe Lahoz Ortiz; Phipps gives the Papal forces at just 3,000–4,000 men but gives their casualties as 400–500 killed. He also has Colli in Rome, 179 miles away at the time of the combat.

349 Phipps, *Italy*, pp.149–151; Smith, *Data Book*, p.133.

of Bernadotte and Delmas. Bernadotte's division gathered around Padua (6 March). In addition, Bonaparte received a further 3,400 men from the west of France. By comparison the Austrians reinforcements, some 30,000–40,000 men, destined to assemble in Fruili, east of Venice, did not leave the Rhine valley until 6 February, and only arrived after the campaign was over.[350]

For the campaign ahead, Bonaparte organised his reinforced army into eight divisions. Bonaparte himself led four divisions, the first under Masséna (9,700 men) was at Bassano del Grappa, the second commanded by Guieu (in place of Augereau who was in France, 10,200 men) was at Treviso, Sérurier commanded the third division (6,500 men) and Bernadotte commanded the fourth division (6,800 men). Together Bonaparte's main body comprised 33,300 men. On his left, Joubert commanded his own fifth division, Rey's sixth division and Delmas's seventh division, in all 14,100 men, around Trento, with his forward posts around Lavis. In addition, Victor's division (6,500 men) was to the south in Foligno, 70 miles north-northeast of Rome and another 8,700 men served in the garrison divisions. Archduke Charles managed to assemble 40,000 men to face Bonaparte's 47,000 men available for the campaign. After some skirmishing at the outposts in the last week of February, on 10 March Bonaparte began his advance, crossing the river Tagliamento, near Valvasone, 37 miles northeast of Treviso (16 March).

Bonaparte (40,000 men) advanced with Bernadotte on the right and Guieu on the left, Dugua's cavalry and Sérurier's division were in reserve. Facing the French, positioned along the two miles between the villages of Gradisca and Gorizia, east of the river, were Archduke Charles's rearguard of 5,000 men. The French advanced in *ordre mixte*, each demi-brigade deploying one battalion in line flanked by two in column, and each division was led by the light infantry flanked by battalions of grenadiers in column. The surprised Austrians at first sent their cavalry to threaten the right of Bernadotte's division but Dugua's cavalry repulsed this attack, and the Austrians later withdrew with losses of 700 men and six guns. French losses amounted to 500 killed and wounded.[351]

Bernadotte then pressed on a further 19 miles, entering Palmanova (18 March) and then, after a further nine miles, approached the Austrian garrison at Gradisca d'Isonzo on the river Soča (or Isonzo). Bernadotte's first assault was defeated but Bonaparte sent Sérurier around the town to the south. Seeing Sérurier's men on the heights to the north and east of the town, the Austrian garrison of four battalions comprising 2,500 men surrendered (19 March).[352]

Meanwhile Masséna was detached from the main army and advanced north from Bassano del Grappa up the valley of the river Piave via Feltre to Belluno, 35 miles north-northeast of Bassano del Grappa. Awaiting him, seven-and-a-half miles further up the river was Lusignan who was posted at Fortogna in an apparently impregnable position between a mountain and the river. Discovering that the river was in fact fordable, Masséna sent his tirailleurs forward before the columns of the 18e Demi-Brigade de Ligne, while his dragoons crossed the river and overthrew the Austrian hussars before attacking the left rear of the Austrian infantry. Most of the Austrian infantry left the

350 Phipps, *Italy*, pp.158–159; Bernadotte was promoted to *général de division* in October 1794.

351 Phipps, *Italy*, pp.162–164; Smith, *Data Book*, pp.133–134; Delmas replaced Dallemagne in early March, see Nafziger's 21 March 1797 order of battle for the Armée d'Italie on the Napoleon Series at <https://www.napoleon-series.org/nafzigger/797CAD.pdf> accessed 18 November 2022.

352 Phipps, *Italy*, p.165; Smith, *Data Book*, p.134.

field in rout, but Lusignan managed to form a square with the remainder and withdraw, but at the head of the Vajont Gorge, three miles further back near Longarone, he surrendered with 660 of his men. This action removed the threat to the rear of the Armée d'Italie, which Lusignan had posed.[353]

When Bonaparte called him to join his main body, Masséna scrambled 25 miles south-southeast across the mountains to Sacile (16 March). Unable to join the initial crossing of the Tagliamento, Bonaparte ordered Masséna 23 miles to the northeast where he crossed the river at Spilimbergo. Once across the Tagliamento, Masséna was detached again and sent up the left bank of the river. When he reached the Forte di Ossopo, 11 miles north of Spilimbergo, he encountered the Austrians removing the stores from the fort. Masséna led his escort of 25 *chasseurs* in a charge on the 50 Austrians covering the operation, drove them off and captured the fort and the stores.

Advancing seven miles further north, Masséna reached the village of Portis, where he continued north along the Fiume Fella a further five miles to reconnoitre Moggio di Soto. Again, the position, held by Ocskay's brigade, seemed impregnable but it was soon turned, and the Austrians were driven 13 miles up the river valley, further north to Pontebba via Chiusaforte. But Ocskay then continued his retreat eastwards a further 14 miles to Tarvis (present day Tarvisio) and then eight miles further east to Wurzen (Podkoren) in the valley of the river Sava.

This move uncovered the line of retreat of Bajalics's column, including cavalry, artillery and the trains of the army, retiring up the river Isonzo, pursued by Bonaparte leading the divisions of Guieu and Sérurier. Bonaparte ordered Masséna to reconnoitre as far north as Tarvis, 24 miles northeast of Portis, (19 March) and then from Goriza, 38 miles to the south, Bonaparte ordered Masséna to occupy Tarvis (21 March). Masséna had followed Ocskay a mile and half beyond Tarvis before falling back to the west of the town, when he learnt that his troops occupying Tarvis had been driven out by Gontroeul's brigade (2,000 men), the advanced guard of Bajalics's column (22 March). Gontroeul occupied a strong position in the narrow valley at Saifnitz (Camporosso), two and a half miles west of Tarvis, and was soon joined by a further 1,700 men from Bajalics's column. At the same time, Archduke Charles ordered Ocskay back to Tarvis, arriving there with him. Masséna attacked at once, the frozen ground impeding his cavalry, but with Motte leading the infantry forward the Austrians were driven back beyond Tarvis, despite Archduke Charles personally leading his escort squadron forward in an attempt stem the retreat. With Masséna now at the head of the gorge up which he was marching and attacked from behind by Gueiu, Bajalics and his column surrendered yielding 3,500–4,000 prisoners, 25 guns and 400 wagons and other wheeled vehicles to the French. The French lost 1,200 men, killed and wounded from their 11,000 engaged men, while the Austrians also lost 1,000 men, killed and wounded, of their 8,000 engaged men.[354]

Following up this victory, Masséna, followed by the divisions of Guieu and Chabot (commanding Sérurier's division), advanced 14 miles northeast to Villach and then 22 miles east to Klagenfurt am Wörthersee, which was captured by a cavalry charge on the Austrian centre, before moving 10 miles north to Sankt Veit an der Glan (31 March). Advancing 17 miles further north Masséna discovered the Austrians deployed in the

353 Phipps, *Italy*, pp.166–167.

354 Phipps, *Italy*, pp.167–172; Smith, *Data Book*, p.134; *Generalmajor* Karl Philipp Vinchant de Gontroeul; *General de Brigade* Robert Motte.

gorges of Dürnstein in der Steiermark, five miles before Neumarkt in der Steiermark (2 April). Putting himself at the head of the 18e and 32e Demi-Brigades de Ligne from Brune's brigade, Masséna led the attack which drove the Austrians back and he entered Neumarkt the next day (3 April). With the Austrians fighting hard to defend the road to their capital, Vienna, Brune led Masséna's advanced guard through combat after combat through Judenburg and down the valley of the river Mur until, approaching Sankt Michael in Obersteiermark, Masséna heard that an armistice had been agreed at Judenburg (7 April). Masséna advanced four miles beyond Sankt Michael to occupy Loeben, 94 miles northeast of Tarvis and only 83 miles southwest of Vienna (9 April). During the negotiations that followed, Masséna moved to Bruck, while Guieu held Loeben and Chabot held Graz further down the valley of the river Mur, where Sérurier joined him to resume command of the division (21 April).[355]

Meanwhile, Bonaparte had sent Bernadotte eastwards from the river Tagliamento to Laibach (present day Ljubljana), 45 miles from Gorizia, where he stayed until 31 March. Bernadotte was then ordered to move to Klagenfurt am Wörthersee (3 April). Setting out the next day he marched to join the main body of the army, halting at Neumarkt in der Steiermark. Dugua who with his cavalry had advanced as far east as Trieste, was also recalled to the main body of the army, to be replaced by Victor's division. Joubert who had been left in the Tyrol around Trento with his own division and those of Delmas and Dumas (previously Dallamagne's and Rey's divisions), a total of 18,000 men, was ordered to cross the river Lavis (17 March).

Advancing 10 miles to Salurn (Salorno) Joubert, in severe fighting, defeated Kerpen (12,000 men) driving him back (20 March), the next day Loudon's brigade was defeated at Egna Neumarkt (21 March). Joubert then managed to divide the Austrians to his front, driving Kerpen, the local Austrian commander to the northeast away from his subordinate Loudon's brigade, which retired through Boltzen (present day Bolzano) northwest through Meran (Merano in Italian). Kerpen was again defeated at Klausen (22 March) and withdrew to Brixen and then 17 miles northwest to Sterzing (Vipiteno in Italian), a total withdrawal of 65 miles, where he re-joined Loudon. Joubert, leaving Delmas to guard his communications at Boltzen, then advanced to Brixen (23 March) and waited there a few days before he advanced again towards Sterzing, where he pushed Kerpen out of the town (28 March). With the Tyrol aflame and militia everywhere, Joubert withdrew to Brixen, where he was attacked by Kerpen reinforced by 5,000 Tyrolean militia (28 March and 31 March). Joubert now decided to leave the Tyrol and Delmas evacuated Boltzen (4 April) and marched to Brixen. Joubert then marched to join the main body of the army (5 April), marching 53 miles east he reached Lienz (8 April) and then Spital an der Drau in the valley of the river Drave, where he made contact with the main body and learnt of the armistice (8 April).

In so doing Joubert had uncovered Verona exposing it to an Austrian counterstroke. Loudon with 3,000 men and another 6,000 Tyrolean militia advanced down the valley of the river Adige retaking Boltzen, Lavis and Trento before advancing to the hills above Verona, just in time to see the people of Verona together with some Venetian troops rise in rebellion against the French, the *Pâques Véronaises* (17 April). Kilmaine responded by rushing troops to support Balland in the forts of Verona, supported by Victor's division who reached Treviso (18 April). From there Victor moved to Isola Della

355 Phipps, *Italy*, pp.172–174; *Général de Brigade* Louis François Jean Chabot.

Scala to the south of Verona, the arrival of the troops put an end to the insurrection which Loudon chose not to directly support. When Kilmaine informed Loudon of the armistice, the fighting was over.[356] Bonaparte could now focus on Venice and Baraguey d'Hilliers (5,000–6,000 men) occupied the city (16 May 1797).[357]

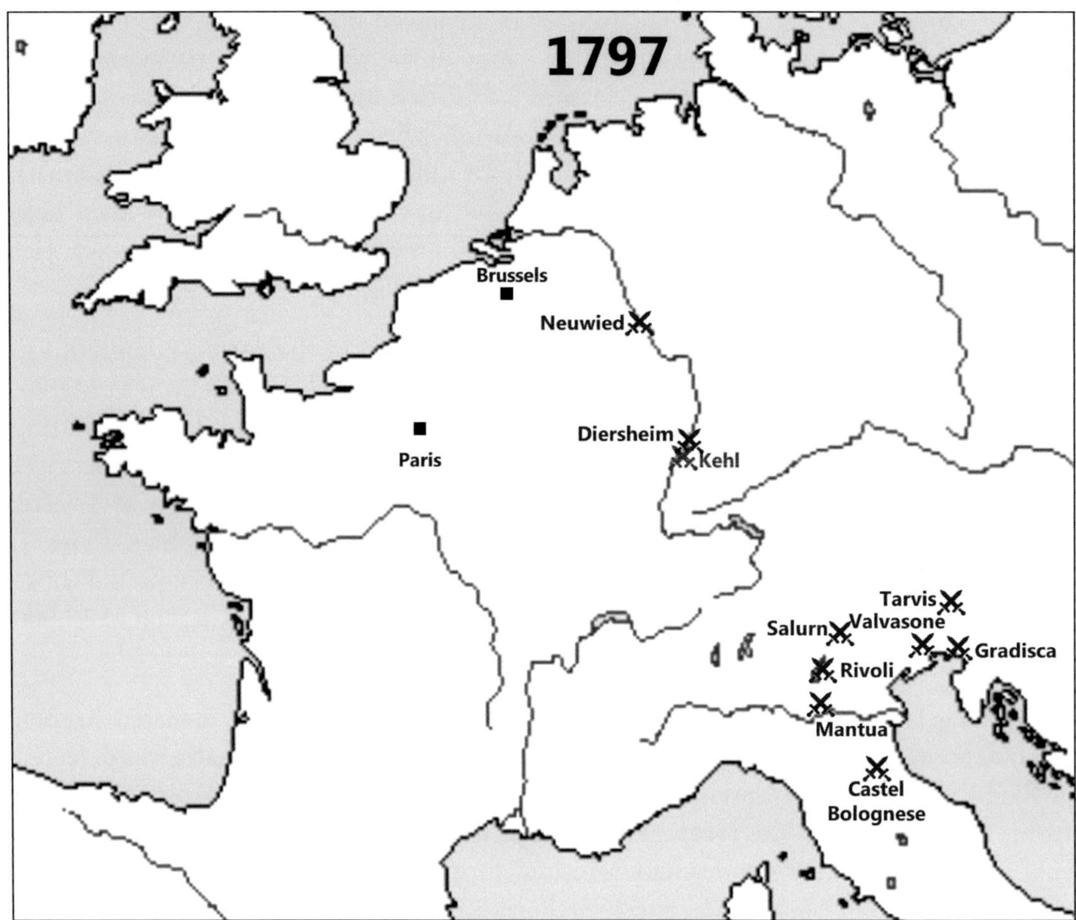

Map 7 – Key actions and battles, 1797

Home Waters

At sea two major engagements were fought in 1797. In the first Jervis intercepted Córdoba's Spanish fleet which was escorting a convoy of quicksilver, off Cape St. Vincent on the Atlantic coast of Spain (14 February). In a foggy morning the 15 British ships of the line met 23 Spanish ships of the line and five transports. The Spanish were in two groups with 18 ships of the line and one transport to windward and the other five ships of the line and four transports detached to leeward. Forming line of battle Jervis cut between the two Spanish groups to attack the Spanish main body from the rear and to windward. However, a counterstroke by the smaller group of Spanish ships disrupted Jervis's manoeuvre. During the ensuing battle, Commodore Nelson distinguished himself by personally leading the boarding parties from his own crippled flagship, HMS *Captain* (74), capturing the much damaged *San Nicolas de Bari* (80) and, from her, boarding and capturing the equally damaged three decker *San Josef* (114).

356 Phipps, *Italy*, pp.174, 179–180; *Feldmarschallleutnant* Wilhelm Lothar Maria von Kerpen; *Generalmajor* Johann Ludwig Alexius von Loudon; *Général de Division* Antoine Belland.

357 Phipps, *Italy*, pp.182–183; *Général de Division* Louis Baraguey d'Hilliers.

In all Jervis's fleet took four prizes with another ship destroyed, gaining a 'complete victory' against a much superior enemy fleet, which was thereafter reluctant to put to sea again.[358]

The second major engagement of 1797 was the Battle of Camperdown (11 October), during which Duncan intercepted de Winter's Batavian fleet, within sight of safety in Texel. A furious action ensued between Duncan's squadron of 16 sail of the line and de Winter's fleet, also comprising 16, albeit slightly lighter, sail of the line. Duncan had no time to form line of battle and sent his ships in two groups to assail the van and rear divisions of de Winter's line and in two and a half hours he captured nine sail of the line and two frigates, including de Winter himself and two other admirals.[359]

Other naval engagements during 1797 include:[360]

358 Rodger, *Command*, pp.438–440; Smith, *Data Book*, p.133; *Contraalmirante* José de Córdoba; Admiral John Jervis.

359 Schomberg, *Naval Chronology*, vol. III, pp.40–43; 46–49; Rodger, *Command*, p.456; Smith, *Data Book*, p.135; Admiral Adam Duncan; *Vice Amiral* Jan Willem de Winter.

360 Schomberg, *Naval Chronology*, vol. III, pp.4–7, 38–40, 49–51, 61–63, 74–77; Rodger, *Command*, 454–455; Norie, *The Naval Gazetteer*, p.413; *La Calliope* is also described as being of 28 guns.

Theatre	Date	Action
Home waters	13–14 January	Sir Edward Pellew in HMS *Indefatigable* (44) and with HMS *Amazon* (32) pursued and engaged 150 miles off Ushant *Les Droits de l'Homme* (74), which was driven ashore and destroyed.
	22 February	1,200 French troops landed at Fishguard from *La Vengeance* (48) and *La Résistance* (48), *La Constance* (22) and *Le Vautour* (16, *Affronteur*-class lugger) but were captured next day.
	9 March	HMS *St. Fiorenzo* (38) and HMS *La Nymphe* (36) met, engaged and captured *La Résistance* (48) and *La Constance* (22) off Brest.
	27 July	Admiral Warren's squadron of five vessels, while cruising off Ushant, intercepted in Audierne Bay a convoy of 14 merchantmen escorted by a frigate and two other sail. The frigate, *La Calliope* (36) was run ashore and destroyed, eight of the convoy taken and two burnt.
	20 August	HMS *Arethusa* (38) en route from the West Indies fell in with and captured *La Gaieté* (20). The brig *L'Espoir* (14) escaped.
	27 August	Warren's squadron attacked a convoy off the mouth of the river Garonne, capturing five sail and driving their escort, *Le Petit Diable* (18) cutter, on shore.
	31 August	Off Ireland, the brig-corvette HMS *Penguin* (14) fell in with and captured *L'Oiseau* (18) and recaptured her prize, the *Express* (12).
	15 December	HMS *Clyde* (38) took the French privateer *La Dorade* (12) but the prize was later lost.
	21 December	HMS *Phoebe* (36) after a fight of 45 minutes captured *La Néréide* (32).
	28 December	In the Bay of Biscay, HMS *Anson* (64) and HMS *Phaeton* (38) fell in with and captured *La Daphne* (30).
Mediterranean	25 July	Rear Admiral Nelson led a squadron in an unsuccessful amphibious assault on Santa Cruz de Tenerife.
West Indies	3 March	HMS *Diligence* (16) captured the Spanish privateer, *La Nativeta* (16), off Cuba.
	15 April	HMS *Thunderer* (74) and HMS *Valiant* (74) drove the French frigate *L'Harmonie* (44) on shore, near Jean-Rabel, Saint Domingue, where it was destroyed by fire.
	17 September	HMS *Pelican* (18) sank the French privateer, *La Trompeuse* (12), off Môle-Saint-Nicolas, Saint Domingue.
	27 December	HMS *Magicienne* (32), HMS *Regulus* (44) and HMS *Diligence* (16) took the French privateer *Le Brutus* (9) and four other sail from under the protection of the forts of Aguadilla Bay, Puerto Rico.

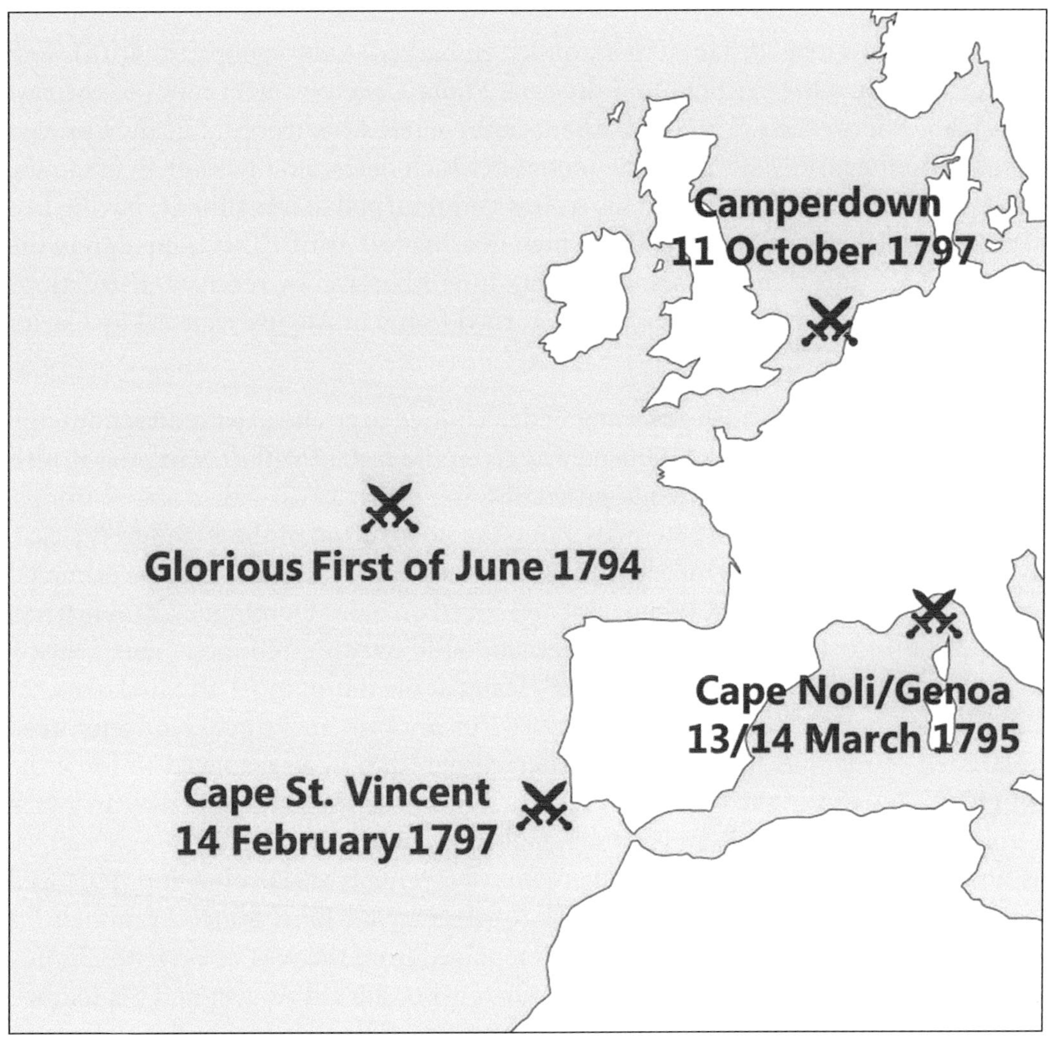

Map 8 – Fleet Actions of the War of the First Coalition

West Indies

In the West Indies, Britain's Abercromby sailed from Portsmouth on 17 November 1796, arriving in Martinique early in January 1797. Ordered to capture the island of Trinidad, Abercromby assembled 4,000 men on the island of Carriacou (130 miles north of Trinidad), comprising the 2nd, 14th and 53rd Foot together with the flank companies of the 3rd Foot and detachments of the 38th and 60th Foot and the foreign contingents of Hompesch and Lowenstein. In conjunction with the naval commander Rear Admiral Henry Hervey, Abercromby sailed for Trinidad 15 February. Arriving off Trinidad the next day through the *Bocas del Dragón* (Dragon's Mouth) to the west of the island, the British fleet discovered four Spanish ships of the line and a frigate at anchor (16 February). While the British prepared for an attack by land and sea at daybreak, the Spanish destroyed their squadron by fire. Abercromby then landed his troops and meeting minimal resistance, with only a single officer killed, captured the island and the garrison of 600 men along with the ships' crews (1,600 men) and a ship of the line which was still intact. Leaving Picton with a thousand men to garrison Trinidad, Abercromby returned to Martinique to prepare an assault on Puerto Rico.[361]

361 Schomberg, *Naval Chronology*, vol. III, pp.70–111; Fortescue, *History*, vol. IV, pt.1, pp.539–540; Lieutenant-Colonel Thomas Picton, 56th Foot, of Waterloo fame.

Reinforced from Great Britain, Abercromby embarked 4,000 troops (8 April) and, after a delay at St. Kitts, anchored off the cape *Punta Congrejo*, eight miles to the east of San Juan, Puerto Rico (17 April). Abercromby landed his troops, but they proved inadequate to the task of storming the redoubts which defended the route to the town. Defeated, Abercromby reembarked his troops and returned to Martinique, having lost 100 men in killed and wounded and 120 men missing (30 April). This campaign in the Windward Isles thus came to an end when in June Abercromby received instructions to remain on the defensive. Abercromby returned home in August replaced by Cuyler and Bowyer.[362]

On Saint Domingue the British government determined to go ahead without reinforcing the British troops on the island. Simcoe was given the task of withdrawing the British troops to Môle-Saint-Nicolas, while protecting the other areas with colonial troops. However, Cap Français, a port 80 miles along the north coast of the island to the east, and the island of Tortuga, 40 miles northeast of Môle-Saint-Nicolas, could be occupied to secure Môle-Saint-Nicolas. When Simcoe arrived on Saint Domingue (20 February) he found the British regiments to be weak and still awaiting reinforcement. During March Toussaint L'Ouverture's Republican levies took the outpost at Mirebalais, 23 miles northeast of Port-au-Prince, and closed in on Port-au-Prince, but, reinforced by 600 men of the 40th Foot and other detachments, Simcoe managed to force the Republicans away from the town. This success for Simcoe was interrupted by an attack on Irois in the south of the island by the Republicans, under Rigaud. The French attack was however defeated when HMS *Magicienne* accidentally discovered and destroyed Rigaud's storeships at anchor off Irois (23 April). During June, Simcoe resumed his offensive and recaptured Mirebalais but was repulsed from the post of Verrettes. In July Simcoe returned home to be replaced by Whyte who, during August and September, resumed the war of outposts as Toussaint L'Ouverture descended from the mountains once more. The British government meanwhile prevaricated over the evacuation of their troops from Port-au-Prince to Môle-Saint-Nicolas, before ultimately evacuating all their troops from Saint Domingue (3 October).[363]

Conclusion

Bonaparte and Johann Ludwig von Cobenzl, representing the Austrian government, signed the Treaty of Campo Formio, 17 October 1797, ceding the Austrian Netherlands to France and recognising French control of the Rhineland and much of Italy (Venice was partitioned between Austria and France), thereby ending the War of the First Coalition, with Great Britain left to fight on alone.[364] The campaign in Italy had been very profitable for the French state, with the widespread requisitions and other state sponsored looting yielding an estimated 58,000,000 Francs by 20 December 1796, while on the Rhine 10,000,000 livres was taken.[365] Furthermore, together with the removal of *représentants en mission* (end of 1795) the requisitions made the generals more independent of the government, a situation which Bonaparte had keenly exploited.

362 Fortescue, *History*, vol. IV, pt.1, pp.540–541; Major-Generals Henry Bowyer and Cornelius Cuyler.

363 Fortescue, *History*, pp.545–552, 563; Major-General John Graves Simcoe; *Général de Division* François-Dominique Toussaint Louverture; *Général de Brigade* Antoine Rigaud.

364 Phipps, *Italy*, pp.182.

365 Blanning, *Revolutionary Wars*, pp.160–161.

As the War of the First Coalition ended the French Republic had 381,000 men to further prosecute its wars beyond its natural frontiers, which were now secure.[366] In 1797 France's armies had fought nine battles involving 20,000 combatants or more, winning eight and losing one, plus four smaller actions, winning three and losing one.[367] At sea the story was very different, Great Britain won the war at sea asserting a superiority that would last for more than one hundred years. The French lost 11,000 sailors in the two fleet actions of the war alone, perhaps 20 percent of the available seamen in France. Similarly, by 1799 the French fleet had been reduced from 88 to 49 ships of the line and from 73 to 54 frigates.[368]

Popular Resistance

The foregoing chronology is focused very much on the direct military conflicts, but it would not be right to move on without emphasising the popular resistance to the revolution both within France and in the territories that the French armies invaded. During the War of the First Coalition local people took up arms against the French republican armies beyond the famous examples in the Vendée, Maine, Brittany, and Toulon. Inside France the introduction of conscription in particular led to popular risings and riots in Brittany, Normandy, Maine, Anjou, Poitou, Limousin and Auvergne. Poverty, rampant inflation, and famine as well as political issues led to risings across France, including Lyon, Etampes, Montauban, the Cévennes. Outside France, resistance was widespread with armed resistance recorded across the Basque country, Navarre and Catalonia in Spain, Luxembourg, the Rhineland, the Tyrol, Lombardy in Italy, including the city of Pavia, as well as in the Venetian city of Verona and, further south, in the cities of Bologna, Ferrara, Forli and Rimini. Likewise, food shortages caused 50 different riots across the occupied Austrian Netherlands, some of which needed to be suppressed by troops.

In resisting the French, the local people included organised village or parish companies commanded by local notables, as well as ad hoc groups of individuals fighting with whatever came to hand, such as the servant girl Catarina Lanz with her pitchfork, in the Tyrol in 1797. To quote Professor Esdaile, 'only one thing could have checked the spread of popular resistance, and that was an occupation policy based on the maintenance of the highest standards of discipline, the strictest respect for the Catholic church and the minimisation of the burdens imposed on the populace. Yet those were the aspirations which no French general could deliver...' Finally, the poor harvests in 1793–1795 and high food prices amid poor economic conditions caused a significant increase in simple brigandage across the French sphere of influence. All these uprisings offer the wargamer a multitude of skirmish scale actions using Sharp Practice, Forager or Chosen men.[369]

366 Jones, *Companion*, p.157.
367 Smith, *Data Book*, pp.131–135.
368 Blanning, *Revolutionary Wars*, p.211.
369 Esdaile, *Wars*, pp.180–227; Jones, *Companion*, pp.284–285; Blanning, *Revolutionary Wars*, pp.167–169.

4

The Protagonists

At the end of the eighteenth-century Europe was dominated by five great powers; Great Britain, Austria, Prussia, Spain, and France. During this period the Russians were more interested in achieving the partition of Poland and consolidating their gains from the war with the Ottoman Empire, which concluded in January 1792. The Russians gained the Crimea and pushed the frontier with the Ottomans back to the river Dniester, however war would be reignited by the Ottomans in 1806. Although Catherine the Great did eventually decide to enter the War of the First Coalition (18 August 1796), after her death, Tsar Paul I immediately recalled his troops (17 November 1796).[1]

Supporting the five major powers were the United Provinces (now the Netherlands) and the kingdoms of Sardinia-Piedmont and Naples. The British also reinforced their own army with contingents from the Electorate of Hanover and the Landgraves of Hesse-Kassel and Hesse-Darmstadt. The new republican government of France had also to contend with the *émigrés*, nobles who left France to various parts of Europe to continue the fight, as well as internal rebellions in the west and south of France.

The following sections will only address armaments by exception. The armies were armed very similarly with smoothbore muskets for the infantry, smoothbore carbines/musketoons for cavalry and the field artillery with smoothbore cannon (ranging in weight of shot from 3, 4, 6, 8, 9 to 12-pdrs) and howitzers (of 5½, 6 and 8 inches). Howitzer nomenclature could be confusing, as some nations measured their howitzers by the weight, in pounds, of the stone projectile they threw rather than iron as in the case of long guns. For example the 7-pdr howitzer's projectile weighed considerably more, in this case 14 to 15 pounds. The 7-pdr howitzer is approximately equivalent to the 5½ inch howitzer. Similarly, the Hanoverian 30-pdr howitzer threw a projectile weighing 60 pounds, equivalent to the 8-inch howitzer.[2] Predominantly the light cavalry carried (curved) sabres and the heavy cavalry (straight) swords. Exceptions such as 1-pdr amusettes, rifles and the use of the lance will be recorded as appropriate. The British use of shrapnel and rocket artillery lies in the wars of the future coalitions. This chapter can only provide a brief overview of the subject matter, but the footnotes provide plenty of opportunities for further study.

1 Blanning, *Revolutionary Wars*, p.136.
2 Otto von Pivka, *Armies of the Napoleonic Era* (Newton Abbot: David and Charles, 1979), p.24.

Austria

When the French declared war on Austria on 21 April 1792 the new Habsburg Emperor Francis II faced a difficult challenge. He was more interested in the Polish question and although his father had warned the French against harming the French king and particularly his Austrian queen, Marie-Antoinette, he was not prepared for war with France. While the French government appealed to nationalist sentiment within its population to drive home its reforms and rally volunteers to its armies, Francis could only respond in a reactionary manner. Although centred on the hereditary lands (*Erblande*) in modern day Austria, the Habsburg empire straddled a vast swathe of Europe including nine major ethnic/national groups and several minor ones. These groups included 6,500,000 Germans, 3,360,000 Czechs, 2,000,000 Flemings and Walloons, 1,000,000 Poles, 900,000 Croats and 700,000 Serbs.[3] His role as Holy Roman Emperor also gave him influence over the many small German states in Central Europe. This diversity is clearly represented in the name of his army, the Kaiserlich-Könichliche Armee, which reflects both Francis's imperial status and his separate role as King of Hungary. Thus, any appeal to national identity in Austria would open Pandora's box.[4] Francis was not a military man and, following an imperial tradition of being wary of the generals, preferred the advice of his civilian ministers, Thugut, Cobenzl and Colloredo. These ministers did not hesitate to interfere in military strategy or operations in the field.[5]

The imperial war machine was managed by the *Hofkriegstat*, a mix of military and civilian officials who planned operations as well as managed the day-to-day administration of the army. With only 30 officers and 100 clerks, the system was notoriously slow and bureaucratic, complicating the administration of the army at all levels. Another mixed military and civilian operation, the *General-Kriegs-Commissariat*, governed the supply system for the army via a network of large supply depots, *Hauptmagazines*, which fed the *Fessungsmagazines,* which in turn directly supplied the army, via substantial supply trains manned by civilian contractors. The Austrian army became notorious for its long and ponderous supply trains, which slowed the army to advances of less than 10 miles per day.[6]

The ranks of the army were filled by a mixture of volunteers and conscripts who served for life. Most conscripts came from the poorest peasants and day labourers, physically tough and resolute men. General officers were mainly drawn from the senior nobility with minor nobles filling the ranks of the regimental officers, via a system of purchase approved by the regiment's colonel up to the rank of major. The emperor approved all promotions to colonel and above. It was also possible, especially during times of war, for commoners to become officers.[7] The Austrian officer corps, with notable exceptions, was not noted for its level of education or interest in intellectual development and as a body fought the War of the First Coalition using the methods learnt during the Seven Years War (1756–1763) and the war against the Turks (1788–1791).

---

3 Gunther E. Rothenberg, *Napoleon's Great Adversaries, The Archduke Charles and the Austrian Army 1792–1814* (London: B.T.Batsford, 1982), p.14.

4 Lee Eysturlid, *The Austrian Army*, pp.64–85, in Frederick C. Schneid (ed.), *European Armies of the French Revolution, 1789–1802* (Norman: University of Oklahoma Press, 2015), pp.64–65.

5 Eysturlid, *Austrian Army*, p.66; Director General of Foreign Affairs (1793–1803) Johann Amadeus Franz de Paula Baron Thugut; Foreign Minister (1792–1794) Johann Ludwig Joseph Count Cobenzl; *Kabinettminister* Franz de Paula Count Colloredo-Wallsee.

6 Eysturlid, *Austrian Army*, pp.67–68.

7 Eysturlid, *Austrian Army*, p.69.

In 1792 the Austrians could field some 230,000 men, three quarters of whom were infantry, significantly lower than the theoretical strength of 300,000.[8]

The infantry regiments were divided into 'German' regiments, which included men recruited from the German, Italian, Czech, Polish, 'Belgian' and other territories, and 'Hungarian' regiments, recruited from Hungary, Romania and Ruthenia (i.e., Austrian Galicia or modern day western Ukraine). The two types were distinguished by the method of recruitment used and the language used for drill and passing of orders et cetera. The wars against the Turks had created the Military Borders (Croatia, Hungary, Slavonia and Transylvania) populated by military colonists known as Grenzers. This resulted in a third group of regiments, the Grenzer regiments. Originally light troops, Empress Maria Theresa reorganised them as line infantry in the 1740's, a controversial move as the century wore on as the introduction of line infantry drill was seen to detract from their abilities as light troops.[9]

There were 57 regiments of line infantry and 17 of Grenzer infantry, 35 regiments of cavalry and three of artillery. The infantry regiments were numbered and named after their colonel, which in 10 cases changed during our period. The line infantry regiments were numbered one to 59. The regiments numbered 5 and 6 were garrison troops. Infantry regiment number 48 was disbanded in 1795. Regiments 60 to 76 were the Grenzer infantry, they were only renumbered 1 to 17 in 1798.[10]

The line infantry regiments comprised two (German) or three (Hungarian) field battalions, each of six companies. The regiments also included a further, garrison, battalion of four companies. In time of war, this battalion in the German regiments was raised to six companies and a separate reserve division raised.[11] Each regiment also had two companies of grenadiers which were detached to form grenadier battalions with those of two other regiments, thus giving battalions of six companies. The Grenzers were organised similarly with two field battalions but had no grenadiers. In general, the field battalions all served together. The garrison regiments (numbers 5 and 6) had two battalions each. At full strength the companies would have four officers and 250 other ranks, but in 1792 the average company had three officers and 120 men. At the outbreak of the war Austrian infantry were armed with the Model 1774 or Model 1784 smoothbore muskets, together with a bayonet and short sabre. These muskets were both one pound, i.e., significantly heavier than the superior Model 1798 musket.[12]

Each field battalion, both line and Grenzer, was supported by two 3-pdr or 6-pdr cannon and their crews. The line battalions of the Rhine armies used 6-pdr guns (including those later sent to Italy), while those in Italy and the Grenzer battalions used 3-pdr guns.[13]

The 35 regiments of cavalry were divided between the heavy cavalry, cuirassiers wearing only a breastplate, the medium cavalry, the dragoons and *chevaulegers*, and the light cavalry, the hussars and uhlans. The cavalry regiments were numbered consecutively

8 Esdaile, *Wars*, p.237.
9 Eysturlid, *Austrian Army*, pp.70–71.
10 Eysturlid, *Austrian Army*, p.71; C.A.Sapherson, *European Armies 1789–1803* (Leeds: Raider Books, 1991), pp.2–3.
11 Voykowitsch, *Castiglione*, p.35.
12 Eysturlid, *Austrian Army*, p.71; Sapherson, *Armies*, p.6; Rothenberg, *Napoleon's Great Adversaries*, pp.25–26.
13 Philip J. Haythornthwaite, Bryan Fosten, *Austrian Specialist Troops of the Napoleonic Wars* (Oxford: Osprey, 2000), p.4; Dave Hollins, Bill Younghusband, *Austrian Auxiliary Troops, 1792–1816* (London: Osprey, 1996), p.5.

Austrian Infantry Crossing a Pontoon Bridge

regardless of type, there were 11 cuirassier regiments (including the two carabinier regiments), seven of dragoons, seven of *chevauleger*, nine of hussars and one lance-armed uhlan regiment. The cavalry regiments were based around the squadron of around 150 troopers, grouped into divisions of two squadrons. The carabiners and hussars had eight squadrons, the uhlans four, and the rest of the cavalry six.[14]

In 1792 the artillery was organised into three field regiments (9,300 men in total), 13 garrison artillery districts (2,200 men), the Bombardeur Corps (845 men, a training unit for both officers and men) and the *Fusilier-bataillon* (959 men). Each field artillery regiment comprised four battalions each of five companies, increasing to six in 1796. The authorised strength of the companies was 170 men, including four officers.[15] In 1790, the field artillery could deploy 948 pieces; 798 guns, 86 howitzers and 64 cavalry pieces.[16] The artillery used 3-pdr, 6-pdr and 12-pdr cannon together with 7-pdr and 10-pdr howitzers from the Lichtenstein system designed in the middle of the century. This system was a good one and was copied by other nations. However, the French Gribeauval system used the heavier 4-pdr, 8-pdr and 12-pdr guns.

The 3-pdrs and some 6-pdrs were used as battalion guns and in support of the cavalry, while the 6-pdrs and 12-pdrs were used as position guns. The reserve or position batteries were usually comprised of four long guns and two howitzers. The Austrian response to horse artillery was the *cavallerie batterien*, in which the crews were mounted on the less mobile *wurst* wagons rather than horses. These batteries were armed with four 6-pdrs and two 7-pdr howitzers. The number of cavalry guns increased to 72 by 1791 and continued to increase throughout the war reaching 120 in 1800. However, as a proportion of the total guns the cavalry guns were relatively few, less than seven percent,

14 Sapherson, *Armies*, pp.4–6; Frister, *Almanach 1796*, pp.45–63.
15 Philip J. Haythornthwaite, Bryan Fosten, *Austrian Specialist Troops*, pp.4–8.
16 Chris McNab (ed.), *Armies of the Napoleonic Wars, An Illustrated History* (Oxford: Osprey, 2009), p.200.

compared to the French organisation of 1795, which had 23 percent of its field artillery companies in the horse artillery regiments. At Castiglione for example only four of the 60 position or reserve guns were cavalry guns. As the name implies these batteries were largely used in support of the cavalry brigades, although the name refers as much to their need for cavalry support as vice versa. They were however unable to advance with the cavalry during a charge. There was no separate horse artillery organisation.[17]

There were also a number of *freikorps*, the Ulanen Freikorps was raised in 1790 (known by their *oberstleutnant* Degelmann 1790, Schwarzenburg 1792, Kegelvich 1793, Vogel 1796), the Osterreichisches Steyer Wurmsersches Freikorps in 1793 including both infantry and light cavalry, (the latter became the Slavonischcroatisches Grenzer Husaren Freikorps in 1794) and the Croatischslavonische Sharfschutzenkorps raised in 1794. There were also eight infantry *freikorps* providing further light infantry capability, the Dandini (Mahony from 1793) Feld-Jägers, De Loup *Feld-Jägers* (Austrian Netherlands), Laudon Freikorps (later known as Grün-Laudon), O'Donnel Freikorps, Gyulai Croat Freikorps, Légion Bourbon, Tyroler *Feld-Jägers* and the Mihaljevich Freikorps (Serbian, Branowatzky Freikorps from 1796)). Four more units were raised during the war: the Carneville Freikorps in 1793, the Legion Erzherzog Karl in 1794 incorporating the Limburger Freiwillige (Volunteers) originally raised in 1792, the Lüttich Freiwillige (Austrian Netherlands) in 1794, and the Wiener Freiwilliger Korps in 1796. Although most French émigrés joined the Légion Bourbon, others joined the Rohan Freikorps comprising both cavalry and infantry, which was raised in 1792 and entered Austrian service in 1796.[18]

Most Austrian infantry were armed with smoothbore muskets, but some carried unusual weapons. The first of these was the 1780 Girandoni (or Girardoni) *Repetier Windbüchse* (repeating air rifle) which could fire 40 balls on one charge of air, the first 20 in only 30 seconds, and was completely smokeless. In combat the range of this rifle matched that of smoothbore muskets, although this declined as the air bottle emptied. With a fully charged air bottle, the first 10 balls could reach 150 metres, the next 10, 125 metres and the third 10, 100 metres.[19] The air bottle was recharged using a handpump, a somewhat tiresome process, although two spare charged bottles were carried. The weapon was in service with the *freikorps/jägers* throughout the War of the First Coalition before being withdrawn due to maintenance issues in 1800. In all 1,100 of these weapons were manufactured.[20]

The 240 sharpshooters in each Grenzer regiment were armed with the double barrelled 1768 and 1795 *doppelstutz*, which had a rifled upper barrel for long range and a smoothbore lower barrel for short ranges. The sharpshooters used a 2.5m *Hackenlanze* pike as a rest for this heavy rifle. This rifle was also carried, along with muskets, by the Mahony Feld-Jägers, which feature in the Castiglione scenario.[21]

On campaign Austrian generals emphasised the need to protect their line of communication and their base of supply, using fortresses as forward depots, and to

17 Philip J. Haythornthwaite, Bryan Fosten, *Austrian Specialist Troops*, pp.4–5; McNab, *Armies*, p.200; Voykowitsch, *Castiglione*, p.74.

18 Sapherson, *Armies*, p.5; Frister, *Almanach* 1796, pp.112–118, 1797, p.118; Dave Hollins, Bill Younghusband, *Austrian Auxiliary Troops*, pp.13–14.

19 Attributed to August Haller in *Die österreichische Militär-Repetier-Windbüchse* (1891).

20 Hollins, *Austrian Auxiliary Troops*, pp.43–44, plate E1; Rothenberg, *Adversaries*, p.52.

21 Hollins, *Austrian Auxiliary Troops*, pp.7–9, 13, plate A1.

avoid risking the main army. Consequently, they employed the 'cordon system', in which an entire region was occupied by many detachments connecting the network of fortresses. The intention was to force the French to besiege the fortresses giving the Austrians time to concentrate a force ready for a countermove. When attacking the Austrian generals liked to launch concentric columns directed to surround the French or at least moving them from their own lines of communication. These columns and their component brigades, of three to six battalions, were only temporary organisations, constantly changing according to the circumstances, and the Austrians had no permanent organisations above the battalion, such as the French divisions with their permanent staffs. Unfortunately, the Austrians did not have the required complement of competent staff officers, below the level of the army, and were rarely swift enough to ensure success. Whether in attack or defence, the faster moving, less encumbered French armies were often able to dislocate such a system.[22]

On the battlefield the Austrian generals looked to deploy their infantry in the centre in two lines (*treffen*) with a third line containing the artillery reserves and grenadiers. This line was divided into three sections: the centre and the left and right flanks. The senior regiments and the senior subordinate general were deployed on the right. Broken terrain significantly disrupted the ability of the generals to coordinate the movement of these three lines. The position batteries were spread along the front reinforcing the fire of the infantry. Despite the infantry advancing into battle with bayonets fixed, the doctrine was focused on creating a wall of fire, with the battalions firing by platoons.[23] Coburg's instructions to his army include the direction that when defending entrenchments, the infantry should open fire on the enemy when they are within 300 paces.[24] The wars with the Turks, who had a large and outnumbering cavalry arm, had taught the Austrian infantry the benefits of the closed column for defence against cavalry.

The cavalry protected the flanks, the squadrons deployed in three ranks with the intention of keeping the enemy cavalry at bay. Despite their high quality, the Austrian cavalry tended to be poorly used, being deployed in small groups disadvantaged by poor coordination, rather than being used en masse. This applied in different ways to all classes of cavalry.

In summary the Austrian military was better suited to the defence than the attack and this suited the aims of the emperor, who never seemed totally committed to the aggressive overthrow of the French Republic and the restoration of the Bourbon monarchy by force. Acting as a solid bulwark against the flood of revolutionary fervour was considered achievement enough.

The Holy Roman Empire

At its heart the Holy Roman Empire, while under the leadership of the Hapsburgs of Austria since 1438, was a decentralised system comprised of 165 secular and 67 ecclesiastical principalities and 51 imperial cities managed by magistrates, each of which could enter into military alliances with other powers provided these alliances were not directed against the Empire. Within this system, power was concentrated in the hands of

22 Eysturlid, *Austrian Army*, pp.75–76; Voykowitsch, *Castiglione 1796*, p.37.
23 Eysturlid, *Austrian Army*, pp.75–76; Rothenberg, *Napoleon's Great Adversaries*, pp.27–29.
24 Fortescue, *History*, vol. IV, pt.1, p.224.

family dynasties. The Hapsburgs controlled five of the largest principalities comprising a third of the empire, while the Hohenzollerns of Prussia controlled 18 territories of different sizes making up 19 percent of the empire. Similarly, the Wittelsbach family controlled 21 territories, including Bavaria and the Palatinate and King George III of Great Britain and Ireland was the Prince Elector of Brunswick-Lüneburg (Hanover).

In 1792, 20 of these territories could supply armed forces greater than 1,000 men, but the four biggest contingents were Saxony (26,773 men), Bavaria (19,696 men), Hanover (17,836 men) and Hessen Kassel (15,000). These four thus contributed 79,000 men out of a military potential of 120,000 men. The next five largest, Hessen-Darmstadt, Würzburg, Württemberg, Mainz and Brunswick-Wolfenbüttel, contributed between 3,000 and 4,000 men, for a total of almost 17,000 men. Coordination of the raising and directing of these troops was achieved by regionally grouping the territories into one of 10 Imperial Circles (*Kreise*). The territories raised men according to a fixed basic quota (*Simplum*), which was fixed in 1681 at 12,000 cavalry and 28,000 infantry, although cavalry could be replaced with three times the number of infantry. The quota could also be fulfilled by cash payments.

This total of 40,000 men across the 10 *Kreise* could be doubled (*duplum*) or tripled (*triplum*). Decisions about the use and particularly the offensive use of this army had to be agreed centrally by the Imperial Diet (*Reichstag*) to be binding on all territories. Following the French invasion of the Rhineland in October 1792, Austria established a majority in the *Reichstag* in favour of declaring an imperial war (*Reichskreig*, 23 March 1793). The Reichstag authorised a triple quota or *triplum* but increased it to a *quintuplum* of 200,000 men (13 October 1794), which remained in force until the end of the War of the First Coalition. Both Austria and Prussia kept their own quota contributions, 36,000 men and 12,000 men respectively, separate from the Imperial army. These two major powers also took payments (*relutions*) from other territories to fulfil the quotas of those territories. Austria contributed 12,000 men from the *triplum* on behalf of 60 minor territories, while Prussia, similarly, contributed a further 10,000 men. The contingents from territories west of the river Rhine were soon lost when the French overran these territories, removing 6,700 men from the Imperial army.

However not all the contingents were available to the Imperial army, as, for example, Brunswick-Wolfenbüttel sent all its troops into Dutch service in 1788 and paid *relutions* rather than raising more troops from 1793. Similarly, Hessen Kassel, having merged all its *Kreise* troops into its main army, sent all its troops to the Austrian Netherlands under British command after 1793. George III, while supporting Hanover's compliance with the Imperial Constitution refused to send Hanover's contingent to the Imperial army because Austria insisted on the overall command. Instead, Hanover's *Kreise* contingent of 3,066 men (in 1792) together with the rest of its army was sent into British pay from 1793, again serving in the Austrian Netherlands. For similar reasons Bavaria sent only a token 2,500 men to the Imperial army in 1793. On the other hand, Salzburg sent its lone regiment directly into Austrian service throughout the war.

Although Saxony fully cooperated with the Imperial army sending 6,000 men in 1793, Prussia proved uncooperative, demanding that the Saxons served with its forces on the Lower Rhine rather than join the rest of the Imperial army with the Austrians. Once Prussia left the First Coalition, Saxony recalled its contingent in July 1796, joining the northern neutral zone that November.

The *relutions* fund was also used to hire and establish *émigré* regiments, such as the Dumouriez corps (1793), the Hohenlohe corps, the Bourbon and Condé regiments. Similarly, Brunswick and Paderborn directly contracted the Rohan corps.

Overall, the Germans were not supporters of the French Revolution, thus just nine of the 90 officers in France's Légion Germanique were German. The only German prince to support the revolution, Friedrich III of Salm-Kyrburg, voted against the declaration of war in 1793 and even took command of a Parisian volunteer battalion before being sent to the guillotine by Robespierre in 1794 alongside Alexandre de Beauharnais.[25]

The Imperial army contingents tended to be organised along similar lines based around the regiment. Hessian, Bavarian and Saxon infantry regiments comprised two battalions while the Hanoverian regiments had only a single battalion. There were four to 10 companies to a battalion. Cavalry regiments comprised two to five squadrons each of two companies. However, the peacetime practice of keeping all regiments with only a cadre rather than reducing the number of regiments, led to a scramble when war came to create contingents for the Imperial army. For example, Bavaria had to combine three regiments to find 787 men in 1794. Most Princes kept guard units, *Garde du Corps* (cavalry), *Garde* or *Leib* (infantry). Saxony, Bavaria, Hanover, and Hessen Kassel all had at least one guard infantry regiment. Several territories had at least one battalion of grenadiers, however Hanover and others retained the practice of including a grenadier company in each regiment which were merged into composite battalions on the battlefield. Most territories also had separate *jäger* (rifle armed) or fusilier units trained to fight as light infantry in extended order; indeed, the small contingents of both Weimar and Trier were primarily *jägers*. Hessen Kassel had a battalion of *jägers* (from 1788) and one of light infantry. Hanover formed a light infantry regiment of two battalions in 1793.

Cavalry was predominantly dragoons and hussars except for the larger contingents. Saxony fielded four cuirassier regiments, Hessen Kassel three and Bavaria two. Hanover had four regiments of heavy cavalry, but these did not wear breastplates.

Artillery amongst the four largest contingents were used in ad hoc organisations in the field. Several states introduced horse artillery.[26]

Alongside the Imperial army itself, the German Principalities also provided contingents to support the other European powers. Great Britain was the principal partner with a long history of employing German auxiliaries to support its own operations. The largest contingents were naturally from Hanover which, in return for £1,390,000, sent 13,900 troops in 1793 and another 5,200 men in 1794. Hessen Kassel supplied 12,535 men in 1793–1794, Hessen-Darmstadt sent a mixed brigade of 2,800 men in October 1793 and Baden sent 754 infantry from October 1793.[27]

Saxony

In 1792 the army of the Electorate of Saxony was made up of four regiments of heavy cavalry (Garde du Korps, Karabiniergarde, Kurfurst Kürassiere and the Zetschwitz

25 Peter H. Wilson, *The Armies of the German Princes*, pp.182–210 in Frederick C. Schneid (ed.), *European Armies of the French Revolution, 1789–1802* (Norman: University of Oklahoma Press, 2015), pp.184–189, 192.

26 Wilson, *Armies of the German Princes*, pp.196–197.

27 Wilson, *Armies of the German Princes*, p.193; Demet, *Duty*, pp.188–189.

Kürassiere), four regiments of chevau-légers, one regiment of hussars, one regiment of guard infantry (Lieb Grenadiergarde) and 12 regiments of line or fusilier infantry. The Garde du Corps had two squadrons each of 365 men and the hussar regiment had eight squadrons each of 132 men. The other cavalry regiments had four squadrons each of 180 men.

The infantry regiments each had two battalions and the fusilier regiments also had two companies of grenadiers which were combined to form six grenadier battalions, each of four companies. Each fusilier company had 130 men and each grenadier company had 160 men.

The artillery comprised 12 companies each with six guns. Each infantry regiment was supported by two light guns. The Saxon ordnance was the Hoyer system of 1772, which followed the Gribeauval system with 4-pdr, 8-pdr and 12-pdr cannon and an 8-pdr howitzer. An interesting weapon was the 4-pdr *Schnellfeuergeschütze* (quick-fire gun), dating from 1766, which was used to support the infantry as regimental guns. The gun had an innovative elevating system and larger windage which could for short periods fire at double the rate of conventional cannon, albeit with reduced range. There was also an early form of gun-howitzer, the 4-pdr *Granatstück* which only fired case shot grenades.[28]

Bavaria

In 1792 the Bavarian cavalry comprised two regiments of *kürassiere* (Minucci and Zweibrücken), two of *dragoners* (Kurfustin and Taxis) and three of *chevau-légers* (Leiningen, La Rosee and Fugger). The cavalry regiments all included four squadrons with a nominal strength of 180 men per squadron but were usually around 110 men per squadron.

The infantry made up four regiments of grenadiers (the Leibregiment Kurfurst, Zedwitz, Ysenburg and Baaden) and 14 regiments of *füsiliers*. There were also two regiments of *feldjägers* (Schwichelt and Salern). Each regiment had two battalions each of four companies, which had a nominal mobilised strength of 168 men.

There were two battalions of artillery each of four companies, each company had a nominal strength of 150 men and served six cannon and two howitzers. In 1795, the artillery adopted Austrian 6-pdr cannon and 7-pdr howitzers.

The contingent serving with the Imperial army in the army of the Upper Rhine comprised the first and sixth *füsilier* regiments and both *feldjäger* regiments, together with a composite cavalry regiment of three squadrons with elements of all three *chevau-léger* regiments. Meanwhile a combined infantry battalion, the fourth *fusilier* regiment and a detachment of 50 troopers from the Zweibrücken Kürassier-Regiment, served on the Lower Rhine.[29]

---

28 Sapherson, *Armies*, pp.45–46; von Pivka, *Armies*, pp.229–234 (for uniform details); Anthony L. Dawson, Paul L. Dawson, Stephen Summerfield, *Napoleonic Artillery* (Marlborough: Crowood Press, 2007), pp.87–89; Stephen Summerfield, *M1766 Quick-Fire Guns*, pp.58–62 in *Smoothbore Ordnance Journal*, 6 (Godmanchester: Ken Trotman, 2013).

29 Sapherson, *Armies*, pp.7–8; Otto von Pivka, *Napoleon's German allies (4): Bavaria* (Oxford: Osprey, 1980), pp.8–9 and pp.5–8 (for uniform details).

Bavarian Infantry and Artillery

Hanover

As the War of the First Coalition began Hanover's army had a theoretical strength of 11,000 infantry and 4,200 cavalry. The infantry was comprised of one *garde* regiment and 13 musketeer regiments, each of two battalions. Each battalion was made up of one grenadier company and five musketeer companies. The 14th regiment of infantry was converted to the 14th Light Infantry regiment when it returned from serving the British East India Company in India in 1792. In its new form the 14th comprised two battalions each of four companies as well as two *jäger* companies.

The cavalry arm comprised one regiment of Guards, the Leibgarde, four regiments of cavalry (numbered 1–4), four of dragoons (5–8) and two of light dragoons (9–10). Each regiment had four squadrons each of two companies. Cavalry squadrons averaged 95 men and infantry companies 66 men.

There were also two battalions of artillery, numbering 10 companies in all. The Hanoverians impressed their British allies in the Austrian Netherlands with their horse artillery which was raised in 1790. The horse artillery had some gunners riding the gun carriages, using a Wurst-style seat, some riding the limbers and some mounted.[30]

30 Dawson, *Napoleonic Artillery*, p.122; Demet, *Duty*, p.125.

Finally, the militia formed 10 *Land* regiments each of five companies of 110 men.

The contingent sent to the Austrian Netherlands, as ordered 4 March 1793, included four cavalry regiments of 16 squadrons in total, a brigade of three battalions of grenadiers, six infantry regiments (the Garde, 4th, 5th, 6th, 10th, and 11th), two divisions of artillery and one of horse artillery. The cavalry field regiments were made up of two squadrons from each of two component regiments. Likewise, the infantry regiments took only eight of their 10 musketeer companies, the other two remaining behind as depot companies. The three grenadier battalions were made up of four companies, two each from two regiments: the first from the Garde and the 10th Regiment, the second from the 5th and 6th Regiments and the third from the 4th and 11th Regiments. The first grenadier battalion was described as a light grenadier battalion, given the shortage of light troops.

Each battalion of infantry was allocated two 3-pdr cannon, battalion guns for close support, served by trained men from the battalion.

The artillery divisions comprised ten 6-pdr cannon, two 30-pdr howitzers and four 7-pdr howitzers, while the horse artillery division had four 3-pdr cannon and two 7-pdr howitzers.

The contingent was commanded by Freytag.[31]

In January 1794 the contingent in British pay was increased by the addition of the 4th Grenadier battalion, 1st and 9th Infantry Regiments and the 14th Light Infantry Regiment, together with an additional division of horse artillery. Rather than 3-pdr cannon, the 14th Light Infantry Regiment was supported by six 1-pdr amusettes, two with each battalion and one with each *jäger* company.[32]

In 1793, the Hanoverian commanders, Freytag (73) and von dem Bussche (67) were understandably seen to lack activity in this campaign, and the *generalmajors* were generally in their late 50s and early 60s. Hammerstein born in 1735 was well regarded and led the Duke of York's advanced guard. The Hanoverian cavalry and artillery were highly regarded, but the infantry, with many young recruits, were seen to be of low quality. The Hanoverian horse artillery were considered the best in Europe.[33]

Demet details the uniforms of the Hanoverian corps.[34]

Hessen Kassel

Hessen Kassel had, in 1792, an army of 14,000 men, including six regiments of cavalry, eight of infantry, the Feldjäger-Korps, the Leichte Infanterie Bataillon Lentz and an artillery regiment.

The heavy cavalry was organised into squadrons of two companies, the Garde du Corps having one squadron and the Gens d'Armes and Carabinier regiments having three. The two dragoon regiments (the Leib Dragoons and Prinz Friedrich's Dragoons) each had five squadrons of one company each, while the hussar regiment had three

31 Demet, *Duty*, pp.125–128, 130–132; *Feldmarschall* Heinrich Wilhelm von Freytag.

32 Demet, *Duty*, pp.136–137.

33 Demet, *Duty*, pp.140–141; Dawson, *Napoleonic Artillery*, p.120; *Generalleutnant* Georg Wilhelm von dem Bussche-Haddenhausen; *Generalmajor* Rudolf Georg Wilhelm von Hammerstein

34 Demet, *Duty*, pp.141–155.

squadrons, each of one company. The heavy cavalry companies averaged 60 men, while the other companies averaged 117 men. The infantry regiments had two battalions each of one grenadier and five musketeer companies, each company averaging 110 men. The grenadier companies were combined, forming four independent battalions each of four companies. Each grenadier battalion was known by the name of its commander. There were also two depot battalions, each of four companies, supplying recruits for the field battalions. Each grenadier and musketeer battalion was supported by two 3-pdr cannon, each served by 11 crew.[35]

In the first half of 1793 Hessen Kassel troops served on the river Rhine in two groups. Firstly, von Biesenrodt commanded the Leib Dragoon Regiment, the Garde Grenadier regiment, the Leib Regiment and their grenadier companies in Bataillon von Dincklage with the Prussians at the siege of Mainz. While the light troops, commanded by Schreiber, comprising the Hussar Regiment, the Feldjäger-Korps and the Leichte Infanterie Bataillon, served separately with the Prussians and then the Austrians.[36]

In April 1793, von Buttlar led the contingent of 7,300 men that served with the British in the Austrian Netherlands, comprising two regiments of heavy cavalry (the Regiment Gens d'Armes and the Carabinier regiment), the Prinz Freidrich Dragoons, four regiments of infantry (the regiments Erb Prinz, Prinz Carl, von Lossberg and von Kospoch), two grenadier battalions (the first and third), the new jäger battalion (two companies each of 98 men plus the battalion staff of six men), and the artillery detachments required to serve the battalion guns. In August 1793, von Hanstein led a further contingent of around 3,600 men into British pay, comprising the Leib Dragoon Regiment, two infantry regiments (the Garde grenadiers and the Leib Regiment), the 2nd Grenadier battalion and the Fusilier battalion, together with the artillery detachments for the battalion guns.[37]

In March 1794 a brigade of artillery was added to the contingent, comprising two companies, each armed with four 12-pdr cannon, four 6-pdr cannon and two 13-pdr howitzers. Each company had 126 men and the brigade also had 231 drivers and 32 other staff.[38]

The Hessen Kassel infantry were rated highly by both British and Prussian observers, although the cavalry and artillery were seen to be of 'indifferent' quality.[39]

Demet details the uniforms of the various corps.[40]

Hesse-Darmstadt

In September 1793 Hesse-Darmstadt provided a corps of three infantry battalions (the two battalions of the Leib Regiment and the 2nd Leibgrenadier battalion) and a company of artillery with six guns. This force was known as the second or Rhein-Brigade and served with the Imperial army on the river Rhine, where it was joined by the second

35 Demet, *Duty*, pp.156–157, 163.

36 Demet, *Duty*, pp.156–158; Paul Demet, personal communication; *Generalleutnant* Hans Bernhard von Biesenrodt; *Oberstleutnant* August Eberhard von Dincklage, succeeded in 1793 by *Oberstleutnant* Friedrich Konstantin August von Germann; *Oberst* Johann Justus Schreiber.

37 Demet, *Duty*, pp.158–159, 162–163, 165; Paul Demet, personal communication; *Generalleutnant* Friedrich Treusch von Buttlar; *Generalmajor* Karl von Hanstein.

38 Demet, *Duty*, pp.167–168.

39 Demet, *Duty*, p.169.

40 Demet, *Duty*, pp.170–178.

battalion of the Landgraf regiment. The first or Nederlandische brigade of 2,807 men, under the command of von Düring, entered British pay in October 1793, comprising the chevau-léger cavalry, the first battalion of the Landgraf infantry regiment, the first Leibgrenadier battalion, the light infantry battalion and the Feldjäger corps together with the artillery detachment for the battalion guns. The chevau-légers comprised four squadrons each of 125 men. The infantry and light infantry battalions comprised four companies each of 169 men, including 10 *schützen*. These battalions were also supported by two 3-pdr cannon, with two more such cannon kept in an artillery reserve. The Feldjäger corps comprised two companies each of approximately 70 men.[41]

Baden

At the end of 1792 Baden had 2,000 men under arms comprising two companies of Garde du Corps cavalry, the Leibinfanterie Regiment and the Fusilier battalions Erbprinz and Rastatt. There was also a small detachment of hussars. The Leibinfanterie Regiment had two battalions, one of grenadiers and one of musketeers, each of four companies. Only one of the grenadier companies went into British pay along with the whole of the musketeer battalion, supported by two 3-pdr cannon. The grenadier company had 110 men and the musketeer companies had 132 men.[42]

France

The debacle for France that was the Seven Years War (1756–1763), the low point in French military history, resulted in a period of intense reflection and reform that produced an army that was capable of playing a significant part in the defeat of Great Britain in the American revolution in 1781. However, in 1789 the French army was still an eighteenth-century army, albeit a professional and volunteer one. It benefited from an effective military administration, developed earlier in the century, which was capable of handling the army as it expanded. However, the Minister of War, initially appointed by the king became a highly politicised role after the revolution. There were eight ministers of war in 1792 alone, while another seven held the role until 1799.[43]

41 Demet, *Duty*, pp.187–192 and 193–198 (for uniform details); *Generalmajor* Georg Emil von Düring.
42 Demet, *Duty*, pp.179–180 and 183–186 (for uniform details).
43 Frederick C. Schneid, *The French Army*, pp.13–35, in Frederick C. Schneid (ed.), *European Armies of the French Revolution, 1789–1802* (Norman: University of Oklahoma Press, 2015), p.23; Jones, *Companion*, pp.78–81.

Minister of War (those in bold had served in the army)	Dates
Louis-Marie Jacques Amalric, Comte de Narbonne-Lara	December 1791–March 1792
Pierre Marie, Marquis de Grave	March–May 1792
Joseph Marie Servan de Gerbey	May–June 1792
Charles-François Dumouriez	June 1792
Pierre Auguste de Lajard	June–July 1792
Charles Xavier Joseph de Francqueville, Baron d'Abancourt	July–August 1792
Étienne Clavière	August 1792
Joseph Marie Servan de Gerbey	August–October 1792
Pierre Henri Hélène Marie Tondu	October 1792
Jean-Nicolas Pache	October–February 1793
Pierre Real de Beurnonville	February–March 1793
Jean-Baptiste Nöel Bouchotte	April 1793–April 1794
Post replaced by a commission	April 1794–November 1795
Jean-Baptiste Annibal Aubert-Dubayet	November 1795–February 1796
Claude Louis Pètiet	February 1796–July 1797
Barthélemy Louis-Joseph Schérer	July 1797–February 1799

The troops of the Royal Household were both infantry and the Maison du Roi cavalry. Within the field army, the infantry comprised 110 regiments which generally had two field battalions and one depot battalion. Six of these regiments served in the colonies and 23 were foreign regiments in French service. Of the foreign regiments 11 were Swiss, eight German, three Irish and one from Liège. Included in the 110 regiments were the two guard regiments, the Gardes Françaises, which had six battalions, and the Gardes Suisses, with four battalions, but these regiments were lost early in the revolution in 1789 and 1792 respectively, the Gardes Suisse were massacred by the mob while defending the king.

Each of the field battalions comprised five companies, four fusilier companies and a grenadier company in the first battalion and four fusilier companies and a chasseur company in the second battalion. The fusilier and chasseur companies each had 171 men, while the grenadier companies were 108 men strong.[44] Each battalion was supported by two 4-pdr guns. The line regiments were numbered 1 to 104, the artillery corps being numbered 64, and the provincial troops numbered 97.[45] From 1 January 1791

44 Schneid, *French Army*, pp.15–16; Sapherson, *Armies*, pp.10–13.

45 Jacques de Roussel, *État Militaire de France* (Paris: Onfroy, 1789), p.285; number 97 covered the Regiments of Royal Grenadiers, the provincial regiments and the garrison troops.

the infantry regiments were to be known only by their numbers.[46] Twelve *chasseur à pied* battalions provided the rest of the light infantry. Each *chasseur* battalion had four *chasseur* companies (154 men each on a war footing). Each company of *chasseurs* included 12 *chasseur-carabiniers*, the most experienced and best marksmen in the company. The title *carabinier* implies that these men were armed with rifled carbines but there is no evidence for this, so these men are better considered as marksmen. Similarly, the *chasseurs* were not specifically recruited from 'mountain men' or regions which might make them suited to the light infantry role.[47]

The cavalry comprised 62 regiments, two regiments of *carabiniers*, 24 of *cavalerie (de bataille)*, 18 of dragoons, 12 of *chasseurs à cheval* and six of hussars. The *carabiniers* and *cavalerie* were the heavy cavalry, the dragoons were the medium cavalry and the *chasseurs à cheval* and hussars the light cavalry. The cavalry and dragoon regiments comprised three squadrons while the hussars and chasseurs à cheval regiments had four squadrons. Each squadron comprised 150 men.[48]

The artillery corps comprised seven regiments plus a colonial regiment, in addition to which were the miners, sappers and engineers. The seven home artillery regiments each comprised two battalions each of 10 companies, seven of field artillery and two of siege artillery and one of sappers. Together these 140 companies comprised 909 officers and 8,204 men. The field artillery companies in total were sufficient to serve 588 guns, although this was raised to 14,000 men and 846 guns when at war. The colonial regiment was similarly organised but without the sappers. The guns largely belonged to the Gribeauval system, the field guns being the 4-pdr, 8-pdr and 12-pdr long guns and 6-inch howitzers.[49]

In January 1792, two companies of *artillerie légère* (horse artillery) were formed, followed in April by the forming of seven more. These companies were divided amongst the existing seven regiments, the first two regiments having two companies and the other five regiments having a single company. The horse artillery companies were initially armed with 4-pdr cannon and 6-inch howitzers, although 8-pdr long guns were later used.[50]

In 1793 the sappers and miners were separated into a separate engineering corps comprised of 12 battalions of sappers and six companies of miners.[51]

In May 1795 the artillery arm was reorganised into eight regiments of foot artillery, eight regiments of horse artillery, 12 companies of *ouvriers* and one battalion of *pontonniers* (eight companies of two officers and 72 men).

46 Terry E. Crowdy, *Napoleon's Infantry Handbook* (Barnsley: Pen and Sword Military, 2015), p.3.

47 Terry Crowdy, *French Light Infantry 1784–1815* (Warwick: Helion, 2021), pp.25–31.

48 John A. Lynn, *The Bayonets of the Republic* (Boulder: Westview Press, 1996), p.195.

49 Louis Susane, *Histoire de l'Artillerie Française* (Paris: J.Hetzel, 1874), pp.192, 203–204, 211–212; the 6 inch howitzer was actually 6.4 English inches.

50 Schneid, *French Army*, pp.15–16; Sapherson, *Armies*, pp.10–13; Susane, *Histoire*, pp.215–216; Louis de Tousard, *American Artillerist's Companion: or Elements of Artillery* (Philadelphia: J. and A. Conrad, 1809), vol. II, pp.38–44; the horse artillery was also called *artillerie volante* (flying artillery), the intention was to mount all the gunners on horses but the shortage of horses meant that some gunners initially rode wurst wagons following the Austrian model.

51 Otto von Pivka, *Armies*, p.129.

French Horse Artillery

The regiments of foot artillery comprised 20 companies, each of two captains, three lieutenants and 88 non-commissioned officers and gunners. The regiments of horse artillery comprised six companies, each of two captains, three lieutenants and 88 non-commissioned officers and gunners.[52]

The revolution unleashed a great deal of disorder in society and consequently the property-owning classes became concerned with restoring order and protecting their property from the unwanted attentions of the unpropertied lower classes. Consequently, initially in Paris and then around the country, the Milices Bourgeoise of the *Ancien Regime* were revived and given a new name, the *Garde Nationale*. This force was a civilian rather than a military force, although it organised itself along military lines. Thus, in summer of 1789, the *Garde Nationale Parisienne* comprised 60 battalions, one for each of the districts in Paris, each of five companies of 100 men (the number of battalions was reduced to 48 in 1792).

The battalions were organised into six divisions each of 10 battalions, a grenadier company was allocated to the first battalion of each division. The total strength was 1,052 officers and 30,006 men, of these men only 6,000 men were salaried. The officers were voted into their positions by their own men. The role of the *garde* was to keep and restore order, including securing food supplies, providing guards at town gates and public buildings, as well as performing ceremonial duties at public festivals and events. As the 'Great Fear' swept France in the summer of 1789, *Garde Nationale* units were formed in cities, towns and villages across the country. Eventually, following the reorganisation in 1791, every district had its own battalion of four companies of *gardes*. Thus, the *Garde Nationale*, the citizen-soldiers, internally secured the constitution, while the army, the soldier-citizens, fought external enemies.[53]

Soon, from the last quarter of 1789, adjacent communities across the country began to organise *fêtes de la fédération* in which the *gardes* of the different communities swore to defend order and fight counter-revolution not only in their own communities but also

52 Susane, *Histoire*, p.222.

53 Bertaud and Palmer, *Army of the French Revolution*, pp.33, 100; a separate paramilitary organisation, the Armée Revolutionnaire (30,000 men, summer 1793 to spring 1794), comprised of sans culottes scoured the countryside securing supplies for both town and country.

in each other's and across France nationally. This mood eventually reached Paris where a national festival was held on the anniversary of the fall of the Bastille (14 July 1790). 15,000 delegates from *Gardes Nationales* all over France came to Paris for the national festival joining 8,000 of their Parisian counterparts. The national festival was held in an arena on the *Champ de Mars*, built in a few months, to hold 300,000 spectators for a religious and 'euphoric' ceremony in front of the king. The event proved to be the apogee of Lafayette, commander-in-chief of the *Garde Nationale Parisienne*, the 'saviour of two worlds', who refused an offer to command all the *Gardes Nationales* across France.

The *Garde Nationale* worked alongside the ancient *Maréchausée*, which in 1791 became the *Gendarmerie Nationale*, the first national police force. As the months and years passed the *Garde Nationale* was not always a purely bourgeois force and, on more than one occasion became part of the problem rather than the solution and its significance diminished after 1795.[54]

In August 1791, the paid companies of the *Garde Nationale Parisienne* were abolished and the now 9,000 men were formed into new units in the line army: 29e Gendarmerie à Pied (912 men), the 30e Gendarmerie à Cheval (912 men), the 102e, 103e and 104e Régiments d'Infanterie (5,634 men) and two battalions of *chasseurs* the *13e* and *14e* (1,682 men in all).[55]

Between 1789 and 1792, instances of mutiny in the Royal army became commonplace and more than 50,000 soldiers of the 180,000 total strength, had left their posts by 1791. The increasing lack of loyalty amongst the Gardes Françaises had already resulted in some of them joining the mob that stormed the Bastille in July 1789, forcing the king to disband the regiment and thereafter to rely heavily on Swiss troops to guard his palaces.[56]

The largely noble officer corps of the royal army was significantly weakened when 6,200 officers, perhaps 60 percent of the total, left France as *émigrés*, some entering the service of France's enemies and some forming *émigré* armies to try to restore the Bourbon monarchy. However clearly 40 percent stayed with significant numbers of former nobles supporting the ideals of the revolution.[57]

Following the Declaration of Pillnitz, the Legislative Assembly needed to do something to ensure that the army was able to repel the soon-to-be-oncoming Prussian and Austrian armies. Although Carnot is held up as the great 'organiser of victory', one of his colleagues Dubois-Crancé was also pivotal in the creation of the resources required by the army, and he was part of the government throughout the War of the First Coalition. He was the primary advocate in the Assemblies and the National Convention for a viable military force based on volunteers rather than conscription. He was also responsible for the *amalgames* of 1794 and 1795–1796, which transformed the organisation of the volunteer army.[58]

54 Pierre-Baptiste Guillemot, *The Garde Nationale, 1789–1815* (Warwick: Helion, 2022), pp.23, 44–47, 154–166, 203, 278; *Lieutenant Général* Marie-Joseph Paul Yves Roch Gilbert du Motier, Marquis de La Fayette.

55 Guillemot, *The Garde Nationale*, p.203.

56 Schneid, *French Army*, pp.16–17.

57 Esdaile, *Wars*, p.67; Digby Smith, *Napoleon's Regiments* (London: Greenhill Books, 2000), p.19; Blanning, *Revolutionary Wars*, p.28; Lynn, *Bayonets*, p.4.

58 Schneid, *French Army*, p.18; Edmond Louis Alexis Dubois-Crancé, a former soldier.

The National Constituent Assembly decreed in August 1791 the creation of 175 battalions of *Volontaires Nationaux*, drawn from the *Garde Nationale* battalions. The *Volontaires Nationaux* battalions would each comprise of eight companies of three officers and 60 men, with a similarly sized company of grenadiers. In total 100,450 men were called forward but across France the response to the call for volunteers was varied, some *departements* on the borders sent more battalions than were asked for, while others were slow or sent nothing at all. Like the *Garde Nationale* battalions the men voted for their officers in these *volontaire nationaux* battalions, with the proviso that one of the *lieutenant colonels* had to have served at least as a *capitaine* in the royal army, while the other officers were expected to have served in the army or at least to have been officers in the *Garde Nationale*. The *volontaires* were expected to pay for their own uniforms and equipment and in return received higher pay than the men already serving in the royal army.[59]

The new battalions were uniformed in the blue coats of the *Garde Nationale* rather than the white coats of the royal army, creating a division between the *bleus* and the *blancs*. The *bleus* were suspicious of the *blancs* because they had stayed with their regiments rather than volunteer into the *Garde Nationale* and were potential counterrevolutionaries, and this mutual suspicion hindered both the training and coordination of the troops.[60]

In May 1792 a further decree raised another 31 battalions of *Volontaires Nationaux* under the motto 'Liberty or Death!', and 20 of these battalions would come from *departements* in central and southern France which had yet to send any battalions. The same decree increased the strength of the battalions from 574 to 800 men. This brought the *Volontaires Nationaux* to a strength of 214 battalions and 171,200 men. As before, the raising of the battalions was spread over the rest of 1792, with some *departements* still showing reluctance until the Brunswick Manifesto, in which the Duke of Brunswick threatened to burn Paris if Louis XVI and his family were harmed, brought war ever closer. Another law in May provided for the raising of 54 *Compagnies Franches* each of 200 light troops.[61]

In preparation for the 1792 *fête de la fédération*, five *Gardes Nationales* from each canton across France were summoned to Paris to police and defend Paris and to take part in the fête, 20,000 men in all. These men were subsequently formed into 18 *bataillon de fédérés* and sent to the front. Consequently, these men were highly politicised, badly equipped, poorly trained and lacking discipline.[62]

The law of 22 July 1792 ordered the raising of 42 battalions of the *Volontaires de 1792*, 33,600 men again drawn from the *Garde Nationale*. The same law called for a further 50,000 men to reinforce the line regiments of the army. The next day a further decree also approved the request of the commander of the Armée du Rhin for 40,000 *Gardes Nationaux* from his area of operations. Furthermore, generals were empowered to request half the grenadiers and chasseurs registered with their local *Gardes Nationale*.

59 Guillemot, *Garde Nationale*, pp.131–133.

60 Schneid, *French Army*, pp.19–20; Guillemot, *Garde Nationale*, p.148; the *Garde Nationale* blue coats briefly had red lapels and white collars, before this was reversed to give the coats that became all too familiar across Europe.

61 Guillemot, *Garde Nationale*, pp.134–141.

62 Lynn, *Bayonets*, p.51.

The initially clear distinction between the army and the *Garde Nationale* was thus blurred. The volunteers of 1792 also tended to be less bourgeois than those of 1791.[63]

In May 1792, the government instructed Kellermann (commander of the camp of Neukirch), Luckner (commanding the Armée du Nord) and Lafayette (commanding the Armée du Centre) to raise three *légions* of light troops, comprising 18 companies of light infantry and eight of light cavalry, each company to be made up of three officers and 105 men. The Légion de Kellermann was built around the troops that remained behind when the 15e Cavalerie regiment and the 4e Hussards chose to become *émigrés* and deserted en masse. In July 1792 a similar *légion* was raised in the Armée du Midi comprised of 18 companies of light infantry and four of light cavalry. Doumouriez (commanding the Armée des Ardennes) raised the Légion des Ardennes, comprising two battalions of light infantry (18 companies) and eight companies of hussars. In August 1792 two further *légions* were raised. The first, the Légion Franche Étrangère was raised from exiles from the Netherlands and other nations, which was to comprise four battalions of line infantry, one of chasseurs, four squadrons of chasseurs à cheval and two companies of artillery, in all 2,822 men. The second, the Légion Franche Allobroge comprised 14 companies of light infantry, four companies of light dragoons and one company of light or horse artillery. In September 1792 two more *légions* were created, the Légion Germanique, comprising 1,000 cavalry in eight squadrons, four each of *cuirassiers légers* and *piquiers à cheval* (lancers), and 2,000 infantry (two battalions of *chasseurs à pied* and one battalion of *arquebusiers*) as well as one company of artillery, and the Légion Nationale des Pyrénées, comprising 1,600 *chasseurs à pied*, 600 *chasseurs à cheval* (4 squadrons) and 300 artillery.[64]

As the war ebbed and flowed in 1793, the government turned its attention to the problem of integrating the new volunteer battalions into the army. In February 1793 Dubois-Crancé proposed the brigading of the two types of battalion, with two of volunteers combined with one regular battalion to form new demi-brigades. The new organisation called for 198 demi-brigades, each of 2,437 men of all ranks. Each demi-brigade was to have three battalions, each of eight fusilier companies and one grenadier company. The infantry was to be supported by a company of 4-pdr guns, two per battalion. Finally, a separate company was to serve as the depot. This *embrigadement* began but had to be suspended in March 1793 before the campaigning season began. These initial demi-brigades were known by the name of the regular battalion.

The government also had to bring the army back up to strength after the losses of the 1792 campaign and the loss of some of the volunteers, who returned home at the end of the campaign. Consequently, it enacted the levy of 300,000 (24 February 1793), although described as volunteers, these men were requisitioned, all single men and widowers between the ages of 18 and 40 were liable for service, each commune was allocated a compulsory number of 'volunteers' to find. By August the levy had only realised 150,000 men and the government enacted the *levée en masse* (23 August 1793), this time calling 450,000 single men and widowers aged between 18 and 25.

The *embrigadement* process began again in February 1794, now known as the first amalgamation, creating the new *demi-brigades de bataille* (line infantry) and *demi-*

63 Guillemot, *Garde Nationale*, pp.134–141.
64 Édouard Desbrière and Maurice Sautai, *La Cavalerie pendant la Révolution — La Crise* (Paris: Berger Levrault, 1907), pp.122–124.

brigades légère (light infantry). The amalgamation gave the men new uniforms based on that of the *Garde Nationale* units and removed the difference in pay. The men were subject to the same code of discipline and the election of officers was generalised, although some promotion based on seniority remained. The amalgamation also mixed the companies of the regular battalions with those of volunteer battalions creating three new battalions, a move which effectively removed the last vestiges of the royal army as a separately identifiable entity. Despite the general thrust of the amalgamation several demi-brigades were also raised entirely from volunteer battalions.[65]

All these actions had a marked impact on the strength of the French army as it fought campaigns on all its borders:[66]

French Army Strength, 1789–1797		Line Infantry Battalions	Light Infantry Battalions
1789	189,000		
1791	138,000	199	14
1792	220,000	199	14
1793	550,000	195	25
1794	750,000	286	52
1795	548,000	484	84
1796	380,000	469	102
1797	380,000		

The decline in these numbers was also due to other factors besides battle casualties and sickness. As the years went by, evasion of the requisitions or drafts became more significant. Similarly, desertion was a significant factor, which in 1793 was eight percent, primarily from newer recruits, four percent in 1794, five percent in 1795 and eight percent again in 1796 and 1797. However, these averages disguise more significant levels in specific units of up to 20 percent.[67]

In total, 205 *demi-brigades de bataille* and 35 *demi-brigades légère* were raised. However, the large number of battalions proved to be unsustainable and in 1796 the second amalgamation began, reducing the number of demi-brigades to 110 *demi-brigades de ligne* and 30 *demi-brigades légère*. After 1795 each demi-brigade had its battalion guns reduced from six pieces to three.[68]

During the War of the First Coalition, the French cavalry were severely handicapped by a lack of good quality horses and firearms, which were not helped by the cavalry's historic links to the aristocracy, the elimination of their depots (1788), the suspension of private horse purchases (1789) and the closure of the state stud farms (1790). Nevertheless, several new regiments were added to the army, raised largely from volunteer units. The

65 Guillemot, *Garde Nationale*, pp.141–144; Lynn, *Bayonets*, pp.57–61; Smith, *Napoleon's Regiments*, pp.305–308.
66 Schneid, *French Army*, p.21; Smith, *Napoleon's Regiments*, p.311.
67 Bertaud and Palmer, *Army of the French Revolution*, pp.259–261, 272–275; data based on a sample of 5,000 men from a selection of volunteer battalions and three *ancien régime* regiments.
68 Smith, *Napoleon's Regiments*, pp.20–21.

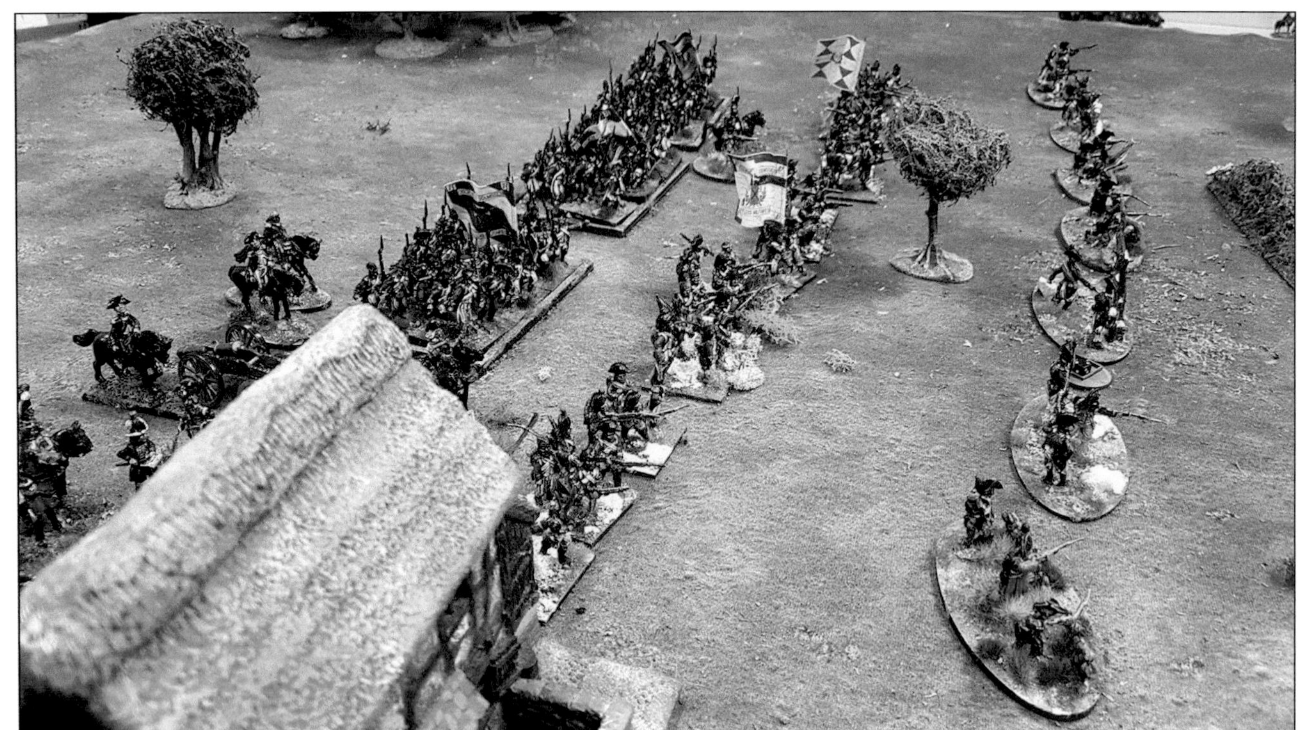

French Demi-Brigade

19e Régiment de Dragons were raised in February 1793 from the Volontaires d'Angers and the Légions du Nord and des Francs. In the same year the 20e Dragons were raised from the Dragons de Jemappes and the 21e Dragons from the Dragons de la Manche and the cavalry of the Légion de Police in December 1796. From 1793 to 1795, 13 new regiments of *chasseurs à cheval*, the *13e* to *25e*, were raised from volunteer units, 11 in 1793 and one each in 1794 (the *13e bis* (which means again or extra)) and 1795 (the *25e*). However, the *17e* and *18e,* originally raised from Belgian cavalry in 1793, including a large number of Austrian deserters, were lost such that the regiments were numbered *1er* to *16e* and *19e* to *25e* plus the *13e bis.*

The 13e and 13e bis Chasseurs à Cheval were converged in April 1795, giving a total of 23 regiments. In November 1792 two volunteer regiments, Régiment de Troupes Légère à Cheval de Boyer and the Hussards de Lamothe became the *7e* and *8e* Hussards, while the Hussards de la Liberté (created in September 1792) became the *7e bis* Hussards. The emigration of the 4e Hussards in 1793, caused the renumbering of regiments *5e* to *8e* to *4e* to *7e*. The Légion d'Eclaireurs à Cheval (Fabrefond's), the *2e* Hussards de la Liberté and Hussards Noir du Nord became the *8e, 9e* and *10e* Hussards in 1793, when the *11e* Hussards was also raised. Two more regiments of hussars were raised, *12e* Hussards in 1794 and the 13e Hussards in 1795 (31 January), for a total of 14 regiments. The *cavalerie* regiments were reduced by one when the *15e* deserted to the opposition to serve the *émigré* cause en masse, causing the renumbering of the regiments *16e* to *24e*. However, there were also three regiments of Cavalerie Nationale raised in Paris at the *Ecole Militaire*, these became the *24e, 25e* and *26e* Cavalerie, by June 1793. Of these *cavalerie* regiments, only the *8e* Cavalerie, formerly the Cuirassiers du Roi, wore the cuirass. In February 1793, the government increased the number of squadrons in the cavalry and dragoon regiments to four and in the light cavalry regiments to six, while the number of men per squadron was increased to 170.[69]

The experience of these men has been sampled by reviewing more than 12,682 individual records of all arms, which suggests that by mid-1794:[70]

When enlisted	Percentage of total sample
Soldiers of the royal army	18.4 } 25% with 2 campaigns
Volunteers of 1791	4.6 } 25% with 2 campaigns
Volunteers of 1792	23.0 } 25% with 2 campaigns
Volunteers of 1793 with 1 campaign	15
Levée en Masse 1794	37 (of whom 62% had received their baptism of fire)
Enlisted before 1789	5.5

Armies are complex organisations which usually confound the use of simplistic labels, such as revolutionary zeal and the cult of the bayonet, which may be better considered as aspirations of the government for their armies, rather than simple statements of factual characteristics.[71] Although the 'volunteers of 1791' may have reflected these attributes, it has been argued that the expansion of the French army in 1792–1794 was driven as much by more favourable terms and hunger as by patriotic fervour. Instilling patriotic fervour into the new recruits was attempted by the political clubs, newspapers, and the pamphleteering that the new army attracted.[72] As a small example, the letters of about one hundred soldiers from the Indre department, included just 15 that gave evidence of republican virtues, while the rest focused on fear, fatigue and despair.[73]

The key to understanding the French army of the War of the First Coalition is to consider it the result of an evolutionary development of eighteenth-century military thought and organisation, rather than a revolution in military practice, in its own right.[74] The revolution ultimately changed the nature and size of the resources available to the French army. However, the 40 percent of officers who stayed with the army brought with them the knowledge of the military schools established earlier in the century. The emigration of the other 60 percent of officers however opened opportunities for promotion to men who would otherwise have missed out under the *ancien régime*. With promotion open to all men of talent, these ambitious men proved better able to relate to and inspire their men, leading from the front more often than not. Of Napoleon's future *Maréchaux de France*, 19 of the 26 were already officers in the army in 1792, and of these six (Berthier,

69 Lynn, *Bayonets*, pp.194–197; Philip Haythornthwaite and Christopher Warner, *Uniforms of the French Revolutionary Wars 1789–1802* (Poole: Blandford Press, 1981), pp.97–98, 124; Smith, *Napoleon's Regiments*, pp.251–252, 272–80, 286–290; Édouard Desbrière and Maurice Sautai, *La Cavalerie pendant la Révolution – La Fin de la Convention* (Paris: Berger Levrault, 1908), pp.74, 76; Desbrière and Sautai, *La Crise*, pp.124–125, 127, 131–133, 154, 193.

70 Bertaud and Palmer, *Army of the French Revolution*, pp.168–169.

71 Esdaile, *Wars*, pp.73–78.

72 Esdaile, *Wars*, p.69; Blanning, *Revolutionary Wars*, pp.85–88.

73 Bertaud and Palmer, *Army of the French Revolution*, p.225.

74 Blanning, *Revolutionary Wars*, pp.17–18; for example, Blanning refers to the Russian army in the eighteenth century having its own 'evolution' mimicking or anticipating the changes that were happening further west.

Moncey, Bernadotte, Davout, Kellermann and Sérurier) were officers in 1789, as was Napoleon himself, and a further five had served in the army at lower ranks.[75]

The Careers of Napoleon's *Maréchaux* during the War of the First Coalition			
Name	Rank 1792	Rank 1797	Armies in which they served
Pierre Augereau	*adjudant major*	*Gén.de Div.*	*Réserve/Ouest, Pyrénées Orientales, Italie*
Jean-Baptiste Bernadotte	*lieutenamt*	*Gén.de Div.*	*Rhin, Nord, Sambre-et-Meuse, Italie*
Louis-Alexandre Berthier	*colonel*	*Gén.de Div.*	*Ouest, Nord, Alpes, Rhin-et-Moselle, Italie*
Jean-Baptiste Bessières	*soldat*	*Chef d'Esc.*	*Midi, Pyrénées Orientales, Italie*
Guillaume Marie-Anne Brune	*adjudant major*	*Gén.de Div.*	*Nord, Intérieur, Italie*
Louis-Nicolas Davout	*2e lt. colonel*	*Gén.de Brig.*	*Nord, Moselle*
Emmanuel de Grouchy	*colonel*	*Gén.de Div.*	*Ouest, Nord, Centre, Alpes*
Jean-Baptiste Jourdan	*lt. colonel*	*Gén.de Div.*	*Nord, Moselle, Sambre-et-Meuse*
François Étienne Ch. de Kellermann	*lieutenant général*	*Gén.de Div.*	*Rhin, Centre, Alpes, Italie*
Jean Lannes	*sous-lieutenant*	*Gén.de Brig.*	*Pyrénées Orientales, Italie*
François Joseph Lefebvre	*capitaine*	*Gén.de Div.*	*Centre, Sambre-et-Meuse*
Jacques Étienne Jos. Alex. Macdonald	*lt. colonel*	*Gén.de Div.*	*Nord*
Auguste F.L.V. de Marmont	*élève sous-lt.*	*Chef de Bat.*	*Alpes, Rhin-et-Moselle, Italie*
André Masséna	*lt. colonel*	*Gén.de Div.*	*Danube, Italie*
Bon-Adrien Jeannot de Moncey	*capitaine*	*Gén.de Div.*	*Midi, Pyrénées Occidentales*
Édouard Mortier	*capitaine*	*Chef de Brig.*	*Nord, Sambre-et-Meuse*
Joachim Murat	*soldat*	*Gén.de Brig.*	*Intérieur, Centre, Nord, Italie*
Michel Ney	*mar. des logis chef*	*Gén.de Brig.*	*Centre, Nord, Sambre-et-Meuse*
Nicolas Charles Oudinot	*2e lt. colonel*	*Gén.de Brig.*	*Nord, Rhin-et-Moselle*
Catherine-Dominique de Pérignon	civilian	*Gén.de Div.*	*Midi, Pyrénées Orientales*
Claude-Victor-Perrin	*adj. sous officier*	*Gén.de Div.*	*Italie, Pyrénées Orientales*
Józef Antoni Poniatowski	major-general	in exile	Kingdom of Poland
Laurent de Gouvion Saint-Cyr	*soldat*	*Gén.de Div.*	*Rhin-et-Moselle*
Jean-Mathieu-Philibert Sérurier	*lt. colonel*	*Gén.de Div.*	*Midi, Italie*
Jean de Dieu Soult	*mar. des logis*	*Gén.de Brig.*	*Sambre-et-Meuse*
Louis Gabriel Suchet	civilian	*Chef de Brig.*	*Italie*

75 Phipps, *Nord*, p.59; Phipps, *Moselle*, p.4; Phipps, *West*, pp.13, 165, 188, 214; Phipps, *Italy*, pp.95, 139, 213–216, 225–226, 240, 269, 289–290; Georges Six, *Les Généraux de la Révolution et de l'Empire, Étude* (Paris: Bernard Giovanangeli, 2008), p.44; *adjuvant major* was a *lieutenant* or *capitaine*.

The wider body of officers were very experienced in 1794:[76]

Officers of 1794	Enlisted before 1789 (%)	Officers in 1789 (%)	NCOs in 1789 (%)	More than 13 years' experience in 1789 (%)
Generals	87.3	41.8	22.9	67.0
Infantry				
Chef de Brigade	86.9	39.7	41	46.0
Chef de Bataillon	73.1			43.0
Capitaines	59.6			29.8 (> 9 years)
Lieutenants	46.2			(average 9 years)
Sous Lieutenants	43.9			
Cavalry	80.0			
Capitaines		>50.0		60.0
Artillery				
Capitaines	84.0			
Lieutenants	73.7			
Sous Lieutenants	80.8			

Esdaile gives improved leadership as the one factor attributable to the revolution.[77] Furthermore the execution of significant numbers of French generals by their own government, 17 in 1793 and a further 67 in 1794, created more opportunities for men of talent and the necessary ambition.[78]

Another example of eighteenth-century evolution is the divisional system, first adopted by Broglie in 1759. While the French organised Military Divisions across France, 23 in 1791, these did not translate into organisations for fighting the war but focused on recruitment and administration.[79] In the field, the division provided a structure above the level of the brigade but below the army level columns. The French implemented these structures as all-arms affairs including cavalry, infantry and artillery. In particular, the French divisions often included an advanced guard brigade of all three arms. This enabled the division to hold its own alone while the other divisions came up in support.

The French structures were more permanent with appropriate staffs, than the Austrian organisations in which even the brigades were ad hoc, and composition depended on the circumstances. Thus, for example, the Austrian order of battle for Castiglione is, above battalion level, hugely different to that of the army as it began the campaign just seven days earlier and their column commanders lacked the staff required to command effectively. Similarly, the Duke of York's army in the Austrian Netherlands operated at brigade level, although his advanced guard usually comprised his German auxiliaries which operated as a division by default. The division was a key organisational

76 Bertaud and Palmer, *Army of the French Revolution*, pp.178–179.
77 Esdaile, *Wars*, pp.141–142.
78 Gunther E. Rothenberg, *The Art of Warfare in the Age of Napoleon* (London: Batsford, 1977), p.36.
79 Griffith, *Art of War*, pp.156–161; emphasises the evolutionary nature of the development of army structures in our period.

development, enabling generals to command the larger armies of the Revolution and Empire periods. The division allowed a more articulated approach to campaigns and battles, than in previous centuries, but placed a greater burden on the commander-in-chief and his staff and could lead to over extension or dispersal of the army. It has been argued that, while 50 years old, the divisional system required a general of the calibre of Bonaparte to reveal its true potential in Italy in 1796, although it is likely that Hoche, Moreau, Moncey, Pichegru, Jourdan, Archduke Charles and Brunswick might have contested this.[80] However, to emphasise the evolutionary nature of these changes, at Pirmasens it was the Prussians who used their divisions (albeit not all-arms divisions) to good effect against a French general who only allocated commands to his generals in the final stages of the advance to contact.[81]

The French army during the War of the First Coalition is sometimes seen to be little more than an untrained rabble thrown at the Coalition forces in a disordered, dispersed and chaotic manner. Certainly, there were many episodes of panic and disorder especially in the early years but throughout the French commanders knew that their very survival depended on the training of the volunteers and the later conscripts joining the armies. Large training camps were established to teach the men the basics of their new profession, generally according the 1791 *Reglement*, over the three months considered necessary to enable a novice to take his place in the battalion. However, even before the war began Rochambeau's training of his Armée du Nord, emphasised using battalion columns for advancing towards the enemy before forming line, rather than the more typical forming of line once within range of the enemy's cannon. The initial training was backed up by sending the recruits on expeditions to harass the Coalition troops in small actions, with a view to gaining combat experience before the big battles came along.[82]

Tactically the debate about whether the French infantry should attack in brigade or division sized columns (*ordre profond*) or in line (*ordre mince*) had been concluded in the last days of the *ancien régime*, coming down firmly on the side of continuing the assault in line with smaller battalion columns used to move reserves and support the first line, as advocated by Guibert and enshrined in the 1791 regulations.[83] In this way the full firepower of the battalion was available if the enemy chose to resist the advance and a firefight ensued. However, the issue arose again when the new, initially poorly trained and inexperienced, *volontaire nationaux* battalions entered the fighting. The inexperience brought panic to many of these battalions in the face of the enemy, while lack of training also limited their tactical options.

In Lynn's famous study of the Armée du Nord, he demonstrates that line and column were both used by the French infantry in attacks during 1792–1794, but the instances of column being used are many more than line (30 versus 7) with only one further case of the attackers advancing in column before deploying into line for the assault,

80 Bertaud and Palmer, *Army of the French Revolution*, pp.232–234.

81 Esdaile, *Wars*, pp.122–123; Rothenberg, *Art of Warfare*, p.23; Gunther Rothenberg, *The Napoleonic Wars* (London: Cassell, 1999), p.22; Voykowitsch, *Castiglione*, pp.37, 43, 74; *Maréchal de France* Victor François de Broglie, 2e Duc de Broglie.

82 Lynn, *Bayonets*, pp.218, 220, 230–232; *Reglement concernant l'exercice et les manoeuvres de l'infanterie du 1er Août 1791* (Paris: Journal Militaire, 1792); Brent Nosworthy, *Battle Tactics of Napoleon and his Enemies* (London: Constable, 1995), p.90; *Maréchal de France* Jean-Baptiste Donatien de Vimeur, Comte de Rochambeau commanded the Armée du Nord from 14 December 1791 to 18 May 1792.

83 Robert B. Bruce, Iain Dickie, Kevin Kiley, Michael F. Pavkovic and Frederick C. Schneid, *Fighting Techniques of the Napoleonic Age 1792–1815* (London: Amber Books, 2008), pp.8–9.

as recommended by Guibert. This use of the column as a direct assault formation, reflected the inability of the *volontaires nationaux* to advance through the last 250 yards to the target, in line formation, without falling into fatal disorder. This however created a firepower deficit, as the column could only deploy a quarter of the firepower of the line. To compensate the French commanders turned to two solutions, dispersed infantry skirmishers and horse artillery in close support.[84]

Light infantry had been an emerging part of the orders of battle of eighteenth-century armies for some time, with the wars in North America from the 1750s through to the 1780s providing British, French and German soldiers plenty of experience in this type of fighting. However, at the advent of the War of the First Coalition light troops were seen as useful mainly in broken ground, woods, forests and mountains, consequently operating on the flanks, while the main battle line remained the province of the line infantry formed in their lines three ranks deep. By using their infantry dispersed in the open ground to support the line infantry in column, the French could fill their firepower deficit at least in part.[85] Acting in this way the *tirailleurs* moved from a supportive role on the flanks of the main battle line to the primary means of delivering fire during an attack. In some cases, this meant that entire battalions dispersed to fight *en tirailleur*, indeed Duhesme wrote that the French infantry, in 1793, could only fight *en tirailleur*. However, this was clearly an exaggeration as Lynn's study identified only five instances of line battalions doing this out of a sample of 39 actions (Esquelsbeque, Tourcoing and Hondschoote in 1793, Mouscron and Courtrai in 1794).[86]

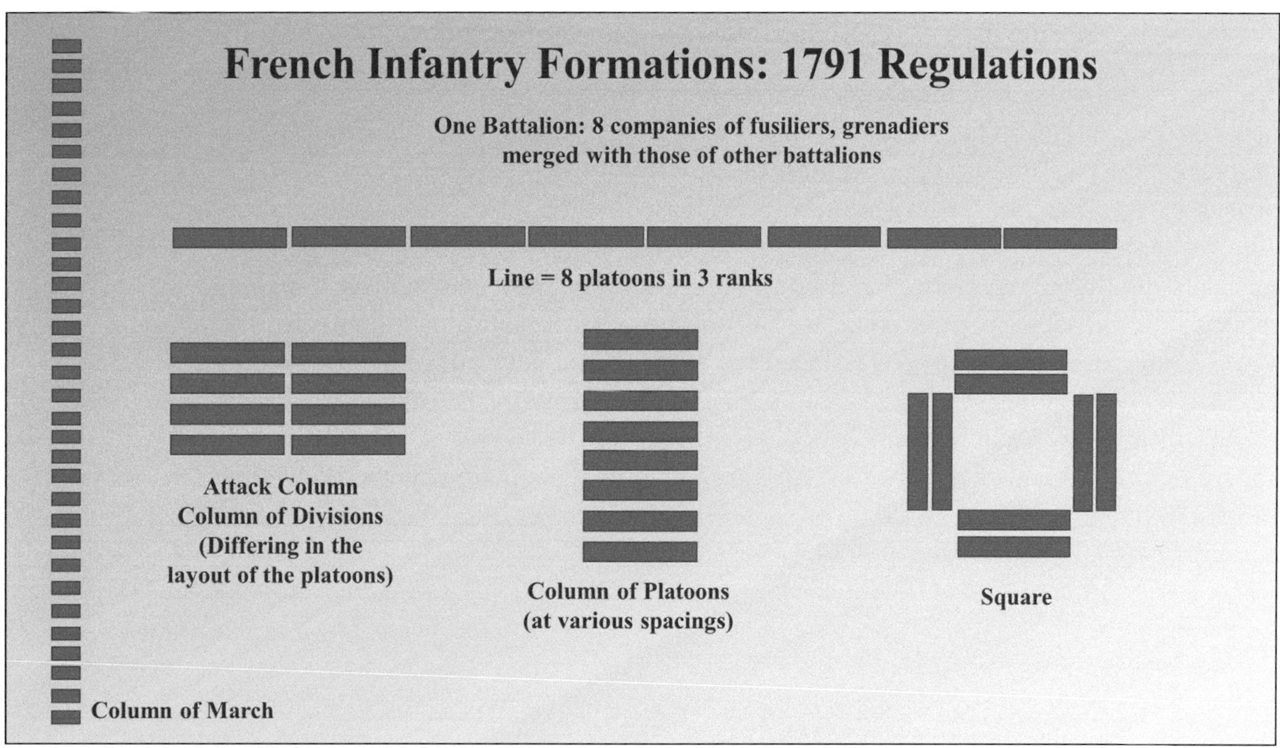

French Infantry Formations: 1791 Regulations

84 Lynn, *Bayonets*, pp.287–291.
85 Bertaud and Palmer, *Army of the French Revolution*, p.239.
86 Lynn, *Bayonets*, pp.241, 270, 292–296: actions where the nature of the action was specified. In 1793, *Général de Brigade* Philibert Guillaume Duhesme was fighting with the Armée du Nord and was later mortally wounded at Waterloo. In 1806 he wrote *Précis Historique de Infanterie Légère*.

Furthermore, during his tenure as commander of the Armée du Nord, in August 1793, Houchard issued instructions to limit the number of *tirailleurs* that each line battalion should deploy to 64, chosen from the bravest men and the best shots. These men would perform this task regularly. Similarly other officers limited the number of *tirailleurs* to 10 per company (80–90 per battalion).[87]

Lynn's study also looked at the different types of light infantry used by the Armée du Nord, differentiating between specialist light infantry from the *chasseur* battalions, and the *demi-brigades légère* that replaced them, from *tirailleurs* drawn from the line battalions. In the sample of 39 specified actions no less than 31 actions involved specialist light infantry units.[88]

This use of large numbers of *tirailleurs* screening the close order columns in more open terrain made them particularly vulnerable to attack by the excellent Allied cavalry. Consequently, it was important that the *tirailleurs* were supported by the close order columns and lines and this was a role that the horse artillery increasingly came to fulfil.[89]

Proper defence against cavalry required the French infantry to be able to form square, which provided all around defence with no flanks. The 1791 *reglement* showed that the square was to be formed from the column of platoons (companies) deployed with two platoons forming each face, one behind the other, which was therefore six ranks deep.[90] The time taken for this formation change depended on the deployment of the column, when deployed at quarter intervals (meaning that the gap between the successive platoons was one quarter of the platoon frontage) the time taken was just 1¼ minutes, but at full distance the time increased to almost 1¾ minutes.

The *reglement* did not describe a separate method of forming square from line formation, instead the battalion in line was to form of column of platoons first; importantly this process could take almost two minutes. During this time a cavalry regiment could probably cover 600 yards over good terrain.[91] Consequently, the brigade and battalion commanders had to be constantly on the alert for cavalry attacks and it perhaps unsurprising that inexperienced and poorly trained *volontaires* were subject to panic, especially in the face of Coalition cavalry. Examples of such panics include Avesnes le Sec (12 September 1793), Lannoy (28 October 1793), Catillon (17 April 1794), Villers-en-Cauchies (24 April 1794) and Beaumont (26 April 1794).[92] Lynn's tactical study could not find any definite examples of the infantry of the Armée du Nord forming square before the end of April 1794. An alternative to the square was to receive the cavalry in line if the flanks could be protected, as done earlier in the century, and this certainly happened during our period.[93]

---

87 ynn, *Bayonets*, p.267; Griffith, *Art of War*, p.210.

88 Lynn, *Bayonets*, pp.292–296.

89 Lynn, *Bayonets*, p.213.

90 Irenée Amelot de Lacroix, *Rules and regulations for the field exercise of the French Infantry* (Boston: Watt and Co., 1810), vol. I, pp.203–208 and plate XIII; being a translation of the 1791 *reglement*.

91 George Nafziger, *Imperial Bayonets* (Warwick: Helion, 2017), pp.49, 53, 180, 194; these are theoretical timings based on the strength of the platoon and the geometry and pace of the *reglement*. Nafziger gives the time as 4.7 minutes based on the battalion in line forming column to the front whereas a simple wheel of each platoon creates the necessary column of platoons much quicker, albeit facing to the left or right, rather than the front.

92 Griffith, *Art of War*, p.210.

93 Lynn, *Bayonets*, pp.259–260, 292.

The French use of massed skirmishers is illustrated by de Rison's account of Saint-Cyr's attack on the village of Berstheim (five miles southwest of Hagenau), during Pichegru's attack on Wurmser's Austrians (2 December 1793):

> ...we see the plain so suddenly covered with an immensity of scattered soldiers, who, starting from the crest of the heights occupied by the Republicans, run towards the village of Berstheim. Scarcely had they got there within pistol range than they formed into platoons, and even into battalions, to hasten the attack on this post which had become so important to them. Our eyes have scarcely time to observe this manoeuvre of which our imagination does not yet conceive the true aim, that Berstheim is in the power of the Republicans. This bold blow rendered almost nil in an instant the whole effect of our cannon.[94]

This account is particularly interesting as the tirailleurs are shown to be capable of reforming into close order.

What has been learnt from the experience of the Armée du Nord cannot be simply extrapolated to all the French armies of the War of the First Coalition. The other armies also had similar problems with the incidence of sudden panics not dissipating in the Armée du Rhin until December 1793. In other armies the commanders followed different approaches, for example, Dugommier in southwestern France kept his untrained men out of combat in the rear. However, it is telling that within these experiences lies the principles that formed the foundation of the tactics of the armies of Napoleon's Empire.[95]

Finally in discussing the French army of the War of the First Coalition it is important to focus on that key weapon of the *ordre profond* school of thought, the bayonet. The bayonet caught the imagination of French political and therefore military leaders, who thought that reliance on the bayonet rather than fire, better suited the temperament or *élan* of the French soldier. This also led to the resurrection, with muskets in short supply, of the pike as a weapon in parts of the *Garde Nationale* and the *Volontaires Nationaux*, but while there is evidence of the pike with the army, there is no evidence of the pike being used in combat.[96] While the bayonet featured strongly in the inspiring rhetoric of the generals and the *Représentants en mission*, actual tactical practice had to be more nuanced.[97] A good account of a French attack has been provided by *Caporal* Jean Claude Vaxelaire (2e Demi-Brigade Légère) remembering his service with the Armée d'Italie:

> The Austrians were waiting for us on a low hill, and we advanced to the attack *en bataille*. As soon as we were within range of their cannon, they fired in great haste, several shots passed by us. But when we arrived within range of their grapeshot, they riddled us from all sides, tree branches were blasted into our faces, pieces of grapeshot cut musket barrels, arms, and legs. On seeing us lashed by fire in this manner, the general ordered the drummers to beat the charge, and we threw ourselves upon them and took their cannon. The cavalry,

94 Phipps, *Moselle*, pp.93, 117; Anon, *Souvenirs d'un Officier Royaliste* (Paris: A.Égron, 1824), vol. II, pt.2, pp.504–505; the author was *Colonel* François-Claude de Rison who was serving in the Condé's army of French émigrés. De Rison had commanded the Régiment d'Artillerie de Metz until 1792. *Chef de Brigade* Laurent de Gouvion Saint-Cyr, future *Maréchal de France*, who was then *chef d'état major* to *Général de Division* Pierre Marie Bartholomé Férino.

95 Lynn, *Bayonets*, p.284; Griffith, *Art of War*, pp.186, 190.

96 Bertaud and Palmer, *Army of the French Revolution*, p.243.

97 Lynn, *Bayonets*, pp.183–193.

> who could only pass or descend via a hollow path, were all taken prisoner. I jumped at the bridle of an officer's horse, he raised his sword to split my head, a sergeant parried the blow, and he was thrown down from his horse, I was left with the horse; the fight over, the Austrians routed, a battalion commander bought my horse for four gold louis. ... 230 of our men were reported as having been killed or wounded.[98]

In summary, the French army was a constantly changing organisation throughout the War of the First Coalition which defies simplistic labels, each scenario needs to be developed with an understanding of which army was involved, which units comprised that army and when the action was being fought. The French army was increasingly fighting in a different way to the Coalition allies, but those differences were evolutions of the shared military thought and experimentation throughout the eighteenth century that was therefore familiar to all the Great Powers of Europe.

Great Britain

Any discussion of the British army during the War of the First Coalition must start with the diversity in the arrangements for its political control. The posts held by military professionals were the commander-in-chief of the forces (General Jeffrey Amherst, Lord Amherst, from January 1793), the Adjutant General (General Sir William Fawcett, in 1793, responsible for orders, regimental returns, reviews, training, discipline, clothing and equipment) and the Quartermaster General (Lieutenant-General George Morrison in 1793, responsible for the movement and quartering of the troops). However, the commander-in-chief did not command those forces sent overseas.

These officers were accountable to their civilian masters, the Secretary at War, Sir George Yonge MP in 1793, responsible for the finances, and the Secretary of State for War Henry Dundas MP from July 1794, responsible for running the war, as well as the Prime Minister, William Pitt the Younger. The technical branches of the army, the artillery, engineers, arms and ammunition supply were separately controlled by the Master General of the Board of Ordnance, General Charles Lennox, 3rd Duke of Richmond in 1793. Another civilian officer, the Paymaster General of His Majesty's Forces, held jointly in 1793 by Dudley Ryder, 1st Earl of Harrowby and Thomas Steele MP, was responsible for the army's pay. King George III as titular head of the army was also involved in the complex process of the management of the army.[99] Just to complete this survey of complexity, the fencibles, militia and volunteers raised for home defence were controlled by the Secretary of State for the Home Department, Henry Dundas MP before July 1794 and then William Henry Cavendish-Bentinck, 3rd Duke of Portland.

In 1793 the basic building block of the army was the infantry regiment of one battalion, each of eight centre companies, one grenadier company and one light company. The

---

98 Esdaile, *Wars*, p.135; citing Jean-C. Vaxelaire, Henri Gauthier-Villars, *Mémoires d'un Vétéran de l'ancienne armée, 1791–1800* (Paris: Delagrave, 1900), pp.38, 42–45; although Esdaile translates *en bataille*, from the original French, as meaning in column, it usually refers to line formation. It is not clear which action Vaxelaire is describing, Esdaile attributes it to Bassano (9 September 1796), but Vaxelaire did not reach Bassano until early 1797, having left Germany 7 January 'Year V' (1797). Consequently, it is more likely to have been part of Masséna's advance from Bassano against Lusignan in March 1797, when Ménard was Vaxelaire's brigade commander.

99 Edward J. Coss, *The British Army*, pp.107–147 in Frederick C. Schneid (ed.), *European Armies of the French Revolution, 1789–1802* (Norman: University of Oklahoma Press, 2015), pp.114–115.

average company had three officers, two drummers and between 60 and 70 non-commissioned officers and privates. There were three Foot Guard Regiments comprised of a total of seven battalions. In 1793, the line infantry comprised 77 numbered regiments and two colonial corps, a total of 81 battalions. Thus, only the 1st and 60th Regiments of Foot had more than one battalion in 1793. The war with France began a process of rapid expansion as the threat of invasion by France was considered very real. Regiments of Foot numbered 78 to 96 were raised during 1793 and those numbered 97 to 135 were raised in 1794. However, in an act of consolidation all regiments numbered 91 and above were disbanded in 1795, those numbered above 100, or 1796, except for the 98th Foot (later the 91st Foot) and the 100th Foot (later the 92nd Foot, the Gordon Highlanders). Similarly, several unnumbered regiments were raised. Of these the Scotch Brigade, the York Rangers and the York Chasseurs, raised in 1793 served throughout the War of the First Coalition, while 10 others raised in 1794 were disbanded in 1795.[100] Twelve West India infantry regiments were raised in 1795.

In 1793, there were 30 regiments of cavalry; two of household cavalry, the Royal Horse Guards, seven of dragoon guards, six of dragoons and 14 of light dragoons.[101] A further 13 regiments of light dragoons were raised in 1794 (five regiments) and 1795 (eight regiments).[102] A typical cavalry regiment comprised four squadrons, each of two troops of 80 men.[103]

The Royal Artillery was a single regiment comprised of four battalions, each of 10 'marching' companies. The establishment of each marching company was five officers, 15 non-commissioned officers, 90 gunners and 15 drivers. Also available was the Royal Artillery Regiment of Ireland which comprised 12 'marching' companies. The greater part of the artillery was made up of the battalion guns, usually light 6-pdr guns, but occasionally also 3-pdr guns and even light howitzers, which were allocated in pairs to each infantry battalion. The heavier field guns, 9-pdrs, 12-pdrs and howitzers were held in reserve or position batteries.[104]

The battalion gun system is much maligned but, although it would ultimately give way to the aggressive use of the new horse artillery, it needs to be viewed in the proper context. Compared to the later Napoleonic period, cannon were relatively numerous in the Duke of York's army in 1793–1795, amounting to approximately 2–3 guns per thousand troops throughout 1794. In April 1794, the battalion guns amounted to only half of the available guns. In October 1794, when the army was much larger, the proportion of guns attached to the infantry battalions rose to 70 percent of the total guns available. Consequently, the field artillery, excluding those guns attached to the infantry battalions, was relatively small, (12 guns and four howitzers in September 1793; 12 guns and two howitzers in April 1794; 20 guns and four howitzers in October 1794) and was often itself only deployed in small groups of two or four guns. By comparison, throughout the Peninsular War Wellington had an average of just over one gun per thousand troops, half the level he enjoyed at Waterloo. Thus, in the Peninsular, Wellington fought his battles with a total artillery that was only 15–20 percent greater than the Duke of

100 Sapherson, *Armies*, pp.14–22; *Army List* 1793, 1796, 1797.

101 Ron McGuigan, *The British Army, 1 February 1793*, the *Napoleon Series*, accessed 10 June 2022, available at: <https://www.napoleon-series.org/military-info/organization/c_britarmy1793.html>.

102 Sapherson, *Armies*, p.15.

103 Coss, *British Army*, pp.121, 125.

104 Garry David Wills, *British Artillery in the Netherlands 1794*, pp.69–75 in *Smoothbore Ordnance Journal*, (Godmanchester: Ken Trotman, 2012), 4, p.69.

York's reserve or position artillery, on a like for like basis. To understand why battalion guns were used in the campaigns of the 1790s – and given a post of honour – it is perhaps worth noting that at least one contemporary commentator viewed them as an 'admirable improvement' on the artillery of the beginning of the eighteenth century and they were often complemented on their battlefield performance.[105]

The Royal Horse Artillery were formed in 1793 and should have been available for service in the campaigns in Flanders and the Netherlands in 1793–1795, however the Duke of Richmond thought otherwise; 'the two Troops of Horse artillery that are in any degree of forwardness are therefore our chief dependence for the defence of this country, and it will be utterly impossible to spare any more artillery men of any kind for foreign service during this year'.[106] Consequently, the Royal Horse Artillery had to wait until almost the turn of the century to see overseas service and in the meantime the Duke of York had to rely on the Hanoverian horse artillery.

The best single descriptor of the British army in 1793 is 'small'. The total British Establishment was 17,344 at home, 18,194 (including 2,495 of the Irish establishment) abroad in the colonies, 10,700 in India with another 3,730 in the artillery. The grand total was approximately 50,992 men.[107] The global dispersion of a relatively small force meant that finding troops for expeditions to Flanders or the West Indies was a challenge and led to some curious decisions. For example, the 8th, 12th, 33rd, 40th, 44th and 55th Regiments of Foot went to Flanders in June 1793 without their flank companies, the grenadiers and light 'bobs', which were sent to the West Indies with Grey.[108]

Separate from the army was the militia, which was raised locally by the Lord Lieutenants of the counties. In England the average strength of the militia during our period was 42,000 men.[109]

In response to the outbreak of war, the Fencible force was created, these units were regular units designed for home defence, such that the Army could be freed up for service overseas. During the War of the First Coalition this force comprised 52 regiments of Fencible infantry and 30 regiments of Fencible cavalry, with at total strength of perhaps 25,000 men.[110]

The threat of invasion by the French also resulted in the creation of the British Volunteer Corps from 1794. In our period (1794–1796) some 99 troops of provisional or Yeomanry Cavalry were raised as well as perhaps 900 companies of Volunteer infantry. Besides these there were the unofficial volunteer Associations of Defence of both cavalry and infantry which have been estimated at up to 500 companies strong. Taking all these forces together Fortescue estimates that the total strength of all the British armed forces, both regular and auxiliary, at any one time was less than 200,000 men.[111]

The war began before the creation the Royal Military College (1801) such that infantry and cavalry officers either received no training or travelled abroad, as did Wellington, to

105 Garry David Wills, *British Battalion Guns in the Netherlands in 1793–1795*, pp.81–98 in *Smoothbore Ordnance Journal*, (Godmanchester: Ken Trotman, 2013), 6, p.84.
106 The National Archives, Kew; WO1/175, p.735; letter to Lord Moira written 10 June 1794.
107 McGuigan, *The British Army, 1 February 1793*.
108 Fortescue, *History*, vol. IV, pt.1, p.296.
109 Fortescue, *History*, vol. IV, pt.2, p.888.
110 Fortescue, *History*, vol. IV, pt.2, p.890; Sapherson, *Armies*, pp.18–19.
111 Fortescue, *History*, vol. IV, pt.2, pp.894–895.

learn their trade. Since 1741 the artillery and engineer officers were trained at the Royal Military Academy at Woolwich. The result was an army which Bunbury described as 'lax in discipline, entirely without a system and very weak in numbers. Each colonel of a regiment managed it according to his own notions or neglected it altogether. There was no uniformity of drill or movement, professional pride was rare and professional knowledge still more so. Never was a kingdom less prepared for a stern and arduous conflict'.[112] A major step towards resolving this issue was the publication in 1788 of Colonel David Dundas's *The Principles of Military Movements chiefly applicable to Infantry*. Dundas's work led to the publication, by the War Office, in 1792 of the *Rules and regulations for the formations, field exercise, and movements, of His Majesty's forces*, which provided each infantry regiment with a system of movement and training that thereby became common across the army. The manual was based on the concept of moving the battalion forward in columns but deploying for battle in a three-deep line. However, the use of two-deep line was trialled in Flanders by the Duke of York, with the encouragement of the Austrian commander-in-chief, the Duke of Coburg.[113]

The equivalent manual for cavalry, *Instructions and Regulations for the Formations and Movements of the Cavalry* was published in 1796, this covered the movement of the regiment on the battlefield and charges but did nothing to distinguish between the differing roles of light and heavy cavalry. However, the 1799 edition also included brief sections on skirmishing, patrols and outposts.[114]

What the manuals did not cover was a core piece of the dominant tactical doctrine of the British infantry, which had been developing throughout the eighteenth century. This doctrine comprised close range musket volleys followed by an immediate bayonet charge and would become a signature of Wellington's Peninsular army.[115]

Another obstacle that the British army faced was the inexperience of many of its field officers, meaning those majors and lieutenant colonels who led the regiments in the field. It was only when the Duke of York became commander-in-chief in Horse Guards in 1795, that he introduced restrictions on the promotion of officers, introducing both minimum ages and minimum service periods before promotion.[116] While good officers such as the Duke of Wellington benefited from the old system, rising from ensign to lieutenant-colonel in 6 years, there were plenty of examples of less successful outcomes. In one such example, the 37th Foot was all but destroyed including losing their battalion guns and a colour, by French cavalry at Druten 19 October 1794. Their commander Lieutenant-Colonel Charles Hope mistook the French cavalry, the 9e Hussards, for his own allies, the 1st Rohan Hussars, despite significant differences in the two uniforms. Although, Hope had enlisted as a cornet in the 3rd Dragoons in 1788, joining the 37th Foot, he rose from captain to lieutenant-colonel in only 16 months (2 March 1793 to 3 June 1794), only four months before Druten. Craig, the Duke of York's, Adjutant

112 Coss, *British Army*, p.124; Lieutenant-General Sir Henry Edward Bunbury, who served in the 1799 campaign in the Netherlands, in Egypt in 1801 and at Maida in 1806. He was Undersecretary of State for War and the Colonies, 1809–1816. The text is taken from the introduction to his book, *Narratives of Some Passages in the Great War with France, from 1799 to 1810* published in 1854.

113 Peter Harrington (ed.), *With the Guards in Flanders: The Diary of Captain Roger Morris 1793–1795* (Warwick: Helion, 2018), p.65; 12 April 1794, the third rank was to be divided into two parties, one on each flank to support each wing as appropriate.

114 Coss, *British Army*, p.126.

115 David Blackmore, *Destructive and Formidable, British Infantry Firepower 1642–1765* (Barnsley: Frontline Books, 2015), pp.172–173; Coss, *British Army*, p.125.

116 Coss, *British Army*, p.116.

General, congratulated Hope on his actions during the attack including his own escape with 50 of his men, but he still bears responsibility for the capture of more than 400 of his men and 10 of his officers.[117] Such problems did not apply to the artillery or engineers who were both trained and promoted based purely on seniority and therefore experience.

The experience of both the French and Indian war (1754–1763) and the American revolution (1775–1783) had brought home to the units involved and the army in general the benefits of fighting in open order (with an increased distance between ranks) and dispersed (meaning increased distance between files) to both facilitate movement and exploit the cover provided by the terrain. Consequently, the introduction of light infantry companies and battalions came about. However, the European as opposed to the American school of thought prevailed and the light infantry companies were abolished following the peace both in 1763 and 1783. Consequently, at the beginning of the War of the First Coalition, there were no light infantry regiments, and the Guards Brigade went to Flanders at the beginning of 1793 without any light companies. Similarly, six of the 22 infantry battalions with the Duke of York in July 1794 went to Flanders without either of their flank companies, which had been sent to the West Indies with Grey.[118]

The practice both in Flanders and in the West Indies was to gather the light companies into ad hoc flank battalions. Grey tended to use his light companies as shock troops very similar to his grenadiers. The publication of de Rottenberg's manual for riflemen and light infantry, the first of its kind in English, was still six years away when hostilities began. Light infantry was largely provided by the Hanoverian and Hessian contingents of the British army in Flanders.[119]

In summary, the British government, giving priority to home defence and policing at the behest of the civil authorities, struggled to find troops for expeditions overseas. Units even arrived in Flanders poorly trained and poorly equipped, with a lack of artillery drivers and crews for their battalion guns.[120] The British performance in the War of the First Coalition was restricted by a lack of numbers and a shortage of experienced field officers and general officers. They were also behind the pace set by Austria and France in the key tactical arenas of light infantry and horse or light artillery. However, when well led the troops proved themselves competent and effective at several of the smaller engagements. This all resulted in the British being a junior partner in Flanders and the Netherlands to the greater Austrian army and being obliged to conform to their movements. Great Britain compensated for these small numbers by its emerging financial muscle which made it a primer mover in the Coalition and enabled it to recruit auxiliary troops to supplement the Duke of York's command. Finally, the Royal Navy, with twice the manpower of the regular army, was the major contribution of the British

117 John Everard Whitting, *Annals of the Thirty Seventh North Hampshire Regiment* (Winchester: Warren and Son, 1878), pp.15–16; Brown, *Flanders Campaign*, pp.226–227; Fortescue, *History*, vol. IV, pt.1, p.311; Brown ref. 20 leads to a dead page, but seems to refer to Verillon's, *Les Trophées de la France*, 1907.

118 Fortescue, *History*, vol. IV, pt.1, p.296; John Frederick Charles Fuller, *British Light Infantry in the Eighteenth Century* (Doncaster: Terence Wise, 1991), pp.124, 155.

119 Fortescue, *History*, vol. IV, pt.2, p.916: note Fortescue misses the point that Grey did not use the light companies as skirmishers but as assault troops. In the Peninsular War, the light companies were again gathered at brigade level in similar converged battalions but were used in a skirmish role.

120 Brown, *Flanders Campaign*, pp.57–58, 227; Harrington, *Morris*, p.123.

government to the war effort, disrupting French trade in the Mediterranean and in the West and East Indies and projecting British power globally.

Prussia

At the outbreak of the War of the First Coalition, King Frederick William II, the nephew of Frederick the Great, commanded an army based around the Foot Guards and 53 regiments of line infantry, with two more added in 1794 and 1795 respectively. The Potsdam regiments were the Grenadier Garde battalion (N.6), the Garde Regiment zu Fuss (N.15), and the Regiment des Königs (N.18). These regiments had one, three and two battalions respectively, each of four companies. The line regiments comprised two battalions, each of four companies of musketeers, for a total of around 800 men per battalion, together with an elite grenadier battalion, also of four companies, which usually operated independently of the regiment.[121] In addition, each regiment was supported by two battalion guns. The regiments were numbered according to their seniority as determined by the date they were originally raised.

The regiments were named after their colonel-in-chief, usually an aristocrat or distinguished general. The drill regulations of 1788 emphasised rapid deployment from the column of march into line formation to deliver rapid musket fire, followed by a bayonet attack on the weakened enemy. The battalion normally deployed in three ranks, over a frontage of approximately 150 yards, with the two battalions deployed side-by-side. To avoid threats to the rear and flanks, the regiments were deployed in a continuous line with a line of supporting regiments behind. Advancing in such a formation presented challenges but the Prussians were renowned for their ability to advance without losing their alignment and were considered superior to all their contemporaries. Above the regiment there was no permanent command structure, brigades were always formed on an ad hoc basis.[122]

The light infantry arm was developed over time, Frederick the Great had, in 1756, raised a corps of rifleman primarily from foresters and huntsmen. By 1792, this Feldjäger-Korps zu Fuß had become a regiment of 1,352 men of all ranks, organised in 10 companies. In 1787 each line infantry company received 10 rifle-armed *schützen*. Although few, these men were chosen for their physical fitness and alertness and given training in marksmanship, skirmishing and skilful use of terrain, according to specific instructions published in 1789. Also in 1787, 20 fusilier battalions were raised to serve as light infantry semi-independently from the line regiments, particularly in wooded or broken terrain, according to their own regulations published in 1788.

The fusilier battalions each comprised four companies, also including 10 *schützen* each, with a total combat strength of 680 men of all ranks. They were designed to fight irregularly against the Croats and Grenzers of the Austrian army. A twenty-first battalion was raised in 1795. The fusilier battalions were organised into six regional brigades. The fusiliers wore green jackets rather than the typical blue jackets of the line and carried a smoothbore musket, the fusilier musket of 1787. The more advanced

121 The grenadier battalions were reduced to two companies in 1799.

122 Sapherson, *Armies*, pp.35–36; Dennis Showalter, *The Prussian Army*, in Frederck C. Schneid (ed.), *European Armies of the French Revolution, 1789–1802* (Norman: University of Oklahoma Press, 2015), pp.36–63; Peter Hofschröer, *Prussian Line Infantry, 1792–1815* (Oxford: Osprey, 1984), pp.4–6.

fusilier musket of 1796 came only after Prussia had left the First Coalition. They fought in two ranks rather than the three of the line infantry, with both ranks thus able to stand while firing. At any one time only a quarter of the battalion was to be deployed to skirmish, the remainder being in close order to provide support and replacement. When in skirmish order they were expected to keep close to one another, advancing in a common direction and to only fire on command. Frederick William II insisted that the fusilier officers be of noble birth but by 1792 a quarter of the officers had no title and, following the 1778 regulations, sergeants could be commissioned as officers.[123]

Prussian cavalry was divided into three categories, *kürassiers*, dragoons and light cavalry. The 13 regiments of *kürassiers* were the heavy cavalry, big men on big horses, wearing breast plates and carrying straight swords – the main cavalry strike force. The 12 regiments of dragoons, originally mounted infantry, had developed into medium cavalry in support of the *kürassiers*. The regiments of *kürassiers* and dragoons were comprised of five squadrons, each of two companies, with a total strength of approximately 800 men in time of war. The exceptions to this strength were the 13th regiment of *kürassiers*, the *Garde du Corps*, which had only three squadrons, with a total strength of 602 men of all ranks. The 5th and 6th dragoons each had 10 squadrons and were therefore double the strength, although they often served on campaign as two battalions each of five squadrons.

The light cavalry was comprised of 11 regiments of hussars. These regiments comprised 10 squadrons with a total strength of 1,550 men. However, the 11th regiment, which was raised in 1792, only had five squadrons. These regiments were all armed with sabres except for the 9th or Bosniaken regiment which was armed with lances and had fewer men per squadron than the other regiments, 112 versus 150. In 1795 a regiment of lance-armed *ulans*, the Tartaren Pulk, was raised, also of five squadrons for a total of around 600 men. The light cavalry served as scouts and raiders away from the main body of the army and were still regarded as irregular cavalry.

The cavalry was trained using the 1790 *Instruction for the Cavalry Regiments* and the 1790 *Regulations for the Royal Prussian Cavalry in the Field.* When attacking enemy cavalry the intention was to close with the enemy at the trot and only gallop in the final stages in order to maintain order and discipline. The need for reserves to allow the charging squadrons to rally and reform was emphasised. A new regulation was published in 1796, after Prussia left the First Coalition.[124]

The artillery comprised four regiments of foot artillery and one of horse artillery, each of 10 companies. Each foot artillery company was armed with eight guns, while the horse artillery companies were armed with six guns.[125] The battalion guns of the grenadier and musketeer battalions were 6-pdr cannon, while the fusilier battalions had 3-pdr cannon. The park or reserve artillery comprised light and heavy 6-pdr and 12-pdr cannon and 7-pdr and 10-pdr howitzers. The light 6-pdr guns were intended for the horse artillery and the heavy 6-pdrs for the foot artillery. The artillery pieces were from the system introduced by General Inspector of Artillery Karl Wilhelm von Dieskau from 1768 (guns) and 1762 (howitzers). In 1790 a light 7-pdr howitzer was

123 Showalter, *Prussian Army*, p.41; Peter Hofschröer, *Prussian Light Infantry, 1792–1815* (Oxford: Osprey, 1984), pp.9, 18.

124 Showalter, *Prussian Army*, p.38; Sapherson, *Armies*, pp.34–35, 37; Peter Hofschröer, *Prussian Cavalry of the Napoleonic Wars (1), 1792–1807* (Oxford: Osprey, 1985), pp.4–6.

125 Sapherson, *Armies*, p.37.

introduced for the horse artillery. The artillery was considered the worst of the three arms of the Prussian army.[126]

Each regiment was assigned a recruiting district or canton, which was further broken down into company areas. All males in each district were entered into the company recruitment rolls at 16 years of age. If there were too few volunteers to fill the gaps in the company's ranks, then eligible candidates from the canton were conscripted. As with similar systems elsewhere there were many exemptions such that only 15 to 20 percent of candidates on the rolls were eligible. Once a conscript had been trained, he could be furloughed back to civilian life for 10 months of each year. Thus, the impact of conscription on the economy was minimised. However, the majority of the force was comprised of volunteers from Prussia and abroad, such that in 1786 some 110,000 of the total force of 190,000 men were *ausländers* (foreigners). This is however a somewhat misleading term as it includes all non-Prussian Germans, but not those from the newly acquired Polish provinces. Prominent *ausländers* included Brunswick (Brunswicker), Blücher (born in Rostock, Mecklenburg-Schwerin), Scharnhorst (Hanoverian) and Gneisenau (Saxon).[127]

Frederick William II was no soldier, but the army was run by the king via a committee separate from the civilian government.[128] In 1790 two Assistant Quartermaster generals were appointed to assist the Quartermaster General von Pfau, one of whom, von Grawert, looked after the Rhineland campaign. Assisting these men were four quartermasters and 10–12 assistant quartermasters. Together these men constituted the general staff of the army.[129]

During Frederick William II's reign the enlightenment in Prussian military circles engendered the broadening and spreading of practical knowledge. Led by the king, Prussia's erstwhile strict approach to disciplining its soldiers was reformed, abolishing the more extreme physical punishments. The King also provided lifelong security for his soldiers, with improved housing and conditions including invalid companies, increased pensions and allowances for the men with children under 13 years of age.[130]

At the outbreak of the War of the First Coalition the Prussian army was a highly respected force across Europe, its reputation further enhanced by its invasion of the United Provinces in September and October 1787, in support of the Stadtholder, who was facing the Patriot revolt. The invasion by 25,000 men under Ferdinand, Duke of Brunswick was smoothly executed, and Utrecht and Amsterdam occupied without significant resistance and order soon restored. Similarly, the army's rapid mobilisation to the border with Poland in 1789, placed Prussia in a strong position relative to both Russia and Austria when it came to the dismemberment of Poland in 1793 and another counterinsurgency operation was undertaken to suppress the Poles. The poor performance of the Prussian army at Valmy where the infantry attack was halted soon after it had begun, in some ways masks the true capability of the army in the later campaign along the Rhine.

126 Dawson, *Napoleonic Artillery*, pp.45, 48.
127 Showalter, *Prussian Army*, p.39; Hofschröer, *Prussian Line Infantry*, pp.9–10.
128 Esdaile, *Wars*, p.233
129 Peter Hofschröer, *Prussian Staff and Specialist Troops, 1792–1815* (Oxford: Osprey, 2003), p.6; Colonel Theodor Phillip von Pfau.
130 Showalter, *Prussian Army*, pp.40–41.

In these campaigns the Prussian light infantry proved to be formidable opponents for their French opposite numbers in the enclosed country of the valley of the river Rhine. Likewise, the line infantry were steady in their execution of the regulation volleys and controlled counterattacks led by a competent officer corps. The Prussian cavalry was well respected, and the light cavalry outperformed the French in the war of outposts. The Prussians in the Rhineland campaign won significant engagements against the French at Pirmasens and Kaiserslautern.[131] Looking at their performance overall, Smith lists 22 actions fought by the Prussians against the French in 1792–1795, of which 12 involved more than 20,000 combatants and of these the Prussians were victorious in eight, while in the 10 smaller actions they were victorious in seven. The Prussian army had thus shown that it could face the challenge of the French republican armies on their own terms.[132] In agreeing the 1795 Peace of Basel and withdrawing from the First Coalition, Frederick William II was choosing an independent course rather than accepting British subsidies with the attendant requirement to serve under British command, in a war which he saw as both less urgent and less ideological. As the War of the First Coalition ended, King Frederick William II died to be succeeded by his son Frederick William III, who would have to deal with Napoleon.[133]

Sardinia-Piedmont

At the outbreak of the war, Italy was divided into 16 states. The Kingdom of Sardinia comprised the island of Sardinia, the Principality of Piedmont, the Duchies of Aosta and Savoy and the County of Nice.[134] Following an invasion of Savoy and the County of Nice by the French in late 1792, the kingdom joined the First Coalition (25 April 1792). The *Regia Armata Sarda* was the largest and most effective army on the Italian peninsula. King Victor Amadeus III had reorganised it in 1786. The strength of the army was fixed at 30,000 men in peacetime, and at 45,000 in wartime. The army was formally divided into two lines, and the lines into two divisions. The division consisted of two wings, which each comprised two brigades. The brigades each had two regiments each of two battalions. This formal organisation was abandoned once the war began, and ad hoc organisations suited to the task in hand became the norm.[135]

There were initially 10 national infantry regiments (*fanteria di ordinanza nazionale*), the Guardie, Monferrato, Piemonte, Saluzzo, Aosta, La Marina, La Regina, Lombardia, Savoia and Sardegna. The regiment Oneglia was created in late 1792 from the crews of the Sardinian navy. There were also four foreign regiments, one German and three Swiss, with a further four Swiss regiments raised in 1792–1793. The foreign regiments were the Real Alemanno, Vallesano (known as de Courten and then de Streng from 1795), Bernese (known as de Rokmondet and then Stettler from 1794), Grigione (known as Christ), Schmidt, Peyer-im-Hoff, Bachmann and Zimmermann. The

131 Showalter, *Prussian Army*, pp.43–47.

132 Smith, *Data Book*, pp.23–26, 32, 41, 44–45, 49, 52, 56, 61–62, 65, 80–81, 87, 92; Showalter, *Prussian Army*, p.57.

133 Showalter, *Prussian Army*, pp.47–48, 55–56.

134 Ciro Paoletti, *The Armies of the Italian States*, pp.211–244 in Frederick C. Schneid (ed.), *European Armies of the French Revolution, 1789-1802* (Norman: University of Oklahoma Press, 2015), p.211.

135 Paoletti, *Italian States*, pp.214, 237, 242; Ferdinando Augusto Pinelli, *Storia militare del Piemonte in continuazione di quella del Saluzo cioè dalla pace d'Aquisgrana sino ai dì nostri, Epoca Primera 1748–1796* (Torino: Degiorgis, 1854), vol. I, pp.47–48.

Chablais regiment was also considered a foreign regiment until 1793 and it became the Alessandria regiment in 1796.[136]

The infantry regiments were formed of two battalions. The regimental staff comprised a *colonnello*, a *tenente-colonnello*, two *maggiori*, two *aiutanti-maggiori*.[137] Each battalion comprised two centuries of *fucilieri* (fusiliers), each of two companies, each of which numbered 12 files in peacetime, and 16 in wartime, for a total of 36 and 48 men respectively. As well as the fusiliers, each battalion had a company of *granatieri* (grenadiers) and a company of *cacciatori* (chasseurs). The officers in each company were a *primo capitano*, a *capitano-tenente*, a *luogotenente* and a *sottotenente*. In wartime, the grenadiers were massed into grenadier regiments with companies from other regiments. The grenadier companies were grouped into four grenadier regiments with a total of eight battalions, and another two grenadier battalions were independent. Battalions numbered I to IX had six companies, while battalion number X had four companies. Two further grenadier battalions comprised the *Reggimento Granatieri Reali*. Sixteen of the 20 chasseur companies were grouped into two battalions of eight companies each, which in turn formed a regiment of 18 companies in March 1796, under the command of Colli-Ricci. There were also depot companies for each regiment.[138]

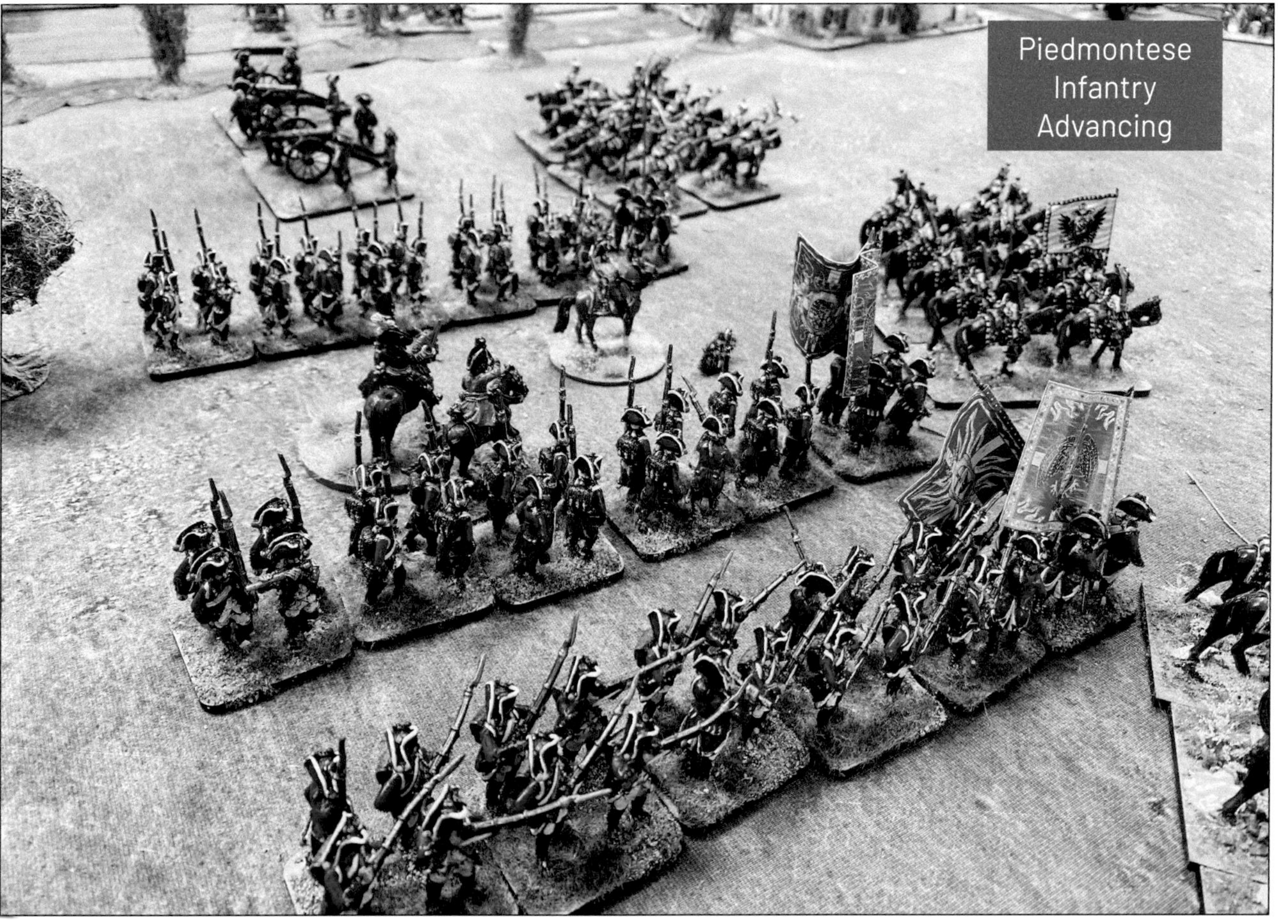
Piedmontese Infantry Advancing

136 Paoletti, *Italian States*, pp.242; Stefano Ales, *Le Regie Truppe Sarde* (Rome: Stato Maggiore Dell'Esercito, 1989), pp.21, 128–130 (for uniform details).

137 Pinelli, *Storia*, p.49.

138 Paoletti, *Italian States*, pp.218, 234–235; *Colonello* Louis Léonard Antoine Joseph Gaspard Venance Colli-Ricci.

Even at their wartime establishments, battalions had only 400 rank-and-file, small by the standards of the time. Despite an additional 207 men being added to the establishment of the regiments in 1793 to give a total establishment of 1,385, in 1794 the average battalion size fell to 325–350 men, with companies and squadrons no stronger than 80 men.[139]

The national infantry was supported by 14 regiments of provincial infantry (*fanteria di ordinanza provinciale*), volunteers, who in peacetime, attended a 14-day review period once a year at camps prepared by the *Legioni dette di Accampamento*.[140] There were two such *Legioni* with a total of four battalions, which in wartime provided pioneers, engineers and flank guards for the army on campaign. The four battalions of the *Legioni* had 825 fusiliers, 200 grenadiers, 50 chasseurs, 50 pioneers and 50 gunners. Four hundred dragoons were also assigned to these *legioni* to assist in the execution of their duties. In 1792 these legions were reformed into two new foot regiments, each of two battalions, the Granatieri Reali and the Pionieri.

In 1793, the provincial troops were reorganised into 32 fusilier battalions (each of 400 men), 28 grenadier companies (100 men), nine chasseur companies (60 men), 14 reserve (depot) companies (270 men) and 448 gunners organised in 16 platoons. The chasseur companies were recruited gradually over 1793, 1794 and 1796. The provincial regiments were Genevese, Moriana, Ivrea, Torino, Nizza, Mondovi, Vercelli, Asti, Pinerolo, Casale, Novara, Tortona, Susa, Acqui, as well as the Granatieri Reali and the Pionieri.[141]

There was also the Legione Reale delle Truppe Leggere (Royal Legion of Light troops), originally deployed as custom troops. The legion had four battalions each of six companies including chasseurs and grenadiers. The legion was later reorganised into two regiments each of two battalions, each of five fusilier, one chasseur and one grenadier companies, for a total of 1,389 men in each regiment (7 April 1795).[142]

The cavalry was organised into two wings, each of two brigades, the first wing comprised three regiments of cavalry and one of light cavalry and the second wing comprised four of dragoons. Each regiment comprised four squadrons of two companies each. In wartime each company had a strength of 48 men. A further regiment of dragoons, of two squadrons, was excluded from this structure as it was based on the island of Sardinia. The cavalry wing comprised three regiments of heavy cavalry and one of *cavalleggeri* (light cavalry). The cavalry regiments were the Piemont Reale, Aosta, Savoia, Dragoni dei Sua Maestà, Dragoni dei Chiabiese, Dragoni di Piemonte, Dragoni della Regina, Dragoni di Sardegna, Cavalleggeri dei Sua Maestà. In each cavalry regiment, one of the companies was an elite one, carabiniers for the cavalry regiments and grenadiers for the dragoon regiments. The cavalry also included three companies of royal bodyguards.[143]

---

139 Leónce Krebs and Henri Moris, *Campagnes dans les Alpes pendant la Revolution 1792–1793* (Paris: E.Plon, Nourrit et Cie, 1891), p.20; Paoletti, *Italian States*, pp.214–215, 225; Ludovic Isnard, *Organisation of the Savoy-Piedmont-Sardinian Armies 1792–1815, Part I: War in the Alps (September 1792–May 1796)*, available on the Napoleon Series at: <https://www.napoleon-series.org/military-info/organization/Piedmont/c_piedmont.html>, accessed 15 June 2022.

140 Pinelli, *Storia*, p.36.

141 Isnard, *Organisation*; Ales, *Truppe Sarde*, pp.26, 65.

142 Paoletti, *Italian States*, p.220; note that Isnard gives each battalion only four fusilier companies.

143 Ales, *Truppe Sarde*, pp.13, 150–151 (for uniform details).

The artillery comprised four battalions which, in 1792, had 2,156 men. The position guns were 8-pdr and 16-pdr smoothbores together with some 7-pdr howitzers manned by 16 artillery companies. The artillery was organised into sections of 16 men plus two guns. The fusiliers and grenadiers were supported by 52 sections with 4-pdr cannon while another four sections with 8-pdr cannon supported the eight battalions in the four grenadier regiments. Thus, each regiment of two battalions was supported by two guns. These weight descriptors for the guns are in the Sardinian weights system and are equivalent to the 3-pdr, 6-pdr, and 12-pdr in the French system.[144] A military corps of drivers was formed in 1793.

In 1794 the army fielded 113 guns in total.[145] An unusual part of the artillery's armament was the M1751 4-pdr *cannone alla Sassone*, which was based on the Saxon quick firing guns. These guns had advanced elevating mechanisms and a greater windage and could be loaded using gravity without the need for ramming. This enabled them to be fired at twice the rate of the more conventional equivalents when firing canister. The increased windage decreased range somewhat. These guns were intended as regimental guns, but they were also used in the War of the First Coalition as mountain guns. The design was not more widely adopted because it was more expensive to manufacture and any slight damage to the mechanism could disable the piece.[146]

The king also declared a general call up of the militia, which was made up volunteers aged from 16 to 60 and comprised, in December 1792, of 391 centuries and 35,602 men. Battalions were comprised of three centuries. Lacking the equipment to arm these troops, only the 10,000 men in the mountains were used in the field, the rest being deployed in garrisons to release the regulars for the field army. However, following a negative report on its training and leadership, the militia was reorganised into 429 town companies. Of these 339 companies were fusiliers (100 men each) and 90 companies were Alpine chasseurs (60 men each). There were also 16 platoons of gunners who served in the mountain batteries, and each platoon comprised 32 gunners and four light guns. Each artillery platoon was allocated to one of the 16 militia regiments. The militia was trained in their garrison duties by a battalion of retired veteran soldiers (*reggimenti di guarnigione*, 740 strong).

In December 1793 the king also established a Free Corps (*Corpo Franco*) of 13 companies with an average of 164 volunteers per company. In 1794, three more companies of Free Corps, one of chasseurs and two of carabiniers were established. In time the chasseurs and one of the carabinier companies were doubled in size to centuries. In 1795 the Free Corps were reorganised into 11 companies of 160 men. These organisations also attracted their fair share of French *émigrés*.[147]

One of the Free Corps companies, the Canale chasseurs, was privately equipped with rifles, but all other infantry were equipped with smoothbore muskets, either the 1752 or 1782 Sardinian models. The Sardinian light infantry had been armed with rifles in the War of the Austrian Succession, but without success, and the experiment was not

144 Dawson, *Napoleonic Artillery*, pp.86–87; Ales, *Truppe Sarde*, p.37; the 7-pdr howitzers are equivalent to 5½-inch howitzers.

145 Paoletti, *Italian States*, pp.225, 244.

146 Giovanni Cerino-Badone, Christian Rogge and Stephen Summerfield, *Piedmont 4-pdr "Cannone alla Sassone"*, p.56–57 in Smoothbore Ordnance Journal, 6, (Godmanchester: Ken Trotman, 2013), available at: <https://www.napoleon-series.org/military-info/OrdnanceJournal/Issue6/SOJ-6-3_Saxon_Quick-fire_Guns.pdf>, accessed 18 June 2022.

147 Paoletti, *Italian States*, pp.219, 243.

repeated.[148] The regional governments of the Vésubia and Roia valleys in the County of Nice also raised volunteer bands, which became the eight companies of the Cacciatori Scelti del Nizzardo in spring 1794.[149]

The army had too many general officers compared to its contemporary equivalents. Four *capitani generali* commanded the four divisions, each of which had under his orders a *generale*, two *tenente generali*, a *maggior generale* and *two brigadieri*. Thus, no less than 28 generals commanded just 45,000 men. Besides these, each place of significance had its own governor.

The army was trained along Frederician lines and was officered by the noble class. The army was a large one relative to its population. It also performed well according to the normal eighteenth-century standards of linear warfare. However, compared to their junior officers the field officers and general officers were slow to understand the challenge brought by the new French army manoeuvring masses in more dispersed formations. The Sardinians had an effective artillery arm and were particularly strong in making the best use of the terrain. At army level command, the agreement that gave Austria supreme command of the Sardinian army, prevented effective attacks on the French, since the Austrians were driven by the need to defend what they held. The Sardinians benefited from a strong antipathy towards the French which made the militia excellent partisans. This was even the case in the county of Nice, where four of André Masséna's relatives fought against the French revolution.[150]

Spain

The Spanish army has the distinction, during the early years of the War of the First Coalition of making larger inroads into France for longer than their allies in the north or east. However, like the armies of the other powers there were similar deficiencies that left them ill-suited to the task in hand. The Spanish army was an integral component of the machinery that kept the absolute monarchy, the ruling Bourbon dynasty, in power. The country was divided into 12 military regions and each region had a *capitán general* and this officer was also president of the regional council (the *audiencias* or *chancillerias*) which governed the administration and law courts of the region.[151] This represented an extreme example of the close integration of the military into the running of the state. King Carlos IV, as commander-in-chief of the army exercised his command through his *Consejo Supremo de Guerra* (Supreme Council of War), which comprised his Minister of War, the senior officers of the combat arms and officers specifically chosen by the king to represent a broad base of military opinion.[152] At the outbreak of war the Supreme Council comprised almost 30 officers.[153] This council originally administered the army and acted as its supreme court, however by the time of the War

148 *Napoleon's Bloody Nose*, accessed 10 March 2023, available at: <https://napoleoninpiedmont.weebly.com/the-sardinian-army-a-survey.html>.

149 Paoletti, *Italian States*, p.220.

150 Paoletti, *Italian States*, p.124; Uniform information provided by Federico Bona is available at: <http://www.bandieresabaude.it/Bandiere033.html>, accessed 19 June 2022.

151 Anon., *Estado Militar de España, año de 1794* (Madrid: Imprenta Real, 1794), pp.72–90.

152 Charles Esdaile, *The Spanish Army*, pp.148–181, in Frederick C. Schneid (ed.), *European Armies of the French Revolution 1789–1802* (Norman: University of Oklahoma Press, 2015), pp.148–150.

153 Anon., *Estado Militar de España, año de 1793* (Madrid: Imprenta Real, 1793), pp.3–5.

of the First Coalition, the minister of war, the Conde del Campo de Alange,[154] had assumed the administrative functions and the transmission of the orders of the king reducing the council to a court of military justice. The instructions of the minister of war were implemented throughout the army by the *inspector generals* of the different arms. The Ministry of Finance however remained primarily responsible for the funding of the military.[155] In 1793, Godoy was the *capitán general* of the army.[156]

Although originally following the French practices of Louis XIV's armies, in 1768 like many others, the Spanish army became enamoured of Frederick the Great's way of war which was codified in the *Ordenanzas* of that year. A third battalion was added to the establishment of the line regiments (22 October 1786), but by 1790 all regiments had only one battalion.[157] In 1787, Carlos III launched a review of the other European armies to determine whether reform was required, but this review determined that no further reforms of the Spanish army were needed.

The organisation of the infantry in our period is somewhat complex and in a state of transition. At the outbreak of the war in 1793, the Spanish infantry comprised two guard regiments (Reales *Guardias de infanteria Española* and *Walona*) and 42 regiments of line infantry (*regimientos de infanteria*), including four regiments of foreign line infantry (*infantería de línea extranjera*: one Flemish, three Irish – Hibernia, Ultonia and Irlanda, and one Italian, Nápoles) and four regiments of Swiss infantry (*infanteria Suiza*; San Gall Ruttiman, Reding, Schwaller and Beschart). The *Estado Militar de España de Año 1793–1798* lists the regiments in order of their seniority based on the date the regiment was first raised, but they were not numbered. During the war a further four regiments were raised, two of line infantry (Granaderos Voluntarios de Estado (1794) and Borbon (1796)) and two Swiss (Yann (1794) and Courten (1796)).[158] As war approached the number of battalions in the line infantry regiments was expanded, such that the total number of battalions rose from 48 in 1790, to 62 in 1792 and then 101 in 1793.[159]

Before the end of 1793, the available light troops comprised nine regiments of light infantry mostly identified as *voluntarios* or *voluntarios de infanteria ligura* (1° and 2° Voluntarios de Infanteria Ligura de Aragón, 1° and 2° Vol. Inf. Lig. de Cataluña, Vol. Inf. Lig. de Tarragona, Vol. Inf. Lig. de Gerona, 1° and 2° Vol. Inf. Lig. de Barcelona, Vol. de Castilla) and two of light cavalry (Voluntarios de España and Maria Luisa Carabinieros).[160] These units had their origins in the need to counter the bandits within the borders of Spain and the coastal raiding of the Barbary corsairs. The light infantry regiments were armed with a lighter musket with a longer barrel for improved accuracy, which suited their role in the *petit guerre* rather than on the main battlefields.[161] Like elsewhere the use of light infantry on the battlefield was being rediscovered in Spain

154 *Estado de 1793*, p.5; Manuel de Negrete y de la Torre, Conde de Alange, *Secretario de Estado y del Despacho Universal de la Guerra de España e Indias, Capitán general de los Ejércitos*.

155 Esdaile, *Spanish Army*, p.150.

156 *Estado de 1794*, p.8.

157 Conde de Clonard, *Historia orgànica de las armas de infanteria y caballeria* (Madrid: Boletin de Jurisprudencia, 1854), vol. V, p.310; Anon., *Estado Militar de España, año de 1790* (Madrid: Imprenta Real, 1790), pp.27–38.

158 Anon., *Estado Militar de España, año de 1798* (Madrid: Imprenta Real, 1798), pp.56, 57, 59; there were also the King's household troops of palace guards, the single company of the Guardias Alabarderos.

159 Anon., *Estado Militar de España, año de 1790, 92, 93* (Madrid: Imprenta Real, 1790, 92, 93); George F. Nafziger, *The Armies of Spain and Portugal, 1808–1814 (3rd Edition)* (West Chester: The Nafziger Collection, 1993), p.6.

160 Anon, *Estado Militar de España, año de 1794* (Madrid: Imprenta Real, 1794), pp.45–47; in 1793, the 1° Vol. Inf. Lig. de Aragón were called the Voluntarios de Aragón (1793, p.41).

161 Sapherson, *Armies*, p.48; Esdaile, *Spanish Army*, p.153; *Estado de 1793*, pp.41–43.

and the first treatise for its use, a translation of Grandmaison's work, was published in Spain in 1794.[162]

That same year, two more light infantry regiments were added, the Vol. de Barbastro (Cazadores Voluntarios de Barbastro in 1798) and the Vol. de Valencia. In 1795 a further regiment was raised, the Cazadores Voluntarios de la Corona.[163] Finally a note in the Estado de 1795, states that seven battalions of such light infantry were raised in Navarre together with the Voluntarios de Guipúzcoa (the province containing San Sebastian), for the duration of the war. These units were obviously based in the seat of the war in the Western Pyrenees and none of these units feature in the subsequent publications of the list, reflecting their disbandment when peace with France was concluded in July 1795.[164]

There were also 43 regiments of provincial militia (*regimiento de milicias provinciales*), which were only raised in times of war by conscription.[165]

Finally, the second reserve of the infantry forces of Spain were the *Milicia Urbanas*, 122 companies recruited from volunteers and via a levy or *quinta*, which operated with many exceptions, in the towns and cities of Spain for defence and garrison duties in time of war, under the command of the governors of the place. There were also other *fija* or stationary companies of similar militia around the country, as well as companies of invalids.[166]

The guard regiments each had six battalions, 37 of the line regiments had three battalions, the other five line regiments and the Swiss regiments had one battalion. The light regiments each had only one battalion, except for the Cazadores Voluntarios de la Corona, which had two. Each provincial militia regiment comprised a single battalion, except that of Mallorca, which had two until 1796.[167]

The regulation of 2 September 1792 described the first and second battalions of the line/national and foreign regiments, but not the Swiss regiments, as comprising eight companies of fusiliers and one of grenadiers. The grenadier company comprised four officers, 13 non-commissioned officers, two drummers and 84 men. The fusilier companies of the first and second battalions, comprised five officers, 21 non-commissioned officers, three drummers and 136 men. The four fusilier companies of the third battalions comprised four officers, 14 non-commissioned officers and 84 men.[168] The Swiss battalions had one company of grenadiers (three officers and 58 men) and

162 Esdaile, *Spanish Army*, p.154; Thomas Auguste LeRoy de Grandmaison, *La petite guerre, ou, Traite du service des troupes legeres en campagne*, originally published in 1756.

163 Anon, *Estado Militar de España, año de 1794* (Madrid: Imprenta Real, 1794), pp.43, 45–47; *Estado de 1798*, p.57.

164 Anon, *Estado Militar de España, año de 1795* (Madrid: Imprenta Real, 1795), p.52; Esdaile, *Spanish Army*, p.154.

165 *Estado de 1793*, pp.31–45.

166 Nafziger, *Armies of Spain and Portugal*, p.76–81.

167 *Estado de 1798*, pp.43–60, 70–77; *Estado de 1796*, p.76; Esdaile, *Spanish Army*, p.152; in 1788, the regiments had two battalions, but the numbers of battalions given here are taken from the Estado entries for each regiment. The *Estado de 1790* and the *Estado de 1792* only records the number of battalions where it was greater than one for the line and guard regiments. This suggests that that five of the line regiments and the Swiss regiments had only one battalion at this time. Conversely, the entries for the light or *voluntarios* regiments, did specify only one battalion.

168 Clonard, *Historia*, vol. VI, pp.54–59.

four of fusiliers (each of five officers and 161 men).[169] The provincial militia battalions comprised one company of grenadiers, one company of *Cazadores* (light infantry) and eight companies of fusiliers.[170] In time of war the grenadiers were detached from the regiments to form converged grenadier battalions. The field officers in the battalions were *coronel* (first battalion), *teniente coronel* (second and third battalions), *sargento mayor* (first battalion) and the *ayudante mayor*.

In June 1791 the battalions of the light infantry regiments comprised four companies, and each company had six officers, 26 non-commissioned officers, three drummers and 175 soldiers, but in 1793 the establishment was increased to 300 men. Each company was divided into six squads. The field officers commanding the battalion were a *comandante* (*teniente coronel*), a *sargento mayor* and two *ayudantes*.[171]

The infantry regiments deployed to confront the French across the Pyrenees were:[172]

Regiments	No. of Battalions per regiment
Guipúzcoa Province: Toledo, Léon, Asturias, América, 2° Vol. de Cataluña Navarra Province: Rey, Principe, Corona, 1°Vol. de Aragón Aragón Province: Murcia, Zarragoza, Aragón, Princesa Cataluña Province: Principe, Saboye, Córdoba, Sevilla, Mallorca, Murcia, Hibernia, Estremadura, Málaga, 1° Vol. de Cataluña, Vol. de Tarragona, Vol. de Gerona	1
Guipúzcoa Province: Reding (Swiss) Cataluña Province: Soria, Granada, Valencia, Burgos, San Gall Ruttiman (Swiss)	2
Cataluña Province: Reales Guardias Walonas, Reina, Navarra	3
Cataluña Province: Reales Guardias Españolas	4

169 Clonard, *Historia*, vol. V, pp.294, 297, 300–301, 302–305; exceptions included the stationary (*fijo*) regiment Ceuta which had 13 companies in each battalion.
170 Esdaile, *Spanish Army*, p.159; Clonard, *Historia*, vol. V, pp.289, 307–309.
171 Clonard, *Historia*, vol. VI, pp.51–54, 61.
172 Clonard, *Historia*, vol. VI, pp.61–62; the table excludes the militia and converged grenadier battalions.

The three-deep line was the standard tactical deployment for the infantry, with the battalions advancing steadily, stopping to fire (beginning at 250 paces), and then advancing again until able to charge with the bayonet. The infantry used the model 1789 smoothbore musket, roughly equivalent to those of other nations. Fire was delivered by files, companies, or half companies in turn. When fighting cavalry, the infantry formed square or a closed battalion column (the *solido*) in which the companies doubled their ranks and closed tightly to deny the cavalry an easy point of attack.[173]

There were 12 regiments of cavalry as well as the two guard regiments, the Guardias de Corps and the Carabineros Reales. Most of these cavalry regiments comprised three squadrons, except the Guardias de Corps and the Carabineros Reales, each of which had four squadrons.[174] Each squadron comprised three companies, each company had three officers, nine non-commissioned officers, six grenadiers and 60 troopers. A further 10 troopers, a *teniente* and a non-commissioned officer were added to each company (7 July 1794). However, in 1795 the 16 regiments of cavalry comprised three squadrons each of four companies but averaged only 34 other ranks per company.[175] These were the heavy cavalry of the army relying on shock action by charging at speed with sword in hand. The cavalry was expected to move and change formation at the trot or gallop.

There were also eight regiments of dragoons. Unlike the heavy cavalry who also had carbines, these regiments were trained to use their carbines both from the saddle and on foot, even forming line like the infantry. These regiments also had three squadrons, each of four companies. The companies comprised three officers, six non-commissioned officers, one trumpeter, four grenadiers and 39 troopers.[176] The companies were later increased to seven non-commissioned officers, 50 mounted troopers and 10 dismounted troopers (24 June 1795).[177]

The light cavalry initially comprised just two regiments, the Costa de Granada and the Voluntarios de España, each of four squadrons.[178] A fifteenth regiment of cavalry, the Carabineros de la Reyna Maria Luisa, also of three squadrons, was raised during 1793, which became the Husares de la Reyna Maria Luisa in 1803.[179] A further regiment, the Husares Españoles, also of three squadrons, was raised in 1795.[180]

Unlike in Northern Europe, Spanish agriculture relied on the hardier mules and oxen rather than the horse, and therefore there was always a shortage of high-quality horses for the cavalry and artillery. Poorly trained officers and a now outdated dragoon doctrine, along with the poor quality of the horse stock, resulted in a reputation for poor combat performance for all 23 regiments of cavalry.[181]

173 Esdaile, *Spanish Army*, p.152; Nafziger, *Armies of Spain and Portugal*, p.24.
174 *Estado de 1793*, pp.47–51; Clonard, *Historica*, vol. XVI, p.79.
175 Clonard, *Historia*, vol. VI, pp.297–278, 300; 13 June 1793 establishment, there were also seven trumpeters divided amongst the nine companies.
176 Clonard, *Historia*, vol. V, p.336; this is the 1763 establishment.
177 Clonard, *Historia*, vol. VI, pp.299; there is no indication in Clonard that the dragoons reduced the number of companies from four to three as happened in the cavalry regiments.
178 Clonard, *Historica*, vol. XVI, pp.73–80, 100–105; the Voluntarios de España are referred to simply as Voluntarios in the Estados.
179 *Estado de 1795*, p.60.
180 *Estado de 1798*, p.66; the Husares Españoles were originally raised in 1742 but disbanded in 1749.
181 Esdaile, *Spanish Army*, p.153.

The artillery comprised six regiments each of eight companies of approximately three officers and 100 men. There was also a company of knight cadets, two provincial companies, three from the provincial militias, and three companies of invalid artillerymen.[182]

The field artillery adopted a French Gribeauval style system after 1783, with the 4-pdr, 8-pdr and 12-pdr guns and 6-*pouce* (6.4-inch) howitzers, of the *Nueva Ordenanza*.[183] In the 1780s, Tomás de Morla y Pacheco, director of the artillery academy in Segovia, writing his seminal treatise on artillery for his student cadets, described the Spanish artillery as being organised in field brigades of nine or 10 guns of the same calibre or mixed with howitzers. The 12-pdr and howitzer brigades had nine guns, while the 8-pdr and 4-pdr brigades had 10. The brigades were allocated to each column of the army with some held in reserve. However, although detachments from the brigades were possible, the artillery was not allocated to individual battalions or regiments, as in some contemporary armies.[184] The numbers of guns per brigade was reduced to six in the early nineteenth century.[185] The Spanish generals made good use of their artillery often behind extensive field fortifications.

Artillery and engineering officers were trained in one of four colleges, consistent with the technical demands of this arm, and promotion was based on seniority. Consequently, the artillery enjoyed a good reputation for their expertise and bravery, but they were severely handicapped by the lack of high-quality horseflesh, which often resulted in the guns being drawn by slower mules or oxen. The artillery was further handicapped, like most contemporaries, by the reliance on civilian contract drivers for the train, which also reduced their mobility on the battlefield. Although experiments with horse artillery were taking place in South America, there was only foot artillery available during the War of the First Coalition. In 1795, Urrutia, *Capitán General* of Cataluña, did order the raising of some 'horse' artillery drawn by mules, but this initiative was overtaken by the declaration of peace.[186]

While the artillery enjoyed a good reputation, the Spanish army laboured against several disadvantages. The guard infantry and cavalry officers were largely noble and received little formal training before joining their regiments and their performance and reputation suffered accordingly. The officers also tended to be absent from their regiments more than was consistent with maintaining unit cohesion and effectiveness. Despite having more than 320 generals in 1792, there was no formal staff system and each field commander had to make ad hoc arrangements at the beginning of each campaign. Although at least a third of the officer corps was promoted from the ranks, these men were disadvantaged by the slowness of promotion to senior ranks for most officers, which depended on political favour and seniority.

---

182 *Estado de 1796*, p.60; there are approximately 48 captains and lieutenants in the battalions, which suggests 48 companies rather than the 42 given by Esdaile.

183 Esdaile, *Spanish Army*, p.154; Stephen Summerfield, *Spanish Gribeauval System 1745–1808*, p.93 in *Spanish Artillery (1745–1808)* in *Smoothbore Ordnance Journal*, (Godmanchester: Ken Trotman, 2012), 4, pp.85–100; these use the French nomenclature for gun calibres.

184 Johann Gottfried von Hoyer, *Lehrbuch der artilleriewissenschaft: Aus dem spanischen des d. Thomas de Morla* (Leipzig: J.A.Barth, 1797), vol. II, p.52.

185 Charles Esdaile, *The Spanish Army in the Peninsular War* (Nottingham: Partizan Press, 2012), p.53.

186 Summerfield, *Spanish Gribeauval System*, p.89; Stephen Summerfield, *Spanish Horse Artillery*, pp.97–98 in *Smoothbore Ordnance Journal*, (Godmanchester: Ken Trotman, 2012), 4, p.98; Ramón de Salas y Cortés, *Memorial histórico de la artillería Española* (Madrid: García, 1831), p.128.

The senior general ranks were dominated by men who had joined at 14 years of age as officer cadets, who had to be amongst the 10 percent of the population that could claim to be noble and have the necessary funds to pay their own expenses. With sufficient favour at court, these men could rise rapidly through the ranks such they could assume important commands while young and inexperienced. Consequently, the commanders of the armies facing the French were men of varied age and experience; the successful Ricardos was 66 years old, Caro y Fontes 62, Urrutia 54, Amarillas 53, La Unión 42, Colomera 71, Castelfranco 45 or 47, Filanguieri 41, Crespo 57, and La Cuesta 52, when assuming command. Despite all these disadvantages, at least to modern eyes, the Spanish officer corps proved capable enough to defeat the French on several occasions during the War of the First Coalition.[187]

Recruitment was always the biggest challenge facing the army and ultimately led to the disbanding of four understrength foreign regiments in 1792–1793 (the regiments Milán, Flandés, Brabante, and Bruselas). The army was intended to be largely recruited from volunteers, but the army was an unpopular occupation and therefore it has been estimated that only a few thousand men volunteered to enlist and during the war against France 1793–1795, and the government had to rely on conscription to fill the ranks. This situation was exacerbated by the peacetime establishment of the infantry regiments, which limited the number of rank and file in each regiment to 400.[188] In 1793 two such mechanisms for conscription were enacted, the *sorteo,* also known as the *quinta,* and the *leva.*[189] The *sorteo* was essentially a ballot, based on a government request for a fixed number of recruits. The provincial authorities then distributed the quota to their municipalities.

The names of the men liable and fit enough for military service were then collated and for each man a ball was drawn by a child to determine their fate, white meant freedom, black meant enlistment. Married men were exempt, but the system was intrinsically unfair based on the large number of exemptions from service, including all nobles and many occupations, which could result in 75 percent of unmarried, fit men being exempt. The system was also corrupt, especially regarding the gaining of medical exemptions. The *sorteo* was therefore hated and made military service still less popular. The *sorteo* was again enacted in 1795.[190]

The *leva* was somewhat more draconian, the authorities were enabled to arrest every man between 17 and 36 years of age who could not demonstrate that they were in permanent employment or who had otherwise been identified as idle, generally causing trouble by drinking or fighting or involved in criminal activity. Those men thus arrested, who were deemed fit for military service, were marched off to the nearest regiment. The net result was a Spanish army full of reluctant men of low quality, including foreign deserters. Furthermore, these manpower difficulties meant that the Spanish armies facing the French in the Roussillon and Cataluña, could still only muster 40,000 men in 1794, with the regiments often being understrength to the extent that some could not field the number of battalions shown in the *Estado.*[191]

187 Esdaile, *Spanish Army*, pp.157–158.
188 Esdaile, *Spanish Army*, p.159.
189 Esdaile, *Spanish Army*, pp.166–167.
190 Esdaile, *Spanish Army*, pp.160–161, 167.
191 Esdaile, *Spanish Army*, pp.159–162, 164.

The regular forces were supported during the war in the Basque provinces, Navarra and Cataluña by irregular forces. The raising of these forces was promoted strongly by the Catholic church raging against Robespierre's alternative cult of the Supreme Being. In Cataluña, the *somatenes* were raised in 1794 by the Conde de La Unión, to undertake harassment of the French in the mountains, while the *tercios de miguelete* were raised to reinforce the regular army on the battlefield. These forces could be gathered in considerable numbers, via a complex system that raised men in proportion to their proximity to the border with France. For example, the *migueletes* numbered up to 14,500 men, large relative to the regular army but far short of the total claimed by Conde de Clonard.[192]

Of less relevance to the War of the First Coalition, there was another military organisation comprising several regiments based in the colonies in the Americas and Cuba.[193]

Portugal preferred to contribute to the War of the First Coalition by adding to the Spanish war effort with British support. Consequently, a division was sent to the Pyrenees to support the campaign in 1793. This force, the Exército Auxiliar à Coroa de Espanha, a force of six regiments of infantry and eight companies of artillery comprising approximately 5,000 men, was commanded by *Tenente-General* John Forbes of Skellater, a Scottish officer in Portuguese service. Forbes's force served with credit until the peace was negotiated in 1795.

In summary, in the first years of the war, despite sharing many of the deficiencies of the other *ancien régime* armies in Europe, the Spanish had fought with distinction both at Toulon and in the Pyrenees, particularly under the excellent Ricardos, gaining some notable successes and could have taken Perpignan at one point. Although liable to outbreaks of panic, in general the Spanish soldiers followed their officers without flinching. In the end Spain's inability to rally sufficient numbers to the colours saw them forced from the war by the weight of numbers as much as French revolutionary fervour.[194]

Naples

The Kingdom of Naples included Naples, Southern Italy (5,000,000 inhabitants) and the island and separate Kingdom of Sicily (1,500,000 inhabitants), which together became the Kingdom of the Two Sicilies in 1816. In southern Italy the two Papal enclaves of Benevento and Pontecorvo were excluded from the territory of the kingdom, which extended south from Abruzzo Ulteriore in the east and Terra di Lavoro in the west. Both kingdoms, each with its own currency and system of measurement, were ruled by the Bourbon King Ferdinand IV and Queen Maria Carolina, the sister of Marie-Antoinette. King Ferdinand also had the right to garrison the fortress of Piombino in Tuscany, 242 miles up the west coast of Italy from Naples, and to appoint the governor of the castle of Ragusa, in Dalmatia on the Adriatic.

The revolution in France interrupted the programme of reform of his armed forces that King Ferdinand and his minister of war (and from 1789 minister of foreign affairs),

192 Esdaile, *Spanish Army*, pp.163.
193 *Estado de 1793*, pp.91–148.
194 Esdaile, *Spanish Army*, pp.168–172; Esdaile, *Peninsular War*, p.28.

Giovanni Acton, had begun in 1786.[195] Reform was necessary because the armed forces had seen little innovation and had not been tested in the field since 1745. From 1787, this reform programme was facilitated by a number of officers from the French service, from the Swiss officer, de Salis, who led the reform of the infantry, O'Reilly, who led that of the cavalry, and de Pommereul, a pupil of Gribeauval, who led the that of the artillery, down to *Sergent* Augereau (later *Maréchal de France*). These men were withdrawn as a consequence of the revolution. The interruption of the reform programme meant that only one brigade of each arm were full beneficiaries of the new methods, the rest of the armed forces being generally hostile to the reforms. The disbanding of the royal guard regiments was particularly disliked by the nobility who formed their officer corps.

With an arguably smaller task and a more receptive officer corps, de Pommereul, who remained until 1793, had more success in reforming the artillery, reorganising it into two regiments, incorporating the engineers, based on the Ordinance of 1788.

In 1788 the reform programme was planned to produce an army that could field 57,587 men in peacetime and 61,543 men when on a war footing, however by 1790 the actual numbers were only 35,734 men and 46,499 men respectively.

Even after the reforms, there was no permanent general staff organisation, instead the term *Stato Maggiore* was simply a collective title for all the general officers. A proper general staff was not established until 1798. In 1797 there were two *capitani generali*, nine *tenenti generali*, 22 *marescialli di campo* and 45 *brigadieri*.[196]

Recruitment into the officer corps was entirely from those men that could prove noble birth, which included members of the aristocracy, but also members of the military with 'personal nobility', therefore including many foreign officers, and those from the families of high-ranking bureaucrats and magistrates. Only in exceptional cases were non-commissioned officers promoted to officer rank. Even then they did not achieve 'personal nobility', allowing their sons to follow their example, unless they reached the unlikely rank of captain. Officers entered the army in one of two ways, either as cadets or from the military academy. Each infantry company offered one place for a cadet and each cavalry squadron offered two. The cadets could be no older than 13 (infantry) or 14 (cavalry) years old. The cadet's parents had to be able to support the cadet during his service. The cadet served as a non-commissioned officer and could be punished by demotion to a private soldier. If they had proved incapable of serving as a non-commissioned officer by their 18th birthday, they were sent home. On the other hand, success could see them – following a successful exam – promoted to the rank *alfiere* (ensign) when vacancies arose, at the discretion of the colonel. If the potential cadet's family could not afford to support them, they could serve in the ranks as *soldati distinti*, distinguished by a collar badge and sabre, who could be promoted to NCO and subsequently officer ranks.

The military academy, based in the Nunziatella in Naples, housed 240 students divided into four brigades, each of which was under the orders of a captain commander, assisted by a second captain, a first and a second lieutenant, two brigadiers and four sub-

195 Giancarlo Boeri and Piero Crociani, *L'Esercito Borbonico dal 1785 al 1815* (Roma: Stato Maggiore dell'Esercito, 1997), pp.6, 10–12, 38, 49–52; Acton was of English descent and had served in the French navy.

196 Boeri and Crociani, *L'Esercito Borbonico*, pp.46–47; *Maréchal de Camp* Baron Rudolph Antoine Hubert de Salis-Marschlins; *Brigadiere* O'Reilly; *Lieutenant-Colonel* François René Jean de Pommereul, appointed *brigadiere* in the service of Naples.

brigadiers chosen from among the students. The students were overseen by a general staff and taught by a staff of 50 instructors. Lessons covered horsemanship, fencing, dancing, chemistry, mathematics, calligraphy, drawing, letters, philosophy, history as well as military subjects. Students entered the academy at between nine and 12 years old and could graduate to become cadets when they had demonstrated an appropriate standard.[197]

In 1789 the infantry comprised 16 national regiments formed into four divisions, each of two brigades, each in turn of two regiments. There was also a fifth division also of two brigades, comprised of the four foreign regiments (1°Estero Re, 2° Estero Regina, 1° Real Macedonia (1° Illirico) and the 2° Real Macedonia). The divisions were numbered 1 to 5 and the brigades 1 to 10:

Regiment	Brigade	Division
Re	1	1
Regina		
Real Borbone	2	
Real Farnese		
Real Italiano	3	2
Real Campania		
Real Napoli	4	
Real Palermo		
Puglia	5	3
Lucania		
Sannio	6	
Messapia		
Calabria	7	4
Agrigento		
Siracusa	8	
Borgogna		
1° Estero Re	9	5
2° Estero Regina		
1° Real Macedonia (Real Illirico)	10	
2° Real Macedonia		

197 Boeri and Crociani, *L'Esercito Borbonico*, pp.123–126.

Throughout our period the infantry regiments were comprised of two field battalions, each of four fusilier companies, and one garrison battalion of two companies. Each field battalion also had a company of grenadiers, but these were normally detached to form separate battalions of grenadiers. Each fusilier company comprised one captain and three other officers plus 140 other ranks, while each grenadier company comprised a captain and two other officers plus 116 other ranks.

Each regiment had an establishment of 1,700 men when on campaign and 1,100 in time of peace. The fusilier companies also included a squad of *cacciatori* (light infantry), which were united to form a division of 20 files, formed in two platoons, usually commanded by a non-commissioned officer. These light infantry platoons were armed with rifled carbines and were designed for reconnaissance and actions in dispersed order. Each battalion carried two flags and was supported by two battalion guns.[198]

The fifth or foreign division, which should have been on a war footing, had only the 9th brigade almost complete (in November 1790 the 2° Estero Regina had only 1,407 men), while its 10th brigade was organised only with difficulty. By the end of 1794, the 10th brigade's first regiment, 1° Real Macedonia had just 1,197 men, divided into the old battalions of 13 companies each, while the second regiment, called temporarily the Real Corpo de Superanti del Reggimento Real Macedonia, had only 13 sergeants and 611 men.[199]

Initially the only light infantry formation was a company of *Fucilieri di montagna* (mountain riflemen), comprising just 150 men. However, after doubling to 300 men, it became a battalion of 10 companies with a total strength of 1,000 men on 14 August 1796. In the final months of the War of the First Coalition, six regiments of light infantry (*Cacciatori* – hunters) were raised (30 January 1797). Each regiment, with a nominal strength of 1,007 men, comprised two battalions, each of four companies.[200]

In 1789, the cavalry comprised eight regiments organised in two divisions each of two brigades, each in turn of two regiments, the whole under the supervision of Spinelli:

Regiment	Brigade	Division
Re	1	1
Regina		
Napoli	2	
Sicilia		
Borbone	3	2
Principe		
Rossiglione	4	
Tarragona		

198 Boeri and Crociani, *L'Esercito Borbonico*, p.193.
199 Boeri and Crociani, *L'Esercito Borbonico*, pp.10–12, 49–52.
200 Boeri and Crociani, *L'Esercito Borbonico*, p.66.

The Tarragona and Rossiglione regiments originated from two Spanish regiments which passed into Neapolitan service in 1737 and still received recruits from Spain. The composition of the regiments was regulated by a royal decree of 14 January 1788. All eight regiments were simply called cavalry regiments, dragoons having been abolished during the reforms. Each regiment comprised four field squadrons and half a squadron which served as the reserve or depot. The field squadrons each comprised four officers, two cadets, nine non-commissioned officers, two trumpeters, one farrier, six *carabinieri*, 108 mounted privates and 12 dismounted privates, giving a total of 145 men of all ranks. The regimental staff comprised one colonel, one lieutenant-colonel, two majors, two adjutants, two standard bearers and nine other staff, a total strength of 674 men (first regiment in the brigade) or 673 men (second regiment), including the reserves. The two reserve half squadrons from each brigade were merged to form a single reserve squadron of 147 men of all ranks (*squadrone di riserba*). Each squadron was divided into four divisions, each led by an officer and a second sergeant or cadet. Each division comprised three squads, which were each led by either a *carabinieri* or a corporal and each comprised nine mounted and one dismounted private. Each squadron was also to include 24 privates, mounted on light Calabrian horses and armed with rifled carbines, to act as flankers or reserves.

The Royal decree was designed to increase the cavalry strength from 3,132 men to 5,392 men, including the brigade commanders. The first brigade, the only 'model' brigade, comprising the Reggimento Re and Reggimento Regina were brought up to strength by drawing men from the four other regiments, Napoli, Principe, Rossiglione and Tarragona. The other six regiments could temporarily only deploy two field squadrons, until the end of 1794, when Reggimento Rossiglione could deploy a third squadron and Reggimento Napoli could deploy all four squadrons.

In January 1796, the regiments Napoli, Sicilia, Borbone, Rossiglione and Tarragona were all ordered to recruit to the planned war establishment strength. In March 1796, Reggimento Napoli, under the orders of *Brigadiere* Prospero Ruiz and *Colonello* Antonio Pinedo, was ordered to join the other three regiments in Lombardy. Later that year, the Corpo dei Volontari Nobili di Cavalleria (Volunteer Noble Cavalry), was formed (27 June 1796), comprising 12 squadrons, one from each province with a total strength of 400 men. A further three squadrons were then raised in Sicily. However, the corps was disbanded in July of the following year.[201]

De Pommereul began his reforms of the artillery by replacing the old organisations with a new Corpo Reale, incorporating all aspects of the artillery and engineering arm. The Corpo Reale comprised a general staff, two artillery regiments, a company of artificers, and various officers assigned to the artillery directorates, commands and armaments factories.

The general staff of the Corpo Reale comprised a director in chief and an inspector (with the rank of general), six directors (colonels), nine sub-directors (lieutenant colonels) and nine *maggiore* (10 in wartime). The inspector had under his command a secretariat composed of a first secretary, two assistants and a draftsman. Three artillery commissaries were also established. The directorates were spread geographically throughout the two kingdoms, including the arsenal at Naples.

201 Boeri and Crociani, *L'Esercito Borbonico*, pp.71–74; *Tenente Generale* Filippo Spinelli.

The two artillery regiments were the Reggimento del Re Artiglieria and the Reggimento della Regina Artiglieria. Each regiment comprised 18 companies, increased to 20 in wartime, of which 16 (18 in wartime) were artillerymen and two were sappers and miners. The staff of each regiment comprised a *colonnello*, a *tenante colonnello*, five *maggiore*, two *aiutante maggiore*, a first and second surgeon, a chaplain, a drum-major, a *profosso* (provost), with the rank of *caporale*, and five bandsmen. The fifth major of the second regiment was to be appointed only in wartime, when the additional companies were formed.

The regiments were divided into two battalions, each of which comprised two brigades of artillery and a half brigade of sappers and miners. The two artillery brigades each comprised four artillery companies and the half brigade of sappers and miners was made up of two companies. The two additional artillery companies completed the third brigade in time of war. Each company had five officers, nine non-commissioned officers, four fireworkers, a drummer, 24 other ranks and eight trainees. In wartime a further 24 trainees were added, bringing the strength of the company to five officers and 72 other ranks. Two volunteers from the nobility were also permitted. Each company was divided into four squads led by a *sergente*. The regiments also had a number of cadets from the military academy serving with the rank of infantry *alfiere*.

One of the artillery regiments was to remain in garrison in Naples where the artillery school had been established. The first battalion of the other regiment was based in the Kingdom of Sicily with garrisons along the coast. The second battalion provided garrisons for the mainland coasts.

There was also an invalid company comprising 100 men in peacetime and 130 men in wartime, each man had to have served no less than 24 years, including 16 in the artillery. The Corpo Reale also included the various civilian roles needed to support the service as well as the artillery school and the necessary supporting schools in mathematics, physics and chemistry.

In 1793 companies of coastal artillerymen were raised by training local inhabitants.

In June 1796 the Corpo Reale was also ordered to serve the artillery of the infantry battalions. A brigade of field engineers for surveying and engineering work was also raised, which was later transferred to the general staff (6 September 1796).

Unsurprisingly, the guns were designed according to the patterns of Gribeauval, according to the *Regolamento 1792*, including 4-pdr, 12-pdr, 16-pdr and 24-pdr long guns, 6-inch and 8-inch howitzers, 8-inch and 12-inch mortars and a light mortar (*petrièro*).[202]

The Kingdom of Naples also had a provincial militia, first raised in 1563 and reorganised in 1782, which comprised 120 companies of 125 men. The men were volunteers aged between 18 and 36 years old, of good conduct, who undertook to provide, for 10 years, a service of Sunday training days, a camp of eight days a year for further training and manoeuvres, as well as any extraordinary service that might be required. The first task of these companies was to maintain public order and defend the coasts from possible incursions. Secondly, they provided a partly trained reserve for the line regiments.

202 Boeri and Crociani, *L'Esercito Borbonico*, pp.79–83.

The royal household troops were provided by the Compagnia delle Reali Guardie del Corpo, the Reale Compagnia Degli Alabardieri and the Cacciatori Reali. The Compagnia delle Reali Guardie del Corpo was initially created in 1734 but reorganised in 1785. The company numbered 160 men in 1790 and 180 men in 1791, under the command of the Prince of Stigliano. In 1794 the company comprised a captain (the Prince of Stigliano), a *tenante*, an *aiutante*, two standard bearers, a surgeon, a chaplain, 10 supernumaries (*esenti*), four brigadiers, five sub-brigadiers, four musicians, a farrier and a saddler, 13 cadets, and 115 guardsmen, divided into two brigades.

Of the men, 15 guardsmen in each brigade served on foot and the rest were mounted. Additionally, 13 boys per brigade were employed to help with the management of the stables.[203] However, masonic infiltration resulted in the dissolution of the company and the forming of a new one (31 October 1795). The new royal corps of guards retained the old officers (with the rank of general officers), but the guards were chosen from among all army officers, who were assigned to this post in turn. The Corps was to be composed of a commanding general (Prince of Stigliano, the previous captain of the company), a general inspector (Prince of Canneto), two major-generals one of whom was supernumerary (Marquis of Arienzo and Don Giuseppe Minutolo), 10 supernumeraries, two major adjutants, a quartermaster, a minor staff of 73 men, and five captains of the army (three of infantry and two cavalry), nine first lieutenants (five infantry and four cavalry), 40 second lieutenants and 24 ensigns from the cavalry who served as horse guards and 80 second lieutenants as infantry, serving as Foot Guards, for a total of 248 men.

The minor staff was composed of a chaplain, a surgeon, four musicians, a farrier and a saddler, a gunsmith, four invalid sergeants (two cavalry and two infantry), 40 cavalry invalids and 20 infantry invalids.

The Reale Compagnia Degli Alabardieri dated back to the beginning of the Bourbon dynasty and wore uniforms based on that of the Swiss Papal Guards. Originally it mounted guard at the palace. As part of Acton's reforms, the old company was replaced in 1785, by a company comprising a captain, two sergeants, four corporals and 36 halberdiers, whose duties involved the transmission of orders and messages. A similar company was based in Palermo, Sicily. In 1790 the two companies were reported to number 86 men. The Cacciatori Reali were formed in 1777 and comprised two companies of 66 men each. These men accompanied the king on his hunting expeditions.[204]

Initially Naples attempted to be neutral as the war began, but reneged on its declaration of neutrality in July 1793, sending an expedition to help the allies hold Toulon. At the beginning of August 1793, a draft of 16,000 men, equal to four per thousand of the population of the continental part of the kingdom, was ordered, destined to serve for the duration of the war comprising 60 battalions and 20 squadrons of volunteers. However, a lack of volunteers and money meant that this draft was not realised in full, even though the purchase of exemptions was banned.

To support the Austrians in their campaigns in northern Italy, 12 squadrons of cavalry were sent to Lombardy from three regiments (5 July 1794). The first brigade formed the bulk of this force which was completed by a third regiment of four squadrons, in the

203 Boeri and Crociani, *L'Esercito Borbonico*, pp.94–95.
204 Boeri and Crociani, *L'Esercito Borbonico*, pp.96–97, 101.

uniform of the Reggimento Principe, but taking men from the regiments Tarragona, Napoli and Sicilia as well as from Reggimento Principe itself. The three regiments were commanded by *Colonello* Barone Abramo de Bock (Re), *Colonello* Henrico Barone di Moetsch (Regina) and *Colonello* Francesco Federici (Principe). The strength of these 12 squadrons was 1,686 men, with each squadron mustering only 110 troopers. A single reserve corps of 120 men, 10 from each squadron was formed in the kingdom for this force, but it was soon dissolved.[205]

The divisional arrangement of the infantry was modified in 1795:[206]

Regiment	Brigade	Division
Re	1	1
Regina		
Real Borbone	2	
Real Farnese		
Real Napoli	3	2
Real Palermo		
Real Italiano	4	
Real Campania		
1° Illirico	5	3
2° Illirico		
Puglia	6	
Lucania		
Sannio	7	4
Messapia		
Calabria	8	
Agrigento		
Siracusa	9	5
Borgogna		

Finally, throughout the period, when threatened with foreign invasion, bodies of volunteers, both infantry and cavalry, were raised, at their own expense, by the nobles or the wealthy across the kingdom, to rush to its defence.

In 1796 and 1797, eight new cavalry regiments were raised, organised similarly to the regulars. These regiments were the Principessa, Real Ferdinando, 1° and 2° Principe Leopoldo, Principe Alberto, Real Carolina, and the 1° and 2° Abbruzzo.[207]

205 Boeri and Crociani, *L'Esercito Borbonico*, pp.73–74.
206 Boeri and Crociani, *L'Esercito Borbonico*, p.52.
207 Boeri and Crociani, *L'Esercito Borbonico*, pp.70, 74.

United Provinces[208]

The United Provinces were a seafaring nation, and this was where the government's priorities lay. Consequently, when the revolution in France began the army of the United Provinces had been somewhat neglected. The component units of the army were actually paid by and in the service of the individual Provinces, rather than the central government. However, the Provinces then placed their units under the command of the Stadtholder, Prince William V of Orange-Nassau, in consultation with the States General. In 1792 the army comprised 44,823 men. The guard infantry comprised the Regiment Hollandsche Gardes (two battalions), Vriesche Gardes (one company), the Garde-Zwitsers (one strong battalion of eight companies) and the Groningsche Gardes (one company).

There were 32 line infantry regiments and five line Swiss regiments. There was also one battalion of Walloon infantry, one battalion of *jagers*, the Amsterdam garrison (400 men) and two regiments of marines. The marine regiments actually served with the field army (regiments N.19 Douglas and N.21 Westerloo) The infantry regiments were numbered (in part) but generally known by the name of their colonel. At this time each regiment (including the marines) comprised two battalions each of a grenadier company and six musketeer companies. However, the Swiss regiments had no separate grenadier company, but each of the six musketeer companies had an allocation of grenadiers. In all there were 36,562 infantry, but the 500 light infantry provided by the *jagers* was woefully inadequate to meet the demands of the coming war.

The cavalry comprised the Garde du Corps, the Regiment Gardes te Paard (Horse Guards), the Regiment Garde Dragonders, six line cavalry regiments, two line dragoon regiments and one regiment of hussars. The cavalry, dragoon and hussar regiments each comprised four squadrons each of two companies, the exception being the Garde du Corps which had only one squadron, giving a total of 4,012 cavalry.

The artillery regiment comprised four battalions, each of five companies of approximately 140 men, each of which served eight guns in the field.

This army was also charged with providing the garrisons for some 40 fortresses and 80 other cities and places. To assist in this task German auxiliaries were taken into Dutch service, the Korps van Mecklenburg (a grenadier battalion and two musketeer battalions, each of four companies, 1,000 men in total), a brigade of Brunswick troops (2,906 men) and the Anspach brigade (two battalions and two companies of grenadiers, fusiliers and *jagers*, 1,389 men in all). Finally, five companies of invalids provided the garrisons for the fortresses of Delft, Woudrichem, Naarden, Klundert and Loevestein.

When war came in 1793, the field army was to be commanded by the son of William V, Willem Frederik the Hereditary Prince of Orange-Nassau (later in 1815, King Willem I). To prepare for war the grenadier companies from the regiments were combined into composite battalions, known by the name of their commanders. Furthermore, the musketeer companies of each regiment were combined into a single battalion of eight companies, although most battalions could field only six companies. Similarly, through lack of horses, the cavalry regiments were initially no stronger than two squadrons. In the artillery four companies of horse artillery were newly raised, each serving eight

208 Geert van Uythoven, *Intermezzo 1787–1793*, First Empire 56, January/February 2001, pp.24–30.

guns. The bulk of the artillery was the forty-eight 3-pdr cannon, allocated in pairs to each infantry battalion. There were also three batteries armed with 6-pdr and 12-pdr cannon and 24-pdr howitzers, albeit with an inadequate number of horses and vehicles. Such was the state of neglect that in February 1793, the field army could only muster 16,000 men and 3,000 horses. The army was also lacking in experience as it had seen no serious action for 45 years and had undertaken no real preparation for war. It could not march for more than two or three days without resting to allow stragglers to re-join their units. Furthermore, the fortresses were in a poor state of defence with garrisons that were too small and with insufficient gunners to man the many guns.

Despite these restrictions, which resulted in them being outnumbered on many occasions the average Dutch soldier fought well and the Hereditary Prince of Orange proved a competent commander.

Royalist French

The Vendéan Rebels

The Armées Catholique et Royale were controlled by the *Conseil Supérieur* which was the civil authority created by the leaders of Royalist rebels (27 May 1793). It comprised three *directoires*, military, ecclesiastical and civil.[209] One of its responsibilities was the election of the *généralissime*, in overall command of the Vendéan armies. Cathelineau was the first appointed on 12 June 1793, but when he died of his wounds on 14 July 1793, he was replaced by d'Elbée who was severely wounded at Cholet on 17 October 1793. The 21-year-old Henri de la Rochejaquelein then took on the role on 20 October 1793.

The preparedness of the rebels to fight varied from group to group. At the end of 1793, there were 30,000 in the ranks, including 2,000 cavalry and 50 guns. Of these, 4,000–5,000 were the *corps d'elite*, always prepared to fight so long as they were led by de la Rochejaquelein or Stofflet. Another *corps d'elite* was comprised of 4,000 men including the Chouans of Cadoudal and Cottereau, Bonchamp's Bretons and Stofflet's 'German Legion'.[210] Another 300–400 men were comprised, amongst others, of Prussians and deserters from the army of the Holy Roman Emperor, as well as those of the French Republic. These men were always ready to run away if the *corps d'elite* failed but were happy to share in the spoils of victory. The Royalist command used these men to carry out the various acts of reprisal, shooting prisoners and massacring civilians. The third group comprised some 20,000 men who only appeared when the battles were over.[211]

Tactically this composition played out in three parts, the first line of troops were the gamekeepers, smugglers and poachers armed with pistols and double-barrelled muskets. These men operated as skirmishers on the front and flanks of the Republican formations. The second line comprised the best armed of the peasants, who could charge the Republicans, once the first line troops had unsettled them. The third group comprised the remainder of the peasants, ill-armed and accompanied by priests and women.[212]

209 Ross, *Banners*, p.129.
210 Georges Cadoudal; Jean Cottereau (also known as Jean Chouan); Charles Melchior Artus de Bonchamps, Marquis de Bonchamps.
211 Ross, *Banners*, p.260–262.
212 Phipps, *West*, pp.6–7.

The Chouannerie

The Royalist rebels north of the river Loire in Brittany, the west of Maine and Normandy were much less organised than those south of the river. These rebels took their name, Chouan, from a nickname of two of their leaders, Jacques Cottereau and his brother. Although organised into *divisions* commanded by a military commander, nominated by the *Émigré* high command in Great Britain, there was no *Chouan* army, the rebels instead formed into small groups of armed rebels whose main method of warfare was to ambush the government troops and their supply convoys as and when the opportunities arose, using the abundant hedgerows as cover. These local groups would vary in size from 50 to a few hundred men. As an example, the Dinan division comprised volunteers from 34 parishes and was commanded by Victor Collas de la Baronnais, previously a lieutenant in the 48e Régiment d'Infanterie de Ligne (Régiment d'Artois).[213]

The Émigré Forces

The emigration of so many officers and indeed whole units from the French army enabled the royal Princes, with financial assistance from their allies, to establish significant Émigré forces on the frontiers of France.

Armée de Condé

Raised and commanded by Louis-Joseph de Bourbon, Prince de Condé, the cousin of Louis XVI of France, this force served throughout the War of the First Coalition. Initially 25,000 men it was soon reduced to 5,000 by the end of 1792. With funding from Britain, it recovered to 10,000 men in 1796. The army fought on the river Rhine with the Austrians.

The following émigré cavalry units were serving with the Austrians: Maison des Princes, Régiment Dragones d'Enghein, Régiment Noble à Cheval d'Angoulème, Chevaliers de la Couronne, Légion de Mirabeau, Hussards de Dauphin, de Salm and de Rohan.[214] The infantry units included the regiments Chasseurs Nobles (became Noble à Pied Condé in 1797, two battalions), Grenadiers Bourbon (two battalions), de Rohan and Durand (one battalion), Légion de Mirabeau (infantry and artillery) and the Brigade de Hohenlohe. The infantry battalions of the Régiment Chasseurs Nobles and Régiment des Grenadiers Bourbon comprised nine companies. The Régiment Durand had a chasseur company a grenadier company and eight fusilier companies. The cavalry had five squadrons each of two companies.[215]

Armée des Princes

This force was raised in Trier by King Louis XVI's brothers, the Comte de Provence and the Duc d'Artois. With a strength of 10,000 men, the army served alongside Brunswick's army in the initial Allied invasion of France. However, after Valmy the army was disbanded (24 November 1792).

---

213 Esdaile, *Wars*, p.192; Jacques de Roussel, *État Militaire de France* (Paris: Onfroy, 1792), p.137.

214 Sapherson, *Armies*, p.6.

215 René Bittard des Portes, *Histoire de l'armée de Condé pendant la Révolution française (1791–1801)* (Paris: Dentu, 1896), pp.25, 388–396.

The infantry regiments included: the Chasseurs Royaux des Princes, Chasseurs Carabiniers de Wittgenstein, Chasseurs Royaux de Provence; Régiments de Dillon, de Walsh, de Vexin,de Wittegnstein, de Berwick, Marine Royale, Hommes d'armes à pied, Coalition de Bretagne, Institution de Saint Louis. There were also several composite units and companies of the officers from a variety of their old Royal regiments.

The cavalry regiments included the Hussards de Bercheny, de Saxe and de Chamorant-Lauzon, Chasseurs Étrangers de Polignac, Hommes d'Armes à Cheval, Compagnies Nobles d'Ordonnance, Grenadiers d'Ordonnance à Cheval, Gardes du Corps du Roi, Gardes du Corps des Princes, Régiment Royale Allemand. As with the infantry there were also several composite units and companies of officers.[216]

Units Serving with the Spanish

Several smaller units were raised in Spain for service in campaigns against France including the Légion de Panetier (400 men raised in 1793), the Légion du Vallespir (raised in 1793), the Légion Royale des Pyrénées (less than 1,000 infantry and cavalry raised in 1794), Royal Roussillon (200 men raised in 1794). After Spain left the First Coalition the remains of these units became the Régiment de Bourbon, a regular unit of the Spanish army.

Units Serving with the Dutch

Several units served with the army of the United Provinces before transferring to British pay in 1795:

Béon: 230 men raised in 1793.

Damas Legion: 596 men comprising two companies of chasseurs and four of fusiliers. Raised in 1793.[217]

Loewenstein's Fusiliers: 700 men raised in 1794.

Lüninick Light Infantry: raised in 1794.

Pfaffenhofen Legion of Germans: 1,200 infantry and 800 hussars raised in 1794.

Wittgenstein Infantry regiment: 900 men raised in 1794.

Units Serving with the British

([Q] denotes units that fought in the Quiberon expedition)

A large number of Émigré units, both large and small, served with the British army during the War of the First Coalition. Several proved relatively insignificant and/or short-lived forces of less than half battalion strength (the 'regiments' of Autichamp, Béthisy, Broglie, Castries, Léon, Trésor, Williamson, Allonville, Carneville, Corsican Chasseurs, Corsican Light Dragoons, Hompesch's Chasseurs, Hompesch's Mounted Rifles, Montmorency-Laval, Mortemart, Périgord Light Infantry[Q], Power's Chasseurs, Royal Louis, Vioménil and Warren's Hussars[Q]).

216 Bazouges and Nichols, *For God and King*, pp.293–295.
217 Bazouges and Nichols, *For God and King*, pp.96–97, 168.

Other units were however more significant, including:

> Raised in 1793: Dresnay Regiment^{Q} (700 men, originally raised as Dresnay's Legion), Loyal Emigrant Regiment^{Q} (720 infantry plus two light guns), Uhlans Britannique (600 men), York Hussars (600 men), York Rangers (600 men).
>
> Raised in 1794: Choiseul's Hussars (682 men in six hussar companies with a horse artillery company), Corsican Gendarmerie (600 men), Hervilly's Regiment^{Q} (1,318 infantry), Hompesch's Hussars (1,100 men), Rohan's Hussars (1,200 men in two regiments), Rohan's Light Infantry (788 men and two battalion guns), Roll's Regiment (1,698 men in two battalions), Rotalier's French Emigrant Artillery^{Q} (600 men), Royal Anglo Corsicans (four battalions reduced to two in 1795), Salm-Kirburg Hussars (912 men including a company of horse artillery, originally served with the Armée du Condé in 1792–1793), Salm-Kirburg Light Infantry^{Q} (850 men).
>
> Raised in 1795: Corsican Regiment (675 infantry), Edward Dillon's Regiment (two battalions, 750 men in each), Hector's Royal Marine^{Q} (700 infantry), Royal Étranger Regiment (1035 infantry with battalion guns), Waldstein's Light Infantry Regiment (800 men).
>
> Raised in 1796: Hompesch's Light Infantry (1,150 men).

These units, while having French officers, recruited widely in the Netherlands, Germany, Switzerland and Spain. Similar units were also raised in the West and East Indies and in South Africa.[218]

Uhlans Britannique Charging a French Column

218 René Chartrand and Patrice Courcelle, *Émigré and Foreign Troops in British Service (1) 1793–1802* (Oxford: Osprey, 1999), pp.6–41.

The Navies of the Major Powers, 1790[219]

	Ships of the line (50 guns or more)	Frigates (20–44 guns)
Austria	0	2
France	81	69
Great Britain	195	210
Prussia	0	0
Spain	72	41
Naples	10	10
United Provinces	44	43
Venice	20	10

The Austrian navy comprised only two 20-gun cutters, based in Ostend, during the War of the First Coalition, after which it acquired the Venetian navy from the Treaty of Campo Formio in 1797.

219 Otto von Pivka, *Navies of the Napoleonic Era* (Newton Abbott: 1980), p.30; based on Fulton's 1810 numbers which do not necessarily focus on just those ships actually in service.

5

Wargaming the Period

For the beginner, setting out to wargame any period in history can be rather daunting as there are so many choices at your fingertips, for which the internet only serves to express the bewildering scope of those choices: What figure scale/size should I use? How many figures will I need? How do I paint the figures? Which rules should I use? What terrain should I use? How big a playing area do I need?

One starting point is to decide which sort of games you want to play? Do you want the game to present the players with the challenges facing an army commander, a corps commander, a division or brigade commander, a battalion commander, or an individual soldier? In this sense the level of the game is determined by the basic manoeuvre unit in the game, which is the smallest common grouping of miniatures that moves and fights together in the game. Thus, *Sharp Practice* is approximately a company level game, with the player acting as a battalion commander, *Black Powder*™ is a battalion level game, with the player acting as a division or corps commander, *Field of Glory Napoleonic* and *Volley and Bayonet* are brigade level games with the player acting as a corps commander, while *De Bellis Napoleonicis* is a division level game, with the player taking the role of the army commander. As you move up this scale of games, the time represented by each turn in the game generally increases from minutes to an hour. For naval games there is a similar distinction between fleet actions, squadron actions and single ship actions.

This distinction between games does not mean that you cannot fight the entirety of large battles with battalion level rulesets such as *Black Powder*™, *Shako* or *Lasalle II*. However, this is usually only achieved using teams of wargamers. Perhaps the best-known recent example is 'The Great Game: Waterloo Replayed' at Glasgow University in June 2019, where 80 wargamers and 40 veterans refought Waterloo in its entirety using *Black Powder*™ rules, over two days, with 22,500 28mm miniatures on three parallel tables each six feet wide and 80 feet long.

Taking one of the scenarios in this volume as an example, the battle of Castiglione in 1796, involved 42 French battalions and 30 Austrian battalions. There is no reason why a single player on each side could not manage this force using a battalion level ruleset such as *Black Powder*™, but it would take a lot of time and require a larger table than most of us could fit into our homes. Thus, to refight Castiglione with every battalion represented, would normally require teams of two or more players on each side, playing on a table of at least 12 feet by six feet. Oftentimes the width of the table required exceeds that which is practical for reaching the centre of the table, this often leads to further compromises in how the battle is represented. The alternative for single players is to refight the battle, on a six by four foot table at division level using, for example, *De Bellis Napoleonicis*, where the players are managing just three and five division sized units or using *Volley and Bayonet* or *Field of Glory Napoleonic* with eight and 13 brigade size units.

An alternative approach to designing scenarios is known as 'bathtubbing', a term coined by Frank Chadwick, one of the authors of *Volley and Bayonet*. In this approach all games are played at the battalion level, by representing larger formations such as brigades and even divisions by single, or at least fewer battalions than the historical reality. This allows the game to be accommodated on a smaller table, using a more reasonable number of figures. The disadvantage of this approach is that the game focuses the gamer's attention on the management of battalions in battle rather than presenting the command challenges of dealing with the higher levels of command.

When forming judgements about different rulesets it is important to recognise what each set was designed to represent and judge it accordingly. There will never be one set of wargame rules that is 100 percent compatible with all the scenarios that we can design and play.

Another dimension to consider is the role of luck in the games. Historically fortune has played and will always play a large part in how battles and wars are fought and resolved. Consequently, most wargames fall somewhere in the middle of a scale of luck between chess at one extreme, where luck is eliminated, to snakes and ladders at the other, where luck is the dominant feature in determining the outcome of the game. Most wargamers are happy to play games where firing and close combat results are driven by die rolls or playing card draws, some are less happy to play games where the movement of units is driven by random factors or even prevented by an unlucky die roll. Particularly in multiplayer games where each player controls only a small number of units, it can be frustrating if those units are prevented from moving throughout the game by an unlucky series of die rolls.

Another choice to be made relates to the degree of complexity involved in playing the game. There tends to be an artificial relationship between the 'realism' offered by the rules and their complexity. Modern rules tend to have all come down on the side of increased playability. An example from a battalion level game will perhaps explain this choice more vividly. If you imagine an infantry battalion approaching another defending battalion. When the attacking battalion gets to within charge range of the defenders, we need to understand whether the attacking unit has the courage to close with their enemy. Assuming they do, we then need to know whether the defending unit will stand to receive the attacker and is able to fire on them as they charge.

After the defenders have fired, we need to know if the attackers have been stopped by the discharge or whether they are able to charge into contact. Finally, we need to know whether the defenders stand against the charge, creating a melee. In total this single incident could require the morale of both the defenders and the attackers to be checked twice each, and there are rulesets which handle the situation in this way. This can massively slow down game play and consequently most modern rulesets tend to abstract this situation. For example, *Black Powder*™ allows the attacking unit to move into contact and then the defenders fire closing fire, which may or may not cause the attackers to take a break test. The melee is then fought. However, if the attackers are beaten off, we do not know when in the process the attack failed, did they simply fail to charge, fail to charge home or were they beaten in the hand-to-hand melee. Likewise, if the defenders lose, we do not know if bayonets were crossed or when they retreated. Consequently, *Black Powder*™ describes this phase of the game as close combat reflecting everything from duels of close-range musket fire to actual melee with sabres and bayonets in action. Similarly, some rulesets will reduce movement by 10 percent for moving uphill, but such detail is superfluous in a game like *Black Powder*™ where a unit can move once, twice or three times in a turn. Wargamers need to understand where they stand on these issues in order to determine the type of game they want to play and to choose their rulesets accordingly.

For all these reasons it is not necessary to worry about settling on just one set of rules as you will soon have a dozen or more different rulesets on your shelf. Each set will perform a different role in your games. The wargamer may choose to play all his games at one level, for example battalion level, or may use different levels of game, with different rulesets, for specific games.

Although enjoyable wargames can be played by simply placing your troops on some random terrain, the best wargames are generally scenario driven. In these games the scenario is designed to let both players understand their forces, objectives, and victory conditions, as well as the impact that the terrain will have on the application of the rules. It is important that these scenarios also address the balance of the game. It is not essential that both sides have the same forces, what is essential is that the victory conditions allow both sides to win. The victory conditions for the side with greater resources will be more difficult to achieve than those for the side with lesser resources. In this sense resources means both the type and number of troops plus any terrain advantages or disadvantages.

I prefer to base my scenarios on either the whole or part of historical battles, such as those included in this volume. In wargames rules today it is common not to tackle the subject of scales, by which I mean ground scale, figure scale and timescale. While this is perfectly acceptable for playing the games, when establishing historical scenarios, it is important to have a grasp of these issues to make the scenarios representative of the historical action. To establish the number of game turns that will make up the scenario, it is obviously important to understand the relationship between the game turn and the time represented on the tabletop. This relationship in most games is often flexible and not fixed, but to establish the game length a general idea of the average needs to be arrived at. Similarly, to plan the terrain on the tabletop it is important to understand the ground scale in the game, that is, what distance is represented by each centimetre or inch on the tabletop.

The relationship between the troops and the terrain it occupies is a significant feature in war and needs to be replicated in our games. In particular, the area taken up by buildings needs to be understood and represented. For example, representing La Haye Sainte by a building on the same scale as that of the miniatures in a battalion level game will result in anomalies in the gameplay, because the total area on the tabletop taken up by the scale model would be many times the reality, due to the difference between the miniature scale and ground scale. Figure scale or the number of real soldiers represented by each miniature, has obvious application to the design of scenarios using the real orders of battle. However, in modern games the figure scale is less important than replicating the frontage of the manoeuvre units. A brigade, battalion or company needs to occupy a realistic frontage on the tabletop, but the number of miniatures is less important. However, games such as *Sharp Practice* still use the removal of miniatures to track casualties.

Rather than using historical events to drive your scenarios, there are a number of published books and online resources with ready-made scenarios that can be converted to most rulesets. 'Tabletop Teasers' are a series of scenarios, which are freely available online.[1] These scenarios, originally published in 1978–1982, have stood the test of time and tend to be relatively small games which are ideal for the beginner. They however can easily be scaled up to larger games and can be easily applied to the War of the First Coalition. These scenarios are inspired by history rather than attempts to recreate history, which has the advantage of the scenario design being focused on creating a good and challenging game for both sides.

Another interesting approach to setting up games is to run a campaign of several linked scenarios, the outcome of one impacting, in some way, the set up for the next scenario. There are several ways to do this, from more complex map movement-based approaches down to simple knockout tournament style campaigns.[2]

There is no perfect wargame, each game or scenario designer wrestles with the compromises entailed in the representation of battle using toy soldiers on a tabletop. Despite having scaled frontages, most wargame units are too deep, taking up more space than necessary, because we do not usually play with one miniature representing one real soldier. The scale buildings will take up more space than they should, and because the ground scale needs to be defined so as to fit a reasonable battlefield on the table, the vertical scale is usually different to the ground scale. Finally, by definition, unlike their historical counterparts, the wargamer can see everything on the table at all times. It is worth understanding these compromises and designing the scenarios with them very much in mind. None of these compromises have prevented wargamers having enjoyable and exciting games.

When choosing a set of wargames rules, personal preference is clearly important. For example, *Shako* and *Lasalle* do not allow cavalry counter charges because to allow it slows down the gameplay. This is a perfectly reasonable choice for the designer to make, even though we know cavalry counter charges have a historical basis, as not every historical event needs to be mimicked in successful wargames. If this design choice does not tally with a wargamer's vision for his/her games, they will look elsewhere.

The foregoing discussion is applicable to most wargames however there are some aspects that are specific to our period.

In his book *War Games through the Ages Vol. III, 1792–1859*, published in 1975, the great wargame pioneer, Donald Featherstone, rated the armies of the War of the First Coalition using a scoring system based on three levels, above average (3), average (2) and below average (1) against a series of criteria judged for each year of the war;[3]

1 Tabletop teasers: < https://steve-the-wargamer.blogspot.com/p/word-document-jpgs-of-original-article.html>, accessed 13 March 2022.

2 See Steve's Balagan website at: < https://balagan.info/wargaming/campaign>, accessed 14 March 2022.

3 Donald F. Featherstone, *War Games through the Ages, Vol. III 1792–1859* (London: Stanley Paul, 1975), pp.87–100.

Donald Featherstone's Ratings of the Armies of the War of the First Coalition						
French						
	1792	1793	1794	1795	1796–1797 Germany	1796–1797 Italy
Commanders	2	3	3	2	2	3
Subordinate Commanders					3	3
Army Composition	2	1	3	3	2	3
Training	1	1	3	3	2	2
Discipline	1	1	2	3	2	3
Morale	3	3	3	2	2	3
Tactical System	1	3	3	3	3	2
Tactical Formation	2	3	3	3	3	2
Speed of Manoeuvre	2	3	3	3	3	3
Arms and Equipment	3	3	3	3	2	2
Weapon Handling	2	2	2	3	3	3
Special factors	1	2	1	-1	-	2
	20	25	29	27	27	31
Allies						
Commanders	2	1	1	2	3	1
Subordinate Commanders					1	1
Army Composition	2	2	2	2	2	3
Training	2	2	2	2	3	2
Discipline	2	2	2	2	2	3
Morale	1	1	1	1	2	2
Tactical System	2	2	1	1	2	1
Tactical Formation	2	2	2	1	2	1
Speed of Manoeuvre	1	1	1	1	2	1
Arms and Equipment	3	3	3	3	2	3
Weapon Handling	2	2	2	3	2	2
Special factors	-	-	-	-	-	-
	19	18	17	18	23	20

Although these ratings show a marked bias towards the French which perhaps owes more to the perception of their strategic victory over the allies rather than their actual battlefield performance, they do offer a useful and visual way of comparing any two forces that we might be bringing together in a scenario. In truth, the quality of the armies was too heterogeneous to allow its reduction to a single number and we need to look at each potential scenario in detail to get an accurate picture. For Featherstone the key features in his analysis of the French were the poor training of the infantry although improving over time, the extensive use of tirailleurs, the lack of cavalry and its poor quality, excellent artillery, the numbers brought to the field armies by the *levée en masse* and excellent commanders and subordinate commanders. Featherstone's view of the allies appears dominated by their average and below average commanders and subordinate commanders, their excellent cavalry, their slow movement, and his belief that the linear tactical system was inferior (average or below average) to the French use of the column for movement and line for fire combat combination (above average). However, it is fair to say that the combat record summarised in chapter three suggests that the two systems were closer in their overall effectiveness than Featherstone's ratings suggest.

The key features of the art of warfare during the War of the First Coalition, semi-permanent all-arms division versus ad hoc columns, differing use of use of skirmishers, increased use of horse artillery, the use of battalion guns, large numbers of poorly trained troops, can be accommodated or emphasised by different rulesets targeting different levels of play. The orders of battle are a key part of creating a wargame force that can behave realistically on the wargames table, but other special rules can be introduced into most rulesets thus ensuring the game has a War of the First Coalition feel to it. For example, in *Black Powder*™ it is sensible to restrict the use of 'attack column' to just the French. This may at first seem odd because other nations had columns of manoeuvre on a platoon or two platoon frontage, but to reflect the way the armies fought, defining the columns of other nations as 'march columns' both encourages historically accurate tactics and discourages anachronistic column-on-column close combat.[4]

The rulesets that have support materials relating to the War of the First Coalition include:

Company Level: *Sharp Practice*

Battalion Level: *Black Powder*™ (with the *Last Argument of Kings* supplement), *Shako II* (the *Fields of Glory* supplement includes scenarios for Castiglione and Rivoli), *Lasalle II.*

Brigade and Higher Level: *Field of Glory Napoleonic 2nd Edition, Volley and Bayonet, De Bellis Napoleonicis, Et Sans Resultat III, Napoleon's Battles 4th Edition.*

Of these *Field of Glory Napoleonics* deals with our period in some detail in the *Emperors and Eagles* volume.[5]

4 Esdaile, *Wars*, pp.46–47.
5 Terry Shaw and Mike Horah, *Emperors and Eagles* (Oxford: Osprey, 2012), pp.9–55.

Although not focused on our period, Paddy Griffith's *Napoleonic Wargaming for Fun* contains several sets of rules which demonstrate the playing of wargames at different unit levels, which can all be adapted to the War of the First Coalition.[6]

Rating Generals

Many wargame rules provide mechanisms for distinguishing between the generals in a game based on their historical performance. For example, *Black Powder*™ uses a system of *staff ratings* which range from five to 10, where five is a 'fool' and 10 is a 'military genius' but most games use the centre of the range; six ('poor'), seven ('average') and eight ('good'). What follows is a list of some of the generals who feature in the military chronology above, rated from poor to excellent, taken from Avalon Hill's *Napoleon's Battles*. The reader is free to use this list with their favourite ruleset or simply use is it as the starting point for a friendly discussion.[7]

Nation	Poor	Average	Good		Excellent
France	Carteaux	Berthier	Augereau	Miranda	Bonaparte
	Dufour	Beurnoville	Beaumont	Miollis	Davout
		Bourcier	Bernadotte	Moncey	Desaix
		Brune	Bon	Moreau	Guieu
		Delaborde	Cervoni	Pichegru	Hoche
		Delmas	Dallemagne	Rampon	Joubert
		Despinoy	Dampierre	Ricard	Lannes
		Doppet	Delaborde	Robert	Lefebvre
		Dugommier	Duhesme	Saint-Cyr	Masséna
		Dumerbion	Dumas	Sauret	Murat
		Fiorella	Dumouriez	Sérurier	Ney
		Garnier	Dupont	Souham	Oudinot
		Jourdan	Grenier	Vaubois	Soult
		Leclerc	Grouchy	Verdier	Vandamme
		Macquard	Kellermann	Victor	
		Marescot	Kilmaine		
		Merle	Kléber		
		Moreaux	Lecourbe		
		Pérignon	Loisin		
		Reynier	Macdonald		
		Rusca	Ménard		
		Schérer	Menou		
		Solignac	Milhaud		
		Valence			
		Wimpffen			

6 Paddy Griffith, *Napoleonic Wargaming for Fun* (London: Ward Lock, 1980).

7 S. Craig Taylor and Robert Coggins, *Napoleon's Battles* (Baltimore: Avalon Hill Game Company, 1989), *Scenario Booklet* pp.32–37.

Nation	Poor	Average	Good	Excellent
Austria	Mack	Davidovich Ferdinand Latour Lipthay Ludwig Mészáros Provera Quosdanovich Vukassovich Wartensleben Werneck	Alvinczi Beaulieu Clerfayt Hohenzollern Kaim Kray Ott Wurmser	Charles Melas
Great Britain			Dundas Duke of York	Abercromby Moore
Netherlands & Belgium				
Prussia		Hohenlohe		Brunswick
Sardinia			Colli	
Spain		Cuesta		

Austrian Commanders

6
Building the Forces

Designing your Miniature Armies

In selecting a wargames army to build there are several factors to consider based on your own interests, resources, availability of space and potential opponents. The best approach to selecting a force to be modelled on the wargames table starts with researching historical orders of battle.[1] The advantage of this approach is that whatever game you play the performance of the army that you are recreating in part reflects its organisation. There are two approaches to take. Firstly, you can choose to recreate a specific organisation at a particular battle by copying the order of battle.

Secondly the historical orders of battle offer an indication of the typical structure of brigades and divisions. The numbers of battalions or squadrons in a brigade are worth noting and whether brigades were purely infantry or cavalry or, as the French and Austrians did during our period, a mix of infantry and cavalry in their advanced guard brigades. The historical orders of battle also show how the army's artillery is organised and allocated to regiments, brigades, or divisions. This must all be viewed in the context of your chosen ruleset and more particularly what each individual base of miniatures represents.

My favoured approach is to identify an historical scenario, either a battle or part of a battle, and build the forces based on this fixed order of battle. This has the advantage of being very straightforward as the scenario is focused on a fixed moment in time. The disadvantage is that the forces maybe less useful in other scenarios, although this is an issue that a bit more painting can usually solve. For example, many units can be reused in other games by painting up another command stand with another, more appropriate flag. This approach is particularly useful for the French as the design of their flags changed quite a bit during the War of the First Coalition. If you already have an opponent obviously you need only create one side of a scenario, however there are advantages to creating both sides. Solo wargaming is a good way of learning the rules and understanding how to best use your new force. A good place to start are the

1 See the Nafiziger collection freely available on The Napoleon Series at: <https://www.napoleon-series.org/resources/the-nafziger-collection-of-napoleonic-orders-of-battle/> accessed 8 March 2022.

scenarios within this volume, which cover a good range of the armies involved in the War of the First Coalition.

Finally, a word about the choice of the size of miniatures for your games. Wargame miniatures are available in many sizes from 2mm to 54mm tall and it is certainly possible to play most wargames with any of these sizes. The larger the miniatures the more skilled a painter you need to be and the larger the playing area you are likely to need to get a good game. The other dimension is that the smaller the miniatures give more of a mass visual effect on a normal sized playing area, with more miniatures in each unit. There is no right answer to this choice, it is really a personal preference based on the finished look and how you relate to the inevitable compromises. For me, the 10–15mm miniatures offer a 'sweet spot' providing good games without compromising the spectacle of the game.

How I Paint 15mm Miniatures

Before discussing the very personal process that is painting miniatures, I need to declare my credentials. I have been painting Napoleonic miniatures, mainly but not exclusively 15mm scale, since 1971. I am not and never have been a professional miniature painter and I have never entered my work into any painting competitions. However, since 1971 I have painted almost 6,000 figures, so I have plenty of experience. Consequently, this section is a description of how I paint miniatures, designed to give the novice some things to think about in embarking on this rewarding aspect of the wargaming hobby.

One of the attractions of wargaming is that it brings together a number of skills and crafts, which together with the wargamer's interests and enthusiasm brings the final product to the tabletop. Different wargamers relate to these different crafts and skills in different ways. Some people prefer to spend all their precious hobby time in playing the games themselves and some people conduct all the research, paint all the figures, build the terrain but rarely if ever actually play any games at all. There is no right place to sit on this spectrum, but for me I love the research, the scenario building, the collecting the miniatures and the painting of the miniatures and terrain, as much as I love playing the games themselves.

Amongst these activities painting miniatures has a special place; it is a very relaxing pastime because it cannot be done without complete focus on the job in hand. Like other aspects of the hobby, I like the painting for its own benefits, and yes, I do have painted miniatures that are patiently waiting, in some cases for years, to get onto a wargames table. The painted miniatures are a very physical expression of our relationship to the period. The choices about which figures to use, what uniform to paint and which flags do the unit carry, are direct expressions of our knowledge of the period and the research we have undertaken. This does not mean that you always have to use miniatures selected and painted specifically for the scenario in question to have a good game, but it is true, nonetheless, as any foray onto Facebook will show you. Following that introduction/disclaimer here is a step-by-step guide to how I paint miniatures.

Workspace

While an individual figure might take 30 minutes to one hour to paint, the truth is that that time is broken down into many 5–10-minute jobs, covering a group of miniatures. For that reason, to make the most of your precious spare time, it is well worth establishing a permanent workstation where you paint. You can then establish the lighting, you can never have too much, and the paints, brushes and other tools on a permanent basis. At a stretch this can be a tray that you take from a cupboard at the key time. This will make it quite easy when you have a spare 15 minutes, to sit down and do some painting. Over the years I have tried several magnifying glasses on fixed stands, but these are not really compatible with the manipulation of the miniature during painting. I find reading glasses perfectly adequate.

Time

Wargames armies can be dozens of figures but are often hundreds of figures, each of which needs painting. In most cases when painting a wargames force, we are dealing with the classic 'elephant task' (How do you eat an elephant? One bite at a time!). The thing to remember is that you always have more time than you think and that it is cumulative, once a figure is painted it stays painted. Try to paint as often as you can, and you will be surprised how it mounts up. This is particularly helped if you are able establish a permanent painting station. Another approach is to build your painted force in such a way that you can play smaller games with them along the way, for example the Castiglione scenario for DBN described below or the Whiff of Grapeshot scenario for Sharp Practice.

Planning

Once you have the painting bug, it is easy to get carried away and dive into painting your favourite unit, to get it done as soon as possible. However, planning is a particularly important step, since the worse outcome is to complete the time-consuming step of painting something, only to discover you have painted the wrong miniature, given it the wrong facings or whatever. It is worth taking time out to plan what to paint and in what order and to ensure you have all your uniform reference material to hand.

Another feature of planning is to decide how many miniatures you are going to paint in each batch. A lot of time is spent opening and closing different paints and cleaning brushes, so it makes sense to paint a batch of miniatures together. By the time you have finished using a colour on the sixth model, the first in the batch will be dry and ready for the next colour. The bigger the batch the more efficient the overall process, but how many you paint in a batch is a matter of personal choice. If you are easily bored you will need smaller batches, at the other end of the scale you will find people using dozens of miniatures in a batch. I use either six or 12 miniatures, which allows the units to grow at a reasonable rate and each painting step is very manageable, but you must find what works for you.

Finally, it is worth studying the miniatures in detail to ensure that you can identify each piece of equipment on the miniature. You will often find actual examples of each piece of kit on the internet, either real museum items or, more often, reproductions produced by or for reenactors. This step will enable you to paint with more confidence. If you are just starting out it is best to avoid painting your elite units first, you will become a better painter with practice.

Some of the best and most readily available uniforms guides are listed in Appendix I.

During the First Coalition there were very many French infantry battalions each of which carried a flag. While the designs of the regular army and the demi-brigades that replaced them are well understood, we do not know the design of all the flags of the early volunteer battalions. However, we do know that the design changed over time as the country transitioned from a monarchy to a republic in a number of steps. One way of solving this issue is to choose a flag based on the date the battalion in question was first raised or by extrapolation from other battalions from the same *department,* which have known designs. Battalions raised in 1791 and early 1792 are likely to have flags featuring the white cross with blue and red corner cantons or with the corner cantons in horizontal tricolour format, while those raised after July 1792 are likely to have the first model of the tricolour flag with the stripes either vertical or horizontal. Battalions raised after August 1793 are likely to have the second model of the tricolour flag, with three vertical stripes, the red nearest the shaft and inscribed with the words '*Le Peuple Française debout contre les tyrans*' in the central white section, the whole flag was edged with a red stripe.[2]

Preparing the Miniatures

As with all painting, preparation of the miniature before painting is an important step. Metal castings often have 'flash', extra metal that is a result of the casting process but not part of the finished model. This needs to be removed carefully with a scalpel and sometimes a pin vice drill. For assembled figures, whether metal or plastic you will also need to ensure any unsightly gaps have been filled. The golden rule with this step is that when you think you have got it all, look again as there is bound to be some you have missed.

During the painting process it is important to be able to manipulate the miniature to achieve the best angle of attack for your paint brush, and this cannot easily be achieved by holding it by its base. I glue my miniatures to five-inch wooden sticks that sit in the hand easily thereby enabling the easy inspection and painting of the miniature from any angle. I use superglue for this purpose because it is fast acting and strong, but brittle enabling the miniatures to be removed from the stick relatively easily once painting is complete. Alternatively, you can purchase commercial painting handles for the same function.

Brushes

After a while you will probably have a dozen or even two dozen brushes at any one time. These will have different functions as they age, like old soldiers, brushes do not die they simply fade away. For detailed painting on a miniature, which for 15mm miniatures is pretty much all of it, you need to buy the best quality natural sable brushes you can afford. In my experience the ingenuity of man has yet to come up with an artificial paint

2 Pierre Charrie, *Drapeaux et Étandards de la Révolution et de l'Empire* (Paris: Copernic, 1982), pp.21–23; Ludovic Letrun *French Infantry Flags from 1786 to the end of the First Empire* (Paris: Histoire et Collections, 2009), pp.9, 50–53.

brush fibre to match the endurance of natural sable. The quality of your painting is strongly linked to your ability to maintain a good tip to your brush as this controls how much paint ends up on the model and where it goes. It may be necessary to clean the brush halfway through painting a colour on your batch. The brushes need to be cleaned thoroughly and recently I have found 'The Masters Brush Cleaner and Preserver' extremely useful for maintaining the shape of my brushes. I tend to do most work with brushes in sizes '000', '1' and '3'. At the other end of the scale, you need economy brushes, the sort that remainder bookshops sell in big packs, to do the undercoating of your miniatures. Old worn brushes are often useful for dry brushing and an old worn stubby brush is also useful for fixing mistakes by removing paint from places on the miniature that it should not be. Dry brushing is the technique of highlighting a part of the miniature using a brush with short bristles, from which most of the paint has been removed using a tissue.

Paints

Most people today use acrylic paints which have the significant advantage of being water based making cleaning up extremely easy. There is consequently a vast range of colours available. However, I started out using enamel paints, which require white spirit as thinners and cleaning agent and are therefore less convenient. Enamels also offer a great range of colours, but they are much less popular, and you will not often see them for sale at wargames shows, for example. I still use enamels as I think they offer better coverage and are more durable than the acrylic equivalents, however this may just be a case of '*grognard*' prejudice. If you are using enamels then you need to ensure that the paint has not 'dried out' too much, as you will have less control of the thicker paint on the miniature, likewise if you do thin paint make sure that control is not lost in the other direction. I also use acrylic washes, dilute paints that will quickly create highlights. For example, I use a flesh wash on my miniatures to highlight or bring out the individual facial features and fingers on hands. The key to mixing enamels and acrylics is to leave the miniature to thoroughly dry between coats, I leave mine overnight.

Undercoating or Priming

Undercoating your miniatures before painting is an essential first step in the painting process. There are various options to choose from, when I started out, I used a white undercoat which has the advantage of making the colours in the finished miniature somewhat brighter. However, I switched to black undercoat, which has the significant advantage that any areas left unpainted for whatever reason will show through as the more acceptable black rather than white. There is a whole style of painting based on this effect of deliberately leaving the black undercoat showing through at the point where colours change, creating a black outline effect. Others use grey undercoats and then there is Zenithal priming which uses all three colours to accentuate the shading and highlighting of the finished miniature. I find that black undercoat works well, particularly for the smaller miniatures.

Inside Out

When starting out it is important not to overload your chosen brush with too much paint as you will lose control of the paint once it touches the miniature. The paint should be in the brush not on it, if you see large drops of paint on the brush just knock them off. Paying attention to how your paint flows from the brush pays dividends. If the paint has dried and thickened, then thinning it appropriately and mixing thoroughly will ensure that that the paint flows such that you have proper control of where the paint goes and where it does not. Always attempt to paint all of the detail on the miniature, a detail may be small such as a buckle on a shoe or a tie on a hair queue, but it will always be obvious if you do not paint it, at least on figures which are 15mm or larger.

The golden rule of painting a miniature is to start from the inside and work outwards. This means that you would start with the flesh on the face and then paint the trousers, the jacket, the collar and then the hair and then the hat, cross belts, and weapons. As you paint the interior layers you will undoubtedly get paint on the outer layers but as you paint these errors will be naturally corrected as you move outwards. I stick to this with one exception, for me the flesh has always been the last thing I paint, since painting the face and hands brings the miniature 'alive'.

Right First Time, Saves Time

Concentrating on the painting task helps to ensure that you make fewer mistakes with your painting. Taking care to get it right first time ensures that you spend less time correcting mistakes. At the same time, it is a question of balance because mistakes can always be corrected, so it is not something to be obsessive about. Ensure your brush is looked after and maintains a good point. As soon as the point on your brush cannot be maintained or becomes bent, change it for a new one.

Avoid Using a Colour More Than Once on a Single Miniature

I try to avoid using the same colour for more than one part of the miniature. If, for example, a miniature has several brown items, for example the backpack, the musket, the hair and perhaps a belt, it is worth using a different shade of brown for each of these items. If you use all the same shade the miniature will look more unnatural than it needs to. My exception to this rule is black. A special case of this feature is the painting of white uniformed troops such as Austrians. The best effects are gained by restricting pure white to the cross belts alone, with the jacket and breeches an off white, either a light cream or light grey colour. White trousers can be achieved by a first coat of a light grey with a dry brush with pure white.

Painting Outer Edges

On smaller miniatures space is a premium and painting the piping on shoulder straps or turnbacks can be a challenge. In these cases, the miniature designer is your friend, the thickness of these items tends to be exaggerated. This enables us to use the edge of the piece to emphasise the colour. Another approach is to paint the piping first and, for example, for the turnbacks on French infantry coats paint the white up to the piping, which may be easier than painting the red piping after the white.

Touching up your Work

Once all the different paints are on the miniature, it is time to inspect each miniature in detail to find the paint that is not where it is supposed to be and those parts of the miniature that have been missed. Normally it is the first paints on the miniature that will need the most touching up. It is more time efficient to do this as a separate step for the whole batch, but if I spot an error during the main painting process that might be overlooked in this step, I will stop and correct it there and then. During this phase it may also be necessary to give a second coat to some of the lighter colours, for example yellow often needs two coats.

Highlighting

Highlighting has a long pedigree in the painting of miniatures, dating back to a time when miniatures were semi-flat. Highlighting a miniature by painting darker tones on the low parts of the miniature, such as at the bottom of creases, and lighter tones on the higher/outer parts of the miniature, was a good way of making those flat miniatures seem more three dimensional than they were. This style of painting has carried over into the painting of today's miniatures, where it emphasises and enhances the natural effect of light on the miniature. The technique is particularly useful on 28mm figures and three-part paint systems are commercially available, and every major colour on the miniature can be painted in three tones. However, the technique is more difficult to do convincingly on the smaller miniatures, consequently I do not use it beyond the occasional bit of dry brushing. As a final step some painters will add mud and dirt to their miniatures to give a more realistic effect, however my miniatures go to the wargames table with clean boots and uniforms.

Painting Horses

Horses need special attention to get them looking their best and you will find plenty of online tutorials to help you. Horses come in many colours and lots of colour combinations and lists of the 12 or 29 most common horse colourings are readily available on the internet. I simplify the process by using the following method. For each horse colour I have a fixed base coat and an accompanying dry brushed topcoat, to highlight the musculature of the miniature. For the mane and tail a darker tone of the base colour is used together with the base coat of the body applied as a dry brushed topcoat to emphasise the major segments of the mane and tail.

	Body		Mane and Tail	
	Base Colour	Dry Brush	Base Colour	Dry Brush
Brown	Dark Brown	Mid Brown	Black	Dark Brown
	Mid Brown	Light Brown	Dark Brown	Mid Brown
	Light Brown	Orange	Mid Brown	Light Brown
Bay	Brown, but with mane, tail and lower legs Black			
Black	Black	Dark Grey	Black	Dark Grey
Grey	Light Grey	White	Mid Grey	Light Grey

You can add more shades of brown in following this scheme, and in total I use five. Having painted these major colours, it is well worth painting some white markings on the face and one or more of the legs. The markings on the face can be small marks on the centre of the face up to a full-face mask in white. The leg markings can be small, up to the fetlock (a sock) or more extensive up to the knee (a stocking). I tend to only mark

Step 0: Preparation and Undercoating
Step 1: Jacket and Breaches Off white (H28)
Step 2: Crossbelts White (H34)
Step 3: Facings Green (H88)
Step 4: Hair Light grey (H64)
Step 5: Haversack Brown (R83)
Step 6: Water Bottle Light brown (H234)
Step 7: Musket Stock etc Dk brown (R84)
Step 8: Hat, cartridge box etc Black (R8)
Step 9: Cockade Yellow (H46)
Step 10: Musket barrel Gunmetal (H27004)
Step 11: Stock plate and bayonet Steel (H27003)
Step 12: Water bottle strap Brown (H26)
Step 13: Brass fittings Brass (H55)
Step 14: Touching up white and facings
Step 15: Musket sling White (H34)
Step 16: Flesh Flesh (H61)
Step 17: Base Grass Green (H80)
Step 18: Flesh wash Vallejo flesh wash
Step 19: Basing
Step 19: Green Grass green (H80)

one leg in this way. The hoof on the marked leg is painted grey, while the remaining hooves the main body colour. I always paint the horses' reins et cetera in black with the bit and some buckles picked out in metallics.

Basing

Napoleonic soldiers in close order were generally formed up close together with the files in elbow-to-elbow touch of each other – the British regulations allowed just 22 inches of frontage for each file. Consequently, my basing philosophy is that the best decoration for a miniatures base is more miniatures! I have spent many years making my own bases out of thick plasticard, with each 15mm miniature occupying 6mm of frontage. I have recently switched to pre-cut 3mm thick MDF bases, from Warbases. These thicker bases have the advantage of making the finished base easy to pick up by the base, rather than by the miniatures themselves. This approach leaves the rest of the base needing little in the way additional decoration. I glue a mixture of flock and grit onto the base at the same time as the miniatures, helping to disguise the miniatures' own base. The base is then painted with two shades of green, picking out the grit in grey, before being finished with an acrylic umber wash. Painting flock may seem odd, but I believe it makes the base and the miniatures fit together. Generally, I try to base my miniatures in company bases for *Black Powder*™ and Battalions for DBN, this usually works out at two, three or four infantry miniatures to a base. I usually base cavalry in pairs.

Flags

I make flags out of tissue paper stiffened by PVA glue and then hand paint so that they match the hand painted miniatures. Occasionally if the flag design is too complex given the size required, I will print them out and give them a light brown wash to make them look less like a printed-out flag.

Varnishing

Once a base of miniatures is thoroughly dry, usually overnight is enough, it is time to varnish them. For enamels it is arguable whether this step is necessary, but I now use a Windsor and Newton Galeria Matt Acrylic Varnish, which delivers a consistent matt finish. The other key benefit of the varnish is that it ensures that all the paint on the model has the same matt finish. The problem with this product is that it foams easily during the very necessary agitation to disperse the matting agent thoroughly before application. I get around this by simply blowing on the miniatures, while ensuring that there is no excess varnish gathered in the nooks and crannies on them. You can also use coloured washes as a varnish, a light brown wash will dull the more vivid colours and give a 'campaign' look. I have tried this on my American Civil War Confederates, and it works quite well, but for the French Revolution and Napoleonic eras, for me, it tends to take away from the spectacle of the game.

7

The Scenarios

Scenario 1:

The Battle of Lincelles 18 August 1793

French vs. Dutch and British. A battalion level action using *Black Powder*™ rules.

This scenario covers both the French assault on the Dutch and the subsequent assault by the British Guards on the French, taking place on 18 August 1793.

Background

The Battle of Lincelles fought on 18 August 1793 was a curious affair. From the British perspective, it involved just the three battalions of the Guards Brigade, with their battalion guns and had no real impact on the course of the campaign, it was, in reality, just an 'affair of posts'. However, it was immediately seen as a glorious affair in which the Guards overthrew three times their own numbers of French Republicans, losing around 15 percent of their own numbers in the process, including one colonel killed and two wounded. It subsequently became the earliest battle honour awarded to British troops in the French Revolutionary and Napoleonic Wars. This makes it a great scenario for a wargame.

However, there is a less well-known story of that day, the story of the tussle between the Dutch and the French for the posts of Linselles and Le Blaton, earlier that same day, which ultimately cost one Dutch commander his life. The story is also illuminated by the involvement of two men who would later be numbered amongst Napoleon's *maréchals*, Jourdan and Macdonald.

In August 1793, Great Britain had been at war with France for six months, as a partner in the First Coalition with Prussia, Austria and the Holy Roman Empire, Spain, Portugal, Sardinia, Naples, and the United Provinces. The Guards Brigade had left England on 25 February 1793.[1] After the 1792 French invasion of the Austrian Netherlands and then Holland in February 1793, the French armies had been pushed back to the borders

1 Frederick William Hamilton, *History and Origins of the First Regiment of Foot Guards* (London: J.Murray, 1874), vol. II, pp.271–272.

of France by May 1793. After the successful siege of Valenciennes in July 1793, rather than advance on Paris directly, the British government chose to divert the Duke of York's army towards the coastal objective of Dunkerque.

For the British government, Dunkerque had always been a primary objective of the expedition.[2] Prime Minister Pitt's view was that the attack on Dunkerque would create additional stress that might cause the collapse of the French, although his critics point to the unwarranted dispersion of the allies in pursuit of individual goals, at a time when a united stroke was required. Similarly, the Austrians preferred to besiege Le Quesnoy.[3]

On 18 August 1793 the Duke of York's army was marching from Tourcoing to Menen. At dawn, covered by the Duke's march, Willem Frederik, Hereditary Prince of Orange-Nassau,[4] with some 5,000 men including the Dutch Guards, had expelled the French outposts from the village of Linselles, 6¾ miles to the northwest of Lille, and the hamlet of Le Blaton.[5] In his memoirs, the future *maréchal*, Étienne Jacques Macdonald, then a *chef de brigade*, stated that he was 'sent to command the frontier from Menen to Armentières' and had command of the French outposts.[6] Having driven off the French, the main Dutch force then retired leaving garrisons in both Le Blaton and Linselles. The garrison of Linselles comprised the Van Breydenbach and Van Plettenberg Grenadier battalions and the single battalion of the De Schepper Infanterie Regiment No.1, with their battalion guns (two 3-pounder guns), two 12-pdr and two 6-pdr guns, as well as two squadrons of the Garde Dragonders.[7] These troops were all under the command of *Generaal-Majoor* Frederik Willem van Nostitz, who had been promoted to this rank earlier in 1793, he was approximately 70 years old.[8] Van Nostitz had a total strength of approximately 1,275 infantry and 165 cavalry.[9]

Général de Brigade Antoine Anne Lecourt de Béru and the future *Maréchal de France*, *Général de Division* Jean-Baptiste Jourdan met at Wambrechies and resolved on a counterattack with a large and overwhelming force. Consequently, while *Chef de Brigade* Macdonald marched from Quesnoy-sur-Deûle, with 2,300 men, to attack the Dutch in Le Blaton,[10] Jourdan attacked Linselles from Wambrechies and Béru from Bondues, with approximately 4,600 men.[11]

---

2 Brown, *Flanders Campaign*, p.60.

3 Harry Verney, *The Journals and Correspondence of General Sir Harry Calvert* (London: Hurst & Blackett, 1853), p.101; Burne, *Noble Duke*, p.66.

4 Willem Frederik, Erfprinz van Oranje-Nassau, the future King William I of the Netherlands, in 1815.

5 The *Carte d'État-major* records two hamlets of similar names, Blaton, ¾ mile from Linselles and Le Blaton, 1¾ miles therefrom. The Cassini map only shows Blaton but calls it Le Blaton, while Le Rouge's map only shows Blaton. Modern maps refer just to the nearer hamlet and call it Le Blaton.

6 Camille Rousset (ed.), *Recollections of Marshal Macdonald, Duke of Tarentum* (London: Bentley, 1893), p.30–31.

7 For the Dutch Army in 1793, see Geert van Uythoven, *First Empire*, 56, 2001, pp.25–30; the infantry regiments, while originally comprising two battalions, were each reorganised into a single battalion of eight companies.

8 Anon., *Nieuwe Nederlandsche Jaarboeken ...*, (Leiden: P. van der Eyk and D. Vygh, and Amsteldam: J. van der Burgh, 1793), pp.1400–1401; Hendrik van der Deyster, *Naamregister der heeren militaire officieren...* (Leiden: author, 1742 and 1746), p.50 and p.59; van Nostitz was an ensign in 1742 and a lieutenant in 1744.

9 Geert van Uythoven, *The Dutch Army of 1793–1794*, available on the *Napoleon Series*, at: <https://www.napoleon-series.org/military-info/organization/c_dutch.html>, accessed 16 August 2021; Strengths estimated from the returns for 21 September 1793 (Geert van Uythoven, personal communication) and the losses for 18 August given by the Prince of Orange on the 22 August, deducting the losses of the Dutch guards (*Jaarboeken*, pp.1409–1410).

10 Camille Rousset, *Recollections of Marshal Macdonald*, p.31.

11 Victor Dupuis, *La campagne de 1793 à l'armée du Nord et des Ardennes, De Valenciennes à Hondtschoote* (Paris: R. Chapelot et Cie, 1906), p.14.

The French infantry was largely organised into *demi-brigades* formed by the *embrigadement,* comprising a regular battalion of the old army combined with two volunteer battalions. These *demi-brigades* were named after the battalion and regiment of the regular army unit.[12] Jourdan himself led the *demi-brigade* comprising the 1/45e Régiment d'Infanterie, the 5e Volontaires des Vosges and the 10e Volontaires de Paris, together with a half company of *artillerie légère* (horse artillery). The 2/12e Régiment d'Infanterie and the 1er Volontaires de l'Allier were also sent by *Adjudant-Général* Pierre Dupont de l'Étang from the *Camp de la Madeleine,* although the third battalion of this *demi-brigade,* was elsewhere.

Béru led the *demi-brigade* comprising the 10e Volontaires de Seine-et-Oise, the 1/47e Régiment d'Infanterie and the 2e Volontaires de la Vienne, together with the 2e Volontaires de Paris. The French sources thus suggest Jourdan and Béru took nine battalions to Linselles.[13] The *Convention Nationale's Représentant du Peuple en Mission,* René Levasseur was also present at Linselles; 'to study the spirit of the soldier and maintain the sacred fire in his soul'.[14]

At Linselles, despite being outnumbered almost three to one and assailed from two different directions, there is clear evidence from the French accounts that the Dutch put up a fight to defend their position.[15] The Prince of Orange's casualty return suggests that the Dutch lost an estimated 220 men at Linselles, some 17 percent of their starting strength.[16] Nevertheless both Linselles and Le Blaton were recaptured by the French.

When the French attacked Linselles, *Generaal-Majoor* van Nostitz wrote to Menen, 4½ miles away, to appeal for help. The Duke of York recorded receiving the request for help at 3:00 p.m., which suggests that the French appeared before Linselles at approximately 1:30–1:45 p.m.[17] In his memoirs, Levasseur stated that the French attacked at 3:00 p.m., however in his despatch Jourdan stated that the French attack was at 4:00 p.m.[18] The French attacks recaptured both villages before any help could arrive.

In response to the Dutch request for help, the Duke of York despatched the Guards Brigade from Geluwe under the command of Major-General Gerard Lake, a veteran of the Battle of Yorktown in 1781, to assist them. From Geluwe, the Guards marched back towards Menen, crossed the river Lys via a pontoon bridge between Bousbecque and Halluin, about a mile from Menen, and then via Colbra and La Vignette, a march of six miles (approximately 2½–3¾ hours), attacking Linselles from the northeast.[19] On

12 Crowdy, *Handbook*, p.4; the *embrigadement* began 21 February 1793, but was then adjourned 31 March 1793. Dupuis's order of battle (pp.14–15) shows its impact in the *Camp de Madeleine.*

13 Dupuis, *Valenciennes*, p.14–15, 199–202.

14 René Levasseur, *Mémoires de R. Levasseur* (Paris: Rapilly, 1829), vol. II, p.34; he was a doctor and a member of the *Montagnards.* 'Sacred Fire' as in '*feu sacré de la liberté*' (sacred fire of freedom) or '*feu sacré de l'amour de la patrie*' (sacred fire of love for the homeland).

15 L.Chassin and L.Hennet, *Les Volontaires Nationaux pendant la Revolution* (Paris: Cerf, Noblet and Quantin, 1902), vol. II, p.114; referencing the archives of the 79e Demi-Brigade.

16 *Jaarboeken*, pp.1409–1410; estimates based on named officer casualties using Oman's proportional method.

17 John Hussey, *Waterloo; the campaign of 1815 from Elba to Ligny and Quatre Bras* (London: Greenhill Books, 2017), p.302–303; cites measured courier speeds based on the Prussian staff logs of 2 miles/hour normally and 3.6 miles/hour in a crisis.

18 Levasseur, *Memoires*, vol. II, p.34; *Service Historique de la Défense*, Paris, SHD B1 17, *Armée du Nord Correspondence, 16-31 Août*, SHD B1 17, 134 & 136; Jourdan has Macdonald attacking from Le Quesnoy which is 38 miles SE of Lille, but Béru has him attacking from Commines. Quesnoy-sur-Deûle is the most likely point of departure.

19 *Jaarboeken*, p.1402; Johann Gottfried von Hoyer, *Neues Militarische Magazin*, (Leipzig: Baumgärtnerischen Buchhandlung, 1801), vol. II, part 2, plate 2; Verney, *Calvert*, p.106; the *Jaarboeken* describes the pontoons as

his arrival Lake found that the Dutch were not able to participate in the retaking the villages, having retired by a different route. Undaunted, 'a firm believer in the attack', he decided to launch an assault himself.[20] Major Jesse Wright, Royal Artillery, who commanded Lake's battalion guns, reported that 'the action began about 6 o'clock in the afternoon and lasted until it was quite dark'.[21]

Lake's force comprised of the 1st Foot Guards, the Coldstream Foot Guards and the 3rd (later Scots) Guards, without their Flank battalion, in all 1,122 rank & file.[22] The battalions were supported by their six light 6-pdr battalion guns, commanded by Major Jesse Wright, Royal Artillery.[23] The 1st Foot Guards were commanded by Colonel Samuel Hulse, the Coldstreams by Colonel Lowther Pennington and the 3rd Foot Guards by Lieutenant-Colonel William Grinfield.[24] The two guns of the 1st Foot Guards were led by First Lieutenant Charles William Lewis de Ginkell (1st Battalion, Royal Artillery), those of the Coldstream Foot Guards by First Lieutenant Alexander Watson (1st Bn, R.A.) and those of the 3rd Foot Guards by First Lieutenant James de Peyster (1st Bn, R.A.).[25]

Prior to the attack of the British Guards, three officers offer evidence that the French at Linselles had received some small reinforcements to the nine battalions that evicted the Dutch. David Hendrik Chassé, then a *capitaine* in the Légion Franche Étrangère, 'was so absorbed by the sight of the fine movement of the English that he was about to be taken captive by their skirmishers; the cry of one of his chasseurs alerted him and awoke him as if from a dream'.[26] A small detachment of the Légion Franche Étrangère (146 men) was stationed on the river Lys, presumably on the stretch from Commines to Wervick.[27] Another Dutch officer from the Légion Franche Étrangère was the then *Lieutenant-Colonel* Hermann Willem Daendels, commander of the Légion, was also almost captured by 'his Dutch (*sic*) compatriots' at Linselles.[28] The third officer, like Chassé, of Waterloo fame, was the Belgian, Joannes Baptista van Merlen, who, as a *capitaine* in the Légion Belge, 'while leading his men into battle, had two of his ribs

being stored at Bousbecque, while the *Neues Militarische Magazin* map shows it closer to Halluin and Calvert puts it 'about a mile above Menin', which places it at Le Malplaquet. For a discussion of the route the Guards took to Linselles see the author's chapter in Andrew Bamford (ed.) *One Hundred Years Of Army Historical Research: Proceedings of the SAHR Centenary Conference* (Solihull: Helion, 2023), pp.70–99.

20 Hugh Wodehouse Pearse, *Memoir of the life and military services of Viscount Lake, Baron Lake of Delhi and Laswaree, 1744–1808* (London: William Blackwood, 1908), p.77.

21 Francis Arthur Whinyates, *The Wright Letters: being a collection of letters written by Major J. Wright, R.A., and others, during the Duke of York's campaigns in the Low Countries, 1793–1794* (London: Eyre, 1902), Letter 18.

22 Frederick Maurice, *The History of the Scots Guards …* (London: Chatto and Windus, 1934), pp.232–233; the total for all ranks would have been approximately 1,250 men, assuming the rank and file are approximately 90 percent of the total, the balance being officers, staff, sergeants, and drummers. For example, the First Guards had 18 officers present at Linselles (Sylvester Urban, *The Gentleman's Magazine*, 1793, vol. LXIII, pt.2, p.780–781) and the Coldstream contingent had 24 officers present in September 1793 (Daniel MacKinnon, *Origin and Services of the Coldstream Guards* (London: Richard Bentley, 1833), vol. II, p.48).

23 Garry David Wills, *Smoothbore Ordnance Journal* (Godmanchester: Ken Trotman, 2013), 6, pp.82–83.

24 *London Gazette Extraordinary*, 13560, 22 August 1793, pp.709–711.

25 Garry David Wills, *Smoothbore Ordnance Journal* (Godmanchester: Ken Trotman, 2013), 6, p.76.

26 Willem Jacobus Del Campo, *Het leven en de krijgsbedrijven van David Hendrik Baron Chassé, in leven Generaal der Infanterie, oud lid der Staten-Generaal, Grootkruis der Militaire Willemsorde, Officier van het Legioen van Eer van Frankrijk* ('s-Hertogenbosch: Muller, 1849), p.11; none of the British accounts mention the Guards deploying skirmishers and the flank battalion, including the light companies, were left at Geluwe.

27 Dupuis, *Valenciennes*, p.14–15; Geert van Uythoven, *First Empire*, 76, 2004, p.23.

28 François de Bas, *Prins Frederik der Nederlanden en zijn tijd* (Schiedam: Roelants, 1887), vol. I, p.202; Geert van Uythoven, *First Empire*, 39, p.5; The Chassé and Daendels stories are similar and raises the question as to whether François de Bas confused his source.

shattered by a bullet'.[29] Dupuis shows this unit as the Bataillon Belge in his order of battle for 30 July 1793 based on the Lys. At that time, the unit had 184 men present under arms.[30]

Dupuis does not include the Légion Franche Étrangère or Bataillon Belge amongst the units that Jourdan and Béru led to Linselles, however both Béru and Levasseur reported that some unidentified French infantry retired from Linselles on Commines. This suggests that like Dellard's unit, which arrived in Le Blaton after the French assault, the Légion Belge/Bataillon Belge and the Légion Franche Étrangère arrived in Linselles after it had been retaken by Jourdan and Béru. These units probably arrived from posts along the Lys from Commines to Wervick.

The strengths of the nine battalions that attacked the Dutch in Linselles and for the two reinforcements can be estimated from the *Situations* reproduced by Dupuis:[31]

	All ranks present under arms	
	30 July 1793	15 October 1793
Initial Assault on the Dutch:		
5e Volontaires des Vosges (formed June 1793)	443	373
1er Bn./45e Régiment d'Infanterie	450	385
10e Volontaires de Paris (23 September 92)	470	444
2e/12e Régiment d'Infanterie	392	
1er Volontaires de l'Allier (9 January 91)	888	518
10e Volontaires de Seine-et-Oise (3 September 92)	457	367
1er/47e Régiment d'Infanterie	471	379
2e Volontaires de la Vienne (5 September 92)	437	381
2e Volontaires de Paris (20 July 91)	813	554
Reinforcement units:		
Légion Belge/Bataillon Belge	184	200
Légion Franche Étrangère	146	

Some of the French infantry would have had their two 4-pdr battalion guns with them. Given the average number of battalion guns for the Armée du Nord at the time, we might

29 *Biografisch Woordenboek van Nederland: 1780–1830*, accessed 10 May 2020, available at; <http://resources.huygens.knaw.nl/bwn1780-1830/lemmata/data/Van%20Merlen>.

30 Dupuis, *Valenciennes*, p.14; Laurent Brayard and Didier Davin, *Les troupes Belges et Liégeoises sous la Révolution, 1792–1803* (SEHRI, 2017), pp.15, 34, available at: < http://assosehri.fr/bibliothequemili/les-troupes-belges-de-1792-1803.pdf >, accessed 30 August 2021; Dupuis names another unit the *1er bataillon belges* but this appears to be the *1er battalion chasseurs belges*.

31 Dupuis, *Valenciennes*, pp.14, 218; Victor Dupuis, *La campagne de 1793 à l'armée du Nord et des Ardennes, De Hondtschoote à Wattignies* (Paris: R. Chapelot et Cie, 1909), pp.100–102.; Georges Armand Louis Dumont, *Bataillons de volontaires nationaux (Cadres et historiques)* (Paris: Henri Charles Lavauzelle, 1914), p.15; 1er d'Allier figure is dated 22–10–1793. Two thirds of 10e Volontaires de Paris were from the March 1793 levy.

expect 11 such cannon.[32] While we know that the French retreated with some of their guns, the British Guards captured seven of these battalion guns plus the two 8-pdrs. Together the evidence suggests that the French at Linselles had the two 8-pdrs and one howitzer from the *artillerie légère* plus from eight to eleven 4-pdrs.[33] The French also had four guns taken from the Dutch that morning, although it appears that two had subsequently been removed.[34] Thus, the French garrisoned Linselles with some 5,000 men and between 11 and 14 guns. Although Jourdan and Béru had difficulty stopping their troops from looting the village, they nonetheless offered a tough nut for Lake to crack.

This data drives the following *Black Powder*™ Playsheet, which also allocates the battalion guns on a 'best guess' approach, given we do not have direct evidence of which battalions had them. The French have separate *tirailleur* units and therefore the infantry battalions cannot use the 'mixed' formation.

32 Dupuis, *Valenciennes*, p.48; cites a report showing that 37 percent of the 4-pdr guns were missing, which suggests 11 guns, while Béru's report to the minister of war confirms that the division had insufficient guns (SHD B1 17, 134).

33 Ditfurth, *Die Hessen*, vol. 1, p.79; Abel Hugo, *France Militaire. Histoire des Armées de Terre et de Mer, 1792 –1832* (Paris: Delloye, 1835), vol. I, p.116; in 1801 *Neues Militarisch Magazin* (p.37) described the guns as twelve 16-pounder cannon, repeated by later sources, however this description does not tally with Congreve's return of the captured guns as published in the *London Gazette*.

34 The British liberated only two of these when they captured the redoubts.

French Division Béru	Figures (1:33)	Size	Armament	Close Combat	Shooting	Morale	Stamina	Special Rules
General de Division Jean-Baptiste Jourdan								
Représentant du Peuple en Mission René Levasseur								
1/45e Demi-Brigade:								
5e Volontaires des Vosges	12	Standard	Musket	5	2	5+	3	Unreliable
1er Bn/45e Régiment d'Infanterie	12	Standard	Musket	5	2	5+	3	Unreliable
Battalion guns, two 4-pdrs	1	1 Model	Lt. S/bore	1	2/1/1	5+	1	
10e Volontaires de Paris	12	Standard	Musket	5	2	5+	3	Unreliable
Battalion guns, two 4-pdrs	1	1 Model	Lt. S/bore	1	2/1/1	5+	1	
2/12e Demi-Brigade:								
2e Bn/12e Régiment d'Infanterie	12	Standard	Musket	5	2	5+	3	Unreliable
Battalion guns, two 4-pdrs	1	1 Model	Lt. S/bore	1	2/1/1	5+	1	
1er Volontaires de l'Allier	18	Large	Musket	7	3	5+	4	Unreliable
Tirailleurs	10	Standard	Musket	5	2	5+	3	Unreliable, Skirmish
Artillerie Légère; 2x 8-pdrs, 1x 6" howitzers	2	1 Model	Smoothbore	1	3/2/1	4+	1	Marauders
Général de Brigade Antoine Anne Lecourt de Béru								
1/47e Demi-Brigade:								
10e Volontaires de Seine-et-Oise	12	Standard	Musket	5	2	5+	3	Unreliable
1er Bn/47e Régiment d'Infanterie	12	Standard	Musket	5	2	5+	3	Unreliable
Battalion guns, two 4-pdrs	1	1 Model	Lt. S/bore	1	2/1/1	5+	1	
2e Volontaires de la Vienne	12	Standard	Musket	5	2	5+	3	Unreliable
Unbrigaded:								
2e Volontaires de Paris	18	Large	Musket	7	3	5+	3	Unreliable
Battalion guns, two 4-pdrs	1	1 Model	Lt. S/bore	1	2/1/1	5+	1	
Tirailleurs	8	Small	Musket	3	1	5+	2	Unreliable, Skirmish
Late Afternoon Reinforcements								
Légion Belge/Bataillon Belge	6	Small	Musket	3	1	5+	2	Unreliable
Légion Franche Étrangère	4	Tiny	Musket	1	1	5+	1	Unreliable

This Dutch and British playsheet for *Black Powder*™ provides the unit profiles for the afternoon defence of Linselles by the Dutch and the evening assault by the British.

Unit	Figures (1:33)	Size	Armament	Close Combat	Shooting	Morale	Stamina	Special Rules
Initial Dutch Garrison								
Generaal-Majoor van Nostitz								
van Breydenbach Grenadiers	12	Standard	Musket	7	3	4+	3	Elite 4+, Reliable
van Plettenberg Grenadiers	12	Standard	Musket	7	3	4+	3	Elite 4+, Reliable
De Schepper Infantry Regt. N.1	12	Standard	Musket	6	3	4+	3	
Artillery: Battalion Guns two 3-pdrs	1	1 Model	Lt. S/bore	1	2/1/1	4+	1	
Artillery; two 12-pdrs	1	1 Model	Smoothbore	1	2/1/1	4+	1	
Artillery; two 6-pdrs	1	1 Model	Lt. S/bore	1	2/1/1	4+	1	
Garde Dragonders (two squadrons)	6	Standard	Sword/carbine	8	0	4+	3	Heavy Cavalry +1, Reliable
British Guards Brigade								
Major-General Gerard Lake								
1st Foot Guards	12	Standard	Musket	7	3	3+	3	Steady, First Fire, Reliable, Elite 3+
Battalion guns; two light 6-pdrs	1	1 Model	Lt. S/bore	1	2/1/1	3+	1	Steady, Reliable, Elite 3+
Coldstream Guards	12	Standard	Musket	7	3	3+	3	Steady, First Fire, Reliable, Elite 3+
Battalion guns; two light 6-pdrs	1	1 Model	Lt. S/bore	1	2/1/1	3+	1	Steady, Reliable, Elite 3+
3rd Foot Guards	16	Large	Musket	9	4	3+	4	Steady, First Fire, Reliable, Elite 3+
Battalion guns; two light 6-pdrs	1	1 Model	Lt. S/bore	1	2/1/1	3+	1	Steady, Reliable, Elite 3+

The Battlefield

The battlefield for the French attack on the Dutch is shown on Map 9, while that for the British attack is shown on Map 10. The battlefield maps represent a wargames table of six by four feet for 15mm and smaller figures, using a 1cm to 20 paces ground scale, or approximately nine by six feet for 28mm figures, using a ground scale of 1 inch to 25 yards. The table could be half these sizes when focussing on just one of the attacks.[35]

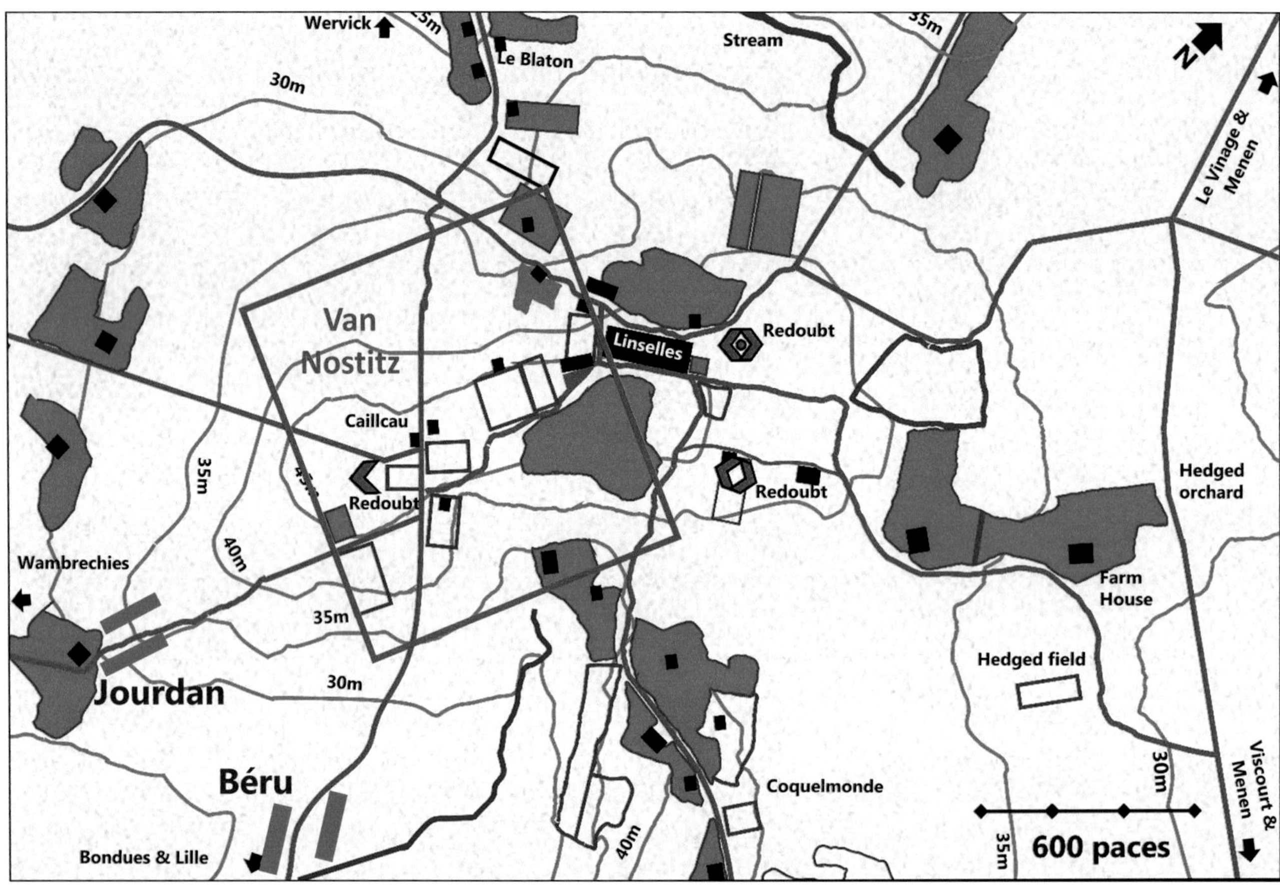

Map 9 – Battle of Lincelles, French Attack

35 For my games I use the centimetre scale for 15mm figures, where all distances in the rules are measured in centimetres rather than inches.

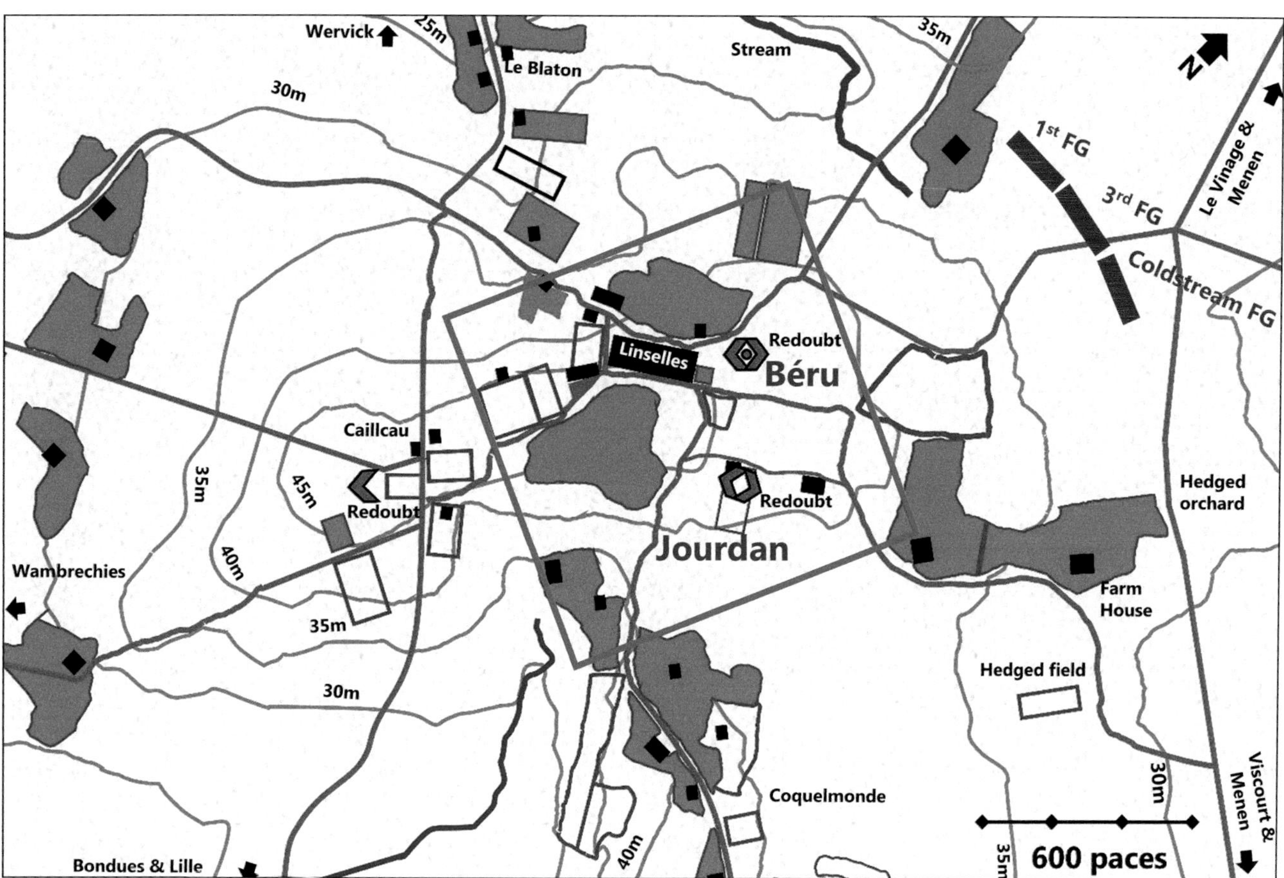

Map 10 – Battle of Lincelles, British Attack

The slopes are gentle (only two to three percent) and do not affect movement. The individual farmhouses on the map are tactically insignificant and cannot be garrisoned by either side.

The orchards block line of sight and count as rough ground. The orchards are all surrounded by hedged enclosures, which count as standard linear obstacles. The hedged field, the Officer of the Guard's 'beanfield', in front of the British start line is treated as rough ground, which blocks line of sight.

The redoubts provide a saving throw modifier of +1, in addition to their garrisons being unclear targets. The redoubts should also be treated as obstacles rather than buildings for the purposes of close combat. Units defending the redoubts cannot be in column formation, but get a free formation change to line formation when occupying them.

Lincelles – The French assaulting the Dutch

Scenario Notes

The staff rating of the French generals should be eight when attacking the Dutch garrison in the afternoon but seven when defending Linselles against the British in the evening, to reflect their difficulty in controlling their men in the evening. At this early stage of the war the French are not allowed to use 'brigade orders' and must order each unit individually.

The staff ratings for the British and Dutch generals are both eight. Lake has one bonus attack and is considered 'aggressive', adding +1 to his staff rating when giving orders to charge.

In the evening, the French generals had difficulty in getting their men to stop pillaging the village and to face the British assault. For this reason, the French will start the scenario with each brigade having some of their battalions deployed in the village. The score of a D6 halved and rounded up is used to determine how many battalions in each brigade must deploy in this way, either one, two or three battalions. Alternatively throw one D6 for each battalion, with a score of 1 or 2 marking them as 'looters'. These battalions would retain any battalion guns with them in the village. Each turn after the first, the 'looter' battalions have a chance of joining the fighting, throw two D6 for each such battalion and on a score of 12, deploy them adjacent to village and they then can act as ordered.

Only the French infantry can form 'attack column', the British and Dutch infantry have the choice of march column or line. This is a simplification to aid gameplay, other nations used wider columns than march columns for manoeuvre, but they always attacked in line in the open field, even, as was the case at Linselles against field works.[36]

However, the French infantry cannot form square and are disordered before delivering closing fire if charged by cavalry.[37]

The battalion gun sections are treated as separate units attached to their parent battalions.

When the battalion guns move, they have the orders of their parent unit provided they are within 6cm/inches of the parent unit. To avoid unrealistically overcrowding the table it is important to remove the limbers when the battalion guns are unlimbered. The battalion guns provide closing fire if in base-to-base contact with their parent battalion when it is charged, but they do not provide support as they are part of the battalion.

The two-gun Dutch sections of 12-pdrs and 6-pdrs can provide support, as can the French light artillery.

If the French infantry columns charge home but fail to force the Dutch or British infantry to retire or break, they become disordered and must be reformed into line as a free compulsory move.

Units defending on a slope can re-roll one failed morale save in the first round of close combat.

Représentant

René Levasseur's influence can be represented by a special rule to reflect his impact on the morale of the troops. When a unit accompanied by the *Représentant* either charges or is charged, a command test is taken before closing fire and the test is completed without the normal modifiers. If the unmodified dice roll (two D6) succeeds by scoring the staff rating or less. the accompanying unit either gets the special rule 'Terrifying Charge' when attacking or 'Stubborn' when defending. On a blunder (a command roll score of 12) the *Représentant* flees the field and is removed from play and the accompanying unit takes a break test immediately. The *Représentant* can only accompany one unit at any one time.

In my games I use the rules from the 'Clash of Eagles' supplement for the replacement of killed or wounded commanders. The replacement commander appears in the next command phase but with a staff rating reduced by one. From the same supplement I also use the rules for penetration of artillery shots at medium and long range. In each range band a line is drawn from the gun barrel through the centre or leader model of the initial target, any unit crossed by this line up to the end of the range band, half range for medium or full range for long range, will also be potentially hit but counting as an unclear target. Separate die rolls are made for each target.

36 Lynn, *Bayonets*, p.2.
37 Lynn, *Bayonets*, pp.259–260.

Victory Conditions

Neither of these games is particularly balanced, the French having approximately 600 points while the Dutch have approximately 300 points and the British 400 points, using the *Black Powder*™ first edition points system. The players are therefore encouraged to play the scenarios twice, swapping sides.

The French Attack

The game starts at 1:45 p.m. and lasts for 12 game turns. To claim victory the French need to break the Dutch brigade. The Dutch breakpoint is three units broken or shaken, excluding the artillery units. For the Dutch to win both French brigades need to be broken, each losing three units broken or shaken.

Lincelles – The Guards attack in 15mm!

The British Attack

The game starts at 6:00 p.m. and ends when darkness fell at 10:00 p.m. – 16 moves in all. To win the British must either take the redoubts or break both French brigades, each losing three units broken or shaken. The French win if they break the British Guards Brigade. Given that the Guards suffered almost 20 percent casualties on the day, the British brigade is only broken if all three Guards battalions are either 'shaken' or 'broken', at the beginning of a British turn. Jourdan described the defeat of the French as a 'rout', therefore any French battalions that leave the table cannot be brought back on.

Lincelles – Gallant Grenadiers Wills Cigarette Card

Historical Outcome

The following day, 19 August 1793, the Duke of York issued an order, 'His Royal Highness the Commander-in-Chief returns his warmest thanks to Major-General Lake, Colonels Hulse, Greenfield, Pennington, Major Wright, and the officers and men belonging to the brigade of Guards and artillery under his command, for the gallantry and intrepidity they so evidently showed in the attack of the French redoubts yesterday afternoon.'[38] The position at Linselles was abandoned on the same day, after the entrenchments had been razed to the ground.[39] Following the action at Linselles, Béru was promoted to *général de division* by the *Représentants en mission* Levasseur and Bentabole. His new rank was confirmed on 19 September 1793, and he was appointed commander of the division at Lille.

This bloody action had little impact on the outcome of the campaign and was overshadowed by the British defeat before Dunkerque.

38 MacKinnon, *Coldstream Guards*, vol. II, pp.43–44.
39 Hoyer, *Neues Militarische Magazin*, 1801, vol. II, part 2, p.39.

Scenario 2:

The Battle of Pirmasens, 14 September 1793

French vs. Prussians. A battalion level action using *Black Powder*™, Lasalle II or General de Brigade rules.

Introduction

In the summer of 1793, the Armée de la Moselle held the line of the river Schwarzbach centred on the town of Zweibrücken (Deux-Ponts) in the Palatinate, some 46 miles west of the river Rhine. Facing them was the Prussian Armee am Rhein, commanded by the Prussian king and the Duke of Brunswick. Brunswick's II Corps was based in the former garrison town of Pirmasens, covering the town of Kaiserslautern.[40]

After a preliminary reconnaissance (12 September), Schauenburg the new commander, in conjunction with the *représentants du peuple*, decided to send Moreaux with the Corps des Vosges to attack Pirmasens. Rather than attack the Prussian defences directly, Moreaux advanced towards Pirmasens from the north. At 10:00 p.m. the Corps des Vosges marched from their camp at Hornbach, 10½ miles west of Pirmasens, leaving three battalions behind to guard the camp. Marching via Monbijou and Walshausen, the French reached Nünschweiler at daybreak where they were spotted by Prussian officers at Bottonbach. The early hopes that the Prussians would be surprised by this indirect approach were dashed, but Brunswick had been warned of the French preparations the day before, and had his troops prepared for immediate action. At 9:00 a.m. Moreaux reached Fehrbach two miles north-northeast of Pirmasens.[41] During a council of war with his generals and the *représentants* Soubrany, Richaud and Ehrmann, Moreaux had a change of heart about the wisdom of an all-out attack, but the *représentants* insisted that he went ahead.[42] Consequently at 10:00 a.m. the French assault on Pirmasens began with a two-hour artillery duel. During this time, belatedly, Moreaux who had only assumed command of his corps a few days before (8 August), divided his force into three columns and allocated commands to his subordinate generals.[43]

The Battlefield

The terrain is shown in Map 11, which is designed for a six by four feet table for use with 15mm figures at a ground scale of 1cm to 20 paces (meaning all distances in the *Black Powder*™ rules are measured in centimetres rather than inches). For 28mm figures you would need a table of approximately nine by six feet, using a ground scale of 1 inch to 25 yards.

40 Julius August Reinhold von Grawert, *Ausführliche Beschreibung der Schlacht bei Pirmasenz, den 14. September 1793 in drei Abschnitten: nebst einem Bataillen-Plan und dazu gehöriger General-Charte* (Potsdam: Horvath, 1796), p.60.

41 Colin, *Campagne de 1793*, vol. I, pp.393, 396–400; *Général de Division* Balthazar Alexis Henri Schauenburg appointed 3 August 1793; *Général de Division* Jean René Moreaux.

42 Arthur Chuquet, *Les Guerres de la Révolution VIII. Wissembourg (1793)* (Paris: Plon, 1890), p.164; Pierre-Amable Soubrany de Macholles, Hyacinthe Richaud and Jean-François Ehrmann.

43 Colin, *Campagne de 1793*, p.399.

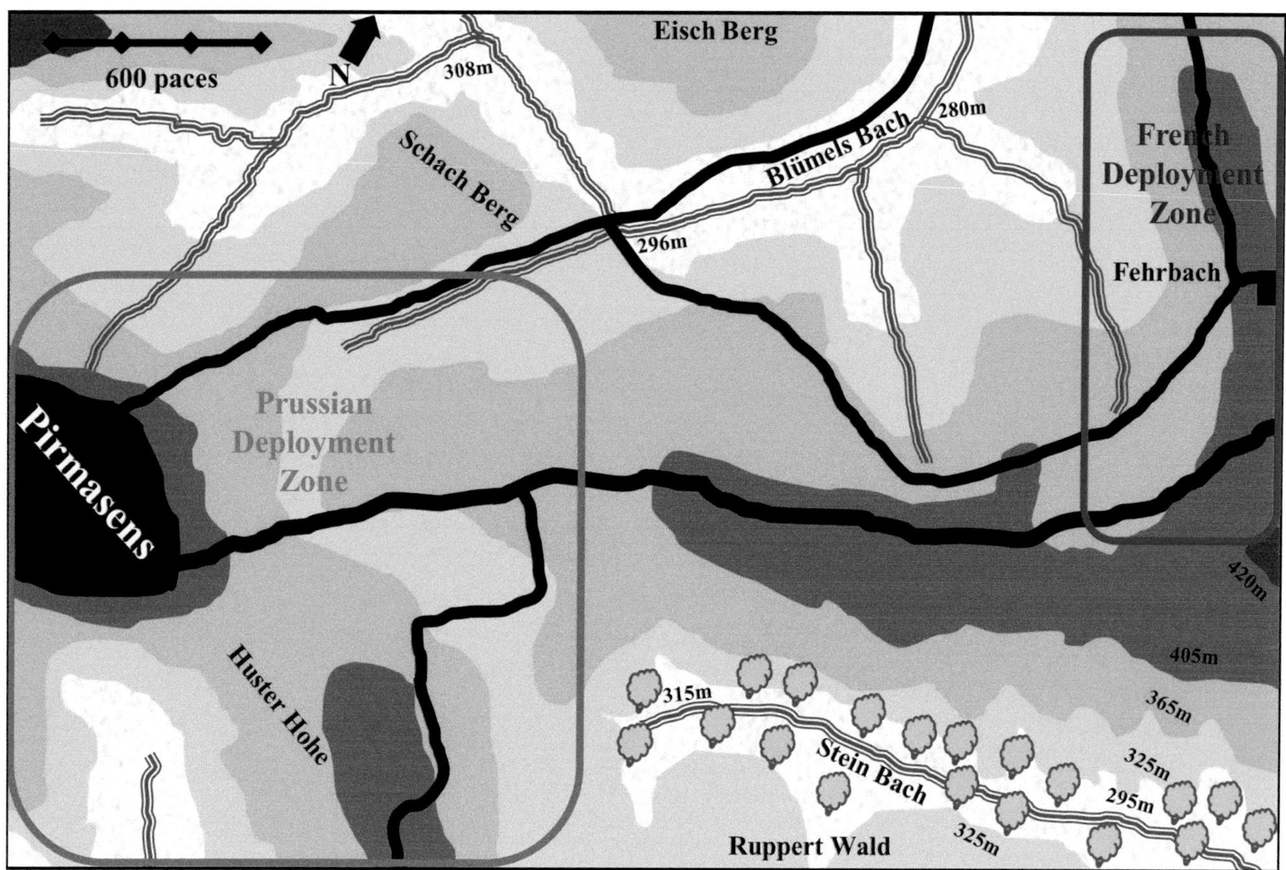

Map 11 – The Battle of Pirmasens

The watercourses run in steep-sided gullies and all the terrain below the 405m contour should be considered rough ground, halving all movement. The ground above the 405m contour allows normal movement. Within this context the streams count as normal linear obstacles but are impassable to artillery. When between the Blumens Bach and the Stein Bach, artillery also cannot descend below the 365m contour except via the roads.

The Forces

The sources give various numbers for the two armies, sometimes depending on the sympathies of the writer. The French army varies between 10,000–15,000 men and the Prussians between 7,000 and 8,000. The following tables give the forces for both sides. For the French we have battalion (infantry) and regiment (cavalry) level detail but for the Prussians we only have the strength of the force as a whole rather than the strengths of the individual units.[44] For the French, I have chosen not to discriminate between the morale of the old royal army battalions and the newer volunteer battalions as it is clear from the battalion strengths that all of the battalions contain large drafts of new men.

For the Prussians I have taken their overall strength at 8,000. Given that Prussian infantry battalions and cavalry regiments have broadly the same establishments, except for the hussars which are twice as large, I have sized the battalions and regiments accordingly. Some data in the source material suggests that a battalion strength of around 600 men

44 Colin, *Campagne de 1793*, pp.84–87, 106–107, 397–378, 400–401; Grawert, *Schlacht bei Pirmasenz*, pp.62–64, 83–85; the Compagnie Franche de Guillaume was also known as the 1er Compagnie Franche de la Moselle.

Preussen.
R. Knötel
Musketier. Unteroffizier. Offiziere.
Infanterie-Regiment v. Wolframsdorf
(1806 v. Tschepe No. 37).
1792.
VINKHUIZEN COLLECTION
DRAPER FUND
Das Regiment wurde 1740 von Friedrich dem Grossen als Füsilier-Regiment errichtet und unter Friedrich Wilhelm II., wie alle früheren Füsilier-Regimenter, zu Musketieren umgewandelt. In der dargestellten Uniform machte es 1792 die sog. »Rheincampagne« mit (Einnahme von Longwy und Verdun, Kanonade von Valmy) und focht 1793 bei Hochheim und vor Mainz, wo es beim Sturme auf die Kostheimer Schanze 2 Kanonen eroberte, ferner vor Landau. In der Schlacht bei Pirmasens machte ein Lieutenant mit 18 Schützen 200 Gefangene. 1794 Gefechte bei Frankenthal, Kaiserslautern und Zweibrücken. 1798 wurden karmoisinrothe Abzeichen eingeführt. 1806 ging das Regiment völlig zu Grunde. Die Architectur im Hintergrunde zeigt das alte, jetzt abgetragene Kommandanturgebäude in Glogau, der damaligen Garnison des Regiments.
Knötel, Uniformenkunde. IX. Band. No. 19.
Verlag von Max Babenzien in Rathenow.

Prussian Line Infantry 1792

is not unreasonable.[45] I prefer to represent the battalion guns on both sides as separate models of reduced firepower but feel free to combine them into six-gun units if you prefer. This is particularly appropriate to this scenario as the Duke of Brunswick did just this on this occasion. The Prussian order of battle includes 11 general officers with commanders at corps, division and brigade levels, while expensive in terms of points, this gives three re-rolls per turn to the Prussians ensuring a more predictable response to orders, as we might expect from the literature.

45 August Wagner, *De Feldzug der K. Preussischen Armee am Rhein im Jahre 1793* (Berlin: G.Reimer, 1831), p.52; citing eight battalions in July 1793.

The Battle of Pirmasens 14 September 1793: *Black Powder*™ Playsheet													
French: Corps des Vosges (Armée de la Moselle)		Type	Armament	Strength	Figures	Figures	Size	Shooting	Melee	Morale	Stamina	Special Rules	Points
					1:33	1:20							1495
Général de Division Jean René Moreaux (SR7 BP=2; 1 re-roll per turn within 12cm)													70
Général de Brigade Paul Guillaume (Reps. du Peuple Soubrany and Dulac) BP=3													70
Right Column	2e/30e Régiment d'Infanterie	Infantry	Musket	644	20	32	Std	3	6	5+	3		32
	Grenadiers/30e Régiment d'Infanterie (2 Coys)	Infantry	Musket	172	5	9	Tiny	1	1	5+	1		15
(Advanced Guard)	4e Bataillon de Haute-Saone Volontaires	Infantry	Musket	476	14	24	Std	2	6	5+	3		30
	Tirailleurs	Infantry	Musket	128	4	6	Tiny	1	1	5+	1	Skirmish	15
	Compagnie Franche de Guillaume (2 coys)	Infantry	Musket	325	10	16	Small	2	4	5+	2	Skirmish	24
	Artillerie Légère (4x 8-pdr, 2x 6" Howitzers)	Artillery	Smoothbore	68	2	3	1 Model	3/2/1	1	5+	2		27
	Battalion guns (4x 4-pdrs)	Artillery	Lt. S/bore		2	4	2 Models	2/1/1	1	5+	1		42
Général de Division François Xavier Jacob Freytag (BP=4)													70
Centre Column	3e Bataillon de la Republique Volontaires	Infantry	Musket	816	25	41	Large	4	8	5+	4		40
	1er Compagnie de l'Observatoire	Infantry	Musket	319	10	16	Small	2	4	5+	2	Skirmish	24
	1er/1er Régiment d'Infanterie	Infantry	Musket	805	24	40	Large	4	8	5+	4		40
	6e Bataillon de la Haute-Saone Volontaires	Infantry	Musket	710	22	36	Large	4	8	5+	4		40
	2e Bataillon de la Moselle Volontaires	Infantry	Musket	779	24	39	Large	4	8	5+	4		40
	1er/96e Régiment d'Infanterie	Infantry	Musket	867	26	43	Large	4	8	5+	4		40
	Tirailleurs	Infantry	Musket	384	12	19	Small	2	4	5+	2	Skirmish	24
	Battalion guns (10x 4-pdrs)	Artillery	Lt. S/bore		5	10	5 Models	2/1/1	1	5+	1		105
Général de Division Louis Lequoy (BP=5)													70
Left Column	9e Régiment de Chasseurs à Cheval I	Cavalry	Sabre	495	8	12	Std	1	6	4+	3		37
	9e Régiment de Chasseurs à Cheval II	Cavalry	Sabre		8	12	Std	1	6	4+	3		37
	l4e Régiment de Dragons I	Cavalry	Sabre	388	6	10	Small	1	6	4+	2		33
	l4e Régiment de Dragons II	Cavalry	Sabre		6	10	Small	1	6	4+	2		33
	1er/24e Régiment d'Infanterie	Infantry	Musket	692	24	40	Large	4	8	5+	4		40
	4e Bataillon de la Manche Volontaires	Infantry	Musket	751	23	38	Large	4	8	5+	4		40
	4e Bataillon de la Seine-Inferieure Volontaires	Infantry	Musket	670	20	34	Large	4	8	5+	4		40
	3e Compagne de Chasseurs du Louvre	Infantry	Musket	319	10	16	Small	2	4	5+	2	Skirmish	24
	3e Bataillon de la Manche Volontaires	Infantry	Musket	515	16	26	Std	3	6	5+	3		32
	9e Bataillon de la Meurthe	Infantry	Musket	952	29	48	Large	4	8	5+	4		40
	Battalion guns (10x 4-pdrs)	Artillery	Lt. S/bore		5	10	5 Models	2/1/1	1	5+	1		105
Général de Brigade Jean-Baptiste Félix de Manscourt du Rozoy (BP=3)													70
Reserve	Park artillery (12x 12-pdrs)	Artillery	Smoothbore	160	6	8	2 Models	3/2/1	1	4+	2		54
	Park artillery (12x 8-pdrs)	Artillery	Smoothbore	160	6	8	2 Models	3/2/1	1	4+	2		54
	Park artillery (6x 6" Howitzers)	Artillery	Howitzers	80	3	4	1 Model	3/2/1	1	4+	2		23
	1er Bataillon de l'Yonne	Infantry	Musket	124	4	6	Tiny	1	1	5+	1		15

The Battle of Pirmasens 14 September 1793: *Black Powder*™ Playsheet

Prussians: Corps II, Armee am Rhein	Type	Armament	Strength	Figures	Figures	Size	Shooting	Melee	Morale	Stamina	Special Rules	Points
				1:33	1:20							2082
Feldmarshall Karl Wilhelm Ferdinand, Duke of Brunswick-Lüneburg (SR 8; 1 re-roll per turn within 12cm)												80
Generalleutnant Wilhelm René de l'Homme de Courbière (1 re-roll per turn within 12cm)												80
Generalmajor Ludwig Prinz zu Baden (BP=2)												80
I/von Borch Regiment zu Fuss	Infantry	Musket	583	16	26	Std	3	6	4+	3		36
II/von Wolframsdorf Regiment zu Fuss	Infantry	Musket		16	26	Std	3	6	4+	3		36
I/von Schladen Regiment zu Fuss	Infantry	Musket		16	26	Std	3	6	4+	3		36
Schützen	Infantry	Rifle	120	4	6	Tiny	1	1	4+	1	Skirmish, S/shooter	23
6-pdr battalion guns	Artillery	Lt. S/bore		4	6	2 models	2/1/1	1	4+	1		42
6-pdr Artillery Coy (Decker, eight guns)	Artillery	Lt. S/bore		4	6	1 model	4/3/1	1	4+	2		31
6-pdr Artillery Coy (Scholten, six guns)	Artillery	Lt. S/bore		4	6	1 model	3/2/1	1	4+	2		23
Generalmajor Friedrich Adrian Dietrich von Roeder (BP=2)												80
(Reserve) II/Garde zu Fuss	Infantry	Musket		16	26	Std	3	6	4+	3		36
III/Garde zu Fuss	Infantry	Musket		16	26	Std	3	6	4+	3		36
6-pdr battalion guns	Artillery	Lt. S/bore		2	3	1 model	2/1/1	1	4+	1		21
10-pdr Howitzer Coy (Alkier, four guns)	Artillery	Lt. S/bore		2	3	1 model	1/1/1	1	4+	2		15
6-pdr Artillery Coy (Wille, six guns)	Artillery	Lt. S/bore		4	6	1 model	3/2/1	1	4+	2		23
Generalleutnant Ludwig Karl von Kalckstein (1 re-roll per turn within 12cm)												80
Generalmajor Karl von Herzberg (BP=2)												80
I/Herzog von Braunschweig Regiment zu Fuss	Infantry	Musket		16	26	Std	3	6	4+	3		36
II/Herzog von Braunschweig Regiment zu Fuss	Infantry	Musket		16	26	Std	3	6	4+	3		36
Grenadiers/Herzog von Braunschweig Regt. zu Fuss	Infantry	Musket		16	26	Std	3	7	4+	3	Elite 4+	43
Schützen	Infantry	Rifle	120	4	6	Tiny	1	1	4+	1	Skirmish, S/shooter	23
6-pdr battalion guns	Artillery	Lt. S/bore		2	3	1 model	2/1/1	1	4+	1		21
6-pdr Artillery Coy (Wundersitz, eight guns)	Artillery	Lt. S/bore		4	6	1 model	4/3/1	1	4+	2		31

Generalmajor Friedrich Gisbert Wilhelm von Romberg (BP=2)													80
	I/Prinz Heinrich Regiment zu Fuss	Infantry	Musket		16	26	Std	3	6	4+	3		36
	II/Prinz Heinrich Regiment zu Fuss	Infantry	Musket		16	26	Std	3	6	4+	3		36
	Grenadiers/Prinz Heinrich Regiment zu Fuss	Infantry	Musket		16	26	Std	3	7	4+	3	Elite 4+	43
	Schützen	Infantry	Rifle	120	4	6	Tiny	1	1	4+	1	Skirmish, S/shooter	23
	6-pdr battalion guns	Artillery	Lt. S/bore		2	3	1 model	2/1/1	1	4+	1		21
	6-pdr Artillery Coy (Pototzky, eight guns)	Artillery	Lt. S/bore		4	6	1 model	4/3/1	1	4+	2		31
Generalleutnant Nikolaus Heinrich von Schönfeld (1 re-roll per turn within 12cm)													80
Generalmajor Johann Friedrich Heinrich Christoph Wilhelm von Katte													80
	Dragoons von Lottum (5 sqdns) I	Cavalry	Sabre/Carbine		8	14	Std	1	8	4+	3	Heavy Cav. +1	45
	Dragoons von Lottum II	Cavalry	Sabre/Carbine		8	14	Std	1	8	4+	3	Heavy Cav. +1	45
	Dragoons von Tschirschky (5 sqdns) I	Cavalry	Sabre/Carbine		8	14	Std	1	8	4+	3	Heavy Cav. +1	45
	Dragoons von Tschirschky II	Cavalry	Sabre/Carbine		8	14	Std	1	8	4+	3	Heavy Cav. +1	45
	½ 6-pdr Horse Artillery Coy (Hahn, three guns)	Artillery	Lt. S/bore		2	3	1 model	2/1/1	1	4+	2		12
Generalmajor Hans Friedrich Heinrich von Borstell													80
	Kürassiers von Borstell (5 sqdns) I	Cavalry	Sabre/Carbine		8	14	Std	1	9	4+	3	Heavy Cav. D3	51
	Kürassiers von Borstell II	Cavalry	Sabre/Carbine		8	14	Std	1	9	4+	3	Heavy Cav. D3	51
	6-pdr Horse Artillery Coy (Meyer, six guns)	Artillery	Lt. S/bore		4	6	1 model	3/2/1	1	4+	2		23
Generalmajor Erich Magnus von Wolffradt													80
	Husaren von Wolffradt (10 sqdns) I	Cavalry	Sabre/Carbine		8	14	Std	1	6	4+	3		37
	Husaren von Wolffradt II	Cavalry	Sabre/Carbine		8	14	Std	1	6	4+	3		37
	Husaren von Wolffradt III	Cavalry	Sabre/Carbine		8	14	Std	1	6	4+	3		37
	Husaren von Wolffradt IV	Cavalry	Sabre/Carbine		8	14	Std	1	6	4+	3		37

Special Scenario Rules

Only the French infantry can form 'attack column'. The Prussian infantry have the choice of march column, line or square, while the schützen can also be deployed as skirmishers. However, the French infantry cannot form square and are disordered before delivering closing fire if charged by cavalry.[46]

The battalion gun sections are treated as separate units attached to their parent battalions. When the battalion guns move, they have the orders of their parent unit provided they are within 6cm/inches of the parent unit. To avoid unrealistically overcrowding the table it is important to remove the limbers when the battalion guns are unlimbered. The battalion guns provide closing fire if in base-to-base contact with their parent battalion when it is charged, but they do not provide support as they are part of the battalion.

If the French infantry columns charge home but fail to force the Prussian infantry to retire or break, they become disordered and must be reformed into line as a free compulsory move.

Units defending on a slope can re-roll one failed morale save in the first round of close combat.

In my games I use the rules from the 'Clash of Eagles' supplement for the replacement of killed or wounded commanders. The replacement commander appears in the next command phase but with a staff rating reduced by one. From the same supplement I also use the rules for penetration of artillery shots at medium and long range. In each range band a line is drawn from the gun barrel through the centre or leader model of the initial target and any unit crossed by this line up to the end of the range band, meaning half range for medium or full range for long range, will also be potentially hit but counting as an unclear target. Separate die rolls are made for each target.

Victory Conditions

The game begins at 10:00 a.m. and ends at 1:00 p.m. which gives a total of 13 turns.

The goal of the Prussian army is to repel the French attack which they can achieve by breaking two of the three French brigades. The French need to capture Pirmasens by breaking four of the Prussian brigades. If neither side has achieved its goal before the end of turn 13, the game is drawn.

The Historical Outcome

In this battle, the Prussian army showed why it was the most feared in Europe at the time. Brunswick had sufficient time to move his forces from their camps to the west of Pirmasens into position creating a killing field based around his artillery and *schützen* beyond the Stein Bach. The hastily arranged French columns were soon thrown into disorder as they veered into the valley of the Blümels Bach (the Blümelsthal) to escape the fire. Although a successful French cavalry charge drove their opposite numbers to the outskirts of Pirmasens itself, it was to no avail and by 1:00 p.m. the Corps des Vosges had been reduced to a 'herd of fugitives'.[47] The French claimed to have lost 1,815

46 Lynn, *Bayonets*, pp.259–260.
47 Chuquet, *Wissembourg*, p.168.

men killed or taken prisoner and 226 wounded. The Prussians however claimed to have taken 1,833 men as prisoners of war and buried a further 800 corpses. Furthermore, the French lost 19 guns (three 12-pdrs, one 8-pdr, thirteen 4-pdrs and two howitzers).[48] Meanwhile the Prussian casualties were approximately 200 men killed and wounded, including six officers.[49] However the Prussians chose not to fully exploit their victory, calling off their pursuit just short of the French camp at Hornbach.

In the aftermath of the defeat, Moreaux blamed the unfortunate Guillaume for leading the army into the poor terrain that was the Blümelsthal. In fact, the wounded Guillaume covered the retreat of the army as best he could in the circumstances, but this did not save him from being summoned before the Revolutionary Tribunal. Despite his failure to recognise the difficulties present by the terrain to the north and east of Pirmasens, Moreaux rose to the command of the Armée de la Moselle (2 July 1794).[50]

Other Rulesets

General de Brigade: If playing the scenario using General de Brigade, the following ratings should be used:

> All the French infantry should be classed as 2nd line, since the *volontaire* battalions were all raised at least a year before the battle, so a conscript rating is probably too harsh.
>
> The Prussian infantry are all rated as line, except for the *garde* battalions which are rated as guard.
>
> The cavalry should all be rated as line, but the French should have 'Inferior mounts'.
>
> The artillery should all be rated as line.
>
> All the rough ground on the table is classified as difficult terrain with steep slopes.

Lasalle: To play the scenario using the Lasalle rules, Greg Savvinos and David Sinclair have provided unit lists which can be found on the Honour Facebook forum, although they recommend that the Prussians use the 1806 statistics from the Army Maker.[51]

48 Colin, *Campagne de 1793*, p.405; also included are the losses recorded for each of the French units (p.406).
49 Grawert, *Schlacht bei Pirmasenz*, p.99.
50 Colin, *Campagne de 1793*, p.406.
51 Greg Savvinos and David Sinclair, *Lasalle II Revolution: Unit lists* available at: <https://www.facebook.com/groups/336901933776882/files/files>, accessed 10/04/2023.

Scenario 3

The Siege of Toulon – the Night Assault on Fort Mulgrave 16–17 December 1793

French vs British, Spanish, Sardinians and Neapolitans. This scenario is a battalion level action using *Black Powder*™ II rules.

Background

By the end of November, the 28,000 inhabitants of the port of Toulon had been joined by a truly multinational force under British command. The initial 1,500 French Federalist troops had been joined by 2,100 British soldiers, seamen and marines, almost 1,600 Sardinians, 4,800 men from the Kingdom of Naples, and 6,800 Spaniards, a total of 16,900 men.[52] The Republican forces besieging Toulon comprised elements of both the Armée d'Italie and the Armée des Alpes and were initially under the command of Carteaux to the west of the port and Lapoype to the east.[53] However the six *Représentants* involved in the siege, Escudier, Fréron, Barras, Gasparin, Roubaud and Albitte, gave Carteaux command over all the forces before Toulon (4 September).[54] Carteaux's command rose from 7,900 men (9 September) to more than 38,000 men (11 December). *Capitaine* Buonaparte, having arrived from Marseilles (16 September), took command of Carteaux's artillery when Dommartin[55] was wounded during the clash at Ollioules, as Carteaux closed in on the port.[56] The *Représentants* then proposed the promotion of Buonaparte to *chef de bataillon*, which was confirmed 18 October.

The siege made slow progress, hampered by an active defence, commanded by Lieutenant-General Charles O'Hara, the Governor of Toulon. Consequently, Carteaux was replaced by Doppet (10 November), who brought with him Du Teil to command the artillery. However, Buonaparte is credited with proposing, to Carteaux and his successors, the plan to take Toulon via the capture of Fort Mulgrave, to the southeast of the harbour guarding the entrance, fire from which would force the Allied fleet to leave the port. Following an abortive assault on Fort Mulgrave (15 November), Doppet was replaced by Dugommier (16 November).[57] During a failed sortie by the Allied garrison, the Allied commander O'Hara was captured (30 November). Buonaparte showed great energy in creating a series of batteries from which Fort Mulgrave and the Allied shipping could be targeted. When all was ready Dugommier launched a night assault on both Fort Mulgrave and Mount Faron (to the northeast of the port), which were successful (17 December). The French assault on Fort Mulgrave was led by two columns, Victor led 2,000 men towards the *Redoute Saint Louis* on the left and Brûlé led another 2,000 men against the right of Fort Mulgrave itself.

---

52 Phipps, *West*, p.110; Robert Forczyk, *Toulon 1793, Napoleon's First Great Victory* (Oxford: Osprey, 2005), pp.31–32.

53 Phipps, *West*, p.112; *Général de Division* Jean-François, Marquis de Lapoype.

54 Jean-François Escudier, Thomas Augustin Gasparin, (*Représentants en Mission* to Var and Bouches-du-Rhône); Jean-Louis Roubaud (Armée d'Italie) and Antoine Louis Albitte (Armée des Alpes).

55 *Général de Brigade* Elzéar-Auguste Cousin de Dommartin.

56 Forczyk, *Toulon*, p.34–35.

57 *Général de Division* Jean Coquille Dugommier.

There is some confusion regarding the interpretation of Dugommier's orders, in his biography of Dugommier, Chuquet reverses the targets of the columns by interpreting left and right from the French perspective whereas the orders are written from Fort Mulgrave's perspective, as indicated by the mention of the 'height of Éguillette' (the *Redoute Saint Louis*) as Victor's target. This is surprising since in his earlier biography of Napoleon he presented it correctly.[58] The *Redoute Saint Louis* was assailed three times by Victor's column before it fell after losing a third of the garrison.[59] Dugommier had to commit both of his reserve columns to take Fort Mulgrave. Buonaparte took part in the assault with these reserves and was wounded in the thigh. A counterattack was organised from the *Redoute Saint Charles* but was called off.[60] In this final assault the British lost 292 men,[61] while their Spanish allies lost 365 men,[62] and the French casualties were reported as 80 dead and 200 wounded.[63] The next day, as predicted by Buonaparte, the allies held a council of war and Vice Admiral Hood decided to withdraw his fleet together with 15,000 inhabitants of Toulon, keen to distance themselves from the vengeful *Représentants* (19 December). In the aftermath nearly 300 citizens of Toulon were either shot or guillotined, overseen by *Représentant* Fréron, but the total number killed in the chaos may have been as high as 2,000. Also involved in the siege were names that would later become famous, Junot, Marmont, Masséna, Suchet and Victor. Amongst the rewards handed out by a grateful republic, Buonaparte was promoted to *Général de Brigade* (22 December, confirmed 6 February 1794).[64]

Spanish Infantry

58 Arthur Chuquet, *Dugommier (1738–1794)* (Paris: A. Fontemoing, 1904), pp.94–95; Félix Alcan (ed.), *Revue Historique* (Paris: Germer Baillère et Cie, 1886), vol. XXX, p.374–376; Arthur Chuquet, *La Jeunesse de Napoléon, III Toulon* (Paris: Armand Colin, 1899), p.216.

59 Indalecio Núñez Iglesias and José María Blanco Núñez, *La Diversion de Tolon* (Madrid: Editorial Naval, 1982) vol. II, pp.166; Victor François Perrin, *Mémoires de Claude-Victor Perrin* (Paris: Dumaine,1847) vol. I, p.184.

60 Chuquet, *Dugommier*, pp.96–102.

61 Anon., *The European magazine, and London review*, vol. XXV (London: J.Sewell, 1794), pp.79–80; due to the confusion of the evacuation of Toulon Dundas reported his casualties as missing; Royal Artificers–3, Royal Artillery–25, 2/1st Foot–20, 18th Foot–3, 30th Foot–150, Marines–62, Royal Navy–29.

62 Iglesias and Núñez, *Tolon*, vol. II, pp.196–197; these numbers exclude the casualties amongst the artillery crews, perhaps a further 10 men, based on *Coronel* Ariz's report.

63 Forczyk, *Toulon*, p.73; Chuquet, *Dugommier*, p.103.

64 Phipps, *West*, pp.110–120; Willis, *Fleet Battle*, p.28; Jones, *Companion*, p.118.

The Game

This scenario refights the night attack on Fort Mulgrave that culminated in the end of the siege and the evacuation of Toulon by the allies. Although Vice Admiral Hood held overall command of the Allied forces in Toulon, the Caire Peninsula, and the *Hauteur de Grasse*, the site of Fort Mulgrave, was predominantly garrisoned by Spanish troops, with British, Sardinian, and Neapolitan contingents in support. Consequently *Marescal de Campo* (Major-General) Don Domingo Izquierdo García was the senior officer present during the French assault.[65]

The Caire Peninsula was fortified by a series of works, some permanent and some temporary, Fort Mulgrave (also known as the *Redoute Anglaise*), *Redoute Saint Charles, Redoute Saint Louis, Fort de Balaguier* and *Fort de l'Éguillette*. The *Redoute Saint Phillipe,* which was designed to hold five guns, was unfinished at the time of the action and remained ungarrisoned.[66]

On 7 November the garrisons of the Caire Peninsula comprised 1,443 Spaniards of all ranks, 265 British, 685 from Naples and 176 from Sardinia-Piedmont, a total of 2,569 men of all ranks.[67]

The different posts the Caire Peninsula were garrisoned as follows:

Fort Mulgrave

The French also called Fort Mulgrave 'Little Gibraltar' implying that it was stronger than it was. However, Dundas admits that it was a temporary position, which could not sustain lasting resistance to determined men. Its profile was weak and its layout defective. 150 metres long, it had parapets clad inside and out with pine trunks placed horizontally, embrasures with openings lined with boards, 20 cannons and four mortars of large calibre formed several batteries separated by numerous traverses [internal barriers], a ditch three metres deep by five metres wide, and, in front of this ditch, a double line of *chevaux-de-frise* and a row of abatis.[68]

Captain William Conolly (18th Foot) was the senior officer, commanding an estimated 635 men.[69] However when the French attack began, Conolly left the redoubt and Captain Philip Vaumorel (30th Foot) took command. These men commanded a British infantry contingent of three companies, 2nd battalion, 1st Foot–107 men,[70] a detachment, 1st battalion 18th Foot–64 men,[71] a detachment, 1st battalion, 30th Foot–94 men,[72] a detachment of His Majesty's Marine Force–67 men. Supporting the British

65 Martinez, *Diccionario*, pp.449–50; Iglesias and Núñez, *Tolon*, vol. II, pp.160–161; Isquierdo was *coronel* of the R.I. Mallorca.

66 Chuquet, *Dugommier*, p.101.

67 Iglesias and Núñez, *Tolon*, vol. II, p.40.

68 Chuquet, *Dugommier*, p.58.

69 *The European magazine*, vol. XXV, pp.77–80; the garrison is based on Dundas' statement of strength and casualty list. The 700 men quoted includes the detachment of British troops on outpost duty(q.v.). Conolly's seniority dated to 26 December 1788.

70 Richard Cannon, *Historical Record of the First or Royal Regiment of Foot* (London: William Clowes and Son, 1837), p.154.

71 Richard Cannon, *Historical record of the Eighteenth, or Royal Irish, Regiment of Foot* (London: Parker, Furnivall and Parker, 1848), p.52; George Le Mesurier Gretton, *The Campaigns and History of the Royal Irish Regiment 1684–1902* (London: W. Blackwood and Sons 1911), pp.91–93.

72 Neil Bannatyne, *History of the Thirtieth Regiment now the First Battalion East Lancashire Regiment 1689–1881* (Liverpool: Littlebury Bros., 1923), pp.181–191; commanded by Captain Philip Vaumorel (Seniority

infantry were two companies, 2° battaglione del Reggimento De Courten (Sardinia-Piedmont)–160 men.[73]

The redoubt held 22 guns which were manned by a mixed detachment comprising, seamen of the Royal Navy–66 men, 2nd battalion, Royal Artillery–66 men, including 10 men from the Royal Artificers.[74] The senior gunner was Lieutenant John Duncan (Thomson's Company, 2nd Battalion, Royal Artillery).[75] However, there were several Royal Navy officers associated with the defence, recorded as either wounded or missing during the French assault, namely Lieutenant Goddard and Midshipman John W. Loring (HMS *Victory*) together with Midshipman Algernon Wilkie (HMS *Princess Royal*).[76]

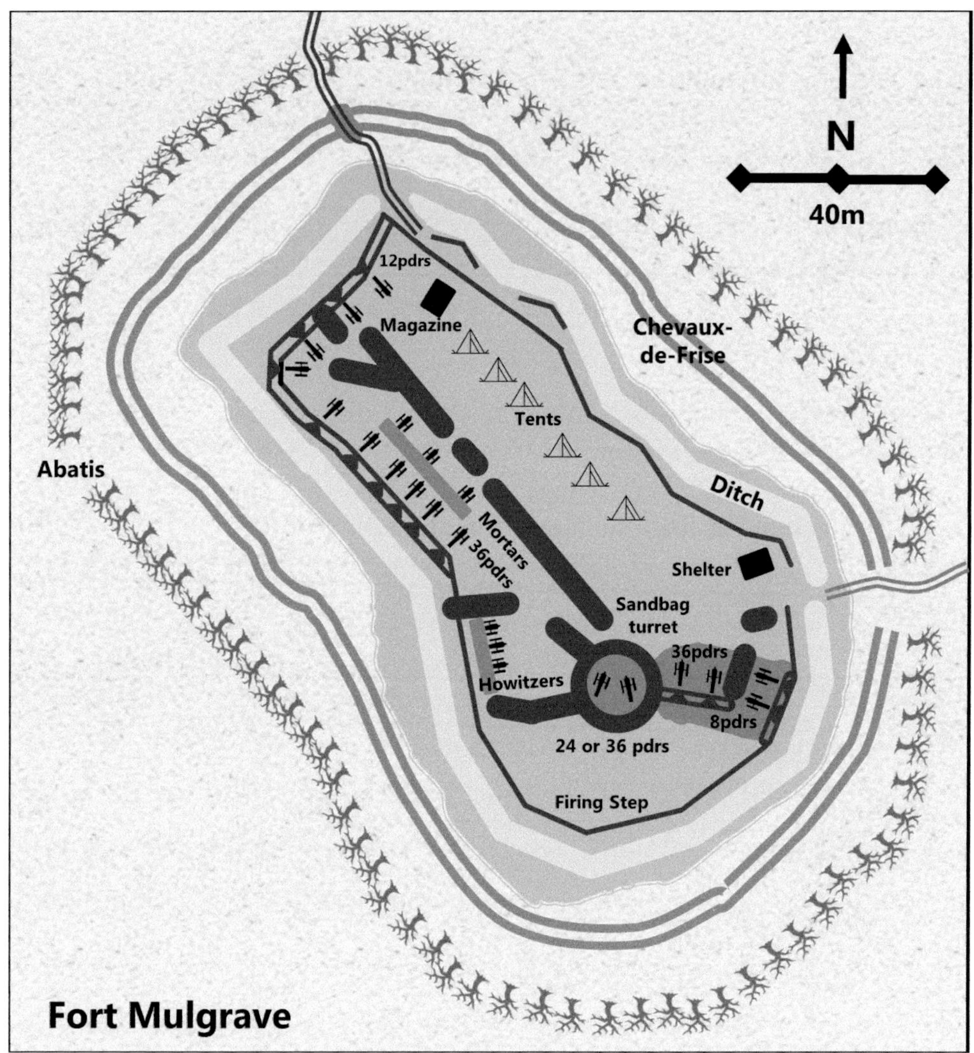

The artillery comprised ten 36-pdrs, two 24-pdrs or two additional 36-pdrs in the sandbag turret, two 12-pdrs, two 8-pdrs, three mortars and three howitzers. Map 12 shows the layout of Fort Mulgrave which was on two levels.[77]

Map 12 – Fort Mulgrave

9 July 1793). Originally four companies of the regiment were deployed to defend Toulon. This number has been reduced to reflect the detachment of some men to the picket line.

73 Revel, *Memoires*, p.168; Forczyk, *Toulon*, p.65; Strength from Iglesias and Núñez, *Tolon*, vol. II, pp.40, 78, this OOB excludes British troops that arrived in late November and early December.

74 Strengths estimated based on the number of guns, divided equally between the Royal Navy and Royal Artillery/Artificers reflecting the reported casualties (29 vs 28 respectively).

75 Francis Duncan, *History of the Royal Artillery* (London: John Murray, 1879), vol. II, p.68; Chuquet, *Dugommier,* p.93; M.E.S.Laws, *Battery Records of the Royal Artillery 1716–1859* (Woolwich: Royal Artillery Institute, 1952), p.80; note the Royal Artillery detachment was made up of three different companies then based in Gibraltar.

76 The National Archives, Kew, (TNA), FO 95 4 6 Corsica Toulon, p.609.

77 National Army Museum, Chelsea, Accession No. 1981-11-17; Hand drawn copy of maps drawn by a Mr. Sardou in 1794; Krebs and Moris, *Campagnes 1792-1793*, Carte three Siège de Toulon en 1793; Forczyk, *Toulon*, p.70; the armament of the redoubt varies in different sources. Krebs and Moris's version of Sardou's map has 24-pdrs on the sandbag turret and has a slightly different layout for the mortars and howitzers. Krebs and Moris attributed the map to *Chef de Bataillon* Armand Samuel de Marescot, Dugommier's chief engineer at Toulon (p.383). Forcyzk gives the armament as two 36-pdrs, four 24-pdrs, two 12-pdrs and two mortars.

Redoute Saint Charles

The garrison of the *Redoute Saint Charles* was commanded by Izquierdo himself.[78] Captain Vaumorel (30th Foot) described the garrison as 700 strong, but this has been reduced here to 644 to accommodate the detachment of men on picket duty.[79] The strengths for the various detachments given below are estimates derived from the order of battle for 23 November 1793, using estimated company strengths where necessary.[80] The Spanish contingent comprised the grenadier companies of both the 1° Batallón del Regimiento de Hibernia (78 men) and the 2° Batallón del Regimiento Suizos de Betschart (108 men), together with the Cazadores de 1° Batallón del Regimiento de Málaga (50 men),[81] a provincial volunteer unit, as well as detachments of the Cuerpo de Batallones de Marina (243 men), Real Cuerpo de Artillería and seaman (66 men). Also present was a detachment of the Reggimento Fanteria di Linea di Borgogna (99 men) provided by the Kingdom of Naples.[82] The artillerymen served four light guns, probably 4-pdr pieces of the Gribeauval design.[83]

Redoute Saint Louis

The Redoute Saint Louis was garrisoned by the Spanish, commanded by the *Coronel* Don Luis Ariza, who would be wounded twice in the assault.[84] He led 437 men comprised of Regimiento de Milicies Provinciale de Chinchilla (84 men), Regimiento de Milicies Provinciale de Lorca (84 men), 2° Batallón del Regimiento de Infanteria de Córdoba (236 men including their grenadiers).[85] A detachment of artillerymen were also present serving two to four light guns, again most likely 4-pdrs.

Piquet Line

The garrisons maintained a line of outposts to give early warning the French attack. This force has been estimated at 300 men, comprising 1° Batallón del Regimiento Málaga (Spain, 132 men), Reggimento Fanteria di Linea di Borgogna (Naples, 99 men)[86] and 1st Battalion, 30th Foot (Britain, 66 men).[87]

78 Iglesias and Núñez, *Tolon*, vol. II, p.189.

79 John Philippart, *The Royal Military Calendar* (London: A.J.Valpy, 1820), vol. IV, p.265.

80 Iglesias and Núñez, *Tolon*, vol. II, pp.71–80.

81 Iglesias and Núñez, *Tolon*, vol. II, p.154; Anon, *Mercurio de España, Enero de 1794* (Madrid: Imprenta Real, 1794), vol. I, p.125; Iglesias and Núñez gives the number of *Cazadores* as an unlikely 500, but the Mercurio gives the strength as 50 men.

82 Luigi del Pozzo, *Cronaca civile e militare delle Due Sicilie sotto la dinastia Borbonica dall'anno 1734 in poi* (Naples: Stamperia Real, 1857), pp.153–154; Iglesias and Núñez, *Tolon*, vol. I, pp.312–313, 315; both battalions of this regiment went to Toulon, the first on 16 September and the second on 21 October. In early October there were detachments of the first battalion deployed on the Caire Peninsula as well as *Fort Saint Antoine* to the north of Toulon.

83 Esdaile, *Spanish Army*, p.154.

84 Iglesias and Núñez, *Tolon*, vol. II, p.195; Martinez, *Diccionario*, p.545; Chuquet, *Dugommier*, p.101; he served in the Córdoba regiment.

85 Iglesias and Núñez, *Tolon*, vol. II, p.189; the total strength of 437 is given in *Amiral* Federico Carlos Gravina y Nápoli's report to Godoy (3 January 1794).

86 Anon., *Gazzetta universale*, 2, 7 January 1794, (publisher not identified) p.15.

87 The sources do not identify the British unit providing the picket line, but, on balance, it was likely to be 30th Foot given the high numbers of men missing from that regiment.

Fort de Balaguier

The fort was garrisoned by 150 men of the Regimiento de Infanteria de Mallorca (Spain) together with perhaps 30 seamen serving the guns.[88]

Fort de l'Éguillette

The fort was garrisoned by a total of 500 men from the Kingdom of Naples, comprising the Reggimento Fanteria di Linea di Borgogna (99 men), Reggimento Fanteria di Linea di Real Macedone (203) and a detachment of the Battaglione de Marinas (209 men).[89] The four guns were served by approximately 30 seamen.

The French

Dugommier gathered his best troops to lead the attack on Fort Mulgrave. The French force was organised into three columns and a reserve. The first column was commanded by *Chef de Brigade* Claude-Victor-Perrin, the future *Maréchal de France*. Victor led three battalions, the 2e bataillon, 23e Régiment d'Infanterie,[90] 1er Volontaires du Gard and the Légion des Volontaires Montagnards.[91] Supporting them was a light infantry detachment from these battalions and a detachment of the Légion des Allobroges. In all Victor led approximately 2,000 men. Victor's column was accompanied by the *Représentants* Saliceti and Augustin Robespierre.[92]

Chef de Brigade Nicolas Brûlé commanded the second column, also of 2,000 men, which comprised three battalions: 2e Volontaires de la Côte D'Or, 11e Volontaires de la Drôme, 4e Volontaires de la Montagne d'Aix, together with the *carabiniers* and *chasseurs* of the 6e Légion de Marseilles.[93] Brûlé was accompanied by the *Représentants* Fréron and Ricord.[94]

Général de Division Henri François Delaborde commanded the third column of 1,500 men comprising three battalions: 5e Volontaires des Haute Alpes,[95] 1er Volontaires de l'Ardèche and the 5e Grenadier Bataillon from the Army of the Alps.[96] Another future

88 Iglesias and Núñez, *Tolon*, vol. I, p.237; the R.I. Mallorca went to Balaguier 21 September, two battalions of the regiment served at Toulon.

89 Forczyk, *Toulon*, p.77, Anon, *Mercurio de España*, p.155, Paul Cottin, *Toulon et les Anglais en 1793* (Paris: P.Ollendorff, 1898), p.310.

90 Forczyk, *Toulon*, p.30; Krebs and Moris, *Campagnes 1792–1793, Piece Just.* 114, 104 and 112; Forczyk has the first battalion, but the 2e/23e was the unit sent to Toulon from Lyon.

91 Victor Louis Jean François Belhomme, *Histoire de l'Infanterie en France* (Paris; Henri Charles Lavauzelle, 1899), vol. IV, 1893–1902, p.55; Balthazar Marie Michel Chastel, *Le sans-culotte Chastel,... à tous ses frères les membres des sociétés populaires de la République, en prenant le commandement des Légionnaires montagnards. (17 brumaire an II.)*(Marseille: J. Mossy, 1793), pp.4, 8; Krebs and Moris (*Campagnes 1792–1793, Piece Just.* 112) describe this unit as the *Bataillon de la Montagne,* but this is the most likely unit, raised in September 1793, comprising two battalions each of eight fusilier companies, one of carabiniers and one of chasseurs.

92 Chuquet, *Dugommier*, p.94; Antoine Christophe Saliceti, Augustin Bon Jos de Robespierre (the younger brother).

93 Krebs and Moris, *Campagnes 1792–1793, Piece Just.* 112; describe this unit as the *6e de Marseille*. The unit was also called the *6e Volontaires des Bouches-du-Rhône*, see <https://revolutionsehrivolontaires.wordpress.com/bouches-du-rhone/>, accessed 25 February 2022.

94 Chuquet, *Dugommier*, p.94; Louis Stanislas Fréron, Jean-François Ricord.

95 Also known as the *2e Chasseurs*.

96 Belhomme, *Histoire*, vol. IV, p.31; formed 4 May 1793 from two regular and four volunteer coys, probably including grenadier company of the 1er/50e *R.Infanterie* (Forczyk, p.76). Furthermore, Étienne-François Girard (10e *R. Infanterie*) was wounded during the attack on Fort Mulgrave, which suggests that the grenadiers of this regiment were also in this battalion.

maréchal, Marmont advanced with Delaborde's column.[97] *Chef de Bataillon* Napoleone di Buonaparte commanded the reserve of 1,700 men, comprised of two battalions, the 4e Volontaires de la Haute Garonne and the 5e Volontaires de la Haute Garonne, these battalions were supported by a detachment of the Chasseurs Allobroges.[98]

Around the Allied positions was a ring of French batteries, established by Buonaparte, which had bombarded Fort Mulgrave in the days before the assault, but which took no part in the assault itself.

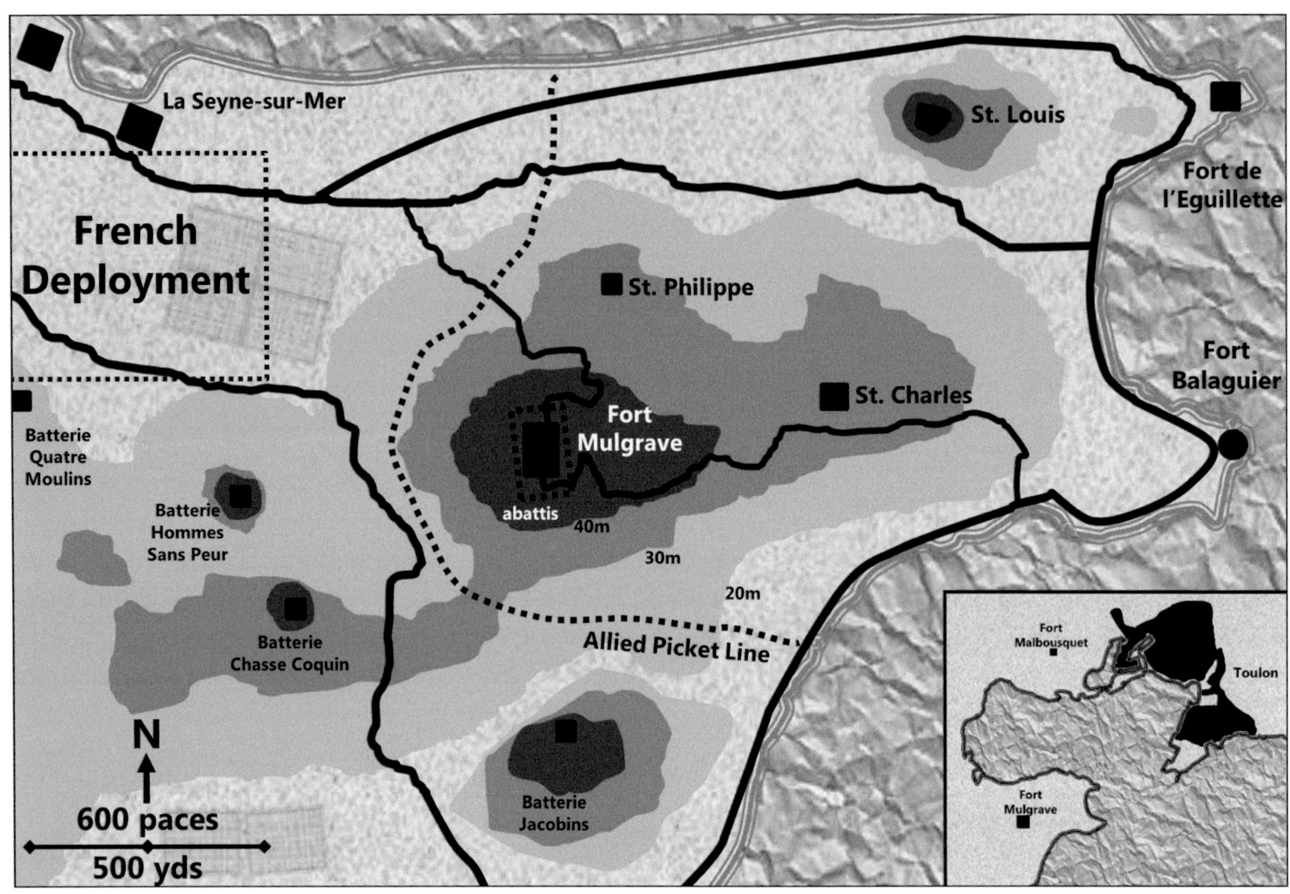

Map 13 – Assault on Fort Mulgrave, Toulon

Deployment

The map is designed for a table of six feet by four feet using a ground scale of 1mm to two paces, using the centimetre scale for *Black Powder*™ (meaning that distances in the rules are read as centimetres rather than inches). For games using 28mm figures (at a scale of one inch represents 25 yards) the same size table will only accommodate the area covering Fort Mulgrave, Fort Saint Charles and Fort Saint Louis and an eight feet long table would be a better choice.

97 Auguste Frédéric Louis Viesse de Marmont, *Mémoires du Maréchal Marmont, Duc de Raguse* (Paris: Perrotin, 1857), vol. I, p.24.

98 Crowdy, *French Light Infantry*, pp.41–42; The *Légion Allobroges* comprised seven companies of *chasseurs*, seven companies of *carabiniers*, three companies of light dragoons and a company of light artillery.

The French should be deployed in the area shown on the map. In the historical deployment Victor's column was on the French left and Brûlé's column was on the French right, with Delaborde's column held back in the centre with the intention of supporting either of the leading columns as required. Buonaparte's reserve force was deployed in the rear.[99]

The allies are deployed within 150mm (12 inches for 28mm) of the redoubts/forts that they are garrisoning.

Scenario Specific Rules for *Black Powder*™

The effect of night on the French attack can be represented by increasing the likelihood of a blunder result in the command tests together with some increased limitations on visibility.

Deployment: It is important that none of the Allied units are deployed in 'march column' at the beginning of the game to reflect the fact that they had no warning of the attack.

Visibility: The night of the 16–17 December 1793 was marked by a full moon; however, the weather was stormy and when Dugommier led the French assault at 1:00 a.m. (17 December) he did so under the cover of a violent rainstorm followed by a misty fog.[100]

Given these conditions it is likely that visibility would have been continually variable and different in individual parts of the battlefield. In this scenario the range of visibility is determined by the score of three D6 measured in centimetres (inches for 28mm scale games). This is determined separately for each command on both sides before they move or shoot, in each turn. D20 die can be used to mark these scores.

Orders: During the night assault Victor's and Brûlé's columns actually ran into one another during the assault, despite being ordered to different flanks of the position.[101] Consequently, in our game, 'Blunders' will be of increased frequency, resulting from command rolls of 2, 3, 11 and 12, thereby increasing blunders at the expense of the 'three move' results. Blunder results are then determined using the score of an Average die (2, 3, 3, 4, 4, 5) on the standard results table.

To reflect the uncertainty as to whether an attack was being launched, the Allied commander cannot issue orders until after the first shooting takes place.

Hills: the slopes on the hills approaching Fort Mulgrave and *Redoute Saint Louis* have a gradient of approximately 15 percent. To reflect this, the ground above the 30m contour should be considered rough ground, halving movement.

Redoubts: All redoubts are governed by the rules for obstacles, the attackers needing 6cm/inches in addition to the movement to make contact. The defenders can claim the protection of the redoubt until they lose a round of combat. Fort Mulgrave can accommodate three artillery models plus one infantry unit. The other redoubts held only two to four guns and therefore could have been quite small; using Fort Mulgrave as

99 Alcan, *Revue Historique*, vol. XXX, p.374–376; Dugommier's orders for the attack.

100 Krebs and Moris, *Campagnes 1792–1793*, p.384; Forczyk, *Toulon*, p.68; David Dundas, *Summary account of the proceeding of the Fleet and Army, employed at Toulon, in 1793* (Brentford: P.Norbury, 1805), p.11; Dundas has the assault beginning at 2:00 a.m. but most other sources give 1:00 a.m.

101 Perrin, *Mémoires*, vol. I, p.183.

the model they needed to be just 50–60 yards square, including the ditch and chevaux-de-frise. In our game, they would therefore be able to hold one artillery model and one small infantry unit.[102] At the point of being charged a redoubt's defenders can chose whether the infantry or the artillery will receive the charge. The chosen unit will then conduct both the closing fire and combat. The redoubts count as defensible positions and therefore broken brigades are not required to abandon them when they become broken.

Troop Quality: the quality of the French troops at this time was very variable given the upheaval caused by the revolution and the rapid expansion of the army using the volunteer battalions. The Légion des Allobroges (raised 13 August 1792) and the 2e Volontaires de la Côte d'Or (raised 1 September 1791) have been described as good troops, consistent with Dugommier's intention to use his best men in the assault.[103] However other battalions involved in the assault were raised very recently; Légion des Volontaires Montagnards (1 November 1793), 11e Volontaires de la Drôme (2 or 7 October 1793), 4e Volontaires de la Montagne d'Aix (after 22 October 1793), 5e Volontaires des Haute Alpes (11 July 1793). The other battalions were raised much earlier; 1er Volontaires du Gard (3 September 1791), 6e Légion de Marseilles (20 August 1792), 4e Volontaires de la Haute Garonne (8 March 1792), 5e Volontaires de la Haute Garonne (10 March 1792).[104]

Chuquet also stated that the volunteers of l'*Ardèche* did not know how to load their muskets, but this is unlikely to apply to the more experienced 1er Volontaires de l'Ardèche (1 July 1792), which had been congratulated on its performance at the recent siege of Lyon.

To reflect these differences the less experienced battalions have been allocated a weaker morale save and the special rules 'unreliable' and 'freshly raised'.

For the allies, the Spanish defenders of the *Redoute Saint Louis* have been given the special rule 'tough fighters' to reflect their stoic performance against Victor's column.

The *Représentants*: The influence of these civilians can be represented by a special rule to reflect their impact on the morale of the troops. When a unit accompanied by a *Représentant* either charges or is charged, a command test is taken before closing fire and the test is completed without the normal modifiers. If the unmodified dice roll (2 D6) succeeds by scoring seven or less. the accompanying unit either gets 'Terrifying Charge' when attacking or 'Stubborn' when defending. On a blunder (a score of 12) the *Représentants* flees the field and is removed from play and the accompanying unit takes a break test immediately. A *Représentant* can only accompany one unit at any one time. This test gives a 42 percent chance of success but if you think the *Représentants* were either more or less inspiring, then use a different staff rating, for example a staff rating of six gives a 28 percent chance of success, while a staff rating of eight gives a 72 percent chance of success.[105]

---

102 The nineteenth century map, the *Carte d'État Major*, shows the *Redoute Saint Louis*, then called the *Redoute de Grasse*, measuring approximately 65x45 metres.

103 Chuquet, *Dugommier*, pp.55–56.

104 Camille Rousset, *Les Volontaires 1791–1794* (Paris: Didier, 1870), p.314; *Bataillons de volontaires nationaux. Un projet de la SEHRI*, available at: <https://revolutionsehrivolontaires.wordpress.com/equipe-et-presentation/>, accessed 1 March 2022.

105 Perrin, *Mémoires*, vol. I, p.183.

Victory Conditions: No artillery units or tiny units count towards brigade break points. The French need to take two or more of the three Allied redoubts (Mulgrave, St. Charles, and St. Louis) to claim victory, and if only one redoubt is taken the result is a draw. All other results are an Allied victory. The scenario will last a maximum of 24 turns, equivalent to six hours.

The following tables are the playsheets for the two sides for the *Black Powder*™ rules. While the number of figures in a unit has no significance in this ruleset, for historical scenarios it can be important to ensure that the units occupy the correct frontage on the tabletop. For this scenario the unit sizes have been defined as follows; LARGE 18–24 figures, STANDARD 12–16 figures, SMALL 6–8 figures and TINY 3–4 figures. These numbers should be doubled if you base your figures in two ranks.

Black Powder™ Playsheet for the Assault on Fort Mulgrave, 16–17 December 1793

		Strength		Unit Size	Armament	Melee	Shooting	Morale	Stamina	Special Rules
		Men	Figures							
French	*Général de Division* Dugommier (Staff Rating 8)									
First Column	*Chef de Brigade* Victor (Breakpoint=2)									
	2/23e Régiment d'Infanterie	587	16*	STANDARD	Musket	6	3	4+	3	
	1er Volontaires du Gard	683	18*	LARGE	Musket	8	4	4+	4	Stubborn
	Légion des Volontaires Montagnards	497	16	STANDARD	Musket	6	3	5+	3	Unreliable, Freshly raised
	Légion des Allobroges and *Tirailleurs*	153	12	STANDARD	Musket	6	3	4+	3	Skirmish
Second Column	*Chef de Brigade* Nicolas Brûlé (BP=2)									
	2e Volontaires de la Côte D'Or	870	22*	LARGE	Musket	8	4	4+	4	
	11e Volontaires de la Drôme	622	16*	STANDARD	Musket	6	3	5+	3	Unreliable, Freshly raised
	4e Volontaires de la Montagne d'Aix and Carabiniers, 6e Légion de Marseilles	340	12	STANDARD	Musket	6	3	5+	3	Unreliable, Freshly raised
	Chasseurs, 6e Légion de Marseilles and *Tirailleurs*	143	12	STANDARD	Musket	6	3	4+	3	Skirmish
Third Column	*Général de Division* Henri François Delaborde (BP=2)									
	5e Volontaires des Haute Alpes	538	14*	STD	Musket	6	3	5+	3	Unreliable
	1er Volontaires de l'Ardèche	501	12*	STD	Musket	6	3	4+	3	
	5e Grenadier Bataillon (Armée des Alpes)	488	12*	STD	Musket	6	3	4+	3	
	Tirailleurs		7	SMALL	Musket	4	2	4+	2	Skirmish
Reserve	*Chef de Bataillon* Napoleone di Buonaparte (BP=2)									
	4e Volontaires de la Haute Garonne	779	18*	LARGE	Musket	8	4	4+	4	
	5e Volontaires de la Haute Garonne	892	21*	LARGE	Musket	8	4	4+	4	
	Chasseurs Allobroges and *Tirailleurs*	160	12	STANDARD	Musket	6	3	4+	3	Skirmish

Note: the asterisk indicates that the unit has contributed some tirailleurs to the combined tirailleur unit in each column at a rate of up to 15 percent of all ranks.

Strengths are taken from Krebs and Moris, *Campagnes 1792–1793, Piece Just.* 112 and are dated 11 December 1793.

Black Powder™ Playsheet for the Assault on Fort Mulgrave, 16–17 December 1793

		Strength		Unit Size	Armament	Melee	Shooting	Morale	Stamina	Special
		Men	Figures							
Spanish and Allied (Staff rating 7)										
Fort Mulgrave (Captains Connolly & Vaumorel)										
	1/30th, 2/1st, 1/18th, Marines (GB), 2/De Courten (Sardinia)	492	15	STANDARD	Musket	6	3	4+	3	First fire
	Royal Artillery/ Royal Artificers (GB)	66	2	1 MODEL	Howitzer	1	2/2/2	4+	2	
	Royal Navy seamen (GB)	66	2	2 MODELS	Std S/bore	1	3/2/1	4+	2	
Redoute Saint Charles (*Marescal de Campo* Don Domingo Izquierdo) (BP=4)										
	1/ R.I. Hib, 2/R.I. Betsch Gren. (Sp), R.F. Borgogna(Naples)	285	8	SMALL	Musket	4	2	4+	2	
	Marinas (Spain)	243	8	SMALL	Musket	4	2	4+	2	
	Caz. R.I. Málaga (Spain)	50	2	TINY	Musket	4	2	4+	2	
	Artillery/Seamen, four 4-pdr guns (Spain)	33	1	1 MODEL	Light S/bore	1	2/1/1	4+	1	
Redoute Saint Louis (Spain)										
	R.M.P. Chinchilla, R.M.P. Lorca, 2/R.I. Córdoba	168	6	SMALL	Musket	4	2	4+	2	Tough Fighters
	R.I. Córdoba	236	8	SMALL	Musket	4	2	4+	2	Tough Fighters
	Two to four 4-pdr guns	33	1	1 MODEL	Light S/bore	1	2/1/1	4+	1	
Picket Line										
	1/R.I. Málaga, R.I. Borgogna, 1/30th Foot (Spain and GB)	297	9	SMALL	Musket	4	2	4+	2	
Fort Balaguier (Spain)										
	R.I. Mallorca, Seamen gunners	165	5	SMALL	Musket	4	2	4+	2	
Fort L'Éguillette (Naples)										
	R.F.L. Real Macedone, R.F.L. Borgogna	302	9	SMALL	Musket	4	2	4+	2	Unreliable
	Marinas, Seamen gunners	209	7	SMALL	Musket	4	2	4+	2	Unreliable

Scenario 4:

The Battle of Boxtel – Abercromby's Attempt to Retake Boxtel, 15 September 1794

(French vs British). A battalion level action using *Black Powder*™ II rules.

Background

Joining the army at the age of eighteen in 1787, the future Duke of Wellington, Arthur Wesley moved through six different regiments on his way from ensign to lieutenant-colonel in the 33rd Foot in 1793. Arthur joined the War of the First Coalition during its second year, arriving in Ostend with his regiment on 25 June 1794. However, this was no glorious debut as the outnumbered allies were forced back by the Armée du Nord on the left and the Armée de Sambre-et-Meuse on the right. Thus, in September, the Duke of York's army found itself on the river Aa, 112 miles northeast of Ostend, hoping that the French would go into winter quarters.

The Hanoverian and Hessian advance guard of the army occupied the line of the river Dommel, around the town of Boxtel, six miles further forward. On 14 September, urged on by Paris, 40,000 men of Pichegru's 60,000-strong Armée du Nord, assailed the 12,000 men of von Hammerstein's advanced guard and threw them out of Boxtel with significant loss, although other posts along the Dommel were retained. The Duke of York's reaction was to send his Corps de Reserve, some 5,000 men, under Lieutenant-General Ralph Abercormby, to retake Boxtel at dawn on the 15 September. At around midnight Arthur Wesley, who commanded the Third Brigade, marched out to fight his first battle. As the sun rose, somewhere along the five-mile-long road between Schyndel and Boxtel, Abercromby's force encountered Delmas's 6e Division and a brief skirmish occurred, Wellington's First Battle.[106] Deciding that the French were too strong, Abercromby determined to retire back to Berlicum. By the time Abercromby

Horse Artillery 1792

106 Charles Antoine Thoumas, *Les grands cavaliers du Premier Empire. Notices biographiques. Series II* (Paris: Berger Levrault, 1892), pp.430–431; Chassin and Hennet, *Volontaires*, vol. II, p.760.

reached Berlicum again, the Duke of York had begun to withdraw his army back to the line of the river Meuse. The retreat continued over the following months until the army was evacuated from Bremen in April 1795. Arthur Wesley had already left the army on leave in February 1795.[107] This scenario assumes that Abercromby was somewhat less cautious and attempted to break through Delmas's division.

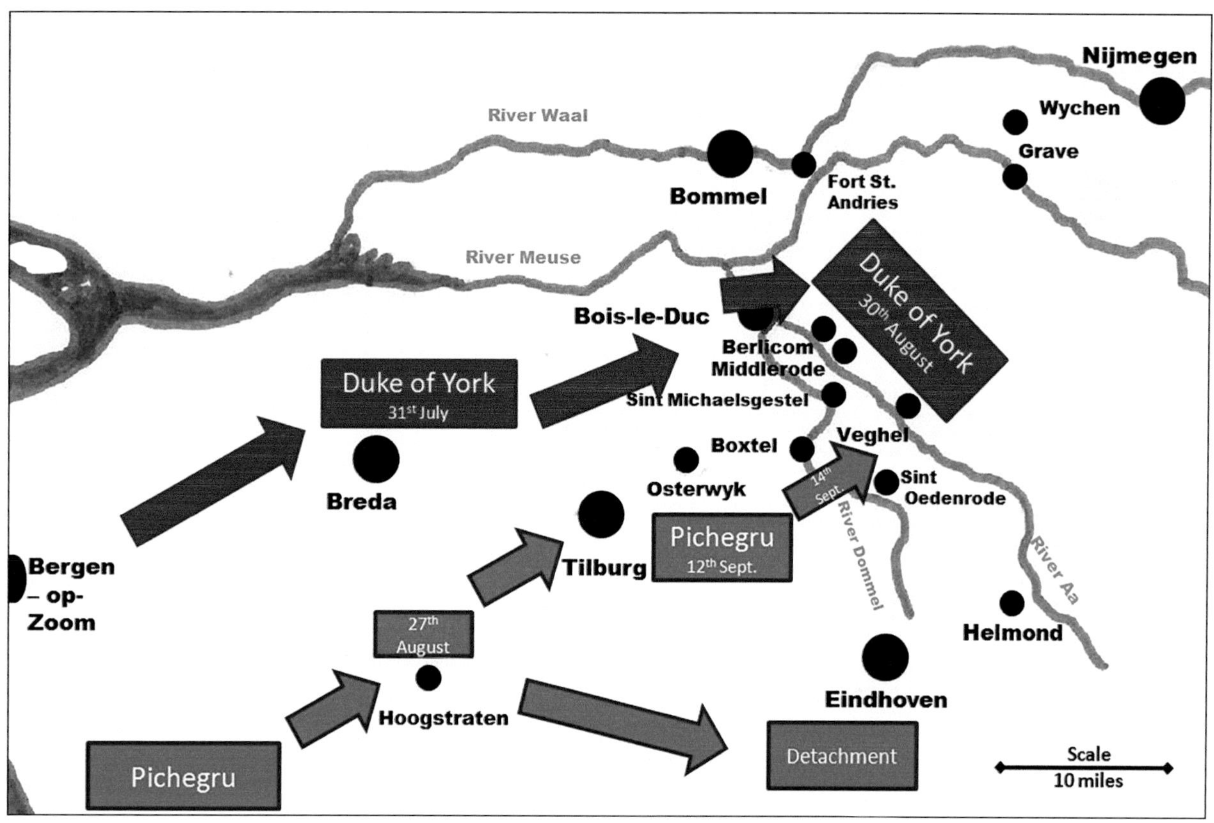

Map 14 – The Battle of Boxtel, Campaign Map

Orders of Battle

Abercromby led the Corps de Reserve of the Duke of York's army. The corps comprised the Guards Brigade commanded by Major-General Samuel Hulse, Major-General Nesbit Balfour's Third Brigade, commanded in his absence by Lieutenant-Colonel Arthur Wesley, and Colonel Richard Vyse's Cavalry Brigade. The Guards were missing the Coldstream Guards, as they were detached to form the left flank guard posted at Erp on the river Aa. Similarly, the Third Brigade had detached the 12th Regiment of Foot, which formed the right flank guard posted at Sint Michelsgestel. The battalions of the 33rd and 44th Foot were also missing their flank companies, which had separately been sent to the West Indies.[108] In the cavalry brigade, the 16th Light Dragoons were a detachment from Laurie's brigade, their strength is estimated by assuming that both squadrons were present with Abercormby.[109] The strengths of the units are given below:[110]

107 Garry David Wills, *First Battle,* pp.8–15.

108 Fortescue, *History*, vol. IV, pt.1, p.296.

109 Richard Cannon, *Historical Record of the Sixteenth or the Queen's Regiment of Light Dragoons, Lancers* (London: John W Parker, 1842), p.44.

110 TNA, WO1/170/555; *1 September 1794 Monthly Returns as sent to Henry Dundas by the Duke of York*; the King's Dragoon Guards had three squadrons divided between Schyndel and Sint Michelsgestel. I have assumed

The Guards Brigade	All ranks fit and present under arms
First Regiment of Foot Guards	666
Third Regiment of Foot Guards	619
Guards Grenadier battalion (four companies)	361
Guards Light Company battalion (eight companies)	702
Artillery	87
Third Brigade	
33rd Regiment of Foot	780
42nd Regiment of Foot	477
44th Regiment of Foot	663
Artillery (Royal Irish Artillery)	99 (est.)
Cavalry Brigade	
1st, The Kings, Dragoon Guards (two squadrons)	200
8th Light Dragoons (two squadrons)	263
14th Light Dragoons (one squadrons)	99
16th Light Dragoons (two squadrons)	300

Six of the infantry battalions, excluding the Guards light infantry battalion, were supported by two battalion guns, light 6-pdrs and 5.5-inch howitzers (44th Foot).[111] The Guards battalion guns were manned by their own men commanded by officers of the Royal Artillery, while those of the Third Brigade were manned and commanded by men of the Royal Irish Artillery. (Lieutenant Augustus Frazer commanded the guns of the Third Regiment of Foot Guards and Captain Robert Crawford commanded those of the 42nd Foot).[112] The force also included two medium 12-pdr cannon from the artillery park, manned by the Royal Artillery.[113]

that only one squadron went to Sint Michelsgestel.

111 Vivien Roworth; personal communication; Vivien Roworth, *Not So Easy Lads, Wearing the Red Coat 1786–1797* (Warwick: Helion and Company, 2023); being the letters of Sergeant-Major William Roworth, 44th Foot, in which he refers to the howitzers by their alternative nomenclature of 24-pdrs (the 5½-inch howitzer shell fits the bore of a 24-pdr long gun). The 33rd Foot may also have had howitzers as they did at Geldermalsen in January 1795.

112 TNA WO1/170/555; Edward Sabine (ed.), *Letters of Colonel Sir Augustus Frazer, K.C.B....* (London: Longman, Brown, Green, Longmans and Roberts, 1859), p.vi; Philippart, *Calendar*, vol. V, p.391.

113 Harrington, *Morris*, p.110; Garry David Wills, *Embarkation return of Lord Moira's Force*, Smoothbore Ordnance Journal, 4, 2013, p.74; Firepower Museum Archives, RA26 *Manuscript Order Book France and Flanders 1793*, see entry for 16 September 1793; the guns were most likely medium 12-pdrs as brought from England by Lord Moira to replace those lost earlier in the campaign.

Delmas's 6e Division of the Armée du Nord was one of the smaller divisions of the army. Some sources give *Chef de Brigade* Jean-Louis Ebénézer Reynier as one of two brigade commanders, but at this time he was still serving as the chief of staff in Souham's division. Instead Delmas had just one brigade commander, *Général de Brigade* Hermann Daendels. The main body of the division was provided by two *demi-brigades de bataille*, the 29e and 199e, each comprised of three battalions, supported by two 4-pdr guns for each battalion. The 199e Demi-Brigade de Bataille became known as the Demi-Brigade des Lombards from March 1795.[114] The division also had an all-arms advanced guard commanded by *Chef de Bataillon* David Hendrik Chassé of Waterloo fame. Chassé's command comprised the 3e bataillon, 30e Demi-Brigade Légère, the 8e Hussards and the 4e compagnie, 9e Régiment d'Artillerie Légère (horse artillery). The light infantry and the horse artillery originated from the Legion Franche Étrangère, recruited from refugees from the United Provinces and the Austrian Netherlands, as well as some Swiss nationals. Since January 1794, the hussar regiments comprised six squadrons each of two companies. The strengths of these units, based on the returns of the 1 September 1794, are given in the following table:[115]

First Foot Guards Centre Company

114 Chassin and Hennet, *Volontaires*, vol. II, p.762.

115 Frederik Henri Alexander Sabron, *De oorlog van 1794–1795 op het grondgebied van de Republiek der Vereenigde Nederlanden* (Breda: Drukk. v. Broese & C. voor rekening v. de Kkl. Milit. Acad., 1892), vol. I, Bijlagen XIII. The 3e/30e Demi-Brigade Légère is known by various names in the sources, e.g. 3e Infanterie Légère.

Advanced Guard	Present under arms (all ranks)
8e Hussards	402
3/30e Demi-Brigade Légère	544
4/9e Régiment d'Artillerie Légère	63
Daendels's Brigade	
29e Demi-brigade de Bataille	
1er bataillon	600
2e bataillon	621
3e bataillon	725
199e Demi-brigade de Bataille	
1er bataillon	918
2e bataillon	542
3e bataillon	688
Battalion guns	180

Two potential battlefields are suggested by the account of the 'Officer of the Guards' on the outskirts of Schyndel and by Captain Roger Morris's diary (Coldstream Guards), more than three miles further down the road to Boxtel. The battlefield was described in various ways by the sources:[116]

Lieutenant-Colonel Edwin Hewgill (Coldstream Guards), 'an Officer of the Guards': 'in front and inclining to the left of Abercromby's Corps ... was a plain skirted by a thick plantation of firs, in which the French had constructed several masked batteries'.

Lieutenant-Colonel Roger Morris (Guards Grenadier battalion): 'we formed our line in a lane leading out to the heath – wood and enclosures to our front and at no great distance on our right flank'.

Sergeant William Roworth (44th Foot): 'Their foot was placed in a very thick wood to our right and left'.

Trumpeter James Russell (1st Kings Dragoon Guards):

> when we began an attack upon the advanced post of the enemy but were repulsed, they having taken up an advantageous position in the woods.

The two potential battlefields have been defined using contemporary maps and are described below.

116 Anon., *An Accurate and Impartial Narrative of the War by an Officer of the Guards* (London: Cadell and Davies, 1795), pp.72–73; Harrington, *Morris*, p.110; Roworth, personal communication; *Diary of James Russell, 1st Kings Dragoon Guards* [the website describes him as a lt. col. but the regimental records suggest that he was in fact a trumpeter], accessed 17 September 2022, available at: <https://web.archive.org/web/20100914101215/http://www.qdg.org.uk/diaries.php?dy=35>

The Schyndel Battlefield

Schyndel lies approximately halfway between the British camp at Berlicum and Abercromby's target of Boxtel. The officer of the guards account suggests that Abercromby spotted the French outposts as he was emerging from Schyndel at about dawn or 6:15 a.m. The chosen battlefield as shown in Map 15 fits some but not all of the terrain clues that we have from the sources but crucially is a better fit to the timeline, given the descriptions of Abercromby's march in the sources. On the other hand, a key source, 'an officer of the guards' is thought to be the Duke of York's Military Secretary, Captain and Lieutenant-Colonel Edwin Hewgill (Coldstream Guards), who was unlikely to have accompanied Abercromby.[117]

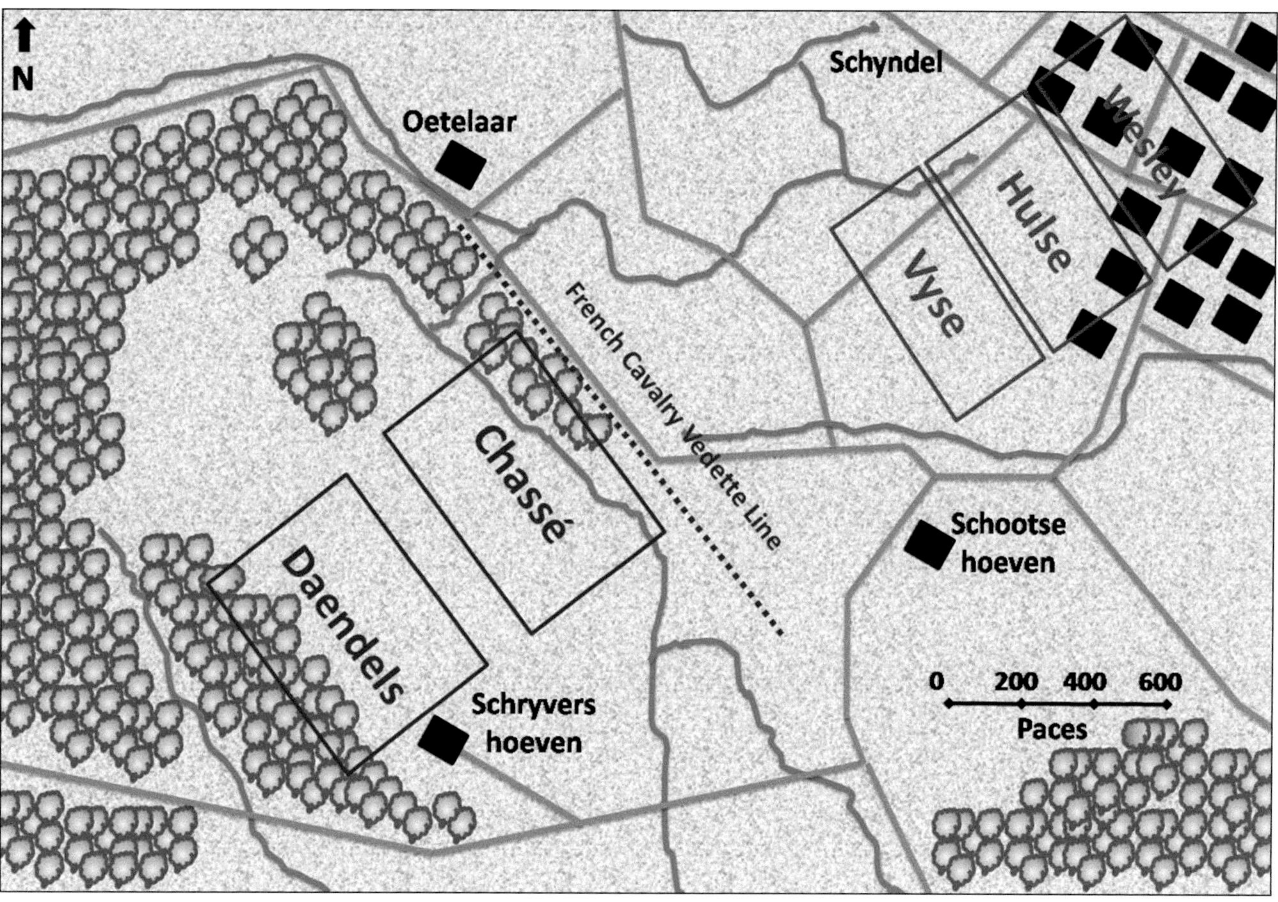

Map 15 – Battle of Boxtel, the Schyndel Battlefield

The 'Lea Common' Battlefield

Regimental Surgeon's Mate John Francis Smet of the 8th Light Dragoons described the battlefield as being close to 'Lea common', while Morris described it as three miles beyond Schyndel and Captain and Lieutenant-Colonel Harry Calvert (Coldstream Guards) described it as 'half a league' or one and a half miles from Boxtel itself. These latter sources place the battlefield close to a small area of common land called Leems Kuyle ('Loamy Pit)', a close approximation to Lea Common.[118] Although this battlefield

117 Stephen George Peregrine Ward, *The Author of 'An accurate and impartial narrative'*, pp.211–223 in *Journal of the Society of Army Historical Research*, vol. LXX, 284, Winter 1992, pp.216, 220.

118 John Francis Smet, *Historical record of the Eighth King's Royal Irish Hussars from its being raised, to 1803* (London: W.Mitchell, 1874), p.63; Verney, *Calvert*, p.325; Harrington, *Morris*, p.110; J.B.Neal, *Extracts from*

fits most of the terrain clues from the various sources, it is rather close to Boxtel and presumes that Delmas's division did not continue its advance towards Schyndel during the last three and half hours of daylight on the 14 September. It also requires that Chassé did not begin his reconnaissance early in the morning of the 15 September, as reported in the French sources. Furthermore, the distance from the camp at Berlicum is too great to fit comfortably into the timeline for the march, given the likely speed of march, as described in Morris's diary and other sources.

Thus, the Schyndel battlefield is perhaps the more likely but both battlefields are provided so that the players can make their own choice.

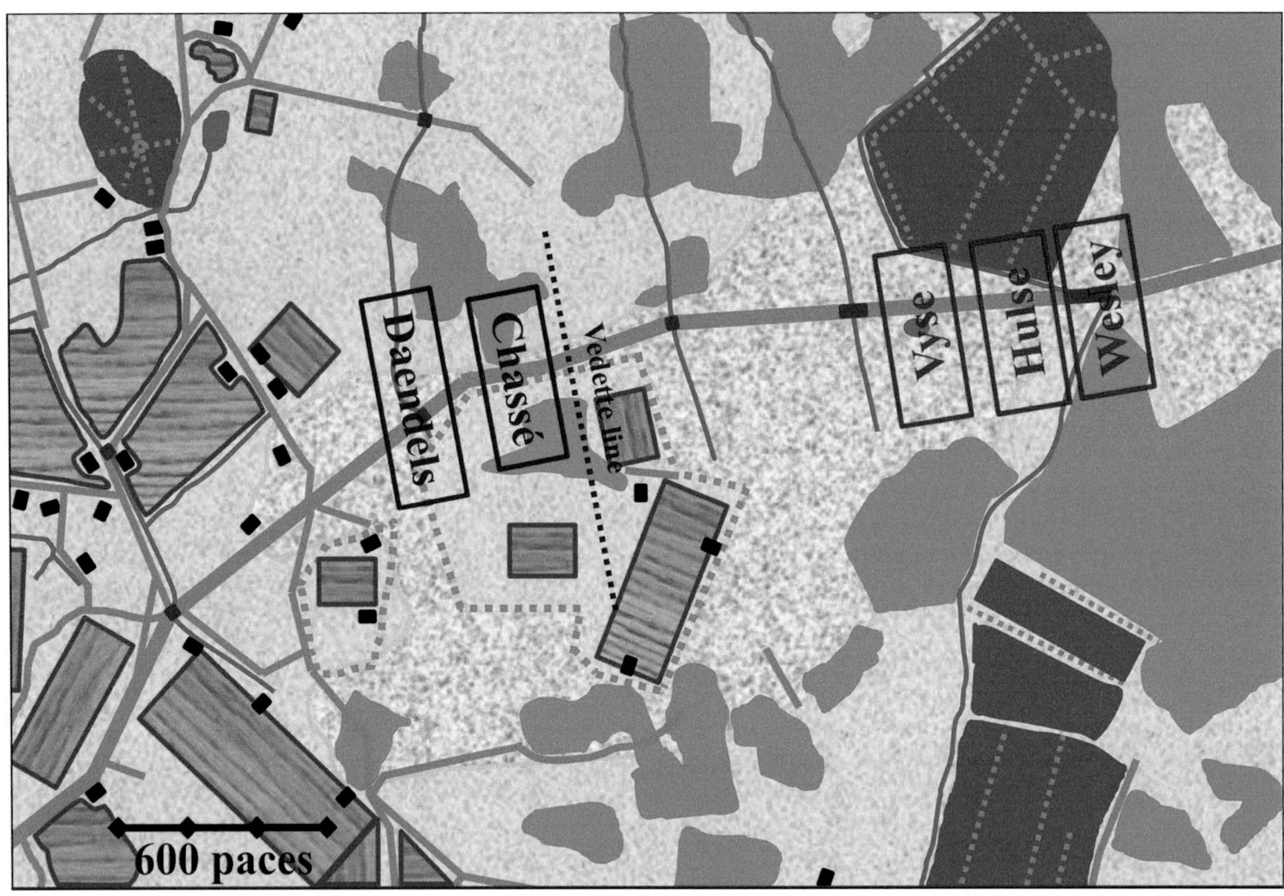

Map 16 - Battle of Boxtel, the Lea Common Battlefield

Deployment & Terrain

Map 15 or 16 should be used to guide the modelling of the battlefield and the deployment of the troops. *Black Powder*™ does not give a specific ground scale, so for 15mm troops I use the 'distances as centimetres' scale with a ground scale of approximately 1cm representing 20 paces. The maps consequently require either a six by four feet table or for 28mm troops approximately a nine by six feet table with 1 inch representing 25 yards. The wooded areas and tree plantations (dark green) should be considered as 'rough ground' which impedes line of sight, rather than 'woods' in order to reflect

the Journals of John Francis Smet, Surgeon of the 8th Hussars, 1815–1825, pp.172–178 in the Journal of the Society for Army Historical Research, vol. XXIX, 120, Winter 1951, p.172; Smet joined the 8th Light Dragoons on 6 October 1794 as regimental surgeon's mate. Throughout Morris's diary are data which suggests that the average march rate of his battalion was 1.6 m.p.h. with a maximum of 2.4 m.p.h.

their open nature. The streams and ditches should all be considered as the standard 'linear obstacle'. The individual farmhouses on either map are too small to be tactically significant and cannot be garrisoned.

Troop Quality

For the purposes of this discussion troops can be in one of three categories based on training and experience, as follows; untrained troops with less than 6 months training, trained troops with more than 6 months training or veteran troops who have experience of two or more campaigns. In addition to this classification some units were also considered as Elite formations.

British: The Foot Guards should be considered elite and trained but not veteran due to the presence with the colours of a large number of recent recruits, especially in the recently raised light companies. By November 1794, the 33rd Foot was considered by Major-General Lord Cathcart to have been one of the better regiments but not the best with respect to their men and equipment, having improved significantly since June 1794. Consequently the 33rd should be considered trained. Although the 42nd Foot had 300 recruits in its ranks and had only been present with the Army since June 1794, it had been together since October 1793, when it had first been sent to Ostend, and so should be considered trained. The 44th Foot had been with the Duke of York since arriving in Flanders in April 1794 from garrison duties in Ireland and should also be considered trained. However, the 33rd and 44th Foot had both been stripped of their elite flank companies, which had been sent to the West Indies.

The 1st King's Dragoon Guards had been with the Duke of York's army since the middle of 1793 but had recently received significant fresh drafts of both men and horses and should therefore be considered trained but not veteran. The 8th Light Dragoons arrived in Ostend in April 1794 and should be considered trained. The 14th Light Dragoons joined the Duke of York's army in June 1794 from Ireland and should be considered trained. The 16th Light Dragoons arrived in Ostend in April 1793 and should also be considered trained.

The battalion guns of the Guards Brigade were partly crewed by the infantry battalions and they should therefore be considered trained. However, the battalion guns of the Third Brigade were manned by a company of the Royal Irish Artillery which arrived in June 1794. These crews were described as recruits by Captain Crawford before he left and were heavily criticised by Major-General Balfour in October 1794, as 'totally unacquainted with any part of their duty'. Thus, these crews should probably be considered untrained.[119]

French: By the end of the 1793 season, the Armée du Nord had acquired significant campaigning experience, with a median service of one to three years. However, these veterans were reinforced over the winter and spring of 1794 by the recruits from the *Levée en Masse* of 1793 with an average of 50 percent of the troops being these conscripts. However, the French were able to provide significant training for the new troops during the summer of 1794. By the autumn most units had had sufficient opportunity to train their recruits. Based on the returns of the 1er Lombard battalion, the 199e Demi-Brigade de Bataille had been brought up to full strength before the

119 Wills, *First Battle*, pp.29–30.

end of February 1794 (and certainly the *demi-brigade* as a whole was at full strength before 19 April) and since then they had sufficient time for training (February to April and August to September) and combat experience (May and June) to be considered trained. The 29e Demi-Brigade de Bataille and the 3/30e Demi-Brigade Légère were both at full strength on 19 April 1794. Based on Coutanceau's figures for the French army as a whole, it is likely that these units were both at least 90 percent of full strength in February. As with the 199e Demi-Brigade de Bataille, it is therefore likely that both of these units were trained by September 1794.

The *artillerie légère* should be considered 'veteran' as this unit had been in existence since 1792 and the *artillerie légère*, in general, attracted the best troops from the foot artillery.

The French cavalry were widely seen to have been mounted on poor quality horses compared to the Allied cavalry during this campaign, which affected their performance throughout, although by September 1794 they should be considered trained. The revolutionary government struggled to provide sufficient carbines for all the cavalry to the extent that at the beginning of the 1794 campaign, the hussars and *chasseurs à cheval* had less than half of the carbines they needed. These shortages persisted, at least in part, into the autumn of 1794. The 8e Hussards apparently kept close to their supporting infantry when approached by the skirmishers of the British 8th Light Dragoons and this suggests that the French cavalry were still affected by this shortage in September 1794.[120]

Victory Conditions

British: Break the Army Morale of the French (two units must be 'lost' from the advanced guard and three from Daendels' Brigade). This is different to the standard rules for ending the game because there are only two French brigades. This modification simply applies the rules for breaking brigades of two units, to the Army level.

Alternatively, the British can win by withdrawing through Schyndel, before the French achieve their victory conditions. However, the main body of Major-General Hulse's Brigade of Foot Guards must first advance to within 200 paces of the initial position of the French Cavalry vedette line, before withdrawing.

French: Break the Army Morale of the British (two units must be 'lost' from each of two or more British Brigades).

The game length will be 16 turns.

Other Options

To play this scenario with General de Brigade®, simply double the number of figures given in the playsheets below. Consider all infantry as first line troops.

A small scenario for Sharp Practice could be constructed around the exploits of Captain George Bristow, First Regiment of Foot Guards, taking his centre company of approximately 80 men (16 figures), to neutralise a French cannon (a 4-pdr battalion gun). The French force would be provided by *Capitaine* Louis-Joseph Bordet with the tirailleurs of the 29e Demi-Brigade de Bataille, approximately 90–120 men (18–24 figures).

120 Wills, *First Battle*, p.30.

Black Powder™ Playsheet for Boxtel, 15 September 1794

French (Staff Rating 8)	Unit Size	Armament	Melee	Shooting	Morale	Stamina	Special	Strength Figures @ 33:1	BP Points 629
6e Division: Général de Division Delmas									80
Advanced Guard (BP=2)									80
8e Hussards	STANDARD	sabres	5		4+	3	Marauders	12	34
3/30e Demi-Brigade Légère	SMALL	s/b musket	4	2	4+	2	Skirmishers	16	28
4e/9e Artillerie Légère	1 MODEL	std s/bore	1	3/2/1	4+	1	Crack, Reliable, Marauders	2	37
Brigade Daendels (BP=3)									80
1/29e Demi-Brigade	SMALL	s/b musket	4	2	4+	2	Reliable attack column	16	28
2/29e Demi-Brigade	STANDARD	s/b musket	6	3	4+	3		17	36
3/29e Demi-Brigade	STANDARD	s/b musket	6	3	4+	3		20	36
Tirailleurs	TINY	s/b musket	2	1	4+	1	Skirmishers	6	20
Battalion guns	3 MODELS	light s/bore	1	1/1/1	4+	1		3	21
1/199e Demi-Brigade	LARGE	s/b musket	8	4	4+	4	Reliable attack column	26	44
2/199e Demi-Brigade	SMALL	s/b musket	4	2	4+	2		14	28
3/199e Demi-Brigade	STANDARD	s/b musket	6	3	4+	3		19	36
Tirailleurs	TINY	s/b musket	2	1	4+	1	Skirmishers	6	20
Battalion guns	3 MODELS	light s/bore	1	1/1/1	4+	1		3	21

Black Powder™ Playsheet for Boxtel, 15 September 1794

British (Staff Rating 7)	Unit Size	Armament	Melee	Shooting	Morale	Stamina	Special	Strength Figures @ 33:1	BP Points 574
Corps de Reserve Lt. Gen. Abercromby									70
Guards: Maj. Gen. Hulse (BP=2)									70
1st Regt. of Foot Guards	STANDARD	s/b musket	7	3	3+	4	Elite 4+, First Fire	20	52
3rd Regt. of Foot Guards	STANDARD	s/b musket	7	3	3+	4	Elite 4+, First Fire	19	52
Guards Grenadier Battalion	SMALL	s/b musket	5	2	3+	3	Elite 4+, First Fire	11	44
Guards Light Battalion	STANDARD	s/b musket	7	3	3+	4	Elite 4+, First Fire	21	52
Battalion guns	3 MODELS	light s/bore	1	1/1/1	3+	1		3	21
3rd Brigade: Lt. Col. Wesley (BP=2)									70
33rd Regiment of Foot	STANDARD	s/b musket	6	3	4+	3		24	36
42nd Regiment of Foot	SMALL	s/b musket	4	2	4+	2		14	28
44th Regiment of Foot	STANDARD	s/b musket	6	3	4+	3		20	36
Battalion guns	3 MODELS	light s/bore	1	1/1/1	4+	1	Unreliable, unclear targets	3	18
Park Artillery	1 MODEL	std s/bore	1	1/1/1	4+	1		1	8
Cavalry Brigade: Col. Vyse (BP=2)									70
1st Kings Dragoon Guards	SMALL	s/b musket	6	1	4+	2	Heavy Cavalry +1	6	37
8th & 14th Light Dragoons	SMALL	s/b musket	4	1	4+	2	Marauders, Skirmish	6	29
16th Light Dragoons	SMALL	s/b musket	4	1	4+	2	Marauders, Skirmish	3	21

Battle of Boxtel in 15mm

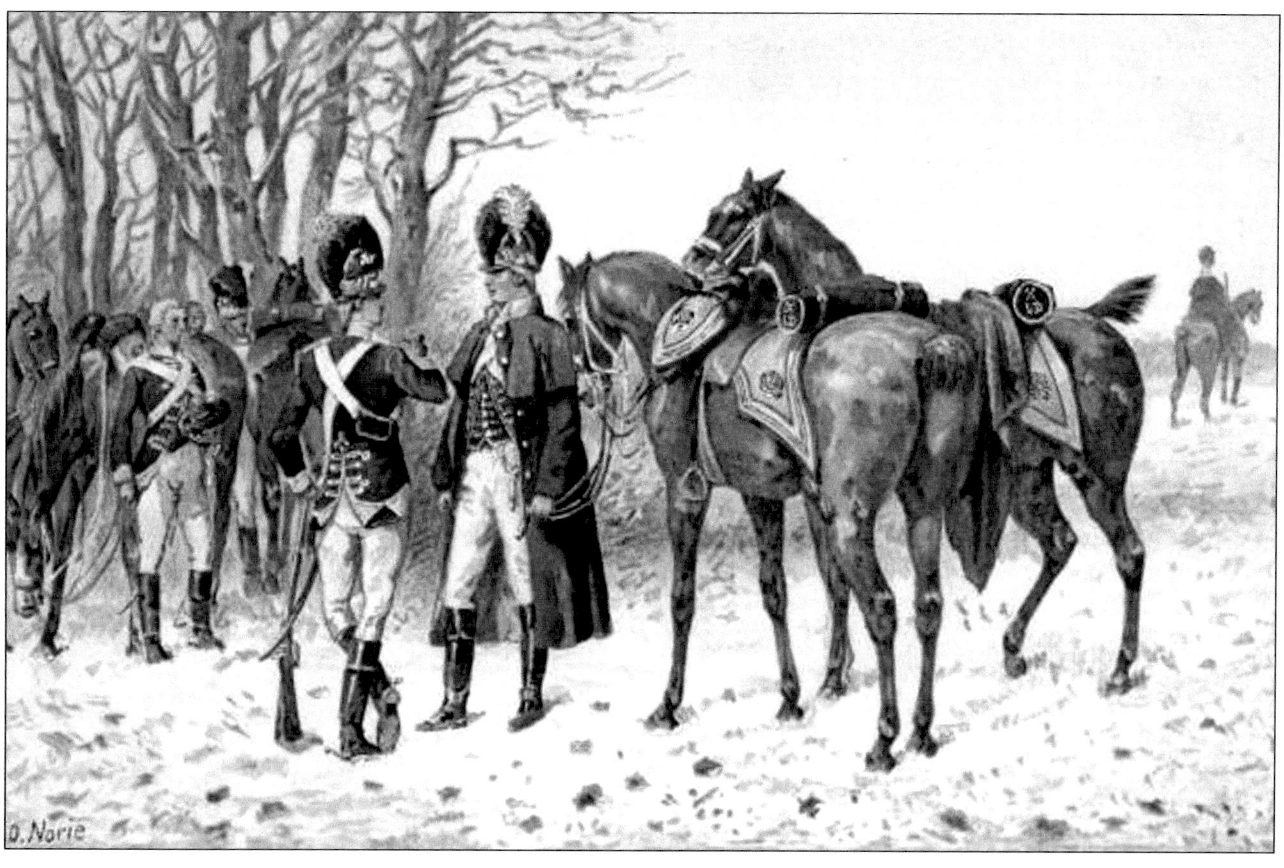

10th Light Dragoons

Scenario 5:

The 13e Vendémiaire or 'the Whiff of Grapeshot', 5 October 1795

French vs 'Royalist' Counter revolutionaries. A company level action using Sharp Practice rules.

Background

Following more bad harvests and bread riots the *Convention Nationale* in Paris was shown to be ineffective in dealing with the problems of France, and a new constitution proved unpopular. Royalist agitators brought about open rebellion in Paris in early October. The rebels were called *Sectionnaires* after the 48 *sections* into which Paris had been divided. Perhaps 16 of the central *sections* of Paris rose in rebellion, led by *Section Le Peletier*. This *section* called Paris to arms to overthrow the *Convention Nationale* (4 October). To coordinate their rebellion the Royalist *Sectionnaires* formed a central commission under the chairmanship of Richer-Sérisy. A military committee was also established including Lafond, Dufaillant, Baron Laporte and Baron Fortisson. Finally, an extraordinary tribunal, the *Comité des Onze*, was created including Richer-Sérisy, Burgurieux, Mésange, Vasselin, Saint Julien, Fitte, Delalot and Girard de Bury. *Général de Brigade* Danican was given command of the Royalist forces.[121]

The headquarters of the *Sectionnaires* was at the convent *Filles Saint Thomas*, in *Section Le Peletier* half a mile north of the Tuileries Palace. Originally Menou was the commander of the Armée de l'Interieur and Durturbie was his artillery commander. This army had been created following earlier disturbances in Paris the same year.[122] Consequently, Menou was sent with troops to quell the rebellion at source, but refusing to use force, he failed and retired. Consequently, Menou was arrested and replaced by Barras,[123] with Duvigneau as his chief of staff.[124] Overnight the Tuileries Palace was stocked with food and turned into a fortress to defend the seat of government, the theatre in the Tuileries Palace, where the *Convention Nationale* met. *Section Le Peletier*'s call to arms resulted in a force of 25,000–30,000 *Sectionnaires*, who were largely comprised of the *Garde Nationale* battalions of the *sections*. Each *section* raised one *Garde Nationale* battalion of 10 companies, eight of fusiliers, each of 77 men, and one each of grenadiers and chasseurs, each of 100 men. The men of these battalions were dressed partly in the national uniform (the grenadiers and chasseurs) and partly in civilian dress.[125]

Despite calling for reinforcements, which arrived too late, the *Convention Nationale*, could count on a force of only 5,000–6,000 men comprised of regulars, armed police,

121 Zivy, *Trieze Vendémiaire*, p.66; Jean Thomas Élisabeth Richer de Sérizy.

122 Zivy, *Le Treize Vendémiaire*, p.79; Six, *Dictionnaire*, vol. II, pp.179, 518–519; *Général de Division* Jacques-François de Menou, Baron de Boussay; *Général de Brigade* Théodore Bernard Simon Durturbie de Rogicourt.

123 Six, *Dictionnaire*, vol. I, p.56; *Général de Division* Paul François Jean-Nicolas Barras, more a politician than a soldier, who had served in the army as a junior officer, 1776–1780, appointed commander of the *Garde Nationale de Paris* in 1794, appointed *général de brigade* 1 August 1795, and *général de division* 4 October 1795.

124 Zivy, *Le Treize Vendémiaire*, p.79; Six, *Dictionnaire*, vol. I, p.419, vol. II, pp.518–519; *Général de Brigade* Bernard Étienne Marie Duvigneau.

125 Guillemot, *The Garde Nationale*, pp.246–247, 264–269.

250 *Gardes Nationales* from the *Montreuil* section, 200 *gendarmes*, pensioners from Les Invalides, and a force of perhaps 1,500 irregulars formed in three battalions in civilian dress, including *Les Patriotes de 89*, *Les Patriotes de* 93 and 48 volunteer gunners.[126] The regular troops were concentrated initially in the *Camp de Marly* (at Trou-d'Enfer, 12 miles west of Paris), and comprised six infantry battalions and two cavalry regiments, forming a strength of 6,965 men of which only 3,907 available for the defence. The artillery was concentrated at the *Camp de Sablons*, guarded by only 200 men.[127]

In June 1795, when the Armée de l'Interieur was created, the infantry comprised the 1er and 3e bataillons, 38e Demi-Brigade de Bataille, 3e bataillon, 128e Demi-Brigade de Bataille, 2e and 3e bataillons, 176e Demi-Brigade de Bataille, 7e bataillon Volontaires de Yonne and the 6e bataillon Volontaires de Soissons. The cavalry comprised the 22e Cavalerie, 3e Dragons and the 21e Chasseurs à Cheval.[128]

With the *Sectionnaires* preparing to march on the Tuileries Palace, Barras, asked his protégé Buonaparte to help defend the *Convention Nationale* (5 October). Buonaparte's role is controversial with 29 other generals known to have been involved in the defence of the *Convention Nationale*. These generals included several men more senior to Buonaparte, indeed Buonaparte ranked only 21st in seniority among the 30. This suggests that Bonaparte was an aide-de-camp. to Barras (as claimed by Barras much later), rather than second in command.[129]

However, Buonaparte wrote to his brother Joseph the next day (6 October), clearly describing his role as Barras's second in command. Second in command is not a normal position in French armies of the time, other than as a result of individual seniority, but a special arrangement may have been put in place, given Barras's lack of command experience. Alternatively, it has also been suggested that Buonaparte was given command of the artillery of the Armée de l'Interieur, presumably in place of the more junior Duturbie. This seems the most likely option, confused by what happened in the aftermath of this day.[130]

Whatever his exact role, Buonaparte sent Murat with 300 cavalry, the 21e Chasseurs à Cheval, to retrieve some artillery from the *Camp des Sablons*, three miles away to the west-northwest. Murat arrived before a competing group of *Sectionnaires* and returned with 40 guns. Lavalette has Buonaparte deploying the guns and infantry around the Tuileries in two lines securing the palace, including near the *Eglise Saint Roch* on the *Rue Saint Honoré*, as shown in Map 17.[131]

---

126 Guillemot, *The Garde Nationale*, p.265; Zivy, *Le Treize Vendémiaire*, pp.19, 20, 40–41, 53, 69; Zivy refers to the *Montreuil section* by its later name the *Faubourg Saint Antoine*. The irregular troops were under the command of *Général de Division* Jean-François Berruyer, who commanded the battalion *Les Patriotes de 93*.

127 Zivy, *Le Treize Vendémiaire*, p.18.

128 Bertaud and Palmer, *Army of the French Revolution*, pp.305–306.

129 Six, *Dictionnaire*, vol. I, pp.50, 89, 114, 122–123, 167, 196, 221–222, 254–255, 408–409, 434; vol. II, p.62–63, 112, 128, 216, 237, 408, 520, 540.

130 Antoine-Marie Chamans, Comte de Lavalette, *Memoirs of Count Lavalette, Adjutant and Private Secretary to Napoleon and Postmaster-general under the Empire* (London: Gibbings, 1894), p.96.

131 Lavalette, *Memoirs*, p.97; Zivy, *Le Treize Vendémiaire*, pp.80–82; this map is based on Zivy's account; Lavalette describes Carteaux's force as including a battalion of regular infantry. Interestingly, Zivy only accounts for 16 of these guns other than the reserve guns, which suggests that many were kept in reserve just to deny them to the *Sectionnaires*.

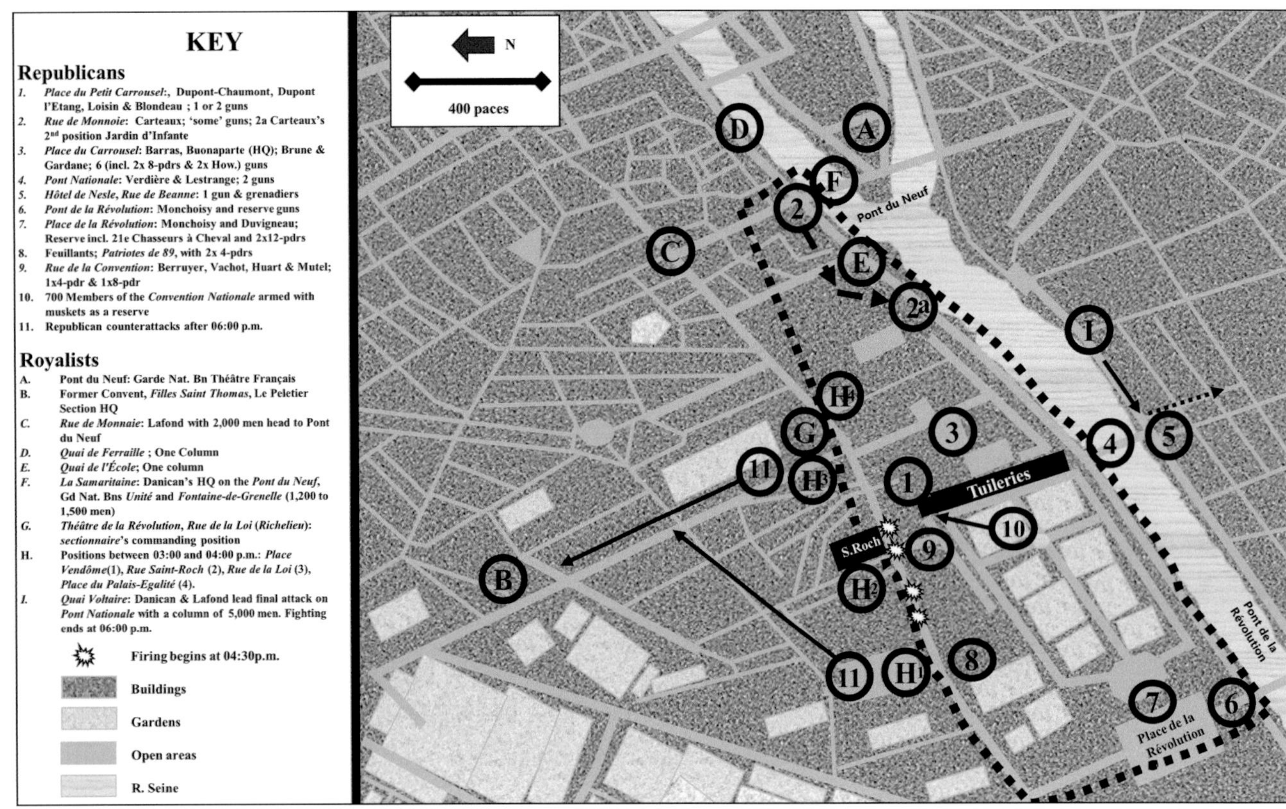

Map 17 – Paris and the 13e Vendémiaire

Most of the *Sectionnaires* remained in their own *sections*, but it is estimated that 7,000–8,000 *Sectionnaires* attempted to march on the Tuileries Palace from various directions. The fighting began at 4:30 p.m. with musket fire ringing out from several places along the *Rue Saint Honoré* close to the *Eglise Saint Roch*. Columns of *Garde Nationale* battalions of several of the central sections of Paris made attacks on the *Pont du Neuf*, the *Rue de la Convention* and the *Pont Nationale*, but were unsuccessful as they were attacking artillery without guns of their own (the *Garde Nationale* battalions had lost their own cannon following previous unrest, 20 May 1795).[132] When the *Sectionnaires* approached, the guns opened fire and the government troops stood firm.

Estimates of casualties vary from 200–300 up to 500–600 *Sectionnaires* killed or wounded, with the Convention Nationale troops losing 300 men, in what Thomas Carlyle, in 1837, christened the 'whiff of grapeshot'. Although the fighting dragged on for two hours, the *Convention Nationale* was saved and a new executive body, the *Directoire* was installed, led by Barras.[133] Buonaparte, now a national figure, was rewarded with promotion to *Général de Division* and the command of the Armée de l'Intérieur (27 October 1795) and subsequently the Armée d'Italie (27 March 1796). For their treasonous behaviour several of the Royalist leaders were sentenced to death although only Lafond was actually executed. Danican managed to escape and live to see the restoration of the Bourbons. This was the first time the regular army had been used in Paris to suppress rebellion against the government since 1789.[134]

132 Zivy, *Le Treize Vendémiaire*, p.38.

133 Guillemot, *The Garde Nationale*, pp.268; Zivy, *Le Treize Vendémiaire*, p.95; Lavalette, *Memoirs*, p.97; Lavalette gives the Royalist casualties as 40 killed and 200 wounded but claims that the Convention's troops lost only four or five men.

134 Zivy, *Le Treize Vendémiaire*, pp.100, 102.

The 30 generals that defended the Tuileries Palace, each of whom could feature in different versions of this scenario, were:[135]

Rank	Name	Seniority
Général de Division	Hilarion P.F.B. du Puget de Barbantane	15 April 1792
	Jean-François Berruyer	1 September 1792
	[Jacques-François de Menou]	15 May 1793
	Jean-François Carteaux	19 August 1793
	Florent Joseph Duquesnoy	3 September 1793
	Philippe-Ambroise-Denis Laronde	30 September 1793
	François Muller	30 September 1793
	Barthélemy François Mousin	7 November 1793
	Pierre Matthieu Parein de Mesnil	3 March 1794
	Louis Bonnaire	9 April 1794
	Pierre Antoine Dupont Chaumont	1 September 1795
	Louis-Antoine C. de Montgay de Montchoisy	1 September 1795
Général de Brigade	Georges Philippe Saboureux de Fontenay	19 September 1792
	Louis C.C. de B. de R. de Lestranges	8 March 1793
	Marie Scipion d'Exéa	9 May 1793
	Joseph Antoine Colomb	15 May 1793
	Jean Lambert Joseph Fyon	15 May 1793
	Guillaume Marie-Anne Brune	18 August 1793
	Pierre Dupont l'Étang	26 August 1793
	René-Bernard Chapuis	12 September 1793
	Nicolas Bertin	2 October 1793
	André Pacifique Peyre	20 October 1793
	Napoleone di Buonaparte	22 December 1793
	Louis Hippolyte Peyron	20 January 1794
	Jacques Denis Boivin	8 February 1794
	François Vachot	9 April 1794
	Jean Henry Tugnot de Lanoye	29 April 1794
	Jean Pierre Thomas Duvigneau	10 December 1794
	Théodore B. S. Durtubie de Rogicourt	20 May 1795
	Jean Christophe Collin (Verdière)	13 June 1795
	Louis Henri Loisin	26 August 1795

135 Six, *Dictionnaire*, vol. I, pp.50, 84, 89, 114, 118, 122–123, 167, 196, 221–222, 254–255, 404–405, 408–409, 419, 434, 482, vol. II, p.62–63, 112, 128, 216, 237, 241, 286, 306–307, 408, 515–516, 518–520, 540; Bertaud and Palmer, *Army of the French Revolution*, p.322; Peyre commanded a company in the first battalion, *Patriotes de 89*; Similarly, Laronde served 'in the ranks' of the second battalion, Patriotes de 89; Tugnot de Lanoye commanded the post at Meudon, five miles southwest of the *Convention Nationale*; Menou is included for completeness but not counted in the 30. Fyon's presence with his Liégeois Legion is mentioned by Bertaud but not by Six.

The events of 13 Vendémiaire were so extraordinary that generals on this list served as battalion and even company commanders. There was one general involved for every 200 men defending the *Convention Nationale*, although Zivy's account only gives 12 of these men prominent roles.

The *Convention Nationale*'s troops were also allocated three *représentants en mission*, Delmas, Goupilleau and Laporte.[136]

The military leaders of the Royalist *Sectionnaires* include:[137]

Rank	Name	Seniority
Général de Division	Charles-François Duhoux	7 September 1792
	Francisco de Miranda	3 October 1792
Général de Brigade	Louis Michel Auguste Thévenet (Danican)	30 September 1793
	Joseph S.F.X.A. Rovére de Fontvielle	13 June 1795
	Nicolas Raffet	8 August 1795
Unknown	Lafond (ex-Garde du Corps)	
	Dufaillant	
	Baron Laporte	
	Baron Fortisson (colonel?)	
	Charles-François Louis Delalot	

Other officers known to be present during *13 Vendémiaire*, who can provide characters for our games, include:[138]

Colonel Adélaïde Biaise François Le Lièvre de Grange et Fourilles
Chef de Brigade Jean-Baptiste Solignac
Adjudant-Général, Chef de Brigade Pierre Devaut
Adjudant-Général, Chef de Brigade François Xavier Octavie Fontaine
Adjudant-Général, Chef de Brigade François Liégard
Adjudant-Général, *Chef de Bataillon* Jacques Blondeau
Chef de Bataillon Louis Robert Bertrand Mutel de Boucheville (engineer)
Chef de Bataillon Louis-Melchior Legrand (previously *Général de Brigade*)
Chef de Bataillon François-Louis Honoré Letourner (engineer)
Chef d'Escadron Claude Mathieu Gardane, 1er Chasseurs à Cheval[139]
Capitaine Antoine-Marie Chamans, Comte de Lavalette

136 Zivy, *Trieze Vendémiaire*, p.69; Jean-François Bertrand Delmas; Jean-François Goupilleau; François Sébastien Christophe Delaporte.

137 Six, *Dictionnaire*, vol. I, pp.281, 389, vol. II, pp.204–205, 343, 403; Zivy, *Trieze Vendémiaire*, p.99; Delalot commanded the grenadiers of *Section Le Peletier*.

138 Six, *Dictionnaire*, vol. I, pp.109, 331, 351, 456, 521, vol. II, pp.39, 97, 114, 124, 399, 462, 493; *Général de Brigade* Charles Alexandre Louis Roussel de St Rémy was suspended from office for not volunteering to defend the *Convention Nationale*.

139 Zivy, *Treize Vendémiaire*, p.80; Six, *Dictionnaire*, vol. I, pp.481–482; Zivy refers to Gardane as 'General Gardane', a rank which Claude achieved only in 1799 (Léonore LH//1071/17; Six calls him Charles), but he may have been referring to *Chef de Brigade* Gaspard-Amédée Gardanne, whom Six has in Italy and was not promoted to general until October.

Capitaine Paul Ferdinand Stanislas Dermoncourt (Eglise Saint Roch)
Capitaine Paul Charles-François Adrien Henri Dieudonné Thiébault
Volontaire François-Antoine Lallemand, a.d.c. to Loisin

The Scenario

This scenario is based on Scenario Five from the Sharp Practice rulebook, 'Attack an Objective'.

In the best spirit of the Sharp Practice rules, this scenario is based on the assumption that Buonaparte was at the *Saint Roch* church and oversaw the defence of the *Convention Nationale* from there, as shown in the famous print by Auguste Raffet.

The government force of 5,000–6,000 men was divided across approximately 10 different positions around the Tuileries Palace, meaning each post had an average of 600 men plus two to three general officers.[140]

The Forces

		Fig. per Group	Points/ group	No. of Groups	Points	Figures
Convention Nationale						
Big Men						
Gén. de Brig. Buonaparte	Level 3	1	9	1	9	1
Gén. de Div. Dupont Chaumont	Level 2	1	6	1	6	1
Gén. de Brig. Loisin	Level 1	1	3	1	3	1
Gén. de Div. Berruyer	Level 2	1	6	1	6	1
Gén. de Brig. Vachot	Level 1	1	3	1	3	1
Groups						
Les bleus 1795	Regulars	8	6	4	24	32
Patriotes de 89	Militia	10	4	2	8	20
Medium artillery		5	7	2	14	10
Totals				8	73	67
Sectionnaires						
Big Men						
Gén. de Brig. Danican	Level 3	1	9	1	9	1
Gén. de Div. Duhoux	Level 2	1	6	1	6	1
Gén. de Brig. Raffet	Level 2	1	6	1	6	1
Baron Laporte	Level 2	1	6	1	6	1
Capitaine Delalot	Level 1	1	3	1	3	1
Groups						
Garde Nationale	Militia	10	4	8	32	80
The Mob	Wallahs	12	3	2	6	24
Totals				10	68	109

140 Zivy, *Treize Vendémiaire*, p.69.

13e Vendémiare Eglise St. Roch

Characteristics

All the regular and militia infantry are armed with muskets.

None of the infantry have the *drill*, *crashing* or *controlled* volley attributes.

All the infantry need two command cards to *step out*.

The artillery has the *controlled* volley attribute and needs three command cards to give a *crashing* volley.

The Terrain

The terrain for the game is shown in Map 18. It is designed for a three by two foot table using 15mm figures with the distances in the rules measured in centimetres. Alternatively, for 28mm figures the map represents seven and half feet by five feet. The dark grey areas are buildings and high walled enclosures, which for the purposes of the scenario are impassable (The *Sectionnaires* took refuge in the buildings only after the initial assaults were defeated). The ground sloped up from the left (the west) to the right towards the *Palais d'Égalité* (formerly the *Palais Royal*), but this has no effect on the game.

Support Options

There are none. For example, barricades were only erected in the streets at the end of the day when the fighting was over.

Deployment

The *Sectionnaires* were quite slow to organise their attack and Barras and Buonaparte had plenty of time to organise their defence. Consequently, the historical deployment would allow the government player to deploy his forces before the game begins, close to the deployment points. However, using the deployment points in the normal way will give a more interesting game.

The Victory Conditions

If the *Sectionnaires* reach the National Convention, capturing either of the Republican deployment points they automatically win the game. Otherwise, the first side to reduce their opponent's Force Morale to zero, wins.

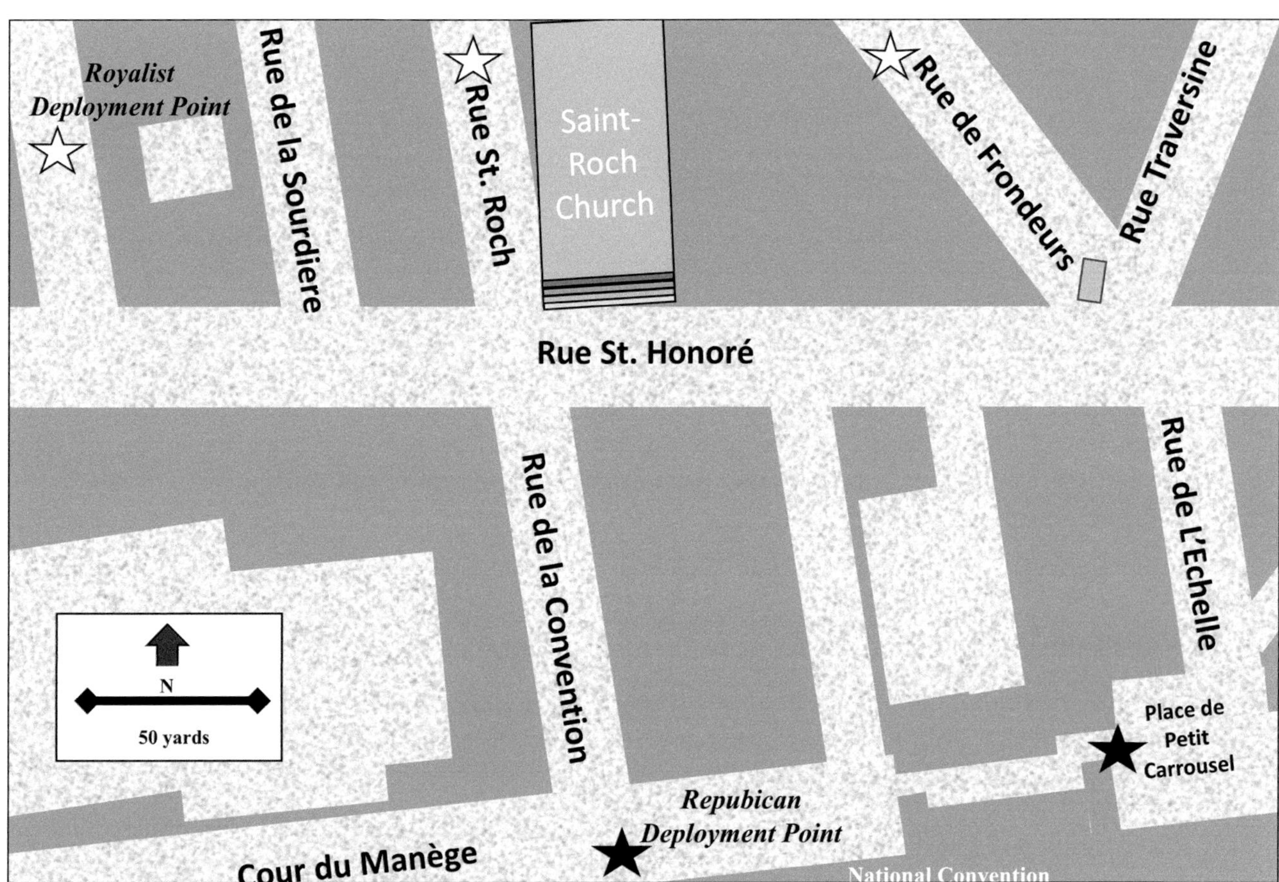

Map 18 – The Whiff of Grapeshot Battlefield Map

Scenario 6:

The Battle of Mondovi, 21 April 1796

France vs Sardinia-Piedmont. A battalion level action using *Black Powder*™.

Background

In the campaign in northern Italy in April 1796, Napoleon Bonaparte provided an excellent demonstration of the strategy of the central position. Although initially surprised by an Austrian attack on his exposed troops at Voltri, Bonaparte first inserted his army between the Austrian and Sardinia-Piedmont armies, separating them at the battles of Montenotte and Dego. Bonaparte then turned on the Sardinia-Piedmont army, determined to knock them out of the war. After two failed French attacks, the Piedmont troops fell back in good order to the town of Mondovi in the angle between the Rio Tanaro and the Torrente Corsaglia. Bonaparte brought some 20,000 men to bear on Colli's 10,000–12,000 men. In response, Colli deployed his light troops along the Torrente Corsaglia, while trying to organise a proper defensive line around Vicoforte, two miles further back towards Mondovi, a further 3 miles to the rear. On the day, Sérurier attacked the Piedmont light troops along the Torrente Corsaglia, quickly pushing them back and through Vicoforte. The speed of the French advance prevented Colli from completing the organisation of his main body sufficiently around the defensive position of *il Brichetto* or *Le Briquet*, just over a mile beyond Vicoforte towards Mondovi. Colli was soon retreating beyond the Torrente Ellero through Mondovi onto the plains of Piedmont. In a few days, Colli was only five miles from Turin and King Victor Amadeus III accepted Bonaparte's terms for an armistice only seven days after Mondovi.

This scenario focuses on the initial fighting as Sérurier's division attacked the line of the Torrente Corsaglia. This is an unbalanced scenario but illustrates some key aspects of the French way of war during the War of the First Coalition and can be rebalanced by placing the French under significant time pressure.

The Terrain

The terrain is shown in Map 19. The map is designed for a six by four feet table for 15mm or smaller figures using a 1mm to two paces ground scale or approximately nine by six feet table for 28mm figures, using a ground scale of 1 inch to 25 yards.

The wooded terrain on the hills counts as rough ground which blocks line of sight and halves all movement when below the 600m contour. Visibility within the woods is limited to 12cms or inches depending on your scale. The central slopes are very steep and where the ground is marked as 'steep slope' on the map, the slope is impassable to artillery and infantry movement is reduced to one quarter until the 600m contour is reached.

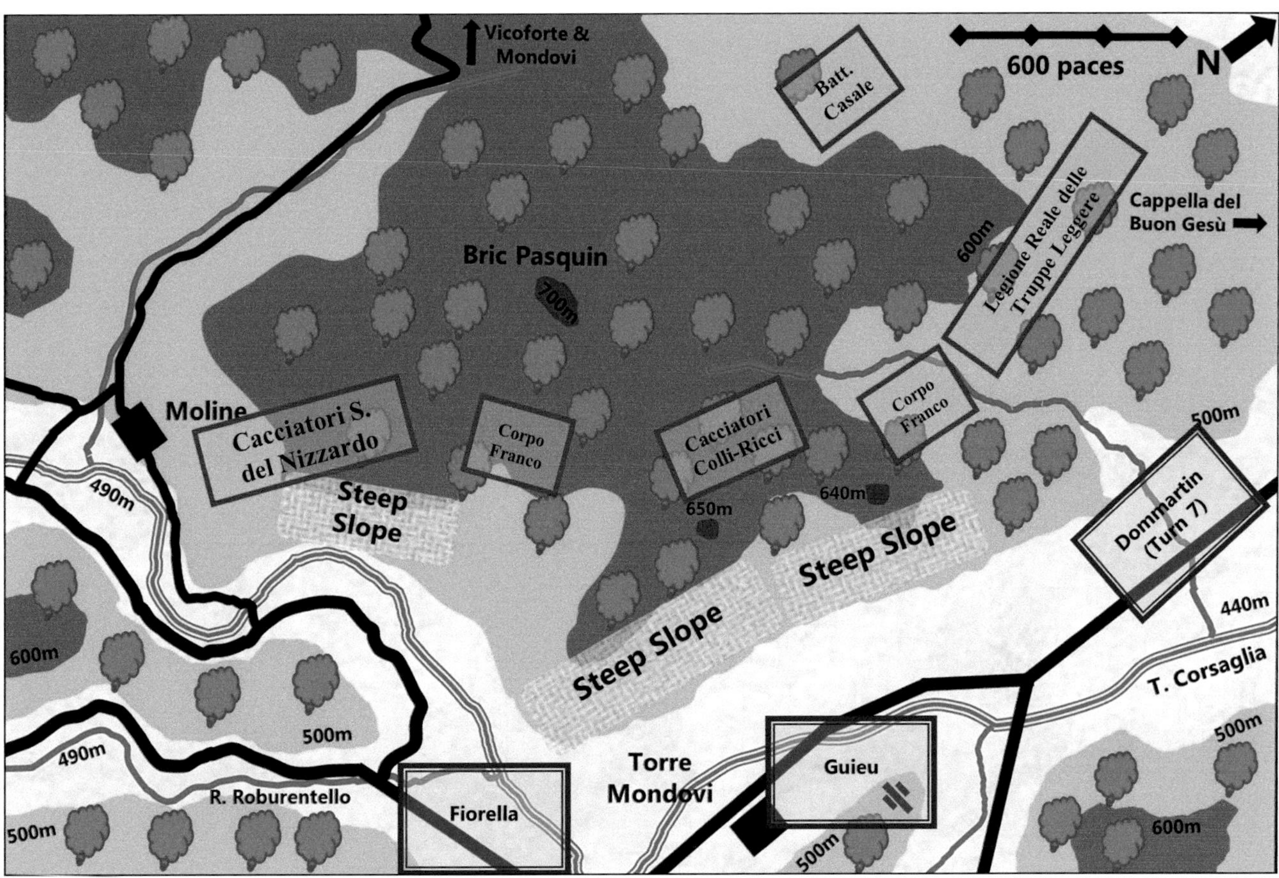

Map 19 – The Battle of Mondovi

The Forces

The troops required are summarised in the following table:[141]

141 Gabriel Fabry, *Mémoires sur la campagne de 1796 en Italie* (Paris: Chapelot, 1905), pp.103, 114, 116; Leónce Krebs and Henri Moris, *Campagnes dans les Alpes pendant la révolution, d'après les archives des états-majors français et austro-sarde, 1794, 1795, 1796* (Paris: Plon, Nourrit et Cie,1895), pp.421–422; Anon., *Ordre de bataille lors de la bataille de Mondovi*, accessed 11 March 2023, available at: <https://fr.wikipedia.org/wiki/Ordre_de_bataille_lors_de_la_bataille_de_Mondovi >; the presence of the Canale battalion in the Piedmontese force is mentioned by Fabry but not by Krebs and Moris. The names of the three battalions of the Legione Leggere vary in the sources, one describing them as the Cacciatori del Bellegarde, the Cacciatori del Balegno and 'six companies of chasseurs and grenadiers of the Legion', but I have gone with Fabry's description. The Corpo Franco units are unidentified in the sources.

Black Powder™ Playsheet for Mondovi, 21 April 1796 – The Piedmontese

Unit	Men	Figures 33:1	Figures 20:1	Unit Size	Armament	Close Combat	Shooting	Morale Save	Stamina	Special Rules	Points
Colonnello Brigadiere Chevalier Civalleri (SR 7)											
Legione Reale delle Truppe Leggere											
1° Batt. 1° Reggimento del Cacciatori	334	10	17	SMALL	Musket	4	2	4+	2		28
1° Batt. 2° Reggimento del Cacciatori	208	11	11	SMALL	Musket	4	2	4+	2		28
2° Batt. 2° Reggimento del Cacciatori	146										
1° Battaglione del Cacciatori Colli-Ricci	178	11	11	SMALL	Musket	4	2	4+	2	Elite 4+	34
2° Battaglione del Cacciatori Colli-Ricci	179										
1° Corpo Franco	250	8	13	SMALL	Musket	4	2	4+	2		28
2° Corpo Franco	250	8	13	SMALL	Musket	4	2	4+	2		28
1° Batt. Cacciatori Scelti del Nizzardo	450	14	23	STD	Musket	6	3	4+	3	Elite 4+	42
1° Batt. Rto. de Casale (Provincial)	220	7	11	SMALL	Musket	4	2	4+	2		28
Totals	2215	67	97								235

Black Powder™ Playsheet for Mondovi, 21 April 1796 – The French											
Unit	Men	Figures 33:1	Figures 20:1	Unit Size	Armament	Close Combat	Shooting	Morale Save	Stamina	Special Rules	Points
Général de Division Sérurier	(SR 8)										
Général de Brigade Fiorella											
Grenadiers, 46e Demi-Brigade	160	5	8	TINY	Musket	1	1	4+	1	Elite 4+	25
1er bataillon, 46e Demi-Brigade	805	24	40	LARGE	Musket	8	4	4+	4		44
2e bataillon, 46e Demi-Brigade	805	24	40	LARGE	Musket	8	4	4+	4		44
3e bataillon, 46e Demi-Brigade	805	24	40	LARGE	Musket	8	4	4+	4		44
Tirailleurs	426	13	21	STD	Musket	6	3	4+	3	Elite 4+	42
Foot Artillery, four 3-pdrs	36	1	2	1 Model	Bn. Guns	1	2/1/1	4+	1		17
Général de Brigade Guieu											
Grenadiers, 19e Demi-Brigade	240	7	12	SMALL	Musket	4	2	4+	2	Elite 4+	34
1er bataillon, 19e Demi-Brigade	782	24	39	LARGE	Musket	8	4	4+	4		44
2e bataillon, 19e Demi-Brigade	782	24	39	LARGE	Musket	8	4	4+	4		44
3e bataillon, 19e Demi-Brigade	782	24	39	LARGE	Musket	8	4	4+	4		44
Tirailleurs	414	13	21	STD	Musket	6	3	4+	3	Elite 4+	42
Foot Artillery, four 4-pdrs	36	1	2	1 Model	Bn. Guns	1	2/1/1	4+	1		17
Général de Brigade Dommartin											
1er bataillon, 84e Demi-Brigade	680	21	34	LARGE	Musket	8	4	4+	4		44
2e bataillon, 84e Demi-Brigade	680	21	34	LARGE	Musket	8	4	4+	4		44
Tirailleurs	240	7	12	SMALL	Musket	4	2	4+	2	Elite 4+	34
Foot Artillery, three 3-pdrs	27	1	1	1 Model	Bn. Guns	1	2/1/1	4+	1		17
Totals	7699	233	385								580

Scenario Notes

The Piedmontese infantry are not allowed to deploy in *Black Powder*™ attack column, but use march column, line or mixed line.

With the exception of the battalion from the Casale Provincial Regiment, all of the Piedmontese infantry are light infantry and the best way to represent their tactical doctrine using the *Black Powder*™ rules is to allow them the 'mixed line' rules but not skirmishers. However, the French tirailleurs and grenadiers can be deployed as skirmishers.

Colli-Ricci's *cacciatori* were the converged chasseur companies from the national regiments. The Piedmontese artillery was all positioned at Vicoforte or further back.

The staff rating of the Piedmontese is seven, that of an 'average' general, but could be reduced to six, for 'poor' depending on your reading of the history. The French staff rating is eight for a 'good' general to reflect the speed of their attack on this day but could alternatively be raised to nine for a 'great' general, which will make the scenario easier for the French.[142]

The size of the Corpo Franco units have been based on Krebs and Moris's assertion that the Piedmont defenders of this position numbered only 2,000 men in total. The alternative order of battle puts them at 420 men each, which would make them both standard sized units.

The full names of the commanders are:

Colonnello Brigadiere Giovanni Battista Civalleri di Masio

Général de Division Jean-Mathieu-Philibert Sérurier

Général de Brigade Pascual Antoine Fiorella

Général de Brigade Jean-Joseph Guieu

Général de Brigade Elzéar-Auguste Cousin de Dommartin

Other unit commanders of note are:[143]

Tenente Colonello Jean, Marchese di Bellegarde (1°/2° Reggimento, Legione Leggere)

Maggiore Santi (2°/2° Reggimento, Legione Leggere)

Tenente Colonello Alessandro,Conti di Malabaila di Antignano (1°/1° Reggimento, Legione Leggere)

Colonello Luigi Leonardo Colli-Ricci, Marquis of Felizzano (Cacciatori Colli-Ricci)

Colonello Chevalier Fea (1° Battaglione Reggimento Casal)

Tenente Colonello d'Auvare (1° Battaglione Cacciatori Scelti del Nizzardo)

Chef de Brigade Rainard (19e Demi-Brigade de Ligne)

142 Paoletti, *Italian States*, pp.224–225.

143 Pietro Crociani and Ciro Paoletti, *La Guerra Delle Alpi (1792–1796)* (Rome: Stato Maggiore Dell'Esercito, 2000), pp.319–349.

Chef de Brigade Jean-Baptiste Venoux (84e (25e) Demi-Brigade de Ligne)[144]

Uniform details for the Sardinia-Piedmont light troops are in *Le Regie Truppe Sarde*.[145]

Game Length

The French begin their attack at sunrise – 6:30 a.m. – and by 10.00 a.m. they were in position to attack Vicoforte itself, before Colli was fully deployed to receive them. Therefore, our game begins at 6:30 a.m., but Dommartin's brigade arrives on game turn seven. The game will end at 9:00 a.m. at the end of game turn 11.

Victory Conditions

The French need to break the Piedmontese brigade and six of the French units need to reach the Piedmontese table edge before the end of game turn 11, all other results are considered a Piedmontese victory.[146]

Scenario 7:

The Battle of Castiglione, 5 August 1796

France vs. Austria. This scenario offers a division or brigade level action, which can be played using De Bellis Napoleonicis or Volley and Bayonet rules.

Background

In this battle, Napoleon Bonaparte's Armée d'Italie faced Wurmer's Kaiserlich-Königliche Lombardische Armee, which had advanced from Austria to relieve the besieged fortress of Mantua. During 1796, in his first campaign as an army commander, *Général de Division* Napoleon Bonaparte had quickly knocked Sardinia-Piedmont out of the war (27 April) following his victory at Mondovi (21 April). The outnumbered Austrians were forced to abandon their own advance on Genoa and retired into Lombardy across the river Po. Outflanking their positions Napoleon crossed the Po (7 May) and forced the Austrians back to the river Adda, a position which was forced at Lodi (10 May). Having taken Milan (12 May) Napoleon then ruthlessly suppressed revolts in Milan and Pavia. The Austrians were forced back from the river Mincio at Borghetto (21 May), following which they retired into the Tyrol, leaving the fortress

144 Krebs and Moris, *Campagnes, 1794, 1795, 1796*, p.368: Anon, *Historique du 25e régiment d'Infanterie de Ligne* (Paris: Charles Lavauzelle, 1887), pp.9, 31; Smith, *Napoleon's Regiments*, pp.69, 76, 94; the army was in the process of executing the second amalgamation which also converted *demi-brigades de bataille* to *demi-brigades de ligne*. The 25e Demi-Brigade de Ligne was one of the six *demi-brigades* in the army that had completed this transformation (28 February 1796) incorporating the 84e Demi-Brigade de Bataille. Although it received the number 25 in the March 1796 lottery, it features in the OOBs using its old number. The 46e DBB became the 39e DBL in October 1796. Contrary to Krebs and Moris, the amalgamation that created the 19e DBL was 8 January 1796.

145 Ales, *Le Regie Truppe Sarde*, Tavole 24–27; reproduced in part at <http://theminiaturespage.com/boards/msg.mv?id=568547>, accessed 11 April 2023.

146 Krebs and Moris, *Campagnes, 1794, 1795, 1796*, pp.422–423; the Piedmontese retired at 7:00 a.m., which suggests the French attacked at sunrise, which was around 6:30 a.m. Dommartin apparently crossed the *Torrente Corsaglia* at 8:00 a.m.

of Mantua in the centre of northern Italy, blockaded. *Feldzeugmeister* Johann Peter de Beaulieu, the Austrian commander, resigned (21 June) and was replaced by the 72-year-old *Feldmarschall* Dagobert Sigismund, Count von Wurmser who was given the task of relieving the fortress, the first of four such attempts. Wurmser also brought 25,000 men from the army on the Rhine to reinforce his new command.

Wurmser was born in Strasbourg and began his military career as a hussar in the service of France, fighting in the War of the Austrian Succession and the Seven Years War before joining the Austrian service (1762) reaching the rank of *feldmarschallleutnant* in 1783. He served with distinction in the War of the Bavarian Succession and in 1787 was promoted to *general der kavallerie*. When the War of the First Coalition broke out, he was appointed commander of the Austrian forces on the Upper Rhine, defeating the French at Rohrbach (29 June 1793), Germersheim (19 and 22 July) and Essingen

1er Hussards, 1795

(27 July) thus preventing them from relieving Mainz. He then stormed the Lines of Lauterbourg and Weissenburg but was forced back across the Rhine by a French counterattack (October 1793), following which he was replaced (January 1794). Wurmser was reappointed to the same command (August 1795) and defeated the French again near Mannheim, capturing that fortress (23 November 1795). Wurmser was promoted to *feldmarschall* (11 December 1795). Thus, when he replaced Beaulieu, he was considered a successful and renowned general, and was considerably more experienced than his opponent.[147]

The siege of Mantua did not commence properly until the fall of Milan's citadel released the necessary siege artillery. The first French batteries opened fire on 18 July. Josef Canto d'Yrles, the commander of the garrison of Mantua, received a letter on 23 July from Wurmser, then at Rovereto, 52 miles to the north in the valley of the river Adige, promising to relieve the fortress by 2 August. This successful exchange of letters illustrates the lack of effectiveness of the French blockade.

British interest in the battle was represented by the presence of the Military Commissioner to the Austrian army in Italy, Colonel Thomas Graham (90th Foot), the future Lord Lynedoch, who was present at Wurmser's headquarters throughout the campaign.[148]

When Wurmser began his offensive to relieve Mantua (29 July) he sent his first column, under Quosdanovich down the west side of Lake Garda with 17,679 men, through the valleys of the Chiese and Mella rivers. Quosdanovich's objective was to seize Brescia. The second, centre right, column under Melas (14,324 men) was to advance down the eastern shore of Lake Garda taking Monte Baldo.[149] The third column, the centre left, under Davidovich, leading 9,486 men, was to advance down the left bank of the Adige. The fourth main column, under Mészáros with 5,021 men was directed via Vincenza on Verona.

Once clear of Lake Garda, the two centre columns were ordered to advance on Mantua, under Wurmser's direct command. In total, Wurmser mustered 46,937 men to face Bonaparte's 35,000 men. Meanwhile the Austrian garrison of Mantua, totalling 10,724 men, were besieged by Sérurier's division of 10,521 men. On Lake Garda itself an Austrian flotilla of local boats armed with field guns faced a French flotilla of six armed boats. Bonaparte had deployed his other divisions such that Despinoy (4,534 men) held Peschiera and Zevio. Augereau (4,749 men) was on the lower Adige occupying Legnano and Ronco. Masséna (15,291 men) was deployed with his right in Verona and his left stretched beyond Rivoli, with his headquarters at Castiglione delle Stiviere. Sauret's division of two brigades (4,293 men) barred the mouth of the valley of the Chiese. Three further divisions with a total of 7,250 men were dispersed in garrisons in the French rear from Lodi and Milan back to France. In total, Bonaparte had 55,120 men in Italy.[150]

147 Voykowitsch, *Castiglione*, pp.21–22.
148 Voykowitsch, *Castiglione*, pp.27–28.
149 *Feldmarschallleutnant* Michael Friedrich Benedikt Freiherr von Melas.
150 Voykowitsch, *Castiglione*, pp.48–50.

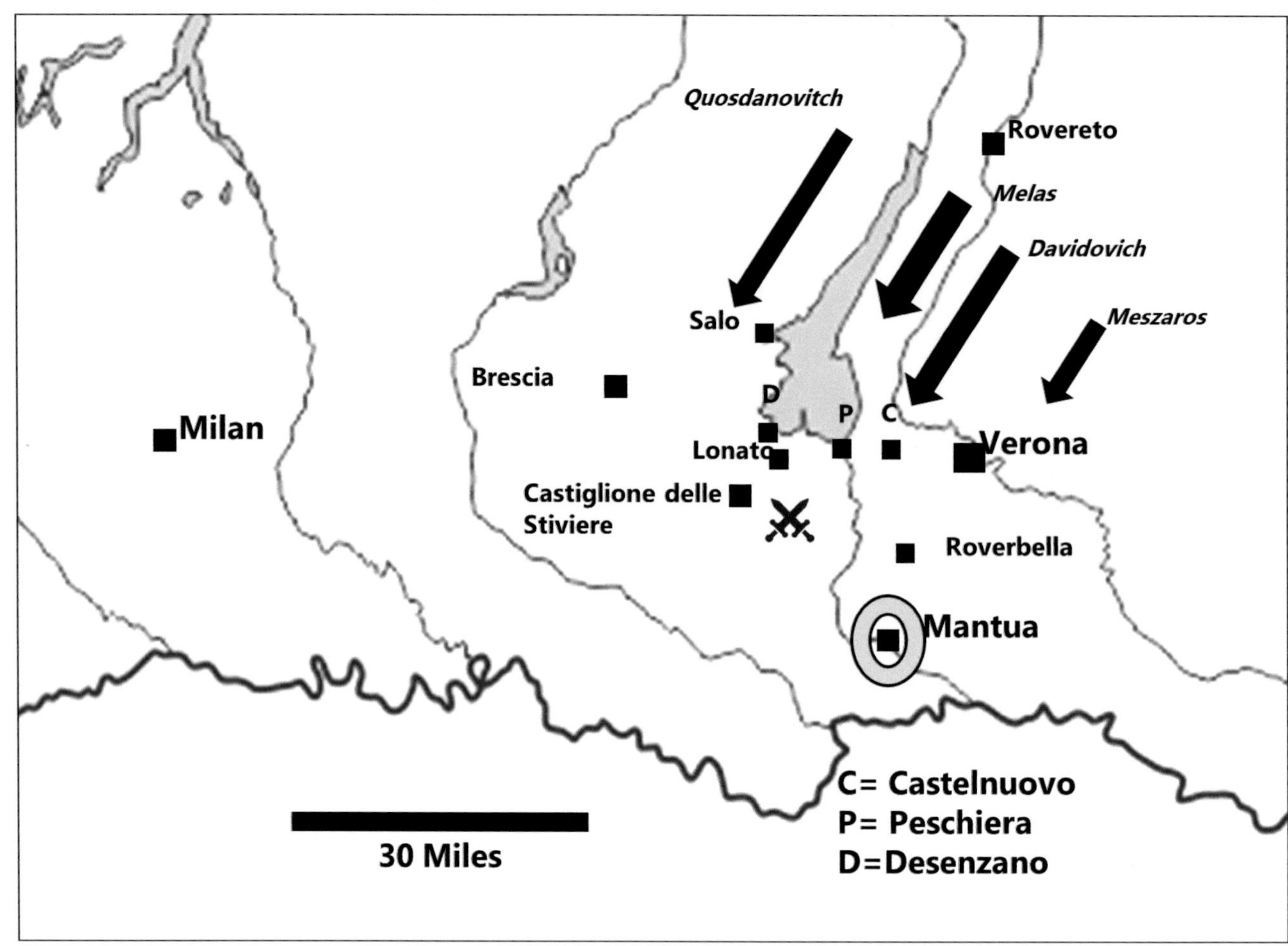

Map 20 – Castiglione campaign map

During the first day of the Austrian offensive (29 July) the central Austrian columns advanced to take the entrenchments on Monte Baldo and Rivoli, storming Brentino along the way, defeating Masséna whose division was holding the valley of the river Adige. In all 1,600 French troops were captured, including most of the 11e Demi-Brigade Légère at Brentino. On the west of Lake Garda, after fierce fighting, Quosdanovich advanced to take Salò and netted a further 500 prisoners, pushing Sauret back to Desenzano. Guieu was left behind by Sauret to hold the castle at Salò.

The next day (30 July) the Austrian advance continued, occupying Brescia – Bonaparte's headquarters as recently as the previous day – in the west and Verona in the east. Meanwhile Bonaparte moved his headquarters to Castelnuovo del Garda, just to the east of Peschiera at the southern end of Lake Garda. His divisions were deployed as follows, Despinoy was at Lonato to the south of Desenzano, Masséna was at Peschiera and Augereau at Roverbella, 12 miles to the south-south-east of Peschiera. Bonaparte then moved to Desenzano and ordered his divisions to the west of the Mincio. Sauret was ordered back to Salò, Masséna to Lonato, Kilmaine and Augereau to Montechiaro. While Sauret advanced to retake Salò, forcing Ocskay back, Ott attacked Despinoy at Lonato but was thrown back when Masséna's division arrived and Lonato was retaken. Quosdanovich with Sauret threatening his line of communication to the Tyrol, cancelled any further advance and focused his efforts on retaking Salò. However, Sauret, aware of his own isolation, withdrew back to Desenzano (31 July).

In response to Wurmser's advance, Sérurier, was ordered to abandon the siege and withdrew west to the line of the river Oglio. Canto d'Yrles celebrated the raising of the siege after his highly active defence. Quosdanovich began the next day at Gavardo, between Brescia and Salò, while the divisions of Masséna, Despinoy and Sauret were in the vicinity of Ponte San Marco, between Desenzano and Brescia. Bonaparte arrived in Brescia sometime after 11:00 a.m. with Augereau's division, where he was joined by Masséna, Despinoy and Guieu (who now commanded Sauret's division). Meanwhile Wurmser was working from the assumption that Bonaparte would be covering the siege of Mantua and had concentrated his central columns around Castelnuovo del Garda, from Peschiera to Roverbella (1 August).[151]

The next day, while Wurmser led his army west across the Mincio, Bonaparte led his army east back towards the Chiese and prepared to attack Quosdanovich, while screening Wurmser's main body (2 August). The next day saw Sauret advancing once more on Salò while Despinoy led his division and d'Allemagne's brigade towards Gavardo.[152] Masséna was directed to attack Desenzano, but his advanced guard, led by Pijon, was attacked itself by Ocksay who both captured Pijon and occupied Lonato. However, when Bonaparte arrived with the rest of Masséna's division, Ocskay was overwhelmed and forced to surrender with most of his brigade, releasing Pijon in the process. *Generalmajor* Reuss advanced with 1,800 men and occupied Desenzano but had to abandon it in the face of overwhelming numbers.

While these combats at Lonato and Desenzano were taking place, Guieu led his men forward and re-occupied Salò. The French did not have it all their own way, Despinoy's attack on Ott's brigade at Gavardo (3 miles to the west of Salò) was a failure with the division panicking and retiring in disorder on Brescia. D'Allemagne managed, however, to seize Gavardo before being driven out by one of Johann Sporck's battalions. This day (3 August) of confused fighting on the Austrian right ended with Quosdanovich's column positioned around Ponte San Marco and Salò. For the French, Guieu's division was at Salò and Masséna's at Desenzano and Lonato. In the Austrian centre, at 2:00 a.m. Augereau had left Montechiaro with his own division and that of Kilmaine (10,000 men in all) marching towards Castigilione delle Stiviere, from whence *Generalmajor* Lipthay was advancing with his brigade (3,700 men) in the opposite direction. The two forces were on different roads and Augereau was consequently positioned on Lipthay's left, or southern, flank.[153] With Lipthay deployed on the heights to the northeast of Castiglione, Augereau advanced to the attack and slowly drove Lipthay's outnumbered force back. However, *Generalmajor* Schubirž's brigade arrived leading the rest of Davidovitch's column.

In all, Lipthay was reinforced by 11,000 men turning the tables on Augereau's force. However, Wurmser decided not to press this advantage and merely held the position that Lipthay had so gallantly defended (3 August). The next day (4 August) Bonaparte, based at Castiglione, sent the combined forces of Guieu from Salò, Masséna from Lonato, Despinoy from Brescia and D'Allemagne's brigade from Rezzato against Quosdanovich's column around Gavardo. In the face of the encircling French attacks, Quosdanovich was forced to withdraw up the Chiese valley. Part of the Austrian rearguard under *Oberst*

151 Voykowitsch, *Castiglione*, pp.18, 20, 51–58.

152 *Général de Brigade* Claude d'Allemagne's brigade was originally part of Sérurier's division besieging Mantua, but when the Austrian offensive began, it was transferred to Masséna's division.

153 Voykowitsch, *Castiglione*, pp.62–69.

Carl Knorr von Rosenroth (Infanterie Regiment N.42),[154] comprising three battalions of infantry and a few hussars, was cut off and attempted to escape east to join the Austrian centre. Finding all routes through and around Lonato blocked by the French, Knorr surrendered. Quosdanovich retired up the valley of the Chiese to Condino (31 miles northeast of Brescia), where he rallied his troops over the next few days. Meanwhile at Solferino, Wurmser deployed his army to prepare for a possible attack on his left flank by Sérurier's division advancing from the Oglio. He also built a redoubt on the Monte Medolano, a hillock 250m long but only 5m above the surrounding plain and another in the hills to the right.

With his rear now secure, Bonaparte brought Masséna's division from Salò, Lonato and Desenzano by forced march to Castiglione.[155]

The Opposing Armies

The forces organised for De Bellis Napoleonicis are as follows:

Austrians

12 bases of muskets, two of light infantry, three of cavalry and six of foot artillery.[156] The rank of the brigade commanders was *generalmajor*, unless stated otherwise.[157] There are two commanders, Wurmser will be the commander-in-chief with Sebottendorf operating as his sub-commander, both men are rated AVERAGE:

French 7e bis Hussards

154 Anon, *Kurze Geschichte der Kais. Koenigl. Regimenter, Corps, Bataillons, und anderen Militaer-Branchen* (Vien: Cath. Gräffer, 1800), vol. I, p.186.

155 Voykowitsch, *Castiglione,* pp.69–73.

156 Voykowitsch, *Castiglione,* pp.22,74.

157 Voykowitsch, *Castiglione,* p.2; Leopold Kudrna, Digby Smith, *Biographical Dictionary of all the Austrian Generals of the Revolutionary and Napoleonic Wars, 1792–1815*, accessed 22 March 2022, available on the Napoleon Series at: <https://www.napoleon-series.org/research/biographies/Austria/AustrianGenerals/c_AustrianGeneralsIndexA.html>.

Austrian	*Feldmarschall* Dagobert Sigmund von Wurmser		
Brigade	Units	Men	Bases (E= elite, M= militia or poor quality)
Feldmarschallleutnant Paul Freiherr (Baron) von Davidovich (Right Wing)			
Anton Schubirž von Chobinin*	Mészáros Ulanen Regiment (1 squadron) Erdödy Husaren Regiment N.11 (2 squadrons)	147 368	1 Light Cavalry (a)
	Szluiner Grenzer Regiment N.63 (6 co.)	1,361	1 Light Infantry (b)
	Mahony Feld-Jägers (2 companies) Oguliner Grenzer Regiment N.62 (2 co.)	317 371	1 Light Infantry (c)
Karl von Spiegel	I,II/Infanterie Regt. N.4 (Deutschmeister)	1,282	1 Musket (d)
	I,II,III/Infanterie Regt. N.45 (Lattermann)*	844	1 Musket (e)
Anton Lipthay de Kisfalud	I,II,III/Infanterie Regiment N.13 (Reisky)	1,428	1 Musket (f)
	I,II/Infanterie Regiment N.8 (Huff)	1,251	1 Musket (g)
	I/Infanterie Regiment N.40 (Mittrowsky) Oguliner Grenzer Regt. N.62 (2 co.)	568 372	1 Musket(M) (h)
Anton von Mittrowsky	III/Infanterie Regiment N.10 (Khuel) Strasoldo Grenadier battalion (2 companies)	1,024 164	1 Musket(M) (i)
	III/Infanterie Regiment N.27 (Strasoldo) III/Infanterie Regiment N.11 (Wallis)	356 887	1 Musket (j)
	I,II/Infanterie Regt. N.25 (Brechainville)*	1,668	1 Musket (k)
FML Karl Philipp Sebottendorf van der Rose (Left Wing)			
Peter von Gummer	I,II/Infanterie Regiment N.19 (Alvinzy)	1,170	1 Musket (l)
	II/Infanterie Regiment N.21 (Gemmingen)	908	1 Musket (m)
Oberst Christoph Karl von Piacsek	Erdödy Husaren Regiment N.11 (4 squadrons)	737	1 Light Cavalry (n)
	Eh. Josef Husaren Regt. N.17 (4 squadrons) Mészáros Ulanen Regiment (1 squadron)	588 147	1 Light Cavalry (o)
Reserve Artillery	18x12-pdrs, 18x6-pdrs, 12x7-pdr howitzers, 8x3-pdrs, two cavalry 6-pdrs and two cavalry 7-pdr howitzers		6 Foot Artillery 12-pdr FA (p,q) 6-pdr FA (r,s,t,u)
Detachment			
Oberst Karl Philippi von Weydenfeld	I,II/Infanterie Regiment N.24 (Preiss)*	2,068	1 Musket (v)
	II/Infanterie Regiment N.27 (Strasoldo) III/Infanterie Regiment N.23 (Toscana) Reserve artillery 2x12-pdrs, 2x7-pdr howitzers	355 587	1 Musket (w)
Each base represents approximately 1000–1250 infantry, 500–625 cavalry or nine guns. (Lower case letter refers to historical deployment on the map) (* indicates that the unit is from the Upper Rhine army) The Oguliner and the Szluiner Grenzer regiments were the third and the fourth regiments of the Carlstädt district.			

In this table the cavalry regiments are numbered as they are in the 1796 *Almanach*, although they are often shown with their post 1798 numbering within each cavalry type. Thus, the Erdödy Husaren N.11 was the second hussar regiment and the Erzherzog Josef Husaren N.17 was the fourth hussar regiment. The single regiment of *ulanen* was unnumbered.[158]

The artillery represents only the reserve artillery of position. The line infantry battalions each had two light guns. Those line battalions that had recently arrived from the Upper Rhine army had 6-pdr battalion guns, while the other line battalions and the *Grenzer* battalions had 3-pdr guns.[159]

The quality of the Austrian infantry was heterogeneous, and the units that came from the interior of Austria were considered to be of poorer quality and are given *militia* status. The Austrian musket units retain their range of 200 paces (50mm) because they have an advantage in the numbers of battalion guns (c.f. page 42 in the rules).[160]

Weydenfeld's detachment is a reinforcement reaching the table at the beginning of turn 20, entering on the road behind Solferino.

Details of the uniforms worn by the Austrians during this campaign are given by von Pivka and others.[161]

French

Fifteen bases of muskets, five of light infantry, five of light cavalry, three of foot artillery and one of horse artillery.[162] The brigade commanders are all *généraux de brigade* unless stated otherwise. There will be three commanders, Bonaparte as commander-in-chief, with Masséna and Fiorella as sub-commanders. Bonaparte and Masséna are both rated as 'Good' commanders. Fiorella reduces all his CAP scores by one to reflect the small size of his command:[163]

158 Frister, *Almanach 1796*, pp.59–60.

159 Voykowitsch, *Castiglione*, pp.36–37, 43.

160 Voykowitsch, *Castiglione*, pp.35–36.

161 von Pivka, *Armies*, pp.79–95; for contemporary facings and button colours see Joseph Frister, *Oesterreichischer Militär Almanach für das Jahr 1793* (Vien: Author, 1793); see also *Napoleon Online, Portal zur Epoche 1792–1815*, accessed 6 April 2022, available at: <http://uniformenportal.de/index.php?/category/60/start-60>.

162 Félix Bouvier, *Bonaparte en Italie, 1796* (Paris: Leopold Cerf, 1899), p.709.

163 DBN rules p.26.

French	*Général de Division* Napoleon Bonaparte		
Brigade	Units	Men	Bases (E= elite, M= militia or poor quality)
Général de Division Hyacinthe François Joseph Despinoy			
Nicolas Bertin	I,II,III/5e Demi-Brigade d'Inf. de Ligne 1x8-pdrs, 1x 6 inch howitzers	1,773	1 Musket (a)
Général de Division André Masséna			
Jean-Joseph Magdeleine Pijon	I,II,III/18e Demi-Brigade d'Inf. de Légère	2,209	2 Light Infantry (b,c)
Antoine Guillaume Rampon	I,III/11e Demi-Brigade d'Inf. de Ligne	1,255	1 Musket (d)
	I,II,III/18e Demi-Brigade d'Inf. de Ligne	2,487	2 Muskets (e,f)
	I,II,III/32e Demi-Brigade d'Inf. de Ligne	2,565	2 Muskets (g,h)
Claude-Victor Perrin	II/11e Demi-Brigade d'Inf. de Ligne I,II,III/4e Demi-Brigade d'Inf. de Légère	722 1,031	1 Light Infantry (i)
	15e Dragons 25e Chasseurs à Cheval	209 209	1 Light Cavalry (M) (j)
Artillery	2x8-pdrs, 2x6 inch howitzers, 1x12-pdr		1 Foot Artillery (k)
Général de Division Charles Pierre François Augereau			
Adjudant-Général Charles Victoire Emmanuel Leclerc	I,II,III/4e Demi-Brigade d'Inf. de Ligne 22e Chasseurs à Cheval	2,097 245	2 Muskets (l,m)
Louis Pelletier	I,II,III/45e Demi-Brigade d'Inf. de Ligne	1,082	1 Musket (n)
	I,II/69e Demi-Brigade d'Inf. de Ligne	1,019	1 Musket (o)
	20e Dragons	351	1 Light Cavalry (p)
Jean Gilles André Robert	I,II,III/51e Demi-Brigade d'Inf. de Ligne	1,738	1 Musket (q)
	I,II,III/17e Demi-Brigade d'Inf. de Légère	1,073	1 Light Infantry (r)
	1er Hussards	358	1 Light Cavalry (M) (s)
Artillery	3x8-pdrs, 3x6 inch howitzers, 1x12-pdr		1 Foot Artillery (t)
Général de Division Charles Édouard Saül Jennings de Kilmaine			
Marc-Antoine Bonin de la Boninière, Comte de Beaumont	5e Dragons 7e Hussards (*bis*)	146 346	1 Light Cavalry (M) (u)
	10e Chasseurs à Cheval	413	1 Light Cavalry (M) (v)
Adjudant Commandant Chef de Brigade Jean Antoine Verdier	5e Bat. Grenadiers 6e/7e Bat. Grenadiers	421 379	1 Musket (E) (w)
Chef de Brigade Auguste de Marmont	4x8-pdrs, 3x6inch howitzers.		1 Horse Artillery (x)
Général de Brigade Pascual Antoine Fiorella (vice *Général de Division* Jean Sérurier)			
Charles-François Charton	I,II,III/19e Demi-Brigade d'Inf. de Ligne 6e Bat. Sappeurs	1,722 546	2 Muskets (y,z)
Emmanuel-Gervais de Roergaz de Serviez	I,II,III/12e Demi-Brigade d'Inf. de Légère	1,376	1 Light Infantry (aa)
	III/69e Demi-Brigade d'Inf. de Ligne 8e Dragons	806 160	1 Musket (bb)
	4x8-pdrs, 3x6 inch howitzers, 4x12-pdrs		1 Foot Artillery (cc)
Each base represents approximately 1000–1250 infantry, 500–625 cavalry or nine guns			

The 5th, 6th and 7th battalions of grenadiers were derived from the *demi-brigades* from the Armée des Alpes, Divisions de la Côte and the Divisions des Pays Conquis. Bonaparte had returned the grenadiers and carabiniers of the Armée d'Italie (1st to 4th battalions of grenadiers and 1st and 2nd battalions of carabiniers) to their parent battalions (2 June).[164]

In theory each battalion of the *demi-brigades de ligne* were to have a single 4-pdr battalion gun. Therefore, at Castiglione, there should have been 27 4-pdr guns supporting the infantry, but as late as June, due to a lack of horses, 89 of the army's 95 4-pdr guns were still back at Nizza, Antibes and Gap. Consequently, at best only a quarter of the infantry battalions would have had their supporting artillery.[165]

The Terrain

The battle was fought around Solferino four miles to the east-south-east of Castiglione delle Stiviere, as shown in Map 21:

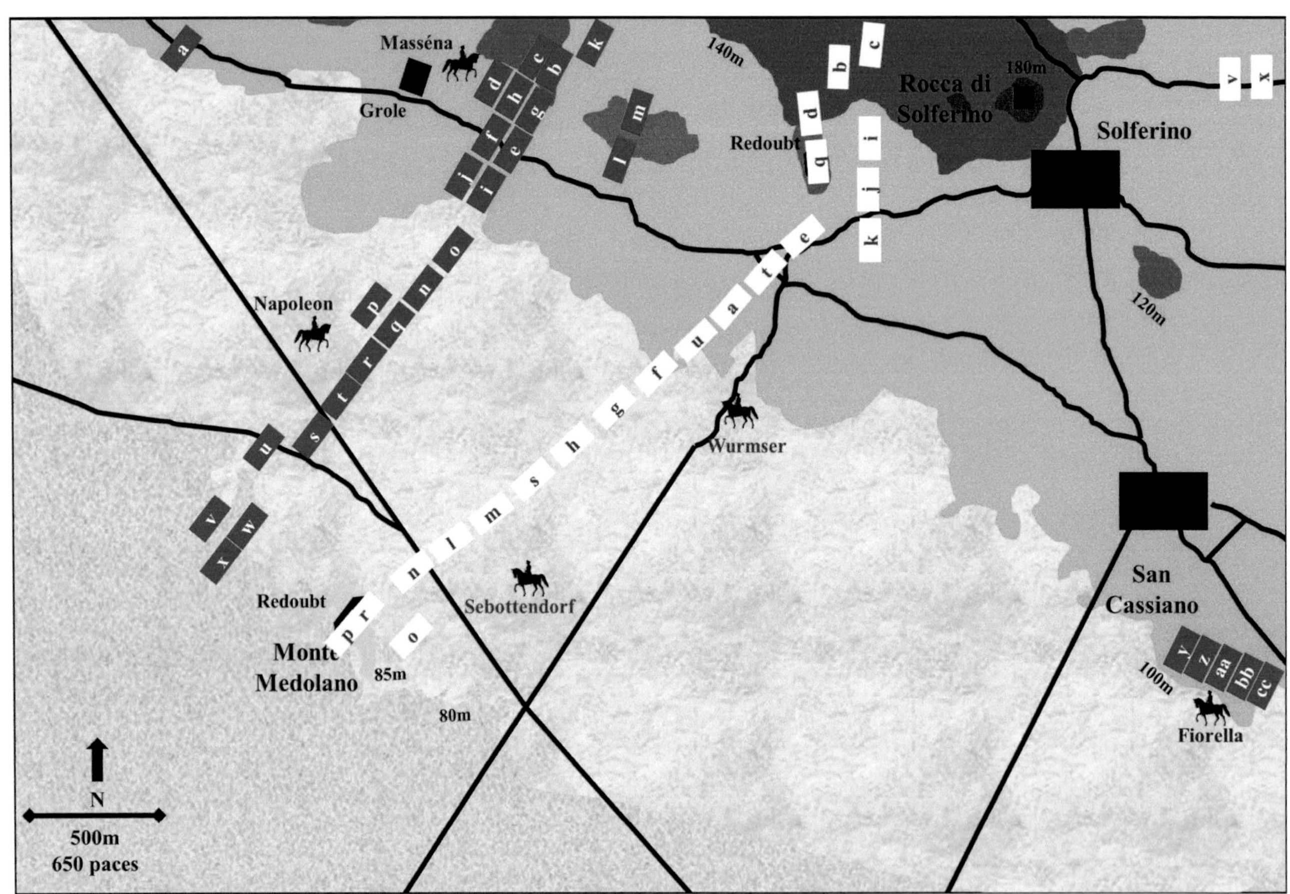

Map 21 – The Battle of Castiglione

Most of the ground is 'good going', but the hills above the 140m contour count as 'bad going'. The redoubts are considered linear fortifications. The southern redoubt can accommodate two artillery units and the northern redoubt can hold one.[166]

164 Voykowitsch, *Castiglione*, p.38.
165 Voykowitsch, *Castiglione*, p.38.
166 Voykowitsch, *Castiglione*, p.72; the illustration shows a contemporary French plan of the battle with 14 and 8 guns respectively in the two redoubts. The purist would class one of the units in the southern redoubt as militia

The map is designed for a six by four foot table, with base widths of six centimetres. This gives a ground scale of 1mm representing four paces and therefore the quick reference sheet will contain the following table:

Troop Type	Range (mm)	Movement (mm)			Combat Factor
		In GG	In BG	Roads	
C-in-C or Sub-Commander	-	100	50	100	+1
Artillery – Foot (FA)	250	50	X	75	+3
Artillery – Horse (HA)	150	75	X	100	+3
Artillery – Rockets (CR)	150	75	X	100	+2 (+3)
Cavalry – Heavy (HC)	-	75	50	100	+3 (+4)
Cavalry – Irregular (IC)	-	125	75	125	+1
Cavalry – Light (LC)	-	100	50	100	+3
Cavalry – Skirmishing (SC)	-	125	50	125	+2
Infantry – Jägers (Jg)	100	75	75	100	+2
Infantry – Light (LI)	75	75	75	100	+3*(+2)
Infantry – Muskets (Ms)	50	50	50	100	+4
Guerrillas (Gs)	50	X	75	-	+2 (+1)
Baggage Train (BT)	-	50	X	75	+1(cc)
*At +4 if garrisoning a built up area (BUA) or Fortification					
(+X) = vs Mounted					
Command radius 300mm					

Victory Conditions

The game starts at an hour after daybreak (6:00 am) and lasts for 24 turns.[167] Either side wins by destroying one third of the opposition's units, so the Austrian's need to destroy 10 units and the French need to destroy eight units. If neither side achieves their victory conditions, the game is drawn. The rules as written suggest that for this sized game an extra two units should be added to each side's goals, i.e. 12 vs 10, but I prefer sticking to one third as this avoids an 'empty battlefield' at the end of the game. Furthermore, the Austrian victory conditions should be 11 or 13, because of the extra French leader, but this has been ignored in the interests of game balance.

Game Balance

The scenario is not balanced if played with the historical setup. The French have 33½ points while the Austrians have 25. Furthermore, the Austrian total includes two points for their reinforcements which do not arrive until turn 20. An option to rebalance the scenario would be to modify the timeline such that Fiorella's division (5 points) is delayed in its approach march to the battlefield. In this option, the French player rolls a D6 at the beginning of each move, Fiorella can be deployed on the table if the score is less than or equal to the turn number.

for being understrength.

167 Phipps, *Italy*, p.71; Boycott-Brown, *Road to Rivoli*, p.400.

Castiglione in 15mm at Salute50

The Smaller Game

For a smaller, faster game, the following organisation, based on the normal unit size in De Bellis Napoleonicis, can be used. In this case, the tabletop will be three by two feet, using six-centimetre base width. The ground scale is now 1mm to eight paces:

Troop Type	Range (mm)	Movement (mm)			Combat Factor
		In GG	In BG	Roads	
C-in-C or Sub-Commander	-	50	25	50	+1
Artillery – Foot (FA)	125	25	X	40	+3
Artillery – Horse (HA)	75	40	X	50	+3
Artillery – Rockets (CR)	75	40	X	50	+2 (+3)
Cavalry – Heavy (HC)	-	40	25	50	+3 (+4)
Cavalry – Irregular (IC)	-	60	40	60	+1
Cavalry – Light (LC)	-	50	25	50	+3
Cavalry – Skirmishing (SC)	-	60	25	60	+2
Infantry – Jägers (Jg)	50	40	40	50	+2
Infantry – Light (LI)	40	40	40	50	+3* (+2)
Infantry – Muskets (Ms)	25	25	25	50	+4
Guerrillas (Gs)	25	X	40	-	+2 (+1)
Baggage Train (BT)	-	25	X	40	+1(cc)

*At +4 if garrisoning a BUA or Fortification

(+X) = vs. Mounted

Command radius 150mm

In this version of the scenario, the Austrians have six musket bases, one light infantry base, two light cavalry bases and three foot artillery bases. In this game, Sebottendorf's CAP die rolls are all reduced by one to reflect the small size of his command.

Austrian	*FM* Dagobert Sigmund von Wurmser	
Brigade	Units	Bases (M= militia or poor quality)
FML Paul Freiherr (Baron) von Davidovich (Right Wing)		
Anton Schubirž von Chobinin*	Mészáros Ulanen Regiment Erdödy Husaren Regiment N.11	1 Light Cavalry (a)
	Szluiner Grenzer Regiment N.63 Mahony Feld-Jägers Oguliner Grenzer Regiment N.62	1 Light Infantry (b)
Karl von Spiegel	I,II/Infanterie Regiment N.4 (Deutschmeister) I,II,III/Infanterie Regiment N.45 (Lattermann)*	1 Musket (c)
Anton Lipthay de Kisfalud	I,II,III/Infanterie Regiment N.13 (Reisky) I,II/Infanterie Regiment N.8 (Huff) I/Infanterie Regiment N.40 (Mittrowsky) Oguliner Grenzer Regiment N.62	1 Musket (d)
Anton von Mittrowsky	III/Infanterie Regiment N.10 (Khuel) Strasoldo Grenadier battalion III/Infanterie Regiment N.27 (Strasoldo)	1 Musket(M) (e)
	III/Infanterie Regiment N.11 (Wallis) I,II/Infanterie Regiment N.25 (Brechainville)*	1 Musket (f)
FML Karl Philipp Sebottendorf van der Rose (Left Wing)		
Peter von Gummer	I,II/Infanterie Regiment N.19 (Alvinzy) II/Infanterie Regiment N.21 (Gemmingen)	1 Musket (g)
Oberst Christoph Karl von Piacsek	Erdödy Husaren Regiment N.11 Eh. Josef Husaren Regiment N.17 Mészáros Ulanen Regiment	1 Light Cavalry (h)
Reserve Artillery	18x12-pdrs, 18x6-pdrs, 12x7-pdr howitzers, 8x3-pdrs, two cavalry 6-pdrs and two cavalry 7-pdr howitzers	3 Foot Artillery (i, j, k)
Detachment		
Oberst Karl Philippi von Weydenfeld	I,II/Infanterie Regiment N.24 (Preiss)* II/Infanterie Regiment N.27 (Strasoldo) III/Infanterie Regiment N.23 (Toscana)	1 Musket (l)
Each base represents approximately 2,000–2,500 infantry, 1,000–1,250 cavalry or 18 guns. (* from the Upper Rhine army)		

For the French, the smaller scenario uses eight musket bases, two light infantry bases, three light cavalry bases, two foot artillery bases and one horse artillery base.[168]

French	*Général de Division* Napoleon Bonaparte	
Brigade	Units	Bases (E= elite, M= militia or poor quality)
Général de Division Hyacinthe François Joseph Despinoy		
Nicolas Bertin	I,II,III/5e Demi-Brigade d'Infanterie de Ligne	1 Musket (a)
Général de Division André Masséna		
Jean-Joseph Magdeleine Pijon	I,II,III/18e Demi-Brigade d'Infanterie de Légère	1 Light Infantry (b)
Antoine Guillaume Rampon	I,III/11e Demi-Brigade d'Infanterie de Ligne	1 Musket (c)
	I,II,III/18e Demi-Brigade d'Infanterie de Ligne I,II,III/32e Demi-Brigade d'Infanterie de Ligne	1 Musket (d)
Claude-Victor Perrin	II/11e Demi-Brigade d'Infanterie de Ligne I,II,III/4e Demi-Brigade d'Infanterie de Légère	1 Light Infantry (e)
	15e Dragons/ 25e Chasseurs à Cheval	1 Light Cavalry (M) (f)
Général de Division Charles Pierre François Augereau		
Adjudant-Général Charles Victoire Emmanuel Leclerc	I,II,III/4e Demi-Brigade d'Infanterie de Ligne 22e Chasseurs à Cheval	1 Musket (g)
Louis Pelletier	I,II,III/45e Demi-Brigade d'Infanterie de Ligne I,II/69e Demi-Brigade d'Infanterie de Ligne	1 Musket (h)
	20e Dragons	1 Light Cavalry (i)
Jean Gilles André Robert	I,II,III/51e Demi-Brigade d'Infanterie de Ligne I,II,III/17e Demi-Brigade d'Infanterie de Légère	1 Musket (j)
	1er Hussards	not represented
	6x8-pdrs, 6x 6 inch How., 2x 12-pdr	1 Foot Artillery (k)
Général de Division Charles Édouard Saül Jennings de Kilmaine		
Marc-Antoine Bonin de La Boninière, Comte de Beaumont	5e Dragons/7e Hussards (*bis*) 10e Chasseurs à Cheval	1 Light Cavalry (M) (l)
Adjudant Commandant Chef de Brigade Jean Antoine Verdier	5e Bat. Grenadiers 6e/7e Bat. Grenadiers	1 Musket (E) (m)
Chef de Brigade Marmont	4x 8-pdrs, 3x 6inch How.	1 Horse Artillery (n)
Général de Brigade Pascual Antoine Fiorella (vice *Général de Division* Jean Sérurier)		
Charles-François Charton	I,II,III/19e Demi-Brigade d'Infanterie de Ligne 6e Bat. Sappeurs	1 Musket (o)
Emmanuel-Gervais de Roergaz de Serviez	I,II,III/12e Demi-Brigade d'Infanterie de Légère III/69e Demi-Brigade d'Infanterie de Ligne 8e Dragons	
	4x8-pdrs, 3x 6 inch How., 4x12-pdrs	1 Foot Artillery (p)
Each base represents approximately 2,000–2,500 infantry, 1,000–1,250 cavalry or 18 guns		

168 Marmont's horse artillery disappears from the OOB at this scale, but they have been kept in due to the key role they played in the battle. If necessary, this can be balanced by removing one of the foot artillery bases or by grading Marmont's unit as militia, as described on p.44 in the rules. In any case the Austrian victory condition has been modified to allow for this.

To win the smaller game the Austrians need to destroy six bases and the French need to destroy five bases.

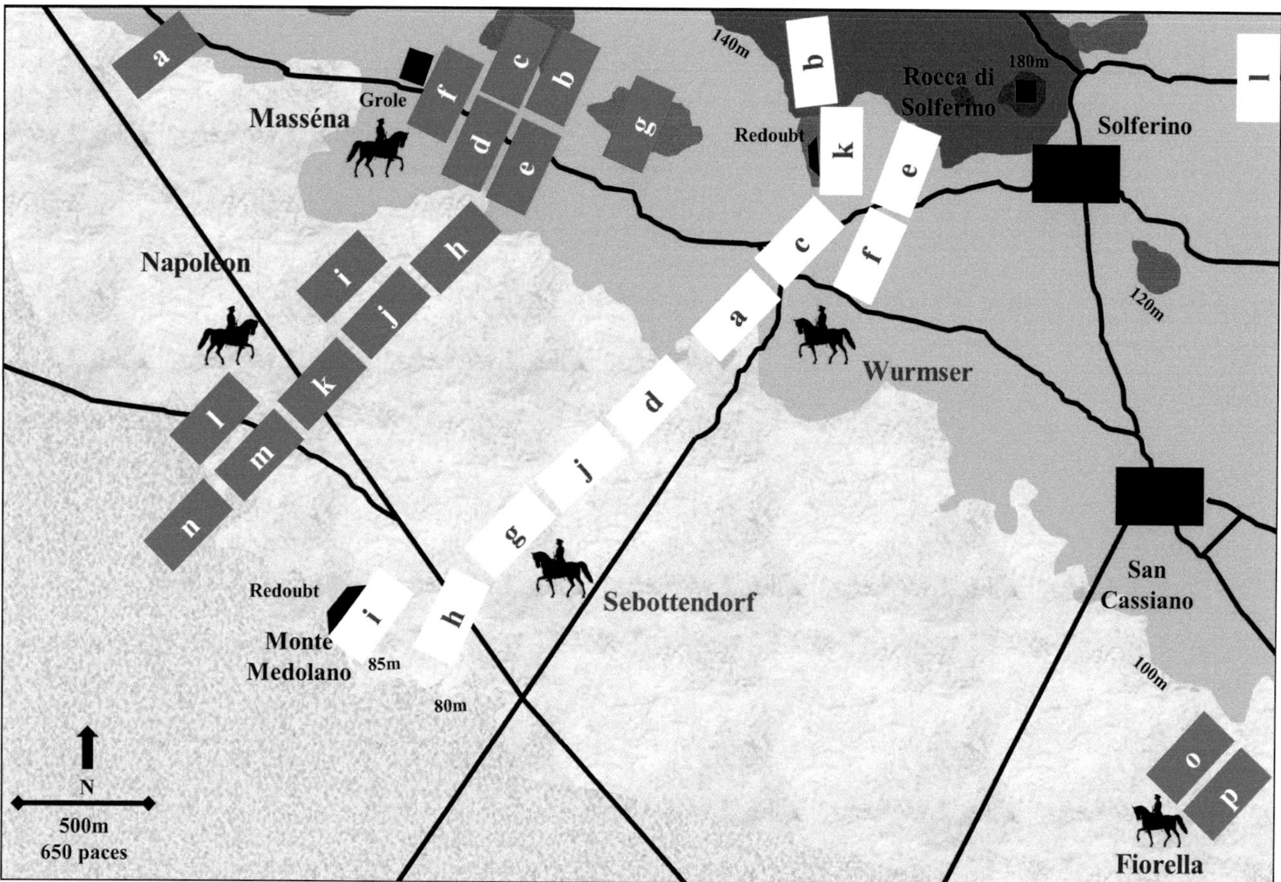

Map 22 – The Battle of Castiglione, Smaller Game

Volley and Bayonet

This smaller scenario can also be played using the popular Volley and Bayonet rules. Using the three by two foot battlefield, all distances in the rules should be halved.

Austrian	*FM* Dagobert Sigmund von Wurmser	
Brigade	Units	V&B Bases (Strength Points)
FML Paul Freiherr (Baron) von Davidovich (Right Wing)		
Anton Schubirž von Chobinin*	Mészáros Ulanen Regiment Erdödy Husaren Regiment N.11	Linear Cav.(1)
	Szluiner Grenzer Regiment N.63 Mahony Feld-Jägers Oguliner Grenzer Regiment N.62	Linear Inf. (3) Inf. Skirmish (1)
Karl von Spiegel	I,II/Infanterie Regiment N.4 (Deutschmeister) I,II,III/Infanterie Regiment N.45 (Lattermann)*	Linear Inf. (4)
Anton Lipthay de Kisfalud	I,II,III/Infanterie Regiment N.13 (Reisky) I,II/Infanterie Regiment N.8 (Huff) I/Infanterie Regiment N.40 (Mittrowsky) Oguliner Grenzer Regiment N.62	Linear Inf. (4) Linear Inf. (3)
Anton von Mittrowsky	III/Infanterie Regiment N.10 (Khuel) Strasoldo Grenadier battalion III/Infanterie Regiment N.27 (Strasoldo)	Linear Inf. (3)
	III/Infanterie Regiment N.11 (Wallis) I,II/Infanterie Regiment N.25 (Brechainville)*	Linear Inf. (5)
FML Karl Philipp Sebottendorf van der Rose (Left Wing)		
Peter von Gummer	I,II/Infanterie Regiment N.19 (Alvinzy) II/Infanterie Regiment N.21 (Gemmingen)	Linear Inf. (4)
Oberst Christoph Karl von Piacsek	Erdödy Husaren Regiment N.11 Eh. Josef Husaren Regiment N.17 Mészáros Ulanen Regiment	Linear Cav.(3)
Reserve Artillery	18x12-pdrs, 18x6-pdrs, 12x7-pdr howitzers, 8x3-pdrs, two cavalry 6-pdrs and two cavalry 7-pdr howitzers	10 Artillery (1)
Detachment		
Oberst Karl Philippi von Weydenfeld	I,II/Infanterie Regiment N.24 (Preiss)* II/Infanterie Regiment N.27 (Strasoldo) III/Infanterie Regiment N.23 (Toscana)	Linear Inf. (6)
Each strength point represents 500 infantry or cavalry, or six guns. (* from the Upper Rhine army)		

The Austrian army is commanded by Wurmser as commander-in-chief, and each division commander is represented, with exhaustion levels (excluding the reserve artillery) of Davidovich (12), Sebottendorf (4) and Weydenfeld (3). All of the Austrian line infantry stands have 'dedicated guns'.

French	*Général de Division* Napoleon Bonaparte	
Brigade	Units	V&B Bases (Strength Points)
Général de Division Hyacinthe François Joseph Despinoy		
Nicolas Bertin	I,II,III/5e Demi-Brigade d'Infanterie de Ligne	Massed Inf. (3)
Général de Division André Masséna		
Jean-Joseph Magdeleine Pijon	I,II,III/18e Demi-Brigade d'Infanterie de Légère	Massed Inf (3) Inf Skirmishers (1)
Antoine Guillaume Rampon	I,III/11e Demi-Brigade d'Infanterie de Ligne	Massed Inf (4)
	I,II,III/18e Demi-Brigade d'Infanterie de Ligne	Massed Inf (4)
	I,II,III/32e Demi-Brigade d'Infanterie de Ligne	Massed Inf (4)
Claude-Victor Perrin	II/11e Demi-Brigade d'Infanterie de Ligne	Massed Inf (2)
	I,II,III/4e Demi-Brigade d'Infanterie de Légère	Inf Skirmishers (1)
	15e Dragons/ 25e Chasseurs à Cheval	Massed Cav. (1)
Général de Division Charles Pierre François Augereau		
Adjudant-Général Charles Victoire Emmanuel Leclerc	I,II,III/4e Demi-Brigade d'Infanterie de Ligne	Massed Inf (4)
	22e Chasseurs à Cheval	Inf Skirmishers (1)
Louis Pelletier	I,II,III/45e Demi-Brigade d'Infanterie de Ligne I,II/69e Demi-Brigade d'Infanterie de Ligne	Massed Inf (4)
	20e Dragons	Massed Cav. (1)
Jean Gilles André Robert	I,II,III/51e Demi-Brigade d'Infanterie de Ligne	Massed Inf (4)
	I,II,III/17e Demi-Brigade d'Infanterie de Légère	Inf Skirmish (1)
	1er Hussards	Massed Cav. (1)
	6x8-pdrs, 6x6 inch Howitzers, 2x12-pdr	2 Artillery (1)
Général de Division Charles Édouard Saül Jennings de Kilmaine		
Marc-Antoine Bonin de La Boninière, Comte de Beaumont	5e Dragons/7e Hussards (*bis*) 10e Chasseurs à Cheval	Massed Cav. (2)
Adjudant Commandant Chef de Brigade Jean Antoine Verdier	5e Bat. Grenadiers 6e/7e Bat. Grenadiers	Massed Inf. (2)
Chef de Brigade Marmont	4x8-pdrs, 3x6inch Howitzers	Artillery (1)
Général de Brigade Pascual Antoine Fiorella (vice *Général de Division* Jean Sérurier)		
Charles-François Charton	I,II,III/19e Demi-Brigade d'Infanterie de Ligne 6e Bat. Sappeurs	Massed Inf. (5)
Emmanuel-Gervais de Roergaz de Serviez	I,II,III/12e Demi-Brigade d'Infanterie de Légère	Massed Inf (4)
	III/69e Demi-Brigade d'Infanterie de Ligne	Inf Skirmishers (1)
	8e Dragons	
	4x8-pdrs, 3x 6 inch How., 4x12-pdrs	2 Artillery (1)
Each strength point represents 500 infantry or cavalry, or six guns.		

The French army is commanded by Bonaparte as commander-in-chief and each division commander is represented. Exhaustion levels are Despinoy (2), Masséna (10), Augereau (9), Kilmaine (3) and Fiorella (6). Three of the massed infantry bases can have 'dedicated' guns.

The game lasts for six one hour turns.

Austrians defending the Northern redoubt

The Battle

The 5 August began with the opposing commanders both playing for time. Wurmser needed to give the garrison of Mantua time to seize the abandoned French siege guns and destroy their works, while Bonaparte awaited Fiorella's advance on the Austrian rear through Guidizollo. Bonaparte was concerned that Wurmser would retire behind the Mincio before his attack and the resulting envelopment could fully develop. Furthermore, Masséna's troops were still arriving on the battlefield.

The Austrian frontline was deployed from the La Rocca hill and tower to the Monte Medolano, with Sebottendorf on the left and Davidovich on the right. To buy time, Bonaparte sent the 4e Ligne to attack the Austrian centre. The Austrians repelled this attack before advancing their right wing to outflank Masséna's division. Bonaparte sent Marmont with 12 guns to bombard the Austrian redoubt on the Monte Medolano, which held 14 guns, Verdier then stormed it with his grenadiers. Augereau, with Kilmaine in support, then attacked the Austrian left and centre, while Masséna attacked their right. Meanwhile Fiorella's division was advancing through Guidizollo into the Austrian rear, Wurmser responded by redeploying battalions from his second line towards Cavriana. In the face of the superior numbers of French, Wurmser ordered his army to retreat via La Volta and Cavriana to Borghetto.

It was at this moment that Despinoy with the 5e Ligne arrived on the battlefield from Brescia. The 5e Ligne was thrown into the assault in support of a renewed attack by Leclerc leading the 4e Ligne. Together they stormed the heights, taking Pozzo Catena, the castle and the tower at Solferino. Schubirž and Mittrowsky from the Austrian right wing covered the withdrawal of the Austrian left. When Masséna attempted to outflank them, Weydenfeld's timely arrival on the battlefield and vigorous assault on Masséna's left forced him to stop. This intervention allowed Davidovich's men to rally and retire to the Mincio. The pursuit of the retiring Austrians was limited to three hours by the exhaustion of the French troops and Bonaparte's shortage of cavalry. The next day (6 August) Masséna forced a crossing of the Mincio near Peschiera, thereby threatening Wurmser's lines of communication back to the Tyrol. Consequently, Wurmser ordered his army to retreat to the Tyrol. Reinforcements and provisions were also sent to Mantua to prepare it for the resumption of the siege. The French then advanced to retake Verona and the heights of Rivoli (7 August).[169]

In conclusion, although Bonaparte had defeated Wurmser and forced him back to the Tyrol, Wurmser had achieved the objective of reinforcing and revictualling Mantua.

There are also opportunities to design scenarios around the smaller actions on the preceding days of the campaign between Masséna and Quosdanovich and between Augereau and Lipthay.

Scenario 8:

A Fleet action based on the Glorious First of June 1794

France vs. Britain. A fleet level action using *Fighting Sail* rules.

A more furious onset was never or more obstinately resisted – *Captain Cuthbert Collingwood, HMS Barfleur*

Background

Sam Willis in the introduction to his book, gives some compelling explanations of the significance of this battle. As wargamers the fact that it was the major fleet action of War of the First Coalition, involved tactical innovation and a hard-fought action are reasons enough for its inclusion in the list of scenarios. It was also the culmination of a week of actions which can provide further wargame scenarios.[170]

169 Voykowitsch, *Castiglione*, pp.73–84.
170 Willis, *Fleet Battle*, pp.xxxiii–xli.

In France the upheaval associated with the revolution had amongst other factors caused a failure of the harvest and with France at war with all its neighbours, she had to look elsewhere to import replacement food supplies. Consequently in 1794 a single large convoy was gathered in Chesapeake Bay to bring grain and other foods, both purchased in the United States and from the French colonies in the Caribbean. It has been estimated that the convoy contained enough food to feed 600,000 to 950,000 people for 4 months, dependent on whether the British estimate (107 ships) or French estimate (170 ships) is believed.[171]

With a French population of approximately 25,000,000 souls the convoy would make a significant contribution, but not enough to make or break the revolution. For Admiral Richard, Viscount Howe, commander of the Royal Navy's Channel Fleet, the major benefit of the French convoy was the opportunity it offered to bring to battle the *Marine Nationale's Grand Flotte*, based in Brest, and destroy it. The French fleet was commanded by 46-year-old *Contre-Amiral* Louis Thomas Villaret de Joyeuse, overseen by the *Représentant en Mission* Jean Bon Saint-André. The *Représentant* was responsible for bringing order and discipline to the French Navy and ending the culture of mutiny justified by the revolution by using the death penalty for a wide range of activities deemed to be treasonous or cowardice.[172] For his part Villaret de Joyeuse received his orders directly from Robespierre, he was not to allow the grain convoy to fall into the hands of the British or else he would lose his head![173]

A great 'what if' scenario is offered by 17 May, when the two fleets sailed past one another in fog, approaching to within 300 yards at one point. In the days leading up to 1 June there were several smaller actions involving the sections of the two fleets together with other convoys of merchantmen, each of which are opportunities for further scenarios. When Howe caught up with the *Grand Flotte* (28 May), both fleets cleared for action, but the French had the weather gauge and Villaret de Joyeuse realised that he had no need to engage the British in order to achieve his goal of protecting the grain fleet, which was now in sight.

Consequently, the British faced the slow task of closing on the French in order to engage. The *Révolutionnaire* (110 guns, formerly the *Bretagne*, launched 1766) was however spoiling for a fight and was engaged by four British 74s from Howe's 'flying squadron', comprised of his four fastest ships of the line, under Rear Admiral Sir Thomas Pasley. The *Révolutionnaire* was severely damaged and ultimately dismasted, but not without inflicting significant damage on the British ships, particularly HMS *Bellepheron* and HMS *Audacious*. When Howe called off the action for the day, and despite having apparently struck its colours, the *Révolutionnaire* was able to limp away and avoid capture, commanded only by its fourth lieutenant, Capitaine Vandoren and the second lieutenant having been killed and the first and third lieutenants having been wounded.[174] Another action was fought the next day (29 May) which became a confused melee between the van of both fleets, as Howe attempted and ultimately succeeded in breaking through the French line to gain the all-important weather gauge, up wind of the French line. Fourteen Royal Navy ships had been engaged and 11 had sustained damage. However, all were ready again for battle on the morning of the 30th.

171 Mark Lardas, *The Glorious First of June 1794* (Oxford: Osprey, 2019), p.38.
172 Willis, *Fleet Battle*, pp.32–35.
173 Willis, *Fleet Battle*, p.121.
174 Willis, *Fleet Battle*, pp.154–155.

The French were harder hit, the *Indomptable* (80 guns) was so badly hit it could not take its place in the line of battle requiring a dockyard refit. The *Tyrannicide* (74) had to be towed for the next three days. Meanwhile the *Terrible* (110) and the *Éole* (74) received significant hull damage. Separately the French also lost their lead ship *Montagnard* (74), which disappeared during the fighting and did not return. Both commanders had something to be pleased about, Howe had gained the precious weather gauge, so that he could attack the French at will, while Villaret de Joyeuse had drawn the British further from the grain convoy and his crews had demonstrated a determination and capacity to fight.

This action also saw the generation of some myths about French gunnery based on the statements of a 13-year-old midshipman, Parker. His claim that the French targeted only the masts and rigging are not borne out by his own later statements or the British damage reports.[175]

The next two days (30–31 May) passed without significant action due to fog which separated Howe from his fleet (31 May). However, he was reassured that the French had already demonstrated a desire to fight rather than run. At dawn on the fateful day, the two fleets were visible to each other, formed in line of battle six nautical miles apart. The wind was moderate from the south-south-east. Howe's flagship HMS *Queen Charlotte* (100) was positioned 563 nautical miles from Brest and 586 nautical miles from Plymouth, thus this would be the only age of sail battle fought so far from land.[176]

At 5:00 a.m., Howe signalled to his fleet to close on the French fleet. Howe's fleet comprised 25 ships of the line, while Villaret de Joyeuse had 28. After breakfast, around 8:30 a.m. the British fleet turned to bear down on the French, Howe having signalled them to engage the enemy closely, break the French line and engage their opposite numbers on the leeward side. Breaking the line enabled the British attackers to rake the French ships and then prevent their escape to leeward, by engaging from that side. The British ships varied in how they interpreted these orders, only six British ships broke the line at the beginning of the action although two others did later. The Van of the British fleet was the first to engage the French, with HMS *Defence* taking the honour of being the first to break through the French line. The rest engaged their opposite numbers to windward, except the leading ship, HMS *Caesar*, which restricted itself to a long-range bombardment of the *Trajan*. The battle degenerated into a melee and lasted for one hour. With 12 of their ships disabled and dismasted and further six seriously damaged, the French survivors formed a line downwind. Both admirals were then more interested in securing their crippled ships and the battle was over. In the end the British took six prizes and the *Vengeur* was sunk after a brutal battle with HMS *Brunswick*. The British lost no ships. The French lost 7,500 killed and wounded and 4,000 prisoners (including some 690 of the wounded). The British casualties were much lighter, 1,150 killed and wounded.

During the fighting leading up to 1 June and during the battle itself, the grain convoy continued its slow but steady progress towards Brest and while the battle raged it was 200 nautical miles away to the east. While Howe was clearly able to claim a 'glorious' tactical victory, Villaret de Joyeuse could be satisfied that he had drawn Howe away

175 Willis, *Fleet Battle*, pp.169–170.
176 Lardas, *Glorious*, p.71; 47°48'N 18°30'W.

from the grain convoy, whose arrival in Brest (12 June), arguably gave him a strategic victory and certainly fulfilled his key campaign objective.

The Game

Famously 20 players met at the Enfilade 2015 convention, Olympia, Washington State in the United States to refight the entire battle using the *Sails of Glory* models and rules. The game involved 71 models, including both the ships of the line and their supporting frigates.[177] More recently eight players met at the *Boards and Swords Hobbies* gaming venue in Derby here in the United Kingdom to refight the battle using the *Black Seas*™ rules and models, on the 228th anniversary in 2022.

To make this scenario more manageable it focuses on the action involving the van (meaning the leading squadrons) of both fleets. This scenario consequently involves seven British ships of the line, five 74-gun ships, one 80-gun ship and one 100-gun flagship, and nine French ships, eight 74-gun ships and one 110-gun ship.

British Ships	Guns/Rating/Class	French Ships	Guns/Rating/Class
HMS *Caesar*	80/3rd/—	*Le Trajan*	74/3rd/*Duquesne*
HMS *Bellepheron*	74/3rd/*Arrogant*	*L'Éole*	74/3rd/*Duquesne*
HMS *Leviathan*	74/3rd/*Courageux*	*L'America*	74/3rd/*Téméraire*
HMS *Russell*	74/3rd/*Ramilles*	*Le Téméraire*	74/3rd/*Téméraire*
HMS *Royal Sovereign* (Flag)	100/1st/ —	*Le Terrible (Flag)*	110/1st/*Terrible*
HMS *Marlborough*	74/3rd/*Ramilles*	*L'Impétueux*	74/3rd/*Téméraire*
HMS *Defence*	74/3rd/*Bellona*	*Le Mucius*	74/3rd/*Téméraire*
		Le Tourville	74/3rd/*Duquesne*
		L'Apollon	74/3rd/*Téméraire*

Notes:

The *Duquesne* class was a sub-class of the *Téméraire* class, the largest class of capital ships ever built.

The *Arrogant*, *Bellona* and *Ramilles* classes all look the same above the waterline.

L'Apollon was renamed the *Gasparin* in February 1794 but reverted to *L'Apollon* in May 1794. She is shown in some orders of battle as the *Gasparin*.[178]

Both fleets were supported by frigates, two or three per squadron, positioned behind the respective line of battle, but these took no direct part in the fighting, other than rescuing crippled ships. However, the frigate HMS *Niger* was particularly allocated to Admiral Graves's flagship, HMS *Royal Sovereign*, to relay signals to and from Lord

177 <https://www.aresgames.eu/14620>

178 Willis, *Fleet Battle*, p.350; <https://en.wikipedia.org/wiki/T%C3%A9m%C3%A9raire-class_ship_of_the_line>, accessed 28 March 2022.

Howe aboard HMS *Queen Charlotte*.[179] Consequently, the frigates are not included in this scenario.

The scenario is designed for *Fighting Sail* rules published by Osprey.[180] These rules give a fast moving and exciting game which works well with the number of ships involved. Since the rules were published, a number of modifications have been published by the author which can be found online.[181] The most significant change is to make the ships more robust to single broadsides, by changing the *damage deck* such that you now need six unsaved hits from one broadside to sink a ship. Five unsaved hits generate a third additional damage token, instead of sinking the ship.

Unsaved hits	The Damage Deck (modified)
0 or less	No effect.
1	Disrupted — the ship gets an Anchor token unless it already had one.
2	Shaken — the ship gets an Anchor token. If it already had one, it gets a Damage token instead.
3	Light Damage — the ship gets an additional Damage token and an Anchor token unless it already has one.
4	Heavy Damage — the ship gets two additional Damage tokens and an Anchor token unless it already has one.
5	Very Heavy Damage — the ship gets three additional Damage tokens and an Anchor token unless it already has one.
6 or more	Catastrophic Damage — the ship is sunk.

Further changes to reduce the effects of cannon fire include restricting 'explosions'/critical hits to raking shots (on hits of 5+) and short range (6+). On the other hand, the hull dice save has been reduced to 5+.

However, for a quicker game, simply use the rules as originally written. The following table gives the game statistics for each ship.

179 Willis, *Fleet Battle*, p.189.

180 Ryan Miller, *Fighting Sail* (Oxford: Osprey Publishing, 2015).

181 Author's amendments to *Fighting Sail* <https://boardgamegeek.com/filepage/171969/rules-update>, accessed 14 March 2022; see also Osprey Wargames gaming resources available at: <https://ospreypublishing.com/gaming-resources-OWG>, accessed 15 February 2022.

Ship	Sailing	Discipline	Boarding	Gunnery	Hull
The British					
HMS *Caesar* (80)	4	6	7	8	7
HMS *Bellepheron* (74)	6	6	7	8	7
HMS *Leviathan* (74)	4	6	7	8	7
HMS *Russell* (74)	4	6	7	8	7
HMS *Royal Sovereign* (100, Flag)	3	8	10	10	10
HMS *Marlborough* (74)	4	6	7	8	7
HMS *Defence* (74)	4	6	7	8	8
Fleet Morale	48				
The French					
Le Trajan (74)	4	5	7	7	7
L'Éole (74)	4	5	7	7	7
L'America (74)	4	5	7	7	7
Le Téméraire (74)	4	5	7	7	7
Le Terrible (110, Flag)	3	7	10	9	10
L'Impétueux (74)	4	5	7	7	7
Le Mucius (74)	4	5	7	7	7
Le Tourville (74)	4	5	7	7	7
L'Apollon (74)	4	5	7	7	7
Fleet Morale	54				

Fighting Sail gives the French 74s a sailing factor of five based on their technically superior hull design, however some historians doubt that this superiority was actually delivered in practice, given British superiority in the amount of sail carried.[182]

The captains of the British ships had vastly more experience of fleet battle than their French opposite numbers, only one of whom had any experience of fleet battle at all.[183]

The ships should be deployed as shown in Map 23. The map is based on an eight by four feet table and is designed for use with my 1:1000 scale *Sails of Glory* models, obviously when using 1:2400 scale models all distances can be halved.

As the battle took place in the middle of the ocean there is no need for any terrain. This opens the possibility of providing more sea room by dividing the playing surface into

182 Lardas, *Glorious*, p.21.
183 Willis, *Fleet Battle*, p.143.

three parts, allowing the rear part of the surface to be moved in front of the line of battle as it moves inexorably forward.

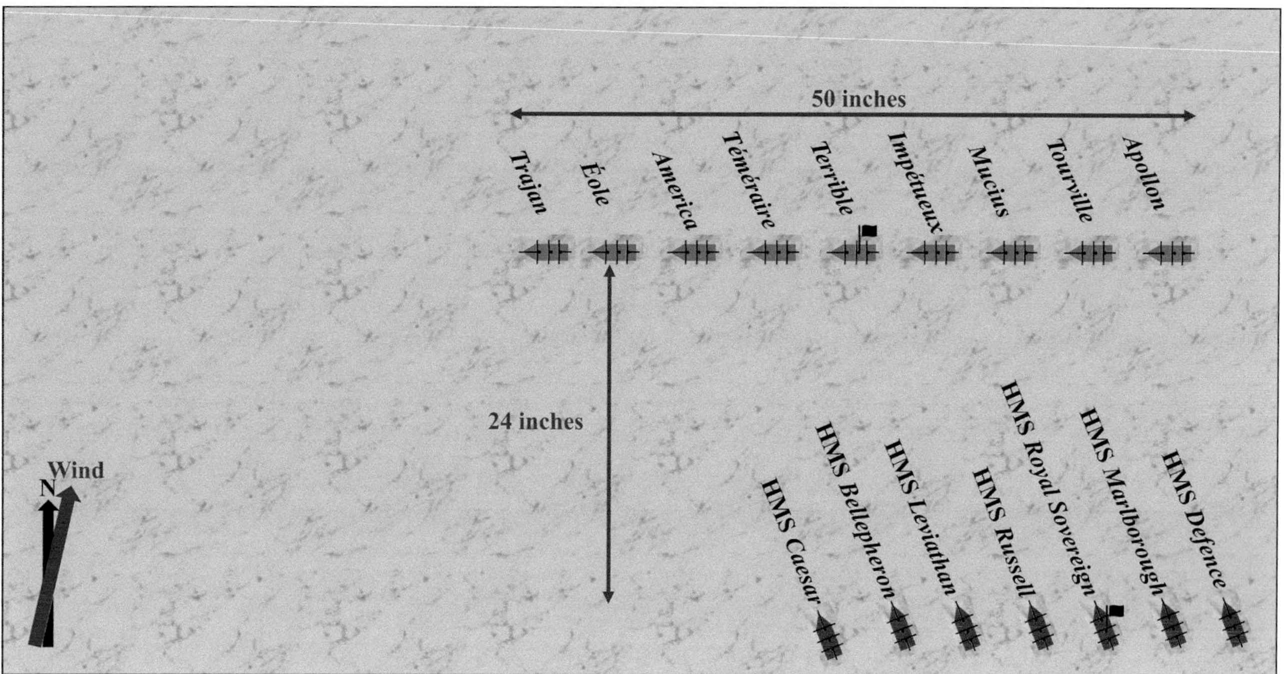

Map 23 – The Glorious First of June, The Van

The game ends immediately when the Fleet Morale of one of the two sides is reduced to zero, the other side is then declared the winner. For a shorter game, base the reduction in Fleet Morale on *unsaved hits*, alternatively for a longer game use *damage tokens* instead.

When playing the scenario, it is tempting to simplify the movement of the lines of battle on, for example, a 'follow my leader' basis. However, this should be discouraged as the effort to maintain the line of battle was a significant feature in this period:

> Maintaining station in a fleet was very difficult. Ships moved at different speeds under similar sail plans and all distances had to be judged by eye. The result was that any 'line' of battle was hardly ever a line as we would conceive it, but more like several lengths of a broken chain. Three, four or five ships might keep close station with each other, but they would be in some measure dissociated from those astern or ahead, and so on.[184]

All the French ships in this scenario flew the early revolutionary flag which was a white flag with a tricolour in the upper left quadrant. At this battle, only Joyeuse de Villerat's flagship, *Le Montagne*, flew the new national tricolour flag.[185]

During the battle the fates of the ships were as follows:[186]

> HMS *Caesar*: 'not materially damaged to outward view but several shot through her sails'. Eighteen killed and 71 wounded (15 percent).
>
> HMS *Bellepheron*: 'fore and main top masts gone and much damaged' by the *Trajan* and the *L' Éole*. She was so damaged that she had to be towed to

184 Willis, *Fleet Battle*, p.48.
185 Willis, *Fleet Battle*, p.204.
186 Willis, *Fleet Battle*, pp.203, 207, 334–337, 356: the quotations are Nicholas Pocock's words.

safety by the frigate HMS *Latona*. Four killed and 27 wounded (6 percent) including Rear Admiral Thomas Pasley who lost a leg.[187] Rear Admiral Pasley was mentioned in Howe's report.

HMS *Leviathan*: 'Foremast and foreyard much wounded, sails and rigging much damaged'. Ten killed and 33 wounded (8 percent). Her captain, Lord Hugh Seymour, was mentioned in Howe's report.

HMS *Russell*: Eight killed and 26 wounded (7 percent). Her captain, John Payne, was mentioned in Howe's report.

HMS *Royal Sovereign*: 'No masts or yards gone … but much shattered'. Fourteen killed and 44 wounded (8 percent). Vice Admiral Thomas Graves was mentioned in Howe's report.[188]

HMS *Marlborough*: 'totally dismasted' and was so damaged she had to be towed to safety by the frigate HMS *Aquilon*. Twenty-nine killed and 90 wounded (22 percent). Her captain, George Berkeley, was mentioned in Howe's report.

HMS *Defence*: the first ship through the French line, was 'totally' dismasted and had to be towed to safety by the frigate HMS *Phaeton*. Eighteen killed and 39 wounded (11 percent). Her captain, James Gambier, was mentioned in Howe's report.

Thus, Captain Anthony Molloy (HMS *Caesar*) was the only commander in the Van not to be recognised by Howe. In response Molloy demanded a court-martial to clear his name, claiming that his ship was too damaged to fully comply with Howe's orders to close with the French and break their line. However, the court found him guilty, and he was removed from his command.[189]

For the French, individual ship casualty figures are hard to come by, but we know that the six captured ships lost 690 killed and 580 wounded.[190] This suggests that, on average the French ships each lost as many as 200 men, killed or wounded. These figures are significantly greater than the British casualties. These differences reflect more efficient British gunnery, based on flexible reloading tools, the more efficient gunlocks, and lighter, more manoeuvrable main guns. To make matters worse for the French, the more fragile hulls of the lighter built French ships resulted in higher casualties, which in turn reduced the firepower of the French ships. The British ships also proved themselves more capable and/or more inclined to come to the support of their own ships.[191] Specific details known for each French ship are:[192]

Le Trajan: *Capitaine* Dumoutier was included in Jeanbon's list of 'treasonous' officers for their 'modest or poor behaviour' during the battle. Dumoutier was sent before the Revolutionary Tribunal, but his trial was cancelled when

187 Willis, *Fleet Battle*, p.212.

188 James, *Naval History*, p.168; has the Royal Sovereign losing its topgallant masts lost.

189 Willis, *Fleet Battle*, pp.262, 269–270.

190 Anon, *Official documents and interesting particulars of the glorious victory obtained over the French Fleet, on Sunday June 1, 1794, by the British Fleet, under the command of Admiral Earl Howe…* (London: J.Debrett, 1794), p.13.

191 Willis, *Fleet Battle*, pp.208–211.

192 Willis, *Fleet Battle*, p.281; Lardas, *Glorious*, pp.28–29; James, *Naval History*, p.168; five of the nine officers on Jeanbon's list were from the Van of the French fleet. Allocation of the captains to their ships taken from Lardas.

Robespierre fell from power.[193] The *Trajan* fought the battle very understrength (240 men sick or missing as prize crews).

L'Éole: *Capitaine* Bertrand Keranguen and *Lieutenant* Benoit, who commanded the ship after Keranguen was killed, were both included in Jeanbon's list of 'treasonous' officers for their 'modest or poor behaviour' during the battle. *Lieutenant* Benoit was dismissed from the service.

L'America: Totally dismasted and captured by the British. One hundred and 34 killed and 110 wounded. Served in the Royal Navy until 1812.[194]

Le Téméraire: unrecorded.

Le Terrible: lost both its main and mizzen masts as shown in Pocock's sketch of HMS *Royal Sovereign* fighting the *Terrible*.

L'Impétueux: Totally dismasted and lost bowsprit. Captured by the British. One hundred killed and 75 wounded. Accidentally burnt at Portsmouth in August 1794, but her design influenced that of two new ships, HMS *Renown* and HMS *Impetueux*.[195]

Le Mucius: Totally dismasted, shown in Pocock's painting with yellow strakes.

Le Tourville: Capitaine Adrien Langlois was included in Jeanbon's list of 'treasonous' officers for their 'modest or poor behaviour' during the battle and was dismissed from the service.

L'Apollon: Capitaine Tardy was included in Jeanbon's list of 'treasonous' officers for their 'modest or poor behaviour' during the battle and was dismissed from the service.

Scenario 9:

Frigate Action Off Banda Aceh, Sumatra in the East Indies, 9 September 1796

French vs British. A squadron level action using *Sails of Glory* or *Fighting Sail* rules.

Background[196]

This scenario pitches two British 74-gun ships of the line against six French frigates of 32–42 guns.

On the 4 March 1796, *Contre-Amiral* Pierre César Charles de Sercey set sail from the roads of La Rochelle at the head of a *division* (squadron) of three frigates – the *Seine* (38),

193 Willis, *Fleet Battle*, p.311.

194 Willis, *Fleet Battle*, p.307.

195 Willis, *Fleet Battle*, pp.307–308.

196 James, *Naval History*, p.387–393; Joseph François Gabriel Hennequin, *Biographie maritime ou notices historiques sur la vie et les campagnes des marins célèbres français et étrangers* (Paris: Regnault, 1836), vol. II, pp.201–205.

Régénérée (40) and the *Forte* (42), the flagship, one ship-corvette – the *Bonne Citoyenne* (20) – and one brig-corvette – the *Mutine* (18) – on his way to the Indian Ocean. On board the squadron were 800 soldiers and two companies of artillery, commanded by *Général de Division* François-Louis Magallon, Comte de la Morlière, together with Civil Commissioners Baco and Burnel destined to bring the benefits of the Revolution, including the abolition of slavery, to the *Île de France* (Mauritius) and the *Île Bourbon* (Réunion).[197] Encountering bad weather in the Bay of Biscay, the *Mutine* was damaged and had to turn back, while the *Bonne Citoyenne* became separated and was captured by a British frigate squadron (10 May). A fourth frigate (*Vertu*) joined the squadron in the Canary Islands having completed its refitting later than the others (29 May). On arrival at the *Île de France* the Civil Commissioners were not well received and provoked an insurrection before being sent home to France by the governor, *Général de Division* Anne Joseph Hippolyte de Maurès, Comte de Malartic. Sercey was now joined by two more frigates the *Prudente* (32) and the *Cybèle* (40) before setting off on a cruise across the Indian Ocean taking 23 merchantmen as prizes. Sercey's commerce raiding took him past Ceylon, the Coromandel Coast and onto the Malacca Straits and Sumatra.[198]

Off the northeast coast of Sumatra, the squadron captured the country-ship *Favourite*, laden with rum and rice (7 September). At daybreak the next day, while off-loading supplies from their prize, the squadron sighted two large ships to leeward. These strangers proved to be the 74-gun third rates, HMS *Arrogant* and HMS *Victorious*, commanded by Captain Richard Lucas and the more junior Captain William Clark respectively. The British spotted the French squadron at 6:00 a.m. when they, the British, were approximately 24 nautical miles to the east of Point Pedro (now Point Batee or Ujung Baka), the northern tip of Sumatra, 10 miles northeast of Banda Aceh.

At 10:00 a.m. Sercey formed his squadron into line of battle astern of his flagship, the *Forte*. At 2:00 p.m. the two British captains met onboard HMS *Victorious* and agreed to engage the French. In the meantime, the French squadron closed with the British ships sufficiently to count their gun ports and at 2:30 p.m., tacked and stood away not wishing to attack the larger British ships. At 4:30 p.m. the British ships turned in pursuit of the French squadron, which was heading to Point Pedro, in the order the *Cybèle, Forte, Seine* and the *Vertu*, the four heaviest frigates, in a single line, with the *Prudente* and the *Régénérée* to windward, prepared to act as a separate light squadron. The French were three nautical miles ahead of the leading British ship, HMS *Arrogant*. At 10:00 p.m. the French tacked in succession, then steered in the direction of east-southeast. At daybreak the next day (9 September), the French squadron was still ahead of the closing British ships, steering to the east in light winds. Assessing that an action was inevitable, at 6:00 a.m. Sercey signalled his fleet to put about, which resulted in the frigates, led by the *Vertu*, sailing on the larboard tack, to the windward of the British ships. At 7:25 a.m. HMS *Arrogant*, on the starboard tack with HMS *Victorious* in attendance, opened fire on the *Vertu* from a range of 700 yards firing two broadsides before the French frigate could reply.

The French fleet was now in the order *Vertu, Seine, Forte, Régénérée,* (a little to the windward of those ahead), *Cybèle*, and lastly the *Prudente* (in line with the *Régénérée*). The action then became intense as the French passed the two British ships in succession. HMS *Victorious* was positioned a cable's length behind and a little to the leeward of

197 René-Gaston Baco de La Chapelle; Étienne Laurent Pierre Burnel.

198 Hennequin, *Biographie maritime*, vol. I, p.241.

HMS *Arrogant*. There followed a confused action in light winds and occasional periods of calm, with the French endeavouring to attack the British ships from positions outside of the arcs of fire of the British broadsides. For example, Tréhouart won praise for launching his boats, during a calm, to tow his ship, the *Cybèle,* into a position where it could rake HMS *Victorious.* At one point HMS *Victorious* was taking fire from all six French frigates at the same time, while HMS *Arrogant* was some distance away. The action lasted until 10:45 a.m. when both fleets limped away without significant result, HMS *Victorious* under tow by HMS *Arrogant* and the *Vertu* under tow by the *Cybèle.*

The Ships

	Guns/Rating/ Class	Armament	Commander
British Ships			
HMS *Arrogant*	74/3rd/*Arrogant*	28x 32-pdr, 28x 18-pdr, 18x 9-pdr	Captain Richard Lucas
HMS *Victorious*	74/3rd/*Culloden*	28x 32-pdr, 28x 18-pdr, 18x 9-pdr	Captain William Clark
French Ships			
La Prudente	32/5th/*Capricieuse*	26x 12-pdr, 2x 6-pdr, 2x *obusiers*	CdV Charles René Magon de Médine
La Seine	38/5th/*Seine*	28x 18-pdr, 12x 9-pdr	LdV Latour
La Cybèle	40/5th/*Nyphme*	28x 18-pdr, 12x 8-pdr, 4x cr	CdF Pierre Julien Tréhouart
La Vertu	40/5th/—	40x 18-pdr	CdF Jean Marthe Adrien L'Hermitte
La Régénérée	40/5th/*Cocarde*	28x 12-pdr, 12x 6-pdr, 4x 36-pdr *ob*	CdV Jean-Baptiste Philibert Willaumez
La Forte(F)	42/5th/*Forte*	28x 24-pdr, 10x 8-pdr, 4x 36-pdr cr	CdV Hubert Le Loup de Beaulieu
CdV *Capitaine de Vaisseau*; CdF *Capitaine de Frégate*; LdV *Lieutenant de Vaisseau*			
(cr = carronade; *obusier* (*de vaisseau*)= French brass 'carronade')			

Although it was unusual for frigates and ships of the line to engage each other, together the French frigates had a superior broadside weight, 3,900 pounds against the British 3,100 pounds.

To represent the 40-gun French frigates ships in my games I have used the *Hébé* class frigates from my *Sails of Glory* collection, the *Carmagnole* (1793) and the *Proserpine* (1785), which were of similarly modern design. The *Prudente* was an older design which used the 12-pdr cannon as its main armament, and this can be represented by the *Embuscade.*

For the British, the HMS *Arrogant* was of similar basic dimensions as the Bellona class 74s and is best represented by HMS *Bellona* or HMS *Defence* from the *Sails of Glory* collection, unless you have the original Kickstarter special edition HMS *Bellepheron,* which was an Arrogant class ship. HMS *Victorious* was a Culloden class ship but can be represented by the similarly sized HMS *Zealous* from the *Sails of Glory* collection.

At the start of the game the ships should be deployed as shown in Map 24. The map is based on a playing area of three *Sails of Glory* mats, joined on the long edge, with a total surface of 78 x 39 inches.

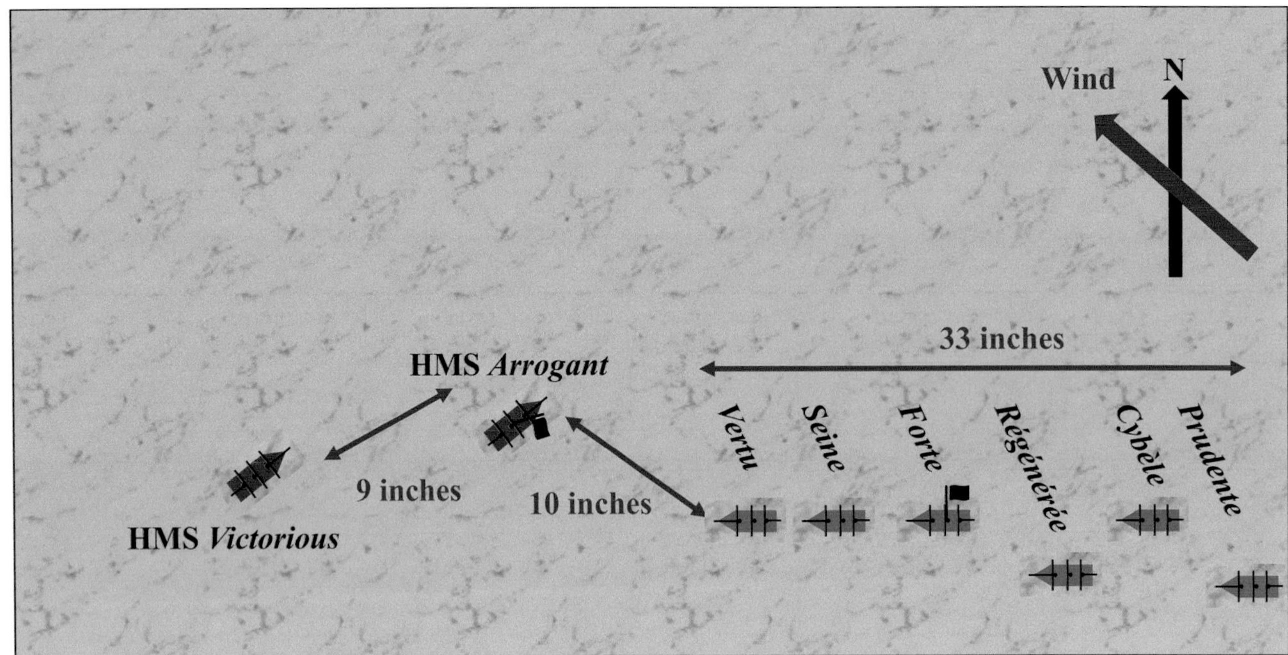

Map 24 – Frigate action off Banda Aceh

The wind strength at the start of the game should be 'low' and can never be stronger than 'low'. To represent the periods of calm, I suggest the following special scenario rule. Use the Variable Wind Strength rules on pages 42–43 of the *Sails of Glory* rulebook, however, use any change in wind strength to swap between becalmed and low wind strength. Thus, if the current wind strength is 'low' any change will result in 'becalmed', and vice versa. This gives approximately a 25 percent chance of the fleets becoming 'becalmed'. When ships are initially becalmed, they will use their current movement card as normal, but their second or planned card is removed. In subsequent moves they can plan moves as normal but cannot act on them until the wind returns.

To win the game the French need to capture or sink one of the British 74s, while the British need to capture or sink three of the French ships. All other outcomes are a draw.

To play the game using *Fighting Sail* from Osprey Games use the following characteristics:

Ship	Sailing	Discipline	Boarding	Gunnery	Hull
The British					
HMS *Arrogant* (74)	4	8	7	8	7
HMS *Victorious* (74)	4	8	7	8	7
Fleet Morale	11				
The French					
La Prudente (32)	7	4	3	3	3
La Seine (38)	7	4	3	3	3
La Cybèle (40)	7	4	3	4	3
La Vertu (40)	7	4	3	4	3
La Régénérée (40)	8	4	3	3	3
La Forte (42, F)	7	4	3	4	3
Fleet Morale	19				

The *Régénérée* was the fastest sailor of the French squadron and has consequently been given an extra sailing die. The 40-gun frigates, the *Cybèle*, the *Vertu* and the *Forte* have been given an extra gunnery die, which is denied the *Régénérée* because of its 12-pdr armament.

Special rule: To reflect the light winds, when the initiative rolls are tied the ships are all becalmed and can only earn sailing points with scores of six.

Use the normal *Fighting Sail* victory conditions based on Fleet Morale.

The Historical Outcome

The French losses were somewhat greater than those of the British, 146 men killed and wounded, as opposed to 108. *Capitaine de Vaisseau* Latour of the *Seine* was amongst the slain, while Captain William Clark of HMS *Victorious* was amongst the wounded.

	Killed and wounded	Damage
British Ships		
HMS *Arrogant*	34 (6 percent of total crew)	4 guns disabled.
HMS *Victorious*	74 (15 percent)	all masts and bowsprit badly damaged, 40 shots through the hull between wind and water.
French Ships		
La Prudente	12	unrecorded
La Seine	62	badly damaged
La Cybèle	17	unrecorded
La Vertu	24	fore topsail yard lost, crippled.
La Régénérée	8	unrecorded
La Forte	23	unrecorded

Sercey clearly felt that he had to engage the British 74s, since this action would have been inconsistent with his mission. The damage inflicted on his ships took them away from commerce raiding to the *Île du Roi*, Mergui Archipelago (the island of Kadan Kyun in far southern Myanmar), for the necessary repairs and resupply. The British captains were criticised for not acting in concert and not capturing some of the French frigates. They also had to seek refuge in Madras for their own essential repairs (6 October), However, they had succeeding in providing the essential trade in the Indian Ocean with a respite from the French commerce raiders.

Scenario 10:

Les Droits de l'Homme, Audierne Bay, 13–14 January 1797

French vs. British. An individual ship action using *Sails of Glory* or *Fighting Sail* rules.

Background

At 12:30 p.m. 13 January 1797 Sir Edward Pellew, aboard HMS *Indefatigable*, was cruising with HMS *Amazon* 150 miles southwest of Ushant in the Atlantic Ocean, when he sighted a large sail in his northwest quarter heading for the coast of France under 'easy sail'. Pellew decided to give chase and by 4:00 p.m. he could identify that his quarry had two decks of guns. He would later discover that it was *Les Droits de l'Homme* and bigger than either of Pellew's ships. The French ship was attempting to return to France, after Hoche's unsuccessful expedition to Ireland in December 1796.

	Guns/Rating/Class	Armament (cr= carronade)	Commander
British Ships			
HMS *Indefatigable* HMS *Amazon*	44/4th/*Ardent* 36/5th/*Amazon*	26x 24-pdr, 20x 12-pdr, 6x 42-pdr cr 28x 18-pdr, 10x 9-pdr, 8x 32-pdr cr	Captain Sir Edward Pellew Captain Robert C. Reynolds
French Ship			
Les Droits de l'Homme	74/3rd/*Téméraire*	28x 36-pdr, 30x 18-pdr, 16x 8-pdr, 4x 36-pdr cr	*Capitaine de Vaisseau* Jean-Baptiste Raymond de Lacrosse

HMS *Indefatigable* was originally a 64-gun third rate ship, one of three such ships which was now a *razee*, a ship with one of its two gundecks removed. This process, which took place in 1794, transformed a small under gunned ship of the line into a more useful large frigate.

At 5:45 p.m. HMS *Indefatigable* was able to engage *Les Droits de l'Homme* and, after an hour, HMS *Amazon* was able to join the fighting in Audierne Bay, 35 miles south of Brest. In the ensuing battle, *La Droits de l'Homme* was severely damaged and wrecked on the French coast. The casualties on the *La Droits de l'Homme* were increased because the ship was carrying troops back from the attempted invasion of Ireland. The masts and rigging of HMS *Amazon* were so damaged that, close to shore, that ship was also lost.[199]

	Killed and wounded
British	
HMS *Indefatigable* HMS *Amazon*	34 (6 percent of total crew) 74 (15 percent)
French	
La Droits de l'Homme	600–1,000 (46 percent)

Sails of Glory Scenario

The ships can be represented by the following *Sails of Glory* models:

British Ships	
HMS *Indefatigable* HMS *Amazon*	HMS *Sybille* HMS *Orpheus* or HMS *Cleopatra*
French Ship	
Les Droits de l'Homme	*Généraux* or *Commerce de Bordeaux*

The ships are deployed as shown in Map 25:

199 Schomberg, *Naval Chronology*, vol. III, pp.4–6, 40; Gardiner (ed.), *Fleet Battle and Blockade*, pp.158–159.

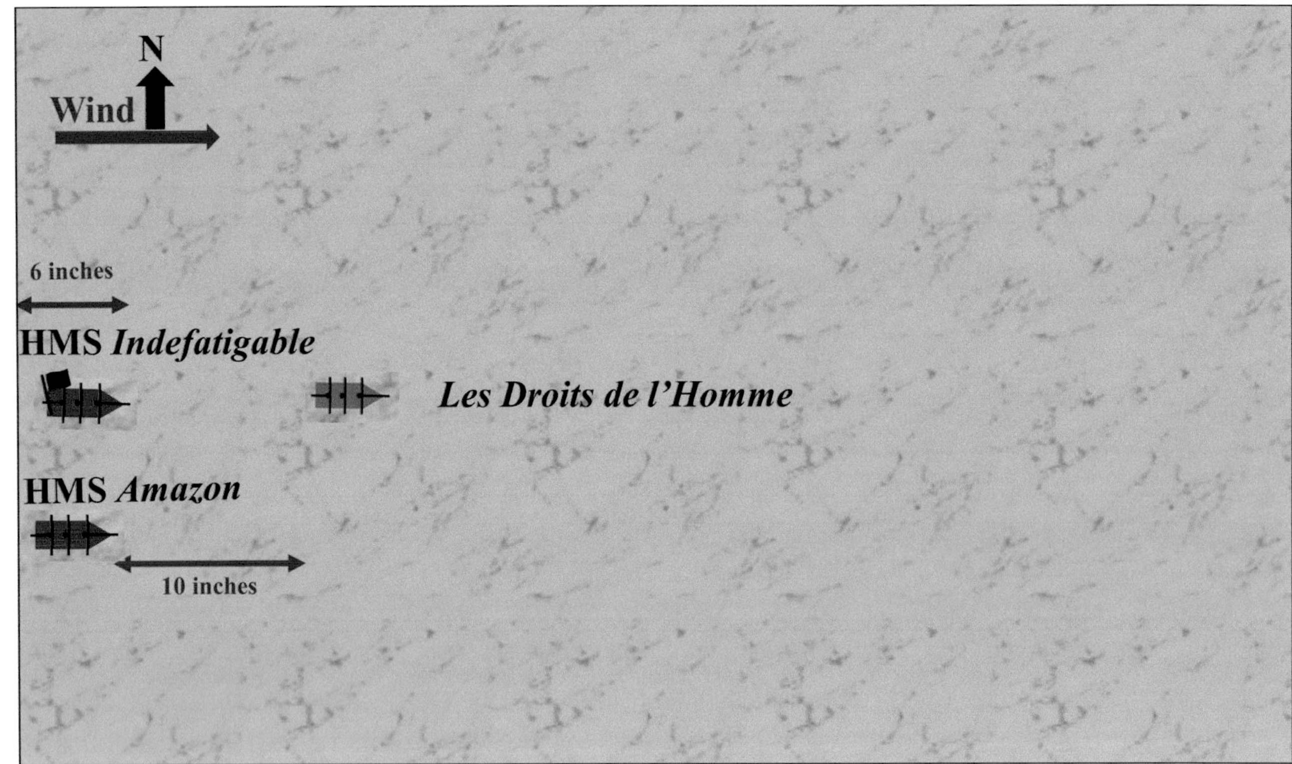

Map 25 – Les Droits de l'Homme

The map is designed for a six foot six inch by three feet three inches table, or the equivalent of three Sails of Glory mats end on end. If different table lengths are chosen the 10-inch spacing between the French and British ships needs to be changed proportionately. However, HMS *Amazon*'s deployment is determined by the drawing of a single damage token from the 'A' damage bag at the beginning of each turn. HMS *Amazon* does not enter the table until the British player draws a 'crew' token.

The wind is of high strength and blowing from the west throughout the scenario, see page 42 in the rulebook. The wind and heavy seas prevented *La Droits de l'Homme* from using its lower deck guns, which is represented by taking its initial broadside from the fifth box from the left of its damage track (3:4:3). However, the broadside will not be further reduced until that fifth box is covered.

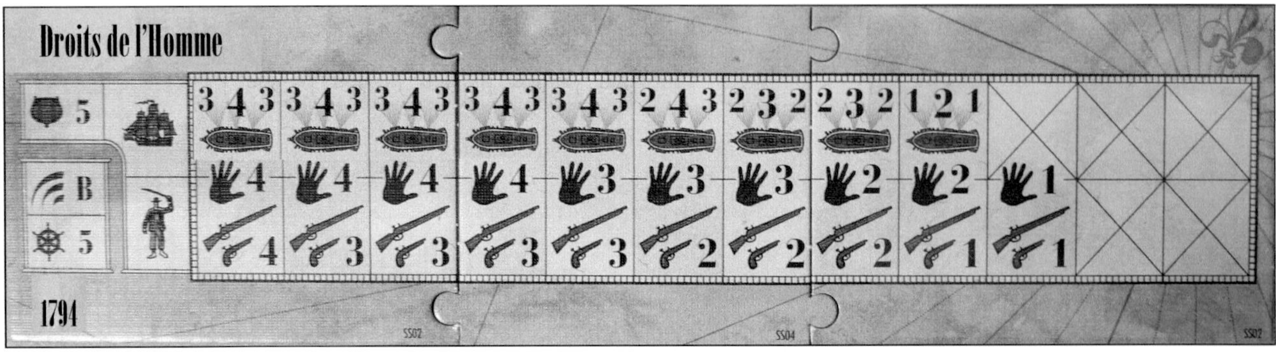

Droits de l'Homme Ship Log

Victory Conditions

The French player wins if the French ship is able to leave the table by the eastern edge or destroys one of more of the British ships. All other results are a British victory.

Fighting Sail Scenario

If playing this scenario using *Fighting Sail*, use the Pursuit and Evasion scenario (#6) in the rulebook (p.58). The ship characteristics would be:

Ship	Cost	Sailing	Discipline	Boarding	Gunnery	Hull
The British						
HMS *Indefatigable* (44)	36	5	5	5	6	5
HMS *Amazon* (36)	26	6	5	3	4	3
Fleet Morale	6					
The French						
Les Droits de l'Homme (74)	55	4	5	7	5	7
Fleet Morale	6					

The winner is the first player to reduce the opposition's Fleet Morale to zero. For a shorter game, base the reduction in Fleet Morale on *unsaved hits*, alternatively for a longer game use *damage tokens* instead.

8

Suppliers of Figures and Terrain

Firstly, a word about figure scales, originally figures scales referred to the height of the figure, but more recently the height to eye level has become the standard, which takes out of the equation differences in headgear, with resulting scale creep. Thus, 15mm became 18mm and 25mm became 28mm. Taller figures allow better proportions of legs and arms, so again it is another trade-off.

For an average man of our period in Europe of 65 inches tall, eye level would be about 62 inches (1,568mm) high. Thus, a 15mm figure is approximately 1:105 in scale; 6mm, 1:261; 10mm, 1:157; 18mm, 1:87; 20mm, 1:78; 25mm, 1:63; 28mm, 1:56; 40mm, 1:39. These differences in scale better illustrate why wargamers are concerned about whether figures from different ranges mix well together on the tabletop.

Irregular Miniatures (6mm) offer a range for our period, based on more generic figure designs that nevertheless would enable you to create British, Dutch and French forces, particularly if you choose carefully from the Napoleonic range.

Pendraken (10mm) offer both French and Austrians for our period in 10mm, although the Austrian range is restricted to 12 packs of infantry and the French to 17 packs of infantry.

Magister Militum (10mm) offer a small range of French infantry in bicornes which will suit the latter part of our period. The Prussians in the range are wearing the later bicorne.

Irregular Miniatures (15mm) offer a small range of generic bicorne clad troops for our period.

Magister Militum (15mm) offer their Chariot Miniatures range in 15mm which includes some especially useful packs for French, Prussians and Austrians. However, while the range includes Austrian infantry wearing the leather *kaskett* from pre-1798, which is suitable for our period, the grenadiers are wearing the post 1798 uniform, although the differences are minor. The artillery crews are wearing the post 1798 bicorne rather than the wide brimmed round hat with a side or the rear folded up in the style of the later *Corsehut*.[1] This whole topic is a bit controversial with little clarity in the source material but can be rectified with a head swap with some *jägers*. The Austrian infantry

1 Haythornthwaite, *Austrian Specialist Troops*, p.14.

range also lacks a suitable figure for the Grenzer and Hungarian regiments, as all the infantry figures have the prominent gaiters of the German infantry. The Grenzers and Hungarian infantry did not wear gaiters instead they wore tight fitting pantaloons to the ankle, otherwise the uniforms are similar. However, the use of a scalpel and a bit of filing can rectify this.

Minitiature Figurines Ltd (15mm) offer a good range of both British and French for our period.

Sho Boki (1:100 or 15/18mm) offer ranges of Austrians, British, Prussians, Hessians and Bavarians. The Austrian range includes some *jägers* in the *kaskett* as well as the *Corsehut*.

Eureka Miniatures (18mm) offer the excellent AB range which provides Austrians for our period. Although the French are designed largely for 1798–1806, some could be used for the later years of our period.

Lancashire Games (18mm) offer a good range of French, Austrians, and Vendéans for our period. The Prussian range, however, is based around infantry wearing the later bicorne headgear.

Old Glory Miniatures (15mm) offer the Blue Moon 15mm range which includes ranges of Austrians, French and Vendéans, these are big 15mm closer to 18mm.

Italeri (1/72 scale or 20mm) offer a wide range of sets of soft plastic, despite the title, the *Austrian Infantry 1798–1805* set includes infantry in the kaskett suitable for our period, as well those in the 1798 helmet. Similarly, the *French Infantry 1798–1805* set could be used for our period.

Irregular Miniatures (25mm) offer a small range of generic bicorne clad troops for our period. The range also includes infantry with Tarleton headgear, so the range is suitable for the French army.

Miniature Figurines (25mm) offer only small range of bicorne clad infantry and cavalry in this scale.

Elite Miniatures (28mm) offer a 28mm *Collector's Range* for the Austrians and French armies in 1796 in Northern Italy.

Emperor Toad's Emporium (28mm) offer a nice and comprehensive range for the War of the First Coalition, including Austrian, British, Dutch, French (including volunteers armed with pikes), French émigrés, Prussian, Sardinia-Piedmont, Vendéan and Chouan rebels.

Eureka Miniatures (28mm) offer an excellent range of 28mm Austrian, French, Sardinia-Piedmontese and Tyrolean militia troops for our period. They also offer a range of AB 18mm French heavy cavalry.

Foundry (28mm) offer an excellent and extensive range of Austrian troops for our period. However, the company took the view that the Austrian artillery crews wore tricorne head gear rather than the early *Corsehut* style designs shown in some sources. Foundry also offer a good range of Prussian and French troops for our period. They also offer an excellent range of rioting French civilians armed in various ways, as well as more well-behaved civilians and complete the range with a guillotine.

Trent Miniatures (28mm), now available through Skytrex (itself part of Warlord Games), offers a nice range of French Republicans, Vendéan/Chouan rebels and Austrians, while the British are available from their 1798 Irish rebellion range. They also have a unique range covering the French, British and Spanish fighting in the Caribbean including the slave revolts on Haiti and elsewhere.

Finally, it is worth noting that other nations such as the Spanish and Sardinia-Piedmont can be represented by cherry-picking from the ranges above or from other more Napoleonic focused ranges. The ranges aimed at the 1799–1803, for example the Old Glory 15s 1799 French range, period may also offer useful figures.

For the naval enthusiasts there are a range of options available *Sails of Glory* offer a range of 1:1,000 scale models that are ready to put on the table straight away, and this is a good option if the naval theatre is a secondary interest. However, there are several options for kits for ships available for our period. The Black Seas range from Warlord Games is a prominent recent entry in 1:700 scale, but other ranges are available including the impressive and extensive Langton Miniatures range in 1:1,200 scale. Navwar offers kits in both 1:1,200 and 1:3,000 scales. GHQ also offers their *Micronauts* range of 1:1,200 scale kits. Magister Militum offer the *Hallmark* range of 1:2,400 ships, while Tumbling Dice offer ships in both 1:2,400 and 1:4,800 scales. In the 3D printed market, Turner Miniatures offer a range of 1:2,400 models, which are ready to paint.

Terrain

Fortunately, we do not need specific terrain for the War of the First Coalition and consequently there is a lot to choose from. Terrain is another one of those very personal choices for wargamers, depending on the particular look for which they are aiming. This relates to the space taken up on the table by the buildings relative to the space occupied by the units in the game. Proper scale models take up too much space and can affect the game, while buildings scaled to the ground scale are much too small and unworkable, so a compromise is often chosen. Fortunately, the wargamer has a choice of both small footprint models and full scale models to choose from. One approach is to select under scaled building models, for example choosing 10/12mm scale buildings for use with 15mm scale figures, this approach is particularly useful if a scenario calls for the representation of single farmhouses or watermills for example, which would otherwise occupy too much space.

Battlescale produce both 6mm and 10mm scale resin buildings for the European theatre, these are nice buildings that I have used to depict single buildings on my 15mm scale games.

Hovels offers a range of reduced footprint resin buildings for our period in 6mm, 10mm, 15mm and 25mm scales.

Magister Militum offer a large range of resin buildings in 6mm, 10mm, 15mm and 28mm scales.

Scale Creep Miniatures offers a range of 6mm European buildings.

Total Battle Miniatures offers two ranges, a *Skirmish range* where the buildings are full scale renderings of the building and a *Big Battalions* range in which the buildings are of the reduced footprint style referred to above. The *Big Battalions* range offers European buildings in 6mm, 10mm, 15mm and 28mm scales. Selected buildings from their WW2 European buildings in the Skirmish range, may also be useful.

Also available are a large number of MDF kits, which tend to be of the full scale design.

4Ground, now sold by Tymeagain, offer a model of La Haye Sainte in both 15mm and 28mm scale, a few other buildings in 15mm and a large southern Europe range in 28mm.

Sarissa Precision offer a range of building kits for Waterloo and other European buildings in 15mm, 20mm and 28mm.

Warbases offer a number of German buildings in their 28mm *Napoleonic Prussia* range, which will work well for the Rhine campaigns. They also have smaller ranges available in 10mm, 15mm and 20mm scales.

Groundworks for your table can by supplied by a range of cloths and mats made from various materials, including neoprene and 'teddy bear fur' or fleece, from suppliers such as Tiny Wargames, Deep-Cut Studio and Cigar Box Battle. Alternatively, very flexible hexagon-based systems are supplied by Kallistra and Geo-Hex.

Dressing the groundwork with roads, rivers/streams, bridges, fences and walls is essential and products are available from many suppliers such as Timecast, Magister Militum, Irregular, Tiny Wargames, 4Ground, Wargamers' Terrain, Battlefield Terrain Concepts.

Trees are another essential component of the tabletop battlefield and can be purchased from many suppliers, including Timecast and specialists such as The Model Tree Shop, K&M Trees and the Model Tree Store. The model railway market, for example, Model Scenery Supplies, has many offerings in this regard including kits to enable the modeller to make his own, and many economy options are available online. On the whole trees are taller than we wargamer's think they are, and the Model Tree Shop has published a handy guide, based on the average British tree of 65 feet, which is approximately equivalent to a model tree of 150mm tall in 15mm scale. The model railway market including Noch, is also the place to start if you want to add crops and flowers to your model battlefields. For battles in the West Indies plastic Aquarium plants are always an option.

3D Printing

The 3D printing world is fast growing and dynamic and offers great potential for our period, although figures for our period are not yet available Aurora Dioramas offers a range of buildings in 15mm scale. Paint and Glue Miniatures also offer a range of 3D printed buildings in a range of scales.

9

Online Resources

Bataillons de volontaires nationaux: A great resource for the volunteer battalions: <https://revolutionsehrivolontaires.wordpress.com/equipe-et-presentation/>

Battles N YouTube channel:

Bonaparte in Italy #1. Start of the 1796 campaign, at: <https://www.youtube.com/watch?v=goPWbXChgy8&ab_channel=BattlesN>

Bonaparte in Italy #2. The Defeat of Piedmont 1796, at: <https://www.youtube.com/watch?v=tqQv-fWQ2Ao&ab_channel=BattlesN>

Bonaparte In Italy #3. Battle of Lodi, at: <https://www.youtube.com/watch?v=7qvGxkGhuTY&ab_channel=BattlesN>

Bonaparte in Italy #4. Battle of Borghetto 1796, at:

<https://www.youtube.com/watch?v=pLtScmpHxT0&t=577s&ab_channel=BattlesN>

French empire.net is great for biographies of the French generals, at:

<https://www.frenchempire.net/biographies/>

Frister, Joseph, *Oesterreichischer Militär Almanach für das Jahr 1796*, available at:

<https://library.hungaricana.hu/en/view/MilitarAlmanachSchematismus_1796/?pg=0&layout=s>

Leopold Kudrna and Digby Smith, *Biographical Dictionary of all Austrian Generals during the French Revolutionary and Napoleonic Wars 1792–1815*, at: <https://www.napoleon-series.org/research/biographies/Austria/AustrianGenerals/c_AustrianGeneralsK.html#K19>

The Nafiziger Orders of Battle collection on The Napoleon Series at: <https://www.napoleon-series.org/resources/the-nafziger-collection-of-napoleonic-orders-of-battle/>

Napoleon Online, Portal zur Epoche 1792–1815 at: <http://uniformenportal.de/index.php?/category/60/start-60>

Napoleon's Bloody Nose, at:< https://napoleoninpiedmont.weebly.com/the-sardinian-army-a-survey.html>.

Steven's Balagan website at: <https://balagan.info/wargaming/campaign>

Tabletop teasers at:

<https://steve-the-wargamer.blogspot.com/p/word-document-jpgs-of-original-article.html>

Three Decks— Warships in the Age of Sail; a great database of all things naval at:

<https://threedecks.org/index.php>

Garry Wills, Playing Historical Scenarios with *Black Powder*™ at: <https://youtu.be/zZwoGHbx8SE>

10

Concluding Remarks

Smith's list of battles and actions for the years 1792–1797, demonstrates that the War of the First Coalition was perhaps closer than we are led to believe. In this period the armies of France fought 144 battles of more than 20,000 combatants, winning 75 and losing 69. They also fought another 139 lesser actions winning 67 and losing 72. It is certainly not the case that the young republican armies, charged by revolutionary fervour, swept away the armies of the *ancien régime* with overwhelming numbers and a completely new way of war. It is certainly true that numerical superiority was achieved at times, especially in the campaigns in the Austrian Netherlands and the United Provinces in 1794, but the battles remained on the same scale or order of magnitude as those of Frederick the Great. The quality of the French commanders who had risen through the ranks and would be made famous for their exploits under the First Empire, does not preclude the existence of generals of equal quality serving the allies. Archduke Charles, Wurmser and Alvinczi all offered significant roadblocks to the French advances and put the outcome in doubt at times. While the operation of war at the strategic and tactical levels was in flux, this was just an exciting waypoint on a journey that had clearly begun earlier in the century.[1]

These data also illustrate the myriad of exciting scenarios that await the wargamer in this period. There are more than 280 historical scenarios to explore and create, which can each provide interesting games. Who would not want to recreate Michel Ney swimming across the river Sieg at the head of a regiment of chasseurs à cheval in the face of Kray's Austrians, to earn his promotion to *général de brigade*?

The art and science of logistics has been given scant attention throughout this work, reflecting the amateur status of most wargamers. Those interested in this vital aspect of war are directed to the excellent work by Martin van Creveld. *Supplying War: Logistics from Wallenstein to Patton*, which suggests that the armies of the War of the First Coalition were more similar in this respect than you might think.[2]

The writing of this guidebook has brought home to this author how personal an endeavour wargaming is, there are many ways to engage with this great hobby and hopefully the reader is inspired to follow their own particular passion for this exciting period of military history.

1 Esdaile, *Wars*, pp.140–141.

2 Martin van Creveld, *Supplying War: Logistics from Wallenstein to Patton* (Cambridge: Cambridge University Press, 1977), pp.35–7, 40–2.

11

Bibliography and Reading List

Archive Sources

Firepower Museum Archives, RA26 *Manuscript Order Book France and Flanders 1793.*

The National Archives, Kew, (TNA):

FO 95 4 6 *Corsica Toulon*, p.609.

WO1/170/555 *1 September 1794 Monthly Returns.*

National Army Museum, Chelsea, Accession No. 1981–11–17; *Hand drawn copy of maps drawn by a Mr. Sardou in 1794.*

Service Historique de la Défense, Paris, SHD B1 17, *Armée du Nord Correspondence, 16–31 Août.*

Online Sources

Biografisch Woordenboek van Nederland: 1780–1830, available at: <http://resources.huygens.knaw.nl/bwn1780-1830/lemmata/data/Van%20Merlen >

Federico Bona, Sardinia-Piedmont Uniforms, available at: <http://www.bandieresabaude.it/Bandiere033.html>. The source for this website is Giorgio Cavalieri, *Uniformi piemontesi 1671–1798*, Edizioni L'Arciere, Cuneo, 2004.

Laurent Brayard and Didier Davin, *Les troupes Belges et Liégeoises sous la Révolution, 1792–1803* (SEHRI, 2017) at: <http://assosehri.fr/bibliothequemili/les-troupes-belges-de-1792-1803.pdf>.

Ludovic Isnard, *Organization of the Savoy-Piedmont-Sardinian Armies 1792–1815, Part I: War in the Alps (September 1792–May 1796)*, available on the Napoleon Series at:
<https://www.napoleon-series.org/military-info/organization/Piedmont/c_piedmont.html>

Leopold Kudna and Digby Smith, *Biographical Dictionary of all Austrian Generals of the French Revolutionary and Napoleonic Wars, 1792–1815*, available via the Napoleon Series at: <https://www.napoleon-series.org/research/biographies/Austria/AustrianGenerals/c_AustrianGeneralsIndexB2.html>.

Maps of France based on the maps at d-maps.com, at: <https://d-maps.com/m/europa/france/france/france06.pdf>

Map of Europe based on the maps at d-maps.com, at: < https://d-maps.com/m/europa/europemin/europemin05.pdf>

Ron McGuigan, *The British Army, 1 February 1793*, available on the *Napoleon Series*, at: <https://www.napoleon-series.org/military-info/organization/c_britarmy1793.html>

Diary of James Russell, 1st Kings Dragoon Guards at: <https://web.archive.org/web/20100914101215/http://www.qdg.org.uk/diaries.php?dy=35>

Geert van Uythoven, *The Dutch Army of 1793–1794*, available on the *Napoleon Series*, at <https://www.napoleon-series.org/military-info/organization/c_dutch.html>.

Wargames Rules and Scenarios

Brown, David, *General de Brigade Deluxe Edition* (Nottingham: Partizan Press, 2010).

Brown, Peter, *Black Powder™ – The Last Argument of Kings* (Nottingham: Warlord Games 2011).

Chadwick, Frank and Novak, Greg, *Volley and Bayonet – Road to Glory* (USA: Test of Battle Games, 2008).

Clarke, Richard, *Sharp Practice: Wargame Rules for large skirmishes in the Era of Black Powder™, 1700–1865* (St. Albans: Too Fat Lardies, 2016).

Conliffe, Arty and Leach, Chris and Waxtel, Dave, *Shako 2nd Edition* (Quantum Printing, 2008).

Gordon, Richard and Preston-Thomas, Brett, *Field of Glory Napoleonic 2nd Edition* (Scotts Valley: Createspace, 2019).

Griffith, Paddy, *Napoleonic Wargaming for Fun* (London: Ward Lock, 1980).

Johnson, Jervis and Priestley, Rick and Stallard, John, *Black Powder™ 2nd Edition* (Nottingham: Warlord Games, 2020).

Miller, Ryan, *Fighting Sail, Fleet Actions 1775–1815* (Oxford: Osprey, 2015).

Angiolino, Andrea and Mainini, Andrea, *Sails of Glory, Napoleonic Wars* (Ares Games, 2013).

Testo, Alex and Carter, Bob, *De Bellis Napoleonicis, Fast Play Rules for the Napoleonic Era, Version 2.1*, (KISR, 2020)

Books and Periodicals

Alcan, Félix (ed.), *Revue Historique* (Paris: Germer Baillère et Cie, 1886).

Ales, Stefano, *Le Regie Truppe Sarde* (Rome: Stato Maggiore Dell'Esercito, 1989).

Anon., *An Accurate and Impartial Narrative of the War by an Officer of the Guards* (London: Cadell and Davies, 1795).

Anon., *Estado Militar de España, año de 1790* (Madrid: Imprenta Real, 1790).

Anon., *Estado Militar de España, año de 1792* (Madrid: Imprenta Real, 1792).

Anon., *Estado Militar de España, año de 1793* (Madrid: Imprenta Real, 1793).

Anon., *Estado Militar de España, año de 1794* (Madrid: Imprenta Real, 1794).

Anon., *Estado Militar de España, año de 1795* (Madrid: Imprenta Real, 1795).

Anon., *Estado Militar de España, año de 1796* (Madrid: Imprenta Real, 1796).

Anon., *Estado Militar de España, año de 1797* (Madrid: Imprenta Real, 1797).

Anon., *Estado Militar de España, año de 1798* (Madrid: Imprenta Real, 1798).

Anon., *Historique du 25e régiment d'Infanterie de Ligne* (Paris: Charles Lavauzelle, 1887).

Anon., *Kurze Geschichte der Kais. Koenigl. Regimenter, Corps, Bataillons, und anderen Militaer-Branchen* (Vien: Cath. Gräffer, 1800), vol.I.

Anon., *Mercurio de España, Enero de 1794* (Madrid: Imprenta Real, 1794).

Anon., *Nieuwe Nederlandsche Jaarboeken …*, (Leiden: P. van der Eyk and D. Vygh, and Amsteldam: J. van der Burgh, 1793).

Anon, *Official documents and interesting particulars of the glorious victory obtained over the French Fleet, on Sunday June 1, 1794, by the British Fleet, under the command of Admiral Earl Howe…* (London: J. Debrett, 1794).

Anon, *Souvenirs d'un Officier Royaliste* (Paris: A.Égron, 1824).

Bamford (ed.), Andrew, *One Hundred Years of Army Historical Research: Proceedings of the SAHR Centenary Conference* (Solihull: Helion, 2023).

Bannatyne, Neil, *History of the Thirtieth Regiment now the First Battalion East Lancashire Regiment 1689–1881* (Liverpool: Littlebury Bros., 1923).

Bas, François de, *Prins Frederik der Nederlanden en zijn tijd* (Schiedam: Roelants, 1887).

Bazouges, Hughes de, and Nichols, Alistair, *For God and King, A History of the Damas Legion (1793–1798): a Case study of the Military Emigration during the French Revolution* (Warwick: Helion and Company, 2021).

Beaulac, Citoyen, *Mémoires sur la Dernière Guerre entre La France et l'Espagne dans les Pyrénées Occidentales* (Paris: Truttel and Würtz, 1801).

Beckett, Ian, *An Honest Man – Moncey* in David G. Chandler (ed.), *Napoleon's Marshals* (London: Weidenfeld and Nicolson, 1987).

Belhomme, Victor Louis Jean François, *Histoire de l'Infanterie en France* (Paris: Henri Charles Lavauzelle, 1899), vol. IV.

Bertaud, Jean Paul, and Palmer, R.R., *The Army of the French Revolution* (Guildford: Princeton University Press, 1988).

Blackmore, David, *Destructive and Formidable, British Infantry Firepower 1642–1765* (Barnsley: Frontline Books, 2015).

Blanning, Timothy Charles William, *The French Revolutionary Wars, 1787–1802* (London: Armold, 1996).

Boeri, Giancarlo, and Crociani, Piero, *L'Esercito Borbonico dal 1785 al 1815* (Roma: Stato Maggiore dell'Esercito, 1997).

Bouvier, Félix, *Bonaparte en Italie, 1796* (Paris: Léopold Cerf, 1899).

Boycott-Brown, Malcolm, *The Road to Rivoli, Napoleon's First Campaign* (London: Cassell, 2001).

Brown, Steve, *By Fire and Bayonet, Grey's West Indies Campaign of 1794* (Solihull: Helion and Company, 2018).

Brown, Steve, *The Duke of York's Flanders Campaign: Fighting the French Revolution 1793–1795* (Barnsley: Frontline Press, 2018).

Bruce, Robert B., and Dickie, Iain, and Kiley, Kevin, and Pavkovic, Michael F., and Frederick C. Schneid, *Fighting Techniques of the Napoleonic Age 1792–1815* (London: Amber Books, 2008).

Cannon, Richard, *Historical record of the Eighteenth, or Royal Irish, Regiment of Foot* (London: Parker, Furnivall and Parker, 1848).

Cannon, Richard, *Historical Record of the First or Royal Regiment of Foot* (London: William Clowes and Son, 1837).

Cannon, Richard, *Historical Record of the Sixteenth or the Queen's Regiment of Light Dragoons, Lancers* (London: John W Parker, 1842).

Cerino-Badone, Giovanni and Rogge, Christian, and Summerfield, Stephen, *Piedmont 4-pdr "Cannone alla Sassone"*, pp.56–57 in *Smoothbore Ordnance Journal*, 6, (Godmanchester: Ken Trotman, 2013).

Charrie, Pierre, *Drapeaux et Étandards de la Révolution et de l'Empire* (Paris: Copernic, 1982).

Chartrand, René, and Courcelle, Patrice, *Émigré and Foreign Troops in British Service (1) 1793–1802* (Oxford: Osprey, 1999).

Chassin L. and Hennet, L., *Les Volontaires Nationaux pendant la Revolution* (Paris: Cerf, Noblet and Quantin, 1902).

Chastel, Balthazar Marie Michel, *Le sans-culotte Chastel,... à tous ses frères les membres des sociétés populaires de la République, en prenant le commandement des Légionnaires montagnards (17 brumaire an II.)* (Marseille: J. Mossy, 1793).

Chuquet, Arthur, *Dugommier (1738–94)* (Paris: A. Fontemoing, 1904).

Chuquet, Arthur, *La Jeunesse de Napoléon, III Toulon* (Paris: Armand Colin, 1899).

Chuquet, Arthur, *Les Guerres de la Révolution VIII. Wissembourg (1793)* (Paris: Plon, 1890).

Clonard, Conde de, *Historia orgànica de las armas de infanteria y caballeria* (Madrid: Boletin de Jurisprudencia, 1854), vol.V.

Clonard, Conde de, *Historia orgànica de las armas de infanteria y caballeria* (Madrid: Castillo, 1854), vol.VI.

Clonard, Conde de, *Historia orgànica de las armas de infanteria y caballeria* (Madrid: D.B.Gonzalez, 1862), vol.XVI.

Colin, Jean, *Campagne de 1793 en Alsace et dans le Palatinat* (Paris: Chapelot, 1902).

Coss, Edward J., *The British Army*, pp.107–147, in Frederick C. Schneid (ed.), *European Armies of the French Revolution, 1789–1802* (Norman: University of Oklahoma Press, 2015).

Cottin, Paul, *Toulon et les Anglais en 1793* (Paris: P.Ollendorff, 1898).

Creveld, Martin van, *Supplying War: Logistics from Wallenstein to Patton* (Cambridge: Cambridge University Press, 1977).

Crociani, Pietro and Paoletti, Ciro, *La Guerra Delle Alpi (1792–1796)* (Rome: Stato Maggiore Dell'Esercito, 2000).

Crowdy, Terry E., *French Light Infantry 1784–1815* (Warwick: Helion, 2021).

Crowdy, Terry E., *Napoleon's Infantry Handbook* (Barnsley: Pen and Sword Military, 2015).

Cust, Edward, *Annals of the Wars of the Eighteenth Century* (London: John Murray, 1869).

David, Pierre, *A history of the campaigns of General Pichegru: containing the operations of the armies of the North, and of the Sambre and the Meuse, from March 1794 to March 1795* (London: G.G.J. and J. Robinson, 1796).

Dawson, Anthony L. and Dawson, Paul L. and Summerfield, Stephen, *Napoleonic Artillery* (Marlborough: Crowood Press, 2007).

Del Campo, Willem Jacobus, *Het leven en de krijgsbedrijven van David Hendrik Baron Chassé, in leven Generaal der Infanterie, oud lid der Staten-Generaal, Grootkruis der Militaire Willemsorde, Officier van het Legioen van Eer van Frankrijk* ('s-Hertogenbosch: Muller, 1849).

Demet, Paul, *We are Accustomed to do our Duty, German Auxiliaries with the British Army 1793–1795* (Warwick: Helion, 2018).

Derksen, G-J.A.N., *De Slag bij Puiflijk, oorlog en politiek overschreden een drempel in het land van Maas en Waal* (Soest: Boekscout, 2015).

Desbrière, Édouard, and Sautai, Maurice, *La Cavalerie pendant la Révolution – La Crise* (Paris: Berger Levrault, 1907).

Desbrière, Édouard, and Sautai, Maurice, *La Cavalerie pendant la Révolution – La Fin de la Convention* (Paris: Berger Levrault, 1908).

Deyster, Hendrik van der, *Naamregister der heeren militaire officieren…* (Leiden: author, 1742 and 1746).

Dumont, Georges Armand Louis, *Bataillons de volontaires nationaux (Cadres et historiques)* (Paris: Henri Charles Lavauzelle, 1914).

Duncan, Francis, *History of the Royal Artillery* (London: John Murray, 1879).

Dundas, David, *Summary account of the proceeding of the Fleet and Army, employed at Toulon, in 1793* (Brentford: P.Norbury, 1805).

Dupuis, Victor, *La campagne de 1793 à l'armée du Nord et des Ardennes, De Hondtschoote à Wattignies* (Paris: R. Chapelot et Cie, 1909).

Dupuis, Victor, *La campagne de 1793 à l'armée du Nord et des Ardennes, De Valenciennes à Hondtschoote* (Paris: R. Chapelot et Cie, 1906).

Esdaile, Charles, *The Spanish Army*, pp.148–181 in Frederick C. Schneid (ed.), *European Armies of the French Revolution 1789–1802* (Norman: University of Oklahoma Press, 2015).

Esdaile, Charles, *The Spanish Army in the Peninsular War* (Nottingham: Partizan Press, 2012).

Esdaile, Charles J., *The Wars of the French Revolution 1792–1801* (Oxon: Routledge, 2019).

Eysturlid, Lee, *The Austrian Army*, pp.64–85 in Frederick C. Schneid (ed.), *European Armies of the French Revolution, 1789–1802* (Norman: University of Oklahoma Press, 2015).

Featherstone, Donald F., *War Games through the Ages, Vol. III 1792–1859* (London: Stanley Paul, 1975).

Forczyk, Robert, *Toulon 1793, Napoleon's First Great Victory* (Oxford: Osprey, 2005).

Fortescue, John William, *A History of the British Army* (Uckfield: The Naval & Military Press Ltd, 2004).

Freemont-Barnes, Gregory, *The French Revolutionary Wars* (Oxford: Osprey, 2001).

Frister, Joseph, *Oesterreichischer Militär Almanach für das Jahr 1793* (Vien: Author, 1793).

Frister, Joseph, *Oesterreichischer Militär Almanach für das Jahr 1796* (Vien: Author, 1796).

Fuller, John Frederick Charles, *British Light Infantry in the Eighteenth Century* (Doncaster: Terence Wise, 1991).

Gardiner, Robert (ed.), *Fleet Battle and Blockade, the French Revolutionary War, 1792–1797* (London: Chatham Publishing, 1996).

Grawert, Julius August Reinhold von, *Ausführliche Beschreibung der Schlacht bei Pirmasenz, den 14. September 1793 in drei Abschnitten: nebst einem Bataillen-Plan und dazu gehöriger General-Charte* (Potsdam: Horvath, 1796).

Gretton, George Le Mesurier, *The Campaigns and History of the Royal Irish Regiment 1684–1902* (London: W. Blackwood and Sons, 1911).

Griffith, Paddy, *The Art of War of Revolutionary France, 1789–1802* (London: Greenhill, 1998).

Guillemot, Pierre-Baptiste, *The Garde Nationale, 1789–1815* (Warwick: Helion, 2022).

Hamilton, Frederick William, *History and Origins of the First Regiment of Foot Guards* (London: J.Murray, 1874).

Harrington, Peter (ed.), *With the Guards in Flanders: The Diary of Captain Roger Morris 1793–1795* (Solihull: Helion, 2018).

Haythornthwaite, Philip J. and Fosten, Bryan, *Austrian Specialist Troops of the Napoleonic Wars* (Oxford: Osprey, 2000).

Haythornthwaite, Philip, and Warner, Christopher, *Uniforms of the French Revolutionary Wars 1789–1802* (Poole: Blandford Press, 1981).

Hennequin, Joseph François Gabriel, *Biographie maritime ou notices historiques sur la vie et les campagnes des marins célèbres français et étrangers* (Paris: Regnault, 1835, Vol. I, 1836 Vol. II).

Hofschröer, Peter, *Prussian Cavalry of the Napoleonic Wars (1), 1792–1807* (Oxford: Osprey, 1985).

Hofschröer, Peter, *Prussian Light Infantry, 1792–1815* (Oxford: Osprey, 1984).

Hofschröer, Peter, *Prussian Line Infantry, 1792–1815* (Oxford: Osprey, 1984).

Hofschröer, Peter, *Prussian Staff and Specialist Troops, 1792–1815* (Oxford: Osprey, 2003).

Hollins, Dave and Younghusband, Bill, *Austrian Auxiliary troops, 1792–1816* (London: Osprey, 1996).

Horne, Alistair, *The French Revolution* (London: Andre Deutsch, 2009).

Hoyer, Johann Gottfried von, *Lehrbuch der artilleriewissenschaft: Aus dem spanischen des d. Thomas de Morla* (Leipzig: J.A.Barth, 1797).

Hoyer, Johann Gottfried von, *Neues Militarische Magazin*, (Leipzig: Baumgärtnerischen Buchhandlung, 1801).

Hussey, John, *Waterloo; the Campaign of 1815 from Elba to Ligny and Quatre Bras* (London: Greenhill Books, 2017).

Hyde, Henry, *The Wargames Compendium* (Barnsley: Pen and Sword Military, 2013).

Iglesias, Indalecio Núñez and Núñez, José María Blanco, *La Diversion de Tolon* (Madrid: Editorial Naval, 1982).

James, William, *The Naval History of Great Britain from the Declaration of War by France in 1793 to the Accession of King George IV* (London: Richard Bentley, 1859).

Jones, Colin, *Longman Companion to the French Revolution* (Harlow: Longman, 1988).

Fabry, Gabriel, *Mémoires sur la campagne de 1796 en Italie* (Paris: Chapelot, 1905).

Krebs, Leónce and Moris, Henri, *Campagnes dans les Alpes pendant la Revolution 1792–1793* (Paris: E.Plon, Nourrit et Cie, 1891).

Krebs, Leónce and Moris, Henri, *Campagnes dans les Alpes pendant la Revolution 1794, 1795, 1796* (Paris: E.Plon, Nourrit et Cie, 1895).

Labouche, Jean H.E., *Le Chef de Brigade Harispe et Les Chasseurs Basques* (Pau: Vve Léon Ribaut, 1894).

Lacroix, Irenée Amelot de, *Rules and regulations for the field exercise of the French Infantry* (Boston: Watt and Co., 1810).

Lardas, Mark, *The Glorious First of June 1794* (Oxford: Osprey, 2019).

Lavalette, Antoine-Marie Chamans, Comte de, *Memoirs of Count Lavalette, Adjutant and Private Secretary to Napoleon and Postmaster-general under the Empire* (London: Gibbings, 1894).

Laws, M.E.S., *Battery Records of the Royal Artillery 1716–1859* (Woolwich: Royal Artillery Institute, 1952).

Letrun, Ludovic, *French Infantry Flags from 1786 to the end of the First Empire* (Paris: Histoire et Collections, 2009).

Levasseur, René, *Mémoires de R. Levasseur* (Paris: Rapilly, 1829).

Lynn, John A., *The Bayonets of the Republic* (Boulder: Westview Press, 1996).

MacKinnon, Daniel, *Origin and Services of the Coldstream Guards* (London: Richard Bentley, 1833).

Marmont, Auguste Frédéric Louis Viesse de, *Mémoires du Maréchal Marmont, Duc de Raguse* (Paris: Perrotin, 1857).

Maurice, Frederick, *The History of the Scots Guards …* (London: Chatto and Windus, 1934).
McNab, Chris (ed.), *Armies of the Napoleonic Wars, An Illustrated History* (Oxford: Osprey, 2009).
Murat, Joachim, *Murat, Lieutenant de l'empereur en Espagne, 1808* (Paris: E. Plon, Nourrit et Cie, 1897).
Nafziger, George, *Imperial Bayonets* (Warwick: Helion, 2017)
Nafziger, George F., *The Armies of Spain and Portugal, 1808–14 (3rd Edition)* (West Chester: The Nafziger Collection, 1993).
Neal, J.B., *Extracts from the Journals of John Francis Smet, Surgeon of the 8th Hussars, 1815–1825*, pp.172–178 in the *Journal of the Society for Army Historical Research*, vol. XXIX, 120,Winter 1951.
Norie, John William, *The Naval Gazetteer, Biographer, and Chronologist; Containing a History of the Late Wars, from Their Commencement in 1793, to Their Conclusion in 1801; and from Their Re-commencement in 1803, to Their Final Conclusion in 1815* (London: Author, 1827).
Nosworthy, Brent, *Battle Tactics of Napoleon and his Enemies* (London: Constable, 1995).
Pajol, Charles-Pierre-Victor, *Kléber, sa vie, sa correspondance* (Paris: Firmin-Didot, 1877).
Paoletti, Ciro, *The Armies of the Italian States*, pp.211–244 in Frederick C. Schneid (ed.), *European Armies of the French Revolution, 1789–1802* (Norman: University of Oklahoma Press, 2015).
Pearse, Hugh Wodehouse, *Memoir of the life and military services of Viscount Lake, Baron Lake of Delhi and Laswaree, 1744–1808* (London: William Blackwood, 1908).
Perrin, Victor François, *Mémoires de Claude-Victor Perrin*, (Paris: Dumaine,1847).
Philippart, John, *The Royal Military Calendar* (London: A.J.Valpy, 1820).
Phipps, Ramsay Weston, *The Armies of the First French Republic, and the Rise of the Marshals of Napoleon I—1. The Armée du Nord* (Godmanchester: Ken Trotman, 2011).
Phipps, Ramsay Weston, *The Armies of the First French Republic, and the Rise of the Marshals of Napoleon I—2. The Armées de la Moselle, du Rhin, de Sambre-et-Meuse, du Rhin-et-Moselle* (Godmanchester: Ken Trotman, 2012).
Phipps, Ramsay Weston, *The Armies of the First French Republic, and the Rise of the Marshals of Napoleon I—3. The Armies in the West 1793 to 1797 and the Armies in the South 1792 to 1796* (Godmanchester: Ken Trotman).
Phipps, Ramsay Weston, *The Armies of the First French Republic, and the Rise of the Marshals of Napoleon I—4. The Army of Italy 1796 to 1797, Paris and the Army of the Interior 1792 to 1797 and the Coup d'État of Fructidor, September 1797* (Godmanchester: Ken Trotman).
Pinelli, Ferdinando Augusto, *Storia militare del Piemonte in continuazione di quella del Saluzo cioè dalla pace d'Aquisgrana sino ai dì nostri, Epoca Primera 1748–1796* (Torino: Degiorgis, 1854).
Pivka, Otto von, *Armies of the Napoleonic Era* (Newton Abbot: David and Charles, 1979).
Pivka, Otto von, *Napoleon's German allies (4): Bavaria* (London: Osprey, 1980).
Pivka, Otto von, *Navies of the Napoleonic Era* (Newton Abbott: 1980).
Poirier de Beauvais, Bertrand, *Mémoires inédits de Bertrand Poirier de Beauvais, commandant général de l'artillerie des armées de la Vendée* (Paris: Plon, 1893).

Portes, René Bittard des, *Histoire de l'armée de Condé pendant la Révolution française (1791–1801)* (Paris: Dentu, 1896).

Pozzo, Luigi del, *Cronaca civile e militare delle Due Sicilie sotto la dinastia Borbonica dall'anno 1734 in poi* (Naples: Stamperia Real, 1857).

Prudhomme, Louis-Marie, *Dictionnaire des individus envoyés a la mort judiciairement, révolutionnairement et contre-révolutionnairement pendant la Révolution...* (Paris: Rue des Marais, No. 20, 1796).

Rodger, Nicholas Andrew Martin, *The Command of the Oceans, A Naval History of Britain, 1649–1815* (London: Penguin, 2006).

Ross, Michael, *Banners of the King, the War of the Vendée 1793–1794* (London: Seeley Service and Co., 1975).

Rothenberg, Gunther E., *Napoleon's Great Adversaries, The Archduke Charles and the Austrian Army 1792–1814* (London: Batsford, 1982).

Rothenberg, Gunther E., *The Art of Warfare in the Age of Napoleon* (London: Batsford, 1977).

Rothenberg, Gunther, *The Napoleonic Wars* (London: Cassell, 1999).

Roussel, Jacques de, *État Militaire de France* (Paris: Onfroy, 1789, 1792 and 1793).

Rousset, Camille, *Les Volontaires 1791–1794* (Paris: Didier, 1870).

Rousset, Camille (ed.), *Recollections of Marshal Macdonald, Duke of Tarentum* (London: Bentley, 1893).

Roworth, Vivien, *Not So Easy Lads, Wearing the Red Coat 1786–1797* (Warwick: Helion and Company, 2023).

Sabine, Edward (ed.), *Letters of Colonel Sir Augustus Frazer, K.C.B....* (London: Longman, Brown, Green, Longmans and Roberts, 1859).

Sagnes Jean (ed.), *L'Espagne et la France à l'époque de la Révolution française (1793–1807)* (Perpignan: Presses Universitaires, 1993).

Salas y Cortés, Ramón de, *Memorial histórico de la artillería Española* (Madrid: García, 1831).

Sapherson, C.A., *European Armies 1789–1803* (Leeds: Raider Books, 1991).

Schneid, Frederick C., *The French Army*, pp.13–35, in Frederick C. Schneid (ed.), *European Armies of the French Revolution, 1789–1802* (Norman: University of Oklahoma Press, 2015).

Schomberg, Isaac, *Naval Chronology or, an Historical Summary of Naval and Maritime Events from the Time of the Romans, to the Treaty of Peace 1802* (London: T. Egerton, 1802).

Six, Georges, *Dictionnaire Bibliographic des Généraux et Amiraux Français de la Révolution et de l'Empire, 1792–1814* (Paris: Librairie Historique et Nobiliaire, 1934).

Six, Georges, *Les Généraux de la Révolution et de l'Empire, Étude* (Paris: Bernard Giovanangeli, 2008).

Smith, Digby, *Napoleon's Regiments* (London: Greenhill Books, 2000).

Smith, Digby, *The Greenhill Napoleonic Wars Data Book* (London: Greenhill Books, 1998).

Summerfield, Stephen, *M1766 Quick-Fire Guns*, pp.58–62 in *Smoothbore Ordnance Journal*, 6, (Godmanchester: Ken Trotman, 2013).

Susane, Louis, *Histoire de l'Artillerie Française* (Paris: J.Hetzel, 1874).

Sydenham, Michael John, *The First French Republic, 1792–1804* (London: Batsford, 1974).

Thaon di Revel, Ignazio and Thaon di Revel, Genova Giovanni, *Memoires sur la Guerre des Alpes et les événemens en Piémont pendant la Révolution française* (Turin: Imprimerie royale Bocca, 1871).

Thoumas, Charles Antoine, *Les grands cavaliers du Premier Empire. Notices biographiques. Series 2: Nansouty, Pajol, Milhaud, Curély, Fournier-Sarlovèze, Chamorin, Sainte-Croix, Exelmans, Marulaz, Franceschi-Delonne* (Paris: Berger Levrault, 1892).

Tousard, Louis de, *American Artillerist's Companion: or Elements of Artillery* (Philadelphia: J. and A. Conrad, 1809).

Townson, Duncan, *France in Revolution* (Sevenoaks: Hodder and Stoughton, 1990).

Uythoven, Geert van, *Dutch Generals of the Napoleonic Wars*, pp.4–11 in *First Empire*, 39, 1998.

Uythoven, Geert van, *Intermezzo 1787–1793*, pp.24–30 in *First Empire*, 56, 2001.

Uythoven, Geert van, *Légion Franche Étrangère*, pp.21–25 in *First Empire*, 76, 2004.

Vaxelaire, Jean-C., and Gauthier-Villars, Henri, *Mémoires d'un Vétéran de l'ancienne armée, 1791–1800* (Paris: Delagrave, 1900).

Verney, Harry, *The Journals and Correspondence of General Sir Harry Calvert* (London: Hurst & Blackett, 1853).

Voykowitsch, Bernhard, *Castiglione 1796* (Maria Enzersdorf: Helmet Military Publications, 1998).

Wagner, August, *De Feldzug der K. Preussischen Armee am Rhein im Jahre 1793*, (Berlin: G.Reimer, 1831).

Ward, Stephen George Peregrine, *The Author of 'An accurate and impartial narrative'*, pp.211–23 in *Journal of the Society of Army Historical Research*, vol. LXX, 284, Winter 1992.

Whinyates, Francis Arthur, *The Wright Letters: being a collection of letters written by Major J. Wright, R.A., and others, during the Duke of York's campaigns in the Low Countries, 1793–4* (London: Eyre, 1902).

Whitting, John Everard, *Annals of the Thirty Seventh North Hampshire Regiment* (Winchester: Warren and Son, 1878).

Willis, Sam, *The Glorious First of June, Fleet Battle in the Reign of Terror* (London: Quercus, 2012).

Wills, Garry David, *British Artillery in the Netherlands 1794*, pp.69–75 in Smoothbore Ordnance Journal, (Godmanchester: Ken Trotman, 2012), 4.

Wills, Garry David, *British Battalion Guns in the Netherlands in 1793–1795*, pp.81–98 in *Smoothbore Ordnance Journal* (Godmanchester: Ken Trotman, 2013), 6.

Wills, Garry David, *Wellington's First Battle, Combat for Boxtel, 15th September 1794*, (Grantham, Caseshot Publishing, 2011).

Wilson, Peter H., *The Armies of the German Princes*, pp.182–210 in Frederick C. Schneid (ed.), *European Armies of the French Revolution, 1789–1802* (Norman: University of Oklahoma Press, 2015).

Zivy, Henry, *Le Trieze Vendémiaire An IV* (Paris: Germer Baillière, 1898).

Appendix I:
Uniform Resources

Terry Crowdy, *French Revolutionary Infantry 1789–1802* (Oxford: Osprey, 2004).

Pierre Charrie, *Drapeaux et Étandards de la Révolution et de l'Empire* (Paris: Copernic, 1982).

Liliane and Fred Funcken, *Les Soldats De La Révolution Française* (Paris: Castermann, 1988).

Haythornthwaite, Philip, and Warner, Christopher, *Uniforms of the French Revolutionary Wars 1789–1802* (Poole: Blandford Press, 1981).

Ludovic Letrun *French Infantry Flags from 1786 to the end of the First Empire* (Paris: Histoire et Collections, 2009).

Otto von Pivka, *Armies of the Napoleonic Era* (Newton Abbot: David and Charles, 1979).

Online

James Hewgill, E. Dayes and J. Turner, *British infantry uniforms 1792* available at: <http://www.napoleon-series.org/military/organization/Britain/Infantry/c_Hewgill.html>.

New York Public Library, Vinkhuijzen Collection of Military prints available at:
<https://digitalcollections.nypl.org/collections/the-vinkhuijzen-collection-of-military-uniforms#/?tab=navigation>.

Anne S.K. Brown Military Collection available at: <https://library.brown.edu/cds/catalog/catalog.php?verb=search&task=setup&colid=13&type=basic>.

Austrian infantry Facing Colours at: <https://www.napoleonguide.com/infantry_austface.htm>

Uniformenportal, an excellent site for the Austrians and Prussians, but also covering other nations available at: <http://uniformenportal.de/index.php?/category/60>.

Richard Knötel, Uniformkunde available at: <https://web.archive.org/web/20070111032014/http://www.grosser-generalstab.de/tafeln/knoetel.html>.